D1699334

Entscheidungen in Kirchensachen

seit 1946

Begründet von

Prof. Dr. Dr. Carl Joseph Hering †   Dr. Hubert Lentz

Herausgegeben von

Prof. Dr. Manfred Baldus   Prof. Dr. Stefan Muckel
Vorsitzender Richter   Universitätsprofessor
am Landgericht Köln a. D.   an der Universität zu Köln

in Verbindung mit dem

Institut für Kirchenrecht
und rheinische Kirchenrechtsgeschichte
der Universität zu Köln

De Gruyter Recht · Berlin

Entscheidungen in Kirchensachen

seit 1946

42. Band

Sonderband
Europäische Entscheidungen

Europäische Kommission für Menschenrechte
Europäischer Gerichtshof für Menschenrechte
Europäischer Gerichtshof

1965 – 2001

De Gruyter Recht · Berlin

Zitierweise
Für diesen Sonderband der „Entscheidungen in Kirchensachen seit 1946"
wird die Abkürzung KirchE-EU empfohlen.

ISBN 978-3-89949-444-0

Druck und buchbinderische Verarbeitung: Hubert & Co., Göttingen
Einbandgestaltung: Christopher Schneider, Berlin

Vorwort und Benutzungshinweise

Die Sammlung „Entscheidungen in Kirchensachen seit 1946" (KirchE) veröffentlicht Judikatur zum Verhältnis von Kirche und Staat und zu weiteren Problemkreisen, die durch die Relevanz religiöser Belange gekennzeichnet sind.

Die Vielfalt der Entscheidungsquellen in allen Gerichtszweigen legte es von vornherein nahe, das Werk in erster Linie als ein möglichst auf Vollständigkeit bedachtes Archiv zu konzipieren und es damit gegenüber Fachzeitschriften abzugrenzen, die nur die aktuell bekannt gewordene Spruchpraxis berücksichtigen können.

Die steigende Bedeutung religionsrechtlich relevanter Fragen in der Rechtsprechung des Europäischen Gerichtshofs für Menschenrechte (EGMR) und des Europäischen Gerichtshofs (EuGH) machte es unerlässlich, auch deren Judikatur in die laufenden Jahrgänge der Entscheidungssammlung aufzunehmen. Dabei werden vornehmlich solche Entscheidungen berücksichtigt, die aus Verfahren in Deutschland hervorgegangen oder sonst von grundsätzlicher Bedeutung sind. Im vorliegenden Sonderband dokumentieren die Herausgeber die einschlägige Rechtsprechung bis Ende 2001. Damit wird dem Benutzer ermöglicht, sich zuverlässig über die Entwicklung der Rechtsprechung auf europäischer Ebene zu informieren und deren Fortführung bis in die Gegenwart zu erkennen. Außer Betracht blieben insbesondere Urteile und Beschlüsse, deren tragende Erwägungen durch spezifische historische oder politische Umstände in dem verfahrensbeteiligten Land bestimmt sind; vgl. z.B. EuGMR, Urteile vom 9.12.1994 - Nr. 10/1993/405/483-484 - (Holy Monasteries ./. Griechenland [Serie A - No. 301A]), vom 10.7.1998 - Nr. 57/1997/841/1047 (Sidiropoulos ./. Griechenland [RJD 1998-IV]), vom 31.7.2001 - Nr. 41340, 41342, 414344/98 (Refah Partisi ./. Türkei [RDJ 2003-II, EuGRZ 2003, 206]).

Die Veröffentlichung erfolgt in einer Amtssprache oder amtlichen Übersetzung, die das Gericht für die Ausgabe der jeweiligen Entscheidung verwendet hat. Ebenso bleibt die von der deutschen Praxis abweichende Form der Entscheidungen und der Abkürzungen gewahrt. Gekürzt wurden die Entscheidungen insbesondere in den Abschnitten zur Prozessgeschichte vor der Kommission bzw. dem Gerichtshof und zu Art. 50 EMRK (Entschädigung etc.). Die Volltexte der Entscheidungen des Europäischen Gerichtshofs für Menschenrechte sind in der Regel über dessen HUDOC-Datenbank (http://hudoc.echr.coe.int.) zugänglich. Dort wurden auch die nicht mit einer amtlichen Quelle nachgewiesenen Entscheidungen der Europäischen Kommission für Menschenrechte recherchiert.

Seit ihrer Gründung (1963) erscheinen die „Entscheidungen in Kirchensachen" in Zusammenarbeit mit dem Institut für Kirchenrecht und rheinische Kirchenrechtsgeschichte der Universität zu Köln und werden

dort auch redaktionell betreut. Unter denen, die die Arbeiten am vorliegenden Sonderband der Entscheidungssammlung durch ihre Mitwirkung
gefördert haben, seien namentlich genannt Dipl.-Bibliothekar Christian
Meyer, Oberregierungsrat Dr. Bernd Eicholt und stud. iur. Kerstin Hal-
verscheid, Daniela Schubert, Kerstin Sieberns, Tobias Kollig und David
Altmaier. Frau Petra Schäfter (Berlin) sei für die druckfertige Erstellung
des Manuskripts gedankt.

Den Benutzern der Sammlung schulden die Herausgeber herzlichen
Dank für Hinweise und die Zusendung bisher unveröffentlichter Entscheidungen; sie werden diese Mithilfe auch weiterhin zu schätzen wissen.

Köln, im Sommer 2007   *Stefan Muckel*   *Manfred Baldus*

Inhaltsverzeichnis

Inhaltsverzeichnis

3. Europäischer Gerichtshof

Abkürzungen und Zitierweise

1. Europäische Kommission für Menschenrechte

Yb	Yearbook of the European Commission on Human Rights (seit 1955)
CD	Collection of Decisions (bis 1974)
DR	Decisions and Reports (ab 1975)

2. Europäischer Gerichtshof für Menschenrechte

Ser. A	Série A des publications de la Cour européenne des droits de l'homme (bis Ende 1995) Der weitere Buchstabenzusatz hinter der Nummer (A-E) erscheint ab 1987.
RJD	Reports bzw. Reports of Judgments and Decisions (seit 1996)
CEDH/ECHR ab 1999	

3. Europäischer Gerichtshof

Slg. Jahr, Seite

4. Weitere Abkürzungen

BayVBl	Bayerische Verwaltungsblätter
DÖV	Die Öffentliche Verwaltung
EuGRZ	Europäische Grundrechte-Zeitschrift
EuR	Europarecht
HRLJ	Human Rights Law Journal
KirchE-EU	Entscheidungen in Kirchensachen seit 1946, Sonderband: Europäische Kommission für Menschenrechte, Europäischer Gerichtshof für Menschenrechte, Europäischer Gerichtshof
KuR	Kirche und Recht
NJW	Neue Juristische Wochenschrift
NVwZ	Neue Zeitschrift für Verwaltungsrecht
öarr	Österreichisches Archiv für Recht und Religion
ÖJZ	Österreichische Juristenzeitung
RUDH	Revue universelle des Droits de l'homme

1. Europäische Kommission für Menschenrechte

1

Zur Aufrechterhaltung der Sicherheit und Ordnung im Strafvollzug kann auch einem Gefangenen, der sich zum Buddhismus bekennt, das Tragen eines Kinnbarts und der Besitz einer Gebetsschnur untersagt werden. Yoga-Übungen, soweit mit der Disziplin in der Anstalt vereinbar, sind ihm gestattet. Ein Anspruch auf Bezug von Schrifttum einer anderen Religionsgemeinschaft und auf Bereitstellung religiöser Literatur in der Gefängnisbücherei besteht nicht.

Art. 9, 27 § 2 a.F. EMRK
EKMR, Teilbeschluss vom 15. Februar 1965
- No. 1753/63 (X. ./. Österreich)[1] -

THE FACTS

The Applicant is an Austrian citizen born in 1921 and at present detained in the prison of Mittersteig serving a sentence of 20 years imprisonment for murder. His application concerns the conditions in the prison of Stein (where he was detained until the spring of 1963) and Garsten (where he was detained until 1964).

The Applicant states that he is of Jewish origin but converted to Buddhism. The prison authorities interfere with the exercise of his religion in that they do not allow him to grow a short and chin beard as prescribed by his religion, that he is prevented from doing contemplative yoga exercises and denied permission to receive the prayer-chain which he had to deposit when transferred to prison. He adds that he did not receive permission to pay 30 Austrian Schillings for a subscription to the „Weltmission" as part of the charity to which he is morally obliged and that he cannot get from the prison library or the book deposit the books necessary for a further development of his philosophy of life (Weltanschauung).
(...)

THE APPLICANT'S ALLEGATIONS

Whereas the Applicant alleges violations:
(1) of art. 9, in respect of the facts set out under point 1 above;
(2) (...)

---

[1] Yb 8, 174.

THE SUBMISSIONS OF THE PARTIES

Whereas the Respondent Government in its observations of 17th September 1964 and the Applicant in his Reply of 2nd October 1964 made the following submissions:

(1) In respect of the alleged violation of art. 9

The Respondent Government submitted that, according to the decision of the Regional Court of Vienna of ... 1958 and to the prison register, the Applicant belongs to no religious faith. He had not during his detention in the prisons of Stein, Garsten and Mittersteig notified the prison authorities concerned that he had joined any religious sect. Consequently, the authorities cannot be said to have interfered with his right to free exercise of religion. It was further submitted that for identification purposes he could not be allowed to grow a beard as he did not have a beard prior to his arrest and conviction. The Applicant was at liberty to do yoga exercises provided that they did not interfere with prison discipline. Consequently the allegations made under art. 9 were manifestly ill-founded.

Finally, it was submitted that the Applicant had not exhausted the remedies available to him as he failed to submit his grievances to the Constitutional Court.

The Applicant submitted that the Austrian authorities refused to recognise Buddhist philosophy and practice as a religion. He maintained that the growing of a beard and the possession of a prayer-chain were necessary elements in practising the Buddhist religion. He contested that identification purposes were relevant as several other prisoners had received permission to grow beards.

(2) (...)

THE LAW

In respect of the alleged violations of art. 9

Whereas art. 9 of the Convention provides as follows:

„(1) Everyone has the right to freedom of thought, conscience and religion; this right includes freedom to change his religion or belief and freedom, either alone or in community with others and in public or private, to manifest his religion or beliefs in worship, teaching, practice and observance.
(2) Freedom to manifest one's religion or beliefs shall be subject only to such limitations as are prescribed by law and are necessary in a democratic society in the interests of public safety, for the protection of public order, health or morals, or for the protection of the rights and freedoms of others."

Whereas the Applicant has maintained that the prison authorities have obstructed his freedom to manifest his religion in five different ways, e.g. by not allowing him to grow a chin beard, by preventing him from doing yoga exercises, by denying him a prayer-chain, by not allowing him to subscribe to a periodical „Weltmission", and by refusing him the books necessary for a further development of his philosophy of life,

Whereas, as to the refusal of permission for the Applicant to grow a chin beard, the Commission has taken note of the submissions of the Respondent Government that this refusal was due to the necessity of being able properly to identify the Applicant; whereas the Commission considers that the refusal is thus justified as being a limitation upon the freedom to manifest one's religion „necessary in a democratic society ... for the protection of public Order ..." within the meaning of par. (2) of art. 9.

Whereas, as to the yoga exercises, the Commission has taken note of the statement in the observations of the Respondent Government of ... 1964 that the Applicant is at liberty to do such exercises, provided that they do not interfere with prison discipline;

Whereas, as to the refusal of permission for the Applicant to obtain a prayer-chain the Commission considers that, even supposing that such chain is an indispensable element in the proper exercise of the Buddhist religion, such limitation is justified under the above par. (2) as a measure „necessary in a democratic society ... for the protection of public Order", in particular, in the interest of the safety of the prisoner and of the maintenance of discipline in the prison;

Whereas, as to the refusal of permission to subscribe to „Weltmission" the Commission has been informed that this periodical is edited by a Roman Catholic organisation; whereas it follows that by the refusal the Applicant, being himself of Buddhist faith, has not been, in any way, restricted in the exercise of his religion;

Whereas, finally, as to the refusal of permission to obtain certain books, art. 9 does not oblige a Contracting Party to put at the disposal of prisoners books which they consider necessary for the exercise of their religion or for the development of their philosophy of life;

Whereas it follows that this part of the Application is manifestly ill-founded and must be rejected in accordance with art. 27, par. (2) of the Convention.

2

Die schutzwürdigen Belange von Unfallbeteiligten rechtfertigen die gesetzliche Einführung einer Kfz-Haftpflichtversicherung oder entsprechender finanzieller Sicherheiten auch für solche Verkehrsteilnehmer, die aus religiösen Gründen den Abschluss von Versicherungen jeder Art ablehnen.

Art. 9 § 2, 27 § 2 a.F. EMRK
EKMR, Beschluss vom 31. Mai 1967 - No. 2988/66 (X. ./.Niederlande)[1] -

THE FACTS

The Applicant is a Netherlands citizen, born in 1939. He is a farmer and merchant residing at B. He states that by reason of his religious beliefs he has objections of conscience to any form of insurance. According to his religious convictions, prosperity and adversity are meted out to human beings by God and it is not permissible to attempt in advance to prevent or reduce the effects of possible disasters. Consequently, the Applicant does not find it possible to accept any systems of compulsory insurance.

In the present case, he refers to one such system introduced by the Act of 30th May, 1963 on Liability Insurance for Motor Vehicles (Wet aansprakelijkheidsverzekoring motorrijtuigen). According to the provisions of this Act, every user of a motor vehicle must be insured against third party liability. As in other Netherlands legislation on compulsory insurance schemes, there are in the Act of 30th May, 1963 special provisions regarding exemption for those who object, on grounds of conscience, to any form of insurance. Persons who are granted exemption under these provisions do not have to pay an insurance premium but are required to pay an equivalent sum of money as income tax and the Applicant states that these tax payments serve, in fact, to cover the same risks as the insurance system is designed to cover. Consequently, there is not, in the Applicant's opinion, any real exemption, and he states that the German term „Etikettenschwindel" (false labelling) has sometimes been used to describe this procedure. The Applicant concludes that the provisions regarding exemption are not acceptable and that, therefore, his objections of conscience also concern the exemption system provided for by the Act.

As the Applicant is a merchant, he urgently needs a car for his business. On 1965, he was convicted by the Magistrate's Court (Kantonrechter) of Harderwijk for driving a motor vehicle without an insurance and he was sentenced to a fine of 50 guilders or, in default, 10 days' detention. The motor vehicle was confiscated with the order that the proceeds from the sale of the vehicle should be handed over to the Applicant. Finally, the Applicant was also disqualified from driving motor vehicles for a period of six months.

On appeal, this judgment was confirmed, on 1966, by the Regional Court (Arrondissementsrechtbank) of Zwolle. The Applicant lodged a further

---

[1] Yb 10, 472. Mit ähnlicher Begründung verneinte die Kommission eine Verletzung von Art. 9 EMRK durch Einführung von Pflichtbeiträgen zur Altersvorsorge; Beschluss vom 14.12.1962 - No. 1497/62 - (Reformierte Kirche von X. ./. Niederlande), Yb 5, 286. Vgl. auch EKMR KirchE-EU S. 66 (Pflichtmitgliedschaft in einer Pensionskasse).

appeal (beroep in cassatie) with the Supreme Court (Hoge Raad), and invoked in particular his objections of conscience to insurance systems. On 1966, this appeal was rejected by the Supreme Court.

The Applicant alleges that the Supreme Court's decision violates the Convention, in particular its art. 9, since for him one of the practices of his religion and religious beliefs is to abstain from participation in the insurance system concerned.

THE LAW

Whereas the Applicant complains of the system of compulsory motor insurance introduced by the Netherlands Act of 30th May, 1963;

Whereas he objects not only to the primary obligation to participate in the insurance scheme but also to the character of the exemption system provided for in the Act in regard to conscientious objectors;

Whereas the Applicant alleges that, as a result of the Act concerned and its application to him, he is the victim of a violation of art. 9 of the Convention;

Whereas art. 9 of the Convention provides as follows:

> „(1) Everyone has the right to freedom of thought, conscience and religion; this right includes freedom to change his religion or belief and freedom, either alone or in community with others and in public or private, to manifest his religion or belief, in worship, teaching practice and observance.
> (2) Freedom to manifest one's religion or beliefs shall be subject only to such limitations as are prescribed by law and are necessary in a democratic society in the interests of public safety, for the protection of public order, health or morals, or for the protection of the rights and freedoms of others."

Whereas the Commission has examined the Application in relation to art. 9 of the Convention and has had regard to its previous decisions in similar cases (see, in particular, Yb 5, pages 278 and 286, CD, Vol. 18, p. 40);

Whereas in the present case the question first arises as to whether the facts alleged could be considered to concern „the right to freedom of thought, conscience and religion" as guaranteed by par. (1) of art. 9;

Whereas, in so far as this provision is involved, the Commission finds it clear that the Netherlands legislation concerned and its application in the present case are justified under par. (2) of art. 9;

Whereas in this respect the Commission has noted that the purpose of the compulsory motor insurance scheme is to safeguard the rights of third parties who may become victims of motor accidents; and whereas par. (2) of art. 9 expressly permits such limitations of the freedom to manifest one's religion or beliefs as are necessary in a democratic society „for the protection of the rights and freedoms of others";

Whereas it follows that the present Application is manifestly ill-founded within the meaning of art. 27, par. (2) of the Convention.
Now therefore the Commission declares this Application inadmissible.

3

Das Recht auf Ehe iSv Art. 12 EMRK begründet keinen Anspruch auf Anerkennung einer nur unter Beachtung religiöser Vorschriften geschlossenen Ehe im weltlichen Rechtskreis.

Art. 9, 12, 27 § 2 a.F. EMRK
EKMR, Beschluss vom 18. Dezember 1974
- No. 6167/73 (X. ./. Deutschland)[1] -

THE FACTS

The applicant is a German citizen born in 1924 and living in Heidelberg.

The applicant complains that the German authorities do not recognise his marriage with Mrs Y. The registrar of marriages refused to make an entry in the family record (Familienbuch) because the applicant had not married under the forms prescribed by Sec. 11 of the Law on Marriages (Ehegesetz). The applicant complained to the competent District Court (Amtsgericht) which rejected his complaint on May 1972. The applicant's appeal (Beschwerde) was rejected by the Regional Court (Landgericht) Heidelberg on September 1972. A further appeal (weitere Beschwerde) was rejected by the Court of Appeal (Oberlandesgericht) Karlsruhe on March 1973. The latter court stated in its decision that in the opinion of the applicant he is married to Y. because he had intercourse with her only after having read out verse 16 of the 22nd chapter of the second book of Moses in the Old Testament. The Court held that the right to marriage as guaranteed under art. 6 (1) of the Constitution (GG) only referred to the conclusion of marriage in the form provided by the legislator in Sec. 11 of the Law on Marriages. In the opinion of the court art. 6 (GG) not only gives the State the right but even creates the obligation for the State to set up regulations for marriages as it is a social institution. Therefore, so the court concluded, the necessity of contracting a marriage in proper form before the registrar of marriages was justified under constitutional law.

The applicant's constitutional appeal was rejected by a group of three judges of the Federal Constitutional Court on June 1973 as being clearly ill-founded.

---

[1] DR 1, 64.

The applicant alleges a violation of most of the articles of the Convention and especially of art. 9 (1).

THE LAW

The applicant has complained that the German authorities do not recognise his marriage contracted according to a special religious ritual and not in the forms prescribed by the Law on Marriages.

It is true that art. 9 (1) of the Convention secures to everyone the right to freedom of religion: However, in this case this provision cannot be considered without having regard to art. 12 which provides that „Men and women of marriageable age have the right to marry and found a family, according to the national laws governing the exercise of this right". Marriage is not considered simply as a form of expression of thought, conscience or religion but is governed by the specific provision of art. 12 which refers to the national laws governing the exercise of the right to marry.

In the present case the applicant was not denied the right to marry. He was only requested to marry under the forms prescribed by German law. There is consequently no appearance of a violation of the Convention, especially of art. 9 (1) and 12.

An examination by the Commission of this complaint as it has been submitted, including an examination made ex officio, does not therefore disclose any appearance of a violation of the rights and freedoms set out in the Convention and in particular in the above article.

It follows that the application is manifestly ill-founded within the meaning of art. 27 (2) of the Convention.

For these reasons, the Commission declares this application inadmissible.

4

Das einem Strafgefangenen auferlegte Verbot, an den Herausgeber einer buddhistischen Zeitschrift Manuskripte zum Zwecke der Veröffentlichung zu übersenden, verletzt nicht die Religionsfreiheit und überschreitet auch nicht das unter den Bedingungen des Strafvollzugs erforderliche Maß an Einschränkungen der Meinungsfreiheit.

Art. 8, 9, 10, 27 § 2 a.F. EMRK
EKMR, Beschluss vom 20. Dezember 1974
- No. 5442/72 (X. ./. Vereinigtes Königreich)[1] -

---

[1] DR 1, 41.

Der in der Amtlichen Sammlung nur stichwortartig wiedergegebene Sachverhalt ist im Wesentlichen folgender:
Der zu einer fünfjährigen Freiheitsstrafe verurteilte Antragsteller ist - wie der Gefängnisbehörde bekannt - buddhistischen Glaubens. Nachdem er dem Herausgeber einer buddhistischen Zeitschrift ein Manuskript zur Veröffentlichung übersandt hatte, untersagte ihm die Behörde die Übermittlung weiterer Manuskripte.
Mit der Beschwerde macht er geltend, die Veröffentlichung der Zeitschriftenartikel diene der Kontaktpflege mit seinen Glaubensgenossen und gehöre damit zur Religionsausübung. Unter diesen Umständen sei auch eine Einschränkung seines Rechts auf Briefverkehr und freie Meinungsäußerung nicht gerechtfertigt.

THE LAW

The applicant, while a prisoner at D., was refused permission to send out articles for publication in a Buddhist magazine. He claims that this constitutes a violation of art. 8, 9 and 10 of the Convention.
The Commission has first examined the complaint in the light of art. 9 of the Convention. Art. 9 provides:

„Everyone has the right to freedom of thought, conscience and religion; this right includes freedom to change his religion or belief and freedom, either alone or in community with others and in public or private, to manifest his religion or belief in worship, teaching, practice and observance.“

However, the Commission notes that, while the applicant was detained in prison, the authorities did what they could to find a Buddhist minister for him (the applicant has not suggested otherwise) and that they eventually allowed him to write an extra letter to a Buddhist every week when it was not possible to find a minister. There is no indication of any interference with the applicant's right to freedom of thought, conscience or religion.
The applicant has produced statements to the effect that communication with other Buddhists is an important part of his religious practice. But he has failed to prove that it was a necessary part of this practice that he should publish articles in a religious magazine. Viewed in the light of art. 9 the complaint is manifestly ill-founded.
The Commission has next considered the complaint within the terms of art. 8 which provides for respect for correspondence. It is not clear whether the applicant originally intended to allege that at one time he had been refused permission to write to Mr Y., the Buddhist publisher. Whether or not this complaint formed part of his original submission, it is clear that the applicant has not pursued it. The respondent Govern-

ment, in their observations, have denied that the applicant was ever refused permission to write and he does not now contradict them.

The applicant was told that he would not be allowed to send out material for publication but there is no indication of interference with his letters, as such, and the complaint is again manifestly ill-founded with respect to this article.

Finally, the Commission has reviewed the matter under art. 10, which provides

> „1. Everyone has the right to freedom of expression. This right shall include freedom to hold opinions and to receive and impart information and ideas without interference by public authority and regardless of frontiers ...
> 2. The exercise of these freedoms, since it carries with it duties and responsibilities, may be subject to such formalities, conditions, restrictions or penalties as are prescribed by law and are necessary in a democratic society, in the interests of national security, territorial integrity or public safety, for the prevention of disorder or crime, for the protection of health or morals, for the protection of the reputation or rights of others, for preventing the disclosure of information received in confidence or for maintaining the authority and impartiality of the judiciary."

The applicant was prevented by Rule 33 of the Prison Rules, as applied by the authorities, from enclosing with his letters to the Buddhist publisher, Mr Y., any material intended for publication, even though he was to receive no money in the event of its publication.

The Commission considers that this might constitute an interference with the applicant's freedom of expression, his right to impart information and ideas without interference.

However, the Commission recognises the extra work and the administrative difficulties of checking all material that might be sent out by prisoners for the purpose of publication and the potential security risk involved without careful control being exercised. The Rule, duly prescribed by law, is necessary for the maintenance of prison discipline and the Commission concludes that the Rule is necessary in a democratic society for the prevention of disorder or crime within the meaning of art. 10 (2).

The Commission considers that, for the same reasons, the application of Rule 33 to the applicant was reasonable. The Commission is not of the opinion that the applicant's situation in the particular circumstances warranted a special exception to the Rule.

The Commission finds therefore that the applicant's complaint does not disclose any appearance of a violation of the rights and. freedoms set out in the Convention and in particular in art. 8, 9 and 10.

It follows that the application is manifestly ill-founded within the meaning of art. 27 (2) of the Convention.

For these reasons, the Commission declares this application inadmissible.

5

Zur Frage des Rechtschutzes für einen Geistlichen gegen Anord-
nungen des staatlichen Kirchenministeriums in religiösen Angelegenheiten (hier: Verbot, die Taufe eines Kindes von der Teilnahme
seiner Eltern am Religionsunterricht abhängig zu machen).
In einem staatskirchlichen System wird der individuellen Religionsfreiheit der Geistlichen durch die freie Entscheidung über den
Eintritt in den Kirchendienst und die Möglichkeit des Kirchenaustritts Rechnung getragen.

Art. 6, 9 EMRK
EKMR, Beschluss vom 8. März 1976 - No. 7374/76 (X. v. Dänemark)[1] -

SUMMARY OF THE RELEVANT FACTS

The applicant is a clergyman in the State church of Denmark (Folke-
kirchen) and the incumbent of a particular parish. He made it a condition
for christening children that the parents attended five religious lessons.

The Church Ministry, being of the opinion that the applicant had no
right to make such conditions, advised him to abandon this practice or to
hand in his resignation. When the applicant refused, the Ministry, set up
a consistory court of an advisory character. The applicant unsuccessfully
requested that the proceedings should take place in public before a consistory court with judicial authority. The public prosecutor's office, however, held the opinion that the case was of a mere disciplinary character
and had no criminal law implications.

The consistory court postponed the examination of the examination of
the case pending the decision of the Commission on the admissibility of
the present case.

The applicant complains in particular of a violation of his freedom of
conscience and claims that he is being denied a right to a fair trial as the
decision is left to the Church Ministry's discretion.

THE LAW (Extract)

1. The applicant first complains that, as a clergyman in the State
Church of Denmark, he has been requested by the Church Ministry under threat of sanctions to abandon a certain practice of christening. He
alleges in this respect a violation of art. 9 of the Convention.

Art. 9 grants to everyone the right to freedom of thought, conscience
and religion including the freedom to manifest his religion or belief in
worship, teaching, practice and observance. The Commission considers it

---

[1] DR 5, 157.

conceivable that a dismissal of a State official for disobedience could in given circumstances raise an issue under this article. However, for the following reasons in the circumstances of the present case no such issue arises.

A church is an organised religious community based on identical or at least substantially similar views. Through the rights granted to its members under art. 9, the church itself is protected in its right to manifest its religion, to organise and carry out worship, teaching practice and observance, and it is free to act out and enforce uniformity in these matters. Further, in a State church system its servants are employed for the purpose of applying and teaching a specific religion. Their individual freedom of thought, conscience or religion is exercised at the moment they accept or refuse employment as clergyman, and their right to leave the church guarantees their freedom of religion in case they oppose its teachings.

In other words, the church is not obliged to provide religious freedom to its servants and members, as is the State as such for everyone within its jurisdiction.

The Commission therefore holds that freedom of religion within the meaning of art. 9 (1) of the Convention does not include the right of a clergyman, in his capacity of a civil servant in a State church system, to set up conditions for baptising, which are contrary to the directives of the highest administrative authority within that church, i.e. the Church Minister.

It follows that the applicant's above complaint does not fall within the scope of art. 9 of the Convention.

2. The applicant further complains that he is being denied access to a court of law or alternatively a consistory court with judicial authority in order to challenge the decision of the Church Ministry to dismiss him if he did not abandon the practice referred to above. He does not accept that the disciplinary proceedings take place before the consistory court which has been constituted in his case, since this court has a fact-finding function only and the determination of the charge will be left to the Church Minister's discretion. In consequence the applicant would allegedly have lesser chances of avoiding dismissal. He also suggests that the purpose behind the choice between these different forms of proceedings is found in the Church Ministry's alleged aims at establishing what it considers to be the correct practice in relation to the christening ritual, rather than simply disciplining him or charging him with a criminal offence.

The applicant refers in this respect to art. 6, par. 1, of the Convention which secures to everyone that in the determination of his civil rights and obligations or of any criminal charge against him he is entitled to a fair and public hearing before an impartial tribunal.

As far as the applicant would like to have issues of faith or religious practice decided by a tribunal, within the meaning of art. 6, par. 1, of the Convention, the Commission is of the opinion that disputes on such issues do not involve the determination of civil rights and obligations of a criminal charge, within the meaning of the said provision.

As far as the applicant claims the right not to be dismissed from his function as a civil servant, the Commission refers to its previous case-law according to which litigation concerning access to or dismissal from civil service falls outside the scope of art. 6, par. 1, of the Convention (see, for example, No. 3937/69, CD 32, p. 61).

It follows that art. 6, par. 1, of the Convention does not apply to this part of the application.

6

Die straßenverkehrsrechtliche Helmpflicht für Motorradfahrer ist als Beschränkung der Religionsfreiheit im Sinne von Art. 9 § 2 EMRK nach wie vor gerechtfertigt, auch nachdem die Gesetzgebung Ausnahmen zugunsten von Sikhs als Turbanträgern zugelassen hat.

Art. 9 § 2 EMRK
EKMR, Beschluss vom 12. Juli 1978
- No. 7992/77 (X. ./. Vereinigtes Königreich)[1] -

SUMMARY OF THE FACTS

The applicant, an Indian citizen, lives in the United Kingdom. The applicant, a sikh, is required by his religion to wear a turban.

Between 1973 and 1976, he was prosecuted, convicted and fined twenty times for failing to wear a crash helmet when riding his motor cycle.

He complains that the requirement to wear a crash helmet, which obliges him to remove his turban, whilst riding his motor cycle interferes with his freedom of religion.

At the end of 1976 an amendment to the legislation exempted sikhs from wearing crash helmets.

THE LAW

The applicant complains that the Motor Cycle (Wearing of Helmets) Regulations 1973 violated his right to freedom of religion by penalising

---

[1] DR 14, 234.

him for failing to remove his turban and put on a crash helmet when riding his motor cycle.

Art. 9 of the Convention provides that

> „1. *Everyone has the right to freedom of thought, conscience and religion; this right includes freedom to change his religion or belief and freedom, either alone or in community with others and in public or in private, to manifest his religion or belief, in worship, teaching, practice and observance.*
> *2. Freedom to manifest one's religion or beliefs shall be subject only to such limitations as are prescribed by law and are necessary in a democratic society in the interests of public safety, for the protection of public order, health or morals, or for the protection of the rights and freedoms of others".*

The Commission considers that the compulsory wearing of crash helmets is a necessary safety measure for motor cyclists. The Commission is of the opinion therefore that any interference that there may have been with the applicant's freedom of religion was justified for the protection of health in Accordance with art. 9 (2).

The facts that Sikhs were later granted an exemption to the traffic regulations does not in the Commission's opinion vitiate the valid health considerations on which the regulations are based.

The Commission concludes therefore that the penalisation of the applicant for failing to comply with these regulations did not constitute a violation of art. 9 of the Convention.

For these reasons, the Commission declares the application inadmissible.

7

Eine Gesellschaft mit beschränkter Haftung kann als ein auf Gewinnerzielung ausgerichtetes Unternehmen nicht in den Schutzbereich des Art. 9 § 1 EMRK fallen.

EKMR, Beschluss vom 27. Februar 1979
- No. 7865/77 (Company X. ./. Schweiz)[1] -

SUMMERY OF THE RELEVANT FACTS

The limited liability company X. runs a printing office in the Canton of Zürich.

The commune in which the company is registered obliges it to pay an ecclesiastical tax both in favour of the Roman Catholic and Protestant Reformed churches, both recognised in the Canton of Zürich. The compe-

---

[1] DR 16, 85.

tent Zürich authorities have confirmed the communal decision. A public law appeal to the Federal Court, lodged by the applicant company was rejected.

THE LAW (Extract)

The applicant, a limited liability company, registered in E. in the Canton of Zürich, complains that the cantonal and federal authorities infringe its rights secured by art. 9 of the Convention, in that they oblige it, as a corporate body to pay ecclesiastical taxes intended for both Christian Churches - the Roman Catholic church and the Protestant Reformed church recognised in the Canton of Zürich.

Art. 9, par. 1 of the Convention, which guarantees to every-one the right to freedom of thought, conscience and religion, stipulates that this right implies the freedom to manifest its religion or belief ... and specifies that this freedom shall be subject to limitations only under the conditions set out under par. 2 of that provision.

Moreover, according to art. 25, par. 1, of the Convention the Commission may receive petitions inter alia from any non-governmental organisation claiming to be the victim of a violation by one of the High Contracting Parties that has recognised the competence of the Commission in this respect, of the rights set forth in the Convention.

Even supposing that the applicant's claim may fall within the ambit of art. 9 of the Convention, the Commission is nevertheless of the opinion that a limited liability company given the fact that it concerns a profit-making corporate body, can neither enjoy nor rely on the rights referred to in art. 9, par. 1, of the Convention.

It follows that in this respect, the application is incompatible with the provisions of the Convention and must be rejected under art. 27, par. 2 of the Convention.

8

Auch an einer weltanschaulich neutralen Schule darf ein Lehrer seine moralische und religiöse Auffassung im Unterricht kundtun, jedoch hat er das Erziehungsrecht der Eltern zu achten und insbesondere ein Verhalten zu meiden, das als aggressiv (*offensive*) verstanden werden oder bei den Schülern Verwirrung stiften kann.

Art. 10 §§ 1, 2 EMRK

EKMR, Beschluss vom 1. März 1979

- No. 8010/77 (X. ./. Vereinigtes Königreich)[1] -

---

[1] DR 16, 101.

SUMMARY OF THE RELEVANT FACTS

From 1971 to 1975 the applicant was a teacher in a public secondary school, in charge of English and mathematics.

He received warnings from the headmaster for having given religious education during class hours, having held „evangelical clubs" on the school premises and for having worn stickers carrying religious and anti-abortion slogans on his clothes or briefcase.

After numerous interviews and exchanges of notes with the headmaster in the course of which the applicant, setting out his strong beliefs, declared himself unwilling to change his behaviour, his dismissal was decided by the competent County authority. The applicant's appeals to the Employment tribunals were unsuccessful.

THE LAW (Extract)

The applicant [also] claims that his dismissal was due to the expression of his views to his headmaster, contrary to art. 10 of the Convention which secures to everyone the right to freedom of expression. However, par. 2 of art. 10 states that „the exercise of these freedoms, since it carries with it duties and responsibilities, may be subject to such formalities, conditions, restrictions or penalties as are prescribed by law and are necessary in a democratic society, in the interests of national security, territorial integrity or public safety, for the prevention of disorder or crime, for the protection of health or morals, for the protection of the reputation or rights of others, for preventing the disclosure of information received in confidence, or for maintaining the authority and impartiality of the judiciary".

It is clear from the documents submitted by the applicant, in particular the decisions of the Industrial Tribunal and the Employment Appeal Tribunal and letters sent to the applicant by his headmaster dated 10 May 1974 and 13 November 1974 that he was dismissed because of his refusal to comply with specific instructions. In particular the letters mentioned above indicate that the only aspect of the applicant's views that were objectionable was his insistence that he should instruct his classes in them. Accordingly, the Commission is satisfied that there is no evidence in support of the complaint that the applicant was dismissed because of the expression of his views to his headmaster.

Nevertheless the Commission notes that an important factor in the dispute between the applicant and the headmaster concerned the latter's instruction to the applicant not to advertise by posters or stickers on school premises his political, moral or religious beliefs.

The Commission considers that this instruction constitutes an interference with the applicant's freedom of expression. However the Commission is of the opinion that school teachers in non-denominational schools should have regard to the rights of parents so as to respect their religious and philosophical convictions in the education of their children. This requirement assumes particular importance in a non-denominational school where the governing legislation provides that parents can seek to have their children excused from attendance at religious instruction and further that any religious instruction given shall not include „any catechism or formulary which is distinctive of any particular religious denomination" (see Education Act 1944, sec. 25 and 26).

In the present case the posters and „stickers" objected to, reflected the applicant's strong Evangelical beliefs and his opposition to abortion. The Commission notes from the observations of the respondent Government that some of the „stickers" worn on the applicant's lapel and on his briefcase were considered offensive to female members of staff and disturbing to children. Having regard to the particular circumstances of the case, the Commission considers that the interference with the applicant's freedom of expression is justified as being necessary in a democratic society for the protection of the rights of others within the meaning of art. 10, par. 2, of the Convention.

9

Eine Kirche (hier: Scientology) ist als solche befähigt, Rechte aus Art. 9 EMRK als Beschwerdeführerin geltend zu machen.

Die Gewährleistung freier Religionsausübung erstreckt sich nicht auf Werbeanzeigen, die - ungeachtet eines religiösen Gegenstandes - nach ihrer Gestaltung auf einen kommerziellen Zweck ausgerichtet sind.

Art. 9, 10, 14, 27 § 2 a.F. EMRK
EKMR, Beschluss vom 5. Mai 1979 - No. 7805/77
(Church of Scientology u.a. ./. Schweden)[1] -

SUMMARY OF THE FACTS

The application was introduced by the „Church of Scientology" in Sweden and by X., one of the ministers.

In 1973, the applicant church placed an advertisement in its periodical which is circulated amongst its members which read as follows:

„Scientology technology of today demands that you have your own E-meter. The E-meter (Hebbard Electrometer) is an electronic instrument for measuring the mental state of an individual and changes of the state.

---

[1] DR 16, 68.

There exists no way to clear without an E-meter. Price: 850 CR. For international members 20% discount: 780 CR."

The applicants define the E-meter as follows „A religious artifact used to measure the state of electrical characteristics of the ‚static field' surrounding the body and believed to reflect or indicate whether or not the confessing person has been relieved of the spiritual impediment of his sins".

Having received various complaints, the Consumer Ombudsman (Konsumentombudsmannen), basing himself on the 1970 Marketing Improper Practices Act (Lagen om otillbörlig marknadsföring) introduced an action before the Market Court (Marknadsomstolen) requesting an injunction against the applicants prohibiting the use of certain passages in the advertisement for the E-meter. After having heard expert witnesses, the Court granted the injunction. A petition for the reopening of the case (Resning) was rejected by the Supreme Court.

THE LAW

[1] The Church of Scientology and Pastor X. claim that the injunction by the Market Court on 19 February 1976 relating to their advertisements of the Hubbard Electrometer (E-meter) violates their freedom of religion and expression in a discriminatory way contrary to art. 9, 10 and 14 of the Convention.

[2] However, before the Commission can consider these complaints two preliminary matters should be clarified. The first matter concerns the question of who can properly be considered as the applicant in the present case.

Under art. 25 (1) of the Convention the Commission may receive petitions from any person, nongovernmental organisation or group of individuals claiming to be the victim of a violation by one of the High Contracting Parties of the rights set forth in the Convention. Pastor X. is such a person.

In respect of the Church, the Commission has previously applied the rule according to which a corporation being a legal and not a natural person is incapable of having or exercising the rights mentioned in art. 9 (1) of the Convention (see Appl.-No. 3796/66, CD 29, p. 70). The Commission has considered that the Church itself is protected in its rights under art. 9 through the rights granted to its members (see Appl.-No. 7374/76, DR 5, p. 157). In accordance with this view it would be open to named individual members of the Church to lodge an application under art. 25, in effect, on the Church's behalf. This would cover for example the five named members of the governing board who decided to lodge the application.

The Commission, however, would take this opportunity to revise its view as expressed in Appl.-No. 3798/68. It is now of the opinion that the above distinction between the Church and its members under art. 9 (1) is essentially artificial. When a church body lodges an application under the Convention, it does so in reality, on behalf of its members. It should therefore be accepted that a church body is capable of possessing and exercising the rights contained in art. 9 (1) in its own capacity as a representative of its members. This interpretation is in part supported from the first paragraph of art. 10 which, through its reference to „enterprises", foresees that a nongovernmental organisation like the applicant Church is capable of having and exercising the right to freedom of expression.

Accordingly, the Church of Scientology, as a nongovernmental organisation, can properly be considered to be an applicant within the meaning of art. 25 of the Convention.

[3] The second preliminary matter relates to whether the applicants have complied with the requirements concerning exhaustion of domestic remedies and with the six months' rule in art. 26. *(wird ausgeführt)*

[4] The applicants complain of an unjustified interference with a right to express a religious opinion in the context of the advertisement for sale of an E-meter.

Art. 9 (1) provides inter alia that everyone has the right to freedom of religion. This right includes the freedom to manifest his religion or belief in worship, teaching, practice and observance.

It is clear that the effect of the Market Court's injunction only concerns the use of certain descriptive words concerning the E-meter, namely that it is „an invaluable aid to measuring man's mental state and changes in it". The Market Court did not prevent the Church from selling the E-meter or even advertising it for sale as such. Nor did the Court restrict in any way the acquisition, possession or use of the E-meter.

The issue, therefore, to be determined is whether the restriction actually imposed on the commercial description of the E-meter could be considered to constitute an interference with the manifestation of a religious belief in practice within the meaning of art. 9 (1).

The Commission is of the opinion that the concept, contained in the first paragraph of art. 9, concerning the manifestation of a belief in practice does not confer protection on statements of purported religious belief which appear as selling „arguments" in advertisements of a purely commercial nature by a religious group. In this connection the Commission would draw a distinction, however, between advertisements which are merely „informational" or „descriptive" in character and commercial advertisements offering objects for sale. Once an advertisement enters into the latter sphere, although it may concern religious objects central to a particular need, statements of religious content represent, in the Commission's view, more the manifestation of a desire to market goods for profit than the manifestation of a belief in practice, within the proper sense of that term. Consequently the Commission considers that the words used in the advertisement under scrutiny fall outside the proper scope of art. 9 (1) and that therefore there has been no interference with the applicants' right to manifest their religion or beliefs in practice under that article.

It follows therefore that this complaint must be rejected as incompatible with the provisions of the Convention within the meaning of art. 27 (2).

[5] The restrictions imposed on the applicants' advertisements rather fall to be considered under art. 10. Art. 10 (1) secures to everyone the right to freedom of expression. This right includes freedom to hold opinions and to receive and impart information and ideas without interference by a public authority.

In the Commission's view the applicants are not prevented from holding their opinion on the religious character of the E-meter. However, they were imparting ideas about that opinion and the Market Court prohibited them from continuing to use a certain wording. This was an interference with the applicants' freedom to impart ideas under art. 10 (1).

Art. 10 (2) permits restrictions on the exercise of these freedoms as are prescribed by law and are necessary in a democratic society, inter alia, for the protection of health or morals and for the protection of the reputation or rights of others.

In assessing whether the requirements of art. 10 (2) have been respected the Commission must have regard to the principles developed in the jurisprudence under the Convention (e.g. Handyside Case, Judgment by the European Court of Human Rights, 7 December 1977, par. 42-59). It observes first, therefore, that the basis in law for the injunction issued by the Market Court was the Marketing (Improper Practices) Act 1970. Consequently, the Commission finds that the restriction imposed on the applicants' freedom to impart ideas was prescribed by law within the meaning of art. 10 (2) of the Convention.

The Marketing Act aimed at protecting the rights of consumers. This aim is a legitimate aim under art. 10 (2), being for the protection of the rights of others in a democratic society.

The remaining question to be examined concerns the „necessity" of the measure challenged by the applicants. It emerges from the case law of the Convention organs that the „necessity" test cannot be applied in absolute terms, but required the assessment of various factors. Such factors include the nature of the right involved, the degree of interference, i.e. whether it was proportionate to the legitimate aim pursued, the nature of the public interest and the degree to which it requires protection in the circumstances of the case.

In considering this question the Commission again attaches significance to the fact that the „ideas" were expressed in the context of a commercial advertisement. Although the Commission is not of the opinion that commercial „speech" as such is outside the protection conferred by art. 10 (1), it considers that the level of protection must be less than that accorded to the expression of „political" ideas, in the broadest sense, with which the values underpinning the concept of freedom of expression in the Convention are chiefly concerned (see Handyside Case, supra cit, par. 49).

Moreover, the Commission has had regard to the fact that most European countries that have ratified the Convention have legislation which restricts the free flow of commercial „ideas" in the interests of protecting consumers from misleading or deceptive practices. Taking both these observations into account the Commission considers that the test of „necessity" in the second paragraph of art. 10 should therefore be a less strict one when applied to restraints imposed on commercial „ideas".

The Commission notes that the applicants' periodical in which the advertisement appeared was circulated in 300 copies to members of the Church. However the Market Court concluded that the advertisements were designed to stimulate the interests both of persons outside the Church as well as its own members in acquiring an E-meter and were thus designed to promote its sales. In arriving at this conclusion the Court had regard to the following factors:

1. that the magazine although distributed only to members might be spread by members to other persons who could be enticed to purchase an E-meter

2. that the advertisement does not appear to limit sale of an E-meter to members only or priests only or those studying for the priesthood.

3. in the advertisements readers are encouraged to seek „international membership" which has the advantage of entitling such members to lower prices for books, tape recordings and E-meters. Such statements were not limited either to priests or those studying for the priesthood.

Finally the Market Court deemed that the advertisements were misleading and that it was important to safeguard the interest of consumers in matters of marketing activities by religious communities and especially in the present case where the consumer would be particularly susceptible to selling arguments.

The Commission considers that in principle it should attach considerable weight to the above analysis and findings of the Market Court.

The Commission further notes that the Market Court did not prohibit the applicants from advertising the E-meter and did not issue the injunction under penalty of a fine. The Court chose what would appear to be the least restrictive measure open to it, namely the prohibition of a certain wording in the advertisements. Consequently, the Commission cannot find that the injunction against the applicants was disproportionate to the aim of consumer protection pursued.

Having regard to the above, the Commission therefore accepts that the injunction granted by the Market Court was necessary in a democratic society for the protection of the rights of others, i.e. consumers.

[6] The applicants claim finally that the injunction by the Market Court was discriminatory and contrary to art. 14 of the Convention. Art. 14 provides as follows:

„The enjoyment of the rights and freedoms set forth in this Convention shall be secured without discrimination on any ground such as sex, race, colour, language, religion, political or other opinion, national or social origin, association with a national minority, property, birth or other status."

It appears that the Consumer Ombudsman had received a number of complaints from the public against the applicant Church in relation to the E-meter and other matters. He therefore instituted proceedings before the Market Court. The case file does not, consequently, disclose that the authorities singled out the applicants for special attention. Nor is there any indication that the authorities have deliberately refrained from intervening against comparable advertisements by other religious communities. The application does not, therefore, disclose that the applicants have been subjected to any differential treatment.

In these circumstances there is no basis for any further examination of the complaint in the light of art. 14.

[7] It follows therefore that the applicants' complaints under art. 10 and art. 14 in conjunction with art. 9 and art. 10 must be rejected as manifestly ill-founded within the meaning of art. 27 (2) of the Convention.

For these reasons, the Commission declares this application inadmissible.

10

Die Gewährleistung von Religionsfreiheit schützt religiöse Bekenntnisse nicht vor jeder Form von Kritik, jedoch kann ein Eingreifen des Staates geboten sein, wenn hierdurch die Entfaltung von Religionsfreiheit in der Öffentlichkeit gefährdet erscheint.

Die Rechtsschutzgarantie eröffnet für eine Personengruppe den Zivilrechtsweg wegen Ansprüchen auf Schutz der eigenen Ehre (right to protect its own reputation) nur, wenn dies auch im nationalen Recht vorgesehen ist.

Eine Kirche oder ihre Mitglieder können, wenn sie sich in ihrer sozialen Geltung beeinträchtigt sehen, aus der Gewährleistung von Religionsfreiheit kein zivilprozessuales Klagerecht wegen Volksverhetzung nach schwedischem Recht („hets mot fokgrupp") herleiten.

Art. 6, 9 EMRK
EKMR, Beschluss vom 14. Juli 1980 - No. 8282/78
(Church of Scientology u.a. ./. Schweden)¹ -

SUMMARY OF THE RELEVANT FACTS

In November 1975, a local Swedish newspaper published certain statements made by a Professor of theology in the course of a lecture, including the following passage: „Scientology in the most untruthful movement
there is. It is the Cholera of spiritual life. That is how dangerous it is".

In May 1976, the Church of Scientology requested the Chancellor of
Justice (Justieiekanselern) to initiate criminal proceedings for „agitation
against a group" („hets mot fokgrupp"). He refused the request pointing
out that a request of that kind ought to be addressed to the public prosecutor in due time and not, as in the present case, four days before the ex-
piring of the period of limitation.

In August 1976, the Church instituted proceedings for damages
against the publisher of the newspaper concerned. After the judge of first
instance and the court of appeal had held that the Church was a competent plaintiff, the Supreme Court held on appeal that it was not qualified
to bring an action since the protection of a group could not be obtained
through the civil proceedings in question.

THE LAW (Extracts)

1. The Commission notes first of all, that this application is brought by
two applicants, namely the Church of Scientology on the one hand, and
128 named applicants, on the other. The Commission recalls that in Application No. 7805/77 (X. and Scientology v. Sweden, DR 16, p. 68;
KirchE-EU S. 18) it recognised the competence of a Church body to lodge
an application in its own capacity.

2. The applicants complain of the decision of the Swedish Supreme
Court to the effect that the Church of Scientology had no competence to
bring either civil or criminal proceedings in respect of alleged „agitation"
against it contrary to Chapter 16, sec. 8, of the Penal Code and Chapter 7, sec. 4, of the Freedom of the Press Act.

3. Art. 9 of the Convention secures the right to „freedom of thought,
conscience and religion". It further states that „this right includes freedom to change his religion or belief and freedom, either alone or in community with others and in public or private, to manifest his religion or
belief, in worship, teaching, practice and observance".

4. The Commission does not consider that it is an element of the concept of freedom of religion, as set forth in this provision that the Church

---

¹ DR 21, 109.

of Scientology or its individual members should be able to bring civil or criminal proceeding based on alleged ‚agitation‘ against it as a group contrary to provisions of the Swedish Criminal law. It considers that this provision seeks to protect the manifestation of religious beliefs in worship, teaching, practice and observance and the freedom to change one's religion.

5. The Commission is not of the opinion that a particular creed or confession can derive from the concept of freedom of religion a right to be free from criticism. Nevertheless the Commission does not exclude the possibility of criticism or ‚agitation‘ against a church or religious group reaching such a level (hat it might endanger freedom of religion and where a tolerance of such behaviour by the authorities could engage State responsibility. However, the Commission does not consider that such an issue arises on the facts of the present case. In reaching this conclusion it notes that the remarks reported in the newspaper article were made in the course of an academic lecture by a professor of theology and not in a context which could render the remarks inflammatory. Moreover, it has not been shown that either the Church of Scientology or its members have been prevented in any way as a consequence of these published remarks from „manifesting their beliefs" in the ways enumerated by this provision.

6. *Accordingly, this complaint must be rejected as manifestly ill-founded under art. 27 (2) of the Convention.*

Art. 6

[16] The applicants have also complained that the inability of the applicant Church of Scientology to institute „civil" proceedings for damages in the present case raises an issue of „access to court" under art. 6 (1) of the Convention.

[17] Art. 6 (1) provides *inter alia* that

„*In the determination of his civil rights and obligations of any criminal charge against him, everyone is entitled to a fair and public hearing within a reasonable time by an independent and impartial tribunal established by law.*"

However, the question arises whether or not the proceedings the applicant sought to bring involved the determination of „civil rights" within the meaning of this provision.

[18] The Commission notes that the European Court of Human Rights in the König case reaffirmed the autonomous nature of the concept of „civil rights" and obligations. However, the Court attached certain weight to the Status and character of the right in question under national law. It stated as follows:

„*... it nevertheless does not consider that, in this context, the legislation of the State concerned is without importance. Whether or not a right is to be regarded* *as civil within the meaning of this expression in the Convention must be determined by reference to the Substantive content and effects of the right - and not its legal classification - under the domestic law of the State concerned. In the exercise of its supervisory function, the Court must also take account of the object and purpose of the Convention and of the national legal system of the other Contracting States ..." (Judgment of 21 June 1978, par. 89).*

[19] The right, whose vindication is sought, in the present case concerns the protection of a group from „expressions of contempt" or protection of the reputation of the group. The Commission notes that national legislation and the Swedish Supreme Court does not recognise such a „right" entitling the group to seek damages in civil proceedings before national courts. Although the Commission has held on several occasions that the right of an individual to protect his reputation can be regarded as a ‚civil right' within the meaning of art. 6 (1), (see e.g. Application No. 7116/75, DR 7. 90) it must attach importance to the characterisation of the right of the group under Swedish law. Moreover, in the exercise of its supervisory jurisdiction, the Commission sees no reason to conclude otherwise. Accordingly, it does not consider that the right of the group in the present case to protect its reputation can be considered a „civil right" under art. 6 (1).

[20] Finally, insofar as this complaint concerns the right of the named individuals in the application to bring proceedings, the Commission notes that under Swedish law it would have been open to them to bring an action for defamation as distinct from the civil proceedings actually instituted on the grounds that the remarks against the Church of Scientology adversely affected their reputation. This it could not be claimed that they were denied access to Court.

[21] *It follows therefore that this part of the application must be rejected as incompatible ratione materiae with the provisions of the Convention, and in respect of the individual applicants, manifestly ill-founded, both under art. 27 (2).*

11

Der Begriff „Ausüben" (practice) in Art. 9 § 1 EMRK deckt nicht jede Handlung, die durch Religion oder Weltanschauung motiviert oder beeinflusst ist. Der persönliche Wunsch, auf dem eigenen Grundstück bestattet zu werden, ist als solcher noch nicht Ausdruck von Religion oder Weltanschauung.

Art. 8, 9 EMRK
EKMR, Beschluss vom 10. März 1981
- No. 8741/79 (X. ./. Deutschland)[1] -

SUMMARY OF THE FACTS

The Hamburg administrative authorities refused the applicant the right to have his ashes scattered on his own land on his death. The Administrative Court quashed this decision allowing the applicant to stipulate that his ashes provided they were contained in an urn, be buried on his land. However the Administrative Court of Appeal quashed this judgment and ruled in the same sense as the administrative authorities. The applicant's subsequent appeals were rejected in last instance by the Federal Constitutional Court. The applicant died in the course of the proceedings before the Commission and his son has continued the proceedings in his own name.

THE LAW

The original applicant complained that he was denied the right to practice his religious belief by having his ashes scattered on his own land after his death and that he was obliged to be buried against his personal convictions in a cemetery with Christian symbols. In this connection, he alleged violations of art. 8 and 9 of the Convention.

1. Art. 9 § 1 of the Convention provides that everyone has the right to freedom of thought, conscience and religion. This right includes the freedom to manifest his religion or belief in worship, practice and observance.

---

[1] DR 24, 137. Die im vorliegenden Beschluss und auch sonst von der EuCommHR und dem EuCHR häufig zitierte Entscheidung in dem Verfahren Arrowsmith ./. Vereinigtes Königreich (Nr. 7050/75, DR 8, 123 u. DR 19, 5 [Report 12.10.1978]) betrifft keine Religionssache, sondern die Frage, ob das Verteilen von Flugblättern pazifistischen Inhalts den Schutz aus Art. 9 EMRK genießt. Sie wird aber offenbar als richtungweisend für die Eingrenzung des Schutzbereichs von Art. 9 EMRK angesehen; vgl. z.B. in diesem Band die Entscheidungen S. 56, S. 66, S. 70, S. 87, S. 110, S. 123, S. 155, S. 169, S. 301. Die Kernstelle EuCommHR DR 19, 5, Ziff. 71, lautet: „The Commission considers that the term 'practice' as employed in Article 9.1. does cover each act which is motivated or influenced by a religion or a belief. It is true that the public declarations proclaiming generally the idea of pacifism and urging the acceptance of a commitment to non-violence may be considered as a normal and recognised manifestation of pacifist belief. However, when the actions of individuals do not actually express the belief concerned they cannot be considered to be as such protected by Article 9.1, even when they are motivated or influenced by it."

The question arises whether the applicant's wish to have his ashes scattered in his garden may fall within the ambit of the right to freedom to religion and may therefore be seen as a belief protected by art. 9 § 1.

The applicant saw a violation of art. 9 in the obligation to be buried in a public cemetery. The Commission observes, however, that the applicant is not obliged to have a religious funeral and a tomb with Christian symbols. On the contrary he is free to have his tomb decorated according to his personal wishes. Art. 9 § 1 of the Convention does not confer on him the right to prevent other people from individually decorating their tombs in a public cemetery including the decoration with religious symbols.

It remains to be determined whether or not the applicant's wish to be buried on his own land according to his religious beliefs is protected by art. 9 § 1 as being the manifestation of a belief in practice. The Commission recalls that the term „practice" as employed in art. 9 § 1 does not cover each act which is motivated or influenced by a religion or a belief (cf. Arrowsmith v. the United Kingdom, Report of the Commission, par. 71).

The Commission considers that in the present case the applicant's wish to be buried on his own land cannot be considered as a manifestation of belief in practice in the sense of art. 9 § 1 of the Convention. The desired action has certainly a strong personal motivation. However, the Commission does not find that it is a manifestation of any belief in the sense that some coherent view on fundamental problems can be seen as being expressed thereby. The decisions of the German authorities and courts did not interfere with the exercise of his rights under this provision.

2. The applicant's complaint must also be examined under art. 8 of the Convention which secures to everyone the right to respect for his private live.

It may be doubted whether or not this right includes the right of a person to choose the place and determine the modalities of his burial. Whilst those arrangements are made for a time after life has come to an end, this does not mean that no issue concerning such arrangements may arise under art. 8 since persons may feel the need to express their personality by the way they arrange how they are buried. The Commission therefore accepts that the refusal of the German authorities to allow the applicant to have his ashes scattered in his garden on his death is so closely related to private life that it comes within the sphere of art. 8 of the Convention.

The next question which must be answered in the present case is whether the contested decision of the German authorities which was in accordance with the legislation on cemeteries constitutes an interference with the right to respect for private life of the original applicant.

While a large proportion of the law existing in a given State has some immediate or remote effect on the individual's possibility of freely pursuing the development and fulfilment of his personality, not all of these can be considered to constitute an interference with the right to respect for private life in the sense of art. 8 of the Convention.

The Commission notes that in the present case the legislation on cemeteries gives everybody a certain freedom in choosing the means of his burial. Although burials of corpses and crematorial ashes out-side cemeteries are generally forbidden, exceptions are permitted in particular cases. Everybody can choose between a burial of his corpse or a cremation. There is no obligation to have a religious funeral and a tomb with Christian symbols.

The legislation concerning cemeteries is intended to protect public interest. The legislator had regard to such factors as to securing a peaceful resting place for human remains, an adequate treatment of corpses and crematorial ashes, the protection of public health and public order and also urban and road planning.

In this respect the Commission observes that there is not one Member State of the Convention which has not, in one way or an-other, set up legal rules in this matter. The German Federal Constitutional Court has referred to the regulation for burials in other European countries. It can be seen therefrom that the choice of the circumstances and of the place of burial is generally not left solely to the individual's discretion. The Commission therefore finds that not every regulation for burials constitutes an interference with the right to respect for private life.

It considers that art. 8 § 1 of the Convention cannot be interpreted as meaning that burials of corpses or crematorial ashes are, as a principle, solely a matter of the persons directly concerned.

In view of this situation the Commission does not find that the legislation on which the refusal of the original applicant's request was based constitutes an interference with his right to respect for his private life.

An examination by the Commission of the application as it has been submitted does not therefore disclose any appearance of a violation of the rights and freedoms set out in the Convention and in particular in the above articles.

It follows that the application is manifestly ill-founded within the meaning of art. 27, par. 2 of the Convention.

For these reasons, the Commission declares this application inadmissible.

12

Die Gewährleistung freier Religionsausübung „allein oder in Gemeinschaft mit anderen" schließt beide Handlungsformen als gleichrangig ein und eröffnet für die Staatsgewalt keine Wahlmöglichkeit.

In Anbetracht der Erfordernisse eines Schulsystems kann ein Lehrer die Berücksichtigung persönlicher Gebetszeiten (hier: Freistellung zur Teilnahme am muslimischen Freitagsgebet) jedenfalls dann nicht verlangen, wenn er das Dienstverhältnis in dieser Hinsicht vorbehaltlos begründet hat.

Art. 9, 14, 27 § 2 a.F. EMRK
EKMR, Beschluss vom 12. März 1981
- No. 8160/78 (X. ./. Vereinigtes Königreich)[1] -

THE FACTS (Auszug)

[1] The applicant, a citizen of the United Kingdom, was born in India in 1940. He is a school teacher by profession and living in London.

[2] The applicant is a devout Muslim. It is the religious duty of every Muslim to offer prayers on Fridays and, if considerations of distance permit, to attend a mosque for this purpose.

[3] From September 1968 until April 1975 the applicant was employed by the Inner London Education Authority (ILEA) as a full-time primary school teacher. His contract did not specify days or hours of attendance. His employment was subject to the rules and regulations of the ILEA which provide for standard school hours of 9.30 a.m. to 12.30 p.m. and 2 p.m. to 4.30 p.m. from Monday to Friday. School governors may, however, vary school hours to suit local circumstance and, in practice, the lunch hour in certain schools is shortened to less than one-and-a-half hours. Accordingly, the extent of the lunch break varies from school to school.

[4] From his appointment in 1968 until 1972 the applicant was employed, in Division 8 of the ILEA, at the W. School for Maladjusted Children, which was some distance away from any mosque. During that period he made no request to be allowed time off for attending a mosque.

[5] After one year's study leave the applicant returned to the W. School and was then advised that he was being moved to another school in the Division. He states that it was at this point that he decided that, if he was to move, then he might sensibly move to a school located near a mosque.

[6] After his transfer, in February 1974, to Division 5 of the ILEA the applicant found himself nearer to mosques. At his first school in that Division, a school for maladjusted children in which he was a supernumerary teacher, the headmaster allowed him to be absent from school for a short period after the mid-day break on Fridays in order to attend prayers at a mosque. The applicant had a teaching period after the Friday mid-day break but his colleagues did not object to his having time off

---

[1] DR 22, 27.

to attend the mosque and were prepared to accommodate him in this respect.

[7] The applicant was next employed, still as a supernumerary teacher, at the C. School. There, according to the judgment of the Court of Appeal, „he did not at first ask for permission to attend a mosque for Friday prayers but the headmistress, Miss G., heard of his intention to do so and obtained advice from the Divisional Office that she could not stop him from going but should not give him permission to do so, and on his later asking for permission to go she gave him these answers and insisted that he should be back by 1.30, at the end of the mid-day break, but he never returned before 2.20 with the result that Friday afternoon teaching periods had to be adjusted until he returned and, although this adjustment was not difficult, the other staff, Miss G. said, had to accommodate him all the time". The applicant states at par. 2 of his petition to the Commission that Friday prayers „took place at 1.00 p.m. and lasted for about one hour, and involved an absence of about three quarters of an hour from the afternoon teaching session".

[8] With regard to the above statement of the Court of Appeal, the applicant has in the present proceedings submitted that he „did inform the headmistress on the Friday that he wished to attend the mosque. Accordingly, it is not quite correct to imply that he did not approach her for permission. At this point the applicant told the headmistress what had happened at other schools. The headmistress stated that it would not be a problem for her to arrange but that she would require the ILEA to consent. It was she who suggested that the applicant write to the ILEA. It is wrong to state that Friday afternoon teaching periods had to be adjusted until the applicant returned because, at this time, the applicant was not a class teacher. He had no timetable. His role was to approach a class with an existing teacher and to pick out a group for special tuition, e.g. to do reading."

[9] According to the Court of Appeal, the applicant „was next employed at the Primary School where he asked for similar permission to attend a mosque for Friday prayers and the headmaster, Mr W., refused this request and reported his refusal to the Divisional Office, but the (applicant) disregarded the refusal and attended the mosque with the result that on one Friday the headmaster had a class without a teacher until the (applicant) returned."

[10] The applicant submits with regard to the above statement of the Court of Appeal that he „was a supernumerary teacher. Each form had a class teacher and, accordingly, it cannot be correct that the headmaster had a class without a teacher until he returned".

[11] The applicant was next employed, still as a supernumerary teacher, at the U. Primary School for one term from September 1974. The headmaster, having previously consulted the Divisional Office, refused his request to be allowed to attend a mosque on Fridays. The applicant

attended the mosque in spite of this refusal, and the deputy headmaster reported that there were grumbles about this from the staff.

[12] Finally, for the first term of 1975, the applicant was employed as a stand-in teacher at a Roman Catholic primary school in U. The headmaster was informed by the Divisional Office that the applicant had been refused permission to be absent during school hours on Fridays. The applicant (who at this school was allowed to use a room for prayers) continued to take time off on Fridays.

[13] During his employment in Division 5 of the ILEA the applicant, by letter of 5 April 1974, formally claimed the right to go to the mosque for Friday prayer. He invoked the Education Act 1944 and requested that the necessary arrangements be made in the school time-table.

[14] By letter of 9 October 1974 the ILEA informed the applicant that his only recourse was to relinquish full-time employment and to apply for appointment as a part -time temporary terminal teacher to work four-and-a-half days a week only. By a further letter of 29 October the ILEA refused to grant the applicant leave of absence „for any part of Friday afternoon sessions".

[15] By letter of 13 January 1975 the ILEA finally informed the applicant that, if he continued to take time off on Friday afternoons, there would be no alternative but to vary his appointment from full-time to four-and-a-half days week.

[16] In response to this letter the applicant wrote on 27 January 1975 that he preferred to be dismissed rather than accept part-time teaching. On 29 January he gave notice of resignation to take effect at the beginning of the Easter holidays.

[17] The applicant was unemployed from April to December 1975. Shortly after his resignation, because of financial pressure, he reapplied to the ILEA to take up their offer of a part-time teaching post. The ILEA refused for the nine months referred to but following the Tribunal hearing agreed to take the applicant on. He became re-employed on the basis of a four-and-a-half day week, spending two-and-a-half days in one school and two days in another school. For the remainder of his old contract salary was deducted for every Friday afternoon that he was absent.

[18] On 7 July 1975 the applicant appealed to an Industrial Tribunal, contending that his resignation, having been brought about by the conduct of the ILEA, constituted unfair dismissal, within the meaning of the Trade Union and Labour Relations Act 1974.

[19] The Tribunal heard evidence from an Islamic religious leader, Dr P., who stated that Friday prayers to the Muslim were like Saturday to the Jew or Sunday to the Christian. To absent oneself from Friday prayer was a sin, so much as that, in an Islamic country like Saudi Arabia, to absent oneself three times running without an excuse was to run the risk of beheading. The only acceptable excuses were to be a woman, a child, a traveller, a slave or to be sick. In fact no beheading for failure to attend

Friday prayers was carried out in Saudi Arabia because everyone complied with this obligation. Dr P. considered that, if there were three other Muslims in the school, the applicant could pray with them, but if not, he was required to attend a mosque, unless it was too far from the school; in that case he could say prayers in a quiet place of worship at the school. Dr P. stated that negotiations were pending with the Department of Employment whereby employees would be allowed to go to the mosque as a matter of right. Some employers in the Midlands apparently allowed it already.

[20] Mr A., Assistant Education Officer of the ILEA, stated in evidence that he knew of no negotiation at national level as mentioned by Dr P. The ILEA must have hundreds of Muslim teachers, and none had ever before complained that the present problem existed.

[21] On 10 November 1975 the Industrial Tribunal dismissed the application, holding „that as a matter of contract the applicant was bound to be in school on Friday afternoons" and that he was required „to work full-time". Clause 9 of the ILEA Staff Code[1] could not in the Tribunal's view cover regular Friday absence to pray in the mosque. Nor could the applicant, for this purpose, rely on sec. 30 of the Education Act 1944.[2] The Tribunal also considered „whether on general grounds the respondents were being unreasonable and whether, despite the contract of employment, they could or should have accommodated him and adjusted his timetable accordingly" and found on balance „that the respondents were not being unreasonable".

---

[1] „Religious observance: teachers other than supply teachers ... who, for reasons of conscience, have objections to working on a particular day in term time, it being a day of special obligation in their religion, shall be allowed leave with pay on the understanding that such leave shall be restricted to days which are generally recognised in their religion as days when no work may be done."

[2] Without a proviso, which does not appear relevant in the present case. Section 30 reads as follows: „Subject as hereinafter provided, no person shall be disqualified by reason of his religious opinions, or of his attending or omitting to attend religious worship, from being a teacher in a county school or in any voluntary school, or from being otherwise employed for the purposes of such a school; and no teacher in any such he school shall be required to give religious instruction or receive any less emolument or be deprived of, or disqualified for, any promotion or other advantage by reason of the fact that he does or does not give religious instruction or by reason of his religious opinions or of his attending or omitting to attend religious worship: Provided that, save in so far as they require that a teacher shall not receive any less emolument or be deprived of, or disqualified for, any promotion or other advantage by reason of the fact that he gives religious instruction or by reason of his religious opinions or of his attending religious worship, the provisions of this Section shall not apply with respect to a teacher in an aided school or with respect to a reserved teacher in any controlled school or special agreement school".

[22] The applicant's petition for a review of this decision was on 10 December 1975 refused by the Tribunal.

[23] The applicant now appealed, on points of law, to the Employment Appeal Tribunal, again relying on the above provisions. He stated *inter alia* that, as he had always been back at school at 2.15 p.m. on Fridays, his attendance at the mosque meant that he missed the first period on those afternoons (from 1.30 to 2.15 p.m.). In the discussions prior to his resignation he had pointed out that, as he had free periods during the week, his time-table could easily be arranged to insert a free period for the first part of Friday afternoon. He thus was asking only for three-quarters of an hour off in every week, and without pay.

[24] The Employment Appeal Tribunal dismissed the appeal on 8 June 1976, substantially on the grounds already given by the Industrial Tribunal in its decision of 10 November 1975.

[25] Leave to appeal to the Court of Appeal (on points of law) was refused by the Employment Appeal Tribunal on 21 July, but granted by the Court of Appeal on 26 July 1976.

[26] On 22 March 1977 the Court of Appeal (Lord Denning, Master of the Rolls, Lord Justice Scarman and Lord Justice Orr) dismissed the appeal. Lord Justice Scarman dissenting.

[41] The Court of Appeal did not give leave to appeal to the House of Lords.

[42] On 14 July 1977 the House of Lords, on report of their Appeal Committee, refused the applicant's petition for leave to appeal to their Court.

COMPLAINT

The applicant contends that the interpretation, by the Tribunals and the Court of Appeal of sec. 30 of the Education Act 1944 contravenes art. 9 of the Convention. The construction of sec. 30 as held by the Court of Appeal „would mean that a Muslim, who took his religious duty seriously, could never accept employment as a full-time teacher, but must be content with the lesser emoluments of part-time service, and would thus also be excluded from opportunities for promotion".

THE LAW

Preliminary observations

[1] The applicant complains that he was forced to resign from his post as a full-time school teacher because he was refused permission to attend a mosque for congressional prayer, and thus to miss about 45 minutes of classwork in the beginning of the afternoon, on those Fridays which are

school days. The Government submit, as a preliminary observation, that the Convention does not protect the right as such to employment.

[2] According to the Commission's case-law, the right to hold a position in public service is not as such guaranteed by the Convention (see Appl.-No. 3788/68, Coll. 35, 56 (71), with further references) but the dismissal of a State official may in certain circumstances raise an issue under specific Convention provisions, such as art. 9 (Appl.-No. 7374/76 - X. v. Denmark, DR 5, 157-158, KirchE-EU S. 12) or art. 10 (Appl.-No. 8010/77 - X v. the United Kingdom DR 16, 101, KirchE-EU S. 16). The Commission considers that this jurisprudence applies also in case of alleged forced resignation, or variation of employment, like that of the present applicant. It here notes that, in the United Kingdom, the legislation prohibiting unfair dismissal may also be invoked by employees who claim that they have been unfairly forced to resign. The Commission has consequently examined the applicant's complaint, that he was forced to resign from full-time employment, under the specific provisions of art. 9 and of art. 14 in conjunction with art. 9 of the Convention.

[3] With regard to the applicant's claim, that the school authorities should have arranged their time-table so that he could attend Friday prayers, the Commission further observes that the object of art. 9 is essentially that of protecting the individual against unjustified interference by the State, but that there may also be positive obligations inherent in an effective „respect" for the individual's freedom of religion *(cf. mutatis mutandis* the judgment of the European Court of Human Rights in the Marckx case, p. 15, par. 31).

As to Art. 9 of the Convention

[4] The freedom of religion guaranteed by art. 9 (1) of the Convention includes the right of everyone to manifest his religion in worship „either alone or in community with others". The applicant's complaint is confined to the freedom to manifest his religion in worship „in community with others". The Government accept that attending the mosque amounts to manifesting religion in worship „in community with others" but suggest that it may suffice to satisfy art. 9 (1) if the right to manifest one's religion „alone" is granted; the interpretation that both possibilities must always be available would have serious implications for the employment of persons belonging to religious minorities which do not have many places of worship. The applicant contests this interpretation.

[5] The Commission has examined the ordinary meaning of the guarantee of the freedom of religion in par. I in the context both of art. 9 of the Convention as a whole, taking into account the object and purpose of the Convention. It notes that the right to manifest one's religion „in community with others" has always been regarded as an essential part of the freedom of religion and finds that the two alternatives „either alone

or in community with others" in art. 9 (1) cannot be considered as mutually exclusive, or as leaving a choice to the authorities, but only as recognising that religion may be practised in either form. It observes at the same time that the freedom of religion is not absolute but under the Convention subject to the limitations of art. 9 (2). The Commission concludes that the applicant may under art. 9 (1) claim the right to manifest his religion „in community with others".

[6] It is, however, disputed between the parties whether the applicant's attendance of Friday prayers at the mosque on school days was during the relevant period-from his transfer to Division 5 of the ILEA until his resignation in 1975-required by Islam and thus a „necessary part" of his religious practice. The Government submit that Islam would have permitted the applicant's absence from the mosque because of his contractual obligation to teach at the school, and that his attendance at the mosque was therefore not „necessary" in the sense of the Commission's case-law (Appl.-No. 5442/74, DR 1, pp, 41-42). The applicant replies that Appl.-No. 5442/74, concerning a prisoner, is not a good analogy for his present application and that, in any case, he was during the relevant period required by Islam to attend prayers at the mosque.

[7] The Commission observes that its decision in Appl.-No. 5442/74 took into account that applicant's situation as a detained person. In the case of a person at liberty, the question of the „necessity" of a religious manifestation, as regards its time and place, will not normally arise under art. 9. Nevertheless, even a person at liberty may, in the exercise of his freedom to manifest his religion, have to take into account his particular professional or contractual position. The parties' submissions in the present case concerning the „necessity" of the applicant's attendance at the mosque are connected with their discussion of his special contractual obligations as a teacher.

[8] The applicant states that it is the religious duty of every Muslim to offer prayers on Fridays and, if considerations of distance permit, to attend a mosque for this purpose. A mere contractual obligation cannot excuse absence - a man cannot willingly put himself into a position where he cannot attend. When the applicant commenced his employment with the ILEA in 1968 there was only one mosque in the London area and it was physically impossible for him to work with the ILEA and to attend Friday prayers. After his transfer, in February 1974, to Division 5 he found himself nearer to mosques. He was then obliged by his religion to attend Friday prayers.

[9] The Commission observes, however, that, in 1968, the applicant, of his own free will, accepted teaching obligations under his contract with the ILEA, and that it was a result of this contract that he found himself unable „to work with the ILEA and to attend Friday prayers". The contract, and the teaching obligations it implied, continued until its termination in 1975. Between 1968 and 1974 the applicant-without ever rais-

ing this issue with the ILEA-accepted that, because of the contract, he was prevented from attending the mosque during school time. The Commission does not consider that the applicant has convincingly shown that, following his transfer in 1974 to a school „nearer to mosques", he was required by Islam to disregard his continuing contractual obligations vis-à-vis the ILEA, entered into six years earlier in 1968 and accepted throughout the years, and to attend the mosque during school time.

[10] In its interpretation and application of art. 9 of the Convention, the Commission does not, however, find it necessary to pursue this matter further - e.g. by obtaining expert evidence as suggested by the applicant - because it considers that, even if such religious obligation were assumed, it could not, for the reasons given below, justify the applicant's claim under this provision in the circumstances of the present case.

[11] The Commission has already stated that the freedom of religion, as guaranteed by art. 9, is not absolute, but subject to the limitations set out in art. 9 (2). Moreover, it may, as regards the modality of a particular religious manifestation, be influenced by the situation of the person claiming that freedom. The Commission has recognised this in the case of a detained person (Appl.-No. 5442/74, DR 1, pp. 41-42) and in the case of a person with special contractual obligations (Appl.-No. 7374/76, DR 5, pp. 157-158, KirchE-EU S. 12). The latter application was brought by a Danish clergyman who had been required by his church to abandon a certain practice of christening. The Commission then stated, with regard to the clergyman's claim to freedom of religion in the performance of his functions, that the freedom of religion of servants of a State church „is exercised at the moment they accept or refuse employment as clergymen, and their right to leave the church guarantees their freedom of religion in case they oppose its teachings" (Application No. 7374/76, loc. cit. p. 158).

[12] The Commission observes that both the present case and Application No. 7374/76 concern persons with special contractual obligations, but that the present case is distinct from Appl.-No. 7374/76 in particular in two respects: firstly, it does not concern religious manifestations in the course of the performance of professional functions, but absence from work for the performance of such manifestations; secondly, it does not relate to a religious dispute but to a coincidence of teaching obligations and religious duties. In 1968 the applicant, by his contract with the ILEA as interpreted by the domestic courts, accepted teaching obligations including duties on Fridays. According to the applicant, the teaching obligations did not from the beginning, but only following his transfer in 1974 conflict with his religious duty to attend congressional prayers at the mosque.

[13] The Commission considers that its reasoning in Appl.-No. 7374/76 cannot automatically be applied in the present case but must be adapted to its particular circumstances. It finds that, in the present case, the

ILEA was during the relevant period (1974/75) in principle entitled to rely on its contract with the applicant. However, the question arises whether, under art. 9 of the Convention, the ILEA had to give due consideration to his religious position.

[14] The Commission here notes that the applicant did not, when he was first interviewed for his teaching position, nor during the first six years of his employment with the ILEA, disclose the fact that he might require time off during normal school hours for attending prayers at the mosque. The Government state that such a disclosure might have resulted in the applicant being offered only part-time employment. The applicant submits that the United Kingdom should not operate a system in which a job applicant must indicate his religion and thus risk not to be appointed because of his religious obligations. The Commission observes that the present case does not raise the general issue of the confidentiality of information concerning one's religion, but the question whether an employee should inform his employer in advance that he will be absent during a part of the time for which he is engaged. It considers it relevant for the appreciation of the parties' position during the relevant period that the applicant had at no time before and during the first six years of his employment brought to the attention of the ILEA his wish to have time off during normal school hours for attending prayers at the mosque.

[15] Referring to its decision on Application No. 7374/76, the Commission further observes that, throughout his employment with the ILEA between 1968 and 1975, the applicant remained free to resign if and when he found that his teaching obligations conflicted with his religious duties. It notes that, in 1975- the applicant did in fact resign from his five-day employment and that he subsequently accepted a four-and-a-half day employment enabling him to comply with his duties as a Muslim on Fridays.

[16] The applicant points out that his present employment means less not only as regards his pay but also concerning his pension rights, chances of promotion and security of employment. He submits that his case could have been better solved by a re-arrangement of the school timetable permitting his absence for about 45 minutes at the beginning of the afternoon sessions on Fridays. The Government contest this possibility.

[17] The Commission, in its consideration of the parties' submissions, has had regard not only to the particular circumstances of the applicant's case but also to its background, as described in the pleadings. It notes that, during the relevant period, the United Kingdom society was with its increasing Muslim community in a period of transition. New and complex problems arose, *inter alia,* in the field of education, both as regards teachers and students. The parties agree that the applicant's case is not an isolated one and that it raises questions of general importance.

[18] The Government state that separate education systems are administered in England, Wales, Scotland and Northern Ireland and that in none of these countries is the system a centralised one. Teachers are employed either by individual local education authorities or by individual schools and there appears to be no generally agreed practice for dealing with requests by teachers of any religious group (including Muslim teachers) for leave of absence from work in order to meet the requirements of their religion. The Council of Local Education Authorities in England and Wales are at present considering whether to issue guidelines on the subject.

[19] The Commission accepts that the school authorities, in their treatment of the applicant's case on the basis of his contract with the ILEA, had to have regard not only to his religious position, but also to the requirements of the education system as a whole; it notes that the complex education system of the United Kingdom was during the relevant time faced with the task of gradual adaptation to new developments in its society. The Commission is not called upon to substitute for the assessment by the national authorities of what might be the best policy in this field but only to examine whether the school authorities, in relying on the applicant's contract, arbitrarily disregarded his freedom of religion.

[20] It is in this perspective that the Commission has considered the parties' conflicting submissions concerning the applicant's conduct, and his treatment by the school authorities, from his transfer to Division 5 of the ILEA in 1974 until his resignation in 1975. It observes that the Government rely on facts as established in the judgment of the Court of Appeal (see above par. 7 and 9 of „The Facts"); that the judgment was submitted by the applicant when he introduced the application: and that the Court's establishment of the facts was not then, but only in 1980, disputed by the applicant (see par. 8 and 10 of „The Facts"). The Commission also notes from the Government's submissions that the Court relied on evidence given in the domestic proceedings and observes that, in the present proceedings, the applicant has offered no evidence to the contrary. It concludes that, in these circumstances, it must base its examination on the facts as established by the domestic court.

[21] The Commission accordingly notes that the applicant, at his first school in Division 5, was allowed to be absent for a short period after the Friday mid-day break in order to attend prayers at the mosque, but that serious difficulties arose as a result of his unauthorised absence, for the same purpose, from the schools at which he was subsequently employed. The Commission further notes the applicant's various suggestions, as to how the school authorities could and should have solved his problem, and the Government's answers thereto.

[22] Having regard also to the requirements of the education system as described by the Government, the Commission does not find that in 1974/75 the ILEA - or, in their independent capacity, the schools of its

Division 5 at which he was employed - in their treatment of the applicant's case on the basis of his contract did not give due consideration to his freedom of religion.

[23] The Commission concludes that there has been no interference with the applicant's freedom of religion under art. 9 (1) of the Convention.

As to Art. 14 in conjunction with Art. 9 of the Convention

[24] When addressing himself to the Commission the applicant only invoked art. 9 of the Convention. The Commission, noting that in the domestic proceedings his case was dealt with under sec. 30 of the Education Act 1944 as one of alleged religious discrimination, has considered the application also under art. 14 in conjunction with art. 9 of the Convention.

[25] It is not the Commission's task in this connection to express any view on the interpretation and application of national legislation, such as the Education Act 1944, by the competent domestic courts, but only to consider whether the result of this application constitutes discrimination in the sense of art. 14 of the Convention.

[26] Art. 14 safeguards individuals or groups of individuals, placed in comparable situations, from all discrimination in the enjoyment of the rights and freedoms set forth in the other normative provisions of the Convention (Judgment of the European Court of Human Rights in the National Union of Belgian Police case, p. 19, par. 44, with further reference).

[27] It does not appear from the applicant's submissions that, as regards the fulfilment of his contractual teaching obligations in 1974/75, he was either individually or as a member of his religious community treated less favourably by the education authorities than individuals or groups of individuals placed in comparable situations. The applicant refers in his submissions to the position of Jewish *children,* but he has not shown that other *teachers* belonging to religious minorities, e.g. Jewish teachers, received a more favourable treatment than he himself.

[28] The Commission further observes in respect of the general question of religious and public holidays, discussed in the parties' submissions, that, in most countries only the religious holidays of the majority of the population are celebrated as public holidays. Thus Protestant holidays are not always public holidays in Catholic countries and vice versa.

[29] The Commission concludes that there is no appearance of a violation of art. 14 in conjunction with art. 9 of the Convention. It follows that the application, both if considered under art. 9 and if examined under art. 14 in conjunction with art. 9, is manifestly ill-founded within the meaning of art. 27 (2) of the Convention.

For these reasons, the Commission declares this application inadmissible.

13

Sind religiöse Vereinigungen vom Geltungsbereich eines staatlichen Vereinsgesetzes ausgenommen, dann begründet ein vereinsrechtlich begründetes Verbot einer solchen Vereinigung keinen Verstoß gegen Art. 9 EMRK.

Art. 9, 11 EMRK

EKMR, Beschluss vom 15. Oktober 1981 - No. 8652/79 (X. ./. Österreich)[1] -

SUMMARY OF THE FACTS

The applicant, a follower of the Moon sect, founded an association in Vienna in 1973 called „Gesellschaft zur Vereinigung des Weltchristentums" (the Society for Uniting World Christianity). It was dissolved on 4 January 1974 by the competent police authority for activities outside the scope of its statutory aims (art. 24 of the Associations Act (Vereinigungsgesetz) and for having the characteristics of a religious community, which communities are not authorised by law to take the form of an association (art. 3 of the Associations Act).

Shortly afterwards the applicant announced the foundation of another association called „Gesellschaft zur Förderung der Vereinigungskirche" (the Society for the Promotion of the Union Church) whose statutory aim had been defined slightly differently.

The notification of this second association was made to the local administration (Magistrat) in Vienna which prohibited it, this decision being upheld by the Ministry of the Interior. However, by a judgment of 10 June 1975 the Constitutional Court quashed the decision because the local authority had no jurisdiction in the matter.

The case e referred to the competent police authority which again prohibited the association under art. 6 (1) of the aforementioned Act, which prohibits the foundation of an association which seeks to continue the illegal activities of an association which has previously been dissolved by the authorities.

Having unsuccessfully appealed to the Ministry of the Interior, the applicant further appealed to the Constitutional Court, invoking, in particular art. 11 and 14 of the Convention. In a decision of 27 September 1978, the Constitutional Court dismissed the appeal noting that the association had been dissolved in accordance with art. 6, par. I of the said Act and not art. 3(a), which had not been applicable to the case. It found the dissolution justified under art. 11, par. 2 of the Convention.

---

[1] DR 26, 89.

THE LAW

1. The applicant who founded and acted as chairman of two associations intended to provide the organisational framework for the Moon sect in Austria complains of the dissolution of these associations by the authorities which he considers to be in violation of his freedom of religion as guaranteed by art. 9 and of his freedom of association as guaranteed by art. 11 of the Convention.

2. As regards the first of these associations, called „Gesellschaft zur Vereinigung des Weltchristentums" (Society for Uniting World Christianity) which was dissolved on 4 January 1974, the applicant has not exhausted the domestic remedies available to him as required by art. 26 of the Convention, and accordingly the applicant's above complaints insofar as they may be understood as relating to the dissolution of this association must be rejected under art. 27 (3) of the Convention.

3. As regards the prohibition of the second association, called „Gesellschaft zur Förderung der Vereinigungskirche" (Society for the Promotion of the Union Church), the applicant has exhausted the domestic remedies available to him by lodging a constitutional appeal. The Constitutional Court's decision was communicated to him on 20 December 1978 and the present application, filed on 12 June 1979, has therefore been brought within the six months period envisaged by art. 26 of the Convention. The Commission is therefore called upon to deal with the substance of the applicant's above complaints insofar as they are related to the prohibition of the second association.

4. The applicant's principal complaint is that there has been an unjustified interference with his freedom of association contrary to art. 11 of the Convention. The relevant parts of this article read as follows:

(1) Everyone has the right to ... freedom of association with others ...
(2) No restrictions shall be placed on the exercise of these rights other than such as are prescribed by law and are necessary in a democratic society in the interests of national security or public safety, for the prevention of disorder or crime, for the protection of health or morals or for the protection of the rights and freedoms of others ...

a) The association founded by the applicant under the name „Gesellschaft zur Förderung der Vereinigungskirche" was prohibited by the authorities. There can therefore be no doubt that there has been interference with the applicant's right to freedom of association within the meaning of the first paragraph of the above article.

b) The question is then whether this interference can be justified under the second paragraph of the article. This paragraph requires, first, that any restriction of the freedom in question should be prescribed by law, secondly, that it should pursue one of the purposes enumerated there, and thirdly, that it should be necessary in a democratic society.

As regards these requirements, the Commission notes that according to the Constitutional Court the decisive reason justifying the prohibition of the association in question was its continuation of the illegal activities of the formerly dissolved association founded by the applicant. This prohibition was based on art. 6 (1) of the Associations Act and hence „prescribed by law" within the meaning of art. 11 (2) of the Convention. The Commission also considers that it is justifiable under this provision, namely as being necessary in a democratic society for the prevention of disorder, to prohibit an association because it unlawfully continues the activities of a dissolved association. The application of art. 6 (1) of the Associations Act does not therefore in itself give rise to a problem under the Convention.

c) The applicant in the present case claims, however, that this provision was wrongly applied to him and that the true reason why the second association founded by him was prohibited was the fact that like the first association it constituted a religious community, excluded from the application of the Associations Act by virtue of its art. 3 (a). This exclusion of religious communities from the application of the Associations Act would have left him without any legal possibility to organise the group represented by him as an entity recognised by law and having legal personality because there are no alternative forms of organisation available for non-recognised religious communities.

In this connection the Commission first notes the Government's argument that it is not open to the applicant to challenge the application of art. 3 (a) of the Associations Act in this case because in the domestic proceedings he failed to do so at the appropriate time, namely in connection with the dissolution of the first association founded by him The Commission considers, however, that it can leave open the difficult question whether or not the applicant has actually exhausted all domestic remedies in this respect. For even assuming that by his constitutional appeal against the prohibition of the second association he did in fact exhaust the domestic remedies in conformity with art. 26 of the Convention, it nevertheless appears from the Constitutional Court's decision itself that art. 3 of the Associations Act was not considered as decisive. The Constitutional Court even stated that in the case before it art. 3 (a) had not been actually applied by the administrative authorities nor had it been applicable („ergibt sich, dass bei der Erlassung des angefochtenen Bescheides § 3 lit. a VG nicht angewendet wurde und auch nicht anzuwenden war").

This decision by the Constitutional Court was the final domestic decision in the applicant's case and therefore the decision which the Commission must take as the starting point for its examination under the Convention. It shows that the Associations Act was applied in such a way as to allow, in principle, for the establishment even of religious organisations as associations under the Act, notwithstanding the terms of art. 3

(a) thereof. The availability of alternative forms of legal organisation is therefore irrelevant. The applicant's complaint that he was barred from having the group represented by him registered as an association because it was a religious community and that his freedom of association as guaranteed by art. 11 of the Convention has thereby been violated is consequently manifestly ill-founded within the meaning of art. 27 (2) of the Convention.

5. The applicant has finally complained that the prohibition of the association founded by him also amounted to an unjustified interference with his and the association's freedom of religion as guaranteed by art. 9 of the Convention.

The Commission observes, however, that in the present case it has not been substantiated by the applicant that there has been any interference with his freedom of religion as a follower of the Moon sect; in particular it has been shown that the dissolution of the association in which the sect wanted to organise itself did as such interfere with the manifestation of his religion or belief in worship, teaching, practice and observance. As the Government have stressed, the practice even of a non-recognised religion is fully guaranteed in Austria by art. 63 (2) of the Treaty of St. Germain independently from any form of registration. The applicant's allegations of harassments by the police cannot be taken into account in this respect because it is clear from his submissions that these allegations, even if they were substantiated, concern the treatment of other persons and not of the applicant himself. It follows that the applicant's complaint of unjustified interferences with his right to freedom of religion as guaranteed by art. 9 of the Convention is also manifestly ill-founded.

For these reasons, the Commission declares the application inadmissible.

14

Eine Regelung des staatlichen Familienrechts, die eine körperliche Züchtigung von Kindern zwar sanktionslos, aber allgemein verbietet, stellt noch keinen Eingriff in das Elternrecht (familiäre und schulische Erziehung u.a. nach der eigenen religiösen oder weltanschaulichen Überzeugung) dar.

Art. 8 § 1, 9 § 2, 27 § 2 a.F. EMRK, 2 Erstes Zusatzprotokoll
EKMR, Beschluss vom 13. Mai 1982 - No. 8811/79 (X. ./. Schweden)[1] -

---

[1] DR 29, 104.

THE FACTS

The applicants, three couples and one divorcee, are all resident in Sweden and have children aged between 20 months and 12 years. They all belong to a Protestant free church congregation in Stockholm. As such the applicants believe in „traditional" means of bringing up their children and in particular, as an aspect of their religious doctrine, they believe in the necessity of physical punishment of their children, which they justify by reference to Biblical texts (e.g. Proverbs 13:12, Hebrews 12:6) and doctrinal works such as Luther's Large Catechism and Summa Theologiae Moralis (Mekkelbach).

The applicants complain at the restrictions which are imposed by Swedish law on the corporal punishment of children, which are as follows:

Under the Swedish Penal Code, Chapter 3, sec. 5 and 6 (Brottsbalken) the offences of assault and aggravated assault are respectively defined.

Sec. 5 provides:

„A person who inflicts bodily injury, illness or pain on another person, or renders him unconscious or otherwise similarly helpless, shall be sentenced for assault to imprisonment for at most two years or in cases where the offence is a petty one, to pay a fine."

Sec. 6 provides:

„If the offence mentioned in sec. 5 is considered grave, the sentence shall be for aggravated assault to imprisonment for at least one and at most ten years".

The applicants contend that the scope of the application of the criminal offence of assault to cases of parental chastisement of their children was uncertain until January 1979 but that it was widely considered and the applicants believe that parents had a degree of immunity in this respect, which excluded chastisement such as boxing a child's ears, from the scope of the offence.

Hence they refer to the decision of a municipal court which in 1975 acquitted a father who had been accused of maltreating his three year old daughter on the grounds that he had not been proved to exceed „the right of corporal chastisement that a guardian has towards a child in his custody."

On 1 January 1979, however, the Swedish Parliament adopted a new second paragraph to Chapter 6, sec. 3, of the Code of Parenthood (Föraldrabalken) as a result of which sec. 3 now reads:

„A custodian shall exercise the necessary supervision over the child with due regard to the child's age and other circumstances.

The child shall not be subjected to corporal punishment or any other form of humiliating treatment".

Although the Code of Parenthood is not part of the Penal Code and its obligations are incomplete, in that no sanction attaches to their breach, the applicants contend that their rights and freedoms under the Convention have been and continue to be prejudiced both by the express terms and effect of the addition to Chapter 6, sec. 3, of the Code of Parenthood and also by the effect which it has had on the interpretation of the criminal law and in particular of Chapter 3, sec. 5, of the Penal Code.

The new legislation was described by the Swedish Standing Committee on Law Procedure in its official commentary (LU 1978/79, p. 5) as removing the uncertainty that existed (as a result of an amendment to the law in 1966) as to the extent to which mild corporal rebukes of children by their guardians are punishable. As a result of this legislation, the applicants contend that the legal position under the criminal law has now been made clear, that acts of chastisement directed at children by their parents are illegal to the same extent that such acts would be if exercised against an adult.

The applicants set out the following analysis of the legal consequences of corporal chastisement of children by their parents:

1. Manhandling to rescue:

These are acts such as pulling a child away from a fire which are, in the words of the Swedish Standing Committee on Law Procedure (1978/9:11, p. 5) „necessary if the parents are to fulfil their obligation to supervise the child". The intention of such acts is never to punish and they have no consequences under criminal law or the Code of Parenthood.

2. Slight forms of chastisement:

These are acts which are covered by the general prohibition in the Code of Parenthood but do not amount to petty assault under the Penal Code. The applicants describe these as utterly lenient physical expressions of disapproval.

3. Ordinary chastisement:

These are acts such as blows, beatings, boxing the ears which the applicants contend must now be regarded as assault contrary to the Penal Code by virtue of its reinterpretation arising from the amendment to the Code of Parenthood.

4. Maltreatment of children:

This category has always been punishable under criminal law and is exemplified by ordinary chastisement which unintentionally causes injury and has exceeded its natural limits.

The applicants maintain that ordinary chastisement has now become included within the scope of ‚assault' as a criminal offence in Sweden and that parents no longer have a greater immunity from criminal sanction in imposing such ordinary chastisement on their children than they have if the same acts were committed on a stranger. They also maintain that slight forms of chastisement, although not criminally punishable, are breaches of the Code of Parenthood which might lead the applicants to lose custody of their children.

The introduction of the 1979 legislation was accompanied by a considerable amount of publicity about its ideological justification and, in particular, the Central Social Board of Stockholm, to whom the legislation was submitted for consideration, maintained that „special efforts of information" should be mounted in respect of „extreme religious groups which have argued for so-called loving chastisement as a systematic part of the upbringing of children".

The applicants also anticipate that they will be faced with a dilemma in the education of their children, who will be taught at school to regard their parents' values as antisocial and criminal. None of the applicants has been prosecuted under the present state of Swedish criminal law nor have any of them lost the custody of their children.

They contend that they are unable to take legal proceedings to challenge the state of the law in Sweden and that therefore they need do no more to comply with the requirements of art. 26 of the Convention.

COMPLAINTS

The applicants complain that the state of Swedish law resulting from the introduction of the 1979 legislation by the Swedish Government makes the corporal punishment and humiliating treatment of children by their parents a criminal offence to the same extent as if such acts were committed against strangers. They maintain that this state of the law violates their rights to respect for family life, to freedom of religion and to respect for their rights to ensure that their children's education and teaching is in conformity with their own religious and philosophical convictions.

The applicants maintain that they are victims of legislation and a state of the law which is incompatible with art. 8 and 9 of the Convention and art. 2 of the First Protocol even though they have not been prosecuted for assaulting their children. They submit that the terms of the legislation and the state of the law are sufficiently precise to re quire them to alter their conduct. Thus the applicants know that if they chastise children as their consciences and religious convictions dictate, they may be liable to criminal prosecution for assault. Accordingly they maintain that they are directly, immediately and individually affected by the mere state of the law.

Furthermore, the applicants point out that they are unable to challenge the 1979 legislation or the state of the criminal law, which are the law of the land and unimpeachable before the Swedish courts. Consequently they are unable to seek domestic remedies. They also refer to the consequences which would follow if they were not regarded as victims under art. 25 in that they would have to wait to be prosecuted under the present state of the law, which they maintain is incompatible with the Convention, and they would risk not only the public ignominy associated with such proceedings, but also the risk of being declared unsatisfactory guardians of their children and losing custody of them for breaching the Code of Parenthood before being able to bring their application to the Commission.

They accordingly submit that they are victims within the terms of art. 25, have no domestic remedies to exhaust and invoke art. 8 and 9 and art. 2 of the First Protocol.

THE LAW

1. Art. 25 of the Convention

The applicants complain that under the Code of Parenthood they are forbidden from corporally punishing their children. They further complain that under Swedish criminal law the boundary of criminal assault is the same whether the act is committed against a stranger or by a parent in chastising its child. They maintain that their ideological disagreement with these provisions results in their being victims of a continuing violation of their rights under art. 8 and 9 of the Convention and art. 2 of the First Protocol.

The respondent Government has raised the question whether the applicants are victims within the meaning of art. 25 of the Convention, without submitting any specific arguments on this question.

The Commission, like the Court, has consistently held in its case-law that the very existence of legislation may justify an applicant in claiming to be a victim within the meaning of art. 25 of the Convention of a violation of one of its normative provisions where the legislation continuously and directly affects him. Hence in the Marckx case (Series A Judgments and Decisions, Vol. 31, p. 13, par. 27) the Court held: „Art. 25 of the Convention entitles individuals to contend that a law violates their rights by itself in the absence of an individual measure of implementation if they run the risk of being directly affected by it".

In the present case the applicants are all parents who have the custody of children. They are therefore all *ipso facto* affected -by the provisions of the Code of Parenthood and, in the light of their firm religious convictions as to the appropriateness of physical chastisement of children by their parents they are, in the Commission's view, clearly directly affected by the provisions of the Code and the state of the criminal law in Sweden which they submit criminalises behaviour which they regard as necessary and proper:

The Commission therefore concludes that the applicants have shown that they may claim to be victims of violations of the rights and freedoms guaranteed by the Convention within the meaning of art. 25 of the Convention.

2. Art. 26 of the Convention

The applicants contend that their application concerns the state of Swedish criminal and parental law. They have not been subjected to proceedings implementing the law but equally have not instituted proceedings themselves to challenge it, since this is not possible in Sweden. They contend that the requirement of art. 26 of the Convention as to the exhaustion of domestic remedies does not apply to them.

The respondent Government have not disputed the applicants' contention and the Commission finds that, since the applicants were unable to challenge the state of Swedish law in Sweden, the requirement of art. 26 of the Convention as to the exhaustion of domestic remedies is therefore inapplicable.

3. Art. 8 of the Convention

The applicants complain that the present state of Swedish criminal law and the amendment of the Code of Parenthood interfere with their right to respect for private and family life as guaranteed by art. 8 which provides:

„1. Everyone has the right to respect for his private and family life, his home and his correspondence.
2. There shall be no interference by a public authority with the exercise of this right except such as in accordance with the law and is necessary in a democratic society in the interests of national security, public safety or the economic wellbeing of the country, for the prevention of disorder or crime, for the protection of health or morals, or for the protection of the rights and freedoms of others. "

In the applicants' view the interference which they allege the criminalisation of the physical chastisement of their children constitutes with their rights under the first paragraph of this article cannot be justified under the terms of the second paragraph. The respondent Government argue however that the present state of the criminal law of assault, like all other normal provisions of the criminal law, cannot be regarded as constituting an interference with the applicants' right to respect for their family and private lives as guaranteed by art. 8, par. 1, of the Convention. Alternatively the respondent Government contend that any interference which arises is justifiable under the terms of its second paragraph.

The applicants further contend that the 1979 amendment of the Code of Parenthood constituted a further interference with their rights under art. 8, par. 1, which is equally unjustifiable under art. 8, par. 2. The Government contend that the amendment in question, which is an incomplete law, with no relevance to criminal law and no accompanying sanction, cannot be regarded as an interference with the applicants' rights, under this article or can be justified under its second paragraph.

The Commission will examine first the applicants' complaints relating to the Code of Parenthood and in particular to the second paragraph to Chapter 6, sec. 3 of the Code. In the applicants' submission this provision makes even slight forms of corporal chastisement illegal. They maintain that the existence and operation of this law constitutes an interference with their right to respect for family life as guaranteed by art. 8, par. 1, of the Convention.

The Commission recalls its analysis of the scope of the concept of interference in its Report on Appl.-No. 7525/76, Dudgeon against the United Kingdom, where it found (par. 90):

„In accordance with the Court's case-law in the Klass case ... an applicant may only complain of the actual effects of the law on him. If in reality it does not affect him at all, he cannot complain. Or its effects may be slight and not such as to interfere with his right to private life. When he complains of the existence of penal legislation, the question whether he runs any risk of prosecution will be relevant in assessing the existence, extent and nature of any actual effects on him. On the other hand the mere fact that a penal law has not been enforced by means of criminal proceedings, or is unlikely to be so enforced, does not of itself negate the possibility that it has effects amounting to interference with private life. A primary purpose of any such law is to prevent the conduct it proscribes, by persuasion or deterrence. It also stigmatises the conduct as unlawful and undesirable. These aspects must also be taken into consideration."

The Commission must examine the scope and operation of the Code of Parenthood on the basis of the parties' submissions in the light of these criteria. It notes first that the applicants do not contend that light corporal rebukes are breaches of the Swedish criminal law of assault (Chapter 3, sec. 5 and 6, of the Penal Code). Nor have they established any instance of such behaviour being regarded as „molestation" (Chapter 4, sec. 7, of the Penal Code).

The present case does not therefore concern the operation of the criminal law. No question arises of a „risk of prosecution" as a result of the operation of the Code of Parenthood as it did in the Dudgeon case referred to above. The Commission must therefore consider the effects of the Code on the applicant's ability to express and implement their own convictions in the upbringing of their children, in the light of the background and aims of the Code.

The Commission notes first that Sweden is the only Member State of the Council of Europe which has introduced legislation prohibiting all corporal punishment of children by their parents including light corporal rebukes.

The Commission's evaluation of the Code's effect must start from the premise that parental rights and choices in the upbringing and education of their children are paramount as against the state. This is inherent in the terms of the guarantee of respect for family life contained in art. 8, par. 1, since the upbringing of children is a central aspect of family life. The same principle is clearly reasserted in art. 2, First Protocol, the text and interpretation of which by the organs of the Convention leaves the primacy of the parental role in no doubt.

The applicants concede that the scope of permissible parental punishment of their children was uncertain before the amendment to the Code in question and the Government sought by this provision to discourage acts of violence against children by the imposition of the Code's general prohibition of corporal punishment of all kinds.

The applicants contend, however, that this prohibition is contrary to their convictions, which support the use of corporal punishment of their children where appropriate.

They have submitted that the amendment of the Code extended the boundary of the criminal law and also increased the risk that parents who merely used light corporal chastisement may lose the custody of their child but they have not been able to submit any details of reported, or unreported, cases before the Swedish courts to substantiate either claim and which relate directly to light corporal rebukes.

The Government on the other hand have described the amendment to the Code as an incomplete law. They have stressed that it has no accompanying sanction and that it has neither directly, nor indirectly, affected the scope or interpretation of Swedish criminal law. For this reason they have not been able to provide the Commission with any concrete example of the operation of the Code or its interpretation and application by Swedish courts or authorities.

The Government have submitted that it was only by complete prohibition of all corporal punishment that criminal acts of violence against children could be effectively discouraged, since these might arise where a parent exceeded the legitimate non-criminal sphere of light corporal rebukes unintentionally or otherwise. Although the legitimacy of non-criminal light corporal rebukes was not challenged in itself, the Government did not wish to encourage corporal punishment even in this sphere, for fear of such excesses.

In recognition of the difference between what may properly be called violence and is prohibited by the criminal law and the legitimate non-criminal sphere, the prohibition imposed by the amendment to the Code of Parenthood is not accompanied by any sanction or other legal implications for the family, which lends support to the Government's contention that the amendment was and is intended to encourage a reappraisal of the corporal punishment of children in order to discourage abuse.

The Commission must therefore decide whether the effects of the amendment of the Code of Parenthood are such as to constitute an interference which amounts to a lack of respect for the applicants' family life which includes respect for parental acts and convictions relating to the upbringing of their children.

The exact practical effects of the provision about which the applicants complain remain obscure. The applicants have not been directly subjected to any enforcement or other procedure a rising from their disagreement with the Code which might constitute an interference with their rights. Nor have they provided any examples of its interpretation or application by the Swedish authorities in other cases. They have further contended that the provisions of the Code may be relied upon in deciding questions as to the custody of children, but again they have not illustrated this submission and the Commission must therefore find from the facts before it that this has not actually occurred. Furthermore the information provided by the Swedish Government tends to confirm that this incomplete law is without any direct practical effect beyond that of attempting to encourage a reappraisal of the treatment of children.

No concrete measures have ever been referred to by the Government to achieve this reappraisal, except for the mere existence of the amendment and the publicity which it has attracted.

In the light of this, the Commission concludes that the actual effects of the law are to encourage a positive review of the punishment of children by their parents, to discourage abuse and prevent excesses which could properly be described as violence against children. In this respect the Commission must distinguish between the expression of differing opinions from those held by the applicants in the context of the public debate on the proposed amendment and the actual implementation and operation of the amendment once enacted.

On the facts as presented by the applicants it does not appear to the Commission that their original fears as to the nature of the amendment were justified. The Commission does not regard the effects of the amendment which are the subject of this application as constituting an interference which amounts to a lack of respect for the applicants' family life.

It follows that this complaint is manifestly ill-founded within the meaning of art. 27, par. 2, of the Convention.

The applicants also allege that the scope of the criminal law of assault and molesting fails to respect their right to respect for private and family life as guaranteed by art. 8.

The Commission recognises that, whilst the upbringing of children remains essentially a parental duty, encapsulated within the concept of family life, it is inevitable that certain aspects of criminal law will affect the relationship between parents and children to a greater or lesser degree. Hence the assault of children by their parents is treated as criminal and although the applicants have drawn attention to the wider prohibition of all corporal punishment of children contained in the Code of Parenthood, they concede that it is not every corporal rebuke which would infringe the Penal Code.

However the applicants have not shown that the provisions of Swedish law criminalising the assault of children are unusual or in anyway draconian. The fact that no distinction is made between the treatment of children by their parents and the same treatment applied to an adult stranger cannot, in the Commission's opinion, constitute ,an interference' with respect for the applicant's private and family lives since the consequences of an assault are equated in both cases.

Nor does the mere fact that legislation, or the state of the law, intervenes to regulate something which pertains to family life constitute a breach of art. 8, par. 1, of the Convention unless the intervention in question violates the applicants' right to respect for their family life. The Commission finds that the scope of the Swedish law of assault and molestation is a normal measure for the control of violence and that its extension to apply to the ordinary physical chastisement of children by their parents is intended to protect potentially weak and vulnerable member of society.

The Commission therefore concludes that the state of Swedish criminal law does not interfere with their right to respect for private and family life within the meaning of art. 8, par. 1, of the Convention. It follows that this aspect of their complaint is manifestly ill-founded within the meaning of art. 27, par. 2, of the Convention.

4. Art. 9 of the Convention

The applicants further complain that the legal position in question fails to respect their right to freedom of religion as guaranteed by art. 9 of the Convention, which provides:

> „1. Everyone has the right to freedom of thought, conscience and religion; this right includes freedom to change his religion or belief and freedom, either alone or in community with others and in public or private, to manifest his religion or belief, in worship, teaching, practice and observance.
> 2. Freedom to manifest one's religion or beliefs shall be subject only to such limitations as are prescribed by law and are necessary in a democratic society in the interests of public safety, for the protection of public order, health or morals, or for the protection of the rights and freedoms of others. "

The respondent Government contend that the state of the law complained of reveals no interference with the applicants' rights under this article, or in the alternative, that such interference as is occasioned is justified under the terms of its second paragraph.

The Commission considers that on the facts of the application before it the same reasoning applies, *mutatis mutandis,* to the applicants' complaints under this article as to those under art. 8. It follows that there has been no interference with the applicants rights as guaranteed by art. 9 and that this aspect of the applicants' complaints is therefore manifestly ill-founded within the meaning of art. 27, par. 2, of the Convention.

5. Art. 2 First Protocol

The applicants further complain that the amendment of the Code of Parenthood is to be incorporated into the school curriculum in order, in their view, to spread the view as widely as possible and even amongst their own children, that the applicants' attitude to corporal punishment is outdated, wrong and reprehensible. They maintain that such an approach fails to respect the guarantee contained in the second sentence of art. 2 First Protocol, which provides:

> „... *In the exercise of any functions which it assumes in relation to education and to teaching, the State shall respect the right of parents to ensure such education and teaching in conformity with their own religious and philosophical convictions".*

The respondent Government has contended first that this provision is inapplicable since the state of the law complained of by the applicants does not concern the exercise of any state functions in relation to education or teaching, such as the organisation of schools or similar institutions. In the alternative, the Government maintain that if this article is applicable, the second sentence must be given a reasonable interpretation and may not be read to protect extraordinary or unusual elements of religious or philosophical doctrine which may conflict with the State's duties to protect children from harm.

Nevertheless the applicants have referred to passages in official documents published in connection with the amendment of the Code of Parenthood which suggest that the amendment in question should be taken into account in educational establishments. The Commission finds therefore that art. 2 is applicable in the present case.

As far as the respondent Government's second contention is concerned, the Commission was faced with a similar argument on behalf of the United Kingdom Government in Appl.-Nos. 7511/76 and 7743/76, concerning the use of corporal punishment in schools in the United Kingdom, where, at par. 97 of that Report, it concluded that, in the light of the unequivocal terms of art. 1 of the Convention and art. 2 and 5 First

Protocol, „it is precisely in their capacity as individual parents that the applicants are entitled to claim the right to respect for their philosophical convictions and this irrespective of whether their claim may conflict with the standards generally accepted by other parents in respect of discipline".

It is true that those applications concerned the respect for philosophical convictions (par. 83, ibid.), but the Commission recognises that the same criteria must equally apply to religious convictions.

However, as the European Court of Human Rights confirmed in its judgment in the Kjeldsen, Busk Madsen and Pedersen Case (Series A: Judgments and Decisions, Vol. 23, par. 53, KirchE-EU S. 181), the second sentence of art. 2, First Protocol does not prevent States from imparting through teaching or education information or knowledge of a directly or indirectly religious or philosophical kind. Nor does it permit parents to object to aspects of teaching on these grounds unless the information or knowledge in question is not conveyed in an objective, critical and pluralistic manner. Thus „the State is forbidden to pursue an aim of indoctrination that might be considered as not respecting parents' religious and philosophical convictions. That is the limit that must not be exceeded" (ibid).

In the present case the applicants have not complained that their children have in fact been subjected to what they regard as indoctrination on the question of the propriety of corporal punishment. They have merely averted to references in official publications that account should be taken of the amendment to the Code of Parenthood in the educational sphere.

The respondent Government have expressly referred to the underlying purpose of the amendment as an attempt to strengthen the rights of children and encourage respect for them as individuals and have stressed that this humanitarian objective is to be pursued by way of a general policy of education in its broadest sense.

Furthermore the Commission recalls that, in accordance with its constant case-law and that of the Court, art. 2, First Protocol must be read as a whole with the Convention and especially in the light of the guarantees contained in art. 8, 9 and 10.

In the present case the Commission has found that no interference with either art. 8 or 9 arises and concludes that the applicants, who have not averted to more than policy statements of a general character, which could in no sense be described as an attempt by the respondent Government to implement a policy of indoctrination in Swedish schools, have failed to show that their right to respect for their religious convictions protected by art. 2, First Protocol has been violated by any concrete provision or practice.

It follows that this aspect of their complaint is manifestly ill-founded within the meaning of art. 27, par. 2, of the Convention.

For these reasons the Commission declares the application inadmissible.

15

Art. 9 EMRK schützt in erster Linie den Bereich persönlicher Überzeugung und religiösen Glaubens (forum internum) und darüber hinaus die hiermit eng verbundenen, als religiöse Praxis allgemein anerkannten insbesondere gottesdienstlichen Handlungsformen. Nicht ohne weiteres ist hierin eingeschlossen die Gewährleistung eines vom religiösen Glauben bestimmten Verhaltens im öffentlichen Bereich (hier: Verweigerung von Steuerzahlung, soweit militärischen Zwecken zufließend). Im Wege der Beschwerde nach Art. 13 EMRK kann kein Anspruch gegen die vertragsstaatliche Gesetzgebung als solche durchgesetzt werden (hier: Verwendung von Steuermitteln zu einem bestimmten Zweck).

Art. 8, 13, 27 § 2 a.F. EMRK
EKMR, Beschluss vom 15. Dezember 1983
- No. 10358/83 (C. ./. Vereinigtes Königreich)[1] -

THE FACTS

The applicant is a British citizen resident in Oxfordshire and a technical writer by profession, born in 1939. He is employed by a publishing house, and further permitted to undertake assignments as a free-lance journalist.

The income tax on his salary is deducted at source by his employer, and the tax due on his free lance work, after deduction of expenses, is payable direct to the Inland Revenue. The applicant's assessment for the tax owing for the financial year 1981/82 amounts to £ 90, which he is willing to pay, but only on receipt of a guarantee that it will not be spent on purposes which are an outrage to his conscience and religious and philosophical beliefs. He therefore accepts both that tax is owing, and the amount that is due to the Inland Revenue.

The applicant is a member of the Religious Society of Friends (Quakers) a central tenet of whose belief is pacifism. He is not prepared to pay that proportion of his taxes which is used to finance armaments weapons' research and allied industries as these purposes are inconsistent with his beliefs. The Peace Campaign has calculated that a sum equivalent to forty per cent of the Revenue raised by direct income tax in 1980/81 was spent on armaments, weapons' research and allied industries and the applicant having paid substantially more than 60 per cent of the income tax due from him in the year 1980/81, wishes to divert the whole of the sum still owing on his free lance earnings to peaceful purposes.

---

[1] DR 37, 142.

The applicant indicated his philosophical convictions to the Inland Revenue and informed them that he was not prepared to pay the sum in question without guarantees as to its destination. The Inland Revenue applied to Oxford County Court for payment of the sum due, and the applicant entered a defence relying upon his freedom of thought, conscience and religion guaranteed by art. 9 of the Convention. The applicant appeared in person before the Registrar of Oxford County Court sitting in Chambers on 22 November 1982, when his defence was rejected but the Registrar refused to award costs to the Inland Revenue, recognising that the defence was not vexatious or an abuse of the processes of the Court. The applicant applied to have the order of the Registrar set aside, which request was refused by the County Court on 6 December 1982. The applicant then sought leave to appeal against that order on 7 January 1983 which was refused. The applicant sought leave to appeal from the Court of Appeal, his application being dismissed on 18 February 1983.

The Inland Revenue has indicated to the applicant that it intends to seek enforcement of the judgment debt and the applicant therefore has to choose between paying a sum which will be used for further purposes which he opposes as a matter of belief and conscience, or having a judgment debt enforced against him. He contends that no procedure exists whereby he can effectively evoke the right to manifest his pacifist beliefs by directing a proportion of his tax to increase the resources available for peaceful purposes. He invokes art. 9 and 13 of the Convention.

COMPLAINTS

The applicant complains that the absence of any procedure whereby he may effectively invoke the right to manifest his pacifist beliefs by directing a proportion of the tax due from him to peaceful purposes represents a breach of art. 9 and 13 of the Convention. He contends that the final decision is either the debt upon which he received notice of the final demand based on the assessment following the preliminary hearing in Oxford County Court on 22 November 1982, or the date of the final refusal of leave to appeal by the Court of Appeal on 18 February 1983. He also points out that he has exhausted the available remedies under domestic law, a view confirmed by the decision in Cheney v. Conn (1968 I ALL ER 779) that English Courts cannot take account of the United Kingdom's international obligations when admissible legislation is clear an unambiguous.

The applicant also contends that he may be considered „a victim" within the meaning of art. 25 (1) of the Convention, since he is not complaining of domestic law in abstracto, but of the fact that a final demand for payment of income tax has been made, and that he is now liable to enforcement of the judgment debt as soon as the Inland Revenue seek a warrant to do so, and notwithstanding the fact that this step has not yet been taken.

The applicant contends that pacifism comes within the scope and ambit of art. 9 of the Convention as a philosophical belief, as was recognised in Appl.-No. 7050/75 (Arrowsmith v. the United Kingdom, DR 19 p. 5 at p. 19). The manifestation in practice of pacifism requires that an adherent should oppose recourse to force in the settlement of disputes and therefore should not support, directly or indirectly, weapon procurement, weapon development and other defence related expenditure. Where forty per cent of the monies raised by taxation are used for such purposes, it is a necessary part of the manifestation of a pacifist's belief in practice and observance that forty per cent of his or her taxes be diverted to different, peaceful purposes. The present case is thus to be distinguished from Appl.-No. 5442/72 (DR 1 p. 41) and the Arrowsmith case referred to above, especially because the diversion of forty per cent of the applicant's taxes to peaceful purposes is not merely consistent with her beliefs, but necessary for the manifestation of them in practice and observance.

The applicant contends furthermore that his submissions are distinguishable from the conscientious objector cases (e.g. 7565/76, DR 9 p. 117 and 7705/76 DR 9 p. 196) since those cases relate to a factual situation where there is a requirement of some form of service, recognised by art. 4 (3) (b) of the Convention. Thus art. 9 has to be read subject to art. 4 (3) (b) where the fulfilment of such an obligation is at issue. But it has nevertheless been recognised in the conscientious objector cases that, where a form of civilian service may be performed, the duties thereof should not interfere with the practice of any religious belief (Appl.-No. 5591/72, Collection 43 p. 161). Hence art. 4 (3) (b) constitutes a limited exception to art. 9, which only applies to a requirement of military or civilian service and not to the manifestation of beliefs, including pacifist beliefs.

Under the terms of the present law, and in particular the Public Accounts Charges Act 1881, sec. 1 (2), Inland Revenue receipts are paid into a single account. The applicant merely requires that a separate account, „earmarked" for peaceful purposes is established, and submits that such a change in the law as this would require is necessary in order to enable him to pay his taxes without thereby acting in a fashion inconsistent with the manifestation of his pacifist beliefs.

The applicant further contends that no justification can be found in art. 9 (2) of the Convention for the interference with his freedom of conscience about which he complains. Although he recognises that the interference under art. 9 (1) of the Convention is „prescribed by law" within the meaning of art. 9 (2), he contends that the only conceivable justifications which could be invoked are either the interests of public safety, the protection of public order, or the protection of the rights and freedoms of others.

As far as an argument may be made with reference to public safety, the applicant stresses that he is willing to pay the full amount of tax due and that his case is distinguishable from that of other groups who for non-religious or non-philosophical reasons may oppose certain categories of public spending. Pacifists would appear to be the only group who can bring their beliefs within the scope of art. 9 and claim that the manifestation of those beliefs entails opposition to all as opposed to certain elements of military expenditure and thus the diversion of forty per cent of their tax to peaceful purposes. Nor is his position to be compared with that of someone who objects to a particular level of military spending, or spending on a particular military project. In these circumstances, given the narrow basis of his objection, it cannot be argued that a massive precedent would be set by recognising the legitimacy of the applicant's objection. The same arguments apply, mutatis mutandis, to a justification based upon the protection of public safety.

Similarly the applicant contends that no justification can be mounted on the basis of the protection of the rights and freedoms of others, since the Government would then have to establish their defence expenditure unequivocally and undeniably did protect the rights and freedoms of its citizens. Levels of military expenditure are however a question of political choice, and no „minimum" level of military expenditure can be established as necessary in order to protect a given population. In this respect the present case is distinguishable from Application No. 2988/66, (10 Yb p. 472), concerning the requirement for compulsory car insurance, where the amount of premiums were related directly to the compensation of victims of motor accidents, a correlation which does not exist in relation to military spending. Furthermore a Government could either take the view that no military spending, or large military spending, would protect its citizens and could not therefore justify imposing its choice in this respect on the proponents of the opposite argument. Finally even assuming that defence expenditure is for the protection of citizens, the Government must establish that it is necessary in a democratic society to raise funds for this expenditure from all citizens. The applicant contends that it is not necessary or proportionate to the aim of the protection of citizens from war by means of military expenditure to require pacifists to help finance something which they disapprove of on account of their philosophical convictions.

Thus it is the necessity of the limitation on the right of pacifists to manifest their philosophical beliefs in observance and practice which must be justified under the terms of the Convention, and not the need for defence expenditure. No choice therefore arises between two conflicting „pressing social needs", namely defence expenditure and non-interference with the right of pacifists to manifest their beliefs in observance and practice. The applicant asks only that a proportion of his taxes which would go towards military expenditure should be diverted to peaceful purposes. In this respect the applicant recalls that the Government allows pacifists not to fight when the state is actually under an immediate threat by permitting conscientious objection, and that it cannot therefore justify forcing pacifists to pay for military expenditure in peace time, since they are thereby being obliged to pay for something which they are not going to be obliged to do since it violates their conscience. Finally it would be possible to earmark tax raised for specific purposes, as is already done in the case of national insurance contributions.

With respect to the application of art. 13 of the Convention the applicant contends that he has had no opportunity for his claim that his rights under art. 9 of the Convention have been violated, in as far as the United Kingdom makes no provision for the diversion of forty per cent of the taxes of pacifists to peaceful purposes, to be considered by a national authority capable of giving an effective remedy.

THE LAW

1. The applicant invokes art. 9 of the Convention in relation to his complaint that he should not be obliged to pay a portion of his taxes without an assurance that they will not be applied for military or related expenditure. Art. 9 provides:

> *„1. Everyone has the right to freedom of thought, conscience and religion; this right includes freedom to change his religion or belief and freedom, either alone or in community with others and in public or private, to manifest his religion or belief, in worship, teaching, practice and observance.*
> *2. Freedom to manifest one's religion or beliefs shall be subject only to such limitations as are prescribed by law and are necessary in a democratic society in the interests of public safety, for the protection of public order, health of morals, or for the protection of the rights and freedoms of others."*

The applicant, who is a Quaker, contends that to compel him to contribute to expenditure for armaments, rather than for peaceful purposes, is an outrage to his conscience and contrary to the requirements of the manifestation of his belief through practice. He contends that the manifestation in practice of his Quaker beliefs requires him to oppose recourse to force in the settlement of disputes and not to support directly or indirectly weapon procurement, weapon development and other defence related expenditure. It is therefore his contention that it is a necessary part of the manifestation of his Quaker belief in practice and observance that forty per cent of his income tax be diverted to different, peaceful purposes. This step is not merely consistent with the Quaker beliefs, but necessary to their manifestation.

Art. 9 primarily protects the sphere of personal beliefs and religious creeds, i.e. the area which is sometimes called the forum internum. In addition, it protects acts which are intimately linked to these attitudes, such as acts of worship or devotion which are aspects of the practice of a religion or belief in a generally recognised form.

However, in protecting this personal sphere, art. 9 of the Convention does not always guarantee the right to behave in the public sphere in a way which is dictated by such a belief - for instance by refusing to pay certain taxes because part of the revenue so raised may be applied for military expenditure. The Commission has so held in Appl.-No. 7050/75 (Arrowsmith v. the United Kingdom, Comm. Report, par. 71, DR 19 p. 5), where it stated that „the term ‚practice‘ as employed in art. 9 (1) does not cover each act which is motivated or influenced by a religion or a belief."

The obligation to pay taxes is a general one which has no specific conscientious implications in itself. Its neutrality in this sense is also illustrated by the fact that no tax payer can influence or determine the purpose for which his or her contributions are applied, once they are collected. Furthermore, the power of taxation is expressly recognised by the Convention system and is ascribed to the State by art. 1, First Protocol. It follows that art. 9 does not confer on the applicant the right to refuse, on the basis of his convictions, to abide by legislation, the operation of which is provided for by the Convention, and which applies neutrally and generally in the public sphere, without impinging on the freedoms guaranteed by art. 9.

If the applicant considers the obligation to contribute through taxation to arms procurement an outrage to his conscience he may advertise his attitude and thereby try to obtain support for it through the democratic process.

The Commission concludes that there has been no interference with the applicant's rights guaranteed by art. 9(I) of the Convention and it follows that this aspect of the applicant's complaint is manifestly ill-founded within the meaning of art. 27 (2) of the Convention.

The applicant has also complained that he has been denied the opportunity to voice his objection to his payment of taxes without an assurance as to their ultimate destination and invokes art. 13 of the Convention which provides „Everyone whose rights and freedoms as set forth in this Convention are violated shall have an effective remedy before a national authority notwithstanding that the violation has been committed by persons acting in an official capacity.".

However, the Commission notes that the right to specify the purpose for which money raised by taxation is to be spent is not expressly guaranteed by the Convention, and cannot, in the light of the Commission's finding in respect of the applicant's complaint under art. 9 of the Convention above, be implied from its terms.

In as far as the applicant complains of the operation of laws to secure the payment of taxes, the liability to which he does not dispute, the Commission recalls the terms of the final paragraph of art. I First Protocol, which provides a wide discretion to Member States in the enforcement of precisely such measures. The applicant complains that the legislation in the United Kingdom does not provide for him to make conscientious objection to the allocation of revenue arising from his taxation to specific purposes, but the Commission recalls that, in accordance with its established case law, art. 13 of the Convention does not guarantee the right to challenge or review legislation for its conformity with the Convention, but merely ensures a machinery whereby individuals may attempt to vindicate their claims of violations of the Convention (judgment of the Court of 25 November 1980 in the case of Young James and Webster, Series A Vol. 44).

In the present case the applicant is not prevented from holding the view that the legislation relating to collection of taxation should be amended to permit his conscientious views in relation to the application of those funds to be taken into account. In these circumstances the Commission concludes that the applicant has not established the absence of a remedy for a complaint concerning a right guaranteed by the Convention as envisaged by art. 13 of the Convention, and it follows that this aspect of the application is manifestly ill-founded within the meaning of art. 27 (2) of the Convention.

For these reasons the Commission declares the application inadmissible.

16

Die durch staatliches Recht begründete Ermächtigung der Kirchen, von den Gläubigen, soweit diese nicht von ihrem Kirchenaustrittsrecht Gebrauch gemacht haben, Finanzbeiträge zu erheben und im Klagewege geltend zu machen, ist mit der EMRK vereinbar.

Art. 9 § 1, 27 § 2 a.F. EMRK, 1 § 1 Erstes Zusatzprotokoll
EKMR, Beschluss vom 14. Mai 1984
- No. 9781/82 (E.U.G.R. ./. Österreich)[1] -

THE FACTS

The applicants, who are both Austrian citizens, are a married couple who reside in Vienna. They are Roman Catholics.

Their complaint relates to the levy of church contributions under Austrian law. The matter is governed by a law (Gesetz über die Erhebung von Kirchenbeiträgen im Lande Österreich, GBlÖ 543/1939) which was enacted during the time of the „Anschluss" of Austria to Germany, but which remained in force as Austrian law after the restoration of the Re-

---

[1] DR 37, 42.

public. The same applies to the implementing regulations (GBlÖ 718 and 1408/1939) issued in pursuance of this law.

These provisions authorise the churches, including the Roman Catholic Church, to levy contributions from their members according to State-approved autonomous regulations (Beitragsordungen) enacted by the churches. The resultant duty of the individual church member to pay the contributions, except in the case where his church membership has been terminated (by a declaration to the competent State authority) is legally recognised by the State, as the churches can enforce this duty by bringing an action in the civil courts.

The applicants, being members of the Roman Catholic Church, were thus repeatedly required to pay church contributions. In one case they were sued by the church, but could not appeal to the Supreme Court due to the small amount of the claim. For this reason, so they claim, it was not possible for them to raise the question of the constitutionality of the above provisions in the judicial proceedings concerned, with a view to having this question determined by the Constitutional Court. Only the Supreme Court itself could have brought the matter before this court in connection with civil proceedings, whereas the individual has no right of appeal to the Constitutional Court against decisions of the ordinary courts.

The applicants, considering that the above provisions were unconstitutional, as being incompatible with freedom of religion and amounting to an unjustified interference with property, therefore tried alternative ways to bring the matter before the Constitutional Court.

When the competent local church office fixed the contributions payable for the year 1980, they filed objections with the Archdiocese of Vienna. The financial department of the Archdiocese wrote to them on 15 May 1981 asking for the submission of certain documents and indicating that the objections would be considered as withdrawn if the said documents were not submitted within a fixed time limit. The contributions would then be enforced as previously fixed.

The applicants then turned to the Constitutional Court complaining of the action of the Archdiocese, which they qualified as an administrative decision. However, the Constitutional Court did not share this view and by a decision of 1 October 1981 declared itself incompetent to receive the complaint. In the reasons it referred to earlier case law of its own and of the Supreme Court according to which the duty to pay church contributions was an obligation under civil law. From this it inferred that the Archdioceses' letter could not be qualified as an administrative decision, and that the Constitutional Court therefore lacked any competence of review. For the same reason, there was no room for referring the matter to the Administrative Court whose competence was equally limited to the review of administrative decisions.

The applicants further tried to challenge the applicable legal provisions directly before the Constitutional Court, under arts. 139 and 140 of the

Constitution. However, on 27 November 1981 the Constitutional Court also rejected this remedy as inadmissible, because the above constitutional provisions can be invoked by an individual only if an interference with his constitutional rights is brought about directly by the challenged legal regulations, without the intervention of a judicial or administrative decision. The regulations in question, however, did not directly affect the applicants as their application involved judicial court proceedings.

COMPLAINTS

The applicants now complain of violations of their right to freedom of religion as guaranteed by art. 9 of the Convention, and of their right to the peaceful enjoyment of possessions as guaranteed by art. 1 of Protocol No. 1 to the Convention.

They submit, in particular, that the provisions applied to them leave them no other choice than either to pay church contributions, or else to terminate their church membership. They consider it incompatible with freedom of religion that the State directly or indirectly compels a person to perform an act of religious relevance, including State assistance to a church to enforce contributions from its members.

The applicants further submit that there is an unjustified interference with their property rights because the levy of the contributions in question is neither necessary in the public interest nor can it be assimilated to taxes in the sense the second paragraph of art. 1 of the Protocol.

THE LAW

The applicants complain of the system of church contributions existing in Austria as it was applied to them. They allege that this system infringes their rights under art. 9 of the Convention (freedom of religion) and art. 1 of Protocol No. 1 (right to the peaceful enjoyment of possessions).

1. The Commission notes that in Austria the individual's duty to pay contributions to a certain church does not arise directly under the State's legislation which merely authorises (but does not require) the churches to prescribe such contributions from their members. The fact that the churches are in this respect subject to State control does not change the nature of the levy of contributions as an autonomous activity of the churches. Under Austrian law, the individual's duty to pay these contributions is considered as an obligation of civil law which the church in question may enforce against the individual by an action in the civil courts. It is thus left to the church's discretion whether or not it wishes to bring such an action against any particular person.

2. Insofar as the applicants invoke their right to freedom of religion as guaranteed by art. 9 of the Convention, the Commission observes that this provision protects in particular the right to manifest one's religion

„in worship, teaching, practice and observance". The Commission finds that the collection of financial contributions from its members by a church does not, as such, interfere with any of these activities. The applicants are entirely free to practise or not to practise their religion as they please. If they are obliged to pay contributions to the Roman Catholic Church, this is a consequence of their continued membership of this church, in the same way as e.g. the duty to pay contributions to a private association would result from their membership of such association. The obligation can be avoided if they choose to leave the church, a possibility for which the State legislation has expressly provided. By making available this possibility, the State has introduced sufficient safeguards to ensure the individual's freedom of religion. The individual cannot reasonably claim, having regard to the terms of art. 9 of the Convention, to remain a member of a particular church and nevertheless be free from the legal obligations, including financial obligations, resulting from this membership according to the autonomous regulations of the church in question. The same considerations would also apply if the matter were to be considered under art. 11 of the Convention (freedom of association).

The Commission therefore concludes that there is no appearance of any interference with the applicants' rights under art. 9 (and/or 11) of the Convention, and their complaint in this respect must accordingly be rejected as being manifestly ill-founded within the meaning of art. 27 (2) of the Convention.

3. Insofar as the applicants invoke their right to the peaceful enjoyment of their possessions, as guaranteed by art. 1 of Protocol No. 1 to the Convention, the Commission notes that the contributions are not levied by the State. Their collection is an autonomous activity of the churches, and the State's activity in this field is limited to the exercise of a power of control. The individual's duty to pay these contributions is considered as an obligation of civil law which the church in question may enforce against the individual concerned by an action in the civil courts. The mere fact that the State courts are available to the church as to any other physical or legal person who wishes to enforce a civil claim does not, in the Commission's view, amount to an interference by the State with the individual's property rights.

As under art. 25 of the Convention an application can on)y be brought by a person who claims that there has been an interference with his Convention rights by one of the High Contracting Parties, i.e. a State authority, and as there has been no interference with the applicants' property rights by such authority, their complaint in this respect is incompatible ratione personae with the provisions of the Convention, and must for this reason be rejected under art. 27 (2) of the Convention.

For these reasons, the Commission declares the application inadmissible.

17

Nicht jede Handlungsweise, die im weltlichen Bereich durch religiöse Motive bestimmt oder beeinflusst ist, genießt den Schutz der Religionsfreiheit.
Die Pflichtmitgliedschaft in einer Pensionskasse ist mit Art. 9 EMRK vereinbar.

Art. 9, 27 § 2 a.F. EMRK
EKMR, Beschluss vom 5. Juli 1984 - No. 10678/83 (V. ./. Niederlande)[1] -

SUMMARY OF THE FACTS

The applicant is a general medical practioner following anthroposophical principles. He works in a mixed practice, in collaboration with other therapists and the patients themselves. His fees are not calculated by reference to services rendered, but are reimbursed in accordance with a plan agreed with the patient on the basis of need.

In the Netherlands, practioners such as the applicant have been obliged since 1973 (Wet betreffende verplichte deelneming in een beroepspensioenregeling) to participate in a professional pensions scheme whereby pensions and contributions are determined by gross income.

The applicant requested exemption from compulsory participation, principally because it was not compatible with his anthroposophical beliefs. His request was rejected, the Minister of Social Affairs noting that compulsory participation had been established well before the applicant joined his mixed practice. An appeal against the Minister's decision was rejected by the Council of State.

THE LAW

The applicant has complained that he is forced to participate in a pension scheme as a general practitioner, despite the fact that such participation is incompatible with the exercise of his profession on the basis of his anthroposophical beliefs. In this respect, the applicant alleges a violation of art. 9 of the Convention, which provides:

„1. Everyone has the right to freedom of thought, conscience and religion; this right includes freedom to change his religion or belief and freedom, either alone or in community with others and in public or private, to manifest his religion or belief, in worship, teaching, practice and observance.
2. Freedom to manifest one's religion or beliefs shall be subject only to such limitations as are prescribed by law and are necessary in a democratic society in the

---

[1] DR 39, 267. Vgl. hierzu auch EKMR, KirchE-EU S. 5.

interests of public safety, for the protection of public order, health or morals, or for the protection of the rights and freedoms of others."

The Commission recalls that art. 9 of the Convention primarily protects the sphere of personal beliefs and religious creeds, i.e. the area which is sometimes called the *forum internum*. In addition, it protects acts which are intimately linked to these attitudes, such as acts of worship or devotion which are aspects of the practice of a religion or belief in a generally recognised form.

However, in protecting this personal sphere, art. 9 of the Convention does not always guarantee the right to behave in the public sphere in a way which is dictated by such a belief. As the Commission held in Application N° 7050/75 (Arrowsmith v. the United Kingdom, Report of the Commission, DR 19 p. 5, par. 71,9) „the term ,practice' as employed in art. 9 par. 1 does not cover each act which is motivated or influenced by a religion or belief". The Commission further stated that „when the actions of individuals do not actually express the belief concerned, they cannot be considered to be as such protected by art. 9 par. 1, even when they are motivated or influenced by it." (ibid.)

The Commission notes that the obligation to participate in a pension fund applies to all general practitioners on a purely neutral basis, and cannot be said to have any close link with their religion or beliefs.

Correspondingly, the refusal to participate in such a pension scheme, although motivated by the applicant's particular belief, cannot, in the view of the Commission, be considered as an actual expression of this belief.

Therefore, the Commission finds that there has been no interference with the applicant's right under art. 9 par. 1 of the Convention to manifest his belief in practice. It follows that the applicant's complaint is manifestly ill-founded within the meaning of art. 27 par. 2 of the Convention.

For this reason, the Commission declares the application inadmissible.

18

Die Erhebung einer staatlichen Kirchensteuer von Kirchenmitgliedern ist mit der EMRK vereinbar, wenn die Möglichkeit eines Kirchenaustritts, evtl. gemäß förmlicher Erklärung, besteht.

Art. 9 § 1, 27 § 2 a.F. EMRK
EKMR, Beschluss vom 4. Dezember 1984
- No. 10616/83 (Gottesmann ./. Schweiz)[1] -

THE FACTS (Extract)

The applicants, Jean Gottesmann, a forestry engineer born in 1943, and his wife Bertha Gottesmann, a pharmacist born in 1944, are both resident at Einsiedeln/ Switzerland. Both applicants were baptised in the Roman Catholic faith and married in Einsiedeln Roman Catholic church in 1970.

On 1 November 1972 they moved from Zurich to Einsiedeln. On arrival at Einsiedeln and enrolment in the municipal roll (Gemeinderatskanzlei - Einwohnerkontrolle), they did not declare any church membership. In their tax returns for the years 1973-1976 they made no statement as to their religion, merely scoring through the relevant space with a double line. In 1977-1978 they entered the word „none". On 24 August 1979 the applicants received a demand for church tax for the tax years 1972-1978. According to the tax authorities they were Roman Catholics and therefore liable for church tax in the municipality in which they lived.

On 15 January 1981, on an appeal by the applicants, the Einsiedeln district council (Bezirksrat) decided that they were indeed liable to pay church tax for the relevant period.

On 20 February 1981 the applicants appealed from that decision to the Government (Regierungsrat) of the Canton of Schwyz on the ground that they were exempt from the general levy, having clearly stated in their tax returns that they did not belong to any religion.

Their application was referred to the Cantonal Administrative Court, which decided on 2 July 1981 that it was only partly founded.

Noting that in Schwyz cantonal law there were no particular formalities for leaving the Roman Catholic Church, the Court allowed the Gottesmanns' application for exemption in respect only of Jean Gottesmann and of the period after 18 April 1977.

It held that only Jean Gottesmann had clearly notified his wish to leave the Roman Catholic Church: not declaring church membership on arrival in the municipality, crossing out the words „Roman Catholic" on voting cards, and scoring through the space for religious details in tax returns were not clear and unambiguous indications of having left a church, but Jean Gottesmann had given sufficiently clear notice of his decision to leave the Roman Catholic Church, when, under „Religion", he had written the word „none" on his tax return of 18 April 1977. His signature could not, however, be taken to indicate his wife's decision to leave in view of the personal and individual nature of such a decision.

---

[1] DR 40, 284.

The court therefore held that Bertha Gottesmann had remained a member of the Church until 27 January 1981, on which date she had explicitly stated her decision to leave the Church.

A public law appeal was entered on 17 August 1981 against the decision of the Schwyz Cantonal Administrative Court on the ground of a breach of art. 49 par. 6 of the Federal Constitution, which provides that no-one may be compelled to pay church tax to a church of which he is not a member. The applicants contended they had never expressly declared membership of the Einsiedeln Roman Catholic Church and that they had shown clearly their wish to leave the Roman Catholic Church.

The Federal Court dismissed the appeal on 18 March 1983. Having set out the constitutional principle laid down in art. 49 par. 6, the Court held that although a declaration of the wish to leave a church might be required, each religious denomination must specify the formalities involved.

Noting that neither Einsiedeln municipal law nor Schwyz cantonal law prescribed any particular declaration formality for leaving religious denomination, it held that to be valid such decision must be clearly and unambiguously intimated. The Administrative Court's finding that words only, not signs, were a clear and unambiguous intimation of such decision was consistent with the spirit of art. 49 par. 2 and par. 6 of the Federal Constitution.

THE LAW (Extract)

The applicants complain that, on the ground of membership of the Roman Catholic Church, they were compelled to make back payments of church tax in respect of a period during which they were no longer members of that church.

They rely on art. 9 of the Convention, which guarantees the right to freedom of religion.

The Commission holds, first, that the obligation to pay a tax by virtue of membership of a given church is not an interference with everyone's right to freedom of religion. It notes, in particular, that such an obligation does not affect the freedom to change or manifest one's religion.

It refers to its case law that a church tax is not in itself contrary to freedom of religion where domestic law allows the individual to leave the church concerned if he so wishes (see No. 9781/82, X. v. Austria, Dec. 14.5.84, DR 37 p. 42, KirchE-EU S. 62).

In the present case the Commission notes that the domestic courts have never disputed everyone's right to leave the Roman Catholic Church. In addition, that right is expressly recognised by art. 49 par. 2 and par. 6 of the Federal Constitution, which provides that no-one may be compelled to pay tax in respect of a church of which he is not member (art. 49 par. 6). The applicants in actual fact complain that the domestic authorities arbitrarily imposed formalities governing notification of their decision to leave the Roman Catholic Church where none were prescribed in national law.

The Commission finds, however, that for the purposes of art. 9 of the Convention the domestic authorities have a wide discretion to decide on what conditions an individual may validly be regarded as having decided to leave a religious denomination.

It accordingly does not consider arbitrary the domestic courts' refusal to recognise a decision lo leave a religious denomination unless such decision is unambiguously intimated, where no formality for that purpose is prescribed in cantonal law.

This part of the application must accordingly be dismissed as manifestly ill-founded within the meaning of art. 27 par. 2 of the Convention.

19

Ein Geistlicher einer evangelischen Staatskirche, der aus seinen staatsbehördlichen Funktionen nach einem Konflikt mit der Regierung wegen der staatlichen Abtreibungsgesetzgebung entlassen worden ist, kann weder die genannte Gesetzgebung als Betroffener (*victim*) angreifen noch mit Erfolg eine Verletzung der Religionsfreiheit rügen.

Art. 2, 9, 27 § 2 EMRK
EKMR, Beschluss vom 8. März 1985
- No. 11045/84 (Knudsen ./. Norwegen)[1] -

THE FACTS

The applicant is a Norwegian citizen, born in 1937. He is a vicar and resides at Balsfjord, Norway.

In Norway, an Act of 16 June 1978 (No. 66) made a number of amendments to the Act of 13 June 1975 (No. 50) concerning interruption of pregnancy - the so-called Abortion Act. The most important amendment was that whereas a pregnant woman could previously have her pregnancy terminated only by decision of a medical committee in accordance with conditions drawn up by the Act, the 1978 amendment authorised the woman herself to make the final decision whether to terminate the pregnancy provided the operation is performed before the end of the twelfth week of pregnancy.

Already on 31 May 1978, the day after the amending Act had been dealt with in the lower house of the Norwegian Parliament, the applicant

---

[1] DR 42, 247.

declared in a letter to the King that he regarded the Act as being „in manifest conflict with God's holy Commandment and the spirit and letter of the Constitution". He declared that he had to regard himself as relieved from his Government appointment and his oath of office as soon as the Act came into force.

On the day the Act came into force, 1 January 1979, the applicant announced in another letter to the King that he considered himself relieved from the oath he had given on taking the office of vicar. A few months later he informed the parish councils that he had withdrawn from his Government appointment in protest against the new Abortion Act.

As a consequence of his opinion he no longer performed the duties which he considered to belong to the State's part of the office of vicar. He performed no marriages, examination of marriage conditions or conciliation in matrimonial cases. He refused to keep the birth register. He refused to receive Government mail which was sent to him by the Ministry, and he refused to receive salary from the Government. However he still considered himself to be the true clergyman of the parish, holding that office by appointment from the Church, and he continued therefore to perform the functions which he regarded as pertaining to the Church's part of the office.

The Ministry of Church and Education confined itself at first to declaring that the applicant, through his statements and his attitude, had revealed an interpretation of his office which was new and unacceptable to the Ministry. Apart from this, the Ministry decided to await developments, and accordingly no measures were taken against him. As the applicant's action continued and the situation gradually became more difficult, however, the Ministry requested by letter of 25 September 1980 the Bishop of Nord-Hålogaland to pass on an order to the applicant to resume promptly the duties of his office which he was not performing, as the Ministry would otherwise consider dismissing him in accordance with art. 10 of the Criminal Code Enforcement Act (Ikrafttraedelsesloven). The applicant maintained his decision. By Royal Decree of 24 October 1980 it was then decided that the Ministry of Church and Education should on behalf of the Government bring legal action against the applicant to have him dismissed from office by court order.

Following unsuccessful conciliation proceedings the Attorney General instituted proceedings before the Malangen District Court on 21 November 1980, moving on behalf of the Government for the dismissal of the applicant from office, and requesting moreover a declaratory judgment to determine certain specific consequences of a dismissal.

The District Court pronounced judgment on 1 February 1982 concluding that the motion against the applicant should be rejected.

The Government represented by the Ministry of Church and Education appealed against this judgment to the Hålogaland Court of Appeal. During the main hearings in the Court of Appeal the Attorney General moved for dismissal of the applicant, in the alternative, a declaratory judgment obliging him to accept dismissal.

The parties' arguments in the Court of Appeal as well as in Supreme Court were largely the same and may be summarised as follows.

The applicant claimed that it was only formally and in its external aspects that the case concerned neglect of duty. Above all it concerned the innermost essence of the pastoral office. A clergyman had by virtue of his ordination received the call of God and the Church and he was bound primarily by the Word of God and the Confession of the Church. In the applicant's opinion he was acting through his protests on behalf of the Church, and this was so whether or not everybody within the Church agreed with the method of action he had chosen.

The reason for his action should be found in the Abortion Act of 1978. The applicant insisted that the Act implied the abandonment of every legal protection of the budding human life and involved in principle a denial of the foetus's human worth. The Act was in conflict with basic Christian values and hence also with art, 2 and 4 of the Norwegian Constitution which establishes the Evangelical Lutheran religion as the State's official faith. It was moreover in conflict with unwritten constitutional principles and with rules of international law for the protection of human rights. His acts of protest were intended to make the courts examine the legality of the Act. The legality of the Act should be examined in relation to the Constitution or to other superior sources of law. If the applicant was right in claiming that the Act was void, this would influence the evaluation of his action and hence the question whether he could be dismissed.

Furthermore the applicant maintained that his actions were justified under an emergency aspect. The Abortion Act created for the Church a state of affairs that could be called a confession situation, where the Church would lose its credibility if it failed actively to take up the struggle against a denial of vital christian and human values. He, as pastor, was committed by church doctrine, and it was not merely his right but also his duty to react on behalf of the Church. The action he chose went no further than was justified by the situation.

Finally the applicant was of the opinion that even if his acts of protest should not be considered justified, there were in his view no grounds for dismissal. He did not contest that art. 10 of the Criminal Code Enforcement Act, under which a Government official may be dismissed when he persistently proves unable adequately to perform his duties, was in principle applicable also to an official who refused to perform his duties. But the official duties that were neglected in this case were so modest that they could not form reasonable grounds for a dismissal.

The Government through the Ministry of Church and Education on the other hand argued that there were three independent grounds for dismissal. First, the applicant had for several years refused to perform functions that were clearly duties of his office. Second, he had revoked his oath of loyalty which he had made under art. 21 of the Constitution on assuming office, and he could thus no longer be regarded as satisfying the validly required conditions for holding that office. Third, he had by written word and deed made it clear that he considered himself to have retired from office. It should thus be justifiable for the Government to take him at his word and to confirm the dismissal which he himself had in reality effected. The conditions for dismissal according to art. 10 of the Criminal Code Enforcement Act were therefore satisfied.

Furthermore, in the Government's view, the case did not justify any discussion of the position of the Abortion Act in relation to the Constitution, to other constitutional rules or to international law. The Government were of the opinion that the decisive point was that the Abortion Act did not interfere with the applicant's terms of employment; the official duties he refused to perform bore no relation to the Abortion Act. The Government moreover contested that the provisions of art. 2 and 4 of the Constitution regarding the Established Church imposed barriers to legislation which did not concern the Established Church's own affairs. If any such barriers should exist, it was doubtful how far the courts might be competent to undertake the constitutional review which the applicant had requested.

The Government finally maintained that the applicant's acts could not be defended on grounds of emergency law. The applicant had every opportunity of battling for his view of the Abortion Act without resorting to unlawful discontinuance of his functions.

The Court of Appeal pronounced judgment on 26 November 1982 in which the applicant was dismissed from his job according to art. 10 of the Criminal Code Enforcement Act. With regard to the applicant's allegations that the Abortion Act violated constitutional and international law the Court found no reason to express itself on these matters since the Abortion Act did not interfere with the terms of employment between the applicant and the State. The Court found no link between the official duties which the applicant had refused to carry out and the Abortion Act.

On 23 September 1983 the Supreme Court upheld the decision of the Court of Appeal. Regarding the question whether the case provided an occasion for examining the validity of the Abortion Act with regard to constitutional and international law Justice Aasland wrote for the unanimous court:

„Although there are strong indications that the case could have been decided on the grounds argued here by the Government with reference to the Appeal Court's judgment, I find it unsatisfactory under the circumstances to ignore the question of the legal validity of the Abortion Act.

...

[The applicant] has also claimed that the Abortion Act should be regarded as invalid because it is incompatible with central legal principles of a constitutional nature and moreover with rules of international law which bind the legislator. Every Government operating under the rule of law must, he claims, be obliged to establish legal protection of human life, including the unborn life. The Human Rights declaration, adopted by the United Nations on 10 December 1948, affirms in art. 3 that everybody has the right to life, freedom and personal safety. And art. 2 of the European Human Rights Convention of 4 November 1950 provides: ‚Everyone's right to life shall be protected by law. No one shall be deprived of life intentionally, save in the execution of a sentence of a court following his conviction of a crime for which this penalty is provided by law.'

In [the applicant's] view, this Convention overrides internal Norwegian legislation. And in addition he claims - as already mentioned - that the Government's obligation to protect the unborn life applies as a constitutional barrier for the legislator whether or not it follows from any written source of law, since every government operating under the rule of law is obliged not to undermine essential human rights. On that basis the Abortion Act, which deprives the foetus of legal protection in its first twelve weeks of life, should be declared void.

I find it obvious that these arguments too fail to lead to the conclusion that the Abortion Act is invalid.

I start with the question of international law, where the provision of art. 2 of the European Human Rights Convention is particularly important. This Convention, to which Norway has acceded, is legally binding on the contracting States. A somewhat controversial question in the literature on international law is whether and to what extent the provision of art. 2 imposes requirements as to the contents of abortion laws. The Austrian Constitutional Court has in a decision of 11 October 1974 considered that the provision according to its contents does not comprise the unborn. I for my pan do not find it necessary to decide whether it is justified to rely on such an absolute interpretation. In any case the provision must be regarded as not imposing any far-reaching restrictions on the legislator's right to set the conditions for abortion. The Norwegian Act, under which the woman herself makes the final decision whether or not to terminate her pregnancy provided the operation can be made before the end of the twelfth week of pregnancy, is similar to the legislation of a number of other countries belonging to the same culture, countries which also have acceded to the European Human Rights Convention. This is hardly immaterial to the consideration of a matter of international law.

I add for the sake of good order that the decision of 25 February 1975 by the Constitutional Court [of the Federal Republic of Germany] which was mentioned by the Court of Appeal, in which a law permitting the woman herself to require an abortion in the first twelve weeks of pregnancy was declared invalid, concerned the application of internal constitutional rules.

The question now remains whether the Abortion Act is incompatible with unwritten principles of law which bind the legislator. It is of course conceivable that such principles of law might impose more far-reaching requirements on the legislator than does the Human Rights Convention. Another matter is that both the Convention and legislative practice in other countries belonging to our culture must be taken into consideration as expressing the margin it is natural for the legislator to have in this area.

The Supreme Court has in certain decisions, see especially Rt. 1961 p. 1350 and Rt. 1966 p. 476, left open the possibility that a law may have to be declared void if it conflicts with certain general principles of law of a constitutional nature, even if it is not contrary to any positive rule of the Constitution. It was made clear in the 1961 decision, however, that this can only be done in extreme cases, and „that quite exceptional circumstances must be present in order for a law, issued by the Storting and sanctioned by the King, to be thus declared void as conflicting with the „spirit and principles" of the Constitution."

Clearly in my opinion, respect for human life, including the unborn life, is one of the legal principles that might be accepted as overriding positive law. In principle it is not difficult to conceive that an abortion law, based for example on nazi race ideology, might infringe human rights in such a way that it would have to be invalidated as contrary to unwritten standards of law of a constitutional nature. However, this example is remote from our reality.

The Abortion Act which is being challenged by [the applicant] is not the reflection of a legislative ideology based on a lack of respect for human life. I refer to the passages I have quoted above from the opinions expressed in the drafting of the said Act. But abortion laws must necessarily be based on a compromise between the respect for the unborn life and other essential and worthy considerations. This compromise has led the legislator to permit self-determined abortion under the circumstances defined by the Act.

Clearly, such a reconciliation of disparate considerations give rise to ethical problems, and clearly too, there will be some disagreement about the system embodied in the Act. The reactions to the Act show that many, like [the applicant], view it as an attack on central ethical principles. But it is equally relevant that others - also from an ethical point of view - regard the Act as having done away with an unacceptable legal situation.

It is not a matter for the courts to decide whether the solution to a difficult legislative problem which the legislator chose when adopting the Abortion Act of 1978, is the best one. On this point, different opinions will be held among judges as among other members of our society. The reconciliation of opposing interests which abortion laws require is the legislator's task and the legislator's responsibility. The legislative power is exercised by the People through the Storting. The Storting majority which adopted the Abortion Act in 1978 had its mandate from the People after an election campaign in which the abortion question had a prominent place. As already mentioned, the Stoning in 1983, after a new election in which the abortion question was again a central issue, decided moreover not to take the initiative towards any statutory amendment. Clearly, the courts must respect the solution chosen by the legislator.

I accordingly find that [the applicant[has been unsuccessful in challenging the legal validity of the Abonion Act. "

By virtue of this judgment the applicant was dismissed from his job. However, by letter of 6 September 1983 from the Ministry of Church and Education, to which a Royal Decree of 15 January 1982 had delegated the competence to grant a dispensation from the loss of pastoral rights following a possible judgment for dismissal, the Ministry decided that the applicant should not forfeit these rights which follow from his ordination.

This meant that the applicant could continue to carry out religious functions, however, no longer as a State employee.

COMPLAINTS

The applicant maintains that the Norwegian Abortion Act in its wording following the amendment of 16 June 1978, is in contravention of art. 2 of the Convention. He also maintains that the Norwegian Supreme Court has arrived at an incorrect result. It is further maintained in this context that the Convention on Human Rights as a rule of international law supersedes national legislation. If, therefore, the Commission finds that Norwegian legislation in this field is in conflict with the Convention, the consequence is that the Norwegian legislation must be amended.

The applicant is of the opinion that he has a direct legal interest in a decision as to whether Norwegian law is in contravention of art. 2. His case is allegedly different from the earlier so-called abortion cases brought before the Commission, in which the applicants approached the subject in their capacity of ordinary citizens with public interests, but without being personally affected by the national legislation which they attacked. The applicant finds that his case is different: he has risked - and lost - his office on the issue of the acceptability of the Norwegian Abortion Act, i.e. in relation to the Convention on Human Rights. And therefore he has a direct and personal interest in the examination of the matter. It cannot be said in his case therefore, that his interest is of an entirely abstract nature. He will resume his functions in the Norwegian State Church, provided his view on the Abortion Act is upheld. It is his belief that it must follow from a decision by the Commission or the Court, based on his conception of the law, that the Norwegian law must be amended.

The applicant's second line of argument is that his dismissal from his office contravenes art. 9 of the Convention. He has been dismissed from his office although his views on the abortion issue are the same as those of the Church. He alleges that his dismissal was against the wishes of the members of his parish and against the advice of his bishop. In this connection it is argued that a minister in the Church has mixed duties, both towards the Church and towards the State, and that his duties towards the Church are of far greater importance than his relatively unimportant duties towards the State. It is therefore submitted that a minister cannot be dismissed against the wishes of the Church, and that a dismissal solely at the request of the State authorities and upheld by the court, constitutes a breach of the Convention.

THE LAW

1. The applicant has first complained that the Norwegian Abortion Act as it was formulated following the amendment of 16 June 1978 contravenes art. 2 of the Convention. He is furthermore of the opinion that he is personally affected by the above legislation in that he has risked - and lost - his office as vicar of Balsfjord within the Norwegian State Church on account of his views on this issue.

Art. 2 of the Convention provides that everyone's right to life shall be protected by law. Deprivation of life is not permitted under the Convention except in certain cases enumerated in the second sentence of art. 2 par. 1, in art. 2 par. 2, and art. 15 par. 2 of the Convention.

However, it is clear from art. 25 par. 1 of the Convention that the Commission can receive an application from a person, non-governmental organisation or group of individuals only if such person, non-governmental organisation or group of individuals can claim to be a victim of a violation by one of the High Contracting Parties of the rights set forth in the Convention.

The Commission recalls in this respect its earlier case-law according to which the Commission is competent to examine the compatibility of domestic legislation with the Convention only with respect to its application in a concrete case, while it is not competent to examine in abstracto its compatibility with the Convention. The Commission refers on this point in particular to No. 867/60, Dec. 29.5.61, Collection 6 p. 34 concerning a similar case with respect to the introduction of new abortion legislation in Norway where the above principle was applied. The Commission also refers to No. 7045/75, Dec. 10.12.76, DR 7 p. 87 in which the Commission found that the applicant could not claim to be affected by the new legislation in a way different to any other citizen.

On the other hand the Commission has also in No. 6959/75, Dec. 19.5.76, DR 5 p. 103 developed the above principle in the sense that application of the law in a concrete case must not necessarily mean its application by a judicial or other authority. It is sufficient that the applicant is immediately concerned by it. Finally the Commission also recalls No. 8416/79, Dec. 13.5.80, DR 19 p. 244 in which the Commission accepted that the applicant, as a potential father, was so closely affected by the termination of his wife's pregnancy that he could claim to be a victim, within the meaning of art. 25 of the Convention, of the legislation complained of.

With regard to the question whether the applicant can be considered a victim of a violation of art. 2 of the Convention within the meaning of art. 25, the Commission has examined this case under the criteria laid down in the decisions mentioned above.

The Commission recalls that the applicant is of the opinion that he has a direct legal interest in a decision as to whether Norwegian law contravenes art. 2. His case is allegedly different from the earlier so-called abortion cases brought before the Commission, in which the applicants approached the subject in their capacity of ordinary citizens with public interests, but without being personally affected by the national legislation which they attacked. He has risked - and lost - his office on the issue of the acceptability of the Norwegian Abortion Act, i.e. in relation to the Convention on Human Rights. He maintains, therefore, that he has a direct and personal interest in the examination of the matter and that it cannot be said in his case that his interest is of an entirely abstract nature. He will resume a position in the Norwegian State Church, provided his view of the Abortion Act is upheld. It is his belief that it must follow from a decision by the Commission or the Court, based on his conception of the law, that the Norwegian law must be amended.

The Commission finds in accordance with its above case-law that a person cannot claim to be a victim of a violation of the Convention unless he can show that he is personally affected by the circumstances of the case. In regard to legislation governing abortion in connection with art. 2 of the Convention this question obviously raises certain questions as to who may claim to be personally affected by the situation. The Commission has accepted that a potential father may claim to be a victim of an alleged violation of art. 2 but has on the other hand rejected applications where, however respectable his motives may be, the applicant cannot show that he has been affected by the new legislation in a way different to any other citizen.

The Commission cannot find that the applicant in the present case was affected differently by the new legislation than other citizens. The amendment to the Abortion Act did not directly affect the applicant in his family life nor did it affect him in his obligations as vicar. It is true that he lost the said office, but this was not due to the Abortion Act as such but to the fact that the applicant, because of his views on the Act, refused to perform functions that were duties of his office. The functions in question were considered by the applicant to belong to the State's part of the office of vicar. He performed no marriages, examination of marriage conditions or conciliation in matrimonial cases. He refused to keep the birth register, refused to receive Government mail and refused to receive salary from the Government.

The Commission finds that even though the applicant's attitude was motivated by his opposition to the Abortion Act, the sanctions imposed upon him cannot lead to the conclusion that he can claim to be a victim within the meaning of art. 25 of the Convention with regard to that Act.

The Commission therefore concludes that the matters raised by the applicant are abstract questions within the meaning of the Commission's constant case-law. It follows that the applicant cannot, with regard to this complaint, claim to be a victim of a violation of the Convention. This part of the application is therefore incompatible *ratione personae* with the provisions of the Convention and must consequently be rejected under art. 27 par. 2 of the Convention.

2. The applicant has also complained that the Norwegian Abortion Act as amended on 16 June 1978 violates his rights under art. 9 of the Convention in that he was dismissed from his office although his views on the abortion issue are the same as those of the Church.

Art. 9 of the Convention provides:

> 1. Everyone has the right to freedom of thought, conscience and religion; this right includes freedom to change his religion or belief and freedom, either alone or in community with others and in public or private, to manifest his religion or belief, in worship, teaching, practice and observance.
>
> 2. Freedom to manifest one's religion or beliefs shall be subject only to such limitations as are prescribed by law and are necessary in a democratic society in the interests of public safety, for the protection of public order, health or morals, or for the protection of the rights and freedoms of others.

The Commission first points out that a right to hold office within the Norwegian State Church or in general is not as such guaranteed by the Convention. Nevertheless the Commission considers it conceivable that a dismissal of a State official for disobedience could in certain circumstances raise an issue under the above article.

However, in the circumstances of the present case no such issue arises for the following reason.

The Commission finds that a clergyman within a State Church system, has not only religious duties, but has also accepted certain obligations towards the State. If the requirements imposed upon him by the State should be in conflict with his convictions. he is free to relinquish his office as clergyman within the State Church, and the Commission regards this as an ultimate guarantee of his right to freedom of thought, conscience and religion.

In the present case the Commission recalls that the applicant refused to carry out functions that were duties of his office and that he lost the said office. The Commission also recalls that the applicant has retained the pastoral rights which follow from his ordination and which allow him to carry out religious functions. Finally, it is recalled that the applicant's religious views, including his views on the abortion issue, were consistent with the views held by the Norwegian State Church.

However, these views expressed by the applicant did not lead to his dismissal which the Commission finds was due to his refusal to perform functions that were administrative duties of his office. The Commission finds that this refusal did not actually express the applicant's belief or religious views and it cannot, therefore, be considered as such to be protected by art. 9 par. 1, even when it was motivated by such views or belief (cf. Arrowsmith v. the United Kingdom, Comm. Report 12.10.78, par. 71, DR 19 p. 19). The applicant has not shown that he has been under any pressure to change his views or that he has been prevented from manifesting his religion or belief. It follows, that the applicant's dismissal did not in any way interfere with the exercise of his rights under art. 9 of the Convention and this part of the application is therefore manifestly ill-founded within the meaning of art. 27 par. 2 of the Convention. For these reasons, the Commission declares the application inadmissible.

20

Ein Arbeitgeber, der bestimmte Überzeugungen und Wertentscheidungen als wesentlich für die Erfüllung seines Auftrags in der Gesellschaft erachtet, darf auch einen entsprechenden Rahmen für die Freiheit der Meinungsäußerung der Arbeitnehmer bestimmen (hier: kirchlicher Krankenhausträger für mediale Äußerungen eines angestellten Arztes).

Art. 10, 27 § 2 a.f. EMRK
EKMR, Beschluss vom 6. September 1989 - No.12242/86
(Rommelfanger ./. Deutschland)[1] -

THE FACTS

The applicant, a German citizen born in 1950, is a physician. As from 1 February 1979 the applicant was employed as an assistant physician in the hospital of a Roman Catholic foundation (kirchliche Stiftung) in E.. The hospital provides medical care for the public in general without distinction of faith. About 80% of its staff of 630 employees, including 60 physicians, are Roman Catholics. Most of the remaining employees belong to other churches.

The position of the Roman Catholic church under constitutional law in the Federal Republic of Germany is governed by art. 140 of the Basic Law (Grundgesetz) read in conjunction with the Weimar Constitution of 11 August 1919.

The applicant's contract contained a clause according to which the employment relationship was to be governed by the guidelines issued by the umbrella organisation of Catholic charities in Germany (Richtlinien für Arbeitsverträge in den Einrichtungen des Deutschen Caritas-Verbandes). Rule 1 of these guidelines refers to the duties which flow from charity (Caritas) as an essential expression of christian life. The employees are required to perform their services in loyalty and to show a behaviour inside and outside their professional functions which, as a whole,

---

[1] DR 62, 151.

corresponds to the responsibility which they have accepted. It is presupposed that in performing their professional duties they will be guided by christian principles. Rule 16 further stipulates that both parties may terminate the contract for important reasons without complying with the period of notice. Important reasons are, in particular, „breaches of loyalty or gross violations of due respect towards members of the Caritas organisation, leading persons or essential institutions of the Catholic church, serious offences against moral principles of the church or against State law, or other gross violations of professional duties under these guidelines". The guidelines are generally used in employment contracts of Catholic institutions.

In September 1979 the applicant, together with some fifty persons including another physician of the same hospital, signed a letter to the editor of the weekly magazine „Stern" which was published in October under the headline „Physicians versus physicians' representatives" („Ärzte gegen Ärztefunktionäre"). It contained criticism of the attitude of leading personalities in the medical professional organisations concerning the abortion legislation introduced in 1976. In its current version sec. 218a of the Criminal Code (Strafgesetzbuch) provides that an abortion performed by a doctor shall not be punishable if it is carried out with the consent of the pregnant woman not later than twelve weeks after conception and if it is indicated according to medical opinion „in order to avert the danger of a distress which a) is so serious that the pregnant woman cannot be required to continue the pregnancy, and b) cannot be averted in any other way she can reasonably be expected to bear".

The letter to the editor was couched in the following words:

„Wir wehren uns mit diesem Aufruf besonders gegen die Angriffe, die von klerikal-konservativer und standesärztlicher Seite gegen die Praxis des derzeitigen Paragraphen 218 geführt werden. So verglich Dr. Holzgartner, CSU-Funktionär und Vorstandsmitglied der Bayrischen Ärztekammer, den legalen Schwangerschaftsabbruch mit den Massenmorden der Nazis in Auschwitz. Dr. Karsten Vilmar, Präsident der Bundesärztekammer, wollte sogar bestreiten, dass es in einem so reichen Staat wie der BRD eine Notwendigkeit zum Schwangerschaftsabbruch aus sozialer Notlage geben könne. Wir sehen unsere Position zum Abtreibungsparagraphen 218 nicht durch die inhumanen Äußerungen des Präsidenten der Bundesärztekammer vertreten und distanzieren uns von diesen und ähnlichen Versuchen, eine notwendige und sinnvolle Entwicklung zu hemmen. Wir kennen aus eigener beruflicher Praxis die z.T. unlösbaren Schwierigkeiten von Frauen in unserem Land, die ungewollt schwanger geworden sind."

On 13 February 1980 the applicant's employer gave him notice of the termination of his employment contract as from 31 March 1980.

The only reason invoked was his having signed the above letter to the editor. This was seen as a violation of the duties under his employment contract as the views expressed therein were diametrically opposed to the opinion of the church concerning the killing of unborn human beings and as he had deliberately published these views in a magazine with a very wide circulation.

On 11 March 1980 the applicant and his colleague of the same hospital, who had also been dismissed, gave a television interview in which they were, inter alia, asked about the consequences which they drew from the dismissal. The applicant replied that the first consequence was not to depart from the views expressed earlier which referred to the position of sec. 218 and approved it. The applicant's colleague declared that another consequence was to take the case to the courts as they had only expressed support for the existing legislation. At this interview, the applicant and his colleague did not repeat the contents of the above letter to the editor which was summarised by the moderator. As a consequence of this interview, the applicant's employer, on 20 March 1980, again gave notice of dismissal to the applicant with effect from 31 March 1980 or subsidiarily 30 June 1980. The reason stated was that in the above television interview he had defended views on sec. 218 of the Penal Code before a wide audience which, as he must have known, were unacceptable for his employer as a Catholic hospital.

The applicant challenged both dismissals before the competent labour courts which conducted two separate proceedings.

I. In the case concerning the dismissal of 13 February 1980, the Labour Court (Arbeitsgericht) of Essen allowed the applicant's action on 15 April 1980, holding that his dismissal was „manifestly invalid". The applicant had acted outside his professional functions when he signed the letter to the editor. The employer's appeal (Berufung) was rejected by the Regional Labour Court (Landesarbeitsgericht) of Düsseldorf on 8 September 1980 (21 Sa 582/80; KirchE 18, 258). Because of the fundamental importance of the case, the employer was granted leave to appeal on a point of law (Revision) to the Federal Labour Court (Bundesarbeitsgericht). However, the employer's appeal was rejected by that Court on 21 October 1982 (2 AZR 591/80; KirchE 20, 160).

II. The proceedings concerning the second dismissal generally followed those concerning the first dismissal. By judgment of 21 May 1980 the Labour Court of Essen held that also the second dismissal was socially unjustified. It was wrong to see a new violation of the applicant's duties in the fact that he had merely confirmed the views previously expressed. On 3 October 1980 the Regional Labour Court (17 Sa 964/80; KirchE 18, 285) confirmed this decision. It considered that the television interview involved a new breach of loyalty, but that it was justified by important interests which the applicant pursued. This latter decision was confirmed by the Federal Labour Court on 21 October 1982 (2 AZR 628/80; EzA § 1 KSchG Tendenzbetrieb Nr. 12; KirchE 20, 160).

III. The employer lodged constitutional complaints (Verfassungsbeschwerden) in both cases, invoking the fundamental right of freedom of religion under art. 4 par. 2 of the Basic Law and the right of church autonomy under art. 140 of the Basic Law read in conjunction with art. 137 par. 3 of the Weimar Constitution. The employer challenged, in particular, the Federal Labour Court's view that the degree of loyalty of church employees differs according to the measure in which they participate in the specific religious functions of the church.

The Federal Constitutional Court (Bundesverfassungsgericht) dealt with the complaints in joint proceedings and allowed them by a decision of 4 June 1985 (2 BvR 1703/83, 1718/83 u. 856/84; KirchE 23, 105).

On 15 January 1986 the Federal Labour Court (7 AZR 545/86; KirchE 24, 7) thereupon rejected the applicant's actions against his first and second dismissal, following the reasoning of the Federal Constitutional Court in conformity with sec. 31 of the Federal Constitutional Court Act.

The applicant's dismissal with effect from 31 March 1980 thus became finally valid. In the meanwhile he had been offered a post in a Catholic hospital in Duisburg as from 1 September 1985. The offer was withdrawn following the judgment of 15 January 1986. As a consequence the applicant remained unemployed for a month. He is now working in a non-Catholic hospital.

COMPLAINT

The applicant alleges a violation of his right to freedom of expression as guaranteed by art. 10 of the Convention.

PROCEEDINGS

(...)

THE LAW

The applicant alleges a violation of his right to freedom of expression as guaranteed by art. 10 of the Convention which reads as follows:

„1. Everyone has the right to freedom of expression. This right shall include freedom to hold opinions and to receive and impart information and ideas without interference by public authority and regardless of frontiers. ...
2. The exercise of these freedoms, since it carries with it duties and responsibilities, may be subject to such formalities, conditions, restrictions or penalties as are prescribed by law and are necessary in a democratic society, in the interests of national security, territorial integrity or public safety, for the prevention of disorder or crime, for the protection of health or morals, for the protection of the reputation or rights of others, for preventing the disclosure of information received in confidence, or for maintaining the authority and impartiality of the judiciary."

The applicant claims that the State is responsible for an interference with his right to freedom of expression as, following his dismissal by a

Catholic foundation because he had expressed a particular opinion, the Federal Constitutional Court, adopting an unreasonably wide interpretation of church autonomy, failed to protect him. The constitutional norms applied did not provide a sufficiently precise, and foreseeable, legal basis for the restriction of his freedom of expression which, moreover, was disproportionate and not necessary in a democratic society for any of the purposes recognised in art. 10 par. 2.

The Government deny that there has been any direct interference by the State with the applicant's freedom of expression. The limitation of this freedom resulted from the applicant's employment contract with a church institution in which he waived this freedom as regards statements contrary to his duty of loyalty. The applicant could freely express his views concerning abortion, but he had no right to do so while being employed in a Catholic hospital where he had assumed special duties and responsibilities. According to the Government the State was not required to protect him vis-à-vis the employer beyond ensuring that the latter did not make unreasonable demands on him. In this respect it was appropriate for the State to adopt a restrictive approach having regard to the church's right to regulate its internal affairs which is recognised not only in German constitutional law, but also in art. 9 of the Convention. The legal basis for the restriction of the applicant's freedom of expression was sufficiently concrete and foreseeable. The restriction was also proportionate, having regard in particular to the applicant's special duties as a physician employed in a Catholic hospital and the State's wide margin of appreciation.

The Commission must first determine whether in the circumstances of the case the applicant is entitled to invoke his freedom of expression under art. 10. The Government claim that he is debarred from doing so because he waived this freedom by assuming certain duties of loyalty towards the Catholic church in his employment contract.

The Commission finds no basis for the assumption that the applicant waived his freedom of expression as such. That he accepted the status of a doctor employed by a Catholic hospital could not deprive him of the protection afforded by art. 10. However, art. 10 can only be violated if there has been a State interference with the applicant's rights under this provision. Unlike the situation in the Kosiek and Glasenapp cases (cf. EuCHR judgments of 28 August 1986, Series A nos. 104 and 105) the dismissal on the ground of the expression of certain opinions was not pronounced by a State authority. The applicant was dismissed by a private employer. The fact that this was a Catholic foundation and that in German law the Catholic church is regarded as a corporation of public law does not make the dismissal an act of the State. Under the Convention the State cannot be held responsible for acts of the Catholic church or its institutions which must be regarded as non-governmental organisations within the meaning of art. 25 of the Convention. There is thus no question of a direct State interference with the applicant's freedom of expression by his dismissal.

The applicant claims that there has been an indirect State interference in that the German courts failed to protect his freedom of expression against the sanction of dismissal. The Government submit that the courts were not required to protect the applicant as he had accepted limitations of his freedom of expression in his employment contract.

The Commission notes that by entering into contractual obligations vis-à-vis his employer the applicant accepted a duty of loyalty towards the Catholic church which limited his freedom of expression to a certain extent. Similar obligations may also be agreed with other employers than the Catholic church or its institutions. In principle, the Convention permits contractual obligations of this kind if they are freely entered into by the person concerned. A violation of such obligations normally entails the legal consequences stipulated in the contract, including dismissal. Their enforcement with the assistance of the competent State authorities does not as such constitute an „interference by public authority" with the rights guaranteed by art. 10 par. 1 of the Convention (cf. Application No. 11142/84, Carrillo and Burgoa v. Spain, Dec. 3.12.86)

It is true that under art. 1 of the Convention the State is required to „secure" the Convention rights to everyone within its jurisdiction. In certain cases it may therefore be necessary for the State to take positive action with a view to effectively securing these rights (cf. EuCHR, Marckx judgment of 13 June 1979, Series A no. 31, p. 15 par. 31; judgment of X and Y v. the Netherlands of 26 March 1985, Series A no. 91, p. 11 par. 23; Abdulaziz, Cabales and Balkandali judgment of 28 May 1985, Series A no. 94, p. 33 par. 67; Plattform „Ärzte für das Leben" judgment of 21 June 1988, Series A no. 139, p. 12 par. 32). In the case of Young, James and Webster it was held that a positive obligation could arise for the State to provide protection against dismissals pronounced because the applicants had refused to join particular trade unions. The compulsion to do so, under sanction of dismissal, was seen as an interference with their right to freedom of association under art. 11 of the Convention (EuCHR, judgment of 13 August 1981, Series A no. 44, p. 23 par. 55), and the State's responsibility was seen as being engaged by the enactment of legislation which made this treatment of the applicants lawful and thus failed to secure them their rights under art. 11 (ibid. p. 20 par. 49).

The Commission has examined whether in the present case a similar obligation existed for the State to secure the applicant's right to freedom of expression against the measure of dismissal taken by his employer. The normal Labour Court procedure was available to the applicant and the competent courts were required to weigh the applicant's interests, including his interest in freedom of expression, against those of his employer. It is true that particular weight was finally given to the views of the church concerning the duties of loyalty of church employees. According to the Federal Constitutional Court this was necessary in order to safeguard the constitutional right of the church to regulate its internal affairs. Nevertheless the Federal Constitutional Court held that there were limits to the right of the church to impose its views on its employees. In particular the State courts were competent to ensure that no unreasonable demands of loyalty were made. The requirement to refrain from making statements on abortion in conflict with the church's views was not seen as an unreasonable demand because of the crucial importance of this issue for the church. In the case of a doctor employed in a Catholic hospital it was also relevant that the church regards the exercise of charitable functions as one of its essential tasks.

The Commission is satisfied that German law, as interpreted by the Federal Constitutional Court, takes account of the necessity to secure an employee's freedom of expression against unreasonable demands of his employer, even if they should result from a valid employment contract. If, as in the present case, the employer is an organisation based on certain convictions and value judgments which it considers as essential for the performance of its functions in society, it is in fact in line with the requirements of the Convention to give appropriate scope also to the freedom of expression of the employer. An employer of this kind would not be able to effectively exercise this freedom without imposing certain duties of loyalty on its employees. As regards employers such as the Catholic foundation which employed the applicant in its hospital, the law in any event ensures that there is a reasonable relationship between the measures affecting freedom of expression and the nature of the employment as well as the importance of the issue for the employer. In this way it protects an employee against compulsion in matters of freedom of expression which would strike at the very substance of this freedom (cf. a contrario Young, James and Webster judgment, loc. cit., p. 23 par. 55). The Commission considers that art. 10 of the Convention does not, in cases like the present one, impose a positive obligation on the State to provide protection beyond this standard.

It follows that there has been no State interference with the applicant's right to freedom of expression as guaranteed in art. 10 par. 1 of the Convention, nor a failure to comply with positive obligations resulting from this provision. The applicant's complaint must therefore be rejected as being manifestly ill-founded within the meaning of art. 27 par. 2 of the Convention.

For these reasons, the Commission declares the application inadmissible.

21

Es erscheint nicht offensichtlich unbegründet, dass die Verknüpfung von Arbeitsverhältnis und Gewerkschaftsmitgliedschaft für einen orthodoxen Hindu eine Beeinträchtigung seiner Religionsfreiheit darstellt.

Art. 9, 11 EMRK
EKMR, Beschluss vom 16. Mai 1990 - No. 11518/85
(Chauhan ./. Vereinigtes Königreich)[1] -

THE FACTS

The applicant is a citizen of the United Kingdom born in 1938 and is an electrician by profession. He resides in London.

The applicant had been employed as an electrician by the Ford Motor Company since 1978. The company had, at that time, a union membership agreement which required an employee to be a member of a union. The applicant had previously been a member of the Transport and General Workers' Union (TGWU) since 1976 but his membership had lapsed. He then joined the Electrical, Electronics, Telecommunication and Plumbing Union (EETPU) as required by the union membership agreement at the beginning of his employment with the Ford Motor Company. In April 1980 he allowed his membership of the EETPU to lapse by failing to keep up his subscriptions. From that date he has not been a member of any trade union. However, he continued to work for the Ford Motor Company and it was not until three years later, early in June 1983, that the fact of his lapsed union membership came to light.

The applicant claimed that he was a devout orthodox Hindu belonging to the Radhaswami sect. He explained that this sect divided its religious activities into four stages and that he had progressed to the third stage. He considered that the religious teaching at this stage of his religion did not permit him to be a member of a trade union. The applicant offered to pay to charity a sum equivalent to his union dues.

The applicant was subsequently invited by the Employee Relations Manager to appeal to an independent panel, as provided for under the union membership agreement, in order to explain the reasons for his refusal. He subsequently refused to have recourse to this appeal procedure since he considered that the panel could not be regarded as independent so long as any member of a trade union was represented upon it.

The applicant was subsequently dismissed from his employment on 21 October 1983.

---

[1] DR 65, 41.

The applicant then filed an application before the Industrial Tribunal. He complained that his dismissal was unfair since he had genuine objections on grounds of conscience justifying his refusal to join a trade union in accordance with sec. 58 (4) of the Employment Protection (Consolidation) Act 1978.

On 23 January 1984 the Industrial Tribunal rejected the applicant's case, finding that he had not proved a genuine and conscientious objection. Accordingly, his dismissal was fair under the 1978 Act. The Tribunal was satisfied that the Employee Relations Manager had explored the applicant's stated religious objections to trade union membership and that he was entitled to conclude that the applicant did not have a genuine conscientious objection. The Tribunal added:

> *„In order to make a judgment on a man's beliefs and motivations, it is necessary to take account of his actions as well as his words. For our own part, we find it extremely hard to reconcile the applicant's three-year silence with his protestations of conscience. "*

The applicant appealed against this decision to the Employment Appeals Tribunal. This appeal was rejected.

Relevant Domestic law and practice

The Employment Protection (Consolidation) Act 1978 consolidated the unfair dismissal provisions of previous legislation, notably the Trade Union and Labour Relations Act 1974, the Employment Protection Act 1975 and the Trade Union and Labour Relations (Amendment) Act 1976. Under this legislation dismissal for not being a trade union member was to be regarded as fair save where the employee genuinely objected on grounds of religious belief to being a member of a trade union.

The Employment Act 1980 provided greater protection for employees who refused to join a trade union. Dismissal was to be regarded as unfair for:

> *(a) employees who genuinely objected on grounds of conscience or other deeply-held personal conviction to being members of any trade union whatsoever or of a particular union;*
> *(b) employees who belonged to the class of employee covered by the closed shop agreement before it took effect and who had at no time subsequently been members of a trade union in accordance with the agreement;*
> *(c) employees working under a closed shop agreement brought into effect after 14 August 1980, but not approved by at least 80% of the employees covered by the agreement voting in favour of the agreement in secret ballot;*
> *(d) employees working under a closed shop agreement brought into effect after 14 August 1980 which had been approved by at least 80% of those employees covered by it in a secret ballot in which the employee was entitled to vote if the employee*

had not at any time since the day on which the ballot was held been a member of the union.

In addition, a Code of Practice was issued with the authority of Parliament and came into effect on 17 December 1980 (subsequently revised in May 1983). It recommended, inter alia, that closed shop agreements should protect basic individual rights, and be applied flexibly and tolerantly and with due regard to the interests of individuals as well as unions and employers. The Code is admissible in evidence, but imposes no legal obligations.

The Employment Act 1982 further increased the protection of union employees working in the closed shop as well as re-enacting the closed shop dismissal provisions of the 1980 Act. In particular, the 1982 Act provides that the dismissal of an employee for not being a member of a trade union, or for refusing to join one, is automatically unfair where the closed shop concerned is not „approved". Up to 31 October 1984 any closed shop agreement which took effect on or before 14 August 1980 counted as „approved". A closed shop agreement which took effect after 14 August 1980 only counts as „approved" if it has been supported in a secret ballot of all employees affected in which 80% or more of those entitled to vote voted in its favour. These were the provisions enforced when the applicant was dismissed on 21 October 1983.

Since 1 November 1984 a closed shop agreement counts as „approved" on a given date only if in the five years preceding that date it has been supported in a secret ballot involving all the employees affected. The required levels of support in the ballot are set out in the 1982 Act.

Where a closed shop agreement is „approved" dismissal for non- membership of a trade union is not automatically fair. The dismissal of certain categories of employee for not being members of a trade union, or for refusing to join one, remains unfair even where the closed shop agreement is an „approved" one. The protected categories are as follows:

(a) employees who genuinely object on grounds of conscience or other deeply-held personal conviction to being members of any trade union whatsoever or of a particular union; (b) employees who belonged to the class of employees covered by the closed shop agreement before it took effect and who have at no time subsequently been members of a trade union in accordance with the agreement; (c) employees who work under an „approved" closed shop agreement which took effect after 14 August 1980, were entitled to vote in the first or only ballot through which the closed shop agreement was approved, and have not since the day when that ballot was held been members of a trade union in accordance with the agreement; (d) employees who at the time of dismissal either had been found by an industrial tribunal to have been unreasonably excluded or expelled from the trade union of which membership was required under the closed shop agreement or who have a complaint of unreasonable exclusion or expulsion by that union lodged with an industrial tribunal under sec. 4 of the 1980 Act; (e) employees who have qualifi-

cations relating to their job which make them subject to a written code of conduct and either have been expelled from the trade union of which membership is required because they refused to strike or take other industrial action on the grounds that this would have breached the code of conduct; or have refused to belong to the union concerned on the grounds that membership would have required them to take industrial action in breach of the code.

If an employee is unfairly dismissed from either an „approved" or an „unapproved" closed shop for not being a member of a trade union, or for refusing to join one, an industrial tribunal can order the employer to re-employ the employee concerned where this is practicable or to pay him compensation. As a result of the 1982 Act, compensation in such cases has been set at substantially higher levels than in most other cases of unfair dismissal so as to act as a deterrent.

COMPLAINTS

The applicant complains that the dismissal from his employment was due exclusively to his refusal to join a trade union because of his religious objections. He alleges that his dismissal was in breach of art. 11 (1) of the Convention.

SUBMISSIONS OF THE PARTIES

The respondent Government

Art. 11 in conjunction with Art. 9 of the Convention

In the Government's submission where the complaint made is not of direct interference by the State of the rights guaranteed by the Convention but of a failure through its legal system to secure the right against interference by the action of others, the Convention requires the striking of a balance between the competing interests of the individual and of society as a whole. A search for this balance is inherent in the whole of the Convention (EuCHR, Sporrong and Lönnroth judgment of 22 September 1980, Series A no. 52, par. 69).

In marked contrast to the position of the applicants in the case of Young, James and Webster (EuCHR, judgment of 13 August 1981, Series A no. 44) the union membership, or closed shop, agreement within the Ford Motor Company was in full effect at the time when the applicant joined that firm. It is also clear that, for a period of over two years, the applicant in fact belonged to a trade union, first the TGWU and thereafter the EETPU.

Quite apart from the personal position of the applicant, the applicable law at the time of the present applicant's dismissal was substantially different from that which was in effect at the time of the dismissal of the applicants in the case of Young, James and Webster and which was found by the Court to provide inadequate protection for the rights and freedoms guaranteed by art. 11 of the Convention. In the submission of the Government, the provisions of the 1980 and 1982 Acts, designed as they were to increase the protection afforded to individual employees against dismissal for refusing to join a union, strike a fair balance between the rights of the individual and the right of other employees to organise through the closed shop system. In contrast to the position under the 1974 and 1976 Acts, which were the subject of the Court's judgment in the case of Young, James and Webster, it is submitted that the form of compulsion which is permitted under the 1982 Act and to which the applicant was subjected does not strike at the very substance of the freedom guaranteed by art. 11 (1) read on its own or in the light of art. 9, art. 10 of the Convention and did not give rise to a breach of that article in the circumstances of his case.

The Government further contest that art. 11 confers a negative right. The Court in the Young, James and Webster case expressly proceeded on the assumption that the negative aspect was not protected on the same footing as the positive aspect and that compulsion to join a particular union was not automatically contrary to this provision. The Court emphasised in that case that the dismissal stemmed from a closed shop agreement which was concluded after the three applicants were employed by British Rail. Such compulsion was imposed on the applicants unilaterally and was not a condition of their employment when they first applied for the job. In the present case the applicant accepted the requirement that he join a union as a condition of his employment by Ford Motor Company from the outset. This was an essential part of his contract of employment which he accepted voluntarily.

Moreover the applicant had an opportunity to submit his case to an internal tribunal which could have granted him an exception on the basis of his religious views. However the applicant withdrew his appeal because he objected to the presence of a union member. The Government do not accept that the presence of a union member in a tribunal of three persons, with an independent chairman, is a good reason for abandoning such an appeal.

Before the Industrial Tribunal the applicant sought to invoke the provisions of sec. 58 (4) of the 1978 Act submitting that he had genuine objections to union membership on the grounds of conscience or other deeply-held personal convictions. The applicant was represented by counsel before the Tribunal and it was open to him to support his case by both written and oral evidence. In the result, the Tribunal concluded from the material before them that the applicant had not established that he had any genuine objection to union membership on grounds of conscience or other deeply-held personal conviction. In so holding, the Tribunal placed particular reliance on the fact that the applicant had not asserted any objections to union membership until challenged some three years after he had allowed his membership to lapse.

In reviewing the decisions of the Industrial Tribunal and the Employment Appeal Tribunal the Commission should limit itself to the question whether such a determination was unfair, perverse, arbitrary or otherwise a denial of the applicants rights (see, mutatis mutandis, No. 8378/78, Dec of 14.5.80, DR 20 p. 168). However, in his application to the Commission, no complaint is made that the applicant was given an unfair hearing before either the Industrial Tribunal or the Employment Appeal Tribunal or that the decision reached by either of the Tribunals was arbitrary. Nor is it suggested that the decisions resulted from a misinterpretation or misapplication of sec. 58 (4) of the 1978 Act or that no Tribunal properly directing itself could reasonably have concluded that the applicant had no genuine objections to union membership on grounds of conscience or other deeply-held personal convictions.

The Government submit that in such circumstances neither the relevant provisions of domestic law nor the application of those provisions by the domestic tribunals upset the fair balance required by art. 11-1 of the Convention.

Art. 14 of the Convention

The Government submit that the applicant was given exactly the same treatment as other persons including members of other religions in a comparable situation. Neither the statutory provisions in force nor the Industrial Tribunal or Employment Appeal Tribunal treated the applicant in any way unfairly or less favourably than an applicant of a different religious persuasion. This complaint should therefore be rejected as manifestly ill-founded.

The Applicant

Art. 11 in conjunction with Art. 9 of the Convention

The present application is made on the basis that United Kingdom domestic law and practice does not afford the applicant protection of his rights and freedoms under art. 11 in conjunction with art. 9 of the Convention. In particular, protection against unfair dismissal does not extend to a situation where: (1) the applicant is a devout orthodox Hindu; (2) the applicant refuses to join a trade union.

The applicant points out that if the union membership agreement at his place of work had come into effect after 14 August 1980 he would have had the opportunity to vote on its application and, moreover, would have been protected from unfair dismissal on the ground of non-membership if he had not been a member of a trade union since the required ballot. The applicant submits that in making this provision the United Kingdom has impliedly recognised that the legal position for union membership agreements made before 14 August 1980 is in breach of the principle of freedom of association. Since the union membership agreement at the applicant's former place of work came into effect before 14 August 1980 he has been denied the opportunity of wider protection from dismissal on the grounds of non-membership of a trade union.

The applicant states that, although he knew the existence of, and understood the provisions of, the union membership agreement when he accepted employment with the Ford Motor Company, this cannot be taken to imply that he either agreed with it, or that, by taking up employment, he thereby waived any right to leave the union and seek protection from dismissal at a later date.

As regards questions of fact, the applicant makes the following points:
- that in his application to the Commission the applicant stated that when he began his employment he joined the union under duress as there was no legislation prevailing at that time which protected those who did not wish to be a member of a trade union;
- that there was at no time any legislative provision which required him to articulate his conscientious objections to union membership either when the membership lapsed in April 1980 or in the period up until June 1983;
- that the religious involvement of the applicant became more intense between the years 1978 to 1983. The fact that the applicant remained a union member for two years from 1978 until 1980 does not imply that he acquiesced to union membership since the consequences of renouncing his membership were likely to involve his dismissal. At the time of seeking employment in March 1978 his religious beliefs made him reluctant to join a trade union but they were not so strong as to amount to an overriding conscientious objection to membership.

However by April 1980 he had progressed to a higher stage in his religious feeling and believed that his religious views were utterly incompatible with trade union membership. These views stressed non-violence, commitment to truth and freedom from any form of extra-legal compulsion. The applicant thus considered himself under an absolute duty never to be associated with any false statement through membership of a group or to be associated with any group that espouses violent actions and, finally, not to be a party to duress over others or to allow himself to be the victim of compulsion;
- that the reason the applicant withdrew his appeal to the independent panel was on the grounds that the panel could not be regarded as independent since it included a trade union representative. Where a member is being judged by a trade union member there must be a reasonable fear of bias when one is submitting that trade union membership may involve departure from the truth and association with acts of violence;

- the applicant remained silent about his decision to leave the union because this was an action taken from private beliefs and because he would have suffered immediate victimisation and job loss.

The applicant submits that the failure on the part of the United Kingdom to protect the applicant against dismissal on the grounds of his refusal to join a trade union is a breach of art. 11 par. 1 of the Convention. Art. 11 confers a negative right not to join a trade union even where a union membership agreement is in force. The freedom to form or join a trade union does not mean that one is obliged to do so. Only that one is permitted to do so.

Accordingly, the freedom to join a trade union must encompass a freedom not to join. A person cannot be free to do something unless he or she is free not to do it. Since freedom presupposes an element of choice, a regime of compulsion is incompatible with the very idea of freedom. The closed shop as applied in the circumstances of the applicant's case afforded him no real choice whether to join a union or not, since his only other option entailed a loss of livelihood.

In this connection, the tenor of the judgment of the Court in the case of Young, James and Webster favours such a negative freedom.

Thus the majority stated that „the situation facing the applicants clearly runs counter to the concept of freedom of association in its negative sense ..." (loc. cit., par. 55). Moreover, the majority reasoned that a threat of dismissal (including loss of livelihood) is a „most serious form of compulsion - striking at the very substance of the freedom guaranteed by art. 11" (loc. cit., par. 57). Such reasoning would make little sense if it was not based on a presupposition that Art. 11 protects non-membership as well as membership of a union or other association. The compulsion suffered by the applicant involved a threat to extinguish his livelihood at a time of high unemployment. In reality, the situation of the applicant was the same as that faced by the applicants Young, James and Webster.

The Court in Young, James and Webster also put much emphasis on the concept of freedom of choice. In particular it held that:

„An individual does not enjoy the right of freedom of association if in reality the freedom of action or choice which remains available to him is either non-existent or so reduced as to be of no practical value" (loc. cit., par. 56).

It is submitted that the applicant's choice, because of his religious beliefs and because of the nature of the union membership agreement, was so reduced as to be of no practical value. This choice was further reduced by the fact that the only alternative open to the applicant involved loss of livelihood. The applicant accepts that under present United Kingdom law protection is afforded to persons not wishing to be members of a trade union if, inter alia, their objection is based on conscience or other deeply held personal conviction. However, protection under present legislation does not extend to the situation in which the applicant finds himself, namely an Orthodox Hindu who refuses to be in a trade union.

In respect of the respondent Government's submission that the applicant should be regarded as having consented to join the union since he was aware that this was a term of his contract of employment, the applicant points out that the Court has indicated in the Young James and Webster case that there might be compulsion even in this situation (loc. cit., par. 53). Furthermore the applicant joined the union under duress in a situation where there was limited statutory protection for persons not wishing to join trade unions.

Since the right not to join a trade union has been recognised the right to leave a union, after the contract of employment is made without the consequent loss of a job, must follow. If the principle of freedom of association is infringed by dismissal from employment on the grounds of non-membership of a union it can make no logical difference whether the union membership agreement on which dismissals are based was concluded before or after the contract. The mere fact that someone has exercised his right of association does not mean that he should forever be bound by it.

The applicant contends that the „balancing" approach proposed by the respondent Government is erroneous. Once there is an infringement of art. 11 par. 1 there is no longer any balance to be struck between competing interests. Unless the Government can bring themselves within the narrowly interpreted exceptions in art. 11 par. 2 - which has not been argued in this case - the applicant must succeed.

As regards art. 11 in conjunction with art. 9 the applicant submits firstly that the requirement that he join a trade union irrespective of any religious beliefs he might hold constitutes a breach of these provisions read together. A rule that obliges an individual to act contrary to the teachings of his religion amounts to an infringement of religious freedom.

Secondly art. 9 of the Convention extends to the freedom to change belief. The applicant changed his belief when he progressed to a higher stage of his faith. It was for this reason that he allowed his membership to lapse in 1980. The applicant submits, in this respect, that a system which allows his dismissal for leaving a trade union unless he can discharge the burden of proving his religious convictions is in breach of these provisions. It is a violation of religious freedom to be required, on pain of having the dismissal upheld, to prove the genuineness of ones private religious views particularly if one is a member of a little-understood religious sect which imposes higher duties in the course of religious advancement. Furthermore it is incompatible with the protection of intimate spiritual beliefs under art. 9 that an individual should be required to expose elders of his sect or church to cross-examination in public about innermost religious feelings, with the risk of being held up to ridicule, as a pre-condition of protecting his freedom of association.

The applicant submits that, after providing an indication of membership of his religion and of the contents of his religious belief in the form of the Ordinances of Manu, the burden of proving that the belief is not a genuine one ought to have been borne by the employer.

In the circumstances of the case it is submitted that the law with regard to unfair dismissal and its application by domestic tribunals in the present case breached art. 11 of the Convention, considered alone or in conjunction with art. 9 of the Convention.

Art. 14 of the Convention

The applicant further submits that he has suffered discrimination in the enjoyment of his rights under art. 9 and 11 contrary to art. 14 of the Convention.

Those who hold religious opinions which preclude them from joining trade unions are placed under two discriminatory burdens. First they are subjected to duress and pressure to compromise their religious faith. Secondly those who are members of little-understood religious faiths, such as the applicant, bear a much heavier burden of explanation and proof of their creed than members of more traditional religions whose views are well understood by tribunals.

THE LAW

The applicant, who was dismissed from his employment because of his refusal to rejoin a trade union, submits that union membership was incompatible with his deeply-held religious beliefs. He complains under art. 9, 11 and 14 of the Convention ...

The applicant first submits that art. 11 par. 1 contains a general negative right to choose not to be a member of a trade union. He points out that although he knew of the existence of a union membership agreement when he accepted employment with the Ford Motor Company, this cannot be taken to apply that he either agreed with it, or that, by taking up employment, he thereby waived any right to leave the union subsequently. He further complains of a breach of art. 11 read in conjunction with art. 9 since the requirement to join a trade union is incompatible with his religious beliefs. The applicant explains that he is a devote orthodox Hindu who belongs to the Radhaswami sect and whose religious beliefs had progressed to a higher stage when he allowed his union membership to lapse in 1980. These religious beliefs involved a rejection of the use of violence, a deep attachment to the truth and freedom from duress. In particular, he complains that the requirement under the law of the United Kingdom, that he should prove the genuineness of his private religious beliefs and expose the elders of his sect to public cross-examination concerning the intimate details of his creed, constitutes a breach of art. 9 and 11 of the Convention read together.

Finally, the applicant complains that he was a victim of discrimination in the enjoyment of his rights under art. 9, art. 11 of the Convention in that firstly he was required to join a union irrespective of his religious beliefs and that he was required to bear a heavier burden of proof before the Industrial Tribunal than other more traditional faiths.

The respondent Government submit that the applicant accepted voluntarily to join a trade union on taking up employment with the Ford Motor Company. They also point out that the applicant was given full opportunity to establish the genuineness of his beliefs and was represented by counsel both before the Industrial Tribunal and the Employment Appeal Tribunal. These bodies concluded on the basis of the evidence before them that the applicant had not established that he had any genuine objection to union membership on grounds of conscience or other deeply held personal convictions. There is no indication that these decisions were perverse or arbitrary or otherwise a denial of the applicant's rights under the Convention. The Government contend, with reference to the case of Young, James and Webster (EuCHR, judgment of 13 August 1981, Series A no. 44), that art. 11 does not guarantee a general negative freedom not to belong to a trade union. Finally, the Government maintain that the applicant has not substantiated his complaint of discrimination and was treated in the same way as a member of any other religion in a comparable situation.

The Commission considers, in the light of the parties' submissions, that the application as a whole raises complex issues of law and fact under the Convention, the determination of which depend on an examination of the merits of the application.

It concludes, therefore, that the application cannot be regarded as manifestly ill-founded within the meaning of art. 27 par. 2 of the Convention and no other ground for declaring it inadmissible has been established.

For these reasons, the Commission declares the application admissible without prejudging the merits of the case.

22

Der Schutzbereich von Religionsfreiheit und Diskriminierungsverbot bietet keine Grundlage für Verfahren gegen Autor und Verleger des Buches „Satanische Verse" wegen Verletzung religiöser Gefühle von Individuen oder bestimmten Personengruppen.

Art. 9, 14, 27 § 2 a.f. EMRK
EKMR, Beschluss vom 5. März 1991 - No. 17439/90
(Choudhury ./. Vereinigtes Königreich)[1] -

THE FACTS

The applicant is a British citizen born in 1954 and resident in London. On 13 March 1989, the applicant, who is a Moslem, applied to the Chief Metropolitan Magistrate of London at Bow Street Magistrates Court for a summons for criminal prosecution of blasphemy against Salman Rushdie (author of the book „Satanic Verses") and the Viking Penguin Publishing Co. (the publisher of the book) on the grounds that the author and publishers unlawfully and wickedly published in the book blasphemous libels against Almighty God (Allah), the Prophet Abraham and his son Ishmad, Mohammed the Holy Prophet of Islam, his wives and companions and the religion of Islam. The application was dismissed on the basis that the offence of blasphemy relates only to Christianity.

On 19 June 1989, the applicant was granted leave to apply for judicial review of the decision in the Divisional Court of the High Court.

On 9 April 1990, the Court refused the application. The Court found as follows:

„We have no doubt that as the law now stands it does not extend to religions other than Christianity. Can it in the light of the present conditions of society be extended by the courts to cover other religions? Mr. Azhar submits that it can and should be on the grounds that it is anomalous and unjust to discriminate in favour of one religion. In our judgment where the law is clear it is not the proper function of this court to extend it; particularly is this so in criminal cases where offences cannot be retrospectively created. It is in that circumstance the function of Parliament alone to change the law."

During the hearing counsel for the publisher said that there might be a breach of art. 9 of the Convention if criticism or agitation against a church or religious group reached such a level that the church or its members were prevented from manifesting their beliefs in the way set out in art. 9. The Court found that „nothing remotely like that had been demonstrated by the applicant".

The applicant's application for leave to appeal to the House of Lords against this decision was refused on 11 July 1990.

The offence of blasphemy was prior to 1660 dealt with in the Ecclesiastical Courts. The offence of blasphemy at common law traces its origin to Taylor's case (1 vent. 293) in 1676. In the 20th century there has only been two prosecutions for blasphemy (R. v. Gott 1922, 16 Cr. App. R. 87,

---

[1] HRLJ 12 (1991) ,172.

and R. v. Lemon 1979 A.C. 67). In 1985, the Law Commission issued a report (No. 145) recommending that the offence be abolished.

COMPLAINT

The applicant complains under art. 9 of the Convention that the United Kingdom has not given the Moslem religion protection against abuse or scurrilous attacks, and that without that protection there will inevitably be a limited enjoyment of the right to freedom of religion provided for by that article. The applicant also complains of the fact that that protection is extended to the Christian religion and not to other religions, contrary to art. 14.

THE LAW

1. The applicant complains that the law fails to protect his religion against abuse, since it is not covered by the offence of blasphemy. He invokes art. 9 of the Convention which provides:

> „1. Everyone has the right to freedom of thought, conscience and religion; this right includes freedom to change his religion or belief and freedom, either alone or in community with others and in public or private, to manifest his religion or belief, in worship, teaching, practice and observance.
> 2. Freedom to manifest one's religion or beliefs shall be subject only to such limitations as are prescribed by law and are necessary in a democratic society in the interests of public safety, for the protection of public order, health or morals, or for the protection of the rights and freedoms of others."

The Commission notes that the applicant sought to have criminal proceedings brought against the author and the publisher of the book „Satanic Verses" in order to vindicate his claim that the book amounted to a scurrilous attack on, inter alia, his religion. He does not claim, and it is clearly not the case, that any State authority, or any body for which the United Kingdom Government may be responsible under the Convention, directly interfered in the applicant's freedom to manifest his religion or belief.

The question in the present case is therefore whether the freedom of art. 9 of the Convention may extend to guarantee a right to bring any specific form of proceedings against those who, by authorship or publication, offend the sensitivities of an individual or of a group of individuals. The Commission finds no indication in the present case of a link between freedom from interference with the freedoms of art. 9 par. 1 of the Convention and the applicant's complaints.

Accordingly, this part of the application must be declared incompatible ratione materiae with the provisions of the Convention within the meaning of art. 27 par. 2.

2. The applicant also alleges a violation of art. 14 of the Convention in connection with his complaints under art. 9. However, as the complaint under art. 9 has been rejected as being incompatible ratione materiae with the provisions of the Convention, the complaints under art. 14 of the Convention also fall to be regarded as incompatible ratione materiae with the provisions of the Convention within the meaning of art. 27 par. 2.

For these reasons, the Commission unanimously declares the application inadmissible.

23

Die im belgischen Schulrecht vorgesehene Einrichtung von konfessionellem Religionsunterricht (cours de religion) und Ethikunterricht (cours de morale) als Wahlpflichtfächer entspricht den Anforderungen der Europäischen Menschenrechtskonvention. Eine kumulative Ablehnungsmöglichkeit für beide Fächer ist insbesondere angesichts der inhaltlichen Konzeption des Ethikunterrichts nicht geboten.

Art. 8-10, 14, 17, 27 § 2 a.F. EMRK, 2 Erstes Zusatzprotokoll
EKMR, Beschluss vom 9. September 1992
- No.17568/90 (Sluis ./. Belgien)[1] -

EN FAITS

Le requérant est un ressortissant belge, né en 1941. Il est commerçant et réside à Lint (Belgique). Le requérant est le père de onze enfants qui, tous, ont suivi ou suivent l'enseignement officiel en Belgique.

De 1972 à 1983, le requérant obtint, sur base d'une lettre du ministre de l'éducation nationale du 8 novembre 1972, une dispense pour ses enfants scolarisés de suivre soit un cours de religion soit un cours de morale, obligation prévue par l'art. 8 de la loi du 29 mai 1959. L'art. 8 de la loi du 29 mai 1959 est rédigé comme suit:

„Dans les établissements officiels [ainsi que dans les établissements pluralistes] d'enseignement primaire et secondaire de plein exercice, l'horaire hebdomadaire comprend au moins deux heures de religion et deux heures de morale. Par enseignement de la religion, il faut entendre l'enseignement de la religion (catholique, protestante, israélite ou islamique) et de la morale inspirée par cette religion. Par enseignement de la morale, il faut entendre l'enseignement de la morale non confessionnelle.

---

[1] HUDOC.

Le chef de famille, le tuteur ou la personne à qui est confiée la garde de l'enfant est tenu, lors de la première inscription d'un enfant, de choisir pour celui-ci par déclaration signée, le cours de religion ou le cours de morale. Si le choix porte sur le cours de religion, cette Déclaration indiquera explicitement la religion choisie.
[...]
Il est loisible à l'auteur de cette dernière de modifier son choix au début de chaque année scolaire."

Par décret du conseil de la Communauté flamande du 5 juillet 1989, la religion orthodoxe a été ajoutée aux quatre religions dont il est question au par. 2 de l'art. 8 de la loi du 29 mai 1959.

Au début de l'année scolaire 1982-1983, le requérant fut invité à choisir entre cours de religion et cours de morale pour sa fille aînée S. qui suivait des études secondaires. Devant le refus du requérant, le litige fut soumis au ministre de l'éducation qui décida, le 19 décembre 1983, qu'à défaut pour le requérant de faire le choix demandé pour sa fille aînée, celle-ci ne pourrait être considérée comme une élève régulière et pourrait en conséquence ne pas recevoir le diplôme normalement délivré à la fin du cycle d'étude qu'elle avait entamé. Cette décision fut communiquée le 6 janvier 1984 au requérant qui fut à nouveau invité à choisir entre les cours de religion et de morale.

Le 26 janvier 1984, le requérant introduisit devant le Conseil d'Etat un recours en annulation de la décision ministérielle du 19 décembre 1983.

Par arrêt du 14 mai 1985, le Conseil d'Etat annula la décision du ministre. Il motiva sa décision comme suit:

„Attendu qu'il ressort d'une analyse du programme d'enseignement pour le cours de morale dans l'enseignement secondaire de l'Etat des premier, deuxième et troisième échelons V.B.S.O. et du deuxième échelon - qualification courte - que le professeur de morale non confessionnelle est, dans la préface, encouragé à veiller à ce qu'un commentaire humaniste soit toujours présent
... Il doit contribuer à la formation d'un individu qui, sortant de sa relation avec les autres et la nature, s'appuyant sur un libre examen ... La morale doit être une matière fondée sur des idées humanistes et scientifiques ... Le professeur pose le témoignage de son engagement humaniste'; que pareille conception implique que le cours de morale non confessionnelle est conçu comme un plaidoyer pour une doctrine philosophique spécifique, de sorte que le programme d'enseignement est en contradiction avec la conception du cours de morale telle qu'elle est décrite dans une résolution de la Commission permanente du pacte scolaire du 8 mai 1963 qui est ainsi rédigée:
,Le cours de morale non confessionnelle est un fil conducteur des actions morales humaines enracinées dans les responsabilités sociologiques, psychologiques et historiques. Il ne fait aucun appel à des interprétations de nature religieuse et est encore moins conçu comme un plaidoyer pour une doctrine philosophique spécifique. Sur certains points cependant - et lorsque les circonstances l'y contraignent - le titulaire doit pouvoir avec circonspection, poser le témoignage de sa conviction morale personnelle et des fondements de celle-ci. Tant le professeur de morale non

confessionnelle que le professeur de religion et le professeur de morale confession-
nelle concevront leur enseignement de manière positive et éviteront de la sorte
toute critique concernant les doctrines exposées dans les autres cours'; qu'il en
ressort que non seulement le cours de morale, tel qu'il a été mis au point dans le
programme d'enseignement ne répond pas aux données que le législateur de la loi
du 29 mai 1959 a voulu rendre obligatoire pour le cours de morale lorsqu'il n'y
avait pas eu d'option pour un cours de religion, mais également que les parents
qui n'avaient pas choisi de cours de religion sont obligés de faire suivre à leurs
enfants un cours de morale qui n'est pas compatible avec leurs convictions philo-
sophiques, ce qui est contraire à l'art. 2 du Protocole additionnel à la Convention;
que, de la sorte, la décision attaquée qui refuse d'accorder une dispense au requé-
rant et l'oblige à choisir pour sa fille entre un cours de morale et un cours de reli-
gion est, sur base de l'art. 2 du Protocole additionnel, irrégulière; que le moyen
est fondé."

Suite à cet arrêt, le ministre de l'enseignement prit une circulaire mo-
difiant les règles d'attribution de dispense pour les cours de morale non
confessionnelle en date du 26 juillet 1985. Sur base de ce document, le
requérant obtint une dispense pour l'année scolaire 1985-1986 pour sa
fille aînée, ainsi que pour ses autres enfants scolarisés. Le 2 juillet 1986,
le ministre de l'enseignement prit une nouvelle circulaire concernant
l'octroi de dispense pour les cours de morale non confessionnelle. Il releva
que suite à l'arrêt du 14 mai 1985 le programme d'enseignement de la
morale non confessionnelle avait été modifié et que ce programme exposait explicitement qu'il ne pouvait jamais être question de mettre les
cours de morale au service d'une conception sociale ou d'une doctrine philosophique spécifique ou de donner ces cours en fonction des prises de position de pareille conception ou doctrine. Le ministre conclut donc qu'en
principe, aucune dispense ne pourrait plus être accordée.

Le 6 septembre 1986, le requérant introduisit des demandes de dispense pour trois de ses enfants (D., E. et G.) inscrits dans l'enseignement
primaire et deux de ses enfants (L. et H.) inscrits dans l'enseignement
secondaire. Le 7 novembre 1986, le ministre de l'enseignement accorda,
pour l'année scolaire 1986-1987, une dispense pour les deux enfants du
requérant inscrits dans l'enseignement secondaire.

Le 4 février 1987, le ministre de l'enseignement refusa d'accorder une
dispense pour les trois enfants du requérant inscrits dans l'enseignement
primaire. Le 23 mars 1987, le requérant introduisit un recours en annulation du refus de dispense du 4 février 1987, invoquant l'art. 2 du Protocole additionnel.

Par arrêt du 10 juillet 1990, le Conseil d'Etat rejeta le recours du requérant. Il motiva sa décision comme suit:

„3.4. Attendu que dans son arrêt Kjeldsen, Busk Madsen et Pedersen du 7 décem-
bre 1976 (Série A, vol 23, KirchE-EU S. 181) la Cour européenne des Droits de
l'Homme a constaté que la seconde phrase de l'art. 2 du Protocole additionnel' ...

n'empêche pas les Etats de répandre par l'enseignement ou l'éducation des informations ou connaissances ayant, directement ou non, un caractère religieux ou philosophique. Elle n'autorise pas même les parents à s'opposer à l'intégration de pareil enseignement ou éducation dans le programme scolaire, sans quoi tout enseignement institutionnalisé courrait le risque de se révéler impraticable. Il paraît en effet très difficile que nombre de disciplines enseignées à l'école n'aient pas, de près ou de loin, une coloration ou incidence, de caractère philosophique. Il en va de même du caractère religieux si l'on tient compte de l'existence de religions formant un ensemble dogmatique et moral très vaste qui a ou peut avoir des réponses à toute question d'ordre philosophique, cosmologique ou éthique (par. 53); qu'elle (la Cour) a poursuivi comme suit: ,La seconde phrase de l'art. 2 implique en revanche que l'Etat, en s'acquittant des fonctions assumées par lui en matière d'éducation et d'enseignement, veille à ce que les informations ou connaissances figurant au programme soient diffusées de manière objective, critique et pluraliste.

Elle lui interdit de poursuivre un but d'endoctrinement qui puisse être considéré comme ne respectant pas les convictions religieuses et philosophiques des parents. Là se place la limite à ne pas dépasser (ibid.); qu'elle a conclu: Une telle interprétation se concilie à la fois avec la première phrase de l'art. 2 du Protocole, avec les art. 8 à 10 de la Convention et avec l'esprit général de celle-ci, destinée à sauvegarder et promouvoir les idéaux et valeurs d'une société démocratique (ibid.);
3.5. Attendu que dans son arrêt Campbell et Cosans du 25 février 1982 (Série A, Vol 48) la Cour européenne a constaté que le terme ,convictions' dans l'art. 2 du Protocole additionnel est applicable ,à des vues atteignant un certain degré de force, de sérieux, de cohérence et d'importance' et qu'il doit s'agir ,des convictions qui méritent respect dans une ,société démocratique' (voir, en dernier lieu, l'arrêt Young, James et Webster du 13 août 1981, série A, n° 44, p. 25, par. 63), ne sont pas incompatibles avec la dignité de la personne et, de plus, ne vont pas à l'encontre du droit fondamental de l'enfant à l'instruction, la première phrase de l'art. 2 dominant l'ensemble de cette disposition (arrêt Kjeldsen, Busk Madsen et Pedersen précité, pp. 25-26, par. 52, KirchE-EU S. 181).
Attendu qu'après avoir cité l'arrêt Campbell et Cosans, la Commission européenne des Droits de l'Homme a estimé, dans sa décision du 13 octobre 1982 dans l'affaire X., Y. et Z. contre le Royaume-Uni, qu'elle '... ne saurait ... dire que les autorités scolaires n'ont pas ,respecté' les opinions des parents sur les châtiments corporels si les intéressés n'ont pas profité des occasions qui se présentaient pour signaler ces opinions aux autorités" (CommEuDH, D.R., vol. 31, p. 56).
3.6. Attendu que le requérant n'a jamais fait connaître, avec un minimum de précision à la partie adverse quelles étaient les convictions religieuses ou philosophiques qui l'empêchaient de faire suivre à ses enfants un cours de religion ou un cours de morale; qu'il a seulement déclaré qu'il avait contre ces cours des ,objections fondamentales parce qu'ils ne sont pas en accord avec mes convictions philosophiques'; qu'il apparaît d'ailleurs de l'exposé de son unique moyen à l'appui de sa demande d'annulation qu'une telle déclaration doit suffire pour obtenir la dispense demandée; qu'il s'avère qu'il a toujours été d'avis que le ministre n'avait pas le droit ,de décider discrétionnairement si l'enseignement philosophique était ou non en accord avec les convictions religieuses ou philosophiques propres des parents', qu'est donc inacceptable un système dans lequel on accorde au ministre la compétence de ,répondre favorablement ou non à une demande motivée de dispense introduite par les parents'; que cela serait même inacceptable lorsque le

cours de morale non confessionnelle serait ‚neutre‘ au sens du pacte scolaire parce que c'est aux parents, et non à une quelconque autorité, qu'il appartient finalement de décider si ce cours est ou n'est pas, à leur avis, neutre et s'il est conforme à leurs convictions religieuses ou philosophiques; qu'un moyen à l'appui de la demande d'annulation d'une portée aussi extrême - le fait que les parents déclarent simplement que l'enseignement philosophique offert ne concorde pas avec leurs propres convictions religieuses ou philosophiques suffit à faire dispenser leurs enfants de cet enseignement, ce qui revient à ce que quiconque puisse obtenir la dispense - ne se concilie pas avec l'interprétation de l'art. 2 du Protocole additionnel selon la jurisprudence de la Cour et de la Commission européenne énoncée aux points 3.4 et 3.5; que le moyen, qui est uniquement fondé sur l'art. 2 précité, doit donc être rejeté, sans avoir égard à la question de savoir si le motif allégué par la partie défenderesse pour rejeter la demande de dispense était légitime puisque de l'avis de la partie demanderesse, la partie défenderesse ne peut jamais faire valoir un motif légitime à l'appui de son refus."

Entre-temps, le secrétaire d'Etat à l'enseignement avait refusé, par décision du 13 octobre 1988, d'accorder au requérant une dispense pour l'année scolaire 1988-1989 pour son enfant H. qui poursuivait ses études secondaires.

Le 11 septembre 1990, le requérant demanda à nouveau une dispense pour son enfant H. pour l'année scolaire 1990-1991. La dispense fut refusée le 28 septembre 1990, en raison du fait que le requérant n'avait fait valoir aucun motif légitime à l'appui de la demande et n'avait donné aucune indication sur les convictions philosophiques et religieuses qui l'empêchaient de laisser son enfant suivre les cours de religion ou de morale. Une demande identique du requérant du 14 septembre 1990 concernant ses enfants G., N. et J. fut refusée le 30 novembre 1990. Par une lettre rectificative du 9 janvier 1991, le ministre de la Communauté flamande signala au requérant que les enfants G., N. et J. étaient, pour l'année scolaire 1990-1991, dispensés d'assister effectivement au cours de religion ou de morale.

Le requérant a, par ailleurs, signalé que ses enfants n'ont jamais suivi les cours de religion ou de morale, même lorsqu'aucune dispense n'avait été accordée.

GRIEFS

1. Le requérant fait valoir que le refus du ministre, en date du 4 février 1987, d'accorder une dispense de suivre les cours de religion ou de morale pour ses enfants D., E. et G. viole l'art. 2 du Protocole additionnel. Il explique qu'il appartient aux parents, et non à l'Etat, de déterminer si l'enseignement offert est ou non conforme à leurs opinions philosophiques et religieuses et, en cas de réponse négative, de décider que les enfants ne suivront pas cet enseignement, sans avoir à justifier leur position. Il ajoute que par un autre arrêt du 10 juillet 1990, le Conseil d'Etat

a annulé un refus du ministre de l'enseignement d'accorder une dispense à un „témoin de Jehova" dont les enfants suivaient les cours de l'enseignement secondaire, au motif que ladite personne pouvait raisonnablement être d'avis que les divers cours proposés ne pouvaient être en conformité avec ses convictions religieuses.

2. Le requérant fait encore valoir que le refus du ministre d'accorder une dispense porte atteinte aux art. 9, 14 et 17 de la Convention, ainsi que, subsidiairement, à ses art. 8 et 10.

3. Le requérant soulève enfin que le fait que le Conseil d'Etat exige que les parents qui demandent pareille dispense fassent connaître avec un minimum de précision quelles sont les convictions philosophiques ou religieuses les empêchant de faire suivre à leurs enfants les cours de religion figurant au programme ou le cours de morale viole les art. 9, 14 et 17 de la Convention et, subsidiairement, ses art. 8 et 10.

EN DROIT

1. Le requérant fait valoir que le refus du ministre, en date du 4 février 1987, d'accorder une dispense de suivre les cours de religion pour ses enfants D., E. et G. viole l'art. 2 du Protocole additionnel. L'art. 2 du Protocole additionnel est libellé comme suit:

„Nul ne peut se voir refuser le droit à l'instruction. L'Etat, dans l'exercice des fonctions qu'il assumera dans le domaine de l'éducation et de l'enseignement, respectera le droit des parents d'assurer cette éducation et cet enseignement conformément à leurs convictions religieuses et philosophiques."

L'art. 2 du Protocole additionnel est gouverné par sa première phrase, qui consacre le droit de l'enfant à l'instruction, alors que la seconde qui la complète, consacre le droit des parents d'assurer à leur enfant l'éducation et l'enseignement conformément à leurs convictions religieuses et philosophiques (cf. CourEuDH, arrêt Campbell et Cosans du 25 février 1982, série A n° 48, pp. 18-19, par. 40).

Dans son arrêt Kjeldsen, Busk Madsen et Pedersen (CourEuDH, arrêt Kjeldsen, Busk Madsen et Pedersen du 7 décembre 1976, Série A, vol. 23, pp. 26-27, par. 53, KirchE-EU S. 181), la Cour a déclaré que:

„la définition et l'aménagement du programme des études relèvent en principe de la compétence des Etats contractants. Il s'agit, dans une large mesure, d'un problème d'opportunité sur lequel la Cour n'a pas à se prononcer et dont la solution peut légitimement varier selon les pays et les époques. En particulier, la seconde phrase de l'art. 2 du Protocole n'empêche pas les Etats de répandre par l'enseignement ou l'éducation des informations ou connaissances ayant, directement ou non, un caractère religieux ou philosophique. Elle n'autorise pas même les parents à s'opposer à l'intégration de pareil enseignement ou éducation dans le programme scolaire, sans quoi tout enseignement institutionnalisé courrait le risque

de se révéler impraticable. Il apparaît en effet très difficile que nombre de disciplines enseignées à l'école n'aient pas, de près ou de loin, une coloration ou incidence de caractère philosophique. Il en va de même du caractère religieux si l'on tient compte de l'existence de religions formant un ensemble dogmatique et moral très vaste qui a ou peut avoir des réponses à toute question d'ordre philosophique, cosmologique ou éthique. La seconde phrase de l'art. 2 implique en revanche que l'Etat, en s'acquittant des fonctions assumées par lui en matière d'éducation et d'enseignement, veille à ce que les informations ou connaissances figurant au programme soient diffusées de manière objective, critique et pluraliste. Elle lui interdit de poursuivre un but d'endoctrinement qui puisse être considéré comme ne respectant pas les convictions religieuses et philosophiques des parents. Là se place la limite à ne pas dépasser. Une telle interprétation se concilie à la fois avec la première phrase de l'art. 2 du Protocole, avec les art. 8, 9, 10 de la Convention et avec l'esprit général de celle-ci, destinée à sauvegarder et promouvoir les idéaux et valeurs d'une société démocratique."

En l'espèce, la Commission relève que suite à l'arrêt du Conseil d'Etat du 14 mai 1985, le programme d'enseignement de la morale non-confessionnelle avait été modifiée et que le programme exposait explicitement qu'il ne pouvait jamais être question de mettre les cours de morale au service d'une conception sociale ou d'une doctrine philosophique spécifique ou de donner ces cours en fonction des prises de position de pareille conception ou doctrine. Il apparaît donc que les autorités belges ont veillé avec le plus grand soin à ce que les convictions religieuses et philosophiques des parents d'élèves fréquentant l'enseignement officiel, ne soient pas heurtées par le contenu du cours de morale non-confessionnelle, même si l'on ne saurait exclure de la part des enseignants certaines appréciations pouvant empiéter sur le domaine religieux ou philosophique. En effet, les directives explicitement émise par le programme d'enseignement de la morale prouve que ce cours ne constitue point une tentative d'endoctrinement, mais au contraire que les autorités ont eu à coeur de veiller à ce que les informations diffusées lors de ce cours le soient de manière objective, critique et pluraliste, en évitant qu'il soit mis au service d'une conception sociale ou doctrine philosophique spécifique. En outre, les autorités ont, de la sorte, veillé à ce que cet enseignement ne touche pas au droit des parents „d'éclairer et conseiller leurs enfants d'exercer envers eux leurs fonctions naturelles d'éducateurs, de les orienter dans une direction conforme à leurs propres convictions religieuses ou philosophiques" (cf. CourEuDH, arrêt Kjeldsen, Busk Madsen et Pedersen précité, p. 28 p. 54, KirchE-EU S. 181).

La Commission estime donc que l'obligation prévue par art. 8 de la loi du 29 mai 1959 ne blesse point en soi les convictions religieuses ou philosophiques du requérant dans une mesure prohibée par la seconde phrase de l'art. 2 du Protocole additionnel.

Elle relève par ailleurs que l'Etat belge réserve encore une importante ressource aux parents qui désireraient soustraire leurs enfants à l'enseignement de la morale non confessionnelle telle qu'il est dispensé dans l'enseignement officiel puisqu'il les laisse libre de les confier à des écoles privées non astreintes au respect de l'art. 8 de la loi du 29 mai 1959 et, du reste, subventionnées par lui dans le respect du principe de l'égalité entre les réseaux d'enseignement libres et officiels consacrés par l'art. 17 de la Constitution. Eu égard à ces circonstances, la Commission estime que la requête est, sur ce point, manifestement mal fondée au sens de l'art. 27 par. 2 de la Convention.

2. Le requérant fait également valoir que le refus du ministre d'accorder une dispense porte atteinte aux art. 9, 14 et 17 de la Convention et, subsidiairement, à ses art. 8 et 10.

La Commission n'est toutefois pas appelée à se prononcer sur la question de savoir si les faits allégués par le requérant révèlent l'apparence d'une violation de cette disposition. En effet, aux termes de l'art. 26 de la Convention, „la Commission ne peut être saisie qu'après l'épuisement des voies de recours internes, tel qu'il est entendu selon les principes du droit international généralement reconnus".

Cette condition ne se trouve pas réalisée par le seul fait que le requérant a soumis son cas aux différentes instances compétentes. Il faut encore que le grief formulé devant la Commission ait été soulevé, au moins en substance, pendant la procédure en question. Sur ce point, la Commission renvoie à sa jurisprudence constante (cf par exemple N° 10307/83, déc. 6.3.84, DR 37 pp. 113, 127).

En l'espèce, le requérant n'a soulevé ni formellement, ni même en substance, au cours de la procédure devant le Conseil d'Etat, les griefs qu'il fait à présent valoir devant la Commission. De plus, l'examen de l'affaire, telle qu'elle a été présentée, n'a permis de déceler aucune circonstance particulière qui aurait pu dispenser le requérant, selon les principes de droit international généralement reconnus, de soulever ces griefs dans la procédure susmentionnée.

Il s'ensuit que le requérant n'a pas satisfait à la condition relative à l'épuisement des voies de recours internes et que la requête doit être rejetée, sur les points considérés, conformément à l'art. 27 par. 3 de la Convention.

3. Le requérant fait enfin valoir que le fait que le Conseil d'Etat ait, dans son arrêt du 10 juillet 1990, décidé que l'octroi d'une dispense était soumis à la condition que les parents fassent connaître avec un minimum de précisions quelles sont les convictions philosophiques ou religieuses les empêchant de faire suivre à leurs enfants lesdits cours viole les art. 9, 14 et 17 de la Convention et, subsidiairement, ses art. 8 et 10.

A supposer que l'interprétation que fait le requérant de l'arrêt du Conseil d'Etat du 10 juillet 1990 doive être suivie, la Commission, se référant aux considérations développées au point 1, ne discerne aucune atteinte aux art. 8 et 9 de la Convention, dont elle a d'ailleurs tenu compte en interprétant l'art. 2 du Protocole additionnel, ni à ses art. 10, 14 et 17.

Il s'ensuit que l'examen du grief, tel qu'il a été présenté, n'a permis de déceler aucune violation des dispositions de la Convention invoquées par le requérant.

Il s'ensuit que la requête est, quant à ce grief, manifestement mal fondée, au sens de l'art. 27 par. 2 de la Convention.

Par ces motifs, la Commission, à l'unanimité, déclare le requète irrecevable.

24

Die Teilnahme an einem Lehrgang des Zivilschutzes kann nicht unter Berufung auf die Glaubens- und Gewissensfreiheit verweigert werden.

Art. 9 EMRK
EKMR, Beschluss vom 8. Januar 1993 - No. 17003/90, 18206/91
(Fadini ./. Schweiz) -

EN FAITS

Le requérant est un ressortissant suisse, né en 1937. Il est chancelier adjoint du tribunal d'appel de Lugano et réside à Mendrisio (Tessin).

Le 7 décembre 1988, le département militaire du canton de Tessin a infligé au requérant une amende de 200 FS pour avoir omis de se présenter et de participer aux cours introductifs de la protection civile qui se sont tenus à Mendrisio du 25 au 26 février 1988. Le requérant avait en fait refusé de participer aux cours introductifs de formation des personnes astreintes à la protection civile depuis 1985. Il avait alors indiqué que le service de la protection civile n'avait, à son avis, d'autre but „que celui de maintenir vivante chez le peuple la conviction que la guerre était un fait inéluctable" et qu'un cours de ce type contribuerait nécessairement et inévitablement à cultiver chez les participants l'idée qu'une guerre chimique ou une guerre atomique serait un fait normal et non une violation des droits fondamentaux de l'homme. Ultérieurement, le requérant a complété sa prise de position en indiquant que la protection civile faisait partie de la défense nationale et que sa conviction religieuse de chrétien lui interdisait d'adhérer à une forme de violence institutionnalisée telle que la défense nationale.

Le 26 septembre 1988, le requérant a présenté un recours au tribunal administratif cantonal de Lugano contre la décision du département militaire cantonal, lui imposant l'amende de 200 FS. Son recours a été rejeté le 21 novembre 1989. Contre ce rejet, le requérant a introduit devant le Tribunal fédéral un recours en nullité et un recours de droit public. Dans le cadre de ce dernier, il a allégué une violation de l'art. 9 de la Convention. Par arrêt du 12 juin 1990, le Tribunal fédéral a rejeté le recours de droit public. Pour autant que le requérant a invoqué l'art. 9 de la Convention, le Tribunal fédéral a estimé que le recours était, sur ce point, manifestement mal fondé, le service de protection civile prévue par la loi suisse ne constituant pas un service civil de remplacement pour objecteurs de conscience au service militaire mais un service de secours à la population civile, le refus duquel ne saurait être accepté pour des motifs religieux ou éthiques.

En février 1989, le requérant a de nouveau refusé de participer aux cours de protection civile. Le 21 mars 1990, le Procureur public du canton de Tessin a infligé au requérant la peine de six jours d'arrêts avec sursis pour infraction à la loi fédérale sur la protection civile. Cette peine a été confirmée par sentence du 15 novembre 1990 du Pretore de Mendrisio-Nord, notifiée au requérant le 23 novembre 1990.

Le 27 mai 1991, le Procureur public du canton de Tessin a infligé au requérant une autre peine de huit jours d'arrêt pour son refus de participer au cours de protection civile en janvier 1991. Il a également révoqué le sursis précédemment accordé au requérant.

GRIEF

Le requérant soutient que les sanctions qui lui ont été infligées pour avoir refusé de participer aux cours de protection civile constituent des ingérences injustifiées dans son droit à la liberté de conscience et de religion. Il invoque l'art. 9 de la Convention.

EN DROIT

1. La Commission observe que les requêtes présentent des éléments de connexité quant aux faits et griefs et décide de les joindre, en application de l'art. 35 du Règlement intérieur.

2. Le requérant se plaint de sanctions qui lui ont été infligées pour son refus de participer aux cours de protection civile et allègue une violation de l'art. 9 de la Convention qui dispose en son paragraphe premier:

„Toute personne a droit à la liberté de pensée, de conscience et de religion; ce droit implique la liberté de changer de religion ou de conviction, ainsi que la liberté de manifester sa religion ou sa conviction individuellement ou collectivement, en public ou en privé, par le culte, l'enseignement, les pratiques et l'accomplissement des rites."

La Commission rappelle que cette disposition protège les comportements qui constituent l'expression directe d'une conviction religieuse ou philosophique mais cette protection ne s'étend pas à tous les actes moti-

vés ou inspirés par celle-ci (No. 7050/75, Arrowsmith c/ Royaume Uni,
rapport Comm. 12.10.78, DR 19 p. 5; No. 10678/83, déc. 5.7.84, DR 39
p. 267). En l'espèce, le requérant refuse de participer aux cours de protection civile au motif que ces cours cultivent chez les participants l'idée
qu'une guerre serait inéluctable et la question pourrait, dès lors, se poser
de savoir dans quelle mesure ce refus peut passer pour un acte constituant l'expression directe des convictions religieuses ou philosophiques
du requérant. La Commission estime toutefois que cette question peut
demeurer indécise car la requête doit être rejetée, en tout état de cause,
pour les motifs suivants.

La Commission a déjà estimé que la disposition invoquée par le requérant, lue à la lumière de l'art. 4 par. 3 b) de la Convention, laisse aux
Etats Contractants la faculté de ne pas reconnaître un droit à l'objection
de conscience ni un droit d'être exempté d'un service civil de remplacement (No. 7705/76, déc. 5.7.77, DR 9 p. 196; No. 10640/83, déc. 9.5.84, DR
38 p. 219). Dans la mesure où le système conventionnel ne garantit pas le
droit d'être exempté de l'obligation d'effectuer un service militaire pour
des raisons de conscience, la Commission estime qu'on ne saurait inter-
préter l'art. 9 de la Convention comme garantissant le droit d'être exempté de cours de protection civile même lorsque, comme le soutient le requérant, les cours en question font partie du système de défense nationale.

Il s'ensuit qu'aucune violation de l'art. 9 de la Convention ne peut être
décelée en l'espèce.

*Par ces motifs, la Commission, à l'unanimité, déclare la requête irrece-
vable.*

25

**Eine Absolventin einer türkischen Universität hat keinen An-
spruch auf Erteilung eines Diplomzeugnisses, dessen Identitätsfoto
sie mit Kopftuch zeigt.**

Art. 9, 27 § 2 a.F. EMRK
EKMR, Beschluss vom 3. Mai 1993 - No. 18783/91 (Bulut ./. Türkei)[1] -

EN FAIT

La requérante, ressortissante turque, née en 1959, a une licence de
français et réside à Ankara. Elle est femme au foyer.

---

[1] Parallelverfahren: EKMR, Beschluss vom 3. Mai 1993 - No. 16278/90 (Kara-
duman ./. Türkei) - DR 74, 93.

La requérante termina ses études universitaires en juin 1980 à la faculté des sciences éducatives de l'université de Gazi d'Ankara et reçut un certificat provisoire attestant qu'elle avait obtenu la licence. Le 27 janvier 1984, la requérante demanda au service de scolarité de l'université de remplacer son certificat provisoire par un diplôme. Elle fournit une photo d'identité sur laquelle elle portait un foulard. Par lettre du 27 février 1984, l'administration de la faculté informa la requérante que son diplôme n'avait pas été signé du fait qu'elle portait un foulard sur sa photo d'identité.

Le 11 avril 1984, la requérante réitéra sa demande de diplôme auprès du ministère de l'Education nationale. Par lettre du 9 mai 1984,celui-ci répondit qu'il n'était pas possible de fournir un diplôme à la requérante sans que celle-ci produise une photo d'identité conforme au règlement sur la tenue vestimentaire devant être adoptée par les étudiants et les fonctionnaires dans les établissements scolaires et universitaires.

Le 30 avril 1984, la requérante introduisit devant le tribunal administratif d'Ankara un recours en annulation de la décision administrative du 27 février 1984. Elle allégua, entre autres, une atteinte à sa liberté de croyance et de conscience telle que garantie par la Constitution turque et la Déclaration Universelle des Droits de l'Homme.

Par jugement du 10 décembre 1987, le tribunal administratif d'Ankara rejeta le recours de la requérante. Il considéra, en premier lieu, que les règles vestimentaires que doivent respecter les étudiants lors de leur scolarité s'appliquent également aux photos d'identité apposées sur les diplômes. Ces règles ont été établies conformément aux principes selon lesquels les établissements scolaires et universitaires sont pour but de former de jeunes „intellectuels, civilisés et républicains".

Le tribunal constata en second lieu que les règlements sur la tenue vestimentaire précisaient que les étudiantes ne devaient rien porter sur la tête.

Le 12 mai 1988, la requérante attaqua ce jugement devant le Conseil d'Etat. Elle invoqua, entre autres, son droit à la liberté de croyance et de religion et se référa notamment à la Convention européenne des Droits de l'Homme. Elle prétendit qu'elle remplissait parfaitement les qualités mentionnées par le tribunal, à savoir qu'elle était „intellectuelle, civilisée et républicaine".

Par arrêt du 12 décembre 1989, notifiée à la requérante le 22 janvier 1990, le Conseil d'Etat confirma, à la majorité, le jugement du 10 décembre 1987, considérant que les motifs invoqués dans celui-ci étaient conformes à la loi et à la procédure. Deux conseillers d'Etat indiquèrent dans leur opinion dissidente que le refus opposé par l'université était entaché de nullité du fait qu'aucune disposition réglementaire ne comportait expressément une description de la photo à apposer sur le diplôme.

La requérante introduisit devant le Conseil d'Etat un recours en rectification de l'arrêt du 12 décembre 1989 rendu par cette juridiction. Elle a invoqué, entre autres, le non-examen de tous les points de son argumentation, le défaut de motivation de l'arrêt attaqué et la non-tenue d'une audience devant le Conseil d'Etat. Elle rappela également que les dispositions réglementaires interdisant le port du foulard dans les universités avaient été abrogées à partir du 28 décembre 1989.

Par arrêt du 14 décembre 1990, notifié à la requérante le 25 janvier 1991, le Conseil d'Etat rejeta le recours au motif que les conditions requises par la loi pour la rectification d'arrêt n'avaient pas été remplies et il condamna la requérante à une amende de 5000 LT (870 LT = 1 FF) pour recours abusif.

GRIEFS

Devant la Commission, la requérante se plaint d'une atteinte à son droit à la liberté de pensée, de conscience et de religion, dans la mesure où elle n'a pas obtenu son diplôme faute d'avoir fourni des photos d'identité à tête nue, cette tenue étant contraire à la manifestation de ses convictions religieuses. La requérante invoque à cet égard les art. 5, 8 et 9 de la Convention et l'art. 2 du Protocole Additionnel.

PROCEDURE DEVANT LA COMMISSION

(...)

EN DROIT

La requérante se plaint d'une atteinte à son droit à la liberté de religion et de conscience, étant donné que la tenue qu'on exige d'elle pour la photo d'identité à apposer sur son diplôme d'université est contraire à ses convictions religieuses. Elle allègue à cet égard une violation des art. 5, 8 et 9 de la Convention et de l'art. 2 du Protocole Additionnel.

La Commission examine la requête sous l'angle de l'art. 9 de la Convention qui reconnaît à toute personne le „droit à la liberté de pensée, de conscience et de religion; ce droit implique la liberté de changer de religion ou de conviction, ainsi que la liberté de manifester sa religion ou sa conviction individuellement ou collectivement, en public ou en privé, par le culte, l'enseignement, les pratiques et l'accomplissement des rites."

1. L'épuisement des voies de recours internes

(...)

2. Sur le bien-fondé

Le Gouvernement soutient en premier lieu que le refus dont se plaint la requérante ne constitue pas une ingérence dans sa liberté de religion et de culte. Il estime que le fait d'avoir la tête non couverte dans les locaux des universités ainsi que le fait de fournir une photo d'identité dans cette tenue afin de se conformer aux règles disciplinaires de l'université n'empêche pas la personne de pratiquer sa religion. Le Gouvernement fait observer par ailleurs que le certificat de fin d'études fourni à la requérante lui procure tous les avantages d'un diplôme.

Le Gouvernement défendeur soutient en deuxième lieu que l'obligation du respect du principe de laïcité imposée aux étudiants de l'université doit être considérée comme étant conforme aux restrictions prévues au par. 2 de l'art. 9 de la Convention. Il fait observer que la Cour constitutionnelle turque, par arrêt du 7 mars 1989, a déclaré inconstitutionnelle une disposition légale permettant le port du foulard dans les établissements d'enseignement au motif que cette disposition enfreignait le principe de laïcité. La Cour constitutionnelle a précisé, ajoute le Gouvernement défendeur, que le port du foulard islamique peut conduire à prétendre que les femmes qui n'en portent pas sont des athées, et ainsi faire naître des conflits dans la société.

En revanche, la requérante fait observer que bien qu'elle ait terminé avec succès ses études universitaires, son diplôme ne peut lui être délivré du fait qu'elle n'a pas fourni de photo d'identité sur laquelle elle doit apparaître la tête non couverte. Elle soutient que le fait de couvrir sa tête par un foulard fait partie de ses convictions religieuses. Elle prétend dès lors que le refus de l'université de lui fournir son diplôme constitue bien une ingérence dans sa liberté de religion et de conviction.

La Commission rappelle que l'art. 9 de la Convention protège expressément „le culte, l'enseignement, les pratiques et l'accomplissement des rites" d'une religion ou d'une croyance.

La Commission a déjà décidé que l'art. 9 de la Convention ne garantit pas toujours le droit de se comporter dans le domaine public d'une manière dictée par cette conviction. Notamment, le terme „pratiques", au sens de l'art. 9 par. 1, ne désigne pas n'importe quel acte motivé ou inspiré par une religion ou une conviction (cf. N° 7050/75 Arrowsmith c/ Royaume-Uni, rapport Comm. par. 71, DR 19, p. 5 et N° 10358/83, déc. du 15.12.83, DR 37, p. 142).

Pour savoir si cette disposition a été méconnue en l'espèce, il faut d'abord rechercher si la mesure litigieuse constituait une ingérence dans l'exercice de la liberté de religion.

La Commission observe que les règles applicables aux photos d'identité à utiliser pour apposer sur les diplômes, bien que ne concernant pas directement les règles disciplinaires régissant la vie quotidienne dans les universités, font cependant partie des règles universitaires établies dans le but de préserver la nature „républicaine", donc „laïque", de l'université ainsi que l'ont constaté les juridictions nationales ayant statué en l'espèce.

La Commission est d'avis qu'en choisissant de faire ses études supérieures dans une université laïque, un étudiant se soumet à cette réglementation universitaire. Celle-ci peut soumettre la liberté des étudiants de manifester leur religion à des limitations de lieu et de forme destinées à assurer la mixité des étudiants de croyances diverses. Notamment, dans les pays où la grande majorité de la population adhère à une religion précise, la manifestation des rites et des symboles de cette religion, sans restriction de lieu et de forme, peut constituer une pression sur les étudiants qui ne pratiquent pas ladite religion ou sur ceux adhérant à une autre religion. Les universités laïques, lorsqu'elles établissent les règles disciplinaires concernant la tenue vestimentaire des étudiants, peuvent veiller à ce que certains courants fondamentalistes religieux ne troublent l'ordre public dans l'enseignement supérieur et ne portent atteinte aux croyances d'autrui.

La Commission note que dans la présente affaire, le règlement de l'université concernant la tenue vestimentaire impose aux étudiants, entre autres, d'avoir la tête non couverte par un foulard. La Commission prend également en considération les observations de la Cour constitutionnelle turque qui estime que le port de foulard islamique dans les universités turques peut constituer un défi à l'égard de ceux qui ne le portent pas.

La Commission rappelle qu'elle avait estimé compatible avec la liberté de religion, protégée par l'art. 9 de la Convention, l'obligation imposée à un enseignant de respecter les heures de travail qui correspondaient, selon lui, à ses heures de prière (N° 8160/78, X. c/ Royaume-Uni, déc. 12.3.81, DR 22, p. 27, KirchE-EU S. 29). Il en est de même pour ce qui est de l'obligation faite à un motocycliste de porter un casque qui était, selon lui, en conflit avec ses devoirs religieux (N° 7992/77, X. c/ Royaume-Uni, déc. du 12.7.78, DR 14, p. 234). La Commission considère que le statut d'étudiant dans une université laïque implique, par nature, la soumission à certaines règles de conduite établies afin d'assurer le respect des droits et libertés d'autrui. Le règlement d'une université laïque peut prévoir également que le diplôme qu'on fournit aux étudiants ne reflète en aucune manière l'identité d'un mouvement s'inspirant d'une religion et auquel peuvent participer ces étudiants.

La Commission est d'avis également qu'un diplôme universitaire a pour but d'attester des capacités professionnelles d'un étudiant et ne constitue pas un document destiné à l'attention du grand public. La photo apposée sur un diplôme a pour fonction d'assurer l'identification de l'intéressé et ne peut être utilisée par celui-ci afin de manifester ses convictions religieuses.

La Commission observe en l'espèce que les autorités administratives ainsi que les juridictions nationales ont constaté que le règlement de l'université exige que la requérante fournisse une photo d'identité conforme à la tenue vestimentaire réglementaire. Elle note par ailleurs que le rejet opposé par l'administration de la faculté à la demande de la requérante d'obtenir son diplôme n'est pas définitif mais circonstancié: la délivrance du diplôme est en effet liée à la condition que la requérante produise une photo conforme au règlement. La Commission tient également compte de ce que la requérante est titulaire d'un certificat de fin d'études qui lui procure tous les avantages d'un diplôme.

La Commission relève en outre que la requérante ne fait aucunement observer avoir été obligée, pendant ses études universitaires, de respecter, contre sa volonté, le règlement concernant la tenue vestimentaire.

La Commission estime, compte tenu des exigences du système de l'université laïque, que le fait de réglementer la tenue vestimentaire des étudiants ainsi que celui de leur refuser les services de l'administration, tels la délivrance d'un diplôme, aussi longtemps qu'ils ne se conforment pas à ce règlement, ne constitue pas en tant que tel une ingérence dans la liberté de religion et de conscience.

La Commission ne relève donc aucune ingérence dans le droit garanti par l'art. 9 par. 1 de la Convention. Il s'ensuit que la requête est manifestement mal fondée au sens de l'art. 27 par.2 de la Convention.

Par ces motifs, la Commission, à la majorité, déclare la requête irrecevable.

26

Der nationale Gesetzgeber kann die Möglichkeit einer Befreiung sowohl vom schulischen Religionsunterricht (cours d'instruction religieuse et morale) als auch vom Ethikunterricht (cours de morale laïque) auf solche Schüler beschränken, die einer nicht am schulischen Religionsunterricht beteiligten Religionsgemeinschaft angehören.

Art. 9, 14, 27 § 2 a.F. EMRK, 2 Erstes Zusatzprotokoll
EKMR, Beschluss vom 8. September 1993 - No. 17187/90
(Bernard u.a. ./. Luxemburg)[1] -

EN FAIT

Les requérants sont domiciliés au Luxembourg.

Par décisions prises le 1er août 1989, le conseil national de la formation morale et sociale refusa aux enfants des requérants la dispense du cours de formation morale et sociale au motif que les demandes de dispense ne faisaient pas état d'une appartenance à une croyance religieuse, seul motif susceptible d'autoriser une dispense, conformément à l'art. 48

---

[1] DR 75, 57.

de la loi du 10 mai 1968 portant réforme de l'enseignement scolaire, et modifié par la loi du 16 novembre 1988.

L'art. 48 de la loi du 10 mai 1968 était rédigé comme suit:

> „*L'enseignement secondaire comporte un cours d'instruction religieuse et morale et un cours de morale laïque.*
> *Sur déclaration écrite adressée au directeur de l'établissement par la personne investie du droit d'éducation, tout élève sera inscrit soit au cours d'instruction religieuse et morale, soit au cours de morale laïque.*
> *Sur déclaration écrite de la même personne, tout élève sera dispensé de la fréquentation de l'un et de l'autre de ces cours.*"

L'article tel que libellé ayant permis une augmentation du nombre des abstentionnistes aux deux cours, le Gouvernement prit l'initiative de modifier cet article qui stipule désormais:

> „*L'enseignement secondaire comporte un cours d'instruction religieuse et morale et un cours de formation morale et sociale.*
> *Sur déclaration écrite adressée au directeur de l'établissement par la personne investie du droit d'éducation ou de l'élève majeur, tout élève sera inscrit, soit au cours d'instruction religieuse et morale, soit au cours de formation morale et sociale. Seront dispensés des deux cours précités, les élèves qui se réclament d'une croyance religieuse dont les adhérents n'assurent pas de cours d'instruction religieuse et morale dans le cadre des horaires scolaires ...*"

Le 19 octobre 1989, les requérants introduisirent un recours en annulation devant le Conseil d'Etat contre les décisions prises par le conseil national de la formation morale et sociale le 1er août 1989. Les requérants faisaient valoir à l'appui de leurs recours que la loi du 16 novembre 1988 précitée était contraire à l'art. 9 de la Convention et à l'art. 2 du Protocole No. 1 dans la mesure où seule une croyance religieuse, c'est-à-dire une conviction basée sur la foi, pouvait justifier une dispense du cours en question, alors qu'une pensée philosophique basée sur la raison ne le pouvait pas. Or, selon eux, les articles précités n'établissent aucune distinction entre la liberté de pensée, de conscience et de religion où entre les convictions religieuses et les convictions philosophiques.

Par arrêt du 21 mars 1990, le Conseil d'Etat rejeta le recours introduit par les requérants. Il se détermina comme suit:

> „*Considérant que les dispositions de l'art. 9, de même que celles des art. 8 et 10 de la Convention européenne des Droits de l'Homme garantissent à toute personne ,le droit au respect de sa vie privée et familiale', ,à la liberté de pensée, de conscience et de religion', ,à la liberté d'expression' et ,à la liberté d'opinion et à la liberté de recevoir ou de communiquer des informations ou des idées';*
> *Que ces mêmes droits sont garantis par l'art. 18 du Pacte international relatif aux droits civils et politiques;*

Considérant que les droits ainsi énoncés ne peuvent faire l'objet d'autres restrictions, aux termes de ces mêmes articles, que celles qui, prévues par la loi, constituent des mesures nécessaires, dans une société démocratique, à la sûreté publique, à la protection de l'ordre, de la santé ou de la morale publiques, ou à la protection des droits et libertés d'autrui;

Considérant que l'Etat doit dans l'organisation des cours se conformer aux dispositions de l'art. 2 du Protocole précité;

Considérant que ces dispositions visent à sauvegarder la possibilité d'un pluralisme éducatif garantissant la diffusion d'une manière objective, critique et pluraliste des informations ou connaissances figurant au programme et écartant tout endoctrinement qui puisse être considéré comme ne respectant pas les convictions religieuses ou philosophiques des parents;

Considérant que les cours de formation morale et sociale tels qu'ils sont prévus par la loi du 16 novembre 1988 doivent être axés sur l'étude des droits de l'homme et qu'ils doivent être organisés de façon à garantir le pluralisme d'opinions;

qu'il convient de conclure que la loi du 16 novembre 1988 ne viole ni les dispositions de la Convention européenne de sauvegarde des Droits de l'Homme, ni l'art. 2 du Protocole additionnel à cette Convention, ni l'art. 18 du Pacte international relatif aux droits civils et politiques;

qu'il en suit que le conseil national de la formation morale et sociale, en rejetant en date du 1er août 1989 les demandes des requérants visant à dispenser leurs enfants du cours de formation morale et sociale, a fait une application correcte de la loi."

GRIEFS

Les requérants considèrent que le rejet par le conseil national de la formation morale et sociale des demandes de dispense du cours de formation morale et sociale aux motifs que l'art. 48 de la loi du 16 novembre 1988 n'autorise une telle dispense que dans le cas où „les élèves se réclament d'une croyance religieuse dont les adhérents n'assurent pas de cours d'instruction religieuse ... dans le cadre des horaires scolaires" favorise les convictions religieuses au détriment des convictions philosophiques, établit ainsi une distorsion entre ces deux catégories de convictions et méconnaît à ce titre les dispositions de l'art. 9 de la Convention et de l'art. 2 du Protocole No. 1.

D'autre part, les requérants estiment que le Conseil d'Etat, en se basant sur le contenu de l'enseignement donné alors que la question posée dans le mémoire visait à contrôler la compatibilité des articles précités de la Convention avec l'art. 48 de la loi du 16 novembre 1988, a également méconnu l'art. 9 de la Convention et l'art. 2 du Protocole No. 1.

PROCEDURE DEVANT LA COMMISSION

...

EN DROIT

Les requérants se plaignent des décisions par lesquelles leurs demandes de dispense du cours de formation morale et sociale qu'ils avaient présentées au nom de leurs enfants, ont été rejetées. Ils considèrent que ces décisions prises en application de l'art. 48 de la loi du 16 novembre 1988 méconnaissent le principe d'égalité entre les libertés de pensée, de conscience et de religion garanti par l'art. 9 de la Convention et l'art. 2 du Protocole No. 1.

Selon eux, l'art. 48 de la loi du 16 novembre 1988 autorise l'Etat à privilégier les convictions religieuses par rapport aux convictions philosophiques, puisque seule une croyance religieuse permet aux élèves qui l'invoquent d'être dispensés des deux cours.

Par conséquent, les requérants considèrent que c'est sous l'angle de la différence de traitement que doit être analysée la question de la prétendue violation des art. 9 de la Convention et 2 du Protocole No. 1.

1. Le Gouvernement excipe en premier lieu du défaut de qualité de victime des requérants. Il fait valoir à ce titre que les requérants ne précisent pas en quoi les décisions prises par le conseil national de la formation morale et sociale constituent une violation des droits garantis par la Convention et notamment de son art. 9 et de l'art. 2 du Protocole No. 1.

Selon le Gouvernement, les requérants qui n'établissent à aucun moment avoir été gênés dans la manifestation de leurs convictions philosophiques rechercheraient plutôt un contrôle général et abstrait de la législation litigieuse à la lumière de la Convention.

Les requérants contestent la thèse du Gouvernement. Ils soutiennent à cet effet que le pluralisme et la tolérance exigent le respect des opinions d'autrui et impliquent une égalité de traitement entre les personnes, que celles-ci se réclament d'une conviction religieuse ou philosophique.

Or, pour les requérants, tel n'est pas le cas en l'espèce puisque leurs enfants, qui invoquaient à l'appui de leur demande de dispense des convictions philosophiques, n'ont pu l'obtenir contrairement aux élèves qui se réclamaient d'une croyance religieuse dont les adhérents n'assuraient pas de cours d'instruction religieuse dans le cadre des horaires scolaires.

La discrimination subie par leurs enfants suffit, selon les requérants, à fonder leur intérêt à agir devant la Commission.

La Commission rappelle qu'elle ne peut être saisie en vertu de l'art. 25 par. 1 de la Convention d'une requête émanant d'une personne physique, d'une organisation non gouvernementale ou d'un groupe de particuliers, que si la personne, l'organisation ou le groupe peut se prétendre victime d'une violation par l'une des Hautes Parties Contractantes des droits reconnus dans la Convention.

Par ailleurs, il ressort de la jurisprudence des organes de la Convention, que la Commission n'est compétente pour examiner la compatibilité de la législation interne avec la Convention qu'en ce qui concerne son application dans un cas concret, et qu'elle n'est pas compétente pour examiner in abstracto cette compatibilité avec la Convention (cf. N° 11036/84, déc. 2.12.85, DR 45 p. 211).

Certes, en l'espèce, les décisions dont se plaignent les requérants ont été prises par le conseil national de la formation morale et sociale en application de l'art. 48 de la loi du 16 novembre 1988. Toutefois, l'art. 25 de la Convention n'interdit pas aux particuliers de soutenir qu'une loi viole leurs droits dans la mesure où ils montrent qu'ils ont été personnellement affectés par l'application de la loi qu'ils critiquent (cf. N° 11036/84 citée ci-dessus).

La Commission estime que les requérants en tant que représentants légaux de leurs enfants peuvent effectivement se prétendre victimes du refus de dispense du cours de formation morale et sociale car cette décision affecte directement leurs enfants.

Elle considère d'autre part que les requérants peuvent également, à titre personnel et en qualité de parents, se prétendre victimes de la décision prise par le conseil national de la formation morale et sociale dans la mesure où cette décision influe sur l'éducation de leurs enfants, domaine dans lequel l'Etat doit respecter le droit des parents.

Il s'ensuit que l'exception d'irrecevabilité tirée du défaut de qualité de victime des requérants ne saurait être retenue.

2. Quant au bien-fondé de la requête, la Commission note que les griefs des requérants concernent pour l'essentiel les conséquences prétendument discriminatoires de la législation sur la réforme de l'enseignement secondaire luxembourgeois. Elle examine dès lors l'affaire sous l'angle de l'art. 14 de la Convention combiné avec son art. 9 et l'art. 2 du Protocole No. 1.

L'art. 14 est ainsi libellé:

„La jouissance des droits et libertés reconnus dans la présente Convention doit être assurée, sans distinction aucune, fondée notamment sur le sexe, la race, la couleur, la langue, la religion, les opinions politiques ou toutes autres opinions, l'origine nationale ou sociale, l'appartenance à une minorité nationale, la fortune, la naissance ou toute autre situation."

L'art. 9 dispose:

*„1) Toute personne a droit à la liberté de pensée, de conscience et de religion; ce droit implique la liberté de changer de religion ou de conviction, ainsi que la liberté de manifester sa religion ou sa conviction individuellement ou collectivement, en public ou en privé, par le culte, l'enseignement, les pratiques et l'accomplissement des rites.
2) (...)"*

Enfin, l'art. 2 du Protocole N° 1 se lit ainsi:

„Nul ne peut se voir refuser le droit à l'instruction. L'Etat, dans l'exercice des fonctions qu'il assumera dans le domaine de l'éducation et de l'enseignement, respectera le droit des parents d'assurer cette éducation et cet enseignement conformément à leurs convictions religieuses et philosophiques."

Le Gouvernement considère que la requête est manifestement mal fondée.

Il rappelle que l'Etat doit dispenser dans l'accomplissement de sa mission d'éducation et de formation des jeunes toutes les connaissances théoriques et pratiques nécessaires au développement de la personne humaine. La mise en place de cours de formation morale entre par conséquent et, selon le Gouvernement, dans l'exercice des fonctions qu'il assume dans le domaine de l'éducation.

Certes, le Gouvernement reconnaît que l'Etat doit dans l'accomplissement de ses fonctions veiller à garantir le pluralisme éducatif en écartant tout endoctrinement qui puisse être considéré comme ne respectant pas les convictions religieuses ou philosophiques des parents.

S'attachant à décrire le contenu du cours de formation morale et sociale dispensé aux élèves de l'enseignement secondaire et de l'enseignement secondaire technique, le Gouvernement rappelle que l'objectif principal est de sensibiliser les élèves aux problèmes qui se posent dans le monde moderne. Dans ce but, les élèves seront amenés à réfléchir aux notions d'égalité et de liberté en se basant notamment sur la Déclaration des Droits de l'Homme.

Par ailleurs, le Gouvernement souligne que le conseil national de la formation morale et sociale a pour mission, en vertu de l'art. 6 de la loi du 16 novembre 1988, de „veiller à ce que le cours de formation morale et sociale soit dispensé dans un esprit d'objectivité philosophique et idéologique".

Pour le Gouvernement, ces éléments suffisent à démontrer que le cours de formation morale et sociale vise à fournir aux élèves des informations sur les diverses religions et philosophies morales. Ne se rattachant à aucune école ou opinion philosophique déterminée, le Gouvernement estime difficile d'établir une quelconque violation par l'Etat défendeur de la liberté de pensée et de conscience ainsi que des convictions philosophiques des requérants.

Enfin, s'agissant du droit pour les élèves „qui se réclament d'une croyance religieuse dont les adhérents n'assurent pas de cours d'instruction religieuse et morale" d'être dispensé du cours d'instruction religieuse et morale et du cours de formation morale et sociale, le Gouvernement estime que cette faculté ne constitue pas, contrairement à ce qu'allèguent les requérants, un bénéfice ou un avantage mais qu'il s'agit plutôt d'un „pis aller".

Les requérants estiment pour leur part que les conclusions du gouvernement se caractérisent par une absence de réponse aux questions qu'ils ont soulevées dans leur requête introductive. Ils rappellent à cet égard que le problème en cause était relatif à la différence de traitement entre les élèves de convictions religieuses et ceux qui, comme leurs enfants, invoquaient des convictions philosophiques.

Selon eux, le Gouvernement, en se fondant sur le contenu du cours de formation morale et sociale, a esquivé le problème de la discrimination.

La Commission rappelle que l'art. 14 n'a pas d'existence autonome, mais joue un rôle important pour compléter les autres dispositions normatives de la Convention. Une mesure qui serait en elle-même compatible avec l'une des dispositions normatives peut cependant enfreindre cette disposition combinée avec l'art. 14 si elle est appliquée de manière discriminatoire; il suffit donc que la „matière" de la requête entre dans le domaine d'application d'un article protégeant une liberté pour que l'on puisse valablement alléguer la violation du principe de non-discrimination (voir notamment, CourEuDH, arrêts Marckx du 13 juin 1979, série A n° 31, pp. 15-16, par. 32, et Inze du 28 octobre 1987, série A n° 126, p. 17, par. 36).

En ce qui concerne les libertés de pensée, de conscience et de religion garanties par l'art. 9 de la Convention, la Commission estime que l'obligation pour les enfants des requérants de suivre un cours de formation morale et sociale ne constitue pas une ingérence dans l'exercice de la liberté de pensée ou de conscience. Elle note par ailleurs que les requérants ne soutiennent pas qu'en participant à ces cours, leurs enfants feraient l'objet d'un endoctrinement religieux ou autre.

Quant à l'obligation de l'Etat de respecter les droits des parents, tels que prévus à l'art. 2 du Protocole N° 1, la Commission note que les requérants ne soutiennent non plus que l'enseignement, tel qu'il est dispensé, heurte leurs convictions philosophiques. Elle relève en outre que les requérants n'ont pas précisé le concept de leurs convictions philosophiques. Or, la Commission rappelle que le mot „convictions" s'applique à des vues atteignant un certain degré de force, de sérieux, de cohérence et d'importance (cf. CourEuDH, arrêt Campbell et Cosans du 25 février 1982, série A n° 48, p. 16, par. 36).

La Commission fait encore observer que les convictions des parents, relevant de l'art. 2 du Protocole N° 1, visent des convictions qui ne vont pas à l'encontre du droit fondamental de l'enfant à l'instruction. Lorsqu'au lieu de le conforter, les droits des parents entrent en conflit avec le droit de l'enfant à l'instruction, les intérêts de l'enfant priment (voir mutatis mutandis N° 10233/83, déc. 6.3.84, DR 37 p. 105).

A supposer même que les faits litigieux entrent dans le domaine d'application de l'art. 9 de la Convention ainsi que de l'art. 2 du Protocole N° 1, et que dès lors l'art. 14 de la Convention trouve à s'appliquer, la Commission rappelle que, dans la jouissance des droits et libertés reconnus par la Convention, l'art. 14 interdit de traiter de manière différente, sauf justification objective et raisonnable, des personnes placées dans des situations comparables (voir, entre autres, CourEuDH, arrêt Sunday Times c/Royaume-Uni (n° 2) du 26 novembre 1991, série A n° 217, p. 32, par. 58, et arrêt Hoffmann c/Autriche du 23 juin 1993, à paraître dans la série A n° 255-C, par. 31, KirchE-EU, S. 232).

Il y a lieu de déterminer d'abord si les requérants peuvent se plaindre d'une telle différence de traitement.

L'art. 48, tel que modifié par la loi du 16 novembre 1988, a transformé la dispense pure et simple, prévue par la loi du 10 mai 1968, en une dispense conditionnelle et spécifique. En effet, seuls les élèves qui se réclament „d'une croyance religieuse dont les adhérents n'assurent pas de cours d'instruction religieuse et morale" pourront désormais obtenir une dispense des deux cours.

La Commission note que la nouvelle législation introduit une différence de traitement entre ceux qui se réclament d'une croyance religieuse et ceux qui invoquent des convictions philosophiques ne constituant pas des convictions religieuses.

Pareille différence de traitement est discriminatoire en l'absence de „justification objective et raisonnable", en d'autres termes si elle ne poursuit pas un „but légitime" et s'il n'y a pas de „rapport raisonnable de proportionnalité entre les moyens employés et le but visé" (voir notamment, CourEuDH, arrêt Darby du 23 octobre 1990, série A n° 187, p. 12, par. 31).

A la lumière de l'exposé des motifs annexé au projet de loi, le but visé par le législateur en 1988 était de réduire le nombre d'élèves abstentionnistes en vue de fournir à tous les jeunes une instruction morale. Le pourcentage d'élèves dispensés des deux cours était en effet passé de 2 % en 1968 à presque 30 % en 1987.

Ce but peut être considéré comme légitime dans la mesure où l'obligation qui est faite aux élèves de choisir entre le cours d'instruction religieuse et morale, d'une part, et le cours de formation morale et sociale, d'autre part, permet de transmettre aux jeunes des règles de vie nécessaires à la sauvegarde d'une société démocratique.

Il y a donc lieu de rechercher si la deuxième condition se trouve elle aussi remplie.

Le législateur national a instauré le principe d'une dispense conditionnelle. Ainsi, contrairement à ce qui était prévu sous l'empire de la loi du 10 mai 1968, seuls les élèves „se réclamant de convictions religieuses dont les adhérents n'assurent pas de cours d'instruction religieuse et morale dans le cadre des horaires scolaires" peuvent obtenir une dispense des deux cours. Toutefois, en établissant comme condition de dispense, l'appartenance à une croyance religieuse, le législateur n'a pas, ainsi que le prétendent les requérants, favorisé la liberté de religion par rapport aux autres libertés énoncées à l'art. 9 de la Convention. La Commission estime que la possibilité de dispense des deux cours en cause offerte à la catégorie d'élèves qui se réclament d'une croyance religieuse, s'inscrit dans l'obligation qui est faite aux Etats de respecter les convictions religieuses et philosophiques.

Or, la Commission ne voit pas dans quelle mesure les convictions philosophiques des requérants pourraient être méconnues par le choix du législateur d'imposer à leurs enfants l'obligation de participer au cours de formation morale et sociale. La Commission se réfère dans ce contexte à l'arrêt du Conseil d'Etat du 21 mars 1990 dans lequel celui-ci a affirmé que les cours de formation morale et sociale, tels qu'ils étaient prévus par la loi du 16 novembre 1988, devaient porter plus particulièrement sur l'étude des droits de l'homme et que ces cours devaient être organisés de façon à garantir le pluralisme d'opinions. La Commission conclut dès lors à l'existence d'un rapport raisonnable de proportionnalité entre les moyens employés et le but visé.

Il s'ensuit que la requête est manifestement mal fondée et doit être rejetée en application de l'art. 27 par. 2 de la Convention.

Par ces motifs, la Commission, à la majorité, déclare la requête irrecevable.

27

Art. 9 EMRK steht der Anwendung planungsrechtlicher Bestimmungen, die die Anzahl der in einem religiösen Zentrum (auch nur zeitweise) anwesenden Personen beschränken, nicht entgegen, wenn diese Vorschrift die Freiheit der Religionsausübung angemessen berücksichtigt.

Art. 9, 27 § 2 a.F. EMRK
EKMR, Beschluss vom 8. März 1994 - No. 20490/92
(ISKCON u.a. ./. Vereinigtes Königreich)[1] -

THE FACTS

The applicants are the International Society for Krishna consciousness Ltd. („ISKCON") and eight individuals who are members and, in part, officers of ISKCON.

ISKCON acquired a 19th century manor in 1973. The local authority had confirmed, by letter of 27 March 1973, that „on the information available the last use of the premises, namely a nurses' residential college, falls squarely within the same use class as a residential theological college in connection with the promotion of the religion of Krishna Con-

---

[1] DR 76, 90.

sciousness. In the circumstances, planning permission is not required. Although the previous use was largely residential, I gather that it was also partly educational and this appears to be the situation with the use now proposed".

On 25 January 1983 ISKCON entered into an agreement („the Section 52 Agreement") with the local authority that, inter alia, ISKCON would not permit more than 1,000 persons to visit the manor on any one day except with the consent of the council; the council granted consent for more than 1,000 persons to be present on six days in the year (festival days), subject to various conditions. The agreement referred to a previous enforcement notice which had been served in 1981 and against which ISKCON had appealed, and was expressed to be without prejudice to the council's rights to serve further enforcement notices. The council withdrew the existing enforcement notice, and ISKCON agreed not to make any claim for costs in the appeal.

On 8 January 1987 the local authority served an enforcement notice on ISKCON alleging that, by using the land for „the purposes of a residential educational college and a religious community and public worship and public entertainment in connection with religious festivals" ISKCON had materially changed the use of the land, and that this material change of use amounted to a breach of planning control. In the annex to the enforcement notice the local authority referred to the Section 52 Agreement, and alleged that, following repeated complaints from the local residents, the local authority had been made aware that the number of persons attending on non-festival days was increasing and had exceeded the 1,000 person limit.

An Inspector held an inquiry into appeals by ISKCON against the enforcement notice (and related matters). The inquiry was held on 9 November 1987, 21 November 1988, 29 November to 2 December, 6 to 9 December, 14 and 19 to 21 December 1988. In the 136 page report of the inquiry the Inspector found, as matters of fact, as follows:

„B. Religious and Social
1. The Krishna Consciousness movement, a traditionalist branch of the Hindu faith, was founded by Srila Prabhupada, a Sanskrit scholar who emigrated to New York from India, in 1966. Its aim is to stimulate interest and convert people world-wide to the spiritual principles of the Vedic culture of India as expounded in the scriptures of the Bhagavad Gita (The Bible of India). There are now 200 ISKCON centres throughout the world.
2. Devotees of Krishna Consciousness regard it not just as a religion, but as a whole way of life, constantly developing their love of god by rendering devotional service („Shakti-Yoga"). This includes the purification of the consciousness by constant chanting of the Holy Names of God. (The Hare Krishna Mantra).
3. Other forms of devotion regularly practised are the study of the scriptures, guided by priests and teachers, the performance of „puja" or acts of devotion to the deities at a shrine or at home, the offering of sanctified food to the deity before

eating, „prasad", and pilgrimages to a shrine or „tirtha" on holy days and festivals.
4. On these occasions it is customary to take „Darshan" or audience of the deities and offer silent private prayers as well as participating in the services performed by the priest, „Arati", and taking part in congregational chanting.
5. Any Hindu shrine contains deities which are regarded as gods themselves in the form of wood or stone. The deities at the Manor are of marble statues, worthy of the highest veneration.
6. Hindu tradition demands that they be moved only to achieve significantly better facilities for worship within their existing „dharma" or area over which they have exercised their influence. Any other move would be an act of desecration.
7. The first ISKCON shrine was set up in London in 1969 in a rented flat in Bury Place, and deities were installed there. In 1979, following enforcement proceedings and subsequent litigation, that temple and the deities were moved to premises in Soho Street, London, where ISKCON still have a temple with deities and resident priests, and a similar type of worship to that at the Manor.
8. Devotees of Krishna Consciousness are required to observe the „regulative principles", strict rules as to diet and temperance. Single persons live a monastic existence. The movement has a strong social conscience and tradition of counselling the distressed and afflicted.
9. The current Hindu population of Britain is estimated at 750,000 with between 120,000 and 200,000 in North London, 55,000 of these being within Brent and Harrow and forming the main catchment area for the temple congregations.
10. There are few Hindu temples in London, compared with Birmingham, which has 4 to serve a population of 40,000. Those in north-west London serve mainly the Swaminarayan faith, whose followers do not worship Radha and Krishna.
C. The Function of the Manor
1. The Manor is said to be the only „Math", or training college for Hindu priests in the United Kingdom. It welcomed as students anyone who wished to devote all or part of their lives to the understanding of the faith and devotion to Krishna.
...
4. It is a „Tirtha" or place of pilgrimage. Coachloads come from Birmingham to worship at the Manor.
...
6. The shrine is essential to the teaching of priests, regardless of any public worship.
...
8. The following are the principal activities at the Manor:
a. A residence (Ashram) for between 40 and 50 single devotees, priests and novices.
b. A centre for the training of full time Hindu priests and missionaries.
...
i. Devotional services in the temple between 0430 and 2115 hrs. daily, with extended programmes on Sundays, to which all members of the public are free to come.
...
l. The conduct of one or two day festivals on the 3 most important festivals in the Hindu calendar, namely Ramnavani (April), Janmasthnmi (July-September), Diwali (October-November), and other minor festivals on less important holy days."

In sec. D of his Report the Inspector set out the history of the events leading up to the service of the enforcement notice, the material part of which may be summarised as follows:

(1) In 1974 a neighbouring resident complained about large numbers of people living at the Manor, and services being advertised. A newspaper article in the summer of 1974 referred to 1,000 people celebrating Krishna's birthday at the Manor. A weekend festival in August 1975 attracted 5,000 visitors on each day and further festivals in November 1975 and August 1976 attracted not more than 2,500 people in any one day. Parking on neighbouring fields ameliorated adverse effects on the village.

(2) On 30 May 1978 planning permission was granted for the construction of a car park with 127 spaces. The application had been made at the request of the planning authority. The work was completed in 1979 at a cost of £20,000.

(3) A newspaper article in August 1979 reported a forecasted attendance of 10,000 people for the Janmasthami festival. A resident reported 600-800 cars parked in the fields and 11 coaches being parked in lay-byes in the area on Sunday 12 August.

(4) The 1980 Janmasthami festival was held on Saturday / Sunday 31 August after notification had been given that it would be on the Sunday and Monday. It was estimated that 14,000 people had attended each day and 15,000 attended a separate evening festival on Tuesday 2 September, when traffic blocked the village for several hours. By 1980 the Manor had become generally known as „The Temple". Counts carried out by Mr Jeffers in September 1980 indicated that on 3 successive Sundays between 498 and 760 vehicles entered the Manor with a flow of through traffic through the village of between 841 and 1,161 vehicles. in the same period. At the same time between 1,127 and 1,502 persons were counted into the Manor. Further counts on 4 Sundays in October 1980 showed between 587 and 1,119 persons entering the Manor.

(5) In July 1984 ISKCON sold their Worcestershire property, Croome Court, for economic reasons.

(6) A handbill inviting visitors to the Janmasthami Festival on 8 September 1985 stated that coach parties should write to the Manor in advance. It also said that every Sunday a special Festival programme was held from 4 pm to 9 pm featuring dramas, video shows, lectures, children's classes. Full Prasad, Bhajans (congregational chanting) and Arati (temple services). It was estimated that 13,000 people attended, over 2 days.

(7) Counts carried out from September 1985 to September 1988 showed that there have regularly been more than 1,000 visitors to the Manor on non-festival Sundays, the average attendance being in the region of 1,500. The 1986 Janmasthami Festival attracted 1,184 vehicles on Sunday 24 August, 682 on Monday 25 August and 1,955 on Wednesday 27 August, with visitors counted at 4,631, 2,339 and 8,781 on those 3 days. A nearby resident described the Festival as seeming to go on all the week and having only 2 1/2 hours sleep on one night.

(8) Previous proposals for a residential farm community in the Midlands and community halls in areas where the Hindu population were concentrated, such as Brent, Southall and East London had not materialised. Following the initial adjournment of the Inquiry into the Enforcement Notice appeal a search was made for an alternative temple site and that at Dagger Lane was identified. ISKCON

indicated they required a site 3 times the site of that at the Manor, and the buildings proposed would cover about 2 1/2 times the floor area. The deities would be moved to the new temple and the Manor would become primarily a place of spiritual retreat with a shrine for the benefit mainly of residents who would number up to 50.

In sec. E of his Report the Inspector found that the main house was a Grade II listed building (having been added to the list in 1985) and the buildings and most of the grounds were within the Letchmore Heath Conservation Area, designated in 1969. The site was within an extensive area of the Metropolitan Green Belt and this notation had not changed since 1954.

Whilst stating that the legal implications of these facts were matters for the Secretary of State, the Inspector set out in detail the conclusions which he had drawn from the above facts. The Inspector noted that it was quite clear that the notice was aimed at discontinuing all festivals, and that there was no intention to include any saving for the 6 days mentioned in the Section 52 Agreement. The Inspector did not consider there was any necessity for it to do this. He concluded that the enforcement notice was valid and that the appeal failed on each of the grounds relied on by ISKCON.

As to Ground (c) (the appeal on the ground that the breach of planning control had not taken place), the Inspector found on the evidence that residents at the Manor lived as a community, in a regime somewhat similar to a monastery, devoted single-mindedly to the service and promotion of their religion. The bond between all the occupants of the Manor was the religion of Krishna Consciousness, and they worked and ate together, and shared the house and its grounds, each resident having only a part of a shared bedroom for his or her sole occupation. That is communal living as the reasonable man would understand it.

As to public worship, the public were permitted to attend services at all times. The Manor was proud to keep open house, and the gates were locked only for a few hours during part of the night. No visitor had to ask for any permission to enter. The services in the temple were conducted on exactly the same basis as in an Anglican or any other church, although there was no parish roll or register of communicants. Members of the public were invited to celebrate weddings, with a religious ceremony after the civil one, and this also could be described as an element of public worship.

As to public entertainment in connection with religious festivals, the publicity given in the past, and attractions promised at the festivals, with references to firework displays, vegetarian feasting, spectacular pandal performances, dances, drama and music and video shows indicated that the visitors did indeed come not just to worship in the temple or offer silent prayers to the deities, but also to be entertained, albeit against a religious background. The festivals had many of the attractions of a fête, and more besides.

As to Ground (b) (the appeal on the ground that the matters alleged did not breach planning control), the Inspector concluded that the primary use of the Manor was fundamentally different in many ways from a residential theological college and that there had been a material change of use.

It was the practice at the Manor to extend open doors to all comers at almost all hours of the day and night in a way which no college would do, and which would not be found at any church, even a major cathedral in a city. It was, as one resident wrote „rather like having Canterbury Cathedral in the middle of a small English village".

The Inspector expressly considered ISKCON's argument that the effect of the Section 52 Agreement was to found an estoppel. He noted that it was an agreement under seal voluntarily entered into and as such the law of contract applied. Furthermore the recital (viii) clearly implied that the parties envisaged that some further enforcement notice might be served if it was deemed expedient. It was in any event clear from the authority cited that a planning authority could not by virtue of a Section 52 Agreement fetter its discretion to carry out its statutory function to serve another enforcement notice in the future. The rights and duties of the parties conferred by the Section 52 Agreement should be determined by the law of contract, the enforcement notice according to the statutory provisions. The existence of the Section 52 Agreement did not estop the planning authority from serving the enforcement notice and the Section 52 Agreement had no bearing on the Ground b. appeal, which failed.

As to Ground (a) (the ground of appeal that planning permission ought to be granted), the Inspector summarised the primary issues, which were in his view all of equal relevance in setting out the conflicting priorities. These included:

„vi. Does the importance of the Manor as a shrine and the need to provide places of worship for the Hindu population:-
a. constitute those very special circumstances which justify development in the Green Belt in any event;
b. outweigh any specific and convincing planning objections on any of the grounds noted above and justify an exception to Green Belt and other Development Plan policies?
vii. Whether, given the long history, the presumption in favour of development and the previous decisions by the planning authority, any injury to amenity can be met by suitable and enforceable conditions."

The Inspector's conclusions on these issues were as follows:

„37.13 I turn next to issue (vi), very special circumstances. I accept that the Manor has become a special place of worship and pilgrimage for the Hindu

community in this country, and that there appear to be very few Hindu places of worship in North London and nearby counties. The Manor is of special importance as the home in Britain of ISKCON's founder. I do not doubt that the traditional religious rites and ceremonies, in sylvan surroundings, bring inspiration and spiritual comfort to many who visit. No one could ignore the national and international concern, and the social issue posed by the possibility of restricting participation in the worship at the Manor and the celebration of the Hindu festivals. Whilst I have not adopted verbatim the findings of fact suggested by Counsel for the appellants in respect of the planning authority's attitude of partial acceptance over the years, I accept the basic thesis behind them, and indeed they are largely borne out by the planning authority's own evidence.

37.14 The appeal of Krishna Consciousness and the Hindu population have both increased substantially in the past 15 years. It is very clear from the voluminous documents that regular attendances at the Manor over and above those at festival times have also increased significantly in recent years. The Manor has become an important place of worship and pilgrimage. This is unfortunate in view of the fact that it is situated in one of the most vulnerable areas of Green Belt, so very close to London, in a village of high profile public activities. The sale of Croome Court and concentration of activities at the Manor seems to have flown in the face of those constraints which should have been obvious in view of the history of concern by the planning authority through the 1970s.

37.15 I take due note that the Manor has been allowed to be used for public worship and public entertainment at festivals for many years. I do not consider however that this implies toleration of the status quo, but rather that the planning authority have been doing everything they can to avoid the confrontation which the present enforcement notice has provoked. I note that some residents accept that they have had less to complain about from noise and disturbance in recent years, but it is in the nature of things that uses which have caused conflict are toned down when there are enforcement proceedings pending. When I bear in mind the numbers of people and vehicles involved, and the type of activities, such as weddings and feasts which have been publicised in the past, I have to take into account that a planning permission for a use which is geared to attracting people is very likely to result in an upsurge of activity.

37.16 The appellants maintain that because the earlier enforcement notice and the Section 52 Agreement provided for a tolerance of up to 1000 visitors on nonfestival days, this figure at any rate should be regarded as acceptable in planning terms. By the same token they imply that the 6 Festivals should be accepted. I do not consider this should necessarily be so. A figure of 1000 visitors, particularly if it is to be regarded as 1000 visitors in addition to the staff and students whose attendance is part and parcel of the determined use of a theological college, is to my view too large a crowd to bring into the village in any event on a Sunday. Taking Mr Campbell's occupancy of 3.85 occupants per car, which seems surprisingly high, it will still generate some 260 in and out vehicle movements, which will certainly have a considerable effect on the Sunday evening peace and quiet for the nearest residents. I conclude therefore that there is no justification for taking 1000 visitors as an acceptable norm.

37.17 I am in no doubt that any church of any faith or denomination in a small village or indeed in any closely built residential area, which regularly attracted 1000-1500 people for late evening services on Sundays, and crowds of up to 12000 for festivals 3 times a year, would encounter objections from the host com-

munity. The intimate small scale closely built character of a home counties village simply cannot accommodate the crowds attracted to a tirtha in the Indian sub-continent, especially when most of the worshippers or pilgrims have to come in their own private transport or in coaches. When religious meetings on this scale are held in the United Kingdom such as those by Billy Graham and other evangelists, Earls Court or Wembley Stadium are booked. I note that Mr Sharman proposes to hold the next Hindu youth festival in such place, acknowledging that the temple premises in Wandsworth are not large enough.

37.18 It also seems to me that the fact that the tenets of Krishna Consciousness prescribe that there must be devotions virtually 24 hours a day, with comings and goings very late at night, are particularly intrusive in a small village. The appellants are not prepared to even consider curbing their night time activities and maintain that it would be contrary to their faith to do so. I understand what they say, but this inevitably makes the use very difficult to fit into a residential village where most people travel some distance to work, and come home expecting a measure of peace and quiet, essentially at weekends when the use of the Manor is at its most active.

37.19 I take due note of the very large number of letters and petitions, addressed to HM the Queen, the Prime Minister and members of HM Government, Members of Parliament, the planning authority and myself relating to this matter. Unfortunately many of these are based on the premise that there is some antipathy to the Hindu religion, which is not the case. Inevitably many of these letters come from people far away from Letchmore Heath who are not aware of the full circumstances and the problems posed by the attraction of crowds into a small English village. I take particular note however that there are also some letters from local residents supporting the appellants, and there was some support for the alternative access, if that had proved a practical proposition.

37.20 In his submissions counsel for the appellants expressly withdrew any allegations of religious or racial prejudice which had been made against the planning authority. In this, as in very many other planning decisions it is necessary to weigh the needs of one group or interest against others, and the needs of religious or ethnic minorities, however important, cannot necessarily be allowed to override those constraints which have to apply to everyone, in planning as in other matters, in the interests of a tolerant and free society in a small and crowded country.

37.21 The appellants appear to have recognised that the attraction provided by the Manor has outgrown the capacity of Letchmore Heath to accommodate those it attracts, with the risk that the very basis of that attraction, a shrine in a peaceful village in the country, could be destroyed. The aims of the proposal for an alternative temple indicates the growth in popularity which is anticipated and the number of worshippers which might have to be catered for. No further consideration seems to have been given however to acquiring a country mansion in a more remote spot, or a redundant ecclesiastical or educational building closer to the centres of the Hindu population. I appreciate that a very high standard of Puja has been developed at the Manor, which is appreciated by a large congregation, but I am not convinced that the Manor is the only place where this can be carried on, and it appears that as recently as 8 years ago a Math could readily be set up at Croome Court and quickly given up when economic conditions so dictated.

37.22 It was suggested that need justified an exception to, or setting aside Green Belt policy altogether in this particular case. However, when I weigh on one side the needs of the appellants and their congregation and on the other not just for the Green Belt policy, but the actual disquiet and inconvenience to residents, and add to that the positive duty which Conservation Area status imposes on the decision maker, not just to preserve but also to enhance the character of Letchmore Heath, I consider that the interests of the village and its residents should prevail, and that there is insufficient justification for setting aside that weight of policy as well as other specific and convincing planning objections.

37.23 The decision on the merits should in my view also take into account the decision in respect of the Dagger Lane site. If planning permission is granted for a new temple, then my conclusions on the merits in respect of the enforcement notice have that much more force, because an alternative site has been provided, in accordance with the advice in Annex B of Circular 22/80. However if there is to be no new temple, it still seems to me that the combination of policy and clearly identifiable physical disadvantages to the use at Letchmore Heath constitute specific and convincing planning objections of such force that they amply outweigh and displace the arguments on the grounds of need, even though those arguments then become that much stronger.

37.24 I turn finally to conditions. Every encouragement is given by Circulars 22/80 and PPG Note 1 to temper enforcement action by granting planning permission subject to suitable conditions. In this case the planning authority have shown themselves willing for at least 10 years to devise some machinery whereby the religious aspirations of the appellants and their devotees can be equated with the interests of the residents. Whilst it is not for me to disagree with the legal interpretation of the Section 52 Agreement, it does seem to me that the appellants have chosen to disregard the spirit if not the letter of it, and I can only conclude that they are unwilling on principle to restrict the number of people attending their premises in the interests of the neighbouring residents.

37.25 It seems to me that a condition limiting numbers would be the only basis on which the damage to amenity caused by the scale of the public worship and public entertainment activities could be remedied. Given the past history however I have the gravest doubts as to whether such a condition could be enforced, and the very fact that such a condition is necessary points to the fundamental unsuitability of the premises for activities of this kind on anything but a purely local scale. I have to agree with the planning authority that restrictions on numbers have already been proved not to work. I can think of no other form of condition which would remedy the damage to the amenities of the village caused by the present activities, and I do not consider therefore that a conditional permission is appropriate ..."

On 20 March 1990 the Secretary of State, bearing in mind the Inspector's report, largely confirmed the enforcement notice (including his conclusions as to estoppels), with the variation that ISKCON had two years rather than six months to cease the prohibited use, and a minor amendment was made to the use to which the Manor and land could be put.

ISKCON exercised their statutory right of appeal under sec. 246 (1) of the Town and Country Planning Act 1971 (now sec. 289 of the Town and Planning Act 1990). Their Notice of Motion included as a ground of appeal that ISKCON were prepared to enter into a new Section 52 Agreement, but did not repeat the estoppel argument. Mr. Justice Kennedy, giving the judgment of the High Court on 31 October 1991, noted that it was no longer challenged by the applicants that there had been a material change of use of the Manor. Instead, the applicants argued, inter alia, (i) that the Inspector and the Secretary of State had failed to have proper regard to the willingness of the applicants to enter into a new Section 52 Agreement and (ii) that the Secretary of State had been wrong to accept the Inspector's conclusion that the planning objections outweighed the arguments of the applicants on the ground of need.

As to the former submission, the Court held that, as was clear from the Inspector's report, negotiations for a further Section 52 Agreement had broken down. There had been an earlier agreement, but for present purposes it was not material. So, even accepting that the appellants were willing to enter into an agreement on their own terms, the position was, as Counsel for the Secretary of State graphically described it, like one hand clapping. There was nothing for the Inspector of the Secretary of State to take into account.

On the latter point, ISKCON criticised the Secretary of State's acceptance of the Inspector's conclusion in par. 37.23 of his report that even if planning permission were not granted in respect of the Dagger Lane site,

> '... the combination of policy and clearly identifiable physical disadvantages to the use at Letchmore Heath constitute specific and convincing planning objections of such force that they amply outweigh and displace the arguments on the grounds of need, even though those arguments then become that much stronger.'

It was argued by ISKCON that the Inspector's conclusion was founded at least in part on misapprehensions. For example, he was wrong to suggest, without any evidential basis, that if a new temple were to be built there would be increased activity at the Manor due to fund raising, or that the appellants might be unable to complete a new temple project within the time scale allowed. The Court rejected ISKCON's submissions on the grounds that the matters on which the Inspector really relied were matters of substance, which permeated his report. This approach was indicated in par. 37.22 of the Report (see above).

The Secretary of State was entitled to regard the Inspector's conclusions as firmly founded, and there was no substance in any of the points which had been argued in support of the appeal.

ISKCON applied for leave to appeal to the Court of Appeal to the Court of Appeal. On 16 March 1992 Lord Justice Glidewell agreed largely with the decision of Mr Justice Kennedy of 31 October 1991. Leave to appeal was refused.

With the refusal of leave to appeal, the two year period for compliance with the enforcement notice began to run.

RELEVANT DOMESTIC LAW

Sec. 174 (2) of the Town and Country Planning Act 1990 provides for the following grounds for appeal to the Secretary of State against an enforcement notice:

„(a) that planning permission ought to be granted for the development to which the notice relates or, as the case may be, that a condition or limitation alleged in the enforcement notice not to have been complied with ought to be discharged:
(b) that the matters alleged in the notice do not constitute a breach of planning control;
(c) that the breach of planning control alleged in the notice has not taken place;
...
(g) that the steps required by the notice to be taken exceed what is necessary to remedy any breach of planning control or to achieve a purpose specified in sec. 173 (4);
(h) that the period specified in the notice as the period within which any step is to be taken falls short of what should reasonably be allowed. "

An appeal against the Secretary of State may be made to the High Court „on a point of law" (sec. 289 (1) of the Town and Country Planning Act 1990).

COMPLAINTS

The complaints made by ISKCON

ISKCON allege a violation of art. 9 of the Convention. ISKCON accept that the enforcement notice appears to satisfy the requirements of lawfulness and legitimate purpose in art. 9 par. 2, but consider that the interference was not „necessary in a democratic society". In particular, they consider that the enforcement notice, subsequent proceedings and the attitude shown by the authorities were unnecessarily harsh and failed to give sufficient weight to the importance of the Manor as a place of worship and inspiration for Hindus. In this respect they also point to a letter of 17 September 1992 from a minister at the Department of the Environment that "[r]eligious aspects of the Society's activities at Bhaktivedanta Manor were not relevant" to the enforcement and planning appeals, and to further letters to the same effect of 26 August and 22 December 1993 from an official and a minister at the Department of the Environment respectively.

They consider that, in an increasingly ethnically diverse Europe, the Commission should not hesitate, in an appropriate case, to adopt a narrow margin of appreciation under art. 9. ISKCON regard the Section 52 Agreement of 25 January 1983 as evidence of what the council then accepted as reasonable, and that without giving good reasons for changing their mind, the council's subsequent enforcement notice and proceedings were disproportionate.

ISKCON also allege a violation of art. 1 of Protocol No. 1, taken alone and in conjunction with art. 14 of the Convention. ISKCON consider that because of the link with religious freedom, a narrower approach should be made to art. 1 of the First Protocol than is normally the case, and they argue that Muslims, Catholics and Protestants have been given permission to use premises for public worship within Green Belt areas where they have not been so permitted.

ISKCON also allege a violation of art. 6 par. 1 of the Convention in that they were entitled to access to a court with the full guarantees of art. 6 in respect neither of their property rights, nor in respect of their right to freedom of religion. They point out that the proceedings before the Planning Inspector were non- judicial, recommendatory in character and subject to alteration or confirmation at the Secretary of State's discretion, and that the scope of review of the appeal to the High Court (and subsequent application for leave to appeal to the Court of Appeal) was not sufficient to comply with art. 6 par. 1 of the Convention.

ISKCON also allege a violation of art. 13 of the Convention to the extent that art. 6 par. 1 may be found not to be applicable.

The complaints made by the 8 individual applicants

The individual applicants have each submitted a statement to the Commission indicating how seriously he or she will be affected if the enforcement notice takes effect. They ask the Commission to construe art. 9 of the Convention according to international standards and developments, with particular reference to the United Nations Declaration on the Elimination of all forms of intolerance and discrimination based on religion or belief, 1981. Those applicants who are parents also rely on art. 2 of Protocol No. 1 in that they are not able to ensure education and teaching in conformity with their religious convictions, and that they are no longer able to ensure this because of the enforcement notice served on ISKCON. The individual applicants also allege violations of art. 6 and 13 of the Convention.

PROCEEDINGS BEFORE THE COMMISSION

...

THE LAW

[1] ...

[2] ISKCON allege a violation of art. 9 of the Convention in that the enforcement proceedings in respect of Bhaktivedanta Manor interfered in

an unjustified way with their freedom of religion. Art. 9 provides as follows:

> „1. Everyone has the right to freedom of thought, conscience and religion; this right includes freedom to change his religion or belief and freedom, either alone or in community with others and in public or in private, to manifest his religion or belief, in worship, teaching, practice and observance.
> 2. Freedom to manifest one's religion or beliefs shall be subject only to such limitations as are prescribed by law and are necessary in a democratic society in the interests of public safety, for the protection of public order, health or morals, or for the protection of the rights and freedoms of others. "

The Government submit that the interest and importance of ISKCON's rights under art. 9 of the Convention were fully taken into account by the Inspector's report and the Secretary of State's decision.

The Commission notes at the outset that ISKCON do not allege that the mere existence of planning legislation violated their rights under the Convention. Indeed, the Convention organs have found on several occasions that contracting States enjoy a wide discretion in regulating planning matters (cf. EuCHR, Sporrong and Lonnröth judgment of 23 September 1982, Series A no. 52, p. 26 par. 69, and, in the context of the United Kingdom legislation, Chater v. the United Kingdom, No. 11723/85, Dec. 7.5.87, DR 52 p. 250, 256). It is against this background that the Commission must assess the compliance with art. 9-2 of any interference with ISKCON's right under art. 9-1 of the Convention.

ISKCON Ltd. is a registered charity in the United Kingdom. It is part of the International Society for Krishna Consciousness, which is the worldwide promoter of Vayishnavism, the worship of Krishna. ISKCON's use of Bhaktivedanta Manor began in 1973 when the Manor was acquired, and developed as the Manor became more successful and better known. The Commission is prepared to assume that the issue of the enforcement notices to limit use of the manor to that which was permitted when ISKCON acquired the manor amounts to an interference with ISKCON's freedom of religion, including the freedom to manifest that religion in worship, teaching, practice and observance.

The Commission finds that the limitation on ISKCON's freedom to manifest its religion was prescribed by law in that the domestic town and country planning legislation was applied. It has not been suggested that that legislation was insufficiently clear or otherwise in conflict with the requirement that it be „prescribed by law".

It has, however, been submitted by ISKCON that the interference was not „necessary in a democratic society" although they accept that the aim of the interference was to protect the rights of others, namely the residents of the nearby village. The Commission in addition finds an element of protection of public order or health in the aim of the interference, in that planning legislation is generally accepted as necessary in modern society to prevent uncontrolled development.

The adjective „necessary" in the second paragraph of art. 8, 9, 10, 11 of the Convention implies the existence of a „pressing social need". Contracting States have a certain margin of appreciation in assessing whether such a need exists but it goes hand in hand with European supervision, embracing both the law and the decisions applying it, even those given by independent courts. The task of the Convention organs is not to substitute their view for that of the competent national authorities, but rather to review under the article at issue the decisions delivered pursuant to their power of appreciation. This does not mean that supervision is limited to ascertaining whether the respondent State exercises its discretion reasonably, carefully and in good faith; what the Convention organs have to do is to look at the interference complained of in the light of the case as a whole and determine whether it was „proportionate to the legitimate aim pursued" and whether the reasons adduced by the national authorities to justify it are „relevant and sufficient" (cf., in the context of art. 10 of the Convention, EuCHR, Sunday Times judgment of 26 November 1991, Series A no. 217, p. 29 par. 50, with further reference).

Applying these principles to the present case, the Commission notes that ISKCON do not in substance contend that the planning law was wrongly applied. Rather, they consider that as the local authority had initially entered into a Section 52 Agreement with ISKCON, the requirement of proportionality would have been better met by imposing additional conditions on the use of the Manor than by serving an enforcement notice prohibiting the established use of the Manor. They also point out that the effect of the enforcement notice was to deprive them of their rights under the Section 52 Agreement to admit up to 1,000 people per day to the Manor. They also lay emphasis on the fact that inadequate weight was given to their freedom of religion in the proceedings.

As to the Section 52 Agreement, the Commission notes that the agreement in the present case was part of continuing attempts by the local authority and ISKCON to resolve their planning differences, in this case by entering into a contract relating to the use of the land. Moreover, as pointed out by the Inspector, it was not only implicit in the Agreement that further enforcement notices might be served if it were deemed expedient, but negotiations for a further Section 52 Agreement had broken down. Even assuming that conditions acceptable to the local authority had been proposed for inclusion in the existing, or in a new, Section 52 Agreement, the Commission does not consider that the decision of the local authority to control the use of the property by recourse to the statutory enforcement powers, rather than by means of contractual provisions, was in the circumstances disproportionate to the legitimate aim. Similarly the decision was not in the Commission's view rendered disproportionate by the fact that on planning grounds, the local authority was no longer prepared to contemplate visits to the Manor by up to 1,000 persons per day.

With regard to the weight given to ISKCON's right to religion in the enforcement proceedings, the Commission notes that although the courts were limited in their review of the Secretary of State's decision to confirm the enforcement notices, the Inspector who held an inquiry into the enforcement notices gave detailed consideration to the special circumstances of the case. Although he came to the conclusion that the special circumstances were not sufficient to outweigh the general planning considerations, the Commission finds that sufficient weight was given to the position of ISKCON and the difficulties faced if the user of Bhaktivedanta Manor was limited to that which was permitted in 1973. In particular, the Commission does not consider that art. 9 of the Convention can be used to circumvent existing planning legislation, provided that in the proceedings under that legislation, adequate weight is given to freedom of religion. In contending that inadequate weight was given to ISKCON's freedom of religion, the applicants rely on statements in letters sent by Ministers and an official of the Department of the Environment to the effect that the decision on ISKCON's appeal against the enforcement notice was based on the relevant land-use planning grounds and that „the religious aspects of the Society's activities at Bhaktivedanta Manor were not relevant". The Commission does not interpret these statements as suggesting that the religious importance of the Manor to the members of ISKCON was not fully taken into account and weighed against the general planning considerations, but rather as making clear that the refusal of planning permission was based on proper planning grounds and not on any objections to the religious aspects of the activities of ISKCON. It is in any event clear from the terms of the Inspector's Report and the decision letter of the Secretary of State that considerable weight was attached to the religious needs and interests of the members of ISKCON and to the importance of the Manor in relation to the religious activities of the members.

Accordingly, the Commission finds that the interference with ISKCON's right to freedom of religion under art. 9 of the Convention can be regarded as „necessary in a democratic society".

It follows that this part of the application is manifestly ill-founded within the meaning of art. 27-2 of the Convention.

(Verletzung des Art. 1 des Protokolls P1 par. 1 wird geprüft, aber ebenso verneint wie eine Verletzung der Art. 6-1, 9, 13, 14, 27-2 EMRK)

For these reasons, the Commission by a majority declares (...) the application inadmissible.

28

Eine Berücksichtigung von Vordienstzeiten in einem Orden bei der Bemessung von Altersrente ist nicht durch die EMRK geboten.

Art. 9, 11, 14, 27 § 2 a.F. EMRK
EKMR, Beschluss vom 17. Januar 1995 - No. 24389/94
(Temprano Gomez ./. Spanien) -

EN FAIT

La requérante est une ressortissante espagnole, ancienne religieuse, née en 1925 et domiciliée à Madrid.

Le 10 septembre 1990, à l'âge de 65 ans, la requérante demanda à être mise au bénéfice d'une pension de retraite. Le 17 octobre 1990, l'Institut national de la Sécurité sociale accorda à la requérante la pension de retraite pour un montant équivalant à 64% de la base de calcul qui était de 83.583 pesetas. La requérante, ancienne religieuse dans la Congrégation S. S.J., avait travaillé comme enseignante dans les écoles de ladite Congrégation à Badajoz, de septembre 1950 à septembre 1971. Elle fut affiliée au régime général de la Sécurité sociale à partir du 12 novembre 1973. Pour la fixation du montant de la pension de retraite de la requérante, seules les 17 années pendant lesquelles, après avoir quitté la Congrégation, elle avait prêté ses services comme enseignante séculière, furent prises en compte par la Sécurité sociale.

La requérante entama, en 1990, de nombreuses actions à l'encontre de l'Institut National de la Sécurité sociale et de la Trésorerie générale de la Sécurité sociale. Le 19 février 1990, elle intenta également, devant l'Institut d'arbitrage de la Sécurité sociale, un acte de conciliation avec son ancien employeur pendant la période objet du litige (1950-1971), la Congrégation S. S.J. Toutes les actions entamées furent rejetées. Le 18 février 1991, la requérante présenta un recours devant le juge du travail de Madrid, à l'encontre de l'Institut et de la Trésorerie de la Sécurité sociale, et de la Congrégation auprès de laquelle elle avait été religieuse et avait travaillé comme enseignante. La requérante demanda à ce que le montant restant de sa pension de retraite lui soit reconnu, jusqu'à 100% de la base de calcul ci-dessus mentionnée. Par arrêt du 28 juin 1991, le recours fut rejeté. Le juge estima que le fait de travailler comme enseignante entre 1950 et 1971 au sein de la Congrégation S. S.J. ne pouvait pas être considéré comme une relation de travail selon les lois en vigueur à l'époque (Loi générale de la Sécurité sociale), car la requérante ne pouvait justifier de l'existence d'un contrat ou d'une déclaration judiciaire dans ce sens ni la perception d'un salaire en échange de ses prestations à un employeur, entraînant obligatoirement son affiliation à la Sécurité sociale.

La requérante saisit alors le Tribunal constitutionnel d'un recours d'"amparo" sur le fondement des art. 14 et 16 (principe de non-discrimination et droit à la liberté religieuse) de la Constitution. Elle estima avoir fait l'objet d'une discrimination par rapport aux enseignants non-religieux dans la même école, qui furent affiliés à la Sécurité sociale. Dans son mémoire devant le Tribunal constitutionnel le ministère public se prononça en faveur de l'octroi de l'„amparo" à la requérante, estimant que la non rémunération des services prêtés au sein de la Congrégation citée, ne pouvait justifier à elle seule un traitement différent de celui accordé aux professeurs séculiers du même centre.

Par arrêt du 28 février 1994, la haute juridiction rejeta le recours en reprenant, pour l'essentiel, les arguments du juge de travail. Le Tribunal constitutionnel nota que la loi générale de la Sécurité sociale n'incluait pas, au moment des faits, dans son champ d'application personnel, les religieuses qui rendaient leurs services au sein d'une communauté religieuse, ni obligeait cette dernière à les affilier au régime de Sécurité sociale. Le tribunal estima, en outre, que vu l'état de religieuse de la requérante pendant la période considérée, ses activités au sein de la Congrégation étaient motivées par la spiritualité, la gratuité et les voeux d'obéissance et de pauvreté, l'intérêt lié à la rémunération économique, essentiel dans une relation contractuelle de travail, étant absent de la relation nouée avec la Congrégation.

DROIT INTERNE PERTINENT

Durant la période où la requérante a été religieuse auprès de la Congrégation en cause, de 1950 à 1971, la loi générale de Sécurité sociale n'incluait pas dans son champ d'application personnel les religieuses qui appartenaient à une communauté religieuse, ni imposait leur affiliation à la Sécurité sociale.

Actuellement la situation est différente. Depuis le décret 3325/81 du 29 décembre 1981, la période de travail effectuée au sein d'une communauté religieuse est prise en compte aux effets de l'obtention de la prestation de sécurité sociale correspondante.

GRIEFS

Invoquant l'art. 14 de la Convention, la requérante estime que le principe de non-discrimination n'a pas été respecté à son égard du fait que sa condition de religieuse dans une Congrégation l'a privée du droit de percevoir une partie du montant de sa pension de retraite et ce alors que les services d'enseignante qu'elle a prêtés de 1950 à 1971 constituaient un travail, similaire à celui des professeurs séculiers n'appartenant pas à la Congrégation.

En invoquant les art. 9 et 11 de la Convention, la requérante se plaint que la liberté de manifester sa propre religion et la liberté d'association à une Congrégation de caractère religieux ont fait l'objet de restrictions.

EN DROIT

La requérante se plaint d'avoir été privée d'une partie de sa pension de retraite du fait de son état de religieuse, alors que les services d'enseignante qu'elle a prêtés de 1950 à 1971 constituaient un travail, similaire à celui des professeurs séculiers. Elle estime avoir fait l'objet d'une discrimination contraire à l'art. 14 de la Convention. Elle considère également que la liberté de manifester sa propre religion et celle de s'associer à une Congrégation de caractère religieux ont fait l'objet de restrictions. La requérante invoque les art. 9 et 11 de la Convention. Les dispositions citées se lisent comme suit:

> *Art. 14*
> *„La jouissance des droits et libertés reconnus dans la présente Convention doit être assurée, sans distinction aucune, fondée notamment sur ... la religion ...“*
> *Art. 9*
> *„1. Toute personne a droit à la liberté de pensée, de conscience et de religion; ce droit implique la liberté de changer de religion ou de conviction, ainsi que la liberté de manifester sa religion ou sa conviction ...*
> *2. La liberté de manifester sa religion ou ses convictions ne peut faire l'objet d'autres restrictions que celles qui, prévues par la loi, constituent des mesures nécessaires, dans une société démocratique, ... à la protection des droits et libertés d'autrui. ...“*
> *Art. 11*
> *„1. Toute personne a droit à la liberté de réunion pacifique et à la liberté d'association ...*
> *2. L'exercice de ces droits ne peut faire l'objet d'autres restrictions que celles qui, prévues par la loi, constituent des mesures nécessaires, dans une société démocratique, ... à la protection des droits et libertés d'autrui. ...“*

La Commission relève que la requérante se plaint du refus des tribunaux internes de prendre en considération, aux fins de la fixation du montant de sa pension de retraite, la période allant de 1950 à 1971 pendant laquelle elle travailla comme enseignante au sein d'une Congrégation religieuse, et ce au motif qu'en étant religieuse, elle ne pouvait pas être affiliée à la Sécurité sociale. Selon la requérante, ce refus constitue une discrimination par rapport aux enseignants séculiers.

La Commission a examiné le grief de la requérante tiré de l'art. 14 de la Convention tant pris isolément que combiné avec les art. 9 et 11 de la Convention invoqués par elle. La Commission rappelle toutefois que l'art. 14 de la Convention n'interdit la discrimination que dans la jouissance des droits et des libertés garantis par la Convention (cf. N° 11278/ 84, déc. 1.7.85, DR 43 p. 216). Or, le droit à se voir accorder une pension de retraite d'un montant déterminé n'est garanti ni par l'art. 9 ni par l'art. 11 de a Convention.

Il s'ensuit que la requête est incompatible ratione materiae avec les dispositions de la Convention et doit être rejetée conformément à l'art. 27 par. 2 de la Convention.

Par ces motifs la Commission, à l'unanimité, declare la requête irrecevable.

29

Der nichteheliche Vater kann die gerichtliche Erlaubnis einer Adoption des Kindes nicht aus eigenem Recht mit der Begründung angreifen, dass der Mutter als Muslima die Befugnis zur Adoptionsfreigabe fehle.

Art. 9, 27 § 2 a.F. EMRK
EKMR, Beschluss vom 22. Februar 1995 - No. 24848/94
(Bellis ./. Griechenland) -

EN FAIT

Le requérant est un ressortissant grec. Il est avocat et réside à Athènes. En 1985, T.B., ressortissante libanaise de religion musulmane, eut une brève liaison avec le requérant et se trouva enceinte. Le requérant fut informé de son état pendant le troisième mois de sa grossesse et n'eut plus par la suite aucun contact avec elle. Le 16 octobre 1986, T.B. donna naissance à un garçon. En décembre 1986, à la requête de la mère, l'enfant fut confié à l'établissement social „Mitera". Le 15 juillet 1987, le tribunal de grande instance (Polymeles Protodikeio) d'Athènes prononça l'adoption de l'enfant par un couple marié. En décembre 1987, le requérant apprit l'existence de l'enfant.

Le 5 janvier 1988, le requérant reconnut par devant notaire la paternité de l'enfant. Le 31 mars 1988, le requérant forma une tierce opposition (tritanakopi) contre la décision d'adoption du 15 juillet 1987. Le 27 juin 1988, le tribunal de grande instance d'Athènes rejeta la tierce opposition du requérant. Le 26 septembre 1988, le requérant interjeta appel de ce jugement. Le 17 avril 1989, la cour d'appel (Efeteio) d'Athènes rejeta l'appel du requérant. Le 14 avril 1992, le requérant se pourvut en cassation (anairesi). Le 8 février 1994, la Cour de cassation (Areios Pagos) rejeta le pourvoi du requérant.

GRIEFS

1. Invoquant l'art. 6 par. 1 de la Convention, le requérant se plaint que les juridictions internes rejetèrent à tort ses actions et que le procès devant elles n'a pas été équitable.

2. Le requérant allègue que les juridictions internes ont violé son droit au respect de sa vie familiale, garanti par l'art. 8 de la Convention.

3. Le requérant allègue que les juridictions internes ont violé l'art. 9 de la Convention qui garantit le droit à la liberté de religion. Il soutient à cet égard que la mère de l'enfant n'avait pas, en tant que musulmane, le droit de donner son consentement pour l'adoption en cause.

4. Le requérant soutient enfin que les décisions des juridictions grecques violent l'art. 17 de la Convention européenne du 24 avril 1967 sur l'adoption.

EN DROIT

3. Le requérant allègue que les juridictions internes ont violé l'art. 9 de la Convention qui garantit le droit à la liberté de religion. Il soutient à cet égard que la mère de l'enfant n'avait pas, en tant que musulmane, le droit de donner son consentement pour l'adoption en cause.

L'art. 9 de la Convention est ainsi libellé:

> *„1. Toute personne a droit à la liberté de pensée, de conscience et de religion; ce droit implique la liberté de changer de religion ou de conviction, ainsi que la liberté de manifester sa religion ou sa conviction individuellement ou collectivement, en public ou en privé, par le culte, l'enseignement, les pratiques et l'accomplissement des rites.*
> *2. La liberté de manifester sa religion ou ses convictions ne peut faire l'objet d'autres restrictions que celles qui, prévues par la loi, constituent des mesures nécessaires, dans une société démocratique, à la sécurité publique, à la protection de l'ordre, de la santé ou de la morale publiques, ou à la protection des droits et libertés d'autrui.“*

La Commission rappelle qu'aux termes de l'art. 25 de la Convention, elle „peut être saisie d'une requête ... par toute personne physique ... qui se prétend victime d'une violation ... des droits reconnus dans la présente Convention ...“

La Commission note sur ce point que le principe général en ce qui concerne la notion de victime veut que la personne qui introduit la requête soit „la personne directement concernée par l'acte ou l'omission litigieux“ (voir CourEuDH, arrêt Eckle du 15 juillet 1982, série A n° 51, par. 66). Cette règle générale souffre cependant des exceptions dans certaines circonstances, comme lorsque la victime directe est un parent proche du requérant, dans des cas où le requérant lui-même peut être considéré comme ayant subi un préjudice du fait des actions contestées et lorsque la victime directe est incapable de porter plainte elle-même (voir N° 10871/84, déc. 10.7.86, DR 48 p. 154).

En l'espèce, la Commission croit comprendre que le présent grief, visant notamment à contester la légalité de l'adoption en cause, est présenté par le requérant au nom de son enfant et/ou de la mère de ce dernier. La Commission note toutefois que le requérant n'a ni l'autorité parentale sur son enfant ni la garde de celui-ci, ces droits ayant été attribués à ses parents adoptifs. Ce sont par conséquent ces derniers qui ont le droit d'agir pour le compte de l'enfant dans l'exercice de l'autorité parentale. En outre, la Commission note que le requérant n'est pas marié à la mère de l'enfant et qu'il n'a plus de relation avec elle. Par ailleurs, le requérant n'a pas démontré qu'il est autorisé à représenter l'enfant ou sa mère en ce qui concerne la présente requête, ni que ceux-ci ont exprimé le moindre voeu de voir le requérant s'adresser en leur nom à la Commission (voir mutatis mutandis N° 8045/77, déc. 4.5.79, DR 16 p. 105).

Il s'ensuit que cette partie de la requête est incompatible ratione personae avec la Convention au sens de l'art. 27 par. 2.

4. ...

Par ces motifs, la Commission, à la majorité déclare la requête irrecevable.

30

Abtreibungsgegnern kann untersagt werden, vor einer Klinik, in der legale Schwangerschaftsabbrüche vorgenommen werden, Besucher anzusprechen und Handzettel zu verteilen.

Art. 9 Abs. 1, 10 Abs. 2, 14, 27 § 2 a.F. EMRK,
2 Viertes Zusatzprototokoll
EKMR, Beschluss vom 22. Februar 1995 - No. 22838/93
(v.d. Dungen ./. Niederlande)[1] -

THE FACTS

The applicant is a Dutch national, born in 1943, and resides at Nijmegen, the Netherlands.

On 29 January 1990 in summary proceedings before the President of the Regional Court (Arrondissementsrechtbank) of Middelburg the S. Foundation requested an injunction against the applicant, prohibiting

---

[1] Vgl. auch EKMR, Beschluss vom 18.2.1993 - No. 20747/92 (Bouessel du Bourg ./. Frankreich), HUDOC: Verwendung von Steuermitteln zur Mitfinanzierung erlaubter Schwangerschaftsabbrüche. Die Beschwerde wurde nicht zur Entscheidung angenommen.

him from finding himself within 250 metres of the abortion clinic which is run by the S. Foundation in the town of Groede, the Netherlands.

The S. Foundation alleged that the applicant, several times per month, addressed visitors and employees, as they walked from the car park to the clinic, trying to persuade them not to have an abortion by way of showing them enlarged photographs of foetal remains in combination with images of Christ, by calling abortion „child murder" and the employees „murderers", and by handing out leaflets which also contained the said photographs. According to the S. Foundation this led to visitors arriving at the clinic shocked and upset, sometimes to such an extent that treatment had to be postponed.

The applicant maintained that he did not hinder the visitors or employees, that he left them alone if they did not accept the leaflets handed out to them, but that in any case he had the right to try and stop women from having an abortion, which he deems a crime against humanity, as part of his right to freedom of expression.

The President, holding that the applicant's conduct towards the visitors, who would in any case be in a very vulnerable state of mind already, was impermissible and caused damage to the S. Foundation, as it had to offer extra assistance to its patients, granted the injunction for a period of six months.

The applicant appealed against this decision to the Court of Appeal (Gerechtshof) of The Hague, arguing that the injunction violated his rights to freedom of expression, freedom to manifest his religion and freedom to liberty of movement. On 24 October 1991 the Court of Appeal upheld the decision of the President of the Regional Court.

Following a hearing on 20 December 1992, the Supreme Court (Hoge Raad) rejected the applicant's appeal in cassation on 26 February 1993.

In the Netherlands abortion is legal if carried out in accordance with the conditions laid down in the Termination of Pregnancy Act (Wet Afbreking Zwangerschap) and the Royal Decree on Termination of Pregnancy (Besluit Afbreking Zwangerschap) based on this Act.

According to art. 1401 of the Netherlands Civil Code (Burgerlijk Wetboek) victims of a tort are entitled to damages, but may also ask for a declaratory judgment or an injunction by which the defendant is either forbidden or ordered to do something. Under art. 289 of the Code of Civil Procedure (Wetboek van Burgerlijke Rechtsvordering) the President of the Regional Court, in cases requiring immediate measures, is competent to grant such injunctions in summary proceedings (kort geding).

COMPLAINTS

The applicant submits that the injunction prohibiting him from handing out leaflets and showing photographs, which aim at expressing the applicant's religiously inspired opinions about abortion, in the vicinity of an abortion clinic violates his rights to freedom of thought, conscience, religion and expression. He invokes art. 9 and 10 of the Convention. The applicant further complains of a breach of art. 2 of Protocol No. 4 to the Convention, as he is of the opinion that the restriction upon his right to liberty of movement cannot be justified.

The applicant finally maintains that, as it is normal in the Netherlands to be addressed and handed leaflets by all kinds of people without the Dutch authorities acting against this, he is discriminated against contrary to art. 14 of the Convention.

THE LAW

1. The applicant complains that the injunction against him prevents him from manifesting his beliefs, invoking art. 9 of the Convention which reads, so far as relevant:

> „1. Everyone has the right to freedom of thought, conscience and religion; this right includes freedom to change his religion or belief and freedom, either alone or in community with others and in public or private, to manifest his religion or belief, in worship, teaching, practice and observance. ..."

The Commission recalls that art. 9 of the Convention primarily protects the sphere of personal beliefs and religious creeds, i.e. the area which is sometimes called the forum internum. In addition, it protects acts which are intimately linked to these attitudes, such as acts of worship or devotion which are aspects of the practice of a religion or belief in a generally recognised form (cf. No. 11308/84, Dec. 13.4.86, DR 46 p. 200).

However, in protecting this personal sphere, art. 9 of the Convention does not always guarantee the right to behave in the public sphere in a way which is dictated by such a belief. The Commission has constantly held that the term ‚practice' in art. 9 par. 1 does not cover each act which is motivated or influenced by a religion or belief (cf. No. 11308/84 supra; No. 10358/83, Dec. 15.12.83, DR 37 p. 142).

The Commission notes that the applicant's activities were primarily aimed at persuading women not to have an abortion. The Commission considers that the activities at issue do not constitute the expression of a belief within the meaning of art. 9 par. 1 of the Convention.

It follows that this part of the application is manifestly ill-founded and must be rejected in accordance with art. 27 par. 2 of the Convention.

2. The applicant also complains that the injunction against him constitutes an interference with his right to freedom of expression under art. 10 of the Convention, and that such interference is not justified under art. 10 par. 2 of the Convention. Art. 10 of the Convention, so far as relevant, provides:

„1. Everyone has the right to freedom of expression. This right shall include free-
dom to hold opinions and to receive and impart information and ideas without
interference by public authority.
...
2. The exercise of these freedoms, since it carries with it duties and responsibili-
ties, may be subject to such formalities, conditions, restrictions or penalties as are
prescribed by law and are necessary in a democratic society, ... for the protection
of the ... rights of others ..."

In the present case the applicant was prohibited from addressing people and handing out leaflets in the direct vicinity of the abortion clinic.
The Commission considers that such a measure constitutes an interference with the applicant's right to freedom of expression under art. 10
par. 1.

The Commission must next consider whether this interference was justified under art. 10 par. 2 of the Convention.

In the first place the Commission considers that the interference was
prescribed by law, in particular by art. 289 of the Code of Civil Procedure
and art. 1401 of the Civil Code, authorising the President of the Regional
Court in summary proceedings to grant injunctions by which the defendant is either forbidden or ordered to do something.

The interference was aimed at the protection of the rights of others,
namely of the S. Foundation and of the visitors to and the employees of
the clinic run by the S. Foundation. The Commission finds therefore that
the interference had a legitimate aim under art. 10 par. 2 of the Convention.

The Commission must finally examine whether the interference was
necessary in a democratic society.

The Commission recalls that the word „necessary" in par. 2 of art. 10
implies the existence of a „pressing social need" and that the Contracting
States have a certain margin of appreciation in assessing whether such a
need exists (cf. EuCHR, Lingens judgment of 8 July 1986, Series A
no. 103, par. 39).

The Commission further recalls that this margin of appreciation is,
however, subject to a European supervision embracing both the legislation and the decisions applying it, even those given by an independent
court. In particular, it must be determined whether in the light of the
case as a whole the interference complained of is „proportionate to the legitimate aim pursued" and whether the reasons adduced by the national
authorities to justify it are „relevant and sufficient" (cf. EuCHR, Sunday
Times judgment of 26 November 199ř, Series A no. 217, par. 50).

The Commission notes that in the present case the injunction against
the applicant was granted for a limited duration and a specified, limited
area. The Commission notes in particular that the injunction was not
aimed at depriving the applicant of his rights under art. 10 of the Con-

vention but merely at restricting them in order to protect the rights of others. Taking these factors together, the Commission finds that the interference was proportionate to the legitimate aim pursued in that it can reasonably be considered „necessary" for the protection of the rights of others.

It follows that this part of the application must also be rejected as manifestly ill-founded within the meaning of art. 27 par. 2 of the Convention.

3. The applicant further alleges a violation of his right to liberty of movement within the meaning of art. 2 of Protocol No. 4 to the Convention, which provides, so far as relevant:

> „1. Everyone lawfully within the territory of a State shall ... have the right to liberty of movement ...
> 3. No restrictions shall be placed on the exercise of these rights other than such as are in accordance with the law and necessary in a democratic society ... for the protection of the rights and freedoms of others. ..."

The Commission finds that the interference with the applicant's right to liberty of movement was justified under par. 3 of this provision on the same grounds as stated in respect of the applicant's complaint under art. 10 of the Convention.

The Commission concludes therefore that this part of the application must likewise be rejected as manifestly ill-founded within the meaning of art. 27 par. 2 of the Convention.

4. Finally, the applicant complains of discrimination in respect of his right to freedom of thought, conscience, religion, expression and liberty of movement in that the Dutch authorities do not stop other persons from addressing people in the street and handing out leaflets. He invokes art. 14 of the Convention in conjunction with art. 9 and 10 and art. 2 of Protocol No. 4 to the Convention.

Art. 14 of the Convention reads as follows:

> „The enjoyment of the rights and freedoms set forth in this Convention shall be secured without discrimination on any ground such as sex, race, colour, language, religion, political or other opinion, national or social origin, association with a national minority, property, birth or other status."

The Commission recalls that art. 14 of the Convention has no independent existence, but plays an important role by supplementing the other provisions of the Convention and the Protocols. Art. 14 safeguards individuals, placed in similar situations, from discrimination in the enjoyment of the rights set forth in those other provisions.

The Commission has found above that there has been no interference with the applicant's right to manifest his belief within the meaning of art. 9 of the Convention. It considers that no question of discrimination arises in this respect.

The Commission furthermore notes that the applicant, when complaining of discrimination as regards his freedom of expression and liberty of movement, does not suggest that activities similar to those carried out by him in the vicinity of the abortion clinic, would not be subject to an injunction if carried out by other people. He only refers to the distribution of leaflets in unspecified circumstances by other kinds of people. He has thus failed to show with sufficient clarity in what respect in his opinion the interference complained of amounted to discrimination contrary to art. 14.

The Commission therefore finds no appearance of a violation of art. 14 of the Convention in conjunction with art. 9 or 10 of the Convention or art. 2 of Protocol No. 4. It follows that this part of the application must again be rejected as manifestly ill-founded within the meaning of art. 27 par. 2 of the Convention.

For these reasons, the Commission by a majority declares the application inadmissible.

31

Zur Frage disziplinärer und strafrechtlicher Folgen bei Weigerung eines Soldaten, an einer militärischen Ehrenformation anlässlich einer religiösen Veranstaltung teilzunehmen.

Art. 9, 27 § 2 a.F. EMRK

EKMR, Beschluss vom 4. September 1996 - No. 30479/96

(Hernandez Sanchez ./. Spanien) -

EN FAIT

Le requérant est un ressortissant espagnol né 1965 et résidant à Valence. Il est sergent dans l'armée espagnole et avocat au barreau de Valence.

En novembre 1993, les forces armées espagnoles organisèrent, pour les 19 et 20 du même mois, un défilé militaire à Valence incluant un défilé en l'honneur de la „Vierge des Désemparés" (Virgen de los Desamparados) auquel devait participer le requérant en tant que membre de la compagnie d'honneur de son unité pour le mois en question. Invoquant son droit à la liberté de religion, le requérant exprima le souhait de ne pas participer aux actes strictement religieux. Nonobstant, le requérant y fut contraint. Au cours du défilé en l'honneur de la „Vierge des Désemparés" du 19 novembre 1993, ce dernier demanda l'autorisation de se retirer de sa formation, demande qui lui fut refusée. Le requérant refusa d'obtempérer et abandonna la formation. Le deuxième jour, il ne participa pas aux cérémonies religieuses.

1. Procédures disciplinaires engagées contre le requérant

Par décision du chef de la région militaire de Levante du 2 décembre 1993, le requérant se vit infliger une sanction de trente jours d'arrêt à domicile pour faute légère.

Par ailleurs, une procédure disciplinaire pour faute grave d'atteinte à la dignité militaire et pour insubordination fut engagée à l'encontre du requérant et s'acheva par l'imposition, le 20 janvier 1994, de deux sanctions disciplinaires respectivement de 60 et 90 jours de mise aux arrêts dans un établissement pénitentiaire militaire. Contre cette sanction, le requérant forma un recours devant le tribunal militaire central enregistré au greffe du tribunal territorial de Valence le 16 février 1996, recours qui est pendant.

2. Procédure pénale engagée contre le requérant

En outre et suite à l'attitude du requérant pendant les cérémonies en question, les autorités militaires engagèrent à son encontre une procédure pénale pour délit de désobéissance prévu à l'art. 102 par. 1 du Code pénal militaire. Par ordonnance en date du 7 mars 1994, le juge militaire N° 17 de Valence rendit une ordonnance de non-lieu définitif en prenant en considération le motif de l'exercice légitime du droit à la liberté de religion. Le 15 juillet 1994, le tribunal militaire territorial de Madrid confirma cette décision. Le requérant forma un pourvoi en cassation contre cette décision. Par décision (auto) de la chambre militaire du Tribunal suprême du 21 février 1995, le pourvoi fut déclaré irrecevable au motif que le non-lieu définitif équivalait à une relaxe de sorte que le requérant n'avait plus qualité pour introduire le pourvoi (carecía de legitimación).

Contre cette décision, le requérant présenta un recours d'amparo en invoquant le droit à un procès équitable (art. 24 par. 1 de la Constitution) et demanda l'adoption d'une mesure provisoire afin de protéger son droit à la liberté de religion (art. 16 de la Constitution) dans les procédures engagées à son encontre.

Par décision du 3 juillet 1995, le Tribunal constitutionnel rejeta le recours pour défaut manifeste de fondement. La haute juridiction releva qu'en l'absence de condamnation pénale, le requérant ne pouvait faire valoir aucun préjudice. Quant aux sanctions disciplinaires, le tribunal nota que le recours était hors délai quant à la première sanction et prématuré pour les autres.

3. Plaintes pénales déposées par le requérant

Dans le contexte des mêmes événements, le requérant déposa le 28 janvier 1994, devant le juge d'instruction de Valence, une plainte pénale à l'encontre de certains militaires pour atteinte à la liberté de religion.

Par décision (auto) du 28 février 1994, le juge d'instruction de Valence déclara que les faits dénoncés relevaient de la compétence de la juridiction militaire et déféra l'affaire au juge militaire (juez togado militar) de Valence. Contre cette décision, le requérant interjeta appel.

Ultérieurement, la chambre militaire du Tribunal suprême se saisit de l'affaire.

Par décision du 7 mai 1994, le magistrat instructeur du Tribunal suprême ordonna le classement de l'affaire en estimant que les faits de la cause n'étaient pas constitutifs d'infraction pénale. Sur appel du requérant, le Tribunal suprême, par décision du 14 juillet 1994, confirma la décision entreprise.

GRIEFS

Le requérant se plaint en substance que les sanctions disciplinaires prises à son encontre constituent une atteinte au respect de son droit à la liberté de religion. Il se plaint également que le Tribunal constitutionnel n'a pas pris de mesures provisoires afin de protéger son droit au respect de sa liberté de religion. Il invoque l'art. 9 de la Convention. Le requérant se plaint aussi qu'il a été privé d'une protection judiciaire effective dans la mesure où les tribunaux espagnols ont classé sans suite ses plaintes pénales. Il invoque les art. 6 et 13 de la Convention.

EN DROIT

1. Le requérant se plaint que les sanctions disciplinaires prises à son encontre constituent une atteinte au respect de son droit à la liberté de religion. Il se plaint également que le Tribunal constitutionnel n'a pas pris de mesures provisoires tendant à la protection du respect de son droit à la liberté de religion. Il invoque l'art. 9 de la Convention.

Dans la mesure où le requérant se plaint que les sanctions disciplinaires prononcées à son encontre portent atteinte au respect de son droit à la liberté de religion, la Commission n'est pas appelée à se prononcer sur le point de savoir si les faits dénoncés par le requérant révèlent l'apparence d'une violation de la disposition invoquée de la Convention. En effet, la Commission constate que, s'agissant des sanctions disciplinaires prononcées à son encontre par les autorités militaires, le requérant a présenté un recours devant le tribunal militaire central, enregistré le 16 février 1996, qui se trouve toujours pendant. Or, aux termes de l'art. 26 de la Convention, la Commission ne peut être saisie qu'après épuisement des voies de recours internes. Il s'ensuit que ce grief doit être rejeté comme étant prématuré, en application de l'art. 27 par. 3 de la Convention.

Dans la mesure où le requérant se plaint que le Tribunal constitutionnel n'a pas pris de mesures provisoires afin de protéger son droit à la liberté de religion, la Commission rappelle que le droit de bénéficier de mesures provisoires n'est pas, en tant que tel, garanti par la Convention de sorte que ce grief doit être rejeté pour incompatibilité ratione materiae avec les dispositions de la Convention en application de son art. 27 par. 2.

2. Le requérant se plaint encore d'avoir été privé d'une protection judiciaire effective dans la mesure où les tribunaux espagnols ont classé sans suite ses plaintes pénales et n'ont pas ordonné la suspension des sanctions prononcées à son encontre, au mépris des art. 6 et 13 de la Convention.

(...)

Par ces motifs, la Commission, à l'unanimité, déclare la requête irrecevable.

32

Im Rahmen seiner Aufgabe, die Öffentlichkeit in Angelegenheiten von allgemeinem Interesse zu informieren, ist der Staat auch befugt, in objektiver, aber kritischer Form über religiöse Gemeinschaften und Sekten zu unterrichten, falls hiermit keine agitatorischen oder indoktrinierenden, die Religionsfreiheit gefährdenden Ziele verfolgt werden.

Art. 9, 27 § 2 a.F. EMRK
EKMR, Beschluss vom 27. November 1996 - No. 29745/96
(Universelles Leben e.V. ./. Deutschland) -

THE FACTS

The applicant is a registered association with seat in Würzburg. It perceives itself as a religious community gathering persons in a new, true Christian faith conveyed by a new prophet sent by God.

On 20 December 1993 the Cologne Administrative Court (Verwaltungsgericht) granted the applicant association's request for an interim injunction (einstweilige Anordnung) prohibiting the German Government from including a reference to the applicant association in a publication on „So-called youth sects and psycho-groups in the Federal Republic of Germany" („Sogenannte Jugendsekten und Psycho-Gruppen in der Bundesrepublik Deutschland") until a decision in the main proceedings to be brought by the association in due course.

The Administrative Court considered that, for the purposes of the interim injunction proceedings, the association had to be treated as a religious community. The incriminated publication would, if the applicant association were to be mentioned, affect its right to freedom of religion, taking into account that the intended publication contained general „warnings" about the sects concerned. While the Government were, in the exercise of their general tasks in informing the public, entitled to warn publicly about dangers arising from the activities of religious or philosophical communities, there were no compelling reasons to warn about the applicant association. In particular, the Government were not entitled to endorse and publish criticism raised by an official of the Protestant Church in Bavaria, competent in sect matters. The previous German court decisions, confirming that this official had been entitled to raise the said criticism, had only been taken with due regard to his freedom of religion.

In January 1994 the applicant association filed the main administrative court proceedings with the Cologne Administrative Court.

On 25 August 1995 the North-Rhine Westphalia Administrative Court of Appeal (OVG.NW KirchE 33, 313), upon the Government's appeal (Beschwerde), dismissed the applicant association's request.

The Administrative Court of Appeal, assuming that the applicant association was in a position to act on behalf of the religious community in question, found that, after the summary examination in the context of the interim injunction proceedings, there was nothing to conclude that the intended publication was unlawful, rather there were important reasons to conclude that the Government were entitled to publish the information in question. In this respect, the Administrative Court of Appeal had regard to the case-law of the Federal Constitutional Court (Bundesverfassungsgericht). It found that the documents produced by the applicant association itself, in particular on the replacement of medical treatment by religious belief, showed a degree of dangerousness for the general public justifying a reference to the applicant association in the envisaged publication including a warning about its activities.

On 13 September 1995 the Federal Constitutional Court refused to entertain the applicant association's constitutional complaint (Verfassungsbeschwerde).

The main proceedings are still pending.

COMPLAINT

The applicant association complains under art. 9 about the publication envisaged by the German Government. As regards art. 26, it considers that it cannot be expected to await the outcome of lengthy court proceedings.

THE LAW

The applicant association complains about the German Government's intention to publish a general information on „So-called youth sects and psycho-groups in the Federal Republic of Germany" with a reference to the applicant association and its activities, as well as a warning about its tendencies. It invokes art. 9 of the Convention.

Art. 9 provides as follows:

>„1. *Everyone has the right to freedom of thought, conscience and religion; this right includes freedom to change his religion or belief and freedom, either alone or in community with others and in public or in private, to manifest his religion or belief, in worship, teaching, practice and observance.*
>2. *Freedom to manifest one's religion or beliefs shall be subject only to such limitations as are prescribed by law and are necessary in a democratic society in the interests of public safety, for the protection of public order, health or morals, or for the protection of the rights and freedoms of others."*

The Commission considers that, as the applicant association was admitted as party to the administrative court proceedings regarding the above complaint, it is also to be regarded as competent to bring the present application under art. 25 of the Convention.

The Commission observes that, in accordance with art. 26 of the Convention, it may only deal with the matter after all domestic remedies have been exhausted, according to the generally recognised rules of international law. The Commission notes that the applicant association requested an interim injunction against the envisaged publication and exhausted the remedies in these proceedings, whereas the main proceedings on the merits of its request for a prohibitory injunction are still pending. In the applicant association's view, it cannot be expected to await the outcome of lengthy court proceedings. The question arises whether the applicant association, in referring to the probable length of the administrative court proceedings, has justified a special circumstance absolving it from the obligation to exhaust this remedy. However, the Commission need not resolve this matter as the application is anyway inadmissible for the following reasons.

The Commission recalls that freedom of thought, conscience and religion, which is safeguarded under art. 9 of the Convention, is one of the foundations of a „democratic society" within the meaning of the Convention. It is, in its religious dimension, one of the most vital elements that go to make up the identity of believers and their conception of life (cf. EuCHR, Kokkinakis v. Greece judgment of 25 May 1993, Series A no. 260-A, p. 17, par. 31, KirchE-EU S. 202; Otto-Preminger-Institut v. Austria judgment of 20 September 1994, Series A no. 295-A, p. 17, par. 47, KirchE-EU S. 248).

However, those who choose to exercise the freedom to manifest their religion, irrespective of whether they do so as members of a religious majority or a minority, cannot reasonably expect to be exempt from all criticism. They must tolerate and accept the denial by others of their religious beliefs and even the propagation by others of doctrines hostile to their faith (cf. EuCHR, Otto-Preminger-Institut judgment, loc. cit., p. 18, par. 47; No. 8282/78, Dec. 14.7.80, DR 21, p. 109, KirchE-EU S. 248). A State may even legitimately consider it necessary to take measures aimed at repressing certain forms of conduct, including the imparting of information and ideas, judged incompatible with the respect for the freedom of thought, conscience and religion of others (EuCHR, Kokkinakis judgment, loc. cit., p. 21, par. 48, KirchE-EU S. 202; Otto-Preminger-Institut judgment, loc. cit.).

The Commission further considers that a State, in fulfilling the functions assumed by it in the information of the public on matters of general concern, is entitled to convey, in an objective, but critical manner, information on religious communities and sects, if such information does not pursue aims of agitation or indoctrination endangering the freedom of religion (cf., mutatis mutandis, EuCHR, Kjeldsen, Busk Madsen and Pedersen v. Denmark judgment of 7 December 1976, p. 26, par. 53, KirchE-EU S. 181).

In the present case, the Commission considers that the reference to the applicant association in the intended publication does not have any direct repercussions on the religious freedom of the association or its members. Indeed, their freedom to manifest their religion was not subjected to any discretionary restrictions on the part of the German State (cf. EuCHR, Manoussakis and others v. Greece judgment of 26 September 1996, par. 47, KirchE-EU S. 263). In this context, the Commission, having regard to the findings of the German administrative courts in the interim injunction proceedings, also notes that the impugned publication reflects, so far as the applicant association is concerned, criticism lawfully raised against it. Furthermore, the Administrative Court of Appeal, in a summary examination, held that the documents produced by the applicant association itself justified a public warning as to its activities. While limited to a summary examination in the context of the interim injunction proceedings, the Administrative Court of Appeal explained that there were good reasons to justify the impugned publication on the applicant association.

In the circumstances of the present case, the Commission finds that the measure in question, if implemented by the German Government, does not amount to an interference with the applicant association's rights to freedom of religion under art. 9.

It follows that the application is manifestly ill-founded within the meaning of art. 27-2 of the Convention.

For these reasons, the Commission, unanimously, declares the application inadmissible.

33

Art. 9 EMRK schützt in erster Linie die Sphäre persönlicher Überzeugungen und religiösen Glaubens, darüber hinaus Verhaltensweisen, die hiermit eng verbunden sind wie Gottesdienst oder Andacht als praktische, allgemein anerkannte Erscheinungsformen von Religion. Zwar genießen auch Angehörige des öffentlichen Dienstes den Schutz der Europäischen Menschenrechtskonvention, jedoch ist ein im Transportbereich tätiger Zivilangestellter der Staatsbahn verpflichtet, den Dienstplan auch dann einzuhalten, wenn seine Religionsgemeinschaft (hier: Sieben-Tags-Adventisten) Feiertagsruhe gebietet.

Art. 9, 14 EMRK
EKMR, Beschluss vom 3. Dezember 1996 - No. 24949/94
(Konttinen ./. Finnland)[1] -

THE FACTS

The applicant is a Finnish citizen, born in 1963. He is unemployed and resides in Hyvinkää.

A. Particular circumstances of the case

In 1986 the applicant joined the State Railways (Valtionrautatiet, Statsjärnvägarna), where he apparently held various posts.

Most recently, he worked in a goods transportation terminal, where he would feed information concerning completed transports into a computer network. As this post did not entail the exercise of public authority, his working hours were governed by the 1946 Act on Working Hours (työaikalaki, arbetstidslag 604/46) and not by *lex specialis* applicable to civil servants. He performed shift work, his evening shift ending at 18.39 hrs. On Saturdays and Sundays no one worked in the terminal.

In the summer of 1991 the applicant joined The Seventh-day Adventist Church in Finland (Suomen Adventtikirkko, Finlands Adventkyrka). An adventist must refrain from working on the Sabbath (Saturday) which starts at sunset on Friday. By ministerial decision of 7 February 1994 (no. 115/94) the Government approved an amendment to the confession of faith and the form of religious worship within this church, considering that these were not contrary to law or good practices.

When the sun set before his Friday shift had ended on 6 March 1992 the applicant, having informed his employer, absented himself from work

---

[1] DR 87, 68.

at 18.00 hrs. At his employer's request the Board of Civil Servants (virkamieslautakunta, tjänstemannanämnden) within the State Railways then issued him with a disciplinary punishment in the form of a caution (varoitus, varning) on the grounds that he had not observed the working hours. The punishment was upheld by the Supreme Administrative Court (korkein hallinto-oikeus, högsta förvaltnings-domstolen) on 29 December 1992.

On 2 and 16 October and 20 November 1992 as well as on 8 January and 26 February 1993 the applicant, having informed his employer, again absented himself from his work place before his Friday evening shift had ended. He left work at 17.49 hrs, 17.08 hrs, 15.39 hrs, 15.36 hrs and 17.39 hrs, respectively. In discussions with superiors he maintained that he would continue to keep the Sabbath in accordance with his religious convictions.

On 23 March 1993 the Head of the relevant district of the State Railways dismissed the applicant as he had, on six occasions in 1992-93, absented himself from his work place before the end of his Friday evening shift, thereby neglecting the rules regulating his working hours. The duty of all staff to respect their working hours was a precondition for effective working. The employer's efforts to transfer him to another post had failed, as no vacancy had been found. He had repeatedly been warned by superiors that further absence from work would inevitably lead to his dismissal. He had nevertheless continued to show a careless and indifferent attitude towards the applicable rules and his superiors' orders. The applicant and the principal employees' representative were heard prior to the dismissal. Following the applicant's request for a re-examination the Board of Civil Servants, on 28 April 1993, upheld his dismissal, noting, inter alia, that he had been obliged to work an evening shift every fifth Friday. On 6 March, 2 and 16 October and 20 November 1992 as well as on 8 January and 26 February 1993 he had absented himself from his work place without permission and in spite of the caution issued in May 1992 and his superiors' orders and warnings. He had stated that he would persist in his behaviour. The Board concluded that he had continuously and fundamentally breached his official duties. Reference was made to sec. 20 and 46 of the 1986 Act on Civil Servants of the State (valtion virkamieslaki, statstjänstemannalag 755/86) and the State Railways' staff regulations.

One out of the eight members of the Board dissented, noting, inter alia, that the applicant's absence during his Friday evening shift had only had minor effects, no damage having been caused either to his employer or any third party. He had undertaken to compensate the relevant number of working hours and to this end he had requested that his shifts be modified. As he was experienced and had been trained in various tasks, he should have been issued with a further caution and transferred to another post. A dismissal was not proportionate to the behaviour shown by him on his particular post and would result in absence from work on religious grounds being punished more severely than, for instance, alcohol problems.

The applicant appealed to the Supreme Administrative Court, arguing that his right to freedom of religion had been violated. His absence had resulted from an irreconcilable conflict between his religious convictions and work duties and not from negligence. The question concerned a maximum of some five Fridays between October and March, when the sun would set at the most three and a half hours before the end of his shift. In return for a permission to finish his shift at sunset on those days he would have been prepared to work a longer shift in the summertime, when the sun would set late. The State Railways had not argued that such an arrangement would have been unreasonably difficult to implement. Instead of showing indifference towards his duties he had honestly informed his employer that he felt obliged to give priority to his religious convictions, though possibly at the price of being dismissed. Although the State Railways could also order its staff to work on Sundays, it had regulated the working hours at the applicant's work place so that no Sunday work was necessary.

On 17 February 1994 the Supreme Administrative Court upheld the Board's decision, finding no reason for amending it.

B. Relevant domestic law

Finland recognises two State Churches, the Evangelical-Lutheran Church and the Orthodox Church of Finland. Approximately 86 per cent of the population belong to the Evangelical-Lutheran Church and about 1 per cent belongs to the Orthodox Church of Finland.

Under the 1919 Constitution Act (Suomen Hallitusmuoto, Regeringsform för Finland 94/19), as in force at the relevant time, a Finnish citizen was entitled to manifest his or her religion both in private and in public, provided this did not violate the law or good practices (sec. 8). The rights and obligations of a Finnish citizen did not depend on whether or not he or she belonged to a certain religious community, if any (sec. 9). As of 1 August 1995 the Constitution Act guarantees the freedom of religion to everyone. This freedom includes the right to confess one's faith, to worship, to manifest one's belief as well as to belong or not to belong to a religious community (sec. 9 of amending Act no. 969/95).

In addition, the 1922 Act on Religious Freedom (uskonnonvapauslaki, religionsfrihetslag 267/22) guarantees the freedom to manifest a religion, again provided this does not violate the law or good practices (sec. 1). Finally, according to a specific Act of 1921 (no. 173/21), a Finnish citizen is qualified for a post as a civil servant regardless of whether or not he or she belongs to a certain religious community, if any.

Under sec. 1 of the 1989 Act on the State Railways (laki Valtionrau-
tateistä, lag om Statsjärnvägarna 747/89), as in force at the relevant
time, the State Railways was a State enterprise subordinated to the Ministry of Transport and Communications (liikenneministeriö, trafikminis-
teriet). The 1989 Act has later been replaced.

According to the 1986 Act on Civil Servants of the State, as in force at
the relevant time, a civil servant was to perform his or her duties properly without delay and behave in accordance with the requirements of
the relevant office (sec. 20). A written warning or a caution could be issued if the civil servant either deliberately or by negligence acted contrary to his or her duties. A third disciplinary punishment was removal
from office. All three disciplinary punishments were to be imposed by decision of a Board of Civil Servants (sec. 57 and 58). One or several boards
existed within a public authority (sec. 75). A superior could also issue
remarks (sec. 63).

A civil servant could also be dismissed if, for instance, he or she had
continuously or significantly breached the duties relating to the relevant
office or continuously had failed to perform those duties (sec. 46, sub-
sec. 2 [3]). On the other hand, for instance his or her religious views did
not constitute such grounds for dismissal (subsec. 3[4]).

On 1 December 1994 the 1986 Act was largely replaced by a 1994 Act
with the same title (no. 750/94).

The Act on Working Hours stipulates that every employee shall be entitled to a weekly rest lasting at least 30 hours. This rest shall be provided on Sunday or, when this is not possible, during another period.
Certain exceptions are possible but are not relevant here (sec. 15).

In a case of the present kind a final appeal lies with the Supreme Administrative Court. No leave to appeal is required.

COMPLAINTS

1. The applicant complains under art. 9 of the Convention that his
right to freedom of religion has been violated on account of his dismissal
by the State Railways. This right allegedly includes the right to have
one's holy day respected as long as this is not unreasonable from the employer's point of view and does not violate the rights of others. Within
reasonable limits art. 9 also implies a right for a civil servant to refuse to
perform duties contrary to his or her religious belief as long as this does
not significantly impinge on the performance of his or her duties as a
whole.

More particularly, the conflict between his duty to respect, on the one
hand, his religious convictions and, on the other hand, his working hours
only arose about five times a year due to the early sunset in the winter-
time. His requests to have his occasional Friday evening shift in the win-
tertime exchanged for the Friday morning shift and to have his Friday

morning shift in the summertime exchanged for the Friday evening shift were not unreasonable and would not have afforded him any advantage in comparison with his colleagues. The State Railways never argued that such working hours would have been impossible to implement or that they would have been unreasonable from the point of view of his employer or colleagues.

2. The applicant furthermore complains that his dismissal discriminated against him, since under the legislation on working hours the weekly holiday falls on Sunday, i.e. the holy day for the main religious communities in Finland. As a result the State Railways respected the right of his colleagues to keep the Sabbath on Sunday but failed to respect his right to keep it on Saturday. He invokes art. 14 of the Convention in conjunction with art. 9.

3. Finally, the applicant complains that he was denied a fair hearing, as the Supreme Administrative Court, the only independent tribunal to decide on his case, gave no reasons for its decision but instead de facto refused him leave to appeal. He invokes art. 6 of the Convention and underlines that his working hours were governed by legislation applicable to private employment contracts. The proceedings therefore involved a determination of a civil right of his.

PROCEEDINGS BEFORTE THE COURT

...

THE LAW

1. The applicant complains that his right to freedom of religion was violated on account of his dismissal. He invokes art. 9 of the Convention which reads, as far as relevant, as follows:

> „1. Everyone has the right to freedom of ... religion; this right includes freedom to change his religion or belief and freedom, either alone or in community with others and in public or in private, to manifest his religion or belief, in worship, teaching, practice and observance.
> 2. Freedom to manifest one's religion or belief shall be subject only to such limitations as are prescribed by law and are necessary in a democratic society in the interests of public safety, for the protection of public order, health or morals, or for the protection of the rights and freedoms of others."

The Government accept that the State Railways' dismissal of the applicant is imputable to the respondent State under the Convention. They also accept that such a dismissal could in certain circumstances raise an issue under art. 9. In the present case, however, this provision has not been violated. The State Railways was entitled to rely on its employment contract which the applicant had signed without reservations in 1986.

Having joined The Seventh-day Adventist Church in 1991, he was free to relinquish his work if he considered that his professional duties were not reconcilable with his religious convictions. He could also have taken those Fridays off when the beginning of the Sabbath obliged him to leave work before his evening shift had ended.

The Government consider, moreover, that when dismissing the applicant the State Railways did not arbitrarily disregard his freedom of religion. Its efforts to transfer him to another post had failed and changing the shift schedule in accordance with his proposal would have led to inconveniences for the employer and the applicant's colleagues. In these circumstances his dismissal did not interfere with his freedom of religion.

Should the Commission find that the applicant's dismissal limited his freedom to manifest his religion, the Government submit that this limitation was justified under art. 9 par. 2. The dismissal was in accordance with law and pursued legitimate aims, namely the protection both of public order and the rights and freedoms of others. Finally, the dismissal was proportionate to the aims pursued and thus necessary in a democratic society. In most countries only the religious holidays of the majority are celebrated as public holidays. In Finland members of different religious denominations are equal before the law governing working hours. Public officials whose presence at work is required on Sundays cannot refuse to perform their duties. Accommodating the rules of different religious denominations in order to respect an employer's wishes in this field would be unreasonable as far as the employer and usually also the other employees are concerned.

The applicant recalls that under art. 9 par. 1 the right to freedom of religion must be secured without qualification. Should, however, the Commission consider art. 9 par. 2 applicable, the applicant submits that the limitation of his freedom to manifest his religion was not „prescribed by law". This notion is independent of whether the domestic procedure as such was governed by Finnish law. In this context it is of relevance that he did not receive a fair trial within the meaning of art. 6 par. 1 of the Convention.

The applicant furthermore contends that his dismissal did not serve any of the legitimate aims referred to by the Government. His manifestation of his religious belief in no way endangered public order. Nor would the proposed minor adjustments of his work schedule have infringed on the rights and freedoms of others. Finally, the State Railways never argued, though the Government does so before the Commission, that the proposed adjustments would have caused inconveniences to his employer or colleagues.

The applicant finally submits that his dismissal was disproportionate to any assumed legitimate aim. Due to the strong position of the Evangelical-Lutheran State Church in Finland toleration of other religious denominations is fairly low, as shown by the State Railways' inflexibility in his case. He was performing ordinary clerical duties of no urgent or otherwise pressing character requiring his physical presence at a specific hour. The proposed adjustments of his work schedule concerned a maximum of three and a half hours on five Friday afternoons per year. His employer was adamantly against any of the arrangements proposed by him, including, for instance, compensating the lost working hours by relinquishing an equivalent part of his vacation or days off. The matter having eventually evolved into an exertion of authority, he was dismissed for an absence lasting 39 minutes. A limitation of the freedom to manifest one's religion must necessarily fit within a narrow margin of appreciation which was overstepped in the applicant's particular case.

The Commission recalls that art. 9 primarily protects the sphere of personal convictions and religious beliefs. In addition, it protects acts which are intimately linked to these attitudes, such as acts of worship or devotion which are aspects of the practice of a religion or belief in a generally recognised form (see, e.g., Kalaç v. Turkey, Comm. Report 27.2.96, KirchE-EU S. 312).

While it is true that a right of recruitment to the public service was deliberately omitted from the Convention, it does not follow that a person designated as a public servant is debarred from challenging his dismissal if it infringes one of the rights guaranteed by the Convention. Public servants do not fall outside the scope of the Convention any more than do other citizens. In art. 1 and 14 the Convention stipulates that „everyone within [the] jurisdiction" of the Contracting States must enjoy the rights and freedoms in sec. I „without discrimination on any ground" (see EuCHR, Vogt v. Germany judgment of 26 September 1995, Series A no. 323, pp. 22-23, par. 43 with further references). The Commission therefore considers it conceivable that a dismissal of a civil servant for disobedience could, in certain circumstances, raise an issue under art. 9 (cf. No. 8160/78, Dec. 12.3.81, DR 22 pp. 27-38 at p. 33; No. 11045/ 84, Dec. 8.3.85, DR 42 pp. 247-258 at pp. 257-258).

In the present case the Commission finds that the applicant, as a civil servant of the State Railways, had a duty to accept certain obligations towards his employer, including the obligation to observe the rules governing his working hours. He was cautioned by his employer, not having relinquished his post after the irreconcilable conflict arose between his religious convictions and his working hours.

In these particular circumstances the Commission finds that the applicant was not dismissed because of his religious convictions but for having refused to respect his working hours. This refusal, even if motivated by his religious convictions, cannot as such be considered protected by art. 9 par. 1. Nor has the applicant shown that he was pressured to change his religious views or prevented from manifesting his religion or belief.

The Commission would add that, having found his working hours to conflict with his religious convictions, the applicant was free to relinquish his post. The Commission regards this as the ultimate guarantee of his right to freedom of religion. In sum, there is no indication that the applicant's dismissal interfered with the exercise of his rights under art. 9 par. 1 (cf. the above-mentioned No. 8160/78, loc. cit.)

It follows that this complaint is manifestly ill-founded within the meaning of art. 27 par. 2 of the Convention.

2. The applicant furthermore complains that he has been discriminated against, since the State Railways respected the right of his colleagues to keep the Sabbath on Sunday but failed to respect his right to keep it on Saturday. He invokes art. 14 of the Convention in conjunction with art. 9. Art. 14 reads, as far as relevant, as follows:

> „The enjoyment of the rights and freedoms set forth in this Convention shall be secured without discrimination on any ground such as ... religion ... or other status."

The Commission recalls that art. 14 of the Convention complements the other substantive provisions of the Convention and the Protocols. It may be applied in an autonomous manner as a breach of art. 14 does not presuppose a breach of those other provisions. On the other hand, it has no independent existence, since it is effective solely in relation to the enjoyment of the rights and freedoms safeguarded by the other substantive provisions (see, e.g., EuCHR, Van der Mussele v. Belgium judgment of 23 November 1983, Series A no. 70, p. 22, par. 43).

Art. 14) does not forbid every difference in treatment in the exercise of the rights and freedoms recognised by the Convention and its Protocols. It safeguards persons, who are placed in analogous situations, against discriminatory differences of treatment. For the purposes of art. 14 a difference of treatment is discriminatory if it has no objective and reasonable justification. The Contracting States enjoy a certain margin of appreciation in assessing whether and to what extent differences in otherwise similar situations justify a different treatment in law (see, e.g., EuCHR, Lithgow v. the United Kingdom judgment of 8 July 1986, Series A no. 102, pp. 66-67, par. 177).

The Commission considers that the present complaint falls to be examined in conjunction with the above-cited art. 9. It is true that the Finnish legislation on working hours provides that the weekly day of rest is usually Sunday. However, this legislation does not contain provisions which would guarantee to members of a certain religious community any absolute right to have a particular day regarded as their holy day. Assuming that the applicant could be considered to be in a situation comparable to that of members of other religious communities, the Commission therefore finds that he has not been treated differently in comparison with such members. Consequently, this complaint does not disclose any appearance of a violation of art. 14 of the Convention taken in conjunction with art. 9.

It follows that this complaint is also manifestly ill-founded within the meaning of art. 27 par. 2 of the Convention.

3. Finally, the applicant complains that his right to a fair hearing was violated on the basis of the inadequate reasons in the decision of the Supreme Administrative Court, the only independent tribunal to examine his case.

(...)

For these reasons, the Commission, by a majority, declares the application inadmissible.

34

Angehörige von Religionsgemeinschaften müssen öffentliche Ablehnung und Angriffe von Gegnern hinnehmen. Die Gewährleistung ungestörter Religionsausübung schließt nicht notwendig und unter allen Umständen das Recht ein, im Klagewege gegen Autoren oder Herausgeber vorzugehen, die die religiösen Empfindungen Einzelner auch als Gruppe beleidigt haben. Es liegt jedoch in der Verantwortlichkeit des Staates, je nach Art und Weise der Auseinandersetzung für eine friedliche Wahrnehmung der Religionsfreiheit Sorge zu tragen. So kann der Respekt vor den religiösen Gefühlen der Gläubigen durch provozierende Darstellungen von Andachtsgegenständen *(hier:* Bildnis der *Muttergottes von Czenstochau* mit Gasmaske) verletzt sein.

Zur Frage, ob im Einzelfall eine rechtliche Handhabe gegen die Verletzung religiöser Empfindungen zu Gebote stand.

Art. 9 § 1 EMRK
EKMR, Beschluss vom 18. April 1997 - No. 33490/96, 34055/96
(Dubowska u.a. ./. Polen) -

THE FACTS

The applicants are Polish citizens. The first applicant, born 1947 is a psychologist and resides in Warsaw, Poland. The second applicant, born in 1921is a gardener and resides in Siedlce, Poland.

On 16 August 1994 the national weekly „Wprost" (dated 21 August 1994) was disseminated in Poland. On its cover, the magazine published an image of the Czenstochowa Madonna and Child. The faces of both figures were replaced by gas-masks. On their left side there was a headline: „Pilgrimage '94: Wandering Fortress". The images were placed on a cloud and over a view of an unspecified city, and another headline: „Death in the air - norms exceeded by 120%".

On 21 August 1994 the Prior of the Czenstochowa Monastery issued an official protest against the publication. On 22 August 1994 the first applicant requested the Warsaw District Prosecutor (Prokurator Rejonowy) to institute criminal proceedings against the editor of the newspaper on suspicion of committing the offence of publicly insulting religious feelings. In the meantime, on an unspecified date, the applicant's request was transferred to the Poznan-Grunwald District Prosecutor (Prokurator Rejonowy) and joined with more than five hundred similar requests.

On 23 August 1994 the second applicant wrote a letter to the editor of „Wprost". He demanded a public apology for the profanation of the image of the Czenstochowa Madonna and Child. He stressed that the Madonna of Czenstochowa has been an object of deep religious veneration in Poland for centuries. He also asserted that the publication in question was vulgar and seriously offensive in view of the fact that the Madonna of Czenstochowa was a symbol of Poland and its independence.

On 21 September 1994 the second applicant requested the Siedlce District Prosecutor to institute criminal proceedings against the editor of the weekly „Wprost" on suspicion of committing the offence of publicly insulting religious feelings. He submitted that he had not received any apology or reply to his letter of 23 August 1994 and that he had no other means of obtaining satisfaction for an affront to objects of his worship.

In the meantime, on an unspecified date, his request was transferred to the Poznan-Grunwald District Prosecutor and joined with, inter alia, the first applicant's request.

On 11 October 1994 the Poznan-Grunwald District Prosecutor, having interviewed the editor-in-chief of the newspaper, is continued the investigations on the ground that the publication of the images had not been aimed at insulting or debasing an unquestionable object of worship for Polish Catholics, i.e. the so-called „Black Madonna of Czenstochowa" but at informing the public about the pollution of the natural environment in Silesia. The decision stated that the existence of an affront to the religious feelings of the persons concerned was obvious, as such an affront fell within the domain of purely subjective perception. It was also stated that the moral and aesthetic aspects of the publication in question fell outside the scope of the criminal law.

On 20 November 1994 the first applicant appealed against the above decision, arguing that she had never been interviewed by the prosecutor and that the publication of the images had in fact been related to an article criticising the phenomenon of pilgrimage in Poland. She referred, in particular, to the fact that the publication in question took place exactly between two important Catholic church holidays: 15 August (the Feast of the Assumption) and 26 August (the Feast of the Czenstochowa Virgin Mary), and that at the same time thousands of people had gone to Czenstochowa on pilgrimage. She insisted that the provocative and malicious character of the publication was intensified by the particular time of the magazine's dissemination.

On 23 November 1994 the second applicant appealed against the decision of the Poznan-Grunwald District Prosecutor of 27 October 1994. He submitted, inter alia, that the publication in question had touched a very delicate and vulnerable matter and that it had amounted to a clear lack of respect for religious feelings.

On 16 January 1995 the Poznan Provincial Prosecutor (Prokurator Wojewódzki) quashed the decision of 11 October 1994 and ordered further investigations.

On 15 September 1995 a media and sociology expert prepared a report assessing the publication of the images in question in the context of the criminal responsibility and intentions of the editor. The expert stated that sacred works of art were used for the purposes of serious journalism. He expressed the opinion that the portrayal of the Madonna had been related to press material concerning the pollution of the environment in Poland.

On 27 October 1995 the Poznan-Grunwald District Prosecutor again discontinued the investigations in view of the fact that the publication complained of had not aimed deliberately at insulting religious feelings and therefore no offence had been committed.

On 23 November 1995 the second applicant appealed against the decision discontinuing the investigations.

On 27 November 1995 the first applicant appealed against the same decision. She again referred to the fact that the Catholic community in Poland had reacted very strongly against the publishing of its images of worship in the manner complained of. She submitted that the representatives of the other religions (i.e. Protestants, Muslims, Jews and the members of the Orthodox Church) had joined the Polish Roman Catholic Church in condemnation of the publication of a deformed image of the Madonna of Czenstochowa. She also submitted that, according to statements given by witnesses in the course of the investigations, the reaction of Polish Roman Catholics to the publication was the following: „shock", „the humiliation of myself and my religious feelings", „insult", „debasement and pain", „profanation", „lack of respect for human beings" and that a publication constituted a „sneer at faith and religion".

On 12 February 1996 the Poznan Provincial Prosecutor upheld the decision discontinuing the investigations and fully upheld the reasons which had been given therefore.

On 26 February 1996 this decision was sent to the applicants.

On 21 March 1996 the second applicant requested the Prosecutor General (Prokurator Generalny) to quash the final decision discontinuing the investigations. He submitted, inter alia, that even such an important topic of public debate as the pollution of the environment might not have justified the use of the sacred icon of Polish Roman Catholics, as the publisher had at his disposal various means of expression.

On 14 April 1996 the first applicant requested the Prosecutor General to quash the final decision of 12 February 1996. She invoked, inter alia, art. 9 and 10 of the Convention and argued that her religious freedom was being violated.

In May 1996, on an unspecified date, the applicants' requests were transferred to the Poznan Provincial Prosecutor and refused on 5 May 1996 with respect to the first applicant and on 30 May 1996 with respect to the second.

RELEVANT DOMESTIC LAW

Art. 82 par. 1 of the Polish Constitution provides that „The Republic of Poland guarantees its citizens freedom of conscience and religion." Art. 83 of the Constitution provides that „The Republic of Poland guarantees its citizens freedom of speech and printed word, assembly and manifestation."

The Press Act of 28 January 1984 provides that in case of a deliberate violation of the so-called „personal rights", the person concerned may claim compensation. In general, persons concerned have a claim for publication of a rectification and a „right to reply" to a contested publication. Solely in the case of a criminal conviction for an offence committed in connection with a given publication, the court may order the forfeiture of the press material in question. Sec. 198 of the Polish Criminal Code provides:

„Everyone who insults the religious feelings of other persons, in particular by publicly insulting an object of religious worship or a place designed for public religious celebration shall be punished by a maximum of two years' imprisonment ... or a fine."

COMPLAINTS

1. The applicants complain under art. 9 of the Convention that the Polish authorities did not provide them with sufficient protection against a violation of their right to freedom of religion, as they failed to protect them against the distorted publication of sacred images of their worship and that the criminal proceedings against the persons who had insulted the objects of their worship were discontinued.

2. The first applicant also complains under art. 10 of the Convention that the provocative publication of images of her worship was contrary to this provision and that the Polish authorities failed to interfere with the publication in question, in particular in order to protect the rights of others (i.e. the right to freedom of religion).

3. Under art. 6 of the Convention the applicants complain that they had no access to court to pursue their claim against the person responsible for the publication in question as a result of the fact that criminal proceedings against him were discontinued.

4. They complain, lastly, under art. 14 of the Convention that they were discriminated against on the ground of their Catholic religion.

THE LAW

1. The Commission finds it necessary to join the applications under Rule 35 of its Rules of Procedure.

2. The applicants complain under art. 9 of the Convention that the Polish authorities did not provide them with sufficient protection against a violation of their right to freedom of religion, as they failed to protect them against the distorted publication of sacred images of their worship and as the criminal proceedings against the persons who had insulted the objects of their worship were discontinued.

Art. 9 of the Convention provides:

> „1. Everyone has the right to freedom of thought, conscience and religion; this right includes freedom to change his religion or belief and freedom, either alone or in community with others and in public or in private, to manifest his religion or belief, in worship, teaching, practice and observance.
>
> 2. Freedom to manifest one's religion or beliefs shall be subject only to such limitations as are prescribed by law and are necessary in a democratic society in the interests of public safety, for the protection of public order, health or morals, or for the protection of the rights and freedoms of others."

The Commission recalls that the members of a religious community must tolerate and accept the denial by others of their religious beliefs and even the propagation by others of doctrines hostile to their faith. Also, the right to freedom from interference with the rights guaranteed in art. 9 par. 1 of the Convention does not necessarily and in all circumstances imply a right to bring any specific form of proceedings against those who, by authorship or publication, offend the sensitivities of an individual or of a group of individuals (see mutatis mutandis No. 17439/90, Dec. 5.3.91,unpublished).

However, the manner in which religious beliefs and doctrines are opposed or denied is a matter which may engage the responsibility of the State to ensure the peaceful enjoyment of the right guaranteed under art. 9 of the Convention to the holders of those beliefs and doctrines. Thus, the respect for the religious feelings of believers as guaranteed in art. 9 may in some cases be violated by provocative portrayals of objects of religious veneration (see EuCHR, Otto-Preminger-Institut v. Austria judgment of 20 September 1994, Series A no. 295-A, p. 18, par. 47, KirchE-EU, S. 248).

As a consequence, there may be certain positive obligations on the part of a State inherent in an effective respect for rights guaranteed under art. 9 of the Convention, which may involve the adoption of measures designed to secure respect for freedom of religion even in the sphere of the relations of individuals between themselves (see, mutatis mutandis, EuCHR, X and Y v. the Netherlands judgment of 26 March 1985, Series A no. 91, p. 11, par. 23). Such measures may, in certain circumstances, constitute a legal means of ensuring that an individual will not be disturbed in his worship by the activities of others.

However, the Commission notes that in the present case the applicants had at their disposal a legal remedy in case of an insult to their religious feelings. The Polish authorities, upon the applicants' request, instituted criminal investigations against the editor of the weekly „Wprost" which had published the distorted image of their object of worship. The investigations were instituted on suspicion of committing the offence of publicly insulting religious feelings, provided by sec. 198 of the Polish Criminal Code. In the course of the proceedings in question, which lasted almost eighteen months, the authorities had a range of evidence admitted, including the report of a media and sociology expert. In their decisions discontinuing the investigations they carefully assessed all circumstances of the case and the importance of the issue at stake.

Thus, the present case is not one in which the applicants were inhibited from exercising their freedom to hold and express their belief (see Otto-Preminger-Institut v. Austria judgment, ibidem).

Moreover, the fact that the authorities eventually found that no offence had been committed does not in itself amount to a failure to protect the applicants' rights guaranteed under art. 9 of the Convention.

It follows that this part of the application is inadmissible as being manifestly ill-founded within the meaning of art. 27 par. 2 of the Convention.

3. The first applicant also complains under art. 10 of the Convention that the provocative publication of images of her worship was contrary to this provision and that the Polish authorities failed to interfere with the publication in question, in particular in order to protect the rights of others. Under art. 14 of the Convention both applicants complain that they were discriminated against on the ground of their Catholic religion. However, the Commission finds that no separate issue arises under these provisions of the Convention.

It follows that this part of the application is also manifestly ill-founded within the meaning of art. 27 par. 2 of the Convention.

4. Under art. 6 of the Convention the applicants also complain that they had no access to court to pursue their claim against the person responsible for the publication in question as a result of the fact that the criminal proceedings against him were discontinued.

However, the Commission recalls that the right of access to a court afforded by art. 6 par. 1 of the Convention does not guarantee a right to have criminal proceedings instituted against a third person (No. 9777/82, Dec. 14.7.83, DR 34 p. 158).

It follows that the remainder of the application is inadmissible as being incompatible ratione materiae with the provisions of the Convention within the meaning of art. 27 par. 2 of the Convention.

For these reasons, the Commission, by a majority, decides to join the applications; declares the applications inadmissible.

35

Zur Frage der Rechtsstellung des Beschwerdeführers als Betroffener (victim of a violation) bei schulbehördlich verbreitete Warnung vor Scientology.

Art. 9, 13, 27 § 2 a.F. EMRK, 2 Erstes Zusatzprotokoll
EKMR, Beschluss vom 4. März 1998 - No. 36283/97
(Keller ./.Deutschland)[1] -

THE FACTS

The applicants are German citizens. The first and the second applicants, born in 1937 and 1950 respectively, are a married couple. The third and fourth applicants, born in 1981 and 1980, are their daughters. The applicants are members of Scientology, a world-wide organisation with its international headquarters in Los Angeles (United States of America), and live in Sch. (Germany).

Members of the Federal Parliament (Bundestag) in Bonn and of the Parliaments of the Länder discussed repeatedly the question of Scientology. They warned that Scientology was particularly dangerous and considered that it did not constitute a church but instead was much more like a commercial enterprise.

The Federal Government and the Governments of the Länder adopted joint strategies with a view to reducing the influence of Scientology organisations. In various Länder measures were taken to reduce the influence of Scientology and to warn of its dangers.

The Government of the Land of Bavaria ordered schools to inform pupils of all ages and their parents about the goals, strategies and operating procedures of Scientology.

In April 1996, the Bavarian Ministry of Education (Bayerisches Staatsministerium für Kultus, Wissenschaft und Kunst) published in the issue

---

[1] EuGRZ 1998, 321.

of the magazine Schulreport (school report) of April 1996 (issue 1/96) on pages 8 to 10 an article entitled „All clear? Information about Scientology" („Alles Clear? Informationen über Scientology"). 90,000 copies of this report were printed and, apart from 2,200 copies, distributed to Bavarian schools. The article about Scientology was also used for teaching purposes in Bavarian schools.

On 23 May and 28 June 1996 the applicants applied to the Munich Administrative Court (Bayerisches Verwaltungsgericht München) for an interim injunction (einstweilige Anordnung) restraining the Bavarian Government (Freistaat Bayern) from disseminating the issue of the magazine Schulreport of April 1996 and, to the extent it had already been disseminated, from any longer using it for teaching purposes or making it accessible to others. Subsidiarily they requested an order restraining the dissemination of this article with the inclusion of various passages quoted by them, including the following:

> „With a crude mixture of science fiction, psychoanalysis and manipulative prac-
> tices of totalitarian systems members of Scientology are made dependent and
> their financial and working capacities are systematically exploited. Scientology
> uses techniques of mental control based on deception and manipulation.
> Recognising a Scientology member:
> In some cases the behaviour of a person changes as a result of the mind control
> exercised over a period of several months, more typically however within a few
> days or weeks. Interestingly, the members develop towards a standard personal-
> ity (standardisation of personality attributes of the sect members). From the
> physical point of view the following signs are identified as the result of member-
> ship of the sect: a change in weight (corpulence, anorexia), loss of strength, al-
> tered beard-growth, exhaustion syndrome and psychosomatic illness. Psychologi-
> cal effects are manifested, inter alia, in a narrowing and weakening of the process
> of thinking (differentiation of language and metaphors or irony, replaced by the
> use of sect-internal cliches), in the changing of the emotional state, in strong
> changes of emotions and in non-characteristic anti-social behaviour. The occur-
> rence of hallucinations can also be observed, because daily excessive auditing can
> make a person psychologically and physically addicted to this psycho-technique.
> This often has damaging side- effects, such as lowering of cognitive abilities, for
> example weak concentration and decision-making. A radical change of personal-
> ity is the most revealing sign that a totalitarian group is at work. ..."

The applicants also refer to comic-strip pictures drawn by schoolchildren and reproduced on page 9 with the title „Scientology" and on page 10 with the title „Scientology No!"

In their submissions to the Munich Administrative Court the applicants argued in particular that the article about Scientology violated the constitutional requirement of State neutrality in matters of religion and that the article was not factual and offensive.

On 29 July 1996, the Munich Administrative Court rejected the applicants' request on the ground that the applicants were not personally affected by the contested passages and pictures which did not concern all the members of the Scientology organisation. The court pointed out that Scientology was an organisation which - according to information in the contested article - had approximately eight million members world-wide. It was therefore an indeterminable group of persons, with regard to which negative statements, which were not directed at individually determinable members, were lost in the general multitude of persons, and which therefore did not have any concrete effect on individual members. The court further noted that some of the passages invoked by the applicants had not been quoted correctly.

On 20 August 1996, the applicants appealed against this decision. They submitted detailed reasons for the appeal on 27 August 1996 and made supplementary submissions on 10 September 1996. The applicants again argued that the article violated their human rights, and more specifically their right as parents to educate their children in accordance with their beliefs, and insofar as their rights as children were concerned, the right of children to respect for their religious beliefs.

On 27 September 1996, the Bavarian Administrative Court of Appeal (Bayerischer Verwaltungsgerichtshof KirchE 34, 368) dismissed the appeal.

On 30 October 1996, the applicants lodged a constitutional appeal with the Federal Constitutional Court. They stressed that injunctive relief was the only effective remedy in cases concerning the education of children, since proceedings in the main action would last for a long period, and would not be terminated until the children had finished their school education.

On the article itself, the applicants submitted that the depiction of Scientologists as standard personalities with characteristics such as obesity/anorexia, loss of strength and altered beard-growth, whose thinking processes were narrowed and weakened, and who were held up as conditioned and brain-washed „zombies" without free will, as well as the assessment of the applicants' beliefs as „a crude mixture of science fiction, psychoanalysis and manipulative practices of totalitarian systems" was not a neutral, factual, true and tolerant informing of schoolchildren.

The applicants further argued that they were directly affected by the contested article, because, like all Scientologists, they were depicted as victims of manipulation, mind control and indoctrination, and as mentally inferior human beings. Their capacity to think for themselves was denied, and their religious beliefs were derided. According to them, the State, through the publication of the article, directly attempted to indoctrinate teachers and school-children, by creating fear and panic. The educational environment of their daughters was no longer characterised by tolerance and peaceful coexistence but by hatred and exclusion. The parents had to fear for an estrangement from their children, under the influence of the State. They emphasised that the article prejudiced their rights as parents to ensure the education and teaching of their children in conformity with their own religious and philosophical convictions and of the children's right to be educated in an environment that was open and tolerant towards their beliefs.

Sitting as a panel of three members, on 19 November 1996 the Federal Constitutional Court declined to accept the case for adjudication.

COMPLAINTS

The applicants complain that they do not have any remedy against the information campaign conducted by the Bavarian authorities and more specifically that they have been denied an effective remedy against the dissemination and promotion of a highly defamatory article in the magazine Schulreport, which was the centre-piece of the overall governmental campaign against Scientology and its members. The applicants maintain that they are victims of a violation of their right to freedom of thought, conscience and religion, and the first and second applicant of their right to ensure the education and teaching of their children in conformity with their own religious and philosophical convictions.

Referring to the cases of Klass and Malone (EuCHR, Klass and others v. Germany judgment of 6 September 1978, Series A no. 28; Malone v. United Kingdom judgment of 2 August 1984, Series A no. 82), they consider themselves to be directly affected by the campaign directly targeted at a specific minority community, in the course of which the members of that community were described as either brain-dead zombies or demonic manipulators of enslaved victims. In their village they are targeted and ostracised. In „enlightenment" evenings and citizen's initiatives against Scientology they are denounced by name and their house is referred to in the local press as a lair of Scientologists.

The applicants allege a violation of art. 9 of the Convention and of art. 2 of Protocol No. 1. They also invoke art. 13 of the Convention.

THE LAW

1. The applicants complain that they are the victims of the information campaign in Bavaria concerning Scientology and in particular of an article published in the April 1996 issue of the magazine Schulreport on this organisation. They submit that the article constitutes a direct attack - couched in prejudiced and unnecessarily offensive terms - on the peaceful enjoyment of their right to thought, conscience and religion as guaranteed by art. 9 of the Convention.

The applicants also complain that the contested article was expressly intended to inculcate in all Bavarian schools an atmosphere of rejection and of intolerance towards the religious beliefs of the first and second applicant and affected their right as parents to ensure the education and teaching of their children in accordance with their own religious and philosophical convictions, as guaranteed by art. 2 of Protocol No. 1.

The Commission has first examined to what extent the conditions laid down in art. 25-1 of the Convention have been met in the present case.

Art. 25-1 of the Convention provides:

> „The Commission may receive petitions addressed to the Secretary General of the Council of Europe from any person, non- governmental organisation or group of individuals claiming to be the victim of a violation by one of the High Contracting Parties of the rights set forth in this Convention, provided that the High Contracting Party against which the complaint has been lodged has declared that it recognises the competence of the Commission to receive such petitions. ..."

The Commission recalls that, in order for applicants to be able to avail themselves of this provision, they must fulfil two conditions: they must fall into one of the categories of applicants referred to in that provision and they must be able to claim to be a victim of a violation of the Convention.

As regards the first condition, the Commission notes that the applicants, as private persons, clearly fall into the categories of applicants mentioned in art. 25 of the Convention.

As for the second condition, the Commission recalls that the concept of „victim" as used in art. 25 of the Convention must be interpreted autonomously and independently of concepts of domestic law.

The Commission further recalls that an applicant cannot claim to be the victim of a breach of the rights or freedoms protected by the Convention unless there is a sufficiently direct connection between the applicant as such and the injury he maintains he suffered as a result of the alleged breach (No. 10733/84, Dec. 11.3.85, DR 41, p. 211).

The Commission observes that the article complained of contains information about Scientology and members of this world-wide organisation in general and is not aimed at any identifiable person belonging to that organisation. Although the applicants refer to the negative attitude of their neighbourhood and the local press towards them, the Commission finds that there is no indication in the file that this conduct is a result of the information disseminated about Scientology, in particular of the article complained of. The Commission therefore finds that the effects of the contested measures are of a too indirect and remote nature as to affect the applicants' rights under art. 9 of the Convention.

Furthermore, there is no indication in the case file that the first and second applicant's children have ever been confronted in the schoolteaching they received with the contested article or that they risk being subjected to indoctrination that might be considered as not respecting parents' religious and philosophical convictions (see EuCHR, Kjeldsen, Busk

Madsen and Pedersen v. Denmark judgment of 7 December 1976, Series A no. 23, p. 26, par. 53, KirchE-EU S. 181).

It follows that this part of the application is incompatible ratione personae with the provisions of the Convention, within the meaning of art. 27-2 of the Convention.

2. The applicants finally complain under art. 13 of the Convention that they do not have any remedy against the information campaign of the German authorities and that they have been denied an effective remedy against the dissemination of the contested article.

Art. 13 reads as follows:

„Everyone whose rights and freedoms as set forth in this Convention are violated shall have an effective remedy before a national authority notwithstanding that the violation has been committed by persons acting in an official capacity."

However, the Commission recalls that art. 13 of the Convention has no application where, as in the present case, the main complaint is outside the scope of the Convention (see No. 9984/82, Dec. 17.10.85, DR 44, p. 54).

It follows that this part of the application is incompatible ratione materiae with the provisions of the Convention, within the meaning of art. 27-2 of the Convention.

For these reasons, the Commission, unanimously, declares the application inadmissible.

36

Die Gewährleistung von Religionsfreiheit begründet für Aktivitäten einer religiösen Vereinigung nicht ohne weiteres einen Anspruch auf Steuerbegünstigung.

Art. 9, 14, 27 § 2 a.F. EMRK
EKMR, Beschluss vom 16. April 1998 - No. 30260/96
(Sivananda de Yoga Vedanta ./. Frankreich) -

EN FAIT

La requérante est une association sans but lucratif qui prône la pratique et l'enseignement du yoga et de la philosophie hindouiste vedanta.

En 1987, elle fit l'objet d'une vérification de comptabilité pour les années 1984 à 1986. Estimant que les cours de yoga dispensés par l'association présentaient un caractère lucratif, les autorités fiscales l'imposèrent au titre de l'impôt sur les sociétés pour ces années.

La requérante introduisit un recours devant le tribunal administratif de Paris, arguant qu'elle n'exerçait aucune activité lucrative. A la demande du fisc, cette instance fut élargie à l'imposition au titre de la taxe à la valeur ajoutée (TVA) et de retenue à la source, qui avait été notifiée dans l'intervalle à la requérante.

Dans un mémoire du 26 janvier 1990, la requérante demanda qu'il soit sursis à statuer dans l'attente de l'issue d'une demande de reconnaissance du caractère de congrégation religieuse qu'elle avait entretemps introduite auprès du ministre de l'Intérieur.

Par jugement du 20 mars 1992, le tribunal rejeta, d'une part, la demande de sursis à statuer au motif que la reconnaissance n'avait aucun effet rétroactif et que la situation du contribuable devait être examinée au moment des exercices d'imposition litigieux. Elle rejeta, d'autre part, la requête en raison du caractère lucratif des activités.

La requérante fit appel. Par arrêt du 14 décembre 1993, la cour administrative d'appel rejeta la demande de sursis à statuer et la requête, en se fondant sur des motifs semblables à ceux du tribunal administratif.

La requérante introduisit une requête en annulation devant le Conseil d'Etat. Elle fit notamment valoir qu'en refusant de surseoir à statuer et n'ayant pas égard à l'argument selon lequel l'objet religieux de l'association devait l'exonérer de tout assujettissement, la cour avait porté atteinte à diverses dispositions internes et internationales, dont les art. 9 et 14 de la Convention.

Par arrêt du 12 avril 1995 notifié le 11 mai 1995, le Conseil d'Etat décida de ne pas admettre le recours de la requérante pour absence de moyens sérieux, au sens de l'art. 11 de la loi n° 87-1127 du 31 décembre 1987.

GRIEFS

1. La requérante allègue que son assujettissement à l'impôt sur les sociétés et à la TVA, ainsi que le principe de retenue à la source porte atteinte aux droits garantis par les art. 9 et 10 de la Convention, d'autant que les juridictions françaises ont systématiquement analysé de manière négative tous les éléments qui contribuaient à conférer un caractère religieux à ses activités.

2. Elle fait aussi valoir que le Conseil d'Etat n'hésite pas à reconnaître un caractère non lucratif aux activités relevant d'une autre religion, notamment en reconnaissant le caractère non lucratif et désintéressé des activités cultuelles de la religion catholique. Elle soutient, en conséquence, qu'en refusant de reconnaître le caractère non lucratif et désintéressé de ses activités de pratique et d'enseignement du yoga, les autorités françaises lui ont fait subir une discrimination, au mépris des prescriptions de l'art. 14 de la Convention.

3. La requérante soutient enfin que l'absence de motivation de la décision de non-admission de leur pourvoi par le Conseil d'Etat constitue une

violation de leur droit à un procès équitable, au sens de l'art. 6 par. 1 de la Convention.

EN DROIT (Auszug)

1. La requérante se plaint en premier lieu d'une atteinte au droit à la liberté de religion, du fait de son assujettissement à l'impôt sur les sociétés et à la TVA, ainsi que de l'application du principe de retenue à la source. Elle invoque les art. 9 et 10 de la Convention.
   a. Dans la mesure où la requérante a apporté des arguments et éléments de preuve de nature à étayer la prétendue atteinte à l'art. 9 de la Convention qui protège le droit à la liberté d'expression, il n'apparaît pas qu'elle ait présenté pareil grief devant le Conseil d'Etat. Elle n'a donc pas épuisé les voies de recours internes qui lui étaient ouvertes en droit français et le grief doit être rejeté sur ce point, conformément à l'art. 27 par. 3 de la Convention.
   b. L'art. 9 de la Convention se lit comme suit:

> „1. Toute personne a droit à la liberté de pensée, de conscience et de religion; ce droit implique la liberté de changer de religion ou de conviction, ainsi que la liberté de manifester sa religion ou sa conviction individuellement ou collectivement, en public ou en privé, par le culte, l'enseignement, les pratiques et l'accomplissement des rites.
> 2. La liberté de manifester sa religion ou ses convictions ne peut faire l'objet d'autres restrictions que celles qui, prévues par la loi, constituent des mesures nécessaires, dans une société démocratique, à la sécurité publique, à la protection de l'ordre, de la santé ou de la morale publiques, ou à la protection des droits et libertés d'autrui.“

La Commission constate qu'aux termes de cette disposition, le droit à la liberté de religion comprend notamment le droit à manifester sa religion en public ou en privé par le culte ou par l'accomplissement des rites. Toutefois, la Commission ne saurait lire dans l'art. 9 de la Convention un droit à ce que toute activité d'une association qui aurait un caractère religieux ou cultuel soit exonérée de tout impôt. Elle estime que le droit à la liberté de religion n'implique nullement que les églises ou leurs fidèles doivent se voir accorder un statut fiscal différent de celui des autres contribuables (N° 17522/90, déc. 11.1.90, DR 72, p. 256).

Il s'ensuit que sous ce rapport, le grief est manifestement mal fondé et doit être rejeté, conformément à l'art. 27 par. 3 de la Convention.

2. La requérante allègue par ailleurs que dans la mesure où les autorités françaises reconnaissent un caractère non lucratif aux activités d'associations cultuelles et notamment celles de la religion catholique, le refus de reconnaître le caractère non lucratif et désintéressé de ses activités de pratique et d'enseignement du yoga constitue une discrimination en violation de l'art. 14 de la Convention, combiné avec son art. 9.

L'art. 14 de la Convention se lit comme suit:

„La jouissance des droits et libertés reconnus dans la présente Convention doit être assurée, sans distinction aucune, fondée notamment sur le sexe, la race, la couleur, la langue, la religion, les opinions politiques ou toutes autres opinions, l'origine nationale ou sociale, l'appartenance à une minorité nationale, la fortune, la naissance ou toute autre situation."

Toutefois, la Commission rappelle que cette disposition n'interdit pas toute distinction de traitement dans l'exercice des droits et libertés reconnues, l'égalité de traitement n'étant violée que si la distinction manque de justification objective et raisonnable (cf. CourEuDH, arrêt Rasmussen c. Danemark du 28 novembre 1984, série A N° 87, pp. 12, 13, par. 29, 35). La Commission est d'avis que l'on ne saurait considérer que la requérante, qui n'avait pas le statut d'association cultuelle, se trouvait dans une situation analogue ou comparable à celle d'organisations cultuelles, telle la religion catholique.

Dans ces conditions, aucune discrimination au sens de l'art. 14 ne saurait être constatée en l'espèce.

Il s'ensuit que ce grief doit également être rejeté comme étant manifestement mal fondé, par application de l'art. 27 par. 2 de la Convention.

3. La requérante soutient enfin que l'absence de motivation de la décision de non-admission de son pourvoi par le Conseil d'Etat constitue une violation de son droit à un procès équitable, au sens de l'art. 6 par. 1 de la Convention.

(...)

Par ces motifs, la Commission, à l'unanimité, déclare la requête irrecevable.

2. Europäischer Gerichtshof für Menschenrechte

37

In allen Bereichen des Schulwesens hat der Staat bei der Umsetzung des Rechts auf Bildung den Anspruch der Eltern zu achten, die Erziehung und den Unterricht entsprechend ihren religiösen und weltanschaulichen Überzeugungen sicherzustellen. Bei der dem Staat grundsätzlich zustehenden Konzeption des schulischen Curriculums ist eine Beeinflussung (indoctrination) der Schüler, die als Missachtung von religiösen und weltanschaulichen Überzeugungen der Eltern aufgefasst werden könnte, zu vermeiden. Diesen Anforderungen werden die schulrechtlichen Bestimmungen in Dänemark über den Sexualkundeunterricht gerecht, zumal Eltern die Möglichkeit haben, auf Privatschulen und Heimunterricht auszuweichen.

Art. 8-10, 14 EMRK, 2 Erstes Zusatzprotokoll
EGMR, Urteil vom 7. Dezember 1976 - No. 5095/71, 5920/72, 5926/72
(Kjeldsen u.a. / Dänemark)[1] -

AS TO THE FACTS

[14] The applicants, who are parents of Danish nationality, reside in Denmark. Mr. Viking Kjeldsen, a galvaniser, and his wife Annemarie, a schoolteacher, live in Varde; Mr. Arne Busk Madsen, a clergyman, and his wife Inger, a schoolteacher, come from Åbenrå; Mr. Hans Pedersen, who is a clergyman, and Mrs. Ellen Pedersen have their home in Ålborg. All three couples, having children of school age, object to integrated, and hence compulsory, sex education as introduced into State primary schools in Denmark by Act No. 235 of 27 May 1970, amending the State Schools Act (Lov om aendring af lov om folkeskolen, hereinafter referred to as „the 1970 Act").

Primary education in general

[15] According to art. 76 of the Danish Constitution, all children have the right to free education in the State primary schools (folkeskolen), although parents are not obliged to enrol them there and may send them to a private school or instruct them at home. During the school year 1970/71, a total of 716,665 pupils were attending 2,471 schools, of which 277 were private with 43,689 pupils. Some parents chose to educate their children at home.

---

[1] Ser. A Nr. 23; EuGRZ 1976, 478; NJW 1977, 487.

[16] At the time of the facts at issue, primary education in State schools was governed by the State Schools Act (Lov om folkeskolen) (a consolidated version of which was set out in Executive Order No. 279 of 8 July 1966), which had been amended on various occasions between 1966 and 1970. Primary education lasted for nine years; a tenth year, as well as a pre-school year for children of five to six years, were voluntary. The subjects taught in the first four years were Danish, writing, arithmetic, knowledge of Christianity (kristendomskundskab), history, geography, biology, physical training, music, creative art and needlework. In the fifth and sixth years, English and woodwork were added, and in the seventh year German, mathematics, natural sciences and domestic science. As from the eighth year the pupils were, to some extent, allowed to choose from these courses the subjects they preferred. Under the Act, the Minister of Education determined the objectives of schooling and the local school authorities fixed the contents of the curriculum and the number of lessons. There were, however, two exceptions to this rule. Firstly, religious instruction was to be in conformity with the Evangelical Lutheran doctrine of the National Church, but children might be exempted therefrom. Secondly, the legislator had directed schools to include in their curricula, often in conjunction with traditional subjects, certain new topics such as road safety, civics, hygiene and sex education.

[17] The administration of State schools in Denmark is largely decentralised. These institutions are run by the municipal council, the highest education authority in each of the some 275 municipalities in that country, as well as by a school commission and a school board. The school commission (skolekommissionen) is as a general rule composed of eleven members of whom six are elected by the municipal council and five by the parents. The commission, in consultation with the teachers' council and within the limits laid down by law, prepares the curriculum for the schools within its district. The curriculum must be approved by the municipal council. To assist these bodies in the performance of their tasks, the Minister of Education issues guidelines prepared by the State Schools' Curriculum Committee (hereinafter referred to as „the Curriculum Committee"), set up in 1958. Each State school has a school board (skolenaevn) which comprises three or five members; one member is chosen by the municipal council, the two or four others by the parents. The board supervises the school and organises co-operation between school and parents. It decides, upon recommendation from the teachers' council, what teaching aids and in particular what books are to be used by the school and it also determines the distribution of lessons among the teachers.

[18] Primary education at private schools or at home must not fall below the standards laid down for State schools; it must cover the same compulsory subjects and be of comparable quality. While a school may be established without any advance approval, it is subsequently supervised

by the school commissions in order to ensure, in particular, that adequate instruction is given in Danish, writing and arithmetic. The same applies to education given in the home; if the school commission finds twice in succession that such teaching is inadequate, the parents are required to send the child to a State or private school. The State supports private schools provided that they have not less than twenty pupils in all and not less than ten pupils per class. The State subsidises 85 per cent of their running costs (principal's and teachers' salaries, maintenance of buildings, heating, electricity, water, cleaning, insurance, etc.). In addition, private schools may be granted government loans on favourable terms for construction and improvement of buildings. As a result, parents who enrol their children at a private school do not in general have to bear school fees in excess of 1,200 Kroner per child per annum; during the 1973/1974 school year their average expenditure scarcely exceeded 1,050 Kroner. The Danish Parliament voted in May 1976 in favour of a proposal which would oblige municipalities to bear a large proportion of the cost of transport for children attending private schools. The statistics on private schools show that, in the school year 1973/74, there were about seventy „free" schools; one hundred and one private grammar schools without special religious background; twenty-five Catholic schools; nineteen German minority schools; ten schools for members of other religious societies; eight „Christian free" schools; and some thirty-five other schools. The applicants claim that there are insufficient private schools and that their pupils frequently have to travel long distances to attend them; moreover, parents wishing to send their children to a private school in Copenhagen have to enter them on waiting lists at least three years in advance.

Sex education

[19] In Denmark, sex education in State schools has been a topic of discussion for thirty-five years. As early as 1945, sex education was introduced in the State schools of Copenhagen and several institutions outside the capital copied this example. Nevertheless, the Minister of Education spoke against compulsory sex education when the question was raised in 1958. In 1960, the Curriculum Committee published a „Guide to teaching in State schools" which distinguished between instruction on the reproduction of man and sex education proper. The Committee recommended that the former be integrated in the biology syllabus while the latter should remain optional for children and teachers and be provided by medical staff. The Committee also advised that guidelines for schools be drawn up on the contents of, and the terminology to be used in, sex education. In a Circular of 8 April 1960, the Minister of Education adopted the Committee's conclusions: as from the school year 1960/61 reproduction of man became a compulsory part of biology lessons whereas an offi-

cial guide issued by the Ministry, dating from September 1961, specified that only those children whose parents had given their express consent should receive sex education proper.

[20] The Danish Government, anxious to reduce the disconcerting increase in the frequency of unwanted pregnancies, instructed a committee in 1961 to examine the problem of sex education (Seksualoplysningsudvalget). The setting up of such a committee had been urged, among others, by the National Council of Danish Women (Danske Kvinders Nationalraad) under the chairmanship of Mrs. Else-Merete Ross, a Member of Parliament, and by the Board of the Mothers' Aid Institutions (Mødrehjaelpsinstitutionernes Bestyrelse). Every year the latter bodies received applications for assistance from about 6,000 young unmarried mothers of whom half were below twenty years of age and a quarter below seventeen. In addition, many children, often of very young parents, were born within the first nine months after marriage. Legal abortions, for their part, numbered about 4,000 every year and, according to expert opinions, illegal abortions about 15,000 whereas the annual birth rate was hardly more than 70,000.

[21] In 1968, after a thorough examination of the problem, the above-mentioned committee, which was composed of doctors, educationalists, lawyers, theologians and government experts, submitted a report (No. 484) entitled „Sex Education in State Schools" (Seksualundervisning i Folkeskolen m.v., Betaenkning Nr. 484). Modelling itself on the system that had been in force in Sweden for some years, the committee recommended in its report that sex education be integrated into compulsory subjects on the curriculum of State schools. However, there should be no obligation for teachers to take part in this teaching. The report was based on the idea that it was essential for sexual instruction to be adapted to the children's different degrees of maturity and to be taught in the natural context of other subjects, for instance when questions by the children presented the appropriate opportunity. This method appeared to the committee particularly suited to prevent the subject from becoming delicate or speculative. The report emphasised that instruction in the matter should take the form of discussions and informal talks between teachers and pupils. Finally it gave an outline of the contents of sex education and recommended the drawing up of a new guide for State schools.

[22] In March 1970, the Minister of Education tabled a Bill before Parliament to amend the State Schools Act. The Bill provided, inter alia, that sex education should become obligatory and an integrated part of general teaching in State primary schools. In this respect, the Bill was based on the recommendations of the committee on sex education, with one exception: following a declaration from the National Teachers' Association, it did not grant teachers a general right of exemption from participation in such instruction. The Bill had received the support not only

of this Association but also of the National Association of School and Society representing on the national level education committees, school boards and parents' associations, and of the National Association of Municipal Councils. Sec. 1 par. 25 of the 1970 Act, which was passed unanimously by Parliament and became law on 27 May 1970, added „library organisation and sex education" to the list of subjects to be taught, set out in sec. 17 par. 6 of the State Schools Act. Accordingly the latter text henceforth read as follows (Bekendtgørelse No. 300 of 12 June 1970):

„In addition to the foregoing, the following shall also apply to teaching in primary schools: road safety, library organisation and sex education shall form an integral part of teaching in the manner specified by the Minister of Education. ...“

The Act entered into force on 1 August 1970. As early as 25 June, a Circular from the Minister of Education (Cirkulaere om aendring af folkeskoleloven) had advised municipal councils, school commissions, school boards, teachers' councils and headmasters of schools outside Copenhagen „that further texts, accompanied by new teaching instructions, on sex education would be issued". The Circular specified that „henceforth, parents (would) still have the possibility of exempting their children from such education and teachers that of not dispensing it".

[23] After the passing of the 1970 Act, the Minister of Education requested the Curriculum Committee to prepare a new guide to sex education in State schools intended to replace the 1961 guide (par. 19 above). The new guide (Vejledning om seksualoplysning i folkeskolen, hereinafter referred to as „the Guide") was completed in April 1971; it set out the objectives of sex education as well as certain general principles that ought to govern it, and suggested detailed curricula for the various classes.

[24] On the basis of the recommendations in the Guide, the Minister of Education laid down in Executive Order No. 274 of 8 June 1971 (Bekendtgørelse om seksualoplysning i folkeskolen) the rules of which he had given notice in his Circular of 25 June 1970. The Executive Order - which applied to primary education and the first level of secondary education in State schools outside Copenhagen - was worded as follows:

„Sec. 1
(1) The objective of sex education shall be to impart to the pupils knowledge which could:
(a) help them avoid such insecurity and apprehension as would otherwise cause them problems;
(b) promote understanding of a connection between sex life, love life and general human relationships;
(c) enable the individual pupil independently to arrive at standpoints which harmonise best with his or her personality;

(d) stress the importance of responsibility and consideration in matters of sex.
(2) Sex education at all levels shall form part of the instruction given, in the general school subjects, in particular Danish, knowledge of Christianity, biology (hygiene), history (civics) and domestic relations. In addition, a general survey of the main topics covered by sex education may be given in the sixth and ninth school years.
Sec. 2
(1) The organisation and scope of sex education shall be laid down in or in accordance with the curriculum. Assistance in this respect is to be obtained from the Guide issued by the State Schools' Curriculum Committee. If the special instruction referred to in the second sentence of sec. 1 par. 2 is provided in the sixth and ninth years, a small number of lessons shall be set aside each year for this purpose.
(2) Restrictions may not be imposed upon the range of matters dealt with in accordance with sub-sec. 1 so as to render impossible the fulfilment of the purpose of sex education.
(3) The restrictions on the carrying out of sex education in schools, as indicated in Part 4 of the Guide, shall apply regardless of the provisions of the curriculum.
Sec. 3
(1) Sex education shall be given by the teachers responsible for giving lessons on the subjects with which it is integrated in the relevant class and in accordance with the directives of the principal of the school. If it is not clear from the curriculum which subjects are linked to the various topics to be taught, the class teachers shall distribute the work, as far as need be, in accordance with the recommendation of the teachers' council; this latter opinion must be approved by the school board pursuant to sec. 27 par. 5 of the School Administration Act.
(2) A teacher cannot be compelled against his will to give the special instruction in the sixth and ninth years referred to in the second sentence of sec. 1 par. 2.
Sec. 4
(1) The present Order shall come into force on 1 August 1971.
(2) At the same time the right of parents to have their children exempted from sex education given at school shall cease. They may nevertheless, on application to the principal of the school, have them exempted from the special instruction referred to in the second sentence of sec. 1 par. 2.
(3) ..."

[25] A Ministry of Education Circular (Cirkulaere om seksualoplysning i folkeskolen), also dated 8 June 1971 and sent to the same authorities as that of 25 June 1970 (par. 22 above), gave the recipients, inter alia, certain particulars on the preparation of State school curricula in this field. It drew, in particular, their attention to the fact that „it was for the school commission, after discussion with the joint council of teachers, to prepare draft provisions governing sex education to be included in the curricula of the schools of the municipality". Recalling that these provisions may take the form of a simple reference to the recommendations in the Guide, the Circular pointed out that the Guide gave, for the fifth to tenth year classes, various possibilities as regards the manner and scope of teaching. Thus, if there were a simple reference to the Guide, „it is for

the institution (teachers' council) to take a decision in this respect with the agreement of the school board".

[26] The objectives set out in the Executive Order of 8 June 1971 were identical with those of the Guide, except that the latter contains an addition to the effect that schools must try to develop in pupils openness with regard to the sexual aspects of human life and to bring about such openness through an attitude that will make them feel secure.

[27] The principle of integration, provided for in par. 2 of sec. 1 of the Executive Order, is explained as follows in the Guide:

> „*The main purpose of integration is to place sex guidance in a context where the sexuality of man does not appear as a special phenomenon. Sexuality is not a purely physical matter ... nor is it a purely technical matter ... On the other hand it is not of such emotional impact that it cannot be taken up for objective and sober discussion. ... The topic should therefore form an integral part of the overall school education ...*"

[28] As for the definition of the manner and scope of sex education (sec. 2 par. 1 of the Executive Order), the Guide indicates the matters that may be included in the State school curricula. In the first to fourth years instruction begins with the concept of the family and then moves on to the difference between the sexes, conception, birth and development of the child, family planning, relations with adults whom the children do not know and puberty. The list of subjects suggested for the fifth to seventh years includes the sexual organs, puberty, hormones, heredity, sexual activities (masturbation, intercourse, orgasm), fertilisation, methods of contraception, venereal diseases, sexual deviations (in particular homosexuality) and pornography. The teaching given in the eighth to tenth years returns to the matters touched on during the previous years but puts the accent on the ethical, social and family aspects of sexual life. The Guide mentions sexual ethics and sexual morals; different views on sexual life before marriage; sexual and marital problems in the light of different religious and political viewpoints; the role of the sexes; love, sex and faithfulness in marriage; divorce, etc.

[29] The Guide advocates an instruction method centred on informal talks between teachers and children on the basis of the latter questions. It emphasises that „the instruction must be so tactful as not to offend or frighten the child" and that it „must respect each child's right to adhere to conceptions it has developed itself". To the extent that the discussion bears on ethical and moral problems of sexual life, the Guide recommends teachers to adopt an objective attitude; it specifies:

> „*The teacher should not identify himself with or dissociate himself from the conceptions dealt with. However, it does not necessarily prevent the teacher from showing his personal view. The demand for objectivity is amplified by the fact*

that the school accepts children from all social classes. It must be possible for all parents to reckon safely on their children not being influenced in a unilateral direction which may deviate from the opinion of the home. It must be possible for the parents to trust that the ethical basic points of view will be presented objectively and soberly."

The Guide also directs teachers not to use vulgar terminology or erotic photographs, not to enter into discussions of sexual matters with a single pupil outside the group and not to impart to pupils information about the technique of sexual intercourse (sec. 2 par. 3 of the Executive Order). The applicants claim, however, that in practice vulgar terminology is used to a very wide extent. They refer to a book by Bent H. Claësson called „Dreng og Pige, Mand og Kvinde" („Boy and Girl, Man and Woman") of which 55,000 copies have been sold in Denmark. According to them it frequently uses vulgar terminology, explains the technique of coitus and shows photographs depicting erotic situations.

[30] On the subject of relations between school and parents, the Guide points out, inter alia:

„In order to achieve an interaction between sex education at the school and at home respectively, it will be expedient to keep parents acquainted with the manner and scope of the sex education given at school. Parent class meetings are a good way of establishing this contact between school and parents. Discussions there will provide the opportunity for emphasising the objective of sexual instruction at the school and for making it clear to parents that it is not the school's intention to take anything away from them but rather ... to establish co-operation for the benefit of all parties. It can also be pointed out to parents that the integrated education allows the topic to be taken up exactly where it arises naturally in the other fields of instruction and that, generally, this is only practicable if sex education is compulsory for pupils. ... Besides, through his contacts with the homes the class teacher will be able to learn enough about the parents' attitude towards the school, towards their own child and towards its special problems. During discussions about the sex education given by the school, sceptical parents will often be led to realise the justification for co-operation between school and home in this field as well. Some children may have special requirements or need special consideration and it will often be the parents of these children who are difficult to contact. The teacher should be aware of this fact. When gradually the teacher, homes and children have come to know each other, a relationship of trust may arise which will make it possible to begin sex education in a way that is satisfactory to all parties."

[31] The Executive Order No. 313 of 15 June 1972, which came into force on 1 August 1972, repealed the Executive Order of 8 June 1971. The new Order reads:

„Sec. 1

(1) The objective of the sex education provided in Folkeskolen shall be to impart to the pupils such knowledge of sex life as will enable them to take care of themselves and show consideration for others in that respect.

(2) Schools are therefore required, as a minimum, to provide instruction on the anatomy of the reproductive organs, on conception and contraception and on venereal diseases to such extent that the pupils will not later in life land themselves or others in difficulties solely on account of lack of knowledge. Additional and more far-reaching goals of instruction may be established within the framework of the objective set out in sub-sec. (1) above.

(3) Sex education shall start not later than in the third school year; it shall form part of the instruction given in the general school subjects, in particular Danish, knowledge of Christianity, biology (hygiene), history (civics) and domestic relations. In addition, a general survey of the main topics covered by sex education may be given in the sixth or seventh and in the ninth school years.

Sec. 2

The organisation and scope of sex education shall be laid down in or in accordance with the curriculum. If the special instruction referred to in the second sentence of sec. 1 par. 3 is provided, a small number of lessons shall be set aside for this purpose in the relevant years.

Sec. 3

(1) Sex education shall be given by the teachers responsible for giving lessons on the subjects with which it is integrated in the relevant class and in accordance with the directives of the principal of the school. If it is not clear from the curriculum which subjects are linked to the various topics to be taught, the class teachers shall distribute the work, as far as need be, in accordance with the recommendation of the teachers' council; this latter opinion must be approved by the school board pursuant to sec. 27 par. 5 of the School Administration Act.

(2) A teacher cannot be compelled against his will to give the special instruction referred to in the second sentence of sec. 1 par. 3. Nor shall it be incumbent upon the teacher to impart to pupils information about coital techniques or to use photographic pictures representing erotic situations.

Sec. 4

On application to the principal of the school, parents may have their children exempted from the special instruction referred to in the second sentence of sec. 1 par. 3. ..."

[32] In a Circular of 15 June 1972 (Cirkulaere om aendring af reglerne om seksualoplysning i folkeskolen), sent to the same authorities as that of 25 June 1970 (par. 22 above), the Minister of Education stated that the aim of the new Executive Order was to enable local school authorities and, consequently, parents to exert greater influence on the organisation of the teaching in question. In addition, sex education, which „remains an integral part of school education, which is to say that it should form part of the instruction given in obligatory subjects", was to have a more confined objective and place greater emphasis on factual information. The Circular pointed out that henceforth sex education could be postponed until the third school year. It also mentioned that, whilst the Ex-

ecutive Order no longer contained a reference to the Guide - which was still in force -, this was to emphasise that the Guide was simply an aid to local school authorities in the drawing up of curricula. Finally, the Circular gave details on the role of teachers. If a teacher thought he would not be able to take care of this instruction in a satisfactory manner, he should be afforded the opportunity of attending one of the information courses provided by the Teachers' Training College. In addition, the Minister expressly recommended that special consideration be given to the personal and professional qualifications of teachers when courses including sex education are distributed amongst them. According to the applicants, the result of the Executive Order of 15 June 1972 was to free teachers from the duty of giving instruction in sex. It was alleged that in fact the Minister of Education issued it because many teachers vigorously protested against this duty.

[33] On 26 June 1975, the Danish Parliament passed a new State Schools Act (Act No. 313), which became fully effective on 1 August 1976. However, it has not amended any of the provisions relevant to the present case; sex education remains an integral and obligatory part of instruction in the elementary school. Neither has the Act changed the former rules on the influence of parents on the management and supervision of State schools. While the Bill was being examined by Parliament, the Christian People's Party tabled an amendment according to which parents would be allowed to ask that their children be exempted from attending sex education. This amendment was rejected by 103 votes to 24.

[34] Although primary education in private schools must in principle cover all the topics obligatory at State schools (par. 18 above), sex education is an exception in this respect. Private schools are free to decide themselves to what extent they wish to align their teaching in this field with the rules applicable to State schools. However, they must include in the biology syllabus a course on the reproduction of man similar to that obligatory in State schools since 1960 (par. 19 above).

[35] The applicants maintain that the introduction of compulsory sex education did not correspond at all with the general wish of the population. A headmaster in Nyborg allegedly collected 36,000 protest signatures in a very short space of time. Similarly, an opinion poll carried out by the Observa Institute and published on 30 January 1972 by a daily newspaper, the Jyllands-Posten, is said to have shown that, of a random sample of 1,532 persons aged eighteen or more, 41 per cent were in favour of an optional system, 15 per cent were against any sex education whatsoever in primary schools and only 35 per cent approved the system instituted by the 1970 Act. According to the authors of two articles, published in 1975 in the medical journal Ugeskrift for Laeger and produced to the Court by the Commission, the introduction of sex education has not, moreover, brought about the results desired by the legislator. On the contrary indeed, the number of unwanted pregnancies and of abortions is

said to have increased substantially between 1970 and 1974. The Government argue that the statistics from 1970 to 1974 cannot be taken as reflecting the effects of legislation whose application in practice began only in August 1973.

Facts relating to the applicants

[36] Mr. and Mrs. Kjeldsen have a daughter called Karen. She was born in December 1962 and attended St. Jacobi municipal school in Varde. All the municipal schools in this town were still using, until the 1972/73 school year, the curricula adopted in 1969, that is, before the 1970 Act entered into force. In Varde the curriculum changed only with effect from the 1973/74 school year.

[37] On 25 April 1971, the applicants asked the Minister of Education to exempt their daughter from sex education, saying they wished to give her this instruction themselves. On 6 May 1971, the Ministry replied to the effect that a new Executive Order on sex education in State schools was in the course of preparation. The applicants complained to the Danish Parliament but without any result. They then approached the Parliamentary Ombudsman (Folketingets ombudsmand) who told them on 2 June 1971 that he had no competence to deal with the matter.

[38] The Ministry of Education, in a letter of 14 July 1971, advised the applicants that Executive Order No. 274 (par. 24 above) had been issued and added that, for practical reasons, it was not possible to exempt children from integrated sex instruction. On 5 August 1971, the applicants wrote again to the Ministry of Education, this time enquiring about sex education in private schools. The Ministry told them on 20 September that private schools were not obliged to provide instruction beyond that which, since 1960, they had been obliged to give within the context of the biology syllabus. Some weeks before, that is, on 31 August 1971, the school commission of Varde had refused a request by the applicants that their daughter should be given free private education.

[39] On 13 October 1971, the Ministry replied to a further letter, dated 6 September, in which the applicants had requested new legislation to provide for free education without sex instruction. The Ministry said that it did not intend to propose such legislation and it also refused to arrange for the applicants' daughter to receive separate education. Referring to the reply given to another person who, in the same field, had invoked art. 2 of Protocol No. 1, the Ministry stated that Danish legislation on sex education complied with this provision, particularly in view of the existence of private schools. On 15 April 1972, the applicants asked the Ministry of Education why the curricula of the Varde municipal schools had not yet been adapted to the new legislation on sex education; the file in the case does not reveal whether the Ministry replied.

[40] Meanwhile, the applicants had withdrawn their daughter from the St. Jacobi school and during the 1971/72 school year they educated her at home. In August 1972 they again sent her to the Varde municipal school (Brorsonskolen). They maintained before the Commission that the nearest private school was nineteen kilometres from their home and that their daughter, who had diabetes, could not be away from home for a long period of time. The Government did not contest these claims.

[41] Mr. and Mrs. Busk Madsen have four children, the eldest of whom began school in 1972 at a State school in Åbenrå. They attempted unsuccessfully to have their children exempted from sex instruction.

[42] Mr. and Mrs. Pedersen have five children, of whom three were of school age in 1972. Two of them, Ester, born in 1957, and Svend, born in 1965, attended private schools in order to avoid having to follow sex education courses; the third, Hans Kristian, born in 1961, was enrolled at the Poul Paghs Gade municipal school in Ålborg. The applicants paid 660 Kroner a month for Ester, who left the latter school in summer 1972 to attend a private boarding school at Korinth (Fyn), and 75 Kroner for Svend. The Pedersens had asked the competent authorities - likewise unsuccessfully - to exempt their children from sex instruction. They stated in their application that they were considering sending their third child as well to a private school, if the Commission could not help them.

[43] In March 1972, the applicants complained about the use of certain books on sex education at the above-mentioned school. These books had apparently been approved by the school board in consultation with the teachers at the school. The Education and Culture Committee of the Northern Jutland County Council (Nordjyllands amtsråds undervisnings - og kulturudvalg) decided, however, on 16 June 1972 to uphold the school board's action and this decision was confirmed by the Minister of Education on 13 March 1973.

PROCEEDINGS BEFORE THE COMMISSION

[44] The present applications were lodged with the Commission on 4 April 1971 by Mr. and Mrs. Kjeldsen and on 7 October 1972 by Mr. and Mrs. Busk Madsen and Mr. and Mrs. Pedersen. As the Busk Madsens and the Pedersens stated that they regarded their applications as closely linked with that of the Kjeldsens, the Commission decided on 19 July 1973 to join the three applications in accordance with the then Rule 39 of its Rules of Procedure. All the applicants maintained that integrated, and hence compulsory, sex education, as introduced into State schools by the 1970 Act, was contrary to the beliefs they hold as Christian parents and constituted a violation of art. 2 of Protocol No. 1. The Commission took its decision on 16 December 1972 on the admissibility of the Kjeldsens' application, and on 29 May (partial decisions) and 19 July 1973 (final decisions) on the admissibility of the Busk Madsens' and the Peder-

sens' applications. They were accepted insofar as the applicants challenged the 1970 Act under art. 2 of Protocol No. 1, but rejected, for failure to exhaust domestic remedies (art. 27 par. 3), insofar as the applicants were complaining about „the directives issued and other administrative measures taken by the Danish authorities" regarding the manner in which sex education should be carried out. In their written pleadings on the merits, Mr. and Mrs. Kjeldsen also invoked art. 9 and 14 of the Convention.

[45] In its report of 21 March 1975, the Commission expressed the opinion:

- that there is no violation of art. 2 of Protocol No. 1 in the existence, per se, of the Danish system of sex education (seven votes against seven, with the President exercising his casting vote in accordance with the then Rule 18 par. 3 of the Commission's Rules of Procedure);
- that there has been no violation of art. 8 of the Convention (unanimously), or of art. 9 (unanimously);
- that no violation of art. 14 of the Convention is disclosed by the facts of the case (seven votes against four, with three abstentions).

The report contains three separate opinions.

FINAL SUBMISSIONS MADE TO THE COURT

[46] At the oral hearings on 2 June 1976 the Commission's delegates invited the Court to

„judge whether the introduction of integrated, and consequently compulsory, sex education in State primary schools by the Danish Act of 27 May 1970 constitutes, in respect of the applicants, a violation of the rights and freedoms guaranteed by the European Convention on Human Rights, and in particular those set out in art. 8, 9 and 14 of the Convention and art. 2 of the First Protocol".

For their part the Government, whilst making no formal submissions, pleaded the absence of any breach of the requirements of the Convention and of Protocol No. 1.

AS TO THE LAW

[47] The Court must first rule on two preliminary questions. The first concerns the declaration of withdrawal and the accessory request for a separate trial of their cause made by Mr. and Mrs. Kjeldsen (par. 11 above). (*wird ablehnend beschieden*)

[48] In the second place, the Court deems it necessary to delimit the object of the examination that it is required to undertake. (*wird ausgeführt mit dem folgenden Ergebnis*)

Under these conditions, the Court considers that it is called upon to ascertain whether or not the Act of 27 May 1970 and the delegated legislation of general application issued thereunder contravenes the Convention and Protocol No. 1, but that the particular measures of implementation decided upon at the level of each municipality or educational institution fall outside the scope of its supervision. Sec. 1 par. 25 of the Act of 27 May 1970 did no more than supplement the list of compulsory „integrated" subjects by adding, among others, sex education. The Minister of Education was entrusted with fixing the manner of implementing the principle thus enacted (par. 22 above). The Executive Orders and Circulars of 8 June 1971 and 15 June 1972, issued in pursuance of this enabling clause, therefore form a whole with the Act itself and only by referring to them can the Court make an appraisal of the Act; if it were otherwise, the reference of the present case to the Court would, moreover, hardly have served any useful purpose. It should nevertheless be pointed out, as is done by the Commission (par. 145 in fine of the report), that the instant case does not extend to the provisions on the special, optional lessons on sex education (sec. 1 par. 2 in fine, 2 par. 1 in fine, 3 par. 2 and 4 par. 2 in fine of the Executive Order of 8 June 1971, and subsequently sec. 1 par. 3 in fine, 2 in fine, 3 par. 2 and 4 of the Executive Order of 15 June 1972); it covers solely those provisions concerned with the sex education integrated in the teaching of compulsory subjects. The „Guide" of April 1971, on the other hand, is not a legislative or regulatory text, but a working document intended to assist and advise the local school authorities; while the Executive Order (sec. 2) and the Circular of 8 June 1971 mentioned it, the same is not true of those of 15 June 1972 (par. 24-25 and 31-32 above). It nevertheless remains in use throughout the whole country and was frequently cited by those appearing before the Court. Consequently, the Court will have regard to the „Guide" insofar as it contributes to an elucidation of the spirit of the legislation in dispute. Act No. 313 of 26 June 1975, which became fully effective on 1 August 1976, does not call for separate examination as it does not amend any of the provisions relevant to this case (par. 33 above).

I. On the alleged violation of Art. 2 of Protocol No. 1

[49] The applicants invoke art. 2 of Protocol No. 1 which provides:

„No person shall be denied the right to education. In the exercise of any functions which it assumes in relation to education and to teaching, the State shall respect the right of parents to ensure such education and teaching in conformity with their own religious and philosophical convictions."

[50] In their main submission before the Commission, the Government maintained that the second sentence of art. 2 does not apply to State

schools (par. 104-107 of the report and the memorial of 29 November 1973), but their arguments have since evolved slightly. In their memorial of 8 March 1976 and at the hearings on 1 and 2 June 1976, they conceded that the existence of private schools perhaps does not necessarily imply in all cases that there is no breach of the said sentence. The Government nevertheless emphasised that Denmark does not force parents to entrust their children to the State schools; it allows parents to educate their children, or to have them educated, at home and, above all, to send them to private institutions to which the State pays very substantial subsidies, thereby assuming a „function in relation to education and to teaching", within the meaning of art. 2. Denmark, it was submitted, thereby discharged the obligations resulting from the second sentence of this provision. The Court notes that in Denmark private schools co-exist with a system of public education. The second sentence of art. 2 is binding upon the Contracting States in the exercise of each and every function - it speaks of „any functions" - that they undertake in the sphere of education and teaching, including that consisting of the organisation and financing of public education. Furthermore, the second sentence of art. 2 must be read together with the first which enshrines the right of everyone to education. It is on to this fundamental right that is grafted the right of parents to respect for their religious and philosophical convictions, and the first sentence does not distinguish, any more than the second, between State and private teaching. The „travaux préparatoires", which are without doubt of particular consequence in the case of a clause that gave rise to such lengthy and impassioned discussions, confirm the interpretation appearing from a first reading of art. 2. Whilst they indisputably demonstrate, as the Government recalled, the importance attached by many members of the Consultative Assembly and a number of governments to freedom of teaching, that is to say, freedom to establish private schools, the „travaux préparatoires" do not for all that reveal the intention to go no further than a guarantee of that freedom. Unlike some earlier versions, the text finally adopted does not expressly enounce that freedom; and numerous interventions and proposals, cited by the delegates of the Commission, show that sight was not lost of the need to ensure, in State teaching, respect for parents' religious and philosophical convictions. The second sentence of art. 2 aims in short at safeguarding the possibility of pluralism in education which possibility is essential for the preservation of the „democratic society" as conceived by the Convention. In view of the power of the modern State, it is above all through State teaching that this aim must be realised. The Court thus concludes, as the Commission did unanimously, that the Danish State schools do not fall outside the province of Protocol No. 1. In its investigation as to whether art. 2 has been violated, the Court cannot forget, however, that the functions assumed by Denmark in relation to education and to teaching include the grant of substantial assistance to private schools. Although recourse to these schools involves parents in sacrifices which were justifiably mentioned by the applicants, the alternative solution it provides constitutes a factor that should not be disregarded in this case. The delegate speaking on behalf of the majority of the Commission recognised that it had not taken sufficient heed of this factor in par. 152 and 153 of the report.

[51] The Government pleaded in the alternative that the second sentence of art. 2, assuming that it governed even the State schools where attendance is not obligatory, implies solely the right for parents to have their children exempted from classes offering „religious instruction of a denominational character". The Court does not share this view.art. 2, which applies to each of the State's functions in relation to education and to teaching, does not permit a distinction to be drawn between religious instruction and other subjects. It enjoins the State to respect parents' convictions, be they religious or philosophical, throughout the entire State education programme.

[52] As is shown by its very structure, art. 2 constitutes a whole that is dominated by its first sentence. By binding themselves not to „deny the right to education", the Contracting States guarantee to anyone within their jurisdiction „a right of access to educational institutions existing at a given time" and „the possibility of drawing", by „official recognition of the studies which he has completed", „profit from the education received" (judgment of 23 July 1968 on the merits of the „Belgian Linguistic" case, Series A no. 6, pp. 30-32, par. 3-5). The right set out in the second sentence of art. 2 is an adjunct of this fundamental right to education (par. 50 above). It is in the discharge of a natural duty towards their children - parents being primarily responsible for the „education and teaching" of their children - that parents may require the State to respect their religious and philosophical convictions. Their right thus corresponds to a responsibility closely linked to the enjoyment and the exercise of the right to education. On the other hand, „the provisions of the Convention and Protocol must be read as a whole" (above-mentioned judgment of 23 July 1968, ibid., p. 30, par. 1). Accordingly, the two sentences of art. 2 must be read not only in the light of each other but also, in particular, of art. 8, 9 and 10 of the Convention which proclaim the right of everyone, including parents and children, „to respect for his private and family life", to „freedom of thought, conscience and religion", and to „freedom ... to receive and impart information and ideas".

[53] It follows in the first place from the preceding paragraph that the setting and planning of the curriculum fall in principle within the competence of the Contracting States. This mainly involves questions of expediency on which it is not for the Court to rule and whose solution may legitimately vary according to the country and the era. In particular, the second sentence of art. 2 of the Protocol does not prevent States from imparting through teaching or education information or knowledge of a di-

rectly or indirectly religious or philosophical kind. It does not even permit parents to object to the integration of such teaching or education in the school curriculum, for otherwise all institutionalised teaching would run the risk of proving impracticable. In fact, it seems very difficult for many subjects taught at school not to have, to a greater or lesser extent, some philosophical complexion or implications. The same is true of religious affinities if one remembers the existence of religions forming a very broad dogmatic and moral entity which has or may have answers to every question of a philosophical, cosmological or moral nature. The second sentence of art. 2 implies on the other hand that the State, in fulfilling the functions assumed by it in regard to education and teaching, must take care that information or knowledge included in the curriculum is conveyed in an objective, critical and pluralistic manner. The State is forbidden to pursue an aim of indoctrination that might be considered as not respecting parents' religious and philosophical convictions. That is the limit that must not be exceeded. Such an interpretation is consistent at one and the same time with the first sentence of art. 2 of the Protocol, with art. 8 to 10 of the Convention and with the general spirit of the Convention itself, an instrument designed to maintain and promote the ideals and values of a democratic society.

[54] In order to examine the disputed legislation under art. 2 of the Protocol, interpreted as above, one must, while avoiding any evaluation of the legislation's expediency, have regard to the material situation that it sought and still seeks to meet. The Danish legislator, who did not neglect to obtain beforehand the advice of qualified experts, clearly took as his starting point the known fact that in Denmark children nowadays discover without difficulty and from several quarters the information that interests them on sexual life. The instruction on the subject given in State schools is aimed less at instilling knowledge they do not have or cannot acquire by other means than at giving them such knowledge more correctly, precisely, objectively and scientifically. The instruction, as provided for and organised by the contested legislation, is principally intended to give pupils better information; this emerges from, inter alia, the preface to the „Guide" of April 1971. Even when circumscribed in this way, such instruction clearly cannot exclude on the part of teachers certain assessments capable of encroaching on the religious or philosophical sphere; for what are involved are matters where appraisals of fact easily lead on to value-judgments. The minority of the Commission rightly emphasised this. The Executive Orders and Circulars of 8 June 1971 and 15 June 1972, the „Guide" of April 1971 and the other material before the Court (par. 20-32 above) plainly show that the Danish State, by providing children in good time with explanations it considers useful, is attempting to warn them against phenomena it views as disturbing, for example, the excessive frequency of births out of wedlock, induced abortions and venereal diseases. The public authorities wish to enable pupils,

when the time comes, „to take care of themselves and show consideration for others in that respect", „not ... [to] land themselves or others in difficulties solely on account of lack of knowledge" (sec. 1 of the Executive Order of 15 June 1972). These considerations are indeed of a moral order, but they are very general in character and do not entail overstepping the bounds of what a democratic State may regard as the public interest. Examination of the legislation in dispute establishes in fact that it in no way amounts to an attempt at indoctrination aimed at advocating a specific kind of sexual behaviour. It does not make a point of exalting sex or inciting pupils to indulge precociously in practices that are dangerous for their stability, health or future or that many parents consider reprehensible. Further, it does not affect the right of parents to enlighten and advise their children, to exercise with regard to their children natural parental functions as educators, or to guide their children on a path in line with the parents' own religious or philosophical convictions. Certainly, abuses can occur as to the manner in which the provisions in force are applied by a given school or teacher and the competent authorities have a duty to take the utmost care to see to it that parents' religious and philosophical convictions are not disregarded at this level by carelessness, lack of judgment or misplaced proselytism. However, it follows from the Commission's decisions on the admissibility of the applications that the Court is not at present seised of a problem of this kind (par. 48 above). The Court consequently reaches the conclusion that the disputed legislation in itself in no way offends the applicants' religious and philosophical convictions to the extent forbidden by the second sentence of art. 2 of the Protocol, interpreted in the light of its first sentence and of the whole of the Convention. Besides, the Danish State preserves an important expedient for parents who, in the name of their creed or opinions, wish to dissociate their children from integrated sex education; it allows parents either to entrust their children to private schools, which are bound by less strict obligations and moreover heavily subsidised by the State (par. 15, 18 and 34 above), or to educate them or have them educated at home, subject to suffering the undeniable sacrifices and inconveniences caused by recourse to one of those alternative solutions.

[55] The applicants also rely on the first sentence of art. 2. In this connection, it suffices to note that the respondent State has not denied and does not deny their children either access to educational institutions existing in Denmark or the right of drawing, by official recognition of their studies, profit from the education received by them (judgment of 23 July 1968 on the merits of the „Belgian Linguistic" case, Series A no. 6, pp. 30-32, par. 3-5).

II. On the alleged violation of Art. 14 of the Convention taken together with Art. 2 of Protocol No. 1

[56] The applicants also claim to be victims, in the enjoyment of the rights protected by art. 2 of Protocol No. 1, of a discrimination, on the ground of religion, contrary to art. 14 of the Convention. They stress that Danish legislation allows parents to have their children exempted from religious instruction classes held in State schools, whilst it offers no similar possibility for integrated sex education (par. 70, 80 and 171-172 of the Commission's report). The Court first points out that art. 14 prohibits, within the ambit of the rights and freedoms guaranteed, discriminatory treatment having as its basis or reason a personal characteristic („status") by which persons or groups of persons are distinguishable from each other. However, there is nothing in the contested legislation which can suggest that it envisaged such treatment. Above all, the Court, like the Commission (par. 173 of the report), finds that there is a difference in kind between religious instruction and the sex education concerned in this case. The former of necessity disseminates tenets and not mere knowledge; the Court has already concluded that the same does not apply to the latter (par. 54 above). Accordingly, the distinction objected to by the applicants is founded on dissimilar factual circumstances and is consistent with the requirements of art. 14.

III. On the alleged violation of Art. 8 and 9 of the Convention

[57] The applicants, without providing many details, finally invoke art. 8 and 9 of the Convention taken together with art. 2 of Protocol No. 1. They allege that the legislation of which they complain interferes with their right to respect for their private and family life and with their right to freedom of thought, conscience and religion (par. 54, 55, 72, 89 and 170 of the Commission's report). However, the Court does not find any breach of art. 8 and 9 which, moreover, it took into account when interpreting art. 2 of Protocol No. 1 (par. 52 and 53 above).

IV. On the application of Art. 50 of the convention

[58] Having found no breach of Protocol No. 1 or of the Convention, the Court notes that the question of the application of art. 50 does not arise in the present case.

For these reasons the Court
1. *Holds by six votes to one that there has been no breach of art. 2 of Protocol No. 1 or of art. 14 of the Convention taken together with the said art. 2;*

2. *Holds unanimously that there has been no breach of art. 8 and 9 of the*
   Convention taken together with art. 2 of Protocol No. 1.

SEPARATE OPINION OF JUDGE VERDROSS

I have approved par. 1 to 52, 55 and 57 of the judgment but, to my
great regret, I have not been able to vote for item 1 of the operative provisions or to accept the grounds given therefore (par. 53-54 and 56). My
reasons are as follows:

I am in agreement with the Danish Government's starting point, which
is upheld in the judgment, namely that no provision in the Convention
prevents the Contracting States from integrating in their school systems
instruction on sexual matters and from thereby making such instruction
in principle compulsory. The second sentence of art. 2 of Protocol No. 1
thus does not prevent the States from disseminating in State schools, by
means of the teaching given, objective information of a religious or philosophical character. However, this freedom enjoyed by the States is limited by the second sentence of art. 2 of Protocol No. 1 according to which
parents may require that their religious and philosophical convictions be
respected in this teaching.

Since the applicants in the present case consider themselves wronged
in relation to their „Christian convictions", we can leave aside the question of how the term „philosophical convictions" is to be understood. It is
sufficient for us to examine whether the Government complained against
has respected the parents' Christian convictions in the context of sex
education.

Admittedly, the applicants' assertions in this respect are not altogether
precise. Their complaints are nevertheless sufficiently clear to show what
is in issue. The applicants are in fact objecting to the State prematurely
giving „detailed" teaching on sexual matters; they contend that the
State's monopoly in the realm of education deprives them of their basic
right „to ensure their children's education in conformity with their own
religious convictions". This makes it quite plain that they are basing
their complaints on a well established Christian doctrine whereby anything affecting the development of children's consciences, that is their
moral guidance, is the responsibility of parents and, consequently, in this
sphere the State may not intervene between parents and their children
against the former's wishes.

The applicants admittedly subscribe to the same religion as the great
majority of the country, but they belong apparently to a group more
faithful to the Christian tradition than their compatriots who are liberal
or indifferent to religion. However, as all the rights protected by the
Convention and its Protocols are rights of individual human beings, the
Court is not called upon to ascertain whether the rights of persons belonging to any given sect are violated or not. The Court has the sole obli-

gation of deciding whether in the instant case the rights of the applicants have been respected or not.

The question thus arises whether the parents concerned in the current proceedings may, in pursuance of art. 2 cited above, oppose compulsory sex education in a State school even if, as in the present circumstances, such education does not constitute an attempt at indoctrination.

To be able to answer this question, it seems to me necessary to distinguish between, on the one hand, factual information on human sexuality that comes within the scope of the natural sciences, above all biology, and, on the other hand, information concerning sexual practices, including contraception. This distinction is required, in my view, by the fact that the former is neutral from the standpoint of morality whereas the latter, even if it is communicated to minors in an objective fashion, always affects the development of their consciences. It follows that even objective information on sexual activity when given too early at school can violate the Christian convictions of parents. The latter accordingly have the right to object.

Art. 10 of the Convention, which embodies the freedom of everyone to receive and impart information, cannot be relied upon so as to counter this opinion, since art. 2 of Protocol No. 1 constitutes a special rule derogating from the general principle in art. 9 of the Convention. Art. 2 of the said Protocol thus gives parents the right to restrict the freedom to impart to their children not yet of age information affecting the development of the latter's consciences.

According to the judgment, it is true, the aforementioned clause of art. 2 prohibits solely education given with the object of indoctrination. However, this clause does not contain any indication justifying a restrictive interpretation of such a kind. On the contrary indeed, it requires the States, in an unqualified manner, to respect parents' religious and philosophical convictions; it makes no distinction at all between the different purposes for which the education is provided. Since the applicants consider themselves wronged in relation to their „Christian convictions" as a result of the obligation on their children to take part in „detailed" teaching on sexual matters, the Court ought to have restricted itself to ascertaining whether, should there have been any doubt, this complaint tallied or not with the beliefs professed by the applicants.

In this respect, the Court's power seems to me to be similar to that possessed by the bodies responsible, in various countries, for verifying the truth of statements made by persons called up for military service who claim that their religion or philosophy prevents them from carrying arms (conscientious objectors). These bodies have to respect the ideology of the persons concerned once such ideology has been clearly made out.

The distinction between information on the knowledge of man's sexuality in general and that concerning sexual practices is recognised under the Danish legislation itself. While private schools are required under the legislation to include in their curricula a biology course on the reproduction of man, they are left the choice whether or not to comply with the other rules compulsory for State schools in sexual matters. The legislature itself is thereby conceding that information on sexual activity may be separated from other information on the subject and that, consequently, an exemption granted to children in respect of a specific course of the first category does not prevent the integration in the school system of scientific knowledge on the subject.

The Danish Act on State schools does not in any way exempt the children of parents having religious convictions at variance with those of the legislature from attending the whole range of classes on sex education. The conclusion must therefore be that the Danish Act, within the limits indicated above, is not in harmony with the second sentence of art. 2 of Protocol No. 1.

This conclusion is not weakened by the entitlement given to parents to send their children to a private school subsidised by the State or to have them taught at home. On the one hand in fact, the parents' right is a strictly individual right, whereas the opening of a private school always presupposes the existence of a certain group of persons sharing certain convictions in common. Since the State should respect parents' religious convictions even if there existed one couple alone whose convictions as to the development of their children's consciences differ from those of the majority of the country or of a particular school, it can discharge this particular duty only by exempting the children from the classes on sexual practices. Moreover, one cannot fail to recognise that education at a private school, even one subsidised by the State, and teaching at home always entail material sacrifices for the parents. Thus, if the applicants were not entitled to have their children exempted from the classes in question, there would exist an unjustified discrimination, contrary to art. 14 of the Convention, prejudicing them in comparison with parents whose religious and moral convictions correspond to those of the Danish legislature.

38

Strafrechtliche Ahndung von Glaubensabwerbung (Proselytismus), begangen von Zeugen Jehovas durch Missionstätigkeit von Haus zu Haus, verstößt gegen die Freiheit der Religionsausübung.

Art. 7, 9, 10, 14 EMRK
EGMR, Urteil vom 25. Mai 1993 - No. 14307/88 -
(Kokkinakis ./. Griechenland)¹ -

AS TO THE FACTS

I. The circumstances of the case

[6] Mr Minos Kokkinakis, a retired businessman of Greek nationality, was born into an Orthodox family at Sitia (Crete) in 1919. After becoming a Jehovah's Witness in 1936, he was arrested more than sixty times for proselytism. He was also interned and imprisoned on several occasions. The periods of internment, which were ordered by the administrative authorities on the grounds of his activities in religious matters, were spent on various islands in the Aegean (thirteen months in Amorgos in 1938, six in Milos in 1940 and twelve in Makronisos in 1949). The periods of imprisonment, to which he was sentenced by the courts, were for acts of proselytism (three sentences of two and a half months in 1939 - he was the first Jehovah's Witness to be convicted under the Laws of the Metaxas Government (see par. 16 below) -, four and a half months in 1949 and two months in 1962), conscientious objection (eighteen and a half months in 1941) and holding a religious meeting in a private house (six months in 1952). Between 1960 and 1970 the applicant was arrested four times and prosecuted but not convicted.

[7] On 2 March 1986 he and his wife called at the home of Mrs Kyriakaki in Sitia and engaged in a discussion with her. Mrs Kyriakaki's husband, who was the cantor at a local Orthodox church, informed the police, who arrested Mr and Mrs Kokkinakis and took them to the local police station, where they spent the night of 2-3 March 1986.

A. Proceedings in the Lasithi Criminal Court

[8] The applicant and his wife were prosecuted under sec. 4 of Law no. 1363/1938 making proselytism an offence (see par. 16 below) and were committed for trial at the Lasithi Criminal Court (trimeles plimmeliodikio), which heard the case on 20 March 1986.

[9] After dismissing an objection that sec. 4 of that Law was unconstitutional, the Criminal Court heard evidence from Mr and Mrs Kyriakaki, a defence witness and the two defendants and gave judgment on the same day:

„[The defendants], who belong to the Jehovah's Witnesses sect, attempted to proselytise and, directly or indirectly, to intrude on the religious beliefs of Ortho-

---

¹ Ser. A 260-A; ÖJZ 1994, 59; RUDH 1993, 251. Vgl. hierzu auch EKMR, Zulassungsbeschluss vom 3.12.1991 - No. 14307/88 (Kokkinakis ./. Griechenland).

dox Christians, with the intention of undermining those beliefs, by taking advantage of their inexperience, their low intellect and their naïvety. In particular, they went to the home of [Mrs Kyriakaki] ... and told her that they brought good news; by insisting in a pressing manner, they gained admittance to the house and began to read from a book on the Scriptures which they interpreted with reference to a king of heaven, to events which had not yet occurred but would occur, etc., encouraging her by means of their judicious, skilful explanations ... to change her Orthodox Christian beliefs."

The court found Mr and Mrs Kokkinakis guilty of proselytism and sentenced each of them to four months' imprisonment, convertible (under art. 82 of the Criminal Code) into a pecuniary penalty of 400 drachmas per day's imprisonment, and a fine of 10,000 drachmas. Under art. 76 of the Criminal Code, it also ordered the confiscation and destruction of four booklets which they had been hoping to sell to Mrs Kyriakaki.

B. The proceedings in the Crete Court of Appeal

[10] Mr and Mrs Kokkinakis appealed against this judgment to the Crete Court of Appeal (Efetio). The Court of Appeal quashed Mrs Kokkinakis's conviction and upheld her husband's but reduced his prison sentence to three months and converted it into a pecuniary penalty of 400 drachmas per day. The following reasons were given for its judgment, which was delivered on 17 March 1987:

„... it was proved that, with the aim of disseminating the articles of faith of the Jehovah's Witnesses sect (airesi), to which the defendant adheres, he attempted, directly and indirectly, to intrude on the religious beliefs of a person of a different religious persuasion from his own, [namely] the Orthodox Christian faith, with the intention of changing those beliefs, by taking advantage of her inexperience, her low intellect and her naïvety. More specifically, at the time and place indicated in the operative provision, he visited Mrs Georgia Kyriakaki and after telling her he brought good news, pressed her to let him into the house, where he began by telling her about the politician Olof Palme and by expounding pacifist views. He then took out a little book containing professions of faith by adherents of the aforementioned sect and began to read out passages from Holy Scripture, which he skilfully analysed in a manner that the Christian woman, for want of adequate grounding in doctrine, could not challenge, and at the same time offered her various similar books and importunately tried, directly and indirectly, to undermine her religious beliefs. He must consequently be declared guilty of the above-mentioned offence, in accordance with the operative provision hereinafter, while the other defendant, his wife Elissavet, must be acquitted, seeing that there is no evidence that she participated in the offence committed by her husband, whom she merely accompanied ..."

One of the appeal judges dissented, and his opinion, which was appended to the judgment, read as follows:

"... the first defendant should also have been acquitted, as none of the evidence shows that Georgia Kyriakaki ... was particularly inexperienced in Orthodox Christian doctrine, being married to a cantor, or of particularly low intellect or particularly naïve, such that the defendant was able to take advantage and ... [thus] induce her to become a member of the Jehovah's Witnesses sect."

According to the record of the hearing of 17 March 1987, Mrs Kyriakaki had given the following evidence:

"They immediately talked to me about Olof Palme, whether he was a pacifist or not, and other subjects that I can't remember. They talked to me about things I did not understand very well. It was not a discussion but a constant monologue by them. ... If they had told me they were Jehovah's Witnesses, I would not have let them in. I don't recall whether they spoke to me about the Kingdom of Heaven. They stayed in the house about ten minutes or a quarter of an hour. What they told me was religious in nature, but I don't know why they told it to me. I could not know at the outset what the purpose of their visit was. They may have said something to me at the time with a view to undermining my religious beliefs ... [However,] the discussion did not influence my beliefs ..."

C. The proceedings in the Court of Cassation

[11] Mr Kokkinakis appealed on points of law. He maintained, inter alia, that the provisions of Law no. 1363/1938 contravened art. 13 of the Constitution (see par. 13 below).

[12] The Court of Cassation (Arios Pagos) dismissed the appeal on 22 April 1988. It rejected the plea of unconstitutionality for the following reasons:

"Sec. 4 of Law no. 1363/1938, substituted by sec. 2 of Law no. 1672/1939 providing for the implementation of art. 1 and 2 of the Constitution and enacted under the 1911 Constitution then in force, art. 1 of which prohibited proselytism and any other interference with the dominant religion in Greece, namely the Christian Eastern Orthodox Church, not only does not contravene art. 13 of the 1975 Constitution but is fully compatible with the Constitution, which recognises the inviolability of freedom of conscience in religious matters and provides for freedom to practise any known religion, subject to a formal provision in the same Constitution prohibiting proselytism in that proselytism is forbidden in general whatever the religion against which it is directed, including therefore the dominant religion in Greece, in accordance with art. 3 of the 1975 Constitution, namely the Christian Eastern Orthodox Church."

It also noted that the Crete Court of Appeal had given detailed reasons for its judgment and had complied with the 1975 Constitution in applying the impugned provisions.

In the opinion of a dissenting member, the Court of Cassation should have quashed the judgment of the court below for having wrongly applied sec. 4 of Law no. 1363/1938 in that it had made no mention of the promises whereby the defendant had allegedly attempted to intrude on Mrs Kyriakaki's religious beliefs and had given no particulars of Mrs Kyriakaki's inexperience and low intellect.

II. Relevant domestic law and practice

A. Statutory provisions

1. The Constitution

[13] The relevant articles of the 1975 Constitution read as follows:

Art. 3
„1. The dominant religion in Greece is that of the Christian Eastern Orthodox Church. The Greek Orthodox Church, which recognises as its head Our Lord Jesus Christ, is indissolubly united, doctrinally, with the Great Church of Constantinople and with any other Christian Church in communion with it (omodoxi), immutably observing, like the other Churches, the holy apostolic and synodical canons and the holy traditions. It is autocephalous and is administered by the Holy Synod, composed of all the bishops in office, and by the standing Holy Synod, which is an emanation of it constituted as laid down in the Charter of the Church and in accordance with the provisions of the Patriarchal Tome of 29 June 1850 and the Synodical Act of 4 September 1928.
2. The ecclesiastical regime in certain regions of the State shall not be deemed contrary to the provisions of the foregoing paragraph.
3. The text of the Holy Scriptures is unalterable. No official translation into any other form of language may be made without the prior consent of the autocephalous Greek Church and the Great Christian Church at Constantinople."
Art. 13
„1. Freedom of conscience in religious matters is inviolable. The enjoyment of personal and political rights hall not depend on an individual's religious beliefs.
2. There shall be freedom to practise any known religion; individuals shall be free to perform their rites of worship without hindrance and under the protection of the law. The performance of rites of worship must not prejudice public order or public morals. Proselytism is prohibited.
3. The ministers of all known religions shall be subject to the same supervision by the State and to the same obligations to it as those of the dominant religion.
4. No one may be exempted from discharging his obligations to the State or refuse to comply with the law by reason of his religious convictions.
5. No oath may be required other than under a law which also determines the form of it."

[14] The Christian Eastern Orthodox Church, which during nearly four centuries of foreign occupation symbolised the maintenance of Greek culture and the Greek language, took an active part in the Greek people's struggle for emancipation, to such an extent that Hellenism is to some extent identified with the Orthodox faith. A royal decree of 23 July 1833

entitled „Proclamation of the Independence of the Greek Church" described the Orthodox Church as „autocephalous". Greece's successive Constitutions have referred to the Church as being „dominant". The overwhelming majority of the population are members of it, and, according to Greek conceptions, it represents de jure and de facto the religion of the State itself, a good number of whose administrative and educational functions (marriage and family law, compulsory religious instruction, oaths sworn by members of the Government, etc.) it moreover carries out. Its role in public life is reflected by, among other things, the presence of the Minister of Education and Religious Affairs at the sessions of the Church hierarchy at which the Archbishop of Athens is elected and by the participation of the Church authorities in all official State events; the President of the Republic takes his oath of office according to Orthodox ritual (art. 33 par. 2 of the Constitution); and the official calendar follows that of the Christian Eastern Orthodox Church.

[15] Under the reign of Otto I (1832-62), the Orthodox Church, which had long complained of a Bible society's propaganda directed at young Orthodox schoolchildren on behalf of the Evangelical Church, managed to get a clause added to the first Constitution (1844) forbidding „proselytism and any other action against the dominant religion". The Constitutions of 1864, 1911 and 1952 reproduced the same clause. The 1975 Constitution prohibits proselytism in general (art. 13 par. 2 in fine - see par. 13 above): the ban covers all „known religions", meaning those whose doctrines are not apocryphal and in which no secret initiation is required of neophytes.

2. Laws nos. 1363/1938 and 1672/1939

[16] During the dictatorship of Metaxas (1936-40) proselytism was made a criminal offence for the first time by sec. 4 of Law (anagastikos nomos) no. 1363/1938. The following year that section was amended by sec. 2 of Law no. 1672/1939, in which the meaning of the term „proselytism" was clarified:

„1. Anyone engaging in proselytism shall be liable to imprisonment and a fine of between 1,000 and 50,000 drachmas; he shall, moreover, be subject to police supervision for a period of between six months and one year to be fixed by the court when convicting the offender.
The term of imprisonment may not be commuted to a fine.
2. By ‚proselytism' is meant, in particular, any direct or indirect attempt to intrude on the religious beliefs of a person of a different religious persuasion (eterodoxos), with the aim of undermining those beliefs, either by any kind of inducement or promise of an inducement or moral support or material assistance, or by fraudulent means or by taking advantage of his inexperience, trust, need, low intellect or naïvety.

3. The commission of such an offence in a school or other educational establishment or a philanthropic institution shall constitute a particularly aggravating circumstance."

B. Case-law

[17] In a judgment numbered 2276/1953 a full court of the Supreme Administrative Court (Symvoulio tis Epikratias) gave the following definition of proselytism:

> „*Art. 1 of the Constitution, which establishes the freedom to practise any known religion and to perform rites of worship without hindrance and prohibits proselytism and all other activities directed against the dominant religion, that of the Christian Eastern Orthodox Church, means that purely spiritual teaching does not amount to proselytism, even if it demonstrates the errors of other religions and entices possible disciples away from them, who abandon their original religions of their own free will; this is because spiritual teaching is in the nature of a rite of worship performed freely and without hindrance. Outside such spiritual teaching, which may be freely given, any determined, importunate attempt to entice disciples away from the dominant religion by means that are unlawful or morally reprehensible constitutes proselytism as prohibited by the aforementioned provision of the Constitution."*

[18] The Greek courts have held that persons were guilty of proselytism who had: likened the saints to „figures adorning the wall", St Gerasimos to „a body stuffed with cotton" and the Church to „a theatre, a market, a cinema"; preached, while displaying a painting showing a crowd of wretched people in rags, that „such are all those who do not embrace my faith" (Court of Cassation, judgment no. 271/1932, Themis XVII, p. 19); promised Orthodox refugees housing on specially favourable terms if they adhered to the Uniate faith (Court of Appeal of the Aegean, judgment no. 2950/1930, Themis B, p. 103); offered a scholarship for study abroad (Court of Cassation, judgment no. 2276/1953); sent Orthodox priests booklets with the recommendation that they should study them and apply their content (Court of Cassation, judgment no. 59/1956, Nomiko Vima, 1956, no. 4, p. 736); distributed „so-called religious" books and booklets free to „illiterate peasants" or to „young schoolchildren" (Court of Cassation, judgment no. 201/1961, Criminal Annals XI, p. 472); or promised a young seamstress an improvement in her position if she left the Orthodox Church, whose priests were alleged to be „exploiters of society" (Court of Cassation, judgment no. 498/1961, Criminal Annals XII, p. 212). The Court of Cassation has ruled that the definition of proselytism in sec. 4 of Law no. 1363/1938 does not contravene the principle that only the law can define a crime and prescribe a penalty. The Piraeus Criminal Court followed it in an order (voulevma) numbered 36/1962 (Greek Lawyers' Journal, 1962, p. 421), adding that the expres-

sion „in particular" in sec. 4 of Law no. 1363/1938 (see par. 16 above) referred to the means used by the person committing the offence and not to the description of the actus reus.

[19] Until 1975 the Court of Cassation held that the list in sec. 4 was not exhaustive. In a judgment numbered 997/1975 (Criminal Annals XXVI, p. 380) it added the following clarification:

> „... it follows from the provisions of sec. 4 ... that proselytism consists in a direct or indirect attempt to impinge on religious beliefs by any of the means separately listed in the Law."

[20] More recently courts have convicted Jehovah's Witnesses for professing the sect's doctrine „importunately" and accusing the Orthodox Church of being a „source of suffering for the world" (Salonika Court of Appeal, judgment no. 2567/1988); for entering other people's homes in the guise of Christians wishing to spread the New Testament (Florina Court of First Instance, judgment no. 128/1989); and for attempting to give books and booklets to an Orthodox priest at the wheel of his car after stopping him (Lasithi Court of First Instance, judgment no. 357/1990). In a judgment numbered 1304/1982 (Criminal Annals XXXII, p. 502), on the other hand, the Court of Cassation quashed a judgment of the Athens Court of Appeal (no. 5434/1981) as having no basis in law because, when convicting a Jehovah's Witness, the Court of Appeal had merely reiterated the words of the indictment and had thus not explained how „the importunate teaching of the doctrines of the Jehovah's Witnesses sect" or „distribution of the sect's booklets at a minimal price" had amounted to an attempt to intrude on the complainants' religious beliefs, or shown how the defendant had taken advantage of their „inexperience" and „low intellect". The Court of Cassation remitted the case to a differently constituted bench of the Court of Appeal, which acquitted the defendant. Similarly, it has been held in several court decisions that the offence of proselytism was not made out where there had merely been a discussion about the beliefs of the Jehovah's Witnesses, where booklets had been distributed from door to door (Patras Court of Appeal, judgment no. 137/1988) or in the street (Larissa Court of Appeal, judgment no. 749/1986) or where the tenets of the sect had been explained without any deception to an Orthodox Christian (Trikkala Criminal Court, judgment no. 186/1986). Lastly, it has been held that being an „illiterate peasant" is not sufficient to establish the „naïvety", referred to in sec. 4, of the person whom the alleged proselytiser is addressing (Court of Cassation, judgment no. 1155/1978).

[21] After the revision of the Constitution in 1975, the Jehovah's Witnesses brought legal proceedings to challenge the constitutionality of sec. 4 of Law no. 1363/1938. They complained that the description of the offence was vague, but above all they objected to the actual title of the

Law, which indicated that the Law was designed to preserve art. 1 and 2 of the Constitution in force at the time (the 1911 Constitution - see par. 12 above), which prohibited proselytism directed against the dominant religion. In the current Constitution this prohibition is extended to all religions and furthermore is no longer included in the chapter concerning religion but in the one dealing with civil and social rights, and more particularly in art. 13, which guarantees freedom of conscience in religious matters. The courts have always dismissed such objections of unconstitutionality, although they have been widely supported in legal literature.

III. The Jehovah's Witnesses in Greece

[22] The Jehovah's Witnesses movement appeared in Greece at the beginning of the twentieth century. Estimates of its membership today vary between 25,000 and 70,000. Members belong to one of 338 congregations, the first of which was formed in Athens in 1922.

[23] Since the revision of the Constitution in 1975 the Supreme Administrative Court has held on several occasions that the Jehovah's Witnesses come within the definition of a „known religion" (judgments nos. 2105 and 2106/1975, 4635/1977, 2484/1980, 4620/1985, 790 and 3533/1986 and 3601/1990). Some first-instance courts, however, continue to rule to the contrary (Heraklion Court of First Instance, judgments nos. 272/1984 and 87/1986). In 1986 the Supreme Administrative Court held (in judgment no. 3533/1986) that a ministerial decision refusing the appointment of a Jehovah's Witness as a literature teacher was contrary to freedom of conscience in religious matters and hence to the Greek Constitution.

[24] According to statistics provided by the applicant, 4,400 Jehovah's Witnesses were arrested between 1975 (when democracy was restored) and 1992, and 1,233 of these were committed for trial and 208 convicted. Earlier, several Jehovah's Witnesses had been convicted under Law no. 117/1936 for the prevention of communism and its effects and Law no. 1075/1938 on preserving the social order. The Government have not challenged the applicant's figures. They have, however, pointed out that there have been signs of a decline in the frequency of convictions of Jehovah's Witnesses, only 7 out of a total of 260 people arrested having been convicted in 1991 and 1992.

PROCEEDINGS BEFORE THE COMMISSION

(...)

AS TO THE LAW

[27] Mr Kokkinakis complained of his conviction for proselytism; he considered it contrary to art. 7, 9 and 10 of the Convention, and to art. 14 taken together with art. 9.

I. Alleged violation of Art. 9

[28] The applicant's complaints mainly concerned a restriction on he exercise of his freedom of religion. The Court will accordingly begin by looking at the issues relating to art. 9, which provides:

> „1. *Everyone has the right to freedom of thought, conscience and religion; this right includes freedom to change his religion or belief and freedom, either alone or in community with others and in public or private, to manifest his religion or belief, in worship, teaching, practice and observance.*
> 2. *Freedom to manifest one's religion or beliefs shall be subject only to such limitations as are prescribed by law and are necessary in a democratic society in the interests of public safety, for the protection of public order, health or morals, or for the protection of the rights and freedoms of others. "*

[29] The applicant did not only challenge what he claimed to be the wrongful application to him of sec. 4 of Law no. 1363/1938. His submission concentrated on the broader problem of whether that enactment was compatible with the right enshrined in art. 9 of the Convention, which, he argued, having been part of Greek law since 1953, took precedence under the Constitution over any contrary statute. He pointed to the logical and legal difficulty of drawing any even remotely clear dividing-line between proselytism and freedom to change one's religion or belief and, either alone or in community with others, in public and in private, to manifest it, which encompassed all forms of teaching, publication and preaching between people. The ban on proselytism, which was made a criminal offence during the Metaxas dictatorship, was not only unconstitutional, Mr Kokkinakis submitted, but it also formed, together with the other clauses of Law no. 1363/1938, „an arsenal of prohibitions and threats of punishment" hanging over the adherents of all beliefs and all creeds. Mr Kokkinakis complained, lastly, of the selective application of this Law by the administrative and judicial authorities; it would surpass „even the wildest academic hypothesis" to imagine, for example, the possibility of a complaint being made by a Catholic priest or by a Protestant clergyman against an Orthodox Christian who had attempted to entice one of his flock away from him. It was even less likely that an Orthodox Christian would be prosecuted for proselytising on behalf of the „dominant religion".

[30] In the Government's submission, there was freedom to practise all religions in Greece; religious adherents enjoyed the right both to express

their beliefs freely and to try to influence the beliefs of others, Christian witness being a duty of all Churches and all Christians. There was, however, a radical difference between bearing witness and „proselytism that is not respectable", the kind that consists in using deceitful, unworthy and immoral means, such as exploiting the destitution, low intellect and inexperience of one's fellow beings. Sec. 4 prohibited this kind of proselytism - the „misplaced" proselytism to which the European Court referred in its Kjeldsen, Busk Madsen and Pedersen v. Denmark judgment of 7 December 1976 (Series A no. 23, p. 28, par. 54) - and not straightforward religious teaching. Furthermore, it was precisely this definition of proselytism that had been adopted by the Greek courts.

A. General principles

[31] As enshrined in art. 9, freedom of thought, conscience and religion is one of the foundations of a „democratic society" within the meaning of the Convention. It is, in its religious dimension, one of the most vital elements that go to make up the identity of believers and their conception of life, but it is also a precious asset for atheists, agnostics, sceptics and the unconcerned. The pluralism indissociable from a democratic society, which has been dearly won over the centuries, depends on it. While religious freedom is primarily a matter of individual conscience, it also implies, inter alia, freedom to „manifest [one's] religion". Bearing witness in words and deeds is bound up with the existence of religious convictions. According to art. 9, freedom to manifest one's religion is not only exercisable in community with others, „in public" and within the circle of those whose faith one shares, but can also be asserted „alone" and „in private"; furthermore, it includes in principle the right to try to convince one's neighbour, for example through „teaching", failing which, moreover, „freedom to change [one's] religion or belief", enshrined in art. 9, would be likely to remain a dead letter.

[32] The requirements of art. 9 are reflected in the Greek Constitution in so far as art. 13 of the latter declares that freedom of conscience in religious matters is inviolable and that there shall be freedom to practise any known religion (see par. 13 above). Jehovah's Witnesses accordingly enjoy both the status of a „known religion" and the advantages flowing from that as regards observance (see par. 22-23 above).

[33] The fundamental nature of the rights guaranteed in art. 9 par. 1 is also reflected in the wording of the paragraph providing for limitations on them. Unlike the second paragraphs of art. 8, 10 and 11 which cover all the rights mentioned in the first paragraphs of those articles, that of art. 9 refers only to „freedom to manifest one's religion or belief". In so doing, it recognises that in democratic societies, in which several religions coexist within one and the same population, it may be necessary to

place restrictions on this freedom in order to reconcile the interests of the various groups and ensure that everyone's beliefs are respected.

[34] According to the Government, such restrictions were to be found in the Greek legal system. Art. 13 of the 1975 Constitution forbade proselytism in respect of all religions without distinction; and sec. 4 of Law no. 1363/1938, which attached a criminal penalty to this prohibition, had been upheld by several successive democratic governments notwithstanding its historical and political origins. The sole aim of sec. 4 was to protect the beliefs of others from activities which undermined their dignity and personality.

[35] The Court will confine its attention as far as possible to the issue raised by the specific case before it. It must nevertheless look at the foregoing provisions, since the action complained of by the applicant arose from the application of them (see, mutatis mutandis, the de Geouffre de la Pradelle v. France judgment of 16 December 1992, Series A no. 253-B, p. 42, par. 31).

B. Application of the principles

[36] The sentence passed by the Lasithi Criminal Court and subsequently reduced by the Crete Court of Appeal (see par. 9-10 above) amounts to an interference with the exercise of Mr Kokkinakis's right to „freedom to manifest [his] religion or belief". Such an interference is contrary to art. 9 unless it is „prescribed by law", directed at one or more of the legitimate aims in par. 2 and „necessary in a democratic society" for achieving them.

1. „Prescribed by law"

[37] The applicant said that his submissions relating to art. 7 also applied to the phrase „prescribed by law". The Court will therefore examine them from this point of view.

[38] Mr Kokkinakis impugned the very wording of sec. 4 of Law No. 1363/1938. He criticised the absence of any description of the objective substance" of the offence of proselytism. He thought this deliberate, as it would tend to make it possible for any kind of religious conversation or communication to be caught by the provision. He referred to the risk of „extendibility" by the police and often by the courts too of the vague terms of the section, such as „in particular" and „indirect attempt" to intrude on the religious beliefs of others. Punishing a non-Orthodox Christian even when he was offering „moral support or material assistance" was tantamount to punishing an act that any religion would prescribe and that the Criminal Code required in certain emergencies. Law no. 1672/1939 (see par. 16 above) had, without more, stripped the initial wording of sec. 4 of its „repetitive verbiage"; it had retained all the „ex-

tendible, catch-all" expressions, merely using a more concise but equally „pedantic" style designed to ensure that non-Orthodox Christians were permanently gagged. Consequently, no citizen could regulate his conduct on the basis of this enactment. Furthermore, sec. 4 of Law no. 1363/1938 was incompatible with art. 13 of the Constitution.

[39] The Government, on the other hand, maintained that sec. 4 defined proselytism precisely and specifically; it listed all the ingredients of the offence. The use of the adverbial phrase „in particular" was of no importance, as it related only to the means by which the offence could be committed; indicative lists of this kind were, moreover, commonly included in criminal statutes. Lastly, the objective substance of the offence was not lacking but consisted in the attempt to change the essentials of the religious beliefs of others.

[40] The Court has already noted that the wording of many statutes is not absolutely precise. The need to avoid excessive rigidity and to keep pace with changing circumstances means that many laws are inevitably couched in terms which, to a greater or lesser extent, are vague (see, for example and mutatis mutandis, the Müller and Others v. Switzerland judgment of 24 May 1988, Series A no. 133, p. 20, par. 29). Criminal-law provisions on proselytism fall within this category. The interpretation and application of such enactments depend on practice. In this instance there existed a body of settled national case-law (see par. 17-20 above). This case-law, which had been published and was accessible, supplemented the letter of sec. 4 and was such as to enable Mr Kokkinakis to regulate his conduct in the matter. As to the constitutionality of sec. 4 of Law no. 1363/1938, the Court reiterates that it is, in the first instance, for the national authorities, and in particular the courts, to interpret and apply domestic law (see, as the most recent authority, the Hadjianastassiou v. Greece judgment of 16 December 1992, Series A no. 252, p. 18, par. 42). And the Greek courts that have had to deal with the issue have ruled that there is no incompatibility (see par. 21 above).

[41] The measure complained of was therefore „prescribed by law" within the meaning of art. 9 par. 2 of the Convention.

2. Legitimate aim

[42] The Government contended that a democratic State had to ensure the peaceful enjoyment of the personal freedoms of all those living on its territory. If, in particular, it was not vigilant to protect a person's religious beliefs and dignity from attempts to influence them by immoral and deceitful means, art. 9 par. 2 would in practice be rendered wholly nugatory.

[43] In the applicant's submission, religion was part of the „constantly renewable flow of human thought" and it was impossible to conceive of its being excluded from public debate. A fair balance of personal rights

made it necessary to accept that others' thought should be subject to a minimum of influence, otherwise the result would be a „strange society of silent animals that [would] think but ... not express themselves, that [would] talk but ... not communicate, and that [would] exist but ... not coexist".

[44] Having regard to the circumstances of the case and the actual terms of the relevant courts' decisions, the Court considers that the impugned measure was in pursuit of a legitimate aim under art. 9-2, namely the protection of the rights and freedoms of others, relied on by the Government.

3. „Necessary in a democratic society"

[45] Mr Kokkinakis did not consider it necessary in a democratic society to prohibit a fellow citizen's right to speak when he came to discuss religion with his neighbour. He was curious to know how a discourse delivered with conviction and based on holy books common to all Christians could infringe the rights of others. Mrs Kyriakaki was an experienced adult woman with intellectual abilities; it was not possible, without flouting fundamental human rights, to make it a criminal offence for a Jehovah's Witness to have a conversation with a cantor's wife. Moreover, the Crete Court of Appeal, although the facts before it were precise and absolutely clear, had not managed to determine the direct or indirect nature of the applicant's attempt to intrude on the complainant's religious beliefs; its reasoning showed that it had convicted the applicant „not for something he had done but for what he was".

The Commission accepted this argument in substance.

[46] The Government maintained, on the contrary, that the Greek courts had based themselves on plain facts which amounted to the offence of proselytism: Mr Kokkinakis's insistence on entering Mrs Kyriakaki's home on a false pretext; the way in which he had approached her in order to gain her trust; and his „skilful" analysis of the Holy Scriptures calculated to „delude" the complainant, who did not possess any „adequate grounding in doctrine" (see par. 9-10 above). They pointed out that if the State remained indifferent to attacks on freedom of religious belief, major unrest would be caused that would probably disturb the social peace.

[47] The Court has consistently held that a certain margin of appreciation is to be left to the Contracting States in assessing the existence and extent of the necessity of an interference, but this margin is subject to European supervision, embracing both the legislation and the decisions applying it, even those given by an independent court. The Court's task is to determine whether the measures taken at national level were justified in principle and proportionate. In order to rule on this latter point, the Court must weigh the requirements of the protection of the rights

and liberties of others against the conduct of which the applicant stood accused. In exercising its supervisory jurisdiction, the Court must look at the impugned judicial decisions against the background of the case as a whole (see, inter alia and mutatis mutandis, the Barfod v. Denmark judgment of 22 February 1989, Series A no. 149, p. 12, par. 28).

[48] First of all, a distinction has to be made between bearing Christian witness and improper proselytism. The former corresponds to true evangelism, which a report drawn up in 1956 under the auspices of the World Council of Churches describes as an essential mission and a responsibility of every Christian and every Church. The latter represents a corruption or deformation of it. It may, according to the same report, take the form of activities offering material or social advantages with a view to gaining new members for a Church or exerting improper pressure on people in distress or in need; it may even entail the use of violence or brainwashing; more generally, it is not compatible with respect for the freedom of thought, conscience and religion of others. Scrutiny of sec. 4 of Law no. 1363/1938 shows that the relevant criteria adopted by the Greek legislature are reconcilable with the foregoing if and in so far as they are designed only to punish improper proselytism, which the Court does not have to define in the abstract in the present case.

[49] The Court notes, however, that in their reasoning the Greek courts established the applicant's liability by merely reproducing the wording of sec. 4 and did not sufficiently specify in what way the accused had attempted to convince his neighbour by improper means. None of the facts they set out warrants that finding. That being so, it has not been shown that the applicant's conviction was justified in the circumstances of the case by a pressing social need. The contested measure therefore does not appear to have been proportionate to the legitimate aim pursued or, consequently, „necessary in a democratic society ... for the protection of the rights and freedoms of others".

[50] In conclusion, there has been a breach of art. 9 of the Convention.

II. Alleged violation of Art. 7

(...)

[53] In conclusion, there has been no breach of art. 7 of the Convention.

III. Alleged violation of Art. 9

[54] The applicant further relied on his freedom of expression, as secured in art. 9. His conviction, he said, struck not only at the dissemination of his religious opinions but also at that of general sociophilosophical opinions, since the Crete Court of Appeal had noted that he had talked to Mrs Kyriakaki about the politician Olof Palme and had expounded pacifist views.

[55] Having regard to its decision on art. 9 (see par. 50 above), the Court, like the Commission, considers it unnecessary to examine this complaint.

IV. Alleged violation of Art. 14 taken together with Art. 9

[56] In his memorial of 5 August 1992 the applicant also claimed to be the victim of discrimination contrary to art. 14 taken together with art. 9. He submitted that discrimination arose from the defects in sec. 4 of Law no. 1363/1938 or from the use made of it.

[57] Although not raised before the Commission, this complaint relates to the same facts as do those made under art. 7 and 9; having regard to the conclusion in par. 50 above, however, the Court holds that it is unnecessary to deal with it.

V. Application of Art. 50 (...)

For these reasons the Court
1. *Holds by six votes to three that there has been a breach of art. 9;*
2. *Holds by eight votes to one that there has been no breach of art. 7;*
3. *Holds unanimously that it is unnecessary to examine the case under art. 9 or under art. 14 taken together with art. 9;*

In accordance with art. 51 par. 2 of the Convention and Rule 53 par. 2 of the Rules of Court, the following separate opinions are annexed to this judgment:
(a) partly concurring opinion of Mr Pettiti;
(b) concurring opinion of Mr De Meyer;
(c) dissenting opinion of Mr Valticos;
(d) partly dissenting opinion of Mr Martens;
(e) joint dissenting opinion of Mr Foighel and Mr Loizou.
(...)

PARTLY CONCURRING OPINION OF JUDGE PETTITI

I was in the majority which voted that there had been a breach of art. 9 but I considered that the reasoning given in the judgment could usefully have been expanded.

Furthermore, I parted company with the majority in that I also took the view that the current criminal legislation in Greece on proselytism was in itself contrary to art. 9.

The Kokkinakis case is of particular importance. It is the first real case concerning freedom of religion to have come before the European Court since it was set up and it has come up for decision at a time when the United Nations and Unesco are preparing a World Year for Tolerance, which is to give further effect to the 1981 United Nations Declaration against all forms of intolerance, which was adopted after twenty years of negotiations.

In the first place, I take the view that what contravenes art. 9 is the Law. I agree with acknowledging its foreseeability. But the definition is such as to make it possible at any moment to punish the slightest attempt by anyone to convince a person he is addressing.

The reasoning adopted by the majority with the intention of confining themselves to the particular case is tantamount to supervising the national court in respect of the degree of severity of the sentence passed, whereas what is in issue is the very principle of the punishment and it is not the European Court's function to rule on the degree of severity of sentences in domestic law. The Court must abide by its decisions in the cases of Dudgeon v. the United Kingdom (judgment of 22 October 1981, Series A no. 45, pp. 18-19, par. 41) and Norris v. Ireland (judgment of 26 October 1988, Series A no. 142, p. 16, par. 33): the mere threat of applying a provision, even one that has fallen into disuse, is sufficient to constitute a breach.

The expression „proselytism that is not respectable", which is a criterion used by the Greek courts when applying the Law, is sufficient for the enactment and the case-law applying it to be regarded as contrary to art. 9.

The Government themselves recognised that the applicant had been prosecuted because he had tried to influence the person he was talking to by taking advantage of her inexperience in matters of doctrine and by exploiting her low intellect. It was therefore not a question of protecting others against physical or psychological coercion but of giving the State the possibility of arrogating to itself the right to assess a person's weakness in order to punish a proselytiser, an interference that could become dangerous if resorted to by an authoritarian State.

The vagueness of the charge and the lack of any clear definition of proselytism increase the misgivings to which the Greek Law gives rise. Even if it is accepted that the foreseeability of the law in Greece as it might apply to proselytes was sufficient, the fact remains that the haziness of the definition leaves too wide a margin of interpretation for determining criminal penalties.

It may be asked whether the very principle of applying a criminal statute to proselytism is compatible with art. 9 of the Convention.

Criminal policy could be implemented by means of the technique of creating specific criminal offences covering coercive acts and the activities of certain sects which truly attack human freedom and dignity. Minors can be protected by means of precise criminal provisions. The protection of adults can be achieved by fiscal and welfare legislation and by the ordinary law on misrepresentation, failure to assist persons in danger and intentional or negligent injury (even physical).

At all events, even if the principle is accepted, it should not lead to the retention of legislation that provides for vague criminal offences which leave it to the court's subjective assessment whether a defendant is convicted or acquitted. In its judgment in the Lingens v. Austria case (8 July 1986, Series A no. 103) concerning freedom of expression the European Court noted its misgivings about the freedom left to the courts to assess the concept of truth.

Interpretation criteria in relation to proselytism that are as unverifiable as „respectable or not respectable" and „misplaced" cannot guarantee legal certainty.

Proselytism is linked to freedom of religion; a believer must be able to communicate his faith and his beliefs in the religious sphere as in the philosophical sphere. Freedom of religion and conscience is a fundamental right and this freedom must be able to be exercised for the benefit of all religions and not for the benefit of a single Church, even if this has traditionally been the established Church or „dominant religion".

Freedom of religion and conscience certainly entails accepting proselytism, even where it is „not respectable". Believers and agnostic philosophers have a right to expound their beliefs, to try to get other people to share them and even to try to convert those whom they are addressing.

The only limits on the exercise of this right are those dictated by respect for the rights of others where there is an attempt to coerce the person into consenting or to use manipulative techniques.

The other types of unacceptable behaviour - such as brainwashing, breaches of labour law, endangering of public health and incitement to immorality, which are found in the practices of certain pseudo-religious groups - must be punished in positive law as ordinary criminal offences. Proselytism cannot be forbidden under cover of punishing such activities.

Certainly proselytism must not be carried on by coercion or by unfair means that take advantage of minors or persons legally incapacitated under civil law, but such lapses can be alleviated by the ordinary civil and criminal law.

In the second place, even if the Court had not found a breach in respect of the statute, it could, in my opinion, have worded its decision differently by adding a few definitions so that the scope of the decision would be properly understood.

Commentators and the member States may regret that, on such a serious matter, on the eve of the United Nations World Year for Tolerance, and given the United Nations Declaration against religious intolerance, the Court has failed to make explicit its interpretation of proselytism in relation to freedom of religion under art. 9.

The reasoning could also have better reflected the fact that art. 9 applies also to non-religious philosophical beliefs and that the application of it must protect people from abuses by certain sects; but here it is for the States to legislate so that any deviation leading to attempts at brain-

washing are regulated by the ordinary law. Non-criminal proselytism
remains the main expression of freedom of religion. Attempting to make
converts is not in itself an attack on the freedom and beliefs of others or
an infringement of their rights.

The Government admitted that Law no. 1363/1938 had not been repealed after the adoption of the 1975 Constitution. They argued that several judgments of the Supreme Administrative Court had afforded religious freedom effective protection, but the fact remains that the courts
can always apply the Law in the same way as it was applied in the Kokkinakis case. The Strasbourg institutions cannot, however, monitor compatibility with art. 9 on the basis of the degree of severity and the proportionality of the penalty.

Even without criticising the Greek courts' decision in itself, in respect
of the content of the conversation and the verification of the evidence,
one may note that in the decisions no dividing line is drawn, in terms of
the law or the Constitution, between bearing witness, proclaiming one's
faith or religious persuasion, and coercion. The two dissenting judges in
the Greek courts drew attention to the thinness of the reasons given for
the decisions.

In his memorial in reply in the proceedings before the Commission, the
applicant made two significant points:

„1. The formal proclamation of freedom of conscience in religious matters and its
manifestations dates from after the prohibition of ‚proselytism‘ in the various
Constitutions. It was introduced in the Constitution of 3 June 1927 (art. 1 par. 1
(c)) and is included today among the ‚personal and social‘ fundamental rights
listed and, as in the Universal Declaration and the European Convention, specifically described as ‚human rights‘ (Constitution of 9 June 1975, art. 13 par. 1,
25 and 28. There is therefore an anomaly, if not a flagrant contradiction, in the
actual text of the Constitution. While the decrees of 1938-39 issued under the dictatorship aggravated matters by making convictions and the purely verbal exercise of a religion a criminal offence - for which no provision has ever been made
in criminal law (as already noted) -, there are cogent reasons for at last acknowledging that these provisions are incompatible with the letter and spirit of the
Constitution in force: the exercise or harmless expression or even the suspicion of
a sentiment which discloses a religious conviction - as in the Kokkinakis case -
cannot amount to an offence! This is how the Constitution should have been applied by the legislature and the administrative and judicial authorities. And this,
without any doubt, is above all how the European Convention must be obeyed,
and applied by its own institutions.
2. The respondent Government point to certain judicial decisions which they
claim show toleration of the existence and religious activities of believers other
than those of the Orthodox Church and, in an isolated case which is ultimately of
secondary importance, of an adherent of the religion professed by the applicant. It
will be noted, firstly, that the existence of such judgments in itself demonstrates
that there are intolerant administrative practices; secondly, that the cases in
point and the solutions adopted under liberal-sounding recitals are not identi-

fied; and thirdly, that no decision has been cited which repudiates this parasitic criminal legislation that allows of sporadic but none the less virulent persecution of non-Orthodox Christians, since unfortunately no such decision has ever been given. All the decisions have recognised the validity and applicability of the 1938 decrees.

There is no question of embarking here on a discussion of the Constitutional merits of ‚proselytism' in Greece as tendentiously defined in the emergency Laws of 1938/39, since the only issue arising before the European Convention institutions is whether the provisions of these enactments and the application made of them to the detriment of the applicant, until domestic remedies were exhausted, amount to breaches of the Convention for which the Greek Government are responsible."

The Greek Government relied on statements of principle supporting freedom of religion.

On this point the European Court's reasoning does not seem to me to provide sufficient criteria for assessing the relationship between legislation on proselytism and art. 9.

Spiritual, religious and philosophical convictions belong to the private sphere of beliefs and call into play the right to express and manifest them. Setting up a system of criminal prosecution and punishment without safeguards is a perilous undertaking, and the authoritarian regimes which, while proclaiming freedom of religion in their Constitutions, have restricted it by means of criminal offences of parasitism, subversion or proselytism have given rise to abuses with which we are all too familiar.

The wording adopted by the majority of the Court in finding a breach, namely that the applicant's conviction was not justified in the circumstances of the case, leaves too much room for a repressive interpretation by the Greek courts in the future, whereas public prosecution must likewise be monitored. In my view, it would have been possible to define impropriety, coercion and duress more clearly and to describe more satisfactorily, in the abstract, the full scope of religious freedom and bearing witness.

The forms of words used by the World Council of Churches, the Second Vatican Council, philosophers and sociologists when referring to coercion, abuse of one's own rights which infringes the rights of others and the manipulation of people by methods which lead to a violation of conscience, all make it possible to define any permissible limits of proselytism. They can provide the member States with positive material for giving effect to the Court's judgment in future and fully implementing the principle and standards of religious freedom under art. 9 of the European Convention.

CONCURRING OPINION OF JUDGE DE MEYER

Proselytism, defined as „zeal in spreading the faith" (Le Petit Robert, vol. 1, 1992 edition, p. 1552, cannot be punishable as such: it is a way - perfectly legitimate in itself - of „manifesting [one's] religion".

In the instant case the applicant was convicted only for having shown such zeal, without any impropriety on his part (par. 49 of the judgment; par. 71 and 73 of the Commission's report).

All that he could be accused of was that he had tried to get Mrs Kyriakaki to share his religious beliefs. Mrs Kyriakaki had let him into her house and there is nothing to show that she asked him at any point to leave; she preferred to listen to what he had to say (par. 9 and 10 of the judgment; par. 22-25 of the Commission's report), while awaiting the arrival of the police, who had been alerted by her husband, the cantor (par. 7 of the judgment; par. 21 of the Commission's report).

DISSENTING OPINION OF JUDGE VALTICOS

I regret that I cannot share the opinion of the majority of the Court and I regret just as much that they could not accept my view. My disagreement concerns both the scope of art. 9 and the assessment of the facts in this case.

As regards the scope of art. 9, I am unable to interpret the words „freedom, either alone or in community with others and in public or private, to manifest [one's] religion or belief, in worship, teaching, practice, and observance" as broadly as the majority do. As with all freedoms, everyone's freedom of religion must end where another person's begins. Freedom „either alone or in community with others and in public or private, to manifest [one's] religion", certainly means freedom to practise and manifest it, but not to attempt persistently to combat and alter the religion of others, to influence minds by active and often unreasonable propaganda. It is designed to ensure religious peace and tolerance, not to permit religious clashes and even wars, particularly at a time when many sects manage to entice simple, naïve souls by doubtful means. But even if the Chamber considers that such is not its purpose, that is, at all events, the direction in which its conception may lead.

At this stage a misunderstanding must be removed: it has been maintained that conversations during which a person merely sets out his religious beliefs cannot constitute an attack on the religion of others. In reality, the position in the instant case is quite different. In another case being heard by another Chamber (the Hoffmann case [Hoffmann v. Austria judgment of 23 June 1993, Series A no. 255-C, KirchE-EU S. 232]) the Commission states in its report (par. 27) that the complainant, who is also a Jehovah's Witness, made visits once a week to spread her faith. In the case of this sect, therefore, what is involved is indeed a systematic attempt at conversion, and consequently an attack on the religious beliefs of others. That has nothing to do with art. 9, which is designed solely to protect the religion of individuals and not their right to attack that of others.

I may add that the term „teaching" in art. 9 undoubtedly refers to religious teaching in school curricula or in religious institutions, and not to personal door-to-door canvassing as in the present case.

This brings me to the present case.

There are three aspects to it: national law, the facts properly speaking and the court decisions.

First of all, the Law: is it precise or does it contain an element of ambiguity, of excessive generality, which might allow of arbitrariness in the application of it as a criminal statute? In my view, there is no room for doubt. The Law deals with, as an offence, „proselytism", which is of course a Greek word and, like so many others, has passed into English and also into French, and which the Petit Robert dictionary defines as „zeal in spreading the faith, and by extension in making converts, winning adherents". This is a far cry from merely manifesting one's belief, as covered by art. 9. Someone who proselytises seeks to convert others; he does not confine himself to affirming his faith but seeks to change that of others to his own. And the Petit Robert clarifies its explanation by giving the following quotation from Paul Valéry: „I consider it unworthy to want others to be of one's own opinion. Proselytism astonishes me."

Whereas the term „proselytism" would, in my view, have sufficed to define the offence and to satisfy the principle that an offence must be defined in law, Greek criminal law, for the avoidance of any ambiguity, gives an illustration of it which, while intended as an explanation and an example (no doubt the commonest one), none the less constitutes a meaningful definition, and that is: „By ‚proselytism' is meant, in particular, any direct or indirect attempt to intrude on the religious beliefs of a person of a different religious persuasion, with the aim of undermining those beliefs, either by any kind of inducement or promise of an inducement or moral support or material assistance, or by fraudulent means or by taking advantage of his inexperience, trust, need, low intellect or naïvety."

This definition of, if one may so term it, rape of the beliefs of others cannot in any way be regarded as contrary to art. 9 of the Convention. On the contrary, it is such as to protect individuals' freedom of religious belief.

Let us look now at the facts of the case. On the one hand, we have a militant Jehovah's Witness, a hardbitten adept of proselytism, a specialist in conversion, a martyr of the criminal courts whose earlier convictions have served only to harden him in his militancy, and, on the other hand, the ideal victim, a naïve woman, the wife of a cantor in the Orthodox Church (if he manages to convert her, what a triumph!). He swoops on her, trumpets that he has good news for her (the play on words is obvious, but no doubt not to her), manages to get himself let in and, as an experienced commercial traveller and cunning purveyor of a faith he wants to spread, expounds to her his intellectual wares cunningly wrapped up in a mantle of universal peace and radiant happiness. Who, indeed, would not like peace and happiness? But is this the mere exposition of Mr Kokkinakis's beliefs or is it not rather an attempt to beguile the simple soul of the cantor's wife? Does the Convention afford its protection to such undertakings? Certainly not.

One further detail must be provided. The Greek Law does not in any way restrict the concept of proselytism to attempts at the intellectual corruption of Orthodox Christians but applies irrespective of the religion concerned. Admittedly, the Government's representative was not able to give concrete examples concerning other religions, but that is not surprising since the Orthodox religion is the religion of nearly the whole population and sects are going to fish for followers in the best-stocked waters.

Probably in recent years there have been rather too many prosecutions and the police have been rather too active, but more recently there has been a substantial drop in the number of such prosecutions, and in the present case there was no official prosecution - it was the victim's husband who, on returning home and discovering what the home preacher was up to, raised his voice, which was a strong one, to call the police.

I should certainly be inclined to recommend the Government to give instructions that prosecutions should be avoided where harmless conversations are involved, but not in the case of systematic, persistent campaigns entailing actions bordering on unlawful entry.

That having been said, I do not consider in any way that there has been a breach of the Convention.

PS. Having read certain separate opinions annexed to the judgment, I must express my regret at a number of exaggerations which go so far as to make reference to totalitarian regimes.

I should also like to sound a note of caution with regard to the opinion that „attempting to make converts is not in itself an attack on the freedom and beliefs of others or an infringement of their rights". Certainly that is an expression of moderation and common sense and the Chamber (perhaps even the plenary Court should have dealt with it) very rightly warned against abuses where proselytism is concerned. But faith can sometimes be blind and attempts to spread it can be overzealous. Acts of faith have sometimes culminated in autos-dafé and questioning on the subject has led to inquisitions, while the names of certain saints have remained associated with excesses committed on their feast days. In matters of faith as in so many other matters, respect for the human person must always be upheld.

At a time when sects enjoying varying degrees of recognition and, sometimes, even adherents of recognised religions resort, under the in-

fluence of fanaticism, to all kinds of tactics to obtain conversions, sometimes with tragic results, as has been seen again recently, it is regrettable that the above judgment should allow proselytising activities on condition only that they should not be „improper". Can a convention on human rights really authorise such an intrusion on people's beliefs, even
where it is not a forceful one?

PARTLY DISSENTING OPINION OF JUDGE MARTENS

Introduction

[1] I concur with the Court that there has been a breach of art. 9, but
for reasons other than those relied on by the Court. I moreover differ
from the Court in that I consider that there has been a breach of art. 7 as
well.

[2] I likewise agree with the Court that the art. 9 issue is by far the
more important one, and I would have welcomed it if the Court had held
- as, in my judgment, it could very well have done - that in view of its
findings with respect to art. 9 it was not necessary to examine the applicant's complaints under art. 7. I would have preferred the Court to have
chosen that course, since that would have enabled me to follow suit;
whereas now, being unable to agree with the Court's findings with respect to art. 7, I am bound to discuss whether that article has been violated by the wording or the application of a criminal provision the very
existence of which, in my opinion, violates art. 9. However theoretical
such an exercise may seem, it cannot be escaped. And since it may serve
as an introduction to my discussion of the art. 9 issue, I will start with
explaining my position with regard to art. 7.

[3] Before doing so I would, however, point out that although both parties have - rightly - elevated the debate to the plane of important principle, it should not be forgotten that what occasioned this debate was a
normal and perfectly inoffensive call by two elderly Jehovah's Witnesses
(the applicant was 77 at the time) trying to sell some of the sect's booklets to a lady who, instead of closing the door, allowed the old couple entry, either because she was no match for their insistence or because she
believed them to be bringing tidings from relatives on the mainland.
There is no trace of violence or of anything that could properly be styled
„coercion"; at the worst there was a trivial lie. If resort to criminal law
was at all warranted, a prosecution for disturbance of domestic peace
would seem the severest possible response.

Has Art. 7 been violated?

[4] In general I subscribe to what the Court says about art. 7 in the
first part of par. 50 of its judgment, albeit that, unlike the Court, I think

that the requirement that a legal definition of a crime be drafted as precisely as possible is not a consequence but part and parcel of the principle enshrined in art. 7 par. 1. I am, furthermore, convinced that this requirement serves not only (as the Court suggests in the second part of par. 50) the aim of enabling the individual to know „what acts and omissions will make him liable", but is intended - in accordance with its historical origin - also and primarily to secure the individual adequate protection against arbitrary prosecution and conviction: art. 7 par. 1 demands that criminal law should be compatible with the rule of law.

[5] The more I have thought about it, the less I have remained satisfied that sec. 4 of Law no. 1363/1938 defines the offence of proselytism with the degree of precision required by art. 7 thus understood. The first - and, as regards protection against arbitrariness, the most suspect - imprecision lies in the words „in particular": those words virtually permit prosecution for acts that fall outside the definition given. Secondly, the punishable act (as defined) is not „intrusion on the religious beliefs" (whatever that may be), but „any direct or indirect attempt" at such intrusion, which not only considerably broadens the definition but also greatly enhances its essential vagueness. A final point to note is the dangerous ambiguity of the requirement „with the aim of undermining those beliefs": is it at all possible to distinguish between proclaiming one's own faith to others and trying to convince those others that their tenets are „wrong"? These deficiencies are such that, in an atmosphere of religious intolerance, sec. 4 of Law no. 1363/1938 provides a perfect and dangerous instrument for repressing heterodox minorities. The file suggests that in the past it has indeed been used for this purpose, whilst at present such use, to put it mildly, does not seem to be wholly excluded. This aspect is all the more serious as the present situation in the south-eastern part of Europe shows that the region is not at all immune to the rise of fierce religious intolerance which is sweeping over our modern world. This is why I am not impressed by the argument that the above deficiencies of the text are „cured" by case-law, especially of the highest Greek courts. It may be, for instance, that since 1975 the Court of Cassation, reversing its former case-law, has eliminated the consequence of the words „in particular" and that the Supreme Administrative Court's definition at least endeavours to take into account the above distinction between proclaiming one's religion and trying to convince another of the shallowness of his own tenets. However, recent history has taught us that if the political or religious atmosphere in a country changes, the case-law of even the highest courts may change too. Such case-law cannot, therefore, supplement guarantees against arbitrariness which the text of the law does not provide.

[6] As the Court points out, art. 7 par. 1 also enshrines the principle that criminal law should be restrictively interpreted. This principle fulfils the role of a secondary safeguard against arbitrariness. Accordingly,

the broader and vaguer the text of the relevant provision, the more important this secondary safeguard. The more important also the supervision by the Convention institutions. As the Commission has consistently stated, the Convention institutions are empowered under art. 7 par. 1 to verify whether, on the facts of the case, the national courts could reasonably have arrived at a conviction under the applicable rule of municipal law: the Convention bodies have to be satisfied that the conviction not only was based on a pre-existing (and sufficiently precisely worded) provision of criminal law but also was compatible with the principle of restrictive interpretation of criminal legislation. The greater the doubt of the Convention institutions as to whether the provision applied meets the requirement of precision, the stricter should be their supervision of its application.

[7] In the present case the applicant complained of „what he claimed to be the wrongful application to him of sec. 4 of Law no. 1363/1938". One of the points in issue was whether the facts established against the applicant justified a conviction under that section (see par. 60 of the Commission's report). It is true that this issue was addressed mainly in the context of art. 9, but, the Court being master of the legal characterisation to be given to the facts before it, there is room for scrutinising whether or not the Greek courts did respect the principle of restrictive interpretation of criminal legislation.

[8] Let me say at once that upon examination of (the translations of) the full texts of the judgments of the Greek courts submitted by the parties, I have come to the conclusion that this question must be answered in the negative. Before developing the three grounds on which my conclusion is mainly based, I cannot help noting one telling, but in the present context immaterial, feature of the file: although both the applicant and his wife have consistently denied the version of the facts given by Mrs Kyriakaki, his conviction was primarily, and without more, based on that version and consequently rests for all practical purposes on the testimony of one sole witness.

[9] The first ground referred to above concerns the following. Sec. 4 of Law no. 1363/1938 requires an intention to convert the victim to the perpetrator's beliefs (as the word „proselytism" implies), or at least to undermine the victim's beliefs. The applicant, however, denied having had that intention. He pointed out that his intention was merely to „witness", that is to proclaim the gospel as understood by his sect. There is, of course, a fundamental and in the present context crucial difference between, on the one hand, acquainting someone with an opinion or a belief and, on the other hand, trying to convince him of its truth. The Greek courts simply ignored this difference, not even troubling to state on what evidence they based their opinion - which is necessarily implied in their finding the applicant guilty of „proselytism" - that he intended to convince Mrs Kyriakaki of the rightness of his beliefs and of the wrongness

of hers. The inevitable conclusion must therefore be that the applicant's conviction was based on the view that the mere proclaiming of religious beliefs differing from those of the person addressed implies intention to convert within the meaning of sec. 4. This is, however, clearly incompatible with the principle of restrictive interpretation of criminal legislation.

[10] My second ground concerns a related point. The relevant judgments reveal that the Greek courts had no more than an extremely vague notion of what the applicant exactly had said to Mrs Kyriakaki. From what both Mrs Kyriakaki and her eavesdropping husband testified before the magistrates at first instance it might be inferred that the applicant had somehow referred to the coming of the heavenly kingdom. On appeal, however, Mrs Kyriakaki could not remember whether this was mentioned and neither did her husband give any particulars about what he had overheard. The evidence included an equally vague reference to the paradise story and Mrs Kyriakaki's testimony that „they talked to me about Christ". One is forced to question how the Greek courts were able to conclude, as they did, that the applicant (intentionally) attempted to make Mrs Kyriakaki change her beliefs without establishing - at the very least - what exactly he had said to her and that what he had told her was incompatible with what she believed. Here again I find that in juxtaposing the facts with the text of sec. 4 one cannot but conclude that the applicant's conviction is incompatible with the principle of restrictive interpretation of criminal legislation.

[11] My third and final ground corresponds to the criticism expressed by the anonymous dissenters in the Greek courts: the sole evidence for the applicant's (intentionally) taking advantage of Mrs Kyriakaki's „inexperience, her low intellect and her naïvety" (as the Crete Court of Appeal put it) was her testimony that she did not fully understand everything that the applicant read to her and told her. On appeal she even said in so many words: „They talked to me about things I did not understand very well." This sufficed for the Greek courts to hold that the applicant had (intentionally) „abused" Mrs Kyriakaki's „inexperience in doctrine" and „exploited" „her spiritual naïvety" (as the Court of Cassation put it). That can only mean that the applicant's conviction was based on the view that the mere proclaiming of one's faith to a heterodox person whose experience in religious matters or whose mental capacities are less than those of the proclaimer makes the latter guilty under sec. 4. Again one is forced to conclude that the manner in which the Greek courts applied sec. 4 was incompatible with the principle of restrictive interpretation of criminal legislation.

[12] My conclusion is that sec. 4 of Law no. 1363/1938 is per se incompatible with art. 7 par. 1 of the Convention and that its application in the present case has given rise to a further violation of that article.

Has Art. 9 been violated?

[13] The Court's judgment touches only incidentally on the question which, in my opinion, is the crucial one in this case: does art. 9 allow member States to make it a criminal offence to attempt to induce somebody to change his religion? From what it said in par. 40-42 and 46 it is clear that the Court answers this question in the affirmative. My answer is in the negative.

[14] The basic principle in human rights is respect for human dignity and human freedom. Essential for that dignity and that freedom are the freedoms of thought, conscience and religion enshrined in art. 9 par. 1. Accordingly, they are absolute. The Convention leaves no room whatsoever for interference by the State. These absolute freedoms explicitly include freedom to change one's religion and beliefs. Whether or not somebody intends to change religion is no concern of the State's and, consequently, neither in principle should it be the State's concern if somebody attempts to induce another to change his religion.

[15] There were good reasons for laying down in art. 9 that freedom of religion includes freedom to teach one's religion: many religious faiths count teaching the faith amongst the principal duties of believers. Admittedly, such teaching may gradually shade off into proselytising. It is true, furthermore, that proselytising creates a possible „conflict" between two subjects of the right to freedom of religion: it sets the rights of those whose religious faith encourages or requires such activity against the rights of those targeted to maintain their beliefs. In principle, however, it is not within the province of the State to interfere in this „conflict" between proselytiser and proselytised. Firstly, because - since respect for human dignity and human freedom implies that the State is bound to accept that in principle everybody is capable of determining his fate in the way that he deems best - there is no justification for the State to use its power „to protect" the proselytised (it may be otherwise in very special situations in which the State has a particular duty of care, but such situations fall outside the present issue). Secondly, because even the „public order" argument cannot justify use of coercive State power in a field where tolerance demands that „free argument and debate" should be decisive. And thirdly, because under the Convention all religions and beliefs should, as far as the State is concerned, be equal. That is also true in a State where, as in the present case, one particular religion has a dominant position: as the drafting history of art. 9 confirms (see, for example, La Convention européenne des Droits de l'Homme, by J. Velu and R. Ergec, Bruylant, 1990, p. 581, par. 708), the fact of one religion having a special position under national law is immaterial to the State's obligation under that article. To allow States to interfere in the „conflict" implied in proselytising by making proselytising a criminal offence would not only run counter to the strict neutrality which the State is required

to maintain in this field but also create the danger of discrimination when there is one dominant religion. The latter point is tellingly illustrated by the file that was before the Court.

[16] In this context the Court suggests that some forms of proselytism are „proper" while others are „improper" and therefore may be criminalised (par. 48). Admittedly, the freedom to proselytise may be abused, but the crucial question is whether that justifies enacting a criminal-law provision generally making punishable what the State considers improper proselytism. There are at least two reasons for answering that question in the negative. The first is that the State, being bound to strict neutrality in religious matters, lacks the necessary touchstone and therefore should not set itself up as the arbiter for assessing whether particular religious behaviour is „proper" or „improper". The absence of such a touchstone cannot be made good (as the Court attempts to do) by resorting to the quasi-neutral test whether or not the proselytism in question is „compatible with respect for the freedom of thought, conscience and religion of others". This is because that very absence implies that the State is lacking intrinsic justification for attributing greater value to the freedom not to be proselytised than to the right to proselytise and, consequently, for introducing a criminal-law provision protecting the former at the cost of the latter. The second reason is that the rising tide of religious intolerance makes it imperative to keep the State's powers in this field within the strictest possible boundaries. However, the Court achieves quite the reverse in attempting to settle those boundaries by means of so elusive a notion as „improper proselytism", a definition of which the Court does not even attempt to give.

[17] Should the judgment be otherwise where proselytism is combined with „coercion"? I do not think so. Coercion in the present context does not refer to conversion by coercion, for people who truly believe do not change their beliefs as a result of coercion; what we are really contemplating is coercion in order to make somebody join a denomination and its counterpart, coercion to prevent somebody from leaving a denomination. Even in such a case of „coercion for religious purposes" it is in principle for those concerned to help themselves. Accordingly, if there is to be a legal remedy, it should be a civil-law remedy. The strict neutrality which the State is bound to observe in religious matters excludes interference in this conflict by means of criminal law. Unless, of course, the coercion, apart from its purpose, constitutes an ordinary crime, such as physical assault. In such cases the State may, of course, prosecute under the applicable provision of (ordinary) criminal law and a defence based on freedom to proselytise may properly be rejected if that freedom is clearly abused. There is, however, no justification for making coercion in religious matters a criminal offence per se.

[18] Is there no such justification even for making proselytism practised by means of serious forms of spiritual coercion a criminal offence?

Cannot such justification be found in the methods of conversion used by some of the numerous new sects which have emerged these last decades, methods which are often said to be akin to brainwashing? Should not the State be entitled to protect its citizens - and especially its minors - against such methods? Even if the use of such objectionable methods of proselytising had been established, I would have hesitated to answer this question in the affirmative, since it is evidently difficult to establish where spiritual means of conversion cross the borderline between insistent and intensive teaching, which should be allowed, and spiritual coercion akin to brainwashing. I am not satisfied, however, that the existence of such offensive methods has been established. In 1984 the author of a study on these new sects, made at the request of the Netherlands Parliament, concluded after extensive research that, as far as the Netherlands were concerned, there was no such evidence. The author stressed that everywhere the new sects had provoked violent reactions including persistent allegations about such methods, but that Governments had up till then declined to take measures. I would add that there probably are methods of spiritual coercion akin to brainwashing which arguably fall within the ambit of art. 3 of the Convention and should therefore be prohibited by making their use an offence under ordinary criminal law. But in this context also I would stress that there is no justification for making a special provision in the law for cases where such methods are used for the purpose of proselytising.

[19] To summarise: even if the Government's thesis that sec. 4 of Law no. 1363/1938 is intended to prevent conversions being made by coercion were compatible with the wording of that provision (which it is not), that justification would fail.

[20] For these reasons I find that Greece, which, as far as I have been able to ascertain, is the only member State to have made proselytism a criminal offence per se, in so doing has violated art. 9 of the Convention.

JOINT DISSENTING OPINION OF JUDGES FOIGHEL AND LOIZOU

We regret that we are unable to agree with the opinion of the majority of the Court as we take a different approach to the issues raised in this case. Art. 9 par. 1 guarantees to everyone the right to freedom of thought, conscience and religion; this right includes freedom to change one's religion or belief and freedom, either alone or in community with others and in public or private, to manifest one's religion or belief, in worship, teaching, practice and observance. We are concerned here with the freedom one has to teach one's own religion.

The relevant Greek law making proselytism a criminal offence reads as follows:

„By ‚proselytism' is meant, in particular, any direct or indirect attempt to intrude on the religious beliefs of a person of a different religious persuasion, with the aim of undermining those beliefs, either by any kind of inducement or promise of an inducement or moral support or material assistance, or by fraudulent means or by taking advantage of his inexperience, trust, need, low intellect or naïvety."

This definition of the offence of „proselytism" cannot, in our view, be considered to constitute a violation of art. 9 par. 1. It is only when it takes this kind of intrusive form as opposed to genuine, open and straightforward teaching of a religion that it is a criminal offence.

The term „teach" entails openness and uprightness and the avoidance of the use of devious or improper means or false pretexts as in this case in order to gain access to a person's home and, once there, by abusing the courtesy and hospitality extended, take advantage of the ignorance or inexperience in theological doctrine of someone who has no specialist training and try to get that person to change his or her religion.

This is all the more so as the term „teach" has to be read in the context of the whole art. 9 and in conjunction with the limitations prescribed by par. 2, in particular that of the protection of the rights and freedoms of others, which no doubt includes a duty imposed on those who are engaged in teaching their religion to respect that of others. Religious tolerance implies respect for the religious beliefs of others.

One cannot be deemed to show respect for the rights and freedoms of others if one employs means that are intended to entrap someone and dominate his mind in order to convert him. This is impermissible in the civilised societies of the Contracting States. The persistent efforts of some fanatics to convert others to their own beliefs by using unacceptable psychological techniques on people, which amount in effect to coercion, cannot in our view come within the ambit of the natural meaning of the term „teach" to be found in par. 1 of this article.

For the above reasons we find in the circumstances of this case that there has been no breach of art. 9.

39

Kann die Zugehörigkeit eines Ehegatten zur Religionsgemeinschaft der Zeugen Jehovas einer Übertragung des Sorgerechts für die gemeinsamen Kinder nach Ehescheidung entgegenstehen?

Art. 8, 8, 14 EMRK, 2 Erstes Zusatzprotokoll
EGMR, Urteil vom 23. Juni 1993 - No. 15/1992/360/434
(Hoffmann ./. Österreich)[1] -

---

[1] Ser. A 255-C; EuGRZ 1996, 648; ÖJZ 1993, 853.

AS TO THE FACTS

I. The particular circumstances of the case

A. Introduction

[6] Mrs Ingrid Hoffmann is an Austrian citizen residing in G. She is a housewife.

[7] In 1980 Mrs Hoffmann - then Miss Berger - married Mr S., a telephone technician. At that time, they were both Roman Catholics. Two children were born to them, a son, Martin, in 1980 and a daughter, Sandra, in 1982. They were baptised as Roman Catholics.

[8] The applicant left the Roman Catholic Church to become a Jehovah's Witness.

[9] On 17 October 1983 the applicant instituted divorce proceedings against Mr S. She left him in August or September 1984 while the proceedings were still pending, taking the children with her. The divorce was pronounced on 12 June 1986.

B. Proceedings before the Innsbruck District Court

[10] Following their separation, both the applicant and Mr S. applied to the Innsbruck District Court (Bezirksgericht) to be granted parental rights (Elternrechte) over the children. Mr S. submitted that if the children were left in the applicant's care, there was a risk that they would be brought up in a way that would do them harm. He claimed that the educational principles of the religious denomination to which the applicant belonged were hostile to society, in that they discouraged all intercourse with non-members, all expressions of patriotism (such as singing the national anthem) and religious tolerance. All this would lead to the children's social isolation. In addition, the Jehovah's Witnesses' ban on blood transfusions might give rise to situations in which their life or their health was endangered. With regard to the son, Martin, Mr S. noted that he would eventually have to refuse to perform military service or even the civilian service exacted in its stead. The applicant claimed that she was better placed to take care of the children, being in a position to devote herself to them completely, and as a mother better able to provide them with the necessary family environment. She alleged that Mr S. did not even provide for their maintenance, as he was both legally and morally bound to do. She acknowledged, however, that she intended to bring the children up in her own faith. The youth office of the Innsbruck District Authority (Bezirkshauptmannschaft, Abteilung Jugendfürsorge) expressed a preference for granting parental rights to the applicant; it referred to, inter alia, the expert opinion of a child psychologist.

[11] By decision of 8 January 1986, the District Court granted parental rights to the applicant and denied them to Mr S. According to its reasoning, only the children's well-being fell to be considered. The material living conditions of both parents were such that either of them would be able to take proper care of the children; however, the father would need his mother's help. The children had stronger emotional ties with the applicant, having lived with her for a year and a half already, and separating them from her might cause them psychological harm. It followed that it was preferable to leave the children with the mother.

The District Court further observed:

> „*As against this, it has been stated by the children's father, essentially as his only argument, that Ingrid S.'s membership of the religious community of the Jehovah's Witnesses has serious detrimental effects on the children. As to this, it ought to be made clear right away that in no case are parents' religious convictions as such a relevant criterion in deciding on parental rights and duties pursuant to art. 177 par. 2 of the Civil Code. These rights cannot be refused to a parent or withheld from him for the sole reason that he or she belongs to a religious minority.*
>
> *However, in the concrete case it needs to be examined whether the mother's religious convictions have a negative influence on her upbringing of the children which should be taken into account and whether their well-being is impaired as a result. It appears in particular that Ingrid S. would not allow blood transfusions to be given to her children; that for herself she rejects communal celebration of such customary holidays as Christmas or Easter; that the children experience a certain tension in relation to an environment which does not correspond to their faith; and that their integration in societal institutions such as kindergarten and school is made more difficult. However, the father's apprehension of complete social isolation as a result of the mother's religion does not appear well-founded in the light of the established facts. In addition, no possible dangers to either child's development have appeared in the course of the establishment of the facts.*
>
> *It is true that the facts adduced (blood transfusions, holidays, impaired social integration) are in principle capable of having detrimental effects on the children. This point must now be examined in the context of the particular case. It appears first of all that the father's argument that Martin and Sandra would be exposed in an emergency to serious danger to their life and health by the refusal of a blood transfusion is not of decisive importance. In the absence of parental permission for a medically necessary blood transfusion to either child, such permission can be replaced by a judicial decision in accordance with art. 176 of the Civil Code (compare the decision of the Innsbruck Regional Court (Landesgericht) of 3 July 1979, 4R 128/79). In any case, according to this legal provision, anyone can apply to the court for an order that is necessary to ensure the welfare of the child when the parent endangers it by his conduct. In view of this possibility of applying to the court, which is available at all times, no danger to the children need be inferred from the mother's attitude to blood transfusions.*
>
> *As for Ingrid S.'s rejection of holidays, notice must be taken of her express agreement to allow the father to take the children on such occasions and celebrate them with the children as he sees fit. The mother's religious convictions thus do not deprive Martin and Sandra of the possibility of celebrating these holidays in*

the usual way, so that no detriment to the children can be found in this regard either.

Of the reservations with regard to the mother's upbringing of the children resulting from her religion the only remaining one of any significance is the circumstance that Martin and Sandra will in later life experience somewhat more difficulty in finding their way in social groups as a result of the religious precepts of the Jehovah's Witnesses and will find themselves to some extent in a special position. However, the court cannot consider this so detrimental to the children's welfare that they should for that reason not be entrusted to their mother, with whom they have such a close psychological relationship and to whose care they are accustomed. Careful consideration must lead to the conclusion that in spite of more difficult social integration, as discussed above, it appears to be more in the interest of the children's welfare to grant parental rights to the mother than to transfer them to the father."

C. Proceedings before the Innsbruck Regional Court

[12] Mr S. appealed against the above decision to the Innsbruck Regional Court (Landesgericht).

[13] The Regional Court rejected the appeal by decision of 14 March 1986. Its grounds for so doing were the following:

„The main thrust of the appeal is to argue that the decision of the first-instance court is incompatible with the children's welfare in view of the mother's membership of the religious community of the Jehovah's Witnesses. In this connection, the appellant discusses the criteria and objectives peculiar to that religious community and the resulting social attitudes, which are in his opinion wrong; it follows, in his view, that both children are bound to suffer harm if the parental rights and duties are assigned to the mother, and in particular that they may be forced into social isolation removed from reality.
The appellant's line of argument in this regard is unsound. The Jehovah's Witnesses, formerly known as Serious Bible Students, a community based upon their own interpretation of the Bible, are not outlawed in Austria; it may therefore be assumed that their objectives neither infringe the law nor offend morality (see art. 16 of the Basic Law in conjunction with art. 9 of the European Convention on Human Rights). Therefore, the mother's membership of that religious community cannot of itself constitute a danger to the children's welfare ...
Admittedly, the mother's religion will in all probability affect the children's care and upbringing, and they may come to experience a certain tension in relation to an environment which does not correspond to their faith. The first-instance court has already dealt at length with part of the appellant's arguments that relate thereto and has given detailed and conclusive reasons why the father's objections against assigning the parental rights and duties to the mother cannot in the final instance be decisive. The new points raised on appeal - relating to a lack of understanding of democracy and a lack of subordination to the State - cannot cast doubt on the first-instance decision as regards the children's welfare; it suffices in this respect to recall the legal recognition of the religious community of the Jehovah's Witnesses, which meant, contrary to the appellant's allegation, that the first-instance court did not in fact need to seek ex officio an expert opinion on the

objectives or the ‚nature' of the Jehovah's Witnesses. Nor were the first-instance proceedings incomplete because no expert medical opinion was sought regarding the question, which was raised anew on appeal, of blood transfusions, which are rejected by the Jehovah's Witnesses; in the event that a judicial remedy (a decision pursuant to art. 176 of the Civil Code) arrives too late, it will in the final instance be up to the physician treating the patient, when confronted with the problem, to reach a decision, with a view in the first place to life-saving medical action and only in the second place taking into account the rejection of blood transfusions which is peculiar to the Jehovah's Witnesses.

The appellant's further line of argument - to the effect that a properly arranged transfer of the children to himself and properly arranged visiting rights for the mother could not cause the same shock as had the mother's forcible removal of the children, and that the decision under appeal had legalised her unilateral action - also fails to convince. The appellant overlooks the fact that, in view of the paramount importance of the children's welfare, the way in which they reached the place where they are currently being taken care of is not necessarily decisive. Even illegal conduct would be of relevance only to the extent that it might, in an individual case, be possible to infer therefrom a lack of suitability for care or upbringing; it is not otherwise decisive for determining the attribution of parental rights and duties whether or not the parent concerned has taken charge of the children without authorisation. It remains true, however, that both children have for a long time developed harmoniously in the mother's care, that there is a closer relationship with her than with the father, and that, whatever the religious or philosophical views of the mother, neither child has suffered any harm in his or her physical or - particularly - psychological development; in fact the appellant could not seriously claim that they had actually suffered in the latter respect."

D. Proceedings before the Supreme Court

[14] Mr S. lodged an appeal on points of law (außerordentlicher Revisionsrekurs) with the Supreme Court (Oberster Gerichtshof).

[15] By decision of 3 September 1986, the Supreme Court overturned the judgment of the Innsbruck Regional Court, granting parental rights to Mr S. instead of the applicant. It gave the following reasons:

„*The appellant has not hitherto claimed that the children belonged to the Roman Catholic faith; however, he has stated, and it has in fact been established, that the mother is bringing them up according to the principles of the Jehovah's Witnesses' teaching. It is also uncontested that the children do not belong to this confession. The lower courts had therefore to examine whether or not the mother's bringing up the children in this way contravened the provisions of the Federal Law of 1985 on the Religious Education of Children (Bundesgesetz über die religiöse Kindererziehung), BGBl (Bundesgesetzblatt, Federal official Gazette) 1985/155 (re-enactment of the Law of 15 July 1921 on the Religious Education of Children, dRGB (deutsches Reichsgesetzblatt, German Reich Gazette) I. 939). According to art. 1 of the 1921 Act the religious education of a child shall be decided upon by an agreement freely entered into by the parents, in so far as the responsibility for his or her care and upbringing is vested in them. Such an agreement may be revoked at any time and is terminated by the death of either spouse.*

art. 2, par. 1, of the 1921 Act lays down that if such an agreement does not or ceases to exist, the provisions of the Civil Code on the care and upbringing of children shall extend to their religious education. However, according to art. 2, par. 2 of the 1921 Act, during the existence of the marriage neither parent may decide without the consent of the other that the child is to be brought up in a faith different from that shared by both parents at the time of the marriage or from that in which he or she has hitherto been brought up.

Since in any case the children do not belong to the faith of the Jehovah's Witnesses, their education according to the principles of this sect (which is not, as the appellant rightly points out, a recognised religious community: see Adamovich-Funk, Österreichisches Verfassungsrecht, [Austrian Constitutional Law], Vol. 3, p. 415) contravenes art. 2, par. 2, of the 1921 Act. The Regional Court's failure to apply this provision is obviously in breach of the law.

Moreover, the lower courts also failed in their decisions to give due consideration to the children's welfare ... That the mother, as has been established, would refuse to consent to the children's receiving a necessary blood transfusion constitutes a danger to their well-being, since requesting a court to substitute its consent for that of the mother ... may in urgent cases involve a life-threatening delay and medical intervention without seeking the approval of the person entitled to take care of the child is considered contrary to the law ... It has also been established that if the children are educated according to the religious teaching of the Jehovah's Witnesses, they will become social outcasts. In the initial decision as to which of the spouses is to have the right to provide care and upbringing, these circumstances cannot be ignored. Although it is preferable for young children to be taken care of by their mother ..., this applies only provided that all other things are equal ... There is no maternal privilege as regards the attribution of parental right ... The stress caused to the children by being transferred to the care of the other parent, which in any case is usually transitory, has to be accepted in their own best interests ... The file contains no documentary basis for the assumption that a change to another carer ,would with a high degree of probability cause the children serious psychological harm' ... Even according to the opinion of the lower courts, the father is able to see to the children's upbringing, since they have a good relationship with him and with their grandmother, who would take charge of their care and upbringing during the father's absence at work; the availability of accommodation for the children in the house of the father's parents is assured. Therefore, only transfer of parental rights and duties to the father is in the children's interest."

II. Jehovah's witnesses

[16] Numbering about four million worldwide not counting uninitiated sympathisers, the Jehovah's Witnesses form a particular religious movement. It originated in America in the 1870s. Formerly known by names such as International Bible Students, the Jehovah's Witnesses took their present name in 1931.

[17] A central feature of Jehovah's Witness doctrine is the belief that the Holy Scriptures in the original Hebrew and Greek are the revealed word of Jehovah God and must therefore be taken as literal truth. The

refusal to accept blood transfusions is based on several scriptural references, most notably Acts 15: 28-29, which reads (New World translation):

„For the holy spirit and we ourselves have favored adding no further burden to you, except these necessary things, to keep abstaining from things sacrificed to idols and from blood and from things strangled and from fornication. If you carefully keep yourselves from these things, you will prosper ...“

III. Relevant domestic law

A. The Civil Code

[18] Art. 177 of the Austrian Civil Code (Allgemeines Bürgerliches Gesetzbuch) deals with the custody of children in an event such as the dissolution of their parents' marriage by divorce. It reads:

„(1) Where the marriage between the parents of a legitimate minor has been dissolved, annulled or declared void, or where the parents are separated other than merely for a temporary period, they may submit to the court an agreement concerning which of them shall in the future have custody of the child. The court shall approve the agreement if it is in the interests of the child's welfare.
(2) Where no agreement is reached within a reasonable time, or if the agreement reached is not in the interest of the child's welfare, the court shall decide which parent is to have sole custody of the child in the future; in the case of a separation of the parents which is not merely temporary, such a decision shall be taken only on application by one of them.“

[19] Both during and after the parents' marriage, the court may be called upon to substitute its approval or consent for that of the parents (or parent). The relevant provision is art. 176, which reads:

„Where the conduct of the parents threatens the welfare of a minor, the court shall be required, irrespective of who has applied to it, to make the orders necessary for the protection of the child's welfare. Such an order may also be made on application by one of the parents when the parents have failed to reach an agreement concerning a matter of importance to the child. In particular the court may withdraw custody of a child, either wholly or in part, including rights of approval and consent provided by law. In individual cases the court is also required to substitute its approval or consent for parental approval or consent required by law, when there is no justified reason for refusal.“

[20] In taking decisions under art. 176 and 177, the courts follow the criteria set out in art. 178a, which reads:

„In assessing the interests of the minor, his or her personality and needs must be duly taken into consideration, particularly his or her talents, abilities, inclina-

tions and developmental opportunities, as well as the material circumstances of the parents.“

B. Regulation of religious life

[21] Religious freedom is guaranteed by art. 14 of the Basic Law (Staatsgrundgesetz), which reads:

„(1) Complete freedom of beliefs and conscience is guaranteed to everyone.

(2) Enjoyment of civil and political rights shall be independent of religious confessions; however, a religious confession may not stand in the way of civic duties.

(3) No one shall be compelled to take any church-related action or to participate in any church-related celebration, except in pursuance of a power conferred by law on another person to whose authority he is subject.“

[22] Austria has a system of recognition of religious communities. It is governed by the Act of 20 May 1874 concerning the Legal Recognition of Religious Communities (Gesetz betreffend die gesetzliche Anerkennung von Religionsgesellschaften), RGBl (Reichsgesetzblatt, Official Gazette of the Austrian Empire) 1874/68. Only five religious communities are so recognised, among them the Roman Catholic Church but not the Jehovah's Witnesses. Religious groupings without legal recognition have legal personality as „societies“ (Vereine) under the general law.

[23] The religious education of children is governed by the Federal Act on the Religious Education of Children, which re-enacted a German law dating from 1921 that was incorporated into Austrian law in 1939 (see par. 15 above).

Art. 1 reads:

„The religious education of a child shall be decided upon by an agreement freely entered into by the parents, in so far as the responsibility for the child's care and upbringing is vested in them. Such an agreement may be revoked at any time and is terminated by the death of either spouse.“

Art. 2 reads:

„(1) If such an agreement does not or ceases to exist, the provisions of the Civil Code on the care and upbringing of children shall extend to their religious education.

(2) During the existence of their marriage neither parent may decide without the consent of the other that the child is to be brought up in a faith different from that shared by both parents at the time of their marriage or from that in which he or she has hitherto been brought up, or that a child is to cease to attend religious education classes.

(3) In the absence of such consent, application may be made for the mediation of, or a decision by, the guardianship court. In any such decision the interests of education shall be paramount even in cases not covered by art. 176 of the Civil

Code. Before the decision is taken the child's parents, and if necessary relatives, relatives by marriage and teachers, must be heard if this is possible without significant delays or disproportionate costs. The child itself must be heard if it has reached the age of ten."

C. Medical action

[24] The need for parental permission for administering blood transfusions to minors follows from the law governing medical action in general. Thus, the Hospitals Act (Krankenanstaltengesetz), BGBl 1/1957, lays down in art. 8:

„(1)...
(2) Hospital patients may be medically treated only in accordance with the principles and recognised methods of medical science.
(3) Special curative treatments including surgical operations may be carried out on a patient only with his consent, but if the patient has not yet reached the age of eighteen or if because he lacks mental maturity or health he cannot assess the necessity or usefulness of the treatment, only with the consent of his legal representative. Consent is not required if the treatment is so urgently necessary that the delay involved in obtaining the consent of the patient or his legal representative or in appointing a legal representative would endanger his life or would entail the danger of serious harm to his health. The medical director of the hospital or the doctor responsible for the management of the hospital department concerned shall decide on the necessity and urgency of treatment."

[25] It is a criminal offence to administer medical treatment without the requisite consent; this follows from art. 110 of the Criminal Code (Strafgesetzbuch), which reads:

„(1) Whoever treats another person, even according to the rules of medical science, without having obtained that person's consent, shall be liable to imprisonment for up to six months or to a fine of up to 360 daily rates.
(2) If the offender has failed to obtain the consent of the patient because he assumed that a delay in the treatment would entail a serious risk for the life or health of the patient, he shall be punished according to par. 1 only if the assumed risk did not exist and if by taking due care ... he could have been aware of this.
3) The offender shall be punished only at the request of the person who underwent unauthorised treatment."

PROCEEDINGS BEFORE THE COMMISSION

(...)

AS TO THE LAW

I. Alleged violation of Art. 8, taken alone and in conjunction with Art. 14

[28] The applicant complained that the Austrian Supreme Court had awarded parental rights over the children Martin and Sandra to their father in preference to herself, because she was a member of the religious community of Jehovah's Witnesses; she claimed a violation of her rights under art. 8 of the Convention, both taken alone and read in conjunction with art. 14. The Government denied that there had been a violation at all, whereas the Commission agreed that there had been a violation of art. 8 taken in conjunction with art. 14.

[29] According to art. 8 par. 1 of the Convention, „Everyone has the right to respect for his private and family life, his home and his correspondence." The Court notes at the outset that the children had lived with the applicant for two years after she had left with them before the judgment of the Supreme Court of 3 September 1986 compelled the applicant to give them up to their father. The Supreme Court's decision therefore constitutes an interference with the applicant's right to respect for her family life and the case thus falls within the ambit of art. 8. The fact relied on by the Government in support of the opposite view, namely that the Supreme Court's decision was taken in the context of a dispute between private individuals, makes no difference in this respect.

A. Alleged violation of Art. 8 taken in conjunction with Art. 14

[30] In view of the nature of the allegations made, the Court, like the Commission, considers it appropriate to examine the present case under art. 8 taken in conjunction with art. 14, which reads as follows:

> „The enjoyment of the rights and freedoms set forth in [the] Convention shall be secured without discrimination on any ground such as sex, race, colour, language, religion, political or other opinion, national or social origin, association with a national minority, property, birth or other status."

[31] In the enjoyment of the rights and freedoms guaranteed by the Convention, art. 14 affords protection against different treatment, without an objective and reasonable justification, of persons in similar situations (see, amongst other authorities, the Sunday Times v. the United Kingdom (no. 2) judgment of 26 November 1991, Series A no. 217, p. 32, par. 58). It must first be determined whether the applicant can claim to have undergone different treatment.

[32] In awarding parental rights - claimed by both parties - to the mother in preference to the father, the Innsbruck District Court and Regional Court had to deal with the question whether the applicant was fit

to bear responsibility for the children's care and upbringing. In so doing they took account of the practical consequences of the religious convictions of the Jehovah's Witnesses, including their rejection of holidays such as Christmas and Easter which are customarily celebrated by the majority of the Austrian population, their opposition to the administration of blood transfusions, and in general their position as a social minority living by its own distinctive rules. The District and Regional Courts took note of the applicant's statement to the effect that she was prepared to allow the children to celebrate holidays with their father, who had remained Roman Catholic, and to allow the administration of blood transfusions to the children if and when required by law; they also considered the psychological relationship existing between the children (who were very young at the time) and the applicant and her general suitability as a carer. In assessing the interests of the children, the Supreme Court considered the possible effects on their social life of being associated with a particular religious minority and the hazards attaching to the applicant's total rejection of blood transfusions not only for herself but - in the absence of a court order - for her children as well; that is, possible negative effects of her membership of the religious community of Jehovah's Witnesses. It weighed them against the possibility that transferring the children to the care of their father might cause them psychological stress, which in its opinion had to be accepted in their own best interests.

[33] This Court does not deny that, depending on the circumstances of the case, the factors relied on by the Austrian Supreme Court in support of its decision may in themselves be capable of tipping the scales in favour of one parent rather than the other. However, the Supreme Court also introduced a new element, namely the Federal Act on the Religious Education of Children (see par. 15 and 23 above). This factor was clearly decisive for the Supreme Court. The European Court therefore accepts that there has been a difference in treatment and that that difference was on the ground of religion; this conclusion is supported by the tone and phrasing of the Supreme Court's considerations regarding the practical consequences of the applicant's religion. Such a difference in treatment is discriminatory in the absence of an „objective and reasonable justification", that is, if it is not justified by a „legitimate aim" and if there is no „reasonable relationship of proportionality between the means employed and the aim sought to be realised" (see, amongst other authorities, the Darby v. Sweden judgment of 23 October 1990, Series A no. 187, p. 12, par. 31).

[34] The aim pursued by the judgment of the Supreme Court was a legitimate one, namely the protection of the health and rights of the children; it must now be examined whether the second requirement was also satisfied.

[35] In the present context, reference may be made to art. 5 of Protocol No. 7, which entered into force for Austria on 1 November 1988; although

it was not prayed in aid in the present proceedings, it provides for the fundamental equality of spouses inter alia as regards parental rights and makes it clear that in cases of this nature the interests of the children are paramount.

[36] In so far as the Austrian Supreme Court did not rely solely on the Federal Act on the Religious Education of Children, it weighed the facts differently from the courts below, whose reasoning was moreover supported by psychological expert opinion. Notwithstanding any possible arguments to the contrary, a distinction based essentially on a difference in religion alone is not acceptable. The Court therefore cannot find that a reasonable relationship of proportionality existed between the means employed and the aim pursued; there has accordingly been a violation of art. 8 taken in conjunction with art. 14.

B. Alleged violation of Art. 8 taken alone

[37] In view of the conclusion reached in par. 36 above, the Court does not consider it necessary to rule on the allegation of a violation of art. 8 taken alone; the arguments advanced in this respect are in any case the same as those examined in respect of art. 8 taken in conjunction with art. 14.

II. Alleged violation of Art. 9

[38] The Court considers, as did the Commission, that no separate issue arises under art. 9 either taken alone or read in conjunction with art. 14, since the factual circumstances relied on as the basis of this complaint are the same as those which are at the root of the complaint under art. 8 taken in conjunction with art. 14, of which a violation has been found.

III. Alleged violation of Art. 2 of Protocol No. 1

[39] The applicant's complaint under art. 2 of Protocol No. 1 was not pursued before the Court, which finds no reason to examine it of its own motion.

IV. Application of Art. 50

[40] According to art. 50,

> „If the Court finds that a decision or a measure taken by a legal authority or any other authority of a High Contracting party is completely or partially in conflict with the obligations arising from the ... Convention, and if the internal law of the said Party allows only partial reparation to be made for the consequences of this

decision or measure, the decision of the Court shall, if necessary, afford just satisfaction to the injured party."

The applicant made no claim in respect of non-pecuniary damages but she claimed ATS 75,000 in respect of costs and expenses actually incurred before the Convention organs and not covered by legal aid.

The Commission expressed no opinion as to this claim. The Government found it acceptable; the Court agrees.

For these reasons the Court
1. *Holds by five votes to four that there has been a violation of art. 8 in conjunction with art. 14;*
2. *Holds unanimously that it is unnecessary to rule on the allegation of a violation of art. 8 taken alone;*
3. *Holds unanimously that no separate issue arises under art. 9, either taken alone or in conjunction with art. 14;*
4. *Holds unanimously that it is not necessary to rule on the allegation of a violation of art. 2 of Protocol No. 1;*
5. *... (Kosten und Auslagen)*

DISSENTING OPINION OF JUDGE MATSCHER

I feel unable to subscribe to the reasoning and the conclusion of the majority as regards the alleged violation of art. 8 taken in conjunction with art. 14.

[1] First of all it is necessary to examine whether there really was an interference by a public authority with the applicant's family life within the meaning of art. 8. When they separated, the parents did not reach agreement on custody of the children, both parties claiming it for themselves in the competent courts. At first instance and on appeal the courts found for the mother, while the Supreme Court decided in favour of the father. The case therefore concerned a private dispute between two individuals - each of whom was equally entitled from the beginning - which the courts, to which the parties turned as they had failed to reach an agreement, had to decide on the basis of the applicable law, since the fact that the mother had - without authorisation - taken the children away with her did not give her any additional rights. Accordingly, the fact that the children were taken back to their father's home following the final decision of the Supreme Court was not in itself an interference with the mother's rights within the meaning of art. 8.

[2] Even assuming that there was an interference, the following should be noted. The only criterion on which the courts should base their decision in a case such as this is the welfare of the children. The Supreme

Court determined the welfare of the children differently from the courts below. It is not for the Strasbourg Court to substitute its assessment for that of the competent State authorities, which enjoy a wide margin of appreciation in the matter. But it is nevertheless the Court's duty to review whether the choice made by these authorities was within the margin of appreciation that the Convention grants them and did not infringe the rights secured in it. In this instance it did not. The Supreme Court attached more importance to the adverse effects on the children's welfare which might result from the mother's membership of the religious community of the Jehovah's Witnesses. It did not therefore discriminate against the mother's religion as such but merely took into consideration certain consequences which belonging to that religion might entail for the well-being of the children, and this would seem to me to be wholly legitimate. Furthermore, the Supreme Court criticised the courts below for neglecting the fact that, in deciding on the children's future religious education unilaterally, the mother had infringed the provisions of the 1921 Act.

[3] Even though I do not find in the present case any violation of art. 8 taken together with art. 14, I have to deprecate the phrasing of some of the reasons given in the Supreme Court's judgment. But as the Court has noted many times, inept and unfortunate phrasing in a judicial decision does not on its own constitute a violation of the Convention.

PARTLY DISSENTING OPINION OF JUDGE WALSH

[1] I do not agree that in this case there was a violation of art. 8 and 14 taken together, or alone, by reason of the Supreme Court's decision which overturned the decision of the lower court by withdrawing from the applicant the custody of her children. The refusal was grounded on the fear that the children's welfare could be put at risk by reason of the applicant's intention not to permit a blood transfusion, if medically necessary, to either of her children should the occasion arise unless ordered to do so by a court.

[2] The mother's attitude was dictated by the tenets of the religious society or sect she had joined subsequent to the birth of her children. She had become a member of Jehovah's Witnesses after quitting the Catholic Church and she had accepted the view that to permit blood transfusion for her children, who were in her custody, would be morally wrong. Her children had remained members of the Catholic Church, as had her husband. Her children had no known objection to a necessary blood transfusion. In effect the applicant was imposing her religious beliefs upon the life and health of her children and in disregard of the rights of the father and of the provisions of the Religious Education of Children Act 1921.

[3] The father's notice of appeal to the Supreme Court specifically mentioned the withholding of possible blood transfusion as the reason for

seeking a reversal of the order of the lower court. That was an objective ground which a court might or might not, in any given case, regard as a sufficient ground for the transfer of custody. That is not a matter upon which this Court could usurp the discretion of the national court. The matter before the Supreme Court was a question of the hazard of the health of the children. In gauging the seriousness of the hazard the Supreme Court recognised that the cause of the hazard was, admittedly, the applicant's new religious views. The reason or motives for the creation of the hazard are but secondary to the objective effect of the existence of the hazard. If the applicant's attitude was not traceable to a religious belief the question before the national court would remain essentially the same. The fact that the hazard was brought into existence by a religious belief not shared by those upon whom it was sought to impose it does not create a situation where the removal of the hazard must necessarily, if at all, be regarded as a discrimination on the grounds of religious belief. The national court's duty was to evaluate or weigh the effects as distinct from the cause.

[4] The appeal to the Supreme Court was heard before the divorce of the parents became final. After that a different legal situation arose which could give rise to a further recourse to the national courts in consequence of the effect of the divorce on the provisions of the Religious Education of Children Act 1921. That is a situation which is not before this Court. 5.

I agree with the decision of the Court in relation to art. 8 taken alone, art. 9 and art. 2 of Protocol No. 1.

DISSENTING OPINION OF JUDGE VALTICOS

I am unable to share the opinion of the majority of the Chamber that there was in the present case a violation of art. 8 and 14 of the Convention, in that the Supreme Court's decision refusing to grant Mrs Hoffmann custody of her children constituted discrimination on the grounds of religion.

It is in fact clear, in my opinion, that the said decision by the Supreme Court was not based on the sole fact that Mrs Hoffmann was a Jehovah's Witness, but essentially on the consequences that this would have had for the children's future. The question would surely not have arisen in the case of a different religion not having the special characteristics of Jehovah's Witnesses. Thus the refusal to have blood transfusions could, whatever has been said, have endangered the children's health and even their lives. The peculiarities of this religion's tenets of faith would have led to the children being set apart from normal social life and would have contributed to marginalising them and restricting their future and their development. The children had admittedly not yet been accepted into the faith of Jehovah's Witnesses, but the mother took them with her to the

Sunday meetings. Since she made weekly visits for spreading her faith (admittedly without being accompanied by her children), it was to be expected that her children would also become objects of her proselytising zeal, it being natural for her to wish to ensure what she regarded as their salvation.

It should thus have been held that the Supreme Court's decision resulted not from „a distinction based essentially on a difference in religion alone", as the majority of the Court declared, but from the legitimate concern to protect the future of the Hoffmann children.

DISSENTING OPINION OF JUDGE MIFSUD BONNICI

I am unable to agree with the five members of the Court who make up the majority. My reasons are the following:

[1] Art. 8 of the Convention prohibits interference by a public authority with the exercise of the right of one's private and family life, home and correspondence.

[2] In my opinion, a fundamental distinction must be made between interference and intervention. Interference implies that action whereby one interposes or meddles in something, without having the right to do so. Intervention, on the other hand, is that action whereby one steps inbetween, to prevent or hinder a harm which otherwise will occur.

[3] Usually, whenever a marriage breaks down, one or both of the parties requests the court to intervene; as did the applicant and her husband, in the instant case. The first necessary intervention therefore came from the Innsbruck District Court. This first decision of the court was appealed from by the husband, to the Regional Court, and a second (extraordinary) appeal was eventually made to the Supreme Court of Austria.

[4] Each one of these courts had to reach a decision with regard to the care and custody of the children of the marriage. Each one of them was by law obliged to intervene and I cannot see how one can consider these decisions to be interferences by a public authority in the private and family life of the applicant. Rather, these were all necessary interventions, the like of which occur in their hundreds in the daily court life of all the States of the Council of Europe.

[5] The Supreme Court's decision reversed the previous two judgments in that it held that those decisions did not conform with the provisions of the Federal Law of 15 July 1921, which regulated the problem of the religious education of children.

[6] This law provides that the question of the religious education of children is to be regulated as follows:

(a) on marriage the question shall be settled by the free agreement of the partners;

(b) the original agreement may be changed by mutual agreement of the parents at any time;
(c) the father or the mother cannot unilaterally change the agreement;
(d) when one of them dies, the agreement lapses.

[7] The Supreme Court of Austria decided that the religious education of the Hoffmann children had to be regulated according to the original agreement freely entered into between the parents. The breakup of the marriage did not authorise either one of the parents, or the court, to change the original agreement.

[8] The appeal to the Supreme Court was lodged on points of law, mainly on the omission of the lower courts to take account of the 1921 law. This could not in fact be disputed, and one cannot see how the Supreme Court could, in its turn, ignore that law as well. It follows that its decision had to be based on both the elements already in the file and the law of 1921. I cannot see how because of this addition the decision violates the Convention. The lawyer of the applicant, in the oral pleadings, submitted that „the decision of the Supreme Court contradicts Austrian law". I do not believe that I am entitled to hear and decide appeals from the Supreme Court of Austria on the provisions of Austrian law and as to whether Austrian court decisions contradict Austrian law.

[9] In view of all this, I consider all the submissions on the merits or demerits of the applicant's religion as being irrelevant to the issue. The only relevant issue is whether the applicant is entitled or not to vary the original agreement on religious instruction which she had reached with her husband, irrespective of the religion to which that agreement referred. And this issue as regulated by Austrian law does not violate the Convention.

[10] For these reasons I cannot find that either the decision of the Supreme Court of Austria or the Austrian Federal Law on Religious Instruction are in violation of the Convention. Since I find the application completely unfounded, I am not prepared to grant anything under art. 50.

40

Die Gewährleistung freier Religionsausübung bietet keinen Schutz vor der Verbreitung religionskritischer Meinungsäußerungen. Nach Art der Darstellung kann jedoch in besonderen Fällen ein Einschreiten des Staates (hier: Beschlagnahme und Einziehung eines als blasphemisch beurteilten Films) zur Wahrung des religiösen Friedens in der Bevölkerung geboten sein. Wegen der Unterschiedlichkeit der örtlichen Verhältnisse entscheiden die nationalen Behörden auf der Grundlage eines Beurteilungsspielraums (certain margin of appreciation), ob und inwieweit religionskritische Äuße-

rungen geeignet sind, den religiösen Frieden zu gefährden und damit eine Einschränkung der Meinungsfreiheit zu rechtfertigen.

Art. 9, 10 EMRK

EGMR, Urteil vom 20. September 1994 - No. 11/1993/406/485 (Otto-Preminger-Institut für audiovisuelle Mediengestaltung ./. Österreich)[1] -

AS TO THE FACTS

I. The particular circumstances of the case

[9] The applicant, Otto-Preminger-Institut für audiovisuelle Mediengestaltung (OPI), is a private association under Austrian law established in Innsbruck. According to its articles of association, it is a non-profit-making organisation, its general aim being to promote creativity, communication and entertainment through the audiovisual media. Its activities include operating a cinema called „Cinematograph" in Innsbruck.

[10] The applicant association announced a series of six showings, which would be accessible to the general public, of the film Das Liebeskonzil („Council in Heaven") by Werner Schroeter (see par. 22 below). The first of these showings was scheduled for 13 May 1985. All were to take place at 10.00 p.m. except for one matinée performance on 19 May at 4 p.m. This announcement was made in an information bulletin distributed by OPI to its 2,700 members and in various display windows in Innsbruck including that of the Cinematograph itself. It was worded as follows:

„Oskar Panizza's satirical tragedy set in Heaven was filmed by Schroeter from a performance by the Teatro Belli in Rome and set in the context of a reconstruction of the writer's trial and conviction in 1895 for blasphemy. Panizza starts from the assumption that syphilis was God's punishment for man's fornication and sinfulness at the time of the Renaissance, especially at the court of the Borgia Pope Alexander VI. In Schroeter's film, God's representatives on Earth carrying the insignia of worldly power closely resemble the heavenly protagonists.
Trivial imagery and absurdities of the Christian creed are targeted in a caricatural mode and the relationship between religious beliefs and worldly mechanisms of oppression is investigated."

In addition, the information bulletin carried a statement to the effect that, in accordance with the Tyrolean Cinemas Act (Tiroler Lichtspielgesetz), persons under seventeen years of age were prohibited from seeing the film. A regional newspaper also announced the title of the film and

---

[1] Ser. A 295-A; Medien und Recht 1995, 3 (LS); ÖJZ 1995, 154.

the date and place of the showing without giving any particulars as to its contents.

[11] At the request of the Innsbruck diocese of the Roman Catholic Church, the public prosecutor instituted criminal proceedings against OPI's manager, Mr Dietmar Zingl, on 10 May 1985. The charge was „disparaging religious doctrines" (Herabwürdigung religiöser Lehren), an act prohibited by sec. 188 of the Penal Code (Strafgesetzbuch - see par. 25 below).

[12] On 12 May 1985, after the film had been shown at a private session in the presence of a duty judge (Journalrichter), the public prosecutor made an application for its seizure under sec. 36 of the Media Act (Mediengesetz - see par. 29 below). This application was granted by the Innsbruck Regional Court (Landesgericht) the same day. As a result, the public showings announced by OPI, the first of which had been scheduled for the next day, could not take place. Those who attended at the time set for the first showing were treated to a reading of the script and a discussion instead. As Mr Zingl had returned the film to the distributor, the „Czerny" company in Vienna, it was in fact seized at the latter's premises on 11 June 1985.

[13] An appeal by Mr Zingl against the seizure order, filed with the Innsbruck Court of Appeal (Oberlandesgericht), was dismissed on 30 July 1985. The Court of Appeal considered that artistic freedom was necessarily limited by the rights of others to freedom of religion and by the duty of the State to safeguard a society based on order and tolerance. It further held that indignation was „justified" for the purposes of sec. 188 of the Penal Code only if its object was such as to offend the religious feelings of an average person with normal religious sensitivity. That condition was fulfilled in the instant case and forfeiture of the film could be ordered in principle, at least in „objective proceedings" (see par. 28 below). The wholesale derision of religious feeling outweighed any interest the general public might have in information or the financial interests of persons wishing to show the film.

[14] On 24 October 1985 the criminal prosecution against Mr Zingl was discontinued and the case was pursued in the form of „objective proceedings" under sec. 33 par. 2 of the Media Act aimed at suppression of the film.

[15] On 10 October 1986 a trial took place before the Innsbruck Regional Court. The film was again shown in closed session; its contents were described in detail in the official record of the hearing. Mr Zingl appears in the official record of the hearing as a witness. He stated that he had sent the film back to the distributor following the seizure order because he wanted nothing more to do with the matter. It appears from the judgment - which was delivered the same day - that Mr Zingl was considered to be a „potentially liable interested party" (Haftungsbeteiligter). The Regional Court found it to be established that the distributor of the

film had waived its right to be heard and had agreed to the destruction of its copy of the film.

[16] In its judgment the Regional Court ordered the forfeiture of the film. It held:

> *„The public projection scheduled for 13 May 1985 of the film Das Liebeskonzil, in which God the Father is presented both in image and in text as a senile, impotent idiot, Christ as a cretin and Mary Mother of God as a wanton lady with a corresponding manner of expression and in which the Eucharist is ridiculed, came within the definition of the criminal offence of disparaging religious precepts as laid down in sec. 188 of the Penal Code."*

The court's reasoning included the following:

> *„The conditions of sec. 188 of the Penal Code are objectively fulfilled by this portrayal of the divine persons - God the Father, Mary Mother of God and Jesus Christ are the central figures in Roman Catholic religious doctrine and practice, being of the most essential importance, also for the religious understanding of the believers - as well as by the above-mentioned expressions concerning the Eucharist, which is one of the most important mysteries of the Roman Catholic religion, the more so in view of the general character of the film as an attack on Christian religions ...*
> *... Art. 17a of the Basic Law (Staatsgrundgesetz) guarantees the freedom of artistic creation and the publication and teaching of art. The scope of artistic freedom was broadened (by the introduction of that article) to the extent that every form of artistic expression is protected and limitations of artistic freedom are no longer possible by way of an express legal provision but may only follow from the limitations inherent in this freedom ... Artistic freedom cannot be unlimited. The limitations on artistic freedom are to be found, firstly, in other basic rights and freedoms guaranteed by the Constitution (such as the freedom of religion and conscience), secondly, in the need for an ordered form of human coexistence based on tolerance, and finally in flagrant and extreme violations of other interests protected by law (Verletzung anderer rechtlich geschützter Güter), the specific circumstances having to be weighed up against each other in each case, taking due account of all relevant considerations ...*
> *The fact that the conditions of sec. 188 of the Penal Code are fulfilled does not automatically mean that the limit of the artistic freedom guaranteed by art. 17a of the Basic Law has been reached. However, in view of the above considerations and the particular gravity in the instant case - which concerned a film primarily intended to be provocative and aimed at the Church - of the multiple and sustained violation of legally protected interests, the basic right of artistic freedom will in the instant case have to come second ..."*

[17] Mr Zingl appealed against the judgment of the Regional Court, submitting a declaration signed by some 350 persons who protested that they had been prevented from having free access to a work of art, and claiming that sec. 188 of the Penal Code had not been interpreted in line with the guarantee of freedom of art laid down by art. 17a of the Basic

Law. The Innsbruck Court of Appeal declared the appeal inadmissible on 25 March 1987. It found that Mr Zingl had no standing, as he was not the owner of the copyright of the film. The judgment was notified to OPI on 7 April 1987.

[18] Prompted by the applicant association's lawyer, the then Minister for Education, Arts and Sports, Dr Hilde Hawlicek, wrote a private letter to the Attorney General (Generalprokurator) suggesting the filing of a plea of nullity for safeguarding the law (Nichtigkeitsbeschwerde zur Wahrung des Gesetzes) with the Supreme Court (Oberster Gerichtshof). The letter was dated 18 May 1987 and mentioned, inter alia, art. 9 of the Convention. The Attorney General decided on 26 July 1988 that there were no grounds for filing such a plea of nullity. The decision mentioned, inter alia, that the Attorney General's Department (Generalprokuratur) had long held the view that artistic freedom was limited by other basic rights and referred to the ruling of the Supreme Court in the case concerning the film Das Gespenst („The Ghost" - see par. 26 below); in the Attorney General's opinion, in that case the Supreme Court had „at least not disapproved" of that view („Diese Auffassung ... wurde vom Obersten Gerichtshof ... zumindest nicht missbilligt").

[19] There have been theatre performances of the original play in Austria since then: in Vienna in November 1991, and in Innsbruck in October 1992. In Vienna the prosecuting authorities took no action. In Innsbruck several criminal complaints (Strafanzeigen) were laid by private persons; preliminary investigations were conducted, following which the prosecuting authorities decided to discontinue the proceedings.

II. The film „Das Liebeskonzil"

[20] The play on which the film is based was written by Oskar Panizza and published in 1894. In 1895 Panizza was found guilty by the Munich Assize Court (Schwurgericht) of „crimes against religion" and sentenced to a term of imprisonment. The play was banned in Germany although it continued in print elsewhere.

[21] The play portrays God the Father as old, infirm and ineffective, Jesus Christ as a „mummy's boy" of low intelligence and the Virgin Mary, who is obviously in charge, as an unprincipled wanton. Together they decide that mankind must be punished for its immorality. They reject the possibility of outright destruction in favour of a form of punishment which will leave it both „in need of salvation" and „capable of redemption". Being unable to think of such a punishment by themselves, they decide to call on the Devil for help. The Devil suggests the idea of a sexually transmitted affliction, so that men and women will infect one another without realising it; he procreates with Salome to produce a daughter who will spread it among mankind. The symptoms as described by the Devil are those of syphilis. As his reward, the Devil claims freedom of

thought; Mary says that she will „think about it". The Devil then dispatches his daughter to do her work, first among those who represent worldly power, then to the court of the Pope, to the bishops, to the convents and monasteries and finally to the common people.

[22] The film, directed by Werner Schroeter, was released in 1981. It begins and ends with scenes purporting to be taken from the trial of Panizza in 1895. In between, it shows a performance of the play by the Teatro Belli in Rome. The film portrays the God of the Jewish religion, the Christian religion and the Islamic religion as an apparently senile old man prostrating himself before the Devil with whom he exchanges a deep kiss and calling the Devil his friend. He is also portrayed as swearing by the Devil. Other scenes show the Virgin Mary permitting an obscene story to be read to her and the manifestation of a degree of erotic tension between the Virgin Mary and the Devil. The adult Jesus Christ is portrayed as a low grade mental defective and in one scene is shown lasciviously attempting to fondle and kiss his mother's breasts, which she is shown as permitting. God, the Virgin Mary and Christ are shown in the film applauding the Devil.

III. Relevant domestic law and practice

[23] Religious freedom is guaranteed by art. 14 of the Basic Law, which reads:

„(1) Complete freedom of beliefs and conscience is guaranteed to everyone.
(2) Enjoyment of civil and political rights shall be independent of religious confessions; however, a religious confession may not stand in the way of civic duties.
(3) No one shall be compelled to take any church-related action or to participate in any church-related celebration, except in pursuance of a power conferred by law on another person to whose authority he is subject."

[24] Artistic freedom is guaranteed by art. 17a of the Basic Law, which provides:

„There shall be freedom of artistic creation and of the publication and teaching of art."

[25] Sec. 188 of the Penal Code reads as follows:

„Whoever, in circumstances where his behaviour is likely to arouse justified indignation, disparages or insults a person who, or an object which, is an object of veneration of a church or religious community established within the country, or a dogma, a lawful custom or a lawful institution of such a church or religious community, shall be liable to a prison sentence of up to six months or a fine of up to 360 daily rates."

[26] The leading judgment of the Supreme Court on the relationship between the above two provisions was delivered after a plea of nullity for safeguarding the law filed by the Attorney General in a case concerning forfeiture of the film Das Gespenst („The Ghost") by Herbert Achternbusch. Although the plea was dismissed on purely formal grounds without any decision on the merits, it appeared obliquely from the judgment that if a work of art impinges on the freedom of religious worship guaranteed by art. 14 of the Basic Law, that may constitute an abuse of the freedom of artistic expression and therefore be contrary to the law (judgment of 19 December 1985, Medien und Recht 1986, no. 2, p. 15).

[27] A media offence (Medieninhaltsdelikt) is defined as "[a]n act entailing liability to a judicial penalty, committed through the content of a publication medium, consisting in a communication or performance aimed at a relatively large number of persons" (sec. 1 par. 12 of the Media Act). Criminal liability for such offences is determined according to the general penal law, in so far as it is not derogated from or added to by special provisions of the Media Act (sec. 28 of the Media Act).

[28] A specific sanction provided for by the Media Act is forfeiture (Einziehung) of the publication concerned (sec. 33). Forfeiture may be ordered in addition to any normal sanction under the Penal Code (sec. 33 par. 1). If prosecution or conviction of any person for a criminal offence is not possible, forfeiture can also be ordered in separate so-called „objective" proceedings for the suppression of a publication, as provided for under sec. 33 par. 2 of the Media Act, by virtue of which:

> „*Forfeiture shall be ordered in separate proceedings at the request of the public prosecutor if a publication in the media satisfies the objective definition of a criminal offence and if the prosecution of a particular person cannot be secured or if conviction of such person is impossible on grounds precluding punishment ...*"

[29] The seizure (Beschlagnahme) of a publication pending the decision on forfeiture may be effected pursuant to sec. 36 of the Media Act, which reads:

> „*1. The court may order the seizure of the copies intended for distribution to the public of a work published through the media if it can be assumed that forfeiture will be ordered under sec. 33 and if the adverse consequences of such seizure are not disproportionate to the legitimate interests served thereby. Seizure may not be effected in any case if such legitimate interests can also be served by publication of a notice concerning the criminal proceedings instituted.*
> *2. Seizure presupposes the prior or simultaneous institution of criminal proceedings or objective proceedings concerning a media offence and an express application to that effect by the public prosecutor or the complainant in separate proceedings.*

3. The decision ordering seizure shall mention the passage or part of the published work and the suspected offence having prompted the seizure ...
4-5. ..."

[30] The general law of criminal procedure applies to the prosecution of media offences and to objective proceedings. Although in objective proceedings the owner or publisher of the published work does not stand accused of any criminal offence, he is treated as a full party, by virtue of sec. 41 par. 5, which reads:

> *„[In criminal proceedings or objective proceedings concerning a media offence] the media owner (publisher) shall be summoned to the hearing. He shall have the rights of the accused; in particular, he shall be entitled to the same defences as the accused and to appeal against the judgment on the merits ..."*

PROCEEDINGS BEFORE THE COMMISSION

(...)
In its report adopted on 14 January 1993 (art. 31), the Commission expressed the opinion that there had been a violation of art. 9:
(a) as regards the seizure of the film (nine votes to five);
(b) as regards the forfeiture of the film (thirteen votes to one).

FINAL SUBMISSIONS TO THE COURT

(...)

AS TO THE LAW

I. The government's preliminary objections

(... [betr. Fristen und Aktivlegitimation])

II. Alleged violation of Art. 9

[42] The applicant association submitted that the seizure and subsequent forfeiture of the film Das Liebeskonzil gave rise to violations of its right to freedom of expression as guaranteed by art. 9 of the Convention, which provides:

> *„1. Everyone has the right to freedom of expression. This right shall include freedom to hold opinions and to receive and impart information and ideas without interference by public authority and regardless of frontiers. This article shall not prevent States from requiring the licensing of broadcasting, television or cinema enterprises.*
> *2. The exercise of these freedoms, since it carries with it duties and responsibilities, may be subject to such formalities, conditions, restrictions or penalties as are*

prescribed by law and are necessary in a democratic society, in the interests of national security, territorial integrity or public safety, for the prevention of disorder or crime, for the protection of health or morals, for the protection of the reputation or rights of others, for preventing the disclosure of information received in confidence, or for maintaining the authority and impartiality of the judiciary."

A. Whether there have been „interferences" with the applicant association's freedom of expression

[43] Although before the Commission the Government had conceded the existence of an interference with the exercise by the applicant association of its right to freedom of expression only with respect to the seizure of the film and although the same point was made in their preliminary objection (see par. 35 above), before the Court it was no longer in dispute that if the preliminary objection were rejected both the seizure and the forfeiture constituted such interferences. Such interferences will entail violation of art. 10 if they do not satisfy the requirements of par. 2. The Court must therefore examine in turn whether the interferences were „prescribed by law", whether they pursued an aim that was legitimate under that paragraph (art. 10-2) and whether they were „necessary in a democratic society" for the achievement of that aim.

B. Whether the interferences were „prescribed by law"

[44] The applicant association denied that the interferences were „prescribed by law", claiming that sec. 188 of the Austrian Penal Code had been wrongly applied. Firstly, it was in its view doubtful whether a work of art dealing in a satirical way with persons or objects of religious veneration could ever be regarded as „disparaging or insulting". Secondly, indignation could not be „justified" in persons who consented of their own free will to see the film or decided not to. Thirdly, the right to artistic freedom, as guaranteed by art. 17a of the Basic Law, had been given insufficient weight.

[45] The Court reiterates that it is primarily for the national authorities, notably the courts, to interpret and apply national law (see, as the most recent authority, the Chorherr v. Austria judgment of 25 August 1993, Series A no. 266-B, p. 36, par. 25). The Innsbruck courts had to strike a balance between the right to artistic freedom and the right to respect for religious beliefs as guaranteed by art. 14 of the Basic Law. The Court, like the Commission, finds that no grounds have been adduced before it for holding that Austrian law was wrongly applied.

C. Whether the interferences had a „legitimate aim"

[46] The Government maintained that the seizure and forfeiture of the film were aimed at „the protection of the rights of others", particularly

the right to respect for one's religious feelings, and at „the prevention of disorder".

[47] As the Court pointed out in its judgment in the case of Kokkinakis v. Greece of 25 May 1993 (Series A no. 260-A, p. 17, par. 31, KirchE-EU S. 202), freedom of thought, conscience and religion, which is safeguarded under art. 9 of the Convention, is one of the foundations of a „democratic society" within the meaning of the Convention. It is, in its religious dimension, one of the most vital elements that go to make up the identity of believers and their conception of life. Those who choose to exercise the freedom to manifest their religion, irrespective of whether they do so as members of a religious majority or a minority, cannot reasonably expect to be exempt from all criticism. They must tolerate and accept the denial by others of their religious beliefs and even the propagation by others of doctrines hostile to their faith. However, the manner in which religious beliefs and doctrines are opposed or denied is a matter which may engage the responsibility of the State, notably its responsibility to ensure the peaceful enjoyment of the right guaranteed under art. 9 to the holders of those beliefs and doctrines. Indeed, in extreme cases the effect of particular methods of opposing or denying religious beliefs can be such as to inhibit those who hold such beliefs from exercising their freedom to hold and express them. In the Kokkinakis judgment the Court held, in the context of art. 9, that a State may legitimately consider it necessary to take measures aimed at repressing certain forms of conduct, including the imparting of information and ideas, judged incompatible with the respect for the freedom of thought, conscience and religion of others (ibid., p. 21, par. 48). The respect for the religious feelings of believers as guaranteed in art. 9 can legitimately be thought to have been violated by provocative portrayals of objects of religious veneration; and such portrayals can be regarded as malicious violation of the spirit of tolerance, which must also be a feature of democratic society. The Convention is to be read as a whole and therefore the interpretation and application of art. 9 in the present case must be in harmony with the logic of the Convention (see, mutatis mutandis, the Klass and Others v. Germany judgment of 6 September 1978, Series A no. 28, p. 31, par. 68).

[48] The measures complained of were based on sec. 188 of the Austrian Penal Code, which is intended to suppress behaviour directed against objects of religious veneration that is likely to cause „justified indignation". It follows that their purpose was to protect the right of citizens not to be insulted in their religious feelings by the public expression of views of other persons. Considering also the terms in which the decisions of the Austrian courts were phrased, the Court accepts that the impugned measures pursued a legitimate aim under art. 10 par. 2, namely „the protection of the rights of others".

D. Whether the seizure and the forfeiture were „necessary in a democratic society"

1. General principles

[49] As the Court has consistently held, freedom of expression constitutes one of the essential foundations of a democratic society, one of the basic conditions for its progress and for the development of everyone. Subject to par. 2 of art. 10, it is applicable not only to „information" or „ideas" that are favourably received or regarded as inoffensive or as a matter of indifference, but also to those that shock, offend or disturb the State or any sector of the population. Such are the demands of that pluralism, tolerance and broadmindedness without which there is no „democratic society" (see, particularly, the Handyside v. the United Kingdom judgment of 7 December 1976, Series A no. 24, p. 23, par. 49). However, as is borne out by the wording itself of art. 10 par. 2, whoever exercises the rights and freedoms enshrined in the first paragraph of that article undertakes „duties and responsibilities". Amongst them - in the context of religious opinions and beliefs - may legitimately be included an obligation to avoid as far as possible expressions that are gratuitously offensive to others and thus an infringement of their rights, and which therefore do not contribute to any form of public debate capable of furthering progress in human affairs. This being so, as a matter of principle it may be considered necessary in certain democratic societies to sanction or even prevent improper attacks on objects of religious veneration, provided always that any „formality", „condition", „restriction" or „penalty" imposed be proportionate to the legitimate aim pursued (see the Handyside judgment referred to above, ibid.).

[50] As in the case of „morals" it is not possible to discern throughout Europe a uniform conception of the significance of religion in society (see the Müller and Others v. Switzerland judgment of 24 May 1988, Series A no. 133, p. 20, par. 30, and p. 22, par. 35); even within a single country such conceptions may vary. For that reason it is not possible to arrive at a comprehensive definition of what constitutes a permissible interference with the exercise of the right to freedom of expression where such expression is directed against the religious feelings of others. A certain margin of appreciation is therefore to be left to the national authorities in assessing the existence and extent of the necessity of such interference. The authorities' margin of appreciation, however, is not unlimited. It goes hand in hand with Convention supervision, the scope of which will vary according to the circumstances. In cases such as the present one, where there has been an interference with the exercise of the freedoms guaranteed in par. 1 of art. 10, the supervision must be strict because of the importance of the freedoms in question. The necessity for any restriction must be convincingly established (see, as the most recent

authority, the Informationsverein Lentia and Others v. Austria judgment
of 24 November 1993, Series A no. 276, p. 15, par. 35).

2. Application of the above principles

[51] The film which was seized and forfeited by judgments of the Austrian courts was based on a theatre play, but the Court is concerned only
with the film production in question.

(a) The seizure

[52] The Government defended the seizure of the film in view of its
character as an attack on the Christian religion, especially Roman Catholicism. They maintained that the placing of the original play in the
setting of its author's trial in 1895 actually served to reinforce the anti-
religious nature of the film, which ended with a violent and abusive denunciation of what was presented as Catholic morality. Furthermore,
they stressed the role of religion in the everyday life of the people of Tyrol. The proportion of Roman Catholic believers among the Austrian
population as a whole was already considerable - 78% - but among Tyroleans it was as high as 87%. Consequently, at the material time at least,
there was a pressing social need for the preservation of religious peace; it
had been necessary to protect public order against the film and the Innsbruck courts had not overstepped their margin of appreciation in this regard.

[53] The applicant association claimed to have acted in a responsible
way aimed at preventing unwarranted offence. It noted that it had
planned to show the film in its cinema, which was accessible to members
of the public only after a fee had been paid; furthermore, its public consisted on the whole of persons with an interest in progressive culture.
Finally, pursuant to the relevant Tyrolean legislation in force, persons
under seventeen years of age were not to be admitted to the film. There
was therefore no real danger of anyone being exposed to objectionable
material against their wishes. The Commission agreed with this position
in substance.

[54] The Court notes first of all that although access to the cinema to
see the film itself was subject to payment of an admission fee and an age-
limit, the film was widely advertised. There was sufficient public knowledge of the subject-matter and basic contents of the film to give a clear
indication of its nature; for these reasons, the proposed screening of the
film must be considered to have been an expression sufficiently „public"
to cause offence.

[55] The issue before the Court involves weighing up the conflicting interests of the exercise of two fundamental freedoms guaranteed under
the Convention, namely the right of the applicant association to impart

to the public controversial views and, by implication, the right of interested persons to take cognisance of such views, on the one hand, and the right of other persons to proper respect for their freedom of thought, conscience and religion, on the other hand. In so doing, regard must be had to the margin of appreciation left to the national authorities, whose duty it is in a democratic society also to consider, within the limits of their jurisdiction, the interests of society as a whole.

[56] The Austrian courts, ordering the seizure and subsequently the forfeiture of the film, held it to be an abusive attack on the Roman Catholic religion according to the conception of the Tyrolean public. Their judgments show that they had due regard to the freedom of artistic expression, which is guaranteed under art. 9 of the Convention (see the Müller and Others judgment referred to above, p. 22, par. 33) and for which art. 17a of the Austrian Basic Law provides specific protection. They did not consider that its merit as a work of art or as a contribution to public debate in Austrian society outweighed those features which made it essentially offensive to the general public within their jurisdiction. The trial courts, after viewing the film, noted the provocative portrayal of God the Father, the Virgin Mary and Jesus Christ (see par. 16 above). The content of the film (see par. 22 above) cannot be said to be incapable of grounding the conclusions arrived at by the Austrian courts. The Court cannot disregard the fact that the Roman Catholic religion is the religion of the overwhelming majority of Tyroleans. In seizing the film, the Austrian authorities acted to ensure religious peace in that region and to prevent that some people should feel the object of attacks on their religious beliefs in an unwarranted and offensive manner. It is in the first place for the national authorities, who are better placed than the international judge, to assess the need for such a measure in the light of the situation obtaining locally at a given time. In all the circumstances of the present case, the Court does not consider that the Austrian authorities can be regarded as having overstepped their margin of appreciation in this respect. No violation of art. 9 can therefore be found as far as the seizure is concerned.

(b) The forfeiture

[57] The foregoing reasoning also applies to the forfeiture, which determined the ultimate legality of the seizure and under Austrian law was the normal sequel thereto. Art. 10 cannot be interpreted as prohibiting the forfeiture in the public interest of items whose use has lawfully been adjudged illicit (see the Handyside judgment referred to above, p. 30, par. 63). Although the forfeiture made it permanently impossible to show the film anywhere in Austria, the Court considers that the means employed were not disproportionate to the legitimate aim pursued and that therefore the national authorities did not exceed their margin of appre-

ciation in this respect. There has accordingly been no violation of art. 9 as regards the forfeiture either.

For these reasons, the Court
(...)
3. *Holds, by six votes to three, that there has been no violation of art. 9 of the Convention as regards either the seizure or the forfeiture of the film.*

JOINT DISSENTING OPINION OF JUDGES PALM, PEKKANEN AND MAKARCZYK

[1] We regret that we are unable to agree with the majority that there has been no violation of art. 9.

[2] The Court is here faced with the necessity of balancing two apparently conflicting Convention rights against each other. In the instant case, of course, the rights to be weighed up against each other are the right to freedom of religion (art. 9), relied on by the Government, and the right to freedom of expression (art. 10), relied on by the applicant association. Since the case concerns restrictions on the latter right, our discussion will centre on whether these were „necessary in a democratic society" and therefore permitted by the second paragraph of art. 10.

[3] As the majority correctly state, echoing the famous passage in the Handyside v. the United Kingdom judgment (7 December 1976, Series A no. 24), freedom of expression is a fundamental feature of a „democratic society"; it is applicable not only to „information" or „ideas" that are favourably received or regarded as inoffensive or as a matter of indifference, but particularly to those that shock, offend or disturb the State or any sector of the population. There is no point in guaranteeing this freedom only as long as it is used in accordance with accepted opinion. It follows that the terms of art. 10 par. 2, within which an interference with the right to freedom of expression may exceptionally be permitted, must be narrowly interpreted; the State's margin of appreciation in this field cannot be a wide one. In particular, it should not be open to the authorities of the State to decide whether a particular statement is capable of „contributing to any form of public debate capable of furthering progress in human affairs"; such a decision cannot but be tainted by the authorities' idea of „progress".

[4] The necessity of a particular interference for achieving a legitimate aim must be convincingly established (see, as the most recent authority, the Informationsverein Lentia and Others v. Austria judgment of 24 November 1993, Series A no. 276, p. 15, par. 35). This is all the more true in cases such as the present, where the interference as regards the seizure takes the form of prior restraint (see, mutatis mutandis, the Observer and Guardian v. the United Kingdom judgment of 26 November 1991,

Series A no. 216, p. 30, par. 60). There is a danger that if applied to protect the perceived interests of a powerful group in society, such prior restraint could be detrimental to that tolerance on which pluralist democracy depends.

[5] The Court has rightly held that those who create, perform, distribute or exhibit works of art contribute to exchange of ideas and opinions and to the personal fulfillment of individuals, which is essential for a democratic society, and that therefore the State is under an obligation not to encroach unduly on their freedom of expression (see the Müller and Others v. Switzerland judgment of 24 May 1988, Series A no. 133, p. 22, par. 33). We also accept that, whether or not any material can be generally considered a work of art, those who make it available to the public are not for that reason exempt from their attendant „duties and responsibilities"; the scope and nature of these depend on the situation and on the means used (see the Müller and Others judgment referred to above, p. 22, par. 34).

[6] The Convention does not, in terms, guarantee a right to protection of religious feelings. More particularly, such a right cannot be derived from the right to freedom of religion, which in effect includes a right to express views critical of the religious opinions of others. Nevertheless, it must be accepted that it may be „legitimate" for the purpose of art. 9 to protect the religious feelings of certain members of society against criticism and abuse to some extent; tolerance works both ways and the democratic character of a society will be affected if violent and abusive attacks on the reputation of a religious group are allowed. Consequently, it must also be accepted that it may be „necessary in a democratic society" to set limits to the public expression of such criticism or abuse. To this extent, but no further, we can agree with the majority.

[7] The duty and the responsibility of a person seeking to avail himself of his freedom of expression should be to limit, as far as he can reasonably be expected to, the offence that his statement may cause to others. Only if he fails to take necessary action, or if such action is shown to be insufficient, may the State step in. Even if the need for repressive action is demonstrated, the measures concerned must be „proportionate to the legitimate aim pursued"; according to the case-law of the Court, which we endorse, this will generally not be the case if another, less restrictive solution was available (see, as the most recent authority, the Informationsverein Lentia and Others judgment referred to above, p. 16, par. 39). The need for repressive action amounting to complete prevention of the exercise of freedom of expression can only be accepted if the behaviour concerned reaches so high a level of abuse, and comes so close to a denial of the freedom of religion of others, as to forfeit for itself the right to be tolerated by society.

[8] As regards the need for any State action at all in this case, we would stress the distinctions between the present case and that of Müller

and Others, in which no violation of art. 9 was found. Mr Müller's paintings were accessible without restriction to the public at large, so that they could be - and in fact were - viewed by persons for whom they were unsuitable.

[9] Unlike the paintings by Mr Müller, the film was to have been shown to a paying audience in an „art cinema" which catered for a relatively small public with a taste for experimental films. It is therefore unlikely that the audience would have included persons not specifically interested in the film. This audience, moreover, had sufficient opportunity of being warned beforehand about the nature of the film. Unlike the majority, we consider that the announcement put out by the applicant association was intended to provide information about the critical way in which the film dealt with the Roman Catholic religion; in fact, it did so sufficiently clearly to enable the religiously sensitive to make an informed decision to stay away. It thus appears that there was little likelihood in the instant case of anyone being confronted with objectionable material unwittingly. We therefore conclude that the applicant association acted responsibly in such a way as to limit, as far as it could reasonably have been expected to, the possible harmful effects of showing the film.

[10] Finally, as was stated by the applicant association and not denied by the Government, it was illegal under Tyrolean law for the film to be seen by persons under seventeen years of age and the announcement put out by the applicant association carried a notice to that effect. Under these circumstances, the danger of the film being seen by persons for whom it was not suitable by reason of their age can be discounted. The Austrian authorities thus had available to them, and actually made use of, a possibility less restrictive than seizure of the film to prevent any unwarranted offence.

[11] We do not deny that the showing of the film might have offended the religious feelings of certain segments of the population in Tyrol. However, taking into account the measures actually taken by the applicant association in order to protect those who might be offended and the protection offered by Austrian legislation to those under seventeen years of age, we are, on balance, of the opinion that the seizure and forfeiture of the film in question were not proportionate to the legitimate aim pursued.

41

Darf die Eröffnung einer Stätte öffentlicher Religionsausübung von einer Genehmigung durch den Staat oder eine andere Religionsgemeinschaft abhängig gemacht werden?

Art. 9 EMRK
EGMR, Urteil vom 26. September 1996 - No. 59/1995/565/651
(Manoussakis u.a. ./. Griechenland)[1] -

AS TO THE FACTS

I. Particular circumstances of the case

A. Background

[6] The applicants are all Jehovah's Witnesses and live in Crete.

[7] On 30 March 1983 Mr Manoussakis rented under a private agreement a room measuring 88 square metres in a building located in the Ghazi district of Heraklion (Crete). The agreement specified that the room would be used „for all kinds of meetings, weddings, etc. of Jehovah's Witnesses".

[8] On 2 June 1983 he laid a complaint against persons unknown at Heraklion police station because the day before the windows of the room had been broken by unidentified persons. On 26 September 1983 he laid a further complaint concerning a similar incident that occurred on 23 September.

[9] By an application of 28 June 1983 lodged with the Minister of Education and Religious Affairs the applicants requested an authorisation to use the room as a place of worship. On the same day they went to the chairman of Ghazi District Council to ask him to certify their signatures on the application. He refused, however, on the grounds that the applicants did not reside in his district and that they had failed to show him the document bearing their signatures. Following the intervention of the prefect of Heraklion, the Deputy Minister of the Interior and the Speaker of the Greek Parliament, the chairman withdrew his opposition and agreed to certify the signatures on a new application lodged on 18 October 1983.

[10] On 30 July 1983 the Ghazi Orthodox Parish Church notified the Heraklion police authorities that the room was being used as an unauthorised place of worship for Jehovah's Witnesses and informed them of the applications made by the applicants to the Minister. The church authorities asked the police to carry out an inspection of the premises, to take punitive measures against those responsible and above all to prohibit any further meetings until the Minister had granted the authorisation in question.

[11] The applicants received five letters from the Ministry of Education and Religious Affairs, dated 25 November 1983 and 17 February, 17 April, 17 June, 16 August and 10 December 1984, informing them that it

---

[1] RJD 1996-IV; ÖJZ 1997, 352.

was not yet in a position to take a decision because it had not received all the necessary information from the other departments concerned.

[12] On 3 March 1986 the Heraklion public prosecutor's office instituted criminal proceedings against the applicants under sec. 1 of Law no. 1363/1938 (anagastikos nomos), as amended by Law no. 1672/1939 (see par. 21 below). In particular they were accused of having „established and operated a place of worship for religious meetings and ceremonies of followers of another denomination and, in particular, of the Jehovah's Witnesses' denomination without authorisation from the recognised ecclesiastical authorities and the Minister of Education and Religious Affairs, such authorisation being required for the construction and operation of a church of any faith".

B. Proceedings in the Heraklion Criminal Court sitting at first instance

[13] On 6 October 1987 the Heraklion Criminal Court sitting at first instance and composed of a single judge (Monomeles Plimmeliodikeio) acquitted the applicants on the ground that „in the absence of any acts of proselytism, followers of any faith are free to meet even if they do not have the requisite authorisation".

C. Proceedings in the Heraklion Criminal Court sitting on appeal

[14] The Heraklion public prosecutor's office took the view that the Criminal Court had incorrectly assessed the facts and accordingly lodged an appeal against the judgment of 6 October 1987.

[15] On 15 February 1990 the Heraklion Criminal Court sitting on appeal and composed of three judges (Trimeles Plimmeliodikeio), sentenced each of the accused to three months' imprisonment convertible into a pecuniary penalty of 400 drachmas per day of detention, and fined them 20,000 drachmas each. It noted as follows:

„... the accused had converted the room that they had rented into a place of worship, in other words a small temple intended to serve as a place of devotion for a limited circle of persons as opposed to a public building in which everyone without distinction is free to worship God. Thus they established this place on 30 July 1983 and made it accessible ... to others, in particular, their fellow Jehovah's Witnesses from the region (limited circle of persons), without the authorisation of the recognised ecclesiastical authority and of the Ministry of Education and Religious Affairs. At this place they worshipped God by engaging in acts of prayer and devotion (preaching, reading of the scriptures, praising and prayers) and did not confine themselves to the mere holding of meetings for followers and the reading of the gospel ..."

D. Proceedings in the Court of Cassation

[16] On 5 March 1990 the applicants appealed on points of law. They argued, inter alia, that the provisions of sec. 1 of Law no. 1363/1938, in particular the obligation to seek an authorisation to establish a place of worship, were contrary to art. 11 and 13 of the Greek Constitution and to art. 9 and 11 of the European Convention.

[17] In a judgment of 19 March 1991 the Court of Cassation dismissed their appeal on the following grounds:

„*The provisions of sec. 1 of Law no. 1363/1938 and of the royal decree of 20 May/2 June 1939 implementing that Law are contrary neither to art. 11 nor to art. 13 of the 1975 Constitution, for the right to freedom of worship is not unlimited and may be subject to control. The exercise of this right is subject to certain conditions set down in the Constitution and at law: it must be a known religion, not a secret religion; there must be no prejudice to public order or morals; neither must there be any acts of proselytism, such acts being expressly prohibited in the second and third sentences of art. 13 par. 2 of the Constitution. These provisions are, moreover, not contrary to the Convention for the Protection of Human Rights and Fundamental Freedoms ..., art. 9 of which guarantees freedom of religion but art. 9 par. 2 of which authorises such limitations as are prescribed by law and are necessary in a democratic society in the interests of public safety, for the protection of public order, health or morals, or for the protection of the rights of others.*

The said provisions ..., which empower the Minister of Education and Religious Affairs, who has responsibility for all denominations and faiths, to investigate whether the above-mentioned conditions are met, are contrary neither to the 1975 Constitution nor to art. 9 of the Convention, which do not in any way prohibit investigations of this type; the purpose of such investigations is moreover merely to ensure that the statutory conditions necessary to grant authorisation are met; if these conditions are met, the Minister is obliged to grant the requested authorisation."

[18] According to the dissenting opinion of one of its members, the Court of Cassation ought to have quashed the impugned judgment since the applicants could not be accused of a punishable offence as sec. 1 of the Law was contrary to art. 13 of the 1975 Constitution.

[19] On 20 September 1993 the Heraklion police placed seals on the front door of the room rented by the applicants.

II. Relevant domestic law

A. The Constitution

[20] The relevant articles of the 1975 Constitution read as follows:

Art. 3

„1. The dominant religion in Greece is that of the Christian Eastern Orthodox Church. The Greek Orthodox Church, which recognises as its head Our Lord Jesus Christ, is indissolubly united, doctrinally, with the Great Church of Constantinople and with any other Christian Church in communion with it (omodoxi), immutably observing, like the other Churches, the holy apostolic and synodical canons and the holy traditions. It is autocephalous and is administered by the Holy Synod, composed of all the bishops in office, and by the standing Holy Synod, which is an emanation of it constituted as laid down in the Charter of the Church and in accordance with the provisions of the Patriarchal Tome of 29 June 1850 and the Synodical Act of 4 September 1928.
2. The ecclesiastical regime in certain regions of the State shall not be deemed contrary to the provisions of the foregoing paragraph.
3. The text of the Holy Scriptures is unalterable. No official translation into any other form of language may be made without the prior consent of the autocephalous Greek Church and the Great Christian Church at Constantinople.“

Art. 13

„1. Freedom of conscience in religious matters is inviolable. The enjoyment of personal and political rights shall not depend on an individual's religious beliefs.
2. There shall be freedom to practise any known religion; individuals shall be free to perform their rites of worship without hindrance and under the protection of the law. The performance of rites of worship must not prejudice public order or public morals. Proselytism is prohibited.
3. The ministers of all known religions shall be subject to the same supervision by the State and to the same obligations to it as those of the dominant religion.
4. No one may be exempted from discharging his obligations to the State or refuse to comply with the law by reason of his religious convictions.
5. No oath may be required other than under a law which also determines the form of it.“

B. Law no. 1363/1938

21. Sec. 1 of Law no. 1363/1938 (as amended by Law no. 1672/1939) provides:

„The construction and operation of temples of any denomination whatsoever shall be subject to authorisation by the recognized ecclesiastical authority and the Ministry of Education and Religious Affairs. This authorisation shall be granted on the terms and conditions specified by royal decree to be adopted on a proposal by the Minister of Education and Religious Affairs.
As of publication of the royal decree referred to in the preceding paragraph, temples or other places of worship which are set up or operated without complying with the decree ... shall be closed and placed under seal by the police and use thereof shall be prohibited; persons who have set up or operated such places of worship shall be fined 50,000 drachmas and sentenced to a non-convertible term of between two and six months' imprisonment.
...
The term „temple“ as referred to in this Law ... shall mean any type of building open to the public for the purpose of divine worship (parish or otherwise, chapels and altars).“

[22] The Court of Cassation has held that the expression „place of worship" within the meaning of these provisions refers to a „temple of a relatively small size, established in a private building and intended to be used for divine worship by a limited circle of persons as opposed to a building open to the public for the worship of God by everyone without distinction. By operation of a temple or a place of worship under the same provisions is meant the actions by which the temple or place of worship are made accessible to others for the purpose of worshipping God" (judgment no. 1107/1985, Pinika Khronika, vol. 56, 1986).

C. The royal decree of 20 May/2 June 1939

[23] Sec. 1 (3) of the royal decree of 20 May/2 June 1939 provides that it is for the Minister of Education and Religious Affairs to verify whether there are „essential reasons" warranting the authorisation to build or operate a place of worship. To this end the persons concerned must submit through their priest an application giving their addresses and bearing their signatures certified by the mayor or the chairman of the district council of their place of residence. More specifically, sec. 1 of the decree provides as follows:

„1. In order to obtain an authorisation for the construction or operation of temples not subject to the legislation on temples and priests of parishes belonging to the Greek Orthodox Church, within the meaning of sec. 1 of the Law (1672/1939), the following steps must be completed:

(a) An application shall be submitted by at least fifty families, from more or less the same neighbourhood and living in an area at a great distance from a temple of the same denomination, it being assumed that the distance makes it difficult for them to observe their religious duties. The requirement of fifty families shall not apply to suburbs or villages.

(b) The application shall be addressed to the local ecclesiastical authorities and must be signed by the heads of the families, who shall indicate their addresses. The authenticity of their signatures shall be certified by the local police authority, which following an inquiry on the ground shall attest that the conditions referred to in the preceding sub-paragraph are satisfied ...

(c) The local police authority shall issue a reasoned opinion on the application. It shall then transmit the application, with its opinion, to the Ministry of Education and Religious Affairs, which may accept or reject the application according to whether it considers that the construction or use of a new temple is justified or whether the provisions of the present decree have been complied with.

2. ...

3. The provisions of par. 1 (a)-(b) above shall not apply to the issue of an authorisation for the construction or operation of a place of worship. It shall be for the Minister of Education and Religious Affairs to determine whether there are essential reasons warranting such authorisation. In this connection the persons concerned shall address to the Ministry of Education and Religious Affairs through their priest a signed application, the authenticity of the signatures being certified by the mayor or the chairman of the district council. The application shall also indicate the addresses of the persons concerned ..."

D. Case-law

[24] The Government communicated to the Court a series of judgments by the Supreme Administrative Court concerning the authorisation to construct or operate temples or places of worship. It appears from these judgments that the Supreme Administrative Court has on several occasions quashed decisions of the Minister of Education and Religious Affairs refusing such authorisation on the ground that Jehovah's Witnesses in general engaged in proselytism (judgment no. 2484/1980); or that some of those seeking the authorisation had been prosecuted for proselytism (judgment no. 4260/1985); or again because there was an Orthodox church close to the proposed place of worship (4km in the same town) (judgment no. 4636/1977) and the limited number of Jehovah's Witnesses (8) compared to the total population (938) (judgment no. 381/1980).

[25] The Supreme Administrative Court has also held that the requirement that the signatures be certified by the relevant municipal authority (royal decree of 20 May/2 June 1939 - see par. 23 above) does not constitute a restriction on the right to freedom of religion guaranteed under the Greek Constitution and the European Convention (judgment no. 4305/1986). On the other hand, failure to comply with that requirement justifies a refusal to grant the authorisation (judgment no. 1211/1986). Finally the silence of the Minister of Education and Religious Affairs for more than three months following the lodging of an application constitutes failure on the part of the authorities to give a decision as required by law and amounts to an implied rejection, which may be challenged by an application for judicial review (judgment no. 3456/ 1985). Authorisation by the local Metropolitan is required only for the construction or operation of temples and not for other places of worship.

[26] In its judgment (no. 721/1969) of 4 February 1969 the Supreme Administrative Court sitting in plenary session stated that art. 13 of the Constitution did not preclude prior verification by the administrative authorities that the conditions laid down by that article for the practice of a faith were satisfied. However, that verification is of a purely declaratory nature. The grant of the authorisation may not be withheld where those conditions are satisfied and the authorities have no discretionary power in this respect. The prior authorisation of the local Metropolitan for the construction of a temple (see par. 25 above) is not an „enforceable administrative decision", but a „preliminary finding" by a representative of the dominant religion who is familiar with the true position regarding religious practice in the locality. The decision rests with the Minister of Education and Religious Affairs who may decide to disregard the Metropolitan's assessment if he considers that it is not supported by reasons in

conformity with the law. The Supreme Administrative Court subsequently confirmed this case-law holding, inter alia, that the „authorisation" of the local Metropolitan was a mere opinion which did not bind the Minister of Education and Religious Affairs (judgment no. 1444/1991 of 28 January 1991).

(...)

PROCEEDINGS BEFORE THE COMMISSION

[28] (...)

[29] On 10 October 1994 the Commission declared the application (no. 18748/91) admissible as regards the complaint based on art. 9, but inadmissible for the rest. In its report of 25 May 1995 (art. 31), it expressed the unanimous opinion that there had been a breach of that art. 9.

AS TO THE LAW

I. (...)

II. Alleged violation of Art. 9 of the convention

[35] The applicants maintained that their conviction by the Heraklion Criminal Court sitting on appeal infringed art. 9 of the Convention, according to which:

> „1. Everyone has the right to freedom of thought, conscience and religion; this right includes freedom to change his religion or belief and freedom, either alone or in community with others and in public or private, to manifest his religion or belief, in worship, teaching, practice and observance.
> 2. Freedom to manifest one's religion or beliefs shall be subject only to such limitations as are prescribed by law and are necessary in a democratic society in the interests of public safety, for the protection of public order, health or morals, or for the protection of the rights and freedoms of others."

A. Whether there was an interference

[36] The validity of the private agreement concluded by the applicants on 30 March 1983 (see par. 7 above) is not in dispute. The applicants' conviction by the Heraklion Criminal Court sitting on appeal for having used the premises in question without the prior authorisation required under Law no. 1363/1938 was therefore an interference with the exercise of their „freedom ..., to manifest [their] religion ..., in worship ... and observance". Such interference breaches art. 9 unless it was „prescribed by law", pursued one or more of the legitimate aims referred to in par. 2 and was „necessary in a democratic society" to attain such aim or aims.

B. Justification of the interference

1. „Prescribed by law"

[37] In the applicants' submission, Law no. 1363/1938 and its implementing decree of 20 May/2 June 1939 lay down a general and permanent prohibition on the establishment of a church or a place of worship of any religion - the law uses the term „faith" - other than the Orthodox religion. They maintained that this prohibition could only be lifted by a formal decision or a specific discretionary measure. This discretionary power was, in their view, clearly derived from sec. 1 of Law no. 1363/ 1938, which empowers the Government to grant or to refuse the authorisation, or to remain silent in response to an application duly submitted, without setting any limit as to time or establishing any substantive condition. They argued that a law which made the practice of a religion subject to the prior grant of an authorisation, whose absence incurred liability to a criminal sanction, constituted an „impediment" to that religion and could not be regarded as a law designed to protect freedom of religion within the meaning of art. 13 of the Constitution. As regards freedom of religion and worship, the Constitution purported to be more, or at least not less, protective than the Convention because the only grounds on which it permitted restrictions to be placed on the practice of any „known religion" were „public order" and „public morals" (see par. 20 above). In addition, the applicants pointed to the unusual character, as regards Greek public and administrative law, of the procedure established by Law no. 1363/1938 for the construction or the operation of a place of worship. It was the only procedure in respect of which provision was made for the intervention of two authorities, administrative and religious. They criticised the manner in which the Supreme Administrative Court interpreted this Law, namely in the context of the restrictions, suggestions and directives of the Constitution, and the importance attached by that court to compliance with the conditions laid down by the royal decree of 20 May/2 June 1939 for submitting in due form applications for authorisation together with all that those conditions entailed in terms of inquisitorial process and the difficulty in obtaining such authorisation. The wording of this decree conferred a number of different discretionary powers, each of which was sufficient basis for a negative response to the application.

[38] The Court notes that the applicants' complaint is directed less against the treatment of which they themselves had been the victims than the general policy of obstruction pursued in relation to Jehovah's Witnesses when they wished to set up a church or a place of worship. They are therefore in substance challenging the provisions of the relevant domestic law. However, the Court does not consider it necessary to rule on the question whether the interference in issue was „prescribed by

law" in this instance because, in any event, it was incompatible with art. 9 of the Convention on other grounds (see, mutatis mutandis, the Funke v. France judgment of 25 February 1993, Series A no. 256-A, p. 23, par. 51, and par. 53 below).

2. Legitimate aim

[39] According to the Government, the penalty imposed on the applicants served to protect public order and the rights and freedoms of others. In the first place, although the notion of public order had features that were common to the democratic societies in Europe, its substance varied on account of national characteristics. In Greece virtually the entire population was of the Christian Orthodox faith, which was closely associated with important moments in the history of the Greek nation. The Orthodox Church had kept alive the national conscience and Greek patriotism during the periods of foreign occupation. Secondly, various sects sought to manifest their ideas and doctrines using all sorts of „unlawful and dishonest" means. The intervention of the State to regulate this area with a view to protecting those whose rights and freedoms were affected by the activities of socially dangerous sects was indispensable to maintain public order on Greek territory.

[40] Like the applicants, the Court recognises that the States are entitled to verify whether a movement or association carries on, ostensibly in pursuit of religious aims, activities which are harmful to the population. Nevertheless, it recalls that Jehovah's Witnesses come within the definition of „known religion" as provided for under Greek law (see the Kokkinakis v. Greece judgment of 25 May 1993, Series A no. 260-A, p. 15, par. 23). This was moreover conceded by the Government. However, having regard to the circumstances of the case and taking the same view as the Commission, the Court considers that the impugned measure pursued a legitimate aim for the purposes of art. 9 par. 2 of the Convention, namely the protection of public order.

3. „Necessary in a democratic society"

[41] The main thrust of the applicants' complaint is that the restrictions imposed on Jehovah's Witnesses by the Greek Government effectively prevent them from exercising their right to freedom of religion. In terms of the legislation and administrative practice, their religion did not, so they claimed, enjoy in Greece the safeguards guaranteed to it in all the other member States of the Council of Europe. The „pluralism, tolerance and broadmindedness without which there is no democratic society" were therefore seriously jeopardised in Greece. They contended that the Jehovah's Witnesses' movement should be presumed - even if the presumption was a rebuttable one - to respect certain moral rules

and not in itself to prejudice public order. Its doctrines and its rites abided by and extolled social order and individual morality. Accordingly, the political authorities should intervene only in the event of abuse or perversion of such doctrines and rites, and should do so punitively rather than preventively. More particularly, their conviction had been persecutory, unjustified and not necessary in a democratic society as it had been „manufactured" by the State. The State had compelled the applicants to commit an offence and to bear the consequences solely because of their religious beliefs. The apparently innocent requirement of an authorisation to operate a place of worship had been transformed from a mere formality into a lethal weapon against the right to freedom of religion. The term „dilatory" used by the Commission to describe the conduct of the Minister of Education and Religious Affairs in relation to their application for an authorisation was euphemistic. The struggle for survival by certain religious communities outside the Eastern Orthodox Church, and specifically by Jehovah's Witnesses, was carried on in a climate of interference and oppression by the State and the dominant church as a result of which art. 9 of the Convention had become a dead letter. That art. 9 was the object of frequent and blatant violations aimed at eliminating freedom of religion. The applicants cited current practice in Greece in support of their contentions, giving numerous examples. They requested the Court to examine their complaints in the context of these other cases.

[42] According to the Government, in order to resolve the question of the necessity of the applicants' conviction, the Court should first examine the necessity of the requirement of prior authorisation, which owed its existence to historical considerations. In their view, the former presupposed the latter. The applicants' true aim was not to complain about their conviction but to fight for the abolition of that requirement. There were essential public-order grounds to justify making the setting up of a place of worship subject to approval by the State. In Greece this control applied to all faiths; otherwise it would be both unconstitutional and contrary to the Convention. Jehovah's Witnesses were not exempt from the requirements of legislation which concerned the whole population. The setting up of a church or a place of worship in Greece was, so the Government affirmed, often used as a means of proselytism, in particular by Jehovah's Witnesses who engaged in intensive proselytism, thereby infringing the law that the Court had itself found to be in conformity with the Convention (see the above-mentioned Kokkinakis judgment). The sanction imposed on the applicants had been light and had been motivated not by the manifestation by them of their religion but by their disobedience to the law and their failure to comply with an administrative procedure. It was the result of the applicants' culpable neglect to have recourse to the remedy available under the Greek legal system. Finally, the Government referred to the fact that various States parties to the

Convention had legislation containing restrictions similar to those enacted in Greece in this field.

[43] The Commission considered that the authorisation requirement introduced by Law no. 1363/1938 might appear open to criticism. In the first place, the intervention of the Greek Orthodox Church in the procedure raised a complex question under par. 2 of art. 9. Secondly, classifying as a criminal offence the operation of a place of worship without the authorities' prior authorisation was disproportionate to the legitimate aim pursued, especially when, as in this case, the underlying cause of the applicants' conviction lay in the dilatory attitude of the relevant authorities.

[44] As a matter of case-law, the Court has consistently left the Contracting States a certain margin of appreciation in assessing the existence and extent of the necessity of an interference, but this margin is subject to European supervision, embracing both the legislation and the decisions applying it. The Court's task is to determine whether the measures taken at national level were justified in principle and proportionate. In delimiting the extent of the margin of appreciation in the present case the Court must have regard to what is at stake, namely the need to secure true religious pluralism, an inherent feature of the notion of a democratic society (see the above-mentioned Kokkinakis judgment, p. 17, par. 31). Further, considerable weight has to be attached to that need when it comes to determining, pursuant to par. 2 of art. 9, whether the restriction was proportionate to the legitimate aim pursued. The restrictions imposed on the freedom to manifest religion by the provisions of Law no. 1363/1938 and of the decree of 20 May/2 June 1939 call for very strict scrutiny by the Court.

[45] The Court notes in the first place that Law no. 1363/1938 and the decree of 20 May/2 June 1939 - which concerns churches and places of worship that are not part of the Greek Orthodox Church - allow far-reaching interference by the political, administrative and ecclesiastical authorities with the exercise of religious freedom. In addition to the numerous formal conditions prescribed in sec. 1 (1) and (3) of the decree, some of which confer a very wide discretion on the police, mayor or chairman of the district council, there exists in practice the possibility for the Minister of Education and Religious Affairs to defer his reply indefinitely - the decree does not lay down any time-limit - or to refuse his authorisation without explanation or without giving a valid reason. In this respect, the Court observes that the decree empowers the Minister - in particular when determining whether the number of those requesting an authorisation corresponds to that mentioned in the decree (sec. 1 (1) (a)) - to assess whether there is a „real need" for the religious community in question to set up a church. This criterion may in itself constitute grounds for refusal, without reference to the conditions laid down in art. 13 par. 2 of the Constitution.

[46] The Government maintained that the power of the Minister of Education and Religious Affairs to grant or refuse the authorisation requested was not discretionary. He was under a duty to grant the authorisation if he found that the three conditions set down in art. 13 par. 2 of the Constitution were satisfied, namely that it must be in respect of a known religion, that there must be no risk of prejudicing public order or public morals and that there is no danger of proselytism.

[47] The Court observes that, in reviewing the lawfulness of refusals to grant the authorisation, the Supreme Administrative Court has developed case-law limiting the Minister's power in this matter and according the local ecclesiastical authority a purely consultative role (see par. 26 above). The right to freedom of religion as guaranteed under the Convention excludes any discretion on the part of the State to determine whether religious beliefs or the means used to express such beliefs are legitimate. Accordingly, the Court takes the view that the authorisation requirement under Law no. 1363/1938 and the decree of 20 May/2 June 1939 is consistent with art. 9 of the Convention only in so far as it is intended to allow the Minister to verify whether the formal conditions laid down in those enactments are satisfied.

[48] It appears from the evidence and from the numerous other cases cited by the applicants and not contested by the Government that the State has tended to use the possibilities afforded by the above-mentioned provisions to impose rigid, or indeed prohibitive, conditions on practice of religious beliefs by certain non-Orthodox movements, in particular Jehovah's Witnesses. Admittedly the Supreme Administrative Court quashes for lack of reasons any unjustified refusal to grant an authorisation, but the extensive case-law in this field seems to show a clear tendency on the part of the administrative and ecclesiastical authorities to use these provisions to restrict the activities of faiths outside the Orthodox Church.

[49] In the instant case the applicants were prosecuted and convicted for having operated a place of worship without first obtaining the authorisations required by law.

[50] In their memorial the Government maintained that under sec. 1 (1) of the decree of 20 May/2 June 1939 an authorisation from the local bishop was necessary only for the construction and operation of a church and not for a place of worship as in the present case. An application to the Minister of Education and Religious Affairs, indeed one such as that submitted by the applicants, was sufficient.

[51] The Court notes, nevertheless, that both the Heraklion public prosecutor's office, when it was bringing proceedings against the applicants (see par. 12 above), and the Heraklion Criminal Court sitting on appeal, in its judgment of 15 February 1990 (see par. 15 above), relied expressly on the lack of the bishop's authorisation as well as the lack of an authorisation from the Minister of Education and Religious Affairs. The latter, in response to five requests made by the applicants between

25 October 1983 and 10 December 1984, replied that he was examining their file. To date, as far as the Court is aware, the applicants have not received an express decision. Moreover, at the hearing a representative of the Government himself described the Minister's conduct as unfair and attributed it to the difficulty that the latter might have had in giving legally valid reasons for an express decision refusing the authorisation or to his fear that he might provide the applicants with grounds for appealing to the Supreme Administrative Court to challenge an express administrative decision.

[52] In these circumstances the Court considers that the Government cannot rely on the applicants' failure to comply with a legal formality to justify their conviction. The degree of severity of the sanction is immaterial.

[53] Like the Commission, the Court is of the opinion that the impugned conviction had such a direct effect on the applicants' freedom of religion that it cannot be regarded as proportionate to the legitimate aim pursued, nor, accordingly, as necessary in a democratic society.

In conclusion, there has been a violation of art. 9.

(...)

CONCURRING OPINION OF JUDGE MARTENS

[1] I completely share the views expressed in the Court's judgment, but I would have preferred to decide the merits on the basis of the „prescribed by law" requirement, that is to decide the issue which the Court leaves open (see par. 38 of its judgment).

[2] The substance of the „necessary in a democratic society" requirement is a balancing exercise of the elements of the individual case. However, as follows from par. 38 of the Court's judgment, the very essence of the applicants' complaints is not one of individual, but one of general injustice: what they complain of is not so much the harassment they have been subjected to, but, basically, the obstruction to setting up a Jehovah's Witnesses chapel in general. The „prescribed by law" requirement is therefore more suitable to do justice to what - also in the Government's opinion - is the essential thesis of the applicants, viz. that the Law of Necessity no. 1363/1938 is incompatible with art. 9, either per se or in any event as consistently applied by the competent authorities.

[3] I suggest that this approach, although perhaps a little innovatory, is in line with the Court's doctrine that part of its task under the „prescribed by law" requirement is to assess the quality of the law invoked as a justification for the interference under examination.

[4] Turning now to the applicants' thesis that the Law of Necessity no. 1363/1938 is incompatible with art. 9, I agree with counsel for the Government that the first question to be discussed is whether under art. 9 there is room at all for „prior restraint" in the form of making the

construction or operation of a place of worship conditional on a prior governmental authorisation and of making such construction or operation without such authorisation a criminal offence.

[5] As in the province of art. 9, I am opposed to answering this question outright in the negative. It is conceivable that the operation - and a fortiori the construction - of a place of worship in a particular area may raise serious public-order questions and that possibility, in my mind, justifies not wholly excluding the acceptability of making such operation or construction depend on a prior governmental authorisation.

[6] Nevertheless, I think that here, where freedom of religion is at stake - even more than in the province of art. 9 -, the question is very delicate, for public-order arguments may easily disguise intolerance. It is all the more sensitive where there is an official State religion. In such cases it should be absolutely clear both from the wording of, and from the practice under the law in question that the requirement of a prior authorisation in no way whatsoever purports to enable the authorities to „evaluate" the tenets of the applicant community; as a matter of principle the requested authorisation should always be given, unless very exceptional, objective and insuperable grounds of public order make that impossible.

[7] The Government have tried to convince us that the Law of Necessity no. 1363/1938 meets these admittedly strict requirements, but in vain. Counsel for the Government has alleged that under that Law there is no room for discretion, but he has at the same time made it clear that it required the authorities to scrutinise whether the application arose from genuine religious needs or as a means of proselytising and, moreover, whether the tenets of the applicant community were acceptable. And indeed, the requirement that there should be at least fifty families from more or less the same neighbourhood illustrates not only that there is ample room for discretion but also that the Law of Necessity no. 1363/ 1938 goes much further than is permissible in respect of prior restraint of freedom of religion. On top of this there is the involvement of the clerical authorities of the dominant religion in the authorisation procedure which - even if they were confined to a strictly advisory role (which I doubt) - implies in itself that the Law in question does not meet the above-mentioned strict requirements and is incompatible with art. 9.

[8] In sum, I find that the applicants rightly say that the Law of Necessity no. 1363/1938 is per se incompatible with art. 9.

42

Der blasphemische Charakter eines medialen Werks, verstanden als Verletzung religiöser Gefühle anderer, kann eine Einschränkung der Meinungsfreiheit (hier: Ablehnung eines Zertifikats des *British board of film classification* für den Video-Film „Visions of Ecstasy") rechtfertigen.
Zur Frage des zulässigen Beurteilungsspielraums.

Art. 10 EMRK
EGMR, Urteil vom 25. November 1996 - No.19/1995/525/611
(Wingrove ./. Vereinigtes Königreich)[1] -

AS TO THE FACTS

I. Circumstances of the case

[7] The applicant, Mr Nigel Wingrove, is a film director. He was born in 1957 and resides in London.

[8] Mr Wingrove wrote the shooting script for, and directed the making of, a video work entitled Visions of Ecstasy. Its running time is approximately eighteen minutes, and it contains no dialogue, only music and moving images. According to the applicant, the idea for the film was derived from the life and writings of St Teresa of Avila, the sixteenth-century Carmelite nun and founder of many convents, who experienced powerful ecstatic visions of Jesus Christ.

[9] The action of the film centres upon a youthful actress dressed as a nun and intended to represent St Teresa. It begins with the nun, dressed loosely in a black habit, stabbing her own hand with a large nail and spreading her blood over her naked breasts and clothing. In her writhing, she spills a chalice of communion wine and proceeds to lick it up from the ground. She loses consciousness. This sequence takes up approximately half of the running time of the video. The second part shows St Teresa dressed in a white habit standing with her arms held above her head by a white cord which is suspended from above and tied around her wrists. The near-naked form of a second female, said to represent St Teresa's psyche, slowly crawls her way along the ground towards her. Upon reaching St Teresa's feet, the psyche begins to caress her feet and legs, then her midriff, then her breasts, and finally exchanges passionate kisses with her. Throughout this sequence, St Teresa appears to be writhing in exquisite erotic sensation. This sequence is intercut at frequent intervals with a second sequence in which one sees the body of Christ, fastened to the cross which is lying upon the ground. St Teresa

---

[1] RJD 1996-V; ÖJZ 1997, 714.

first kisses the stigmata of his feet before moving up his body and kissing or licking the gaping wound in his right side. Then she sits astride him, seemingly naked under her habit, all the while moving in a motion reflecting intense erotic arousal, and kisses his lips. For a few seconds, it appears that he responds to her kisses. This action is intercut with the passionate kisses of the psyche already described. Finally, St Teresa runs her hand down to the fixed hand of Christ and entwines his fingers in hers. As she does so, the fingers of Christ seem to curl upwards to hold with hers, whereupon the video ends.

[10] Apart from the cast list which appears on the screen for a few seconds, the viewer has no means of knowing from the film itself that the person dressed as a nun in the video is intended to be St Teresa or that the other woman who appears is intended to be her psyche. No attempt is made in the video to explain its historical background.

[11] Visions of Ecstasy was submitted to the British Board of Film Classification („the Board"), being the authority designated by the Home Secretary under sec. 4 (1) of the Video Recordings Act 1984 („the 1984 Act" - see par. 24 below) as

> „the authority responsible for making arrangements
> (a) for determining, for the purposes of [the] Act whether or not video works are suitable for classification certificates to be issued in respect of them, having special regard to the likelihood of video works in respect of which such certificates have been issued being viewed in the home,
> (b) in the case of works which are determined in accordance with the arrangements to be so suitable
> (i) for making such other determinations as are required for the issue of classification certificates, and
> (ii) for issuing such certificates ...
> ..."

[12] The applicant submitted the video to the Board in order that it might lawfully be sold, hired out or otherwise supplied to the general public or a section thereof.

[13] The Board rejected the application for a classification certificate on 18 September 1989 in the following terms:

> „Further to your application for a classification certificate ..., you are already aware that under the Video Recordings Act 1984 the Board must determine first of all whether or not a video work is suitable for such a certificate to be issued to it, having special regard to the likelihood of video works being viewed in the home. In making this judgment, the Board must have regard to the Home Secretary's Letter of Designation in which we are enjoined to ‚continue to seek to avoid classifying works which are obscene within the meaning of the Obscene Publications Acts 1959 and 1964 or which infringe other provisions of the criminal law'. Amongst these provisions is the criminal law of blasphemy, as tested recently in the House of Lords in R. v. Lemon (1979), commonly known as the Gay News

case. The definition of blasphemy cited therein is ,any contemptuous, reviling, scurrilous or ludicrous matter relating to God, Jesus Christ or the Bible ... It is not blasphemous to speak or publish opinions hostile to the Christian religion' if the publication is ,decent and temperate'. The question is not one of the matter expressed, but of its manner, i.e. ,the tone, style and spirit', in which it is presented.

The video work submitted by you depicts the mingling of religious ecstasy and sexual passion, a matter which may be of legitimate concern to the artist. It becomes subject to the law of blasphemy, however, if the manner of its presentation is bound to give rise to outrage at the unacceptable treatment of a sacred subject. Because the wounded body of the crucified Christ is presented solely as the focus of, and at certain moments a participant in, the erotic desire of St Teresa, with no attempt to explore the meaning of the imagery beyond engaging the viewer in an erotic experience, it is the Board's view, and that of its legal advisers, that a reasonable jury properly directed would find that the work infringes the criminal law of blasphemy.

To summarise, it is not the case that the sexual imagery in Visions of Ecstasy lies beyond the parameters of the ,18' category; it is simply that for a major proportion of the work's duration that sexual imagery is focused on the figure of the crucified Christ. If the male figure were not Christ, the problem would not arise. Cuts of a fairly radical nature in the overt expressions of sexuality between St Teresa and the Christ figure might be practicable, but I understand that you do not wish to attempt this course of action. In consequence, we have concluded that it would not be suitable for a classification certificate to be issued to this video work."

[14] The applicant appealed against the Board's determination to the Video Appeals Committee („the VAC" - see par. 25 below), established pursuant to sec. 4 (3) of the 1984 Act. His notice of appeal, prepared by his legal representatives at the time, contained the following grounds:

„(i) that the Board was wrong to conclude that the video infringes the criminal law of blasphemy, and that a reasonable jury properly directed would so find;
(ii) in particular, the Appellant will contend that upon a proper understanding of the serious nature of the video as an artistic and imaginative interpretation of the ,ecstasy' or ,rapture' of the sixteenth-century Carmelite nun, St Teresa of Avila, it would not be taken by a reasonable person as contemptuous, reviling, scurrilous or ludicrous or otherwise disparaging in relation to God, Jesus Christ or the Bible. The appeal will raise the question of mixed fact and law, namely whether publication of the video, even to a restricted degree, would contravene the existing criminal law of blasphemy."

[15] The Board submitted a formal reply to the VAC explaining its decision in relation to its functions under sec. 4 of the 1984 Act:

„The Act does not expressly set out the principles to be applied by the authority in determining whether or not a video work is suitable for a classification certificate to be issued in respect of it. In these circumstances, the Board has exercised its

*discretion to formulate principles for classifying video works in a manner which
it believes to be both reasonable and suited to carrying out the broad objectives of
the Act. Amongst these principles, the Board has concluded that an overriding
test of suitability for classification is the determination that the video work in
question does not infringe the criminal law. In formulating and applying this
principle, the Board has consistently had regard to the Home Secretary's Letter of
Designation under the Video Recordings Act ...
The Board has concluded on the advice of leading Counsel that the video work in
question infringes the criminal law of blasphemy and that a reasonable jury
properly directed on the law would convict accordingly. The Board submits and
is advised that in Britain the offence of blasphemy is committed if a video work
treats a religious subject (in particular God, Jesus Christ or the Bible) in such a
manner as to be calculated (that is, bound, not intended) to outrage those who
have an understanding of, sympathy towards and support for the Christian story
and ethic, because of the contemptuous, reviling, insulting, scurrilous or ludicrous tone, style and spirit in which the subject is presented.
The video work under appeal purports to depict the erotic fantasies of a character
described in the credits as St Teresa of Avila. The 14-minute second section of the
video work portrays ,St Teresa' having an erotic fantasy involving the crucified
figure of Christ, and also a Lesbian erotic fantasy involving the ,Psyche of St
Teresa'. No attempt is made to place what is shown in any historical, religious or
dramatic context: the figures of St Teresa and her psyche are both clearly modern
in appearance and the erotic images are accompanied by a rock music backing.
The work contains no dialogue or evidence of an interest in exploring the psychology or even the sexuality of the character purporting to be St Teresa of Avila. Instead, this character and her supposed fantasies about lesbianism and the body
and blood of Christ are presented as the occasion for a series of erotic images of a
kind familiar from ,soft-core' pornography.
In support of its contentions, the Board refers to an interview given by the appellant and published in Midweek magazine on 14 September 1989. In this interview, the appellant attempts to draw a distinction between pornography and
,erotica', denying that the video work in question is pornographic but stating that
,all my own work is actually erotica'. Further on, the interviewer comments:
,In many ways, though, Visions calls upon the standard lexicon of lust found in
down market porn: nuns, lesbianism, women tied up (Gay Nuns in Bondage
could have been an alternative title in fact). Nigel Wingrove flashes a wicked
grin. ,That's right, and I'm not denying it. I don't know what it is about nuns, it's
the same sort of thing as white stocking tops I suppose.' So why does he not consider Visions to be pornography, or at least soft porn? ,I hope it is gentler, subtler
than that. I suppose most people think pornography shows the sex act, and this
doesn't.'
It is clear from the appellant's own admissions that, whether or not the video
work can rightly be described as pornographic, it is solely erotic in content, and it
focuses this erotic imagery for much of its duration on the body and blood of
Christ, who is even shown to respond to the sexual attentions of the principal
character. Moreover, the manner in which such imagery is treated places the focus of the work less on the erotic feelings of the character than on those of the audience, which is the primary function of pornography whether or not it shows the
sex act explicitly. Because there is no attempt, in the Board's view, to explore the
meaning of the imagery beyond engaging the viewer in a voyeuristic erotic experi-*

ence, the Board considers that the public distribution of such a video work would outrage and insult the feelings of believing Christians ...

...

The Board ... submits that the appeal should be dismissed and its determination upheld."

[16] The applicant then made further representations to the VAC, stating, inter alia:

„*The definition of the offence of blasphemy set out in ... the reply is too wide, being significantly wider than the test approved in the only modern authority - see Lemon & Gay News Ltd v. Whitehouse [1979] Appeal Cases 617, per Lord Scarman at 665. For example, there is no uniform law of blasphemy in Britain; the last recorded prosecution for blasphemy under the law of Scotland was in 1843 - see Thos Paterson [1843] I Brown 629. Nor is any religious subject protected - the reviling matter must be in relation to God, Jesus Christ or the Bible, or the formularies of the Church of England as by law established.*

In the Appellant's contention, these limitations are of the utmost significance in this case since the video is not concerned with anything which God or Jesus Christ did, or thought or might have approved of. It is about the erotic visions and imaginings of a sixteenth-century Carmelite nun - namely St Teresa of Avila. It is quite plain that the Christ figure exists in her fantasy as the Board expressly accepts ... The scurrilous and/or erotic treatment of religious subject matter has received the Board's classification without attempted prosecution in recent years, e.g. Monty Python's Life of Brian and Mr Scorsese's The Last Temptation of Christ.

... The Board argues that the video is purely erotic or ,soft-core' pornographic, without historical, religious, dramatic or other artistic merit. The implication is that, had it possessed such merit the Board's decision might very well have been otherwise. The Appellant will seek to argue and call evidence to the effect that the video work is a serious treatment of the subject of the ecstatic raptures of St Teresa well chronicled in her own works and those of commentators) from a twentieth-century point of view.

The so-called ,rock music backing' was in fact specially commissioned from the respected composer Steven Severin, after discussion of the Director's desired artistic and emotional impact. The Board has based its decision upon the narrowest, most disparaging, critical appreciation of the work. The Appellant will contend that a very much more favourable assessment of his aims and achievement in making Visions of Ecstasy is, at the very least, tenable and that then Board ought not to refuse a certificate on a mere matter of interpretation.

The Appellant takes objection to the Board's quotation ... of comments attributed to him from an article by one Rob Ryan published in Midweek magazine 14th September 1989. The remarks are pure hearsay so far as the Board is concerned. That aside, the piece quoted is in large part the comments of the author of the article. An entirely misleading impression of what the Appellant said to the author is conveyed by the interpolation of the words attributed to him, and by taking this passage out of context.

Above all, the Appellant disputes the key assertion by the Board that the video work is solely erotic in content."

[17] The appeal was heard by a five-member panel of the VAC („the Panel") on 6 and 7 December 1989; oral and affidavit evidence was submitted. By a majority of three to two, a written decision rejecting the appeal was given on 23 December 1989. The Panel also considered itself bound by the criteria set out in the designation notice (see par. 24 below). It had difficulty, however, in ascertaining and applying the present law of blasphemy. It commented as follows:

> „*The authorities on this Common Law offence were reviewed by the House of Lords in the case of Lemon and Gay News Ltd v. Whitehouse which concerned a magazine called Gay News, the readership of which consisted mainly of homosexuals although it was on sale to the general public at some bookstalls. One edition contained a poem entitled The Love that Dares to Speak its Name accompanied by a drawing illustrating its subject matter.*
>
> *In his judgment Lord Scarman said that it was unnecessary to speculate whether an outraged Christian would feel provoked by the words and illustration to commit a breach of the peace, the true test being whether the words are calculated to outrage and insult the Christian's religious feelings, the material in question being contemptuous, reviling, scurrilous or ludicrous matter relating to God, Jesus Christ or the Bible, or the formularies of the Church of England. It should perhaps be added that the word ‚calculated' should be read in the dictionary sense of ‚estimated' or ‚likely' as it was decided that intent (other than an intent to publish) is not an element in the offence.*
>
> *In the same case Lord Diplock said that the material must be ‚likely to arouse a sense of outrage among those who believe in or respect the Christian faith'.*
>
> *In the present case the Board's Director ... said in evidence that the Board's view was that the video was ‚contemptuous of the divinity of Christ'. He added that although the Board's decision was based upon its view that the video is blasphemous (blasphemy being an offence which relates only to the Christian religion), it would take just the same stance if it were asked to grant a Certificate to a video which, for instance, was contemptuous of Mohammed or Buddha.*"

[18] The Panel went on to review the content of the video and accepted that the applicant had in mind St Teresa, a nun, „who is known to have had ecstatic visions of Christ although, incidentally, these did not start until she was 39 years of age - in marked contrast to the obvious youthfulness of the actress who plays the part".

[19] The Panel reached the following conclusion:

> „*From the writings of St Teresa herself, and the subsequent writings of others, there seems no reason to doubt that some of her visions were of seeing the glorified body of Christ and being shown his wounds but, even so, it seems clear that Mr Wingrove has taken considerable artistic licence with his subject.*
>
> *Apart from the age discrepancy - a comparatively minor matter - we were made aware of nothing which would suggest that Teresa ever did anything to injure her hand or that any element of lesbianism ever entered into her visions. More importantly, there seems nothing to suggest that Teresa, in her visions, ever saw herself as being in any bodily contact with the glorified Christ. As one author, Mr*

Stephen Clissold, puts it ,Teresa experienced ecstasy as a form of prayer in which she herself played almost no part'.

So, in view of the extent of the artistic licence, we think it would be reasonable to look upon the video as centring upon any nun of any century who, like many others down the ages, had ecstatic visions.

There is also another reason for taking this stance: unless the viewer happens to read the cast list which appears on the screen for a few seconds, he or she has no means of knowing that the nun is supposed to be St Teresa, nor that the figure of the second woman is supposed to be her psyche. And he or she in any event may well be unaware that Teresa was a real-life nun who had ecstatic visions.

It is true that Mr Wingrove says that it is intended that the sleeve or jacket for the video will provide ,basic historical information to assist the viewer', but we feel bound to regard this as irrelevant. Firstly because it by no means follows that every viewer will read any such description; and secondly because the Board's and the Appeal Panel's decision must be based solely upon the video itself, quite apart from the fact that at the time of making a decision the sleeve or jacket is usually - as in the present instance - not even in existence.

However, although we have thought it proper to dwell at some length with the ,St Teresa' aspect, we are of the opinion that in practice, when considering whether or not the video is blasphemous, it makes little or no difference whether one looks upon the central character as being St Teresa or any other nun.

The appellant, in his written statement, lays stress upon the undoubted fact that the whole of the second half consists of Teresa's vision or dream. Hence he says the video says nothing about Christ, his figure being used only as a projection of St Teresa's mind, nor was it his intention to make that figure an active participant in any overt sexual act.

He goes on to say ,Rather the very mild responses are those of St Teresa's conjecture: the kiss, hand clasp and ultimately the tears of Christ. To show no response to a creation of her own mind would be nonsense; no woman (nor man) whose deep love could cause such visions/ecstasies would imagine the object of that love coldly to ignore their caresses'.

Although we quite appreciate the logic of this point of view, we have reservations about the extent to which a vision or dream sequence can affect the question of whether what is pictured or said is blasphemous.

It would, for instance, be possible to produce a film or video which was most extremely contemptuous, reviling, scurrilous or ludicrous in relation to Christ, all dressed up in the context of someone's imaginings. In such circumstances we find it hard to envisage that, by such a simple device, it could reasonably be said that no offence had been committed. If in our opinion the viewer, after making proper allowance for the scene being in the form of a dream, nevertheless reasonably feels that it would cause a sense of outrage and insult to a Christian's feelings, the offence would be established.

We should perhaps also deal, albeit briefly, with a further submission made on behalf of the appellant, namely that the crime of blasphemy may extend only to the written or spoken word and hence that a court might rule that no film or video, and perhaps nothing shown on television, could become the subject of such a charge. Suffice it to say that in our view this is too unlikely to cause it to be taken into account by the Board or a panel of the Appeals Committee when reaching a decision

In the opinion of a majority of the Panel the video did not, as the appellant claims, explore St Teresa's struggles against her visions but exploited a devotion to Christ in purely carnal terms. Furthermore they considered that it lacked the seriousness and depth of The Last Temptation of Christ with which Counsel for the appellant sought to compare it.

Indeed the majority took the view that the video's message was that the nun was moved not by religious ecstasy but rather by sexual ecstasy, this ecstasy being of a perverse kind - full of images of blood, sado-masochism, lesbianism (or perhaps auto-erotism) and bondage. Although there was evidence of some element of repressed sexuality in St Teresa's devotion to Christ, they did not consider that this gave any ground for portraying her as taking the initiative in indulged sexuality. They considered the over-all tone and spirit of the video to be indecent and had little doubt that all the above factors, coupled with the motions of the nun whilst astride the body of Christ and the response to her kisses and the intertwining of the fingers would outrage the feelings of Christians, who would reasonably look upon it as being contemptuous of the divinity of Christ.

In these circumstances the majority were satisfied that the video is blasphemous, that a reasonable and properly directed jury would be likely to convict and therefore that the Board was right to refuse to grant a Certificate. Hence this appeal is accordingly dismissed.

It should perhaps be added that the minority on the Panel, whilst being in no doubt that many people would find the video to be extremely distasteful, would have allowed the appeal because in their view it is unlikely that a reasonable and properly directed jury would convict."

[20] As a result of the Board's determination, as upheld by the Panel, the applicant would commit an offence under sec. 9 of the 1984 Act (see par. 23 below) if he were to supply the video in any manner, whether or not for reward.

[21] The applicant received legal advice that his case was not suitable for judicial review (see par. 30-31 below) on the grounds that the formulation of the law of blasphemy, as accepted by the Panel, was an „accurate statement of the present law".

II. Situation of the video industry in the United Kingdom

[22] According to statistics submitted by the Government, in 1994 there were 21.5 million video-recorders in the United Kingdom. Out of approximately 20.75 million households in the United Kingdom, 18 million contained at least one video-recorder. There were approximately 15,000 video outlets in the United Kingdom. Videos were available for hire in between 4,000 and 5,000 video rental shops. They were also available for sale in 3,000 „high street" shops and in between 7,000 and 8,000 „secondary" outlets such as supermarkets, corner shops and petrol stations. In 1994 there were 194 million video rentals and 66 million video purchases in the United Kingdom. It is estimated that a further 65 million illegal copies („pirate videos") were distributed during that year.

III. Relevant domestic law

A. The regulation of video works

[23] The Video Recordings Act 1984 („the 1984 Act") regulates the distribution of video works. Subject to certain exemptions, it is an offence under sec. 9 (1) of that Act for a person to supply or offer to supply a video work in respect of which no classification certificate has been issued. Under sec. 7 there are three categories of classification: works deemed suitable for general viewing (and to which a parental guidance reference may be added); works for which the viewing is restricted to people who have attained a specified age; and works which may only be supplied by licensed sex shops. The Secretary of State for the Home Department may require that the content of certain works be labelled (sec. 8). It is an offence to ignore such conditions, for example by supplying someone under 18 years of age with an „18" classified work (sec. 11).

[24] Under sec. 4 (1) of the 1984 Act the Secretary of State may by notice designate any person or body as the authority for making arrangements for determining whether or not video works are suitable for classification certificates to be issued in respect of them (having special regard to the likelihood of certified video works being viewed in the home). By a notice dated 26 July 1985 the British Board of Film Classification was so designated. In the case of works which are determined in accordance with the arrangements described above to be suitable for classification certificates, the Board is responsible under sec. 4 (1) for making arrangements for the issue of certificates and making other determinations relating to their use. The Secretary of State's notice enjoined the Board „to continue to seek to avoid classifying works which are obscene within the meaning of the Obscene Publications Acts 1959 and 1964 or which infringe other provisions of the criminal law".

[25] Pursuant to sec. 4 (3) of the 1984 Act arrangements were made for the establishment of the Video Appeals Committee to determine appeals against decisions by the Board.

B. The law of blasphemy

[26] Blasphemy and blasphemous libel are common law offences triable on indictment and punishable by fine or imprisonment. Blasphemy consists in speaking and blasphemous libel in otherwise publishing blasphemous matter. Libel involves a publication in a permanent form, but that form may consist of moving pictures.

[27] In the case of Whitehouse v. Gay News Ltd and Lemon [1979] Appeal Cases 617 at 665, which concerned the law of blasphemy in England, Lord Scarman held that the modern law of blasphemy was correctly

formulated in art. 214 of Stephen's Digest of the Criminal Law, 9th edition (1950). This states as follows:

„Every publication is said to be blasphemous which contains any contemptuous, reviling, scurrilous or ludicrous matter relating to God, Jesus Christ or the Bible, or the formularies of the Church of England as by law established. It is not blasphemous to speak or publish opinions hostile to the Christian religion, or to deny the existence of God, if the publication is couched in decent and temperate language. The test to be applied is as to the manner in which the doctrines are advocated and not to the substance of the doctrines themselves."

The House of Lords in that case also decided that the mental element in the offence (mens rea) did not depend upon the accused having an intent to blaspheme. It was sufficient for the prosecution to prove that the publication had been intentional and that the matter published was blasphemous. The Gay News case, which had been brought by a private prosecutor, had been the first prosecution for blasphemy since 1922.

[28] As stated above, the law of blasphemy only protects the Christian religion and, more specifically, the established Church of England. This was confirmed by the Divisional Court in 1991. Ruling on an application for judicial review of a magistrate's refusal to issue a summons for blasphemy against Salman Rushdie and the publishers of The Satanic Verses, Lord Watkins stated:

„We have no doubt that as the law now stands it does not extend to religions other than Christianity ...

...

We think it right to say that, were it open to us to extend the law to cover religions other than Christianity, we should refrain from doing so. Considerations of public policy are extremely difficult and complex. It would be virtually impossible by judicial decision to set sufficiently clear limits to the offence, and other problems involved are formidable." (R. v. Chief Metropolitan Stipendiary Magistrate, ex parte Choudhury [1991] 1 All England Law Reports 306 at 318)

[29] On 4 July 1989 the then Minister of State at the Home Department, Mr John Patten, had sent a letter to a number of influential British Muslims, in which he stated inter alia that:

„Many Muslims have argued that the law of blasphemy should be amended to take books such as [The Satanic Verses] outside the boundary of what is legally acceptable. We have considered their arguments carefully and reached the conclusion that it would be unwise for a variety of reasons to amend the law of blasphemy, not the least the clear lack of agreement over whether the law should be reformed or repealed.

...

... an alteration in the law could lead to a rush of litigation which would damage relations between faiths. I hope you can appreciate how divisive and how damag-

ing such litigation might be, and how inappropriate our legal mechanisms are for dealing with matters of faith and individual belief. Indeed, the Christian faith no longer relies on it, preferring to recognise that the strength of their own belief is the best armour against mockers and blasphemers."

C. The availability of judicial review as a remedy

[30] Decisions by public bodies which have consequences which affect some person or body of persons are susceptible to challenge in the High Court on an application for judicial review. Amongst the grounds on which such a challenge may be brought is that the body in question misdirected itself on a point of law. The Video Appeals Committee is such a public body because it is established pursuant to an Act of Parliament (see par. 25 above). Furthermore, its decisions affect the rights of persons who make video works because confirmation of a decision that a video work cannot receive a classification certificate would mean that copies of that work could not be lawfully supplied to members of the public.

[31] On an application for judicial review a court would not normally look at the merits of any decision made by such a body, except where the decision was so unreasonable that no reasonable body, properly instructed, could have reached it. However, where the decision is based on a point of law and it is alleged that the body has misdirected itself on that point, the decision could be challenged by an application for judicial review. In the case of C.C.S.U. v. Minister for the Civil Service [1984] 3 All England Law Reports at 950, Lord Diplock, in the House of Lords, classified under three heads the grounds on which administrative action is subject to control by judicial review. He called the first ground „illegality" and described it as follows:

> „By ‚illegality' as a ground for judicial review I mean that the decision-maker must understand correctly the law that regulates his decision-making power and must give effect to it. Whether he has or not is par excellence a justiciable question to be decided, in the event of a dispute, by those persons, the judges, by whom the judicial power of the State is exercisable."

PROCEEDINGS BEFORE THE COMMISSION

(...)

FINAL SUBMISSIONS TO THE COURT

(...)

AS TO THE LAW

I. Alleged violation of Art. 10 of the convention

[35] The applicant alleged a violation of his right to freedom of expression, as guaranteed by art. 10 of the Convention, which, in so far as relevant, provides:

> „1. *Everyone has the right to freedom of expression. This right shall include freedom to hold opinions and to receive and impart information and ideas without interference by public authority and regardless of frontiers ...*
> *2. The exercise of these freedoms, since it carries with it duties and responsibilities, may be subject to such formalities, conditions, restrictions or penalties as are prescribed by law and are necessary in a democratic society, in the interests of national security, territorial integrity or public safety, for the prevention of disorder or crime, for the protection of health or morals, for the protection of the reputation or rights of others, for preventing the disclosure of information received in confidence, or for maintaining the authority and impartiality of the judiciary."*

[36] The refusal by the British Board of Film Classification to grant a certificate for the applicant's video work Visions of Ecstasy, seen in conjunction with the statutory provisions making it a criminal offence to distribute a video work without this certificate (see par. 23 above), amounted to an interference by a public authority with the applicant's right to impart ideas. This was common ground between the participants in the proceedings. To determine whether such an interference entails a violation of the Convention, the Court must examine whether or not it was justified under art. 10 par. 2 by reason of being a restriction „prescribed by law", which pursued an aim that was legitimate under that provision (art. 10-2) and was „necessary in a democratic society".

A. Whether the interference was „prescribed by law"

[37] The applicant considered that the law of blasphemy was so uncertain that it was inordinately difficult to establish in advance whether in the eyes of a jury a particular publication would constitute an offence. Moreover, it was practically impossible to know what predictions an administrative body - the British Board of Film Classification - would make as to the outcome of a hypothetical prosecution. In these circumstances, the applicant could not reasonably be expected to foresee the result of the Board's speculations. The requirement of foreseeability which flows from the expression „prescribed by law" was therefore not fulfilled.

[38] The Government contested this claim: it was a feature common to most laws and legal systems that tribunals may reach different conclusions even when applying the same law to the same facts. This did not necessarily make these laws inaccessible or unforeseeable. Given the in-

finite variety of ways of publishing „contemptuous, reviling, scurrilous or ludicrous matter relating to God, Jesus Christ or the Bible" (see par. 27 above), it would not be appropriate for the law to seek to define in detail which images would or would not be potentially blasphemous.

[39] The Commission, noting that considerable legal advice was available to the applicant, was of the view that he could reasonably have foreseen the restrictions to which his video work was liable.

[40] The Court reiterates that, according to its case-law, the relevant national „law", which includes both statute and common law (see, inter alia, the Sunday Times v. the United Kingdom (no. 1) judgment of 26 April 1979, Series A no. 30, p. 30, par. 47), must be formulated with sufficient precision to enable those concerned - if need be, with appropriate legal advice - to foresee, to a degree that is reasonable in the circumstances, the consequences which a given action may entail. A law that confers a discretion is not in itself inconsistent with this requirement, provided that the scope of the discretion and the manner of its exercise are indicated with sufficient clarity, having regard to the legitimate aim in question, to give the individual adequate protection against arbitrary interference (see, for instance, the Tolstoy Miloslavsky v. the United Kingdom judgment of 13 July 1995, Series A no. 316-B, pp. 71-72, par. 37, and the Goodwin v. the United Kingdom judgment of 27 March 1996, RJD 1996-II, pp. 496-97, par. 31).

[41] It is observed that, in refusing a certificate for distribution of the applicant's video on the basis that it infringed a provision of the criminal law of blasphemy, the British Board of Film Classification acted within its powers under sec. 4 (1) of the 1984 Act (see par. 24 above).

[42] The Court recognises that the offence of blasphemy cannot by its very nature lend itself to precise legal definition. National authorities must therefore be afforded a degree of flexibility in assessing whether the facts of a particular case fall within the accepted definition of the offence (see, mutatis mutandis, the Tolstoy Miloslavsky judgment cited above at par. 40, p. 73, par. 41).

[43] There appears to be no general uncertainty or disagreement between those appearing before the Court as to the definition in English law of the offence of blasphemy, as formulated by the House of Lords in the case of Whitehouse v. Gay News Ltd and Lemon (see par. 27 above). Having seen for itself the content of the video work, the Court is satisfied that the applicant could reasonably have foreseen with appropriate legal advice that the film, particularly those scenes involving the crucified figure of Christ, could fall within the scope of the offence of blasphemy. The above conclusion is borne out by the applicant's decision not to initiate proceedings for judicial review on the basis of counsel's advice that the Panel's formulation of the law of blasphemy represented an accurate statement of the law (see, mutatis mutandis, the Open Door and Dublin

Well Woman v. Ireland judgment of 29 October 1992, Series A no. 246-A, p. 27, par. 60).

[44] Against this background it cannot be said that the law in question did not afford the applicant adequate protection against arbitrary interference. The Court therefore concludes that the impugned restriction was „prescribed by law".

B. Whether the interference pursued a legitimate aim

[45] The applicant contested the Government's assertion that his video work was refused a certificate for distribution in order to „protect the right of citizens not to be offended in their religious feelings". In his submission, the expression „rights of others" in the present context only refers to an actual, positive right not to be offended. It does not include a hypothetical right held by some Christians to avoid disturbance at the prospect of other people's viewing the video work without being shocked. In any event - the applicant further submitted - the restriction on the film's distribution could not pursue a legitimate aim since it was based on a discriminatory law, limited to the protection of Christians, and specifically, those of the Anglican faith.

[46] The Government referred to the case of Otto-Preminger-Institut v. Austria (judgment of 20 September 1994, Series A no. 295-A, pp. 17-18, par. 47-48, KirchE-EU S. 248) where the Court had accepted that respect for the religious feelings of believers can move a State legitimately to restrict the publication of provocative portrayals of objects of religious veneration.

[47] The Commission considered that the English law of blasphemy is intended to suppress behaviour directed against objects of religious veneration that is likely to cause justified indignation amongst believing Christians. It follows that the application of this law in the present case was intended to protect the right of citizens not to be insulted in their religious feelings.

[48] The Court notes at the outset that, as stated by the Board, the aim of the interference was to protect against the treatment of a religious subject in such a manner „as to be calculated (that is, bound, not intended) to outrage those who have an understanding of, sympathy towards and support for the Christian story and ethic, because of the contemptuous, reviling, insulting, scurrilous or ludicrous tone, style and spirit in which the subject is presented" (see par. 15 above). This is an aim which undoubtedly corresponds to that of the protection of „the rights of others" within the meaning of par. 2 of art. 10. It is also fully consonant with the aim of the protections afforded by art. 9 to religious freedom.

[49] Whether or not there was a real need for protection against expo-
sure to the film in question is a matter which must be addressed below
when assessing the „necessity" of the interference.

[50] It is true that the English law of blasphemy only extends to the
Christian faith. Indeed the anomaly of this state of affairs in a multide-
nominational society was recognised by the Divisional Court in R. v.
Chief Metropolitan Stipendiary Magistrate, ex parte Choudhury [1991] 1
All England Law Reports 306 at 317 (see par. 28 above). However, it is
not for the European Court to rule in abstracto as to the compatibility of
domestic law with the Convention. The extent to which English law protects other beliefs is not in issue before the Court which must confine its
attention to the case before it (see, for example, the Klass and Others v.
Germany judgment of 6 September 1978, Series A no. 28, p. 18, par. 33).
The uncontested fact that the law of blasphemy does not treat on an
equal footing the different religions practised in the United Kingdom
does not detract from the legitimacy of the aim pursued in the present
context.

[51] The refusal to grant a certificate for the distribution of Visions of
Ecstasy consequently had a legitimate aim under art. 10 par. 2.

C. Whether the interference was „necessary in a democratic society"

[52] The Court recalls that freedom of expression constitutes one of the
essential foundations of a democratic society. As par. 2 of art. 10 expressly recognises, however, the exercise of that freedom carries with it
duties and responsibilities. Amongst them, in the context of religious beliefs, may legitimately be included a duty to avoid as far as possible an
expression that is, in regard to objects of veneration, gratuitously offensive to others and profanatory (see the Otto-Preminger-Institut judgment
cited above at par. 46, pp. 18-19, par. 47 and 49).

[53] No restriction on freedom of expression, whether in the context of
religious beliefs or in any other, can be compatible with art. 9 unless it
satisfies, inter alia, the test of necessity as required by the second paragraph of that art. 10. In examining whether restrictions to the rights and
freedoms guaranteed by the Convention can be considered „necessary in
a democratic society" the Court has, however, consistently held that the
Contracting States enjoy a certain but not unlimited margin of appreciation. It is, in any event, for the European Court to give a final ruling on
the restriction's compatibility with the Convention and it will do so by
assessing in the circumstances of a particular case, inter alia, whether
the interference corresponded to a „pressing social need" and whether it
was „proportionate to the legitimate aim pursued" (see, mutatis mutandis, among many other authorities, the Goodwin judgment cited above at
par. 40, pp. 500-01, par. 40).

[54] According to the applicant, there was no „pressing social need" to ban a video work on the uncertain assumption that it would breach the law of blasphemy; indeed, the overriding social need was to allow it to be distributed. Furthermore, since adequate protection was already provided by a panoply of laws - concerning, inter alia, obscenity, public order and disturbances to places of religious worship - blasphemy laws, which are incompatible with the European idea of freedom of expression, were also superfluous in practice. In any event, the complete prohibition of a video work that contained no obscenity, no pornography and no element of vilification of Christ was disproportionate to the aim pursued.

[55] For the Commission, the fact that Visions of Ecstasy was a short video work and not a feature film meant that its distribution would have been more limited and less likely to attract publicity. The Commission came to the same conclusion as the applicant.

[56] The Government contended that the applicant's video work was clearly a provocative and indecent portrayal of an object of religious veneration, that its distribution would have been sufficiently public and widespread to cause offence and that it amounted to an attack on the religious beliefs of Christians which was insulting and offensive. In those circumstances, in refusing to grant a classification certificate for the applicant's video work, the national authorities only acted within their margin of appreciation.

[57] The Court observes that the refusal to grant Visions of Ecstasy a distribution certificate was intended to protect „the rights of others", and more specifically to provide protection against seriously offensive attacks on matters regarded as sacred by Christians (see par. 48 above). The laws to which the applicant made reference (see par. 54 above) and which pursue related but distinct aims are thus not relevant in this context. As the observations filed by the intervenors (see par. 5 above) show, blasphemy legislation is still in force in various European countries. It is true that the application of these laws has become increasingly rare and that several States have recently repealed them altogether. In the United Kingdom only two prosecutions concerning blasphemy have been brought in the last seventy years (see par. 27 above). Strong arguments have been advanced in favour of the abolition of blasphemy laws, for example, that such laws may discriminate against different faiths or denominations - as put forward by the applicant - or that legal mechanisms are inadequate to deal with matters of faith or individual belief - as recognised by the Minister of State at the Home Department in his letter of 4 July 1989 (see par. 29 above). However, the fact remains that there is as yet not sufficient common ground in the legal and social orders of the member States of the Council of Europe to conclude that a system whereby a State can impose restrictions on the propagation of material on the basis that it is blasphemous is, in itself, unnecessary in a democratic society

and thus incompatible with the Convention (see, mutatis mutandis, the Otto-Preminger-Institut judgment cited above at par. 46, p. 19, par. 49).
[58] Whereas there is little scope under art. 10 par. 2 of the Convention for restrictions on political speech or on debate of questions of public interest (see, mutatis mutandis, among many other authorities, the Lingens v. Austria judgment of 8 July 1986, Series A no. 103, p. 26, par. 42; the Castells v. Spain judgment of 23 April 1992, Series A no. 236, p. 23, par. 43; and the Thorgeir Thorgeirson v. Iceland judgment of 25 June 1992, Series A no. 239, p. 27, par. 63), a wider margin of appreciation is generally available to the Contracting States when regulating freedom of expression in relation to matters liable to offend intimate personal convictions within the sphere of morals or, especially, religion. Moreover, as in the field of morals, and perhaps to an even greater degree, there is no uniform European conception of the requirements of „the protection of the rights of others" in relation to attacks on their religious convictions. What is likely to cause substantial offence to persons of a particular religious persuasion will vary significantly from time to time and from place to place, especially in an era characterised by an ever growing array of faiths and denominations. By reason of their direct and continuous contact with the vital forces of their countries, State authorities are in principle in a better position than the international judge to give an opinion on the exact content of these requirements with regard to the rights of others as well as on the „necessity" of a „restriction" intended to protect from such material those whose deepest feelings and convictions would be seriously offended (see, mutatis mutandis, the Müller and Others v. Switzerland judgment of 24 May 1988, Series A no. 133, p. 22, par. 35). This does not of course exclude final European supervision. Such supervision is all the more necessary given the breadth and open-endedness of the notion of blasphemy and the risks of arbitrary or excessive interferences with freedom of expression under the guise of action taken against allegedly blasphemous material. In this regard the scope of the offence of blasphemy and the safeguards inherent in the legislation are especially important. Moreover the fact that the present case involves prior restraint calls for special scrutiny by the Court (see, mutatis mutandis, the Observer and Guardian v. the United Kingdom judgment of 26 November 1991, Series A no. 216, p. 30, par. 60).
[59] The Court's task in this case is to determine whether the reasons relied on by the national authorities to justify the measures interfering with the applicant's freedom of expression are relevant and sufficient for the purposes of art. 10 par. 2 of the Convention.
[60] As regards the content of the law itself, the Court observes that the English law of blasphemy does not prohibit the expression, in any form, of views hostile to the Christian religion. Nor can it be said that opinions which are offensive to Christians necessarily fall within its ambit. As the English courts have indicated (see par. 27 above), it is the

manner in which views are advocated rather than the views themselves which the law seeks to control. The extent of insult to religious feelings must be significant, as is clear from the use by the courts of the adjectives „contemptuous", „reviling", „scurrilous", „ludicrous" to depict material of a sufficient degree of offensiveness. The high degree of profanation that must be attained constitutes, in itself, a safeguard against arbitrariness. It is against this background that the asserted justification under art. 10 par. 2 in the decisions of the national authorities must be considered.

[61] Visions of Ecstasy portrays, inter alia, a female character astride the recumbent body of the crucified Christ engaged in an act of an overtly sexual nature (see par. 9 above). The national authorities, using powers that are not themselves incompatible with the Convention (see par. 57 above), considered that the manner in which such imagery was treated placed the focus of the work „less on the erotic feelings of the character than on those of the audience, which is the primary function of pornography" (see par. 15 above). They further held that since no attempt was made in the film to explore the meaning of the imagery beyond engaging the viewer in a „voyeuristic erotic experience", the public distribution of such a video could outrage and insult the feelings of believing Christians and constitute the criminal offence of blasphemy. This view was reached by both the Board of Film Classification and the Video Appeals Committee following a careful consideration of the arguments in defence of his work presented by the applicant in the course of two sets of proceedings. Moreover, it was open to the applicant to challenge the decision of the Appeals Committee in proceedings for judicial review (see par. 30 above). Bearing in mind the safeguard of the high threshold of profanation embodied in the definition of the offence of blasphemy under English law as well as the State's margin of appreciation in this area (see par. 58 above), the reasons given to justify the measures taken can be considered as both relevant and sufficient for the purposes of art. 10 par. 2. Furthermore, having viewed the film for itself, the Court is satisfied that the decisions by the national authorities cannot be said to be arbitrary or excessive.

[62] It was submitted by both the applicant and the Delegate of the Commission that a short experimental video work would reach a smaller audience than a major feature film, such as the one at issue in the Otto-Preminger-Institut case (cited above at par. 46). The risk that any Christian would unwittingly view the video was therefore substantially reduced and so was the need to impose restrictions on its distribution. Furthermore, this risk could have been reduced further by restricting the distribution of the film to licensed sex shops (see par. 23 above). Since the film would have been dispensed in video boxes which would have included a description of its content, only consenting adults would ever have been confronted with it.

[63] The Court notes, however, that it is in the nature of video works that once they become available on the market they can, in practice, be copied, lent, rented, sold and viewed in different homes, thereby easily escaping any form of control by the authorities.

In these circumstances, it was not unreasonable for the national authorities, bearing in mind the development of the video industry in the United Kingdom (see par. 22 above), to consider that the film could have reached a public to whom it would have caused offence. The use of a box including a warning as to the film's content (see par. 62 above) would have had only limited efficiency given the varied forms of transmission of video works mentioned above. In any event, here too the national authorities are in a better position than the European Court to make an assessment as to the likely impact of such a video, taking into account the difficulties in protecting the public.

[64] It is true that the measures taken by the authorities amounted to a complete ban on the film's distribution. However, this was an understandable consequence of the opinion of the competent authorities that the distribution of the video would infringe the criminal law and of the refusal of the applicant to amend or cut out the objectionable sequences (see par. 13 above). Having reached the conclusion that they did as to the blasphemous content of the film it cannot be said that the authorities overstepped their margin of appreciation.

D. Conclusion

[65] Against this background the national authorities were entitled to consider that the impugned measure was justified as being necessary in a democratic society within the meaning of par. 2 of art. 10. There has therefore been no violation of art. 10 of the Convention.

For these reasons the Court
Holds by seven votes to two that there has been no breach of art. 10 of the Convention.

CONCURRING OPINION OF JUDGE BERNHARDT

Personally, I am not convinced that the video film Visions of Ecstasy should have been banned by the refusal of a classification certificate, and this conviction is, inter alia, based on my impression when seeing the film. But it is the essence of the national margin of appreciation that, when different opinions are possible and do exist, the international judge should only intervene if the national decision cannot be reasonably justified.

I have finally voted with the majority for the following reasons:

(1) A prior control and classification of video films is not excluded in this most sensitive area and in view of the dangers involved, especially for young persons and the rights of others.

(2) Such a control requires a proper procedure and a careful weighing of the interests involved whenever a classification certificate is refused. In this respect, the present judgment describes in detail (par. s 11-19) the considerations and reasons in the decisions of the British authorities.

(3) In respect of the question whether the interference was „necessary in a democratic society", I am convinced that the national authorities have a considerable margin of appreciation, and they have made use of it in the present case in a manner acceptable under Convention standards.

CONCURRING OPINION OF JUDGE PETTITI

I voted with the majority, but for reasons which are substantially different in structure and content from those given in the judgment; I have not followed the reasoning in the Otto-Preminger-Institut case (judgment of 20 September 1994, Series A no. 295-A, KirchE-EU S. 248).

The first problem considered concerned the British legislation making blasphemy a criminal offence.

Admittedly, it is regrettable that the protection afforded by this legislation does not apply to other religions, for such a limitation makes no sense in 1996 now that we have the United Nations and UNESCO instruments on tolerance. However, the European Convention on Human Rights does not, on the one hand, prohibit legislation of this type, which is found in a number of member States, and, on the other hand, it leaves scope for review under art. 14. In the present case no complaint had been made to the European Court under that article.

The Court had to decide the case under art. 10. To my mind, the law on blasphemy provides a basis for consideration of the case under par. 2 of art. 10 and cannot automatically justify a ban on distribution.

Art. 9 is not in issue in the instant case and cannot be invoked. Certainly the Court rightly based its analysis under art. 10 on the rights of others and did not, as it had done in the Otto-Preminger-Institut judgment combine art. 9 and 10, morals and the rights of others, for which it had been criticised by legal writers. However, the wording adopted by the Chamber in par. 50 and 53 creates, in my opinion, too direct a link between the law of blasphemy and the criteria justifying a ban or restriction on the distribution of video-cassettes.

The fact that under the legislation on blasphemy, profanation or defamation may give rise to a prosecution does not in itself justify, under art. 10 of the European Convention, a total ban on the distribution of a book or video.

In my view, the Court ought to have made that clear. There can be no automatic response where freedom of expression is concerned.

The Court should, I think, have set out in its reasoning the facts that led the Video Appeals Committee - to which the applicant appealed against the determination of the British Board of Film Classification - to prohibit distribution of the video.

I consider that the same decision could have been reached under par. 2 of art. 10on grounds other than blasphemy, for example the profanation of symbols, including secular ones (the national flag) or jeopardising or prejudicing public order (but not for the benefit of a religious majority in the territory concerned).

The reasoning should, in my opinion have been expressed in terms both of religious beliefs and of philosophical convictions. It is only in par. 53 of the judgment that the words „any other" are cited.

Profanation and serious attacks on the deeply held feelings of others or on religious or secular ideals can be relied on under art. 10 par. 2 in addition to blasphemy.

What was particularly shocking in the Wingrove case was the combination of an ostensibly philosophical message and wholly irrelevant obscene or pornographic images.

In this case, the use of obscenity for commercial ends may justify restrictions under art. 10 par. 2; but the use of a figure of symbolic value as a great thinker in the history of mankind (such as Moses, Dante or Tolstoy) in a portrayal which seriously offends the deeply held feelings of those who respect their works or thought may, in some cases, justify judicial supervision so that the public can be alerted through the reporting of court decisions.

But the possibility of prosecution does not suffice to make a total ban legitimate. That question has been raised recently: can a breach of rules of professional conduct (medical confidentiality) in itself justify a total ban on a book?

Mr Wingrove's own argument and the contradictions it contained could even have been used to supplement the Court's reasoning.

In his application he claimed that intellectual works should be protected against censorship on exclusively moral or religious grounds. In an article which is not reproduced in the video Mr Wingrove indicated that he was seeking to interpret St Teresa's writings explaining her ecstasies. In his submission, they amounted practically to a Voltairean work or one having anti-religious connotations. The film is quite different. Mr Wingrove did not even agree to cut (which he was entitled to do as the filmmaker) the „simulated copulation" scene which was quite unnecessary, even in the context of the film. Indeed, he acknowledged that as the video stood, it could have been called Gay Nuns in Bondage, like a pornographic film (see the Commission's report, decision on admissibility, p. 32).

The use of the word „ecstasy" in the title was a source of ambiguity, as much for people interested in literary works as for those interested in

pornography. The sale in hypermarkets and supermarkets of videos inciting pornographic or obscene behaviour is even more dangerous than the
sale of books, as it is more difficult to ensure that the public are protected.

The recent world-wide conference in Stockholm on the protection of
children highlighted the harmful social consequences of distributing mil-
lions of copies of obscene or pornographic videos to the public without
even minimal checking of their identification marks. Disguising content
is a commercial technique that is used to circumvent bans (for example,
videos for paedophiles that use adolescent girls, who have only just attained their majority, dressed up as little girls).

Admittedly, before it was edited, Mr Wingrove's film was presented as
having literary rather than obscene ambitions, but its maker chose not to
dispel the ambiguity he had created. Nor did he seek judicial review, as it
was open to him to do, of the Video Appeals Committee's dismissal of his
appeal against the Board of Film Classification's refusal to grant a classification certificate.

It is true that sec. 7 of the Video Recordings Act 1984 contains a variety of provisions regulating the grant and use of certificates, ranging
from outright bans to restrictions on viewing, identification requirements
(in sales centres and on the cover) or measures to protect minors. On this
point, British and North American case-law, particularly in Canada, contains a wealth of definitions of the boundaries between literature, obscenity and pornography (see the Revue du Barreau du Québec and the Supreme Court's case-law review).

The majority of the Video Appeals Committee took the view that the
imagery led not to a religious perception, but to a perverse one, the ecstasy being furthermore of a perverse kind. That analysis was in conformity with the approach of the House of Lords, which moreover did not
discuss the author's intention with respect to the moral element of the offence. The Board's Director said that it would have taken just the same
stance in respect of a film that was contemptuous of Mohammed or Bud-
dha.

The decision not to grant a certificate might possibly have been justifiable and justified if, instead of St Teresa's ecstasies, what had been in issue had been a video showing, for example, the anti-clerical Voltaire having sexual relations with some prince or king. In such a case, the decision
of the European Court might well have been similar to that in the Wingrove case. The rights of others under art. 10 par. 2 cannot be restricted
solely to the protection of the rights of others in a single category of religious believers or philosophers, or a majority of them.

The Court was quite right to base its decision on the protection of the
rights of others pursuant to art. 9, but to my mind it could have done so
on broader grounds, inspired to a greater extent by the concern to protect

the context of religious beliefs „or ... any other", as is rightly pointed out in par. 53 of the judgment.

In the difficult balancing exercise that has to be carried out in these situations where religious and philosophical sensibilities are confronted by freedom of expression, it is important that the inspiration provided by the European Convention and its interpretation should be based both on pluralism and a sense of values.

DISSENTING OPINION OF JUDGE DE MEYER

[1] This was a pure case of prior restraint, a form of interference which is, in my view, unacceptable in the field of freedom of expression. What I have written on that subject, with four other judges, in the case of Observer and Guardian v. the United Kingdom (Judgment of 26 November 1991, Series A no. 216, p. 46) applies not only to the press, but also, mutatis mutandis, to other forms of expression, including video works.

[2] It is quite legitimate that those wishing to supply video works be obliged to obtain from some administrative authority a classification certificate stating whether the works concerned may be supplied to the general public or only to persons who have attained a specified age, and whether, in the latter case, they are to be supplied only in certain places (sec. 7 of the Video Recordings Act 1984). Of course, anything so decided by such authority needs reasonable justification and must not be arbitrary. It must, if contested, be subject to judicial review, and it must not have the effect of preventing the courts from deciding, as the case may be, whether the work concerned deserves, or does not deserve, any sanction under existing law.

[3] Under the system established by the Video Recordings Act 1984 the British Board of Film Classification and the Video Appeals Committee may determine that certain video works are not suitable for being classified in any of its three categories (sec. 4 of the Act), and they can thus ban them absolutely ab initio. This was indeed what actually happened in respect of the piece in issue in the present case. It certainly goes too far.

[4] To the extent that the criminal law of blasphemy might have been infringed by the applicant, I would observe that the necessity of such laws is very much open to question. I would rather join Mr Patten's remark that for the faithful „the strength of their own belief is the best armour against mockers and blasphemers" (See par. 29 of the present judgment).

DISSENTING OPINION OF JUDGE LOHMUS

[1] I am unable to agree with the conclusion of the majority that the interference with the applicant's right to freedom of expression was „necessary in a democratic society".

[2] The British Board of Film Classification and the five-member panel of the VAC took the view that the applicant would commit an offence of blasphemy if his video work Visions of Ecstasy were to be distributed (see par. 20 of the judgment).

[3] In cases of prior restraint (censorship) there is interference by the authorities with freedom of expression even though the members of the society whose feelings they seek to protect have not called for such interference. The interference is based on the opinion of the authorities that they understand correctly the feelings they claim to protect. The actual opinion of believers remains unknown. I think that this is why we cannot conclude that the interference corresponded to a „pressing social need".

[4] The law of blasphemy only protects the Christian religion and, more specifically, the established Church of England (see par. 28 of the judgment). The aim of the interference was therefore to protect the Christian faith alone and not other beliefs. This in itself raises the question whether the interference was „necessary in a democratic society".

[5] As the Court has consistently held, the guarantees enshrined in art. 9 apply not only to information or ideas that are favourably received or regarded as inoffensive, but also to those that shock or disturb. Artistic impressions are often conveyed through images and situations which may shock or disturb the feelings of a person of average sensitivity. In my view, the makers of the film in issue did not exceed the reasonable limit beyond which it can be said that objects of religious veneration have been reviled or ridiculed.

[6] The majority has found that in the field of morals the national authorities have a wide margin of appreciation. As in that field, „there is no uniform European conception of the requirements of ‚the protection of the rights of others' in relation to attacks on their religious convictions" (see par. 58 of the judgment). The Court makes distinctions within art. 9 when applying its doctrine on the States' margin of appreciation. Whereas, in some cases, the margin of appreciation applied is wide, in other cases it is more limited. However, it is difficult to ascertain what principles determine the scope of that margin of appreciation.

43

Zur Frage, ob eine Schülerin, die der Religionsgemeinschaft der Zeugen Jehovas angehört, zur Teilnahme an einer Schülerparade zum Nationalfeiertag verpflichtet ist.

Art. 9 EMRK, 2 Erstes Zusatzprotokoll
EGMR, Urteil vom 18. Dezember 1996 - No. 74/1995/580/666
(Valsamis ./. Griechenland)[1] -

THE FACTS

I. Circumstances of the case

[6] The three applicants are Jehovah's Witnesses. Elias and Maria Valsamis are the parents of Victoria, who was born in 1980 and is currently a pupil in the last three years of State secondary education at a school in Melissia, Athens. According to them, pacifism is a fundamental tenet of their religion and forbids any conduct or practice associated with war or violence, even indirectly. It is for this reason that Jehovah's Witnesses refuse to carry out their military service or to take part in any events with military overtones.

[7] On 20 September 1992 Mr and Mrs Valsamis submitted a written declaration in order that their daughter Victoria, who was then 12 and in the first three years of secondary education at a school in Melissia, should be exempted from attending school religious-education lessons, Orthodox Mass and any other event that was contrary to her religious beliefs, including national-holiday celebrations and public processions.

[8] Victoria was exempted from attendance at religious-education lessons and Orthodox Mass. In October 1992, however, she, in common with the other pupils at her school, was asked to take part in the celebration of the National Day on 28 October, when the outbreak of war between Greece and Fascist Italy on 28 October 1940 is commemorated with school and military parades. On this occasion school parades take place in nearly all towns and villages. In the capital there is no military parade on 28 October, and in Salonika the school parade is held on a different day from the military parade. The school and military parades are only held simultaneously in a small number of municipalities.

[9] Victoria informed the headmaster that her religious beliefs forbade her joining in the commemoration of a war by taking part, in front of the civil, Church and military authorities, in a school parade that would follow an official Mass and would be held on the same day as a military parade. According to the applicants, the school authorities refused to accept her statement. In the Government's opinion, it was imprecise and muddled and did not make clear the religious beliefs in question. At all events, her request to be excused attendance was refused but she nevertheless did not take part in the school's parade.

---

[1] RJD 1996-VI; ÖJZ 1997, 714. Vgl. auch EGMR, Urteil vom 23.1.1996 - No. 77/1996/696/888 (Efstratiou ./. Griechenland), RJD 1996-VI.

[10] On 29 October 1992 the headmaster of the school punished her for her failure to attend with one day's suspension from school. That decision was taken in accordance with Circular no. C1/1/1 of 2 January 1990 issued by the Ministry of Education and Religious Affairs (see par. 13 below).

II. Relevant domestic law and practice

A. On religion

[11] The 1975 Constitution contains the following provisions:

Art. 3

„*1. The dominant religion in Greece is that of the Christian Eastern Orthodox Church. The Greek Orthodox Church, which recognises as its head Our Lord Jesus Christ, is indissolubly united, doctrinally, with the Great Church of Constantinople and with any other Christian Church in communion with it [omodoxi], immutably observing, like the other Churches, the holy apostolic and synodical canons and the holy traditions. It is autocephalous and is administered by the Holy Synod, composed of all the bishops in office, and by the standing Holy Synod, which is an emanation of it constituted as laid down in the Charter of the Church and in accordance with the provisions of the Patriarchal Tome of 29 June 1850 and the Synodical Act of 4 September 1928.*

2. The ecclesiastical regime in certain regions of the State shall not be deemed contrary to the provisions of the foregoing paragraph.

3. The text of the Holy Scriptures is unalterable. No official translation into any other form of language may be made without the prior consent of the autocephalous

Art. 13

„*1. Freedom of conscience in religious matters is inviolable. The enjoyment of personal and political rights shall not depend on an individual's religious beliefs.*

2. There shall be freedom to practise any known religion; individuals shall be free to perform their rites of worship without hindrance and under the protection of the law. The performance of rites of worship must not prejudice public order or public morals. Proselytism is prohibited.

3. The ministers of all known religions shall be subject to the same supervision by the State and to the same obligations to it as those of the dominant religion.

4. No one may be exempted from discharging his obligations to the State or refuse to comply with the law by reason of his religious convictions.

5. No oath may be required other than under a law which also determines the form of it."

[12] A royal decree of 23 July 1833 entitled „Proclamation of the Independence of the Greek Church" described the Orthodox Church as „autocephalous". Greece's successive Constitutions have referred to the Church as being „dominant". According to Greek conceptions, the Orthodox Church represents de jure and de facto the religion of the State itself, a good number of whose administrative and educational functions (mar-

riage and family law, compulsory religious instruction, oaths sworn by members of the Government, etc.) it moreover carries out. Its role in public life is reflected by, among other things, the presence of the Minister of Education and Religious Affairs at the sessions of the Church hierarchy at which the Archbishop of Athens is elected and by the participation of the Church authorities in all official State events; the President of the Republic takes his oath of office according to Orthodox ritual (art. 33 par. 2 of the Constitution); and the official calendar follows that of the Christian Eastern Orthodox Church.

B. On school matters

[13] Circular no. C1/1/1 of 2 January 1990 issued by the Ministry of Education and Religious Affairs provides:

> *„Schoolchildren who are Jehovah's Witnesses shall be exempted from attending religious-education lessons, school prayers and Mass.*
> *...*
> *In order for a schoolchild to benefit from this exemption, both parents (or, in the case of divorced parents, the parent in whom parental authority has been vested by court order, or the person having custody of the child) shall lodge a written declaration to the effect that they and their child (or the child of whom they have custody) are Jehovah's Witnesses.*
> *...*
> *No schoolchild shall be exempted from taking part in other school activities, such as national events."*

[14] The relevant articles of Presidential Decree no. 104/1979 of 29 January and 7 February 1979 are the following:

> *Art. 2*
> *„1. The behaviour of pupils inside and outside the school shall constitute their conduct, irrespective of the manner - by act or by omission - in which they express it. Pupils shall be required to conduct themselves suitably, that is to say in accordance with the rules governing school life and the moral principles governing the social context in which they live, and any act or omission in contravention of the rules and principles in question shall be dealt with according to the procedures provided in the educational system and may, if necessary, give rise to the disciplinary measures provided in this decree."*
> *The disciplinary measures laid down in art. 27 of the same decree are, in increasing order of severity, a warning, a reprimand, exclusion from lessons for an hour, suspension from school for up to five days and transfer to another school.*
> *Art. 28 par. 3*
> *„Suspended pupils may remain at school during teaching hours and take part in various activities, under the responsibility of the headmaster."*

C. Appeals

1. The right of petition

[15] Art. 10 of the Constitution provides:

„*Any person, or persons acting jointly, shall be entitled, subject to compliance with the laws of the State, to submit written petitions to the authorities. The latter shall be required to act as quickly as possible in accordance with the provisions in force and to give the petitioner a reasoned written reply in accordance with the statutory provisions.*"

Art. 4 of Legislative Decree no. 796/1971 provides:

„*Once the authorities have received the petition [provided for in art. 10 of the Constitution], they must reply in writing and give the petitioner all necessary explanations, within the time deemed absolutely necessary, which shall not exceed thirty days from service of the petition.*"

2. Judicial review

[16] Art. 95 of the Constitution is worded as follows:

„*The following shall in principle lie within the jurisdiction of the Supreme Administrative Court:*
(a) the setting aside, on application, of enforceable acts of the administrative authorities for misuse of authority or error of law.
..."

According to the settled case-law of the Supreme Administrative Court, „decisions of school authorities to impose on pupils the penalties provided in art. 27 of Presidential Decree no. 104/1979 are intended to maintain the necessary discipline within schools and contribute to their smooth running; they are internal measures which cannot be enforced through the courts, and no application lies to have them set aside by the courts" (judgments nos. 1820/1989, 1821/1989 and 1651/1990). Only transfer to another school has been held to be enforceable and amenable to being quashed by the Supreme Administrative Court (judgment no. 1821/1989).

3. Actions for damages

(...)

PROCEEDINGS BEFORE THE COMMISSION

(...)

AS TO THE LAW

[21] Relying on art. 2 of Protocol No. 1 and art. 3, 9 and 13 of the Convention, the applicants complained of the penalty of one day's suspension from school that was imposed on the pupil Victoria, who had refused to take part in the school parade on 28 October, a national day in Greece. Since, owing to their religious beliefs, Mr and Mrs Valsamis were opposed to any event with military overtones, they had sought an exemption for their daughter, but in vain. They relied on the Commission's opinion in the case of Arrowsmith v. the United Kingdom (application no. 7050/75, DR 19, p. 19, par. 69), according to which pacifism as a philosophy fell within the ambit of the right to freedom of thought and conscience, and the attitude of pacifism could thus be seen as a belief protected by art. 9 par. 1. They therefore claimed recognition of their pacifism under the head of religious beliefs, since all Jehovah's Witnesses were bound to practise pacifism in daily life.

I. Alleged violation of Art. 2 of Protocol No. 1

[22] Mr and Mrs Valsamis alleged that they were the victims of a breach of art. 2 of Protocol No. 1, which provides:

> *„No person shall be denied the right to education. In the exercise of any functions which it assumes in relation to education and to teaching, the State shall respect the right of parents to ensure such education and teaching in conformity with their own religious and philosophical convictions."*

The parents did not allege any breach of Victoria's right to education. On the other hand, they considered that the above provision prohibited requiring their daughter to take part in events extolling patriotic ideals to which they did not subscribe; pupils' education should be provided through history lessons rather than school parades.

[23] The Government contested the parents' submission, arguing that the school parade on 28 October had no military overtones such as to offend pacifist convictions. They disputed that Mr and Mrs Valsamis's belief could count as a conviction for the purposes of art. 2 of Protocol No. 1. They added that the State's educational function, which had to be understood in a broad sense, allowed it to include in pupils' school curriculum the requirement to parade on 28 October. The National Day commemorated Greece's attachment to the values of democracy, liberty and human rights which had provided the foundation for the post-war legal order. It was not an expression of bellicose feelings, nor did it glorify military conflict. Communal celebration of it retained today an idealistic and pacifist character that was strengthened by the presence of school parades. Lastly, a pupil's temporary suspension had a negligible effect on the an-

nual programme of study and could not be regarded as a denial of the right to education.

[24] In the Commission's view, the convictions of Jehovah's Witnesses were protected by art. 2 of Protocol No. 1 and the school parade in question was not of a military character incompatible with pacifist convictions. At the hearing the Delegate added that the scope of art. 2 of Protocol No. 1 was limited; the provision must enable parents to obtain exemption from religious-education lessons if the religious instruction was contrary to their convictions, but it did not require the State to guarantee that all their wishes, even if they were founded on their convictions, should be acceded to in educational and related matters. In this instance, the pupil had not been refused the right to education by being suspended for only a short time.

[25] The Court does not consider that it must rule of its own motion on the question whether the pupil Victoria's right to education was respected. It reiterates that „the two sentences of art. 2 [of Protocol No. 1] must be read not only in the light of each other but also, in particular, of art. 8, 9 and 10 of the Convention" (see the Kjeldsen, Busk Madsen and Pedersen v. Denmark judgment of 7 December 1976, Series A no. 23, p. 26, par. 52, KirchE-EU S. 181). The term „belief" („conviction") appears in art. 9 in the context of the right to freedom of thought, conscience and religion. The concept of „religious and philosophical convictions" appears in art. 2 of Protocol No. 1. When applying that provision, the Court has held that in its ordinary meaning „convictions", taken on its own, is not synonymous with the words „opinions" and „ideas". It denotes „views that attain a certain level of cogency, seriousness, cohesion and importance" (see the Campbell and Cosans v. the United Kingdom judgment of 25 February 1982, Series A no. 48, p. 16, par. 36).

[26] As the Court observed in its judgment of 25 May 1993 in the case of Kokkinakis v. Greece (Series A no. 260-A, p. 18, par. 32, KirchE-EU S. 202), Jehovah's Witnesses enjoy both the status of a „known religion" and the advantages flowing from that as regards observance. Mr and Mrs Valsamis were accordingly entitled to rely on the right to respect for their religious convictions within the meaning of this provision. It remains to be ascertained whether the State failed to discharge its obligations to respect those convictions in the applicants' case.

[27] The Court reiterates that art. 2 of Protocol No. 1 enjoins the State to respect parents' convictions, be they religious or philosophical, throughout the entire State education programme (see the Kjeldsen, Busk Madsen and Pedersen judgment cited above, p. 25, par. 51). That duty is broad in its extent as it applies not only to the content of education and the manner of its provision but also to the performance of all the „functions" assumed by the State. The verb „respect" means more than „acknowledge" or „take into account". In addition to a primarily negative undertaking, it implies some positive obligation on the part of the State

(see the Campbell and Cosans judgment cited above, p. 17, par. 37). The Court has also held that „although individual interests must on occasion be subordinated to those of a group, democracy does not simply mean that the views of a majority must always prevail: a balance must be achieved which ensures the fair and proper treatment of minorities and avoids any abuse of a dominant position" (Young, James and Webster v. the United Kingdom judgment of 13 August 1981, Series A no. 44, p. 25, par. 63).

[28] However, „the setting and planning of the curriculum fall in principle within the competence of the Contracting States. This mainly involves questions of expediency on which it is not for the Court to rule and whose solution may legitimately vary according to the country and the era" (see the Kjeldsen, Busk Madsen and Pedersen judgment cited above, p. 26, par. 53). Given that discretion, the Court has held that the second sentence of art. 2 of Protocol No. 1 forbids the State „to pursue an aim of indoctrination that might be regarded as not respecting parents' religious and philosophical convictions. That is the limit that must not be exceeded" (ibid.).

[29] The imposition of disciplinary penalties is an integral part of the process whereby a school seeks to achieve the object for which it was established, including the development and moulding of the character and mental powers of its pupils (see the Campbell and Cosans judgment cited above, p. 14, par. 33).

[30] In the first place, the Court notes that Miss Valsamis was exempted from religious-education lessons and the Orthodox Mass, as had been requested by her parents. The latter also wished to have her exempted from having to parade during the national commemoration on 28 October.

[31] While it is not for the Court to rule on the Greek State's decisions as regards the setting and planning of the school curriculum, it is surprised that pupils can be required on pain of suspension from school - even if only for a day - to parade outside the school precincts on a holiday. Nevertheless, it can discern nothing, either in the purpose of the parade or in the arrangements for it, which could offend the applicants' pacifist convictions to an extent prohibited by the second sentence of art. 2 of Protocol No. 1. Such commemorations of national events serve, in their way, both pacifist objectives and the public interest. The presence of military representatives at some of the parades which take place in Greece on the day in question does not in itself alter the nature of the parades. Furthermore, the obligation on the pupil does not deprive her parents of their right „to enlighten and advise their children, to exercise with regard to their children natural parental functions as educators, or to guide their children on a path in line with the parents' own religious or philosophical convictions" (see, mutatis mutandis, the Kjeldsen, Busk Madsen and Pedersen judgment cited above, p. 28, par. 54).

[32] It is not for the Court to rule on the expediency of other educational methods which, in the applicants' view, would be better suited to the aim of perpetuating historical memory among the younger generation. It notes, however, that the penalty of suspension, which cannot be regarded as an exclusively educational measure and may have some psychological impact on the pupil on whom it is imposed, is nevertheless of limited duration and does not require the exclusion of the pupil from the school premises (art. 28 par. 3 of Decree no. 104/1979 - see par. 14 above).

[33] In conclusion, there has not been a breach of art. 2 of Protocol No. 1.

II. Alleged violation of Art. 9 of the convention

[34] Miss Valsamis relied on art. 9 of the Convention, which provides:

„*1. Everyone has the right to freedom of thought, conscience and religion; this right includes freedom to change his religion or belief and freedom, either alone or in community with others and in public or private, to manifest his religion or belief, in worship, teaching, practice and observance.*
2. Freedom to manifest one's religion or beliefs shall be subject only to such limitations as are prescribed by law and are necessary in a democratic society in the interests of public safety, for the protection of public order, health or morals, or for the protection of the rights and freedoms of others."

She asserted that the provision (art. 9) guaranteed her right to the negative freedom not to manifest, by gestures of support, any convictions or opinions contrary to her own. She disputed both the necessity and the proportionality of the interference, having regard to the seriousness of the penalty, which stigmatised her and marginalised her.

[35] In the Government's submission, art. 9 protected only aspects of religious practice in a generally recognised form that were strictly a matter of conscience. The State was not under an obligation to take positive measures to adapt its activities to the various manifestations of its citizens' philosophical or religious beliefs.

[36] The Commission considered that art. 9 did not confer a right to exemption from disciplinary rules which applied generally and in a neutral manner and that in the instant case there had been no interference with the applicant's right to freedom to manifest her religion or belief.

[37] The Court notes at the outset that Miss Valsamis was exempted from religious education and the Orthodox Mass, as she had requested on the grounds of her own religious beliefs. It has already held, in par. 31-33 above, that the obligation to take part in the school parade was not such as to offend her parents' religious convictions. The impugned measure therefore did not amount to an interference with her right to freedom of religion either (see, in particular, the Johnston and Others v. Ireland judgment of 18 December 1986, Series A no. 112, p. 27, par. 63).

[38] There has consequently not been a breach of art. 9 of the Convention.

III. Alleged violation of Art. 3 of the convention

[39] Miss Valsamis went on to allege, without giving any particulars, that her suspension from school was contrary to art. 3 of the Convention, which provides:

„*No one shall be subjected to torture or to inhuman or degrading treatment or punishment.*"

[40] The Government did not express a view.

[41] The Court reiterates that ill-treatment must attain a minimum level of severity if it is to fall within the scope of art. 3 (see, in particular, the Ireland v. the United Kingdom judgment of 18 January 1978, Series A no. 25, p. 65, par. 162, and the Campbell and Cosans judgment cited above, pp. 12-13, par. 27-28). Like the Commission, it perceives no infringement of this provision (art. 3).

[42] In conclusion, there has been no breach of art. 3 of the Convention.

IV. Alleged violation of Art. 13 of the convention

(...)

V. Application of Art. 50 of the convention (...)

For these reasons, the Court
1. *Holds by seven votes to two that there has not been a breach of art. 2 of Protocol No. 1;*
2. *Holds by seven votes to two that there has not been a breach of art. 9 of the Convention;*
3. *Holds unanimously that there has not been a breach of art. 3 of the Convention;*
4. *Holds unanimously that there has been a breach of art. 13 of the Convention taken together with art. 2 of Protocol No. 1 and art. 9 of the Convention, but not taken together with art. 3 of the Convention;*

JOINT DISSENTING OPINION OF JUDGES THÓR VILHJÁLMSSON AND JAMBREK

In this case we find a violation both of art. 2 of Protocol No. 1 to the Convention and of art. 9 of the Convention. In this we disagree with the judgment. On the other points set out in the operative provisions of the judgment we voted in the same way as the majority of the judges.

Art. 2 of Protocol No. 1

Mr and Mrs Valsamis alleged that there is a breach of this article where pupils, like their daughter Victoria, are forced as part of their school duties to take part in organised events imbued with a symbolism that is contrary to the most deeply held religious and philosophical convictions of their parents. This applies even more where the events are held in a public place, outside school, on a national holiday with the intention of delivering a message to the community concerned. According to Mr and Mrs Valsamis, the pupils are thus obliged to show publicly, by their acts, that they adhere to beliefs contrary to those of their parents.

In our opinion, Mr and Mrs Valsamis's perception of the symbolism of the school parade and its religious and philosophical connotations has to be accepted by the Court unless it is obviously unfounded and unreasonable.

We do not think that the opinions of Mr and Mrs Valsamis were obviously unfounded and unreasonable. Even if their daughter's participation in the parade would only have taken up part of one day and the punishment for not attending was, in objective terms, not severe, the episode was capable of disturbing both the parents and the girl and humiliating Victoria. Commemorations of national events are valuable to most people, but the Valsamis family was under no obligation to hold that opinion with regard to the parade at issue in this case. Neither is it an argument against finding a violation that the participation was part of Victoria's education, because the nature of such school activities is not neutral and they do not form part of the usual school curriculum.

For these reasons we find a violation of art. 2 of Protocol No. 1.

Art. 9

Victoria Valsamis stated that the parade she did not participate in had a character and symbolism that were clearly contrary to her neutralist, pacifist, and thus religious, beliefs. We are of the opinion that the Court has to accept that and we find no basis for seeing Victoria's participation in this parade as necessary in a democratic society, even if this public event clearly was for most people an expression of national values and unity.

We therefore find a violation of art. 9.

44

Aktive Mitgliedschaft eines Angehörigen der türkischen Militärjustiz in einer islamisch-fundamentalistischen Sekte kann als Ausdruck eines anti-laizistischen und damit gesetzwidrigen Verhaltens die Entlassung aus dem Dienst rechtfertigen.

Art. 9 EMRK
EGMR, Urteil vom 1. Juli 1997 - No. 61/1996/680/870
(Kalaç ./. Türkei)[1] -

AS TO THE FACTS

I. Circumstances of the case

7. Mr Faruk Kalaç, a Turkish citizen born in 1939, pursued a career as judge advocate in the air force. In 1990 he was serving, with the rank of group captain, as the high command's director of legal affairs.

8. By an order of 1 August 1990 the Supreme Military Council (Yüksek Askeri Sûrasi), composed of the Prime Minister, the Minister of Defence, the Chief of Staff and the eleven highest-ranking generals in the armed forces, ordered the compulsory retirement of three officers, including Mr Kalaç, and twenty-eight non-commissioned officers for breaches of discipline and scandalous conduct. The decision, which was based on sec. 50 (c) of the Military Personnel Act, sec. 22 (c) of the Military Legal Service Act and art. 99 (e) of the Regulations on assessment of officers and non-commissioned officers, made the specific criticism, in the applicant's case, that his conduct and attitude „revealed that he had adopted unlawful fundamentalist opinions".

9. In a decision of 22 August 1990 the President of the Republic, the Prime Minister and the Minister of Defence approved the above order, which was served on the applicant on 3 September. The Minister of Defence ordered the forfeiture of the applicant's social security (health insurance) card, his military identity card and his licence to bear arms.

10. On 21 September 1990 Mr Kalaç asked the Supreme Administrative Court of the Armed Forces (Askeri Yüksek idare Mahkemesi) to set aside the order of 1 August 1990 and the measures ordered by the Ministry of Defence.

---

[1] RDJ 1997-IV. Vgl. auch EKMR, Beschluss vom 1.6.1993 - Appl.-No. 14524/89 (Yanasik ./. Türkei); EGMR, Beschlüsse vom 10.9.2001 in den Verfahren Appl.-No. 31990 u. 32359/1996, 34479, 3508, 35081, 36196, 36198, 36200, 36594, 37960 u. 38603/1997, Beschluss vom 11.9.2001 - Appl.-No. 31876/96. Diese gegen die Türkei gerichteten Beschwerden wurden nicht zur Entscheidung angenommen.

11. In a judgment of 30 May 1991 the Supreme Administrative Court of the Armed Forces ruled by four votes to three that it did not have jurisdiction to entertain the application to set aside the order of 1 August 1990, on the ground that under art. 125 of the Constitution the decisions of the Supreme Military Council were final and not subject to judicial review. In that connection it observed that under the Military Legal Service Act members of the military legal service had the status of military personnel. Their compulsory retirement for breaches of discipline was regulated in the same manner as that of other army officers.

In their dissenting opinion the three members of the minority referred to the principle of the independence of the judiciary enunciated in art. 139 of the Constitution. They expressed the view that security of tenure for both civilian and military judges, which was protected by that article, formed a lex specialis in relation to the other provisions of the Constitution and that decisions of the Supreme Military Council which infringed that principle should therefore be subject to review by the Supreme Administrative Court of the Armed Forces.

The court set aside, however, the refusal to issue social security cards to the applicant and his family.

12. On 9 January 1992 the court dismissed an application for rectification lodged by Mr Kalaç.

II. Relevant domestic law

A. The Constitution

13. The relevant provisions of the Constitution are as follows:

Art. 14 par. 1
„None of the rights and freedoms set forth in the Constitution may be exercised with the aim of undermining the territorial integrity of the State or the indivisible unity of its people, imperilling the existence of the Turkish State and the Republic, abolishing fundamental rights and freedoms, handing over control of the State to a single individual or group or bringing about the dominance of one social class over the others, establishing discrimination on the grounds of language, race, religion or adherence to a religious sect or setting up by any other means a State order based on such beliefs and opinions."
Art. 24
„Everyone shall have the right to freedom of conscience, faith and religious belief. Prayers, worship and religious services shall be conducted freely, provided that they do not violate the provisions of art. 14. No one shall be compelled to participate in prayers, worship or religious services or to reveal his religious beliefs and convictions; nor shall he be censured or prosecuted because of his religious beliefs or convictions. ...
No one may exploit or abuse religion, religious feelings or things held sacred by religion in any manner whatsoever with a view to causing the social, economic,

political or legal order of the State to be based on religious precepts, even if only in part, or for the purpose of securing political or personal influence thereby."

Art. 125
"All acts or decisions of the administration are subject to judicial review ...

Decisions of the President of the Republic concerning matters within his sole jurisdiction and decisions of the Supreme Military Council shall not be subject to judicial review.
...*"*

Art. 139
"Judges and public prosecutors shall not be removed from office or compelled to retire without their consent before the age prescribed by the Constitution; nor shall they be deprived of their salaries, allowances or other rights relating to their status, even as a result of the abolition of a court or post.

The exceptions laid down by law concerning judges or public prosecutors who have been convicted of an offence requiring their dismissal from the service, those whose unfitness to carry out their duties for medical reasons has been finally established or those whose continued service has been adjudged undesirable shall remain in force."

Art. 144
"Supervision of judges and public prosecutors as regards the performance of their duties in accordance with laws, regulations, subordinate legislation and circulars (administrative circulars, in the case of judges), investigations into whether they have committed offences in connection with, or in the course of, their duties, or whether their conduct and attitude are compatible with the obligations arising from their status and duties and, if necessary, inquiries concerning them shall be made by judicial inspectors with the permission of the Ministry of Justice. The Minister of Justice may also ask a judge or public prosecutor senior to the judge or public prosecutor in question to conduct the investigation or inquiry."

Art. 145, fourth paragraph *"The organisation and functions of military judicial organs, the personal status of military judges and the relations between judges acting as military prosecutors and the commanders under whom they serve shall be regulated by law in accordance with the principles of the independence of the courts and the security of tenure of the judiciary and with the requirements of military service. Relations between military judges and the commanders under whom they serve as regards their non-judicial duties shall also be regulated by law in accordance with the requirements of military service."*

B. Law no. 357 („the Military Legal Service Act")

14. Sec. 22 (c) of the Military Legal Service Act provides:

"Irrespective of length of service, servicemen whose continued presence in the armed forces is adjudged to be inappropriate on account of breaches of discipline or immoral behaviour on one of the grounds set out below, as established in one or more documents drawn up during their service in the last military rank they held, shall be subject to the provisions of the Turkish Pensions Act.

...

Where their conduct and attitude reveal that they have adopted unlawful opinions."

C. Law no. 926 („the Military Personnel Act")

15. Sec. 50 (c) of the Military Personnel Act provides:

„Irrespective of length of service, servicemen whose continued presence in the armed forces is adjudged inappropriate on account of breaches of discipline and immoral behaviour shall be subject to the provisions of the Turkish Pensions Act.

The Regulations for Military Personnel shall lay down which authorities have jurisdiction to commence proceedings, to examine, monitor and draw conclusions from personnel assessment files and to carry out any other act or formality in such proceedings. A decision of the Supreme Military Council is required to discharge an officer whose case has been submitted by the Chief of Staff to the Supreme Military Council."

D. The Regulations on assessment of officers and non-commissioned officers

16. Art. 99 of the Regulations on assessment of officers and non-commissioned officers provides:

„Irrespective of length of service, the compulsory retirement procedure shall be applied to all servicemen whose continued presence in the armed forces is adjudged to be inappropriate on account of breaches of discipline or immoral behaviour on one of the grounds set out below, as established in one or more documents drawn up during their service in the last military rank they held:

...

(e) where by his conduct and attitude the serviceman concerned has provided evidence that he holds unlawful, subversive, separatist, fundamentalist and ideological political opinions or takes an active part in the propagation of such opinions."

PROCEEDINGS BEFORE THE COMMISSION

(...)

AS TO THE LAW

I. Scope of the case

19. In his memorial to the Court the applicant, in addition to his complaint under art. 9 of the Convention, also relied on art. 6 par. 1 on the ground that he had not had a hearing by a tribunal in connection with the facts held against him.

20. The Court notes that this last complaint lies outside the compass of the case as delimited by the Commission's decision on admissibility, since it was not dealt with either in that decision or in the Commission's report (see, among other authorities, the Scollo v. Italy judgment of 28 September 1995, Series A no. 315-C, p. 51, par. 24; and the Hussain v. the

United Kingdom judgment of 21 February 1996, RJD 1996-I, p. 266, par. 44).
The scope of the case is therefore limited to the questions raised under art. 9.

II. Alleged violation of Art. 9 of the convention

A. The Government's preliminary objection

21. The Government submitted to the Commission a preliminary objection divided into three limbs, but in their memorial to the Court they resubmitted only the limb concerning failure to exhaust domestic remedies, leaving aside the other two, which concerned the Commission's lack of competence ratione materiae and the application's late submission. At the hearing on 17 February 1997 the Government presented argument on the first limb and in addition pleaded the Court's lack of jurisdiction ratione materiae.

The Court considers that the latter objection calls for no decision as it was submitted to the Court out of time for the purposes of Rule 48 par. 1 of Rules of Court A.

22. As for the argument which was repeated in the memorial of December 1996 and at the hearing, it amounts to an assertion that the applicant did not explicitly allege to the Turkish authorities that his right to freedom of conscience and religion had been infringed. The Government maintained that, in accordance with the principle laid down by the Court in its judgment of 15 November 1996 in the case of Ahmet Sadik v. Greece (RJD 1996-V, p. 1654, par. 33), the applicant should have relied on art. 9 of the Convention, which formed an integral part of Turkish law.

23. Like the Delegate of the Commission, the Court considers that the objection of failure to exhaust domestic remedies must be dismissed because, under art. 125 of the Constitution, and as the Supreme Administrative Court of the Armed Forces held in its judgment of 30 May 1991, the Supreme Military Council's decision against Mr Kalaç was not subject to judicial review.

B. Merits of the complaint

24. The applicant submitted that his compulsory retirement from his judge advocate's post infringed his freedom of religion on the ground that it was based on his religious beliefs and practices. He relied on art. 9 of the Convention, which provides:

„1. Everyone has the right to freedom of thought, conscience and religion; this right includes freedom to change his religion or belief and freedom, either alone

or in community with others and in public or in private, to manifest his religion or belief, in worship, teaching, practice and observance.
2. Freedom to manifest one's religion or beliefs shall be subject only to such limitations as are prescribed by law and are necessary in a democratic society in the interests of public safety, for the protection of public order, health or morals, or for the protection of the rights and freedoms of others. "

The applicant argued that domestic law gave no indication of what the expression „unlawful fundamentalist opinions", given as grounds for his compulsory retirement (see par. 8 above), should be understood to mean. As a practising Muslim, he prayed five times a day and kept the fast of Ramadan. The documents produced by the Government for the first time when the proceedings were already before the Court did not constitute evidence of his alleged membership of the Muslim fundamentalist Süleyman sect (Süleymancilik tarikati), whose existence he had been unaware of. Moreover, the Supreme Military Council's decision infringed the principle of judges' security of tenure, which was set forth in art. 139 of the Constitution.

25. The Government argued that the question whether Mr Kalaç should be allowed to remain a member of the armed forces lay at the heart of the problem submitted to the Court. His compulsory retirement was not an interference with his freedom of conscience, religion or belief but was intended to remove from the military legal service a person who had manifested his lack of loyalty to the foundation of the Turkish nation, namely secularism, which it was the task of the armed forces to guarantee. The applicant belonged to the Süleyman sect, as a matter of fact, if not formally, and participated in the activities of the Süleyman community, which was known to have unlawful fundamentalist tendencies. Various documents annexed to the memorial to the Court showed that the applicant had given it legal assistance, had taken part in training sessions and had intervened on a number of occasions in the appointment of servicemen who were members of the sect. On the basis of those documents, a committee of five officers drawn from the highest echelons of the military had concluded that by taking and carrying out instructions from the leaders of the sect Group Captain Kalaç had breached military discipline and should accordingly be compulsorily retired pursuant to sec. 50 (c) of the Military Personnel Act. The Supreme Military Council had based its decision on this opinion, which had been approved by the high command and the air force chief of staff. Lastly, facilities to practise one's religion within the armed forces were provided in Turkey for both Muslims and the adherents of other faiths. However, the protection of art. 9 could not extend, in the case of a serviceman, to membership of a fundamentalist movement, in so far as its members' activities were likely to upset the army's hierarchical equilibrium.

26. The Commission, basing its opinion on the documents submitted to it by the Government, took the view that the applicant's compulsory retirement constituted interference with the right guaranteed by art. 9 par. 1 and concluded that there had been a breach of that provision (art. 9-1) on the ground that the interference in question was not prescribed by law within the meaning of the second paragraph (art. 9-2), finding that the relevant provisions did not afford adequate protection against arbitrary decisions. The Delegate observed that, in support of their memorial to the Court, the Government had produced documents which, during the proceedings before the Commission, had been said to be „secret in the interests of national security". In any event, these documents did not support the argument that Mr Kalaç had any links with a sect.

27. The Court reiterates that while religious freedom is primarily a matter of individual conscience, it also implies, inter alia, freedom to manifest one's religion not only in community with others, in public and within the circle of those whose faith one shares, but also alone and in private (see the Kokkinakis v. Greece judgment of 25 May 1993, Series A no. 260-A, p. 17, par. 31, KirchE-EU S. 202). Art. 9 lists a number of forms which manifestation of one's religion or belief may take, namely worship, teaching, practice and observance. Nevertheless, art. 9 does not protect every act motivated or inspired by a religion or belief. Moreover, in exercising his freedom to manifest his religion, an individual may need to take his specific situation into account.

28. In choosing to pursue a military career Mr Kalaç was accepting of his own accord a system of military discipline that by its very nature implied the possibility of placing on certain of the rights and freedoms of members of the armed forces limitations incapable of being imposed on civilians (see the Engel and Others v. the Netherlands judgment of 8 June 1976, Series A no. 22, p. 24, par. 57). States may adopt for their armies disciplinary regulations forbidding this or that type of conduct, in particular an attitude inimical to an established order reflecting the requirements of military service.

29. It is not contested that the applicant, within the limits imposed by the requirements of military life, was able to fulfil the obligations which constitute the normal forms through which a Muslim practises his religion. For example, he was in particular permitted to pray five times a day and to perform his other religious duties, such as keeping the fast of Ramadan and attending Friday prayers at the mosque.

30. The Supreme Military Council's order was, moreover, not based on Group Captain Kalaç's religious opinions and beliefs or the way he had performed his religious duties but on his conduct and attitude (see par. 8 and 25 above). According to the Turkish authorities, this conduct breached military discipline and infringed the principle of secularism.

31. The Court accordingly concludes that the applicant's compulsory retirement did not amount to an interference with the right guaranteed by art. 9 since it was not prompted by the way the applicant manifested his religion. There has therefore been no breach of art. 9.

For these reasons, the Court unanimously
1. *Dismisses the Government's preliminary objection;*
2. *Holds that there has been no breach of art. 9 of the Convention.*

45

Die Rechtspersönlichkeit und Prozessfähigkeit einer Kirchengemeinde kann auch auf gewohnheitsrechtlicher Grundlage entstehen und ist insoweit nicht von der Erfüllung staatlicher Vorschriften über die Entstehung juristischer Personen oder Personengesamtheiten abhängig.
Zur Frage der Gleichbehandlung von Religionsgemeinschaften im Rechtsverkehr.

Art. 6 § 1, 9, 14 EMRK
EGMR, Urteil vom 16. Dezember 1997 - No. 25528/94 -
(Kath. Kirche von Canea ./. Griechenland)[1] -

AS TO THE FACTS

I. Circumstances of the case

[1] The Roman Catholic Church of the Virgin Mary (*Tis Panagias*) in Canea is the cathedral of the Roman Catholic diocese of Crete. Built in the thirteenth century, it adjoins a former Capuchin convent and it has been used as a place of worship continuously since at least 1879. The building was acquired by the church by adverse possession (*ektakti khrissiktissia*).

[2] In June 1987 two people living next to the church, Mr I.N. and Mr A.K., demolished one of its surrounding walls, which was 1.20 metres high, and made a window looking onto the church in the wall of their own building.

A. Proceedings in the Canea District Court

[3] On 2 February 1988 the church, represented by the abbot, the Right Reverend Giorgios Roussos, applied to the Canea District Court seeking

---

[1] RJD 1997-VIII; ÖJZ 1998, 750.

a declaration that it was the owner of the wall in question and orders
that the defendants must cease the nuisance and restore the previously
existing situation, that the judgment should be provisionally enforceable
and that the defendants should be liable to a fine of 100,000 drachmas
and six months' imprisonment if they did not comply with the judgment.
The defendants raised an objection to admissibility on the ground that
Catholic churches in Greece had no legal personality and were thus prevented from bringing legal proceedings. The plaintiff church answered
the objection by stating that it was a cloister church, founded and authorised before 1830 and recognised under the Protocol of London of
3 February 1830. More particularly, it stated that it was a Capuchin
cloister that had been authorised before 1830 and belonged to the diocese
of Syros and Thera, which did have legal personality (*aftotelia*).

[4] On 18 October 1988 the District Court held that the wall was owned
by the church and ordered the defendants to rebuild it to its original
height. As to the objection to admissibility, the court held that it was unfounded, accepting the plaintiff church's submissions, which - it found -
were substantiated by the papal seal of 20 June 1974 that was in the file;
the court also noted that the abbot was the manager of its wealth and
was therefore entitled to represent it in legal proceedings.

B. Proceedings in the Canea Court of First Instance sitting as an appellate court

[5] The defendants appealed against that judgment to the Canea Court
of First Instance on 8 December 1988.

[6] On 18 May 1989 the Court of First Instance, allowing the appeal,
quashed the judgment of the court below for the following reasons:

> „The provisions of the Treaty of Sèvres of 10 August 1920, which remains in force
> by virtue of Protocol No. 16 annexed to the Treaty of Lausanne of 24 July 1923,
> require Greece to ensure Greeks' freedom of religion, freedom of worship and
> equality before the law irrespective of their religious denomination - freedoms
> which are, moreover, guaranteed in art. 4, 5 and 13 of the current Constitution -
> but do not provide that religious or other establishments founded by a religious
> minority may acquire legal personality without complying with the State's laws
> on the acquisition of legal personality. Furthermore, the Third Protocol of Lon-
> don adopted by the protecting powers on 3 February 1830, and ratified in Greece
> by the Greek Senate's Memorandum of 10 April 1830, ... did not confer on the
> bishops of the Western Church any jurisdiction other than spiritual and adminis-
> trative, that is to say relating to that Church's domestic order, and the provisions
> of the canon law that governs the Roman Catholic Church which attribute legal
> personality to convents and other Church establishments founded by decisions of
> the bishops of that Church were not adopted.
> In the instant case the Holy Church and Holy Convent of the Capuchins, whose
> date of foundation is not apparent from the evidence, did not acquire legal per-
> sonality from the sole fact of being founded by the competent bishop in Greece

without the formalities laid down in Greek laws on the acquisition of legal personality having been complied with. Consequently, they have no legal standing and their action must be dismissed for that reason in accordance with art. 62 of the Code of Civil Procedure. The failure to comply with the State's laws on the acquisition of legal personality is admitted by the plaintiffs themselves. It must be noted that even if this church was founded before 1830, it accordingly did not acquire legal personality, having failed to comply with the laws of the State."

C. Proceedings in the Court of Cassation

[7] On 14 December 1990 the church appealed on points of law, alleging a breach of the Protocol of London of 3 February 1830 taken together with the Greek Senate's Memorandum of 10 April 1830, art. 8 of the Treaty of Sèvres of 1920, art. 13 of the Civil Code, art. 13 and 20 of the Constitution and art. 9 of the European Convention on Human Rights. In his opinion of 10 December 1992 the reporting judge of the Court of Cassation indicated that he thought the judgment of 18 May 1989 should be quashed; he pointed out that under art. 13 § 2 of the Constitution and art. 8 of the Treaty of Sèvres, Greek nationals belonging to religious minorities enjoyed the same protection in law and in fact and the same safeguards as other Greek nationals and, in particular, had an equal right to establish religious foundations and practise their religion freely; furthermore, under the canon law of the Roman Catholic Church, churches, convents and monasteries established with the approval of the Holy See had legal personality without it being necessary to comply with the formalities laid down in Greek laws. Such a restriction would be contrary to art. 13 of the Constitution and art. 8 of the Treaty of Sèvres.

[8] In a judgment of 2 March 1994 the Court of Cassation dismissed the appeal in the following terms:

„*[The Treaty of Sèvres], having been ratified in a statute, was kept in force as domestic law, but inasmuch as its content is covered by the Convention for the Protection of Human Rights and Fundamental Freedoms, which is much wider in scope, the treaty must be regarded as having been abrogated by this subsequent Convention, which pursues the same objective. However, the special provisions of the treaty which are not reproduced in the Rome Convention and do not conflict with it must be regarded as still being in force. By means of the Convention Greece protects, inter alia, the religious freedom not only of minorities but of any person within its jurisdiction, irrespective of religion, national origin, membership of an ethnic minority, etc. Art. 13 § 2 of the Constitution, which provides for freedom to practise any ‚known' religion and for freedom to perform religious obligations without hindrance, likewise corresponds to the content [of the Convention].*

Regard being had to the foregoing, it is clear that the above-mentioned provisions guarantee to religious minorities freedom of religion, freedom of worship and religious equality and, by extension, the right to found religious associations and establishments, which acquire legal personality as of right but only after comply-

ing with the State's laws on such acquisition ... It is even provided (in art. 13 § 4 of the Constitution) that the religious convictions of minorities cannot constitute a legal ground exempting them from complying with the above-mentioned laws on the acquisition of legal personality, which, by the first sentence of art. 62 of the Code of Civil Procedure, is a condition of being able to bring or defend legal proceedings ... Consequently, if art. 20 of the Constitution, whereby everyone is entitled to seek legal protection from the courts, is to apply, the above-mentioned statutory conditions must be satisfied. Furthermore, since sec. 13 of the Introductory Law to the Civil Code ... provides that only legal persons ,lawfully constituted' at the date of adoption of the Civil Code continue to exist, the court below rightly held that art. 20 of the Constitution did not apply in the instant case as the formalities required by Greece's laws for the acquisition of legal personality had not been complied with by the appellants."

II. Relevant domestic law and practice

A. Statutory provisions

1. The Constitution

[9] The relevant articles of the Constitution provide:

Art. 3
„1. The dominant religion in Greece is that of the Christian Eastern Orthodox Church. The Greek Orthodox Church, which recognises as its head Our Lord Jesus Christ, is indissolubly united, doctrinally, with the Great Church of Constantinople and with any other Christian Church in communion with it (omodoxi), immutably observing, like the other Churches, the holy apostolic and synodical canons and the holy traditions. It is autocephalous and is administered by the Holy Synod, composed of all the bishops in office, and by the standing Holy Synod, which is an emanation of it constituted as laid down in the Charter of the Church and in accordance with the provisions of the Patriarchal Tome of 29 June 1850 and the Synodical Act of 4 September 1928.
2. The ecclesiastical regime in certain regions of the State shall not be deemed contrary to the provisions of the foregoing paragraph.
3. The text of the Holy Scriptures is unalterable. No official translation into any other form of language may be made without the prior consent of the autocephalous Greek Church and the Great Christian Church at Constantinople."
Art. 13
„1. Freedom of conscience in religious matters is inviolable. The enjoyment of personal and political rights shall not depend on an individual's religious beliefs.
2. There shall be freedom to practise any known religion; individuals shall be free to perform their rites of worship without hindrance and under the protection of the law. The performance of rites of worship must not prejudice public order or public morals. Proselytism is prohibited.
3. The ministers of all known religions shall be subject to the same supervision by the State and to the same obligations to it as those of the dominant religion.
4. No one may be exempted from discharging his obligations to the State or refuse to comply with the law by reason of his religious convictions.

5. No oath may be required other than under a law which also determines the form of it."

2. The Civil Code

[10] Sec. 13 of the Introductory Law to the Civil Code provides:

„*Legal persons that were lawfully constituted at the date of adoption of the Civil Code [23 February 1946] shall continue to exist. As regards their legal capacity, administration or functioning, the relevant provisions of the Code shall apply.*"

[111] Art. 61 of the Civil Code gives the following definition of a legal person in general:

„*A union of persons for the purpose of pursuing a given aim or a group of assets assigned to the service of a given aim may acquire legal personality if the requirements laid down by law are satisfied.*"

[12] The legal persons provided for in the Civil Code are associations (art. 78 et seq.), foundations (art. 108 et seq.) and charitable fund-raising committees (art. 122 et seq.). Non-commercial partnerships only acquire legal personality after taking the publicity measures laid down by law for commercial partnerships (art. 741 et seq. and art. 784). It must also be noted that the Civil Code makes the provisions on partnerships applicable to unions of persons that have been created to pursue a given aim but are not associations (art. 107).

3. The Code of Civil Procedure

[13] By art. 62 of the Code of Civil Procedure, „A person who has the capacity to possess rights and be bound by obligations shall also be entitled to bring or defend legal proceedings. Unions of persons which pursue a specified aim without being associations and also partnerships that do not have legal personality may bring or defend legal proceedings." This concept of a union of persons seems to approximate to the concept of a common-interest group in Greek law, since the courts have applied the concept to co-ownership of a seagoing vessel, to a political party and to an association of co-owners of a building.

4. Law no. 590/1977 on the Charter of the Church of Greece

[14] Sec. 1 (4) of Law no. 590/1977 on the Charter of the Church of Greece confers personality in public law on the Orthodox Church and on a number of its institutions, at least as regards „their legal relations".

5. The Treaty of Sèvres of 10 August 1920

[15] Art. 8 of the Treaty of Sèvres of 10 August 1920 provides:

> „*Greek nationals who belong to racial, religious or linguistic minorities shall enjoy the same treatment and security in law and in fact as the other Greek nationals. In particular they shall have an equal right to establish, manage and control, at their own expense, charitable, religious and social institutions, schools and other educational establishments, with the right to use their own language and to exercise their religion freely therein.*"

B. Case-law

[16] The applicant church annexed to the memorial it filed with the Court a series of judgments given by the highest courts in the land which, it submitted, substantiated its assertion that neither the legal personality of the Catholic Church in Greece nor its capacity to bring or defend legal proceedings had ever been called in question. The decisions were the following:

(a) judgment no. 142/1889 of the Court of Cassation, in which the court held that the appropriate Catholic bishop represented the legal person of the Catholic Church and its parish churches in legal proceedings for the protection of their property, and did so by virtue of the Catholic canon law, which was wholly applicable in Greece in so far as it did not conflict with any provisions of national law;

(b) judgment no. 1437/1896 of the Athens Court of Appeal, in which the court ruled similarly, holding that the canon law of the Catholic Church had been recognised in the Protocol of 3 February 1830 „as having the force of law" in Greece;

(c) judgment no. 256/1902 of the Athens Court of Appeal, in which the court held that it was for the Pope to appoint local administrators of the Catholic Church's property and, moreover, that there was no need for Catholic parish churches „once established and lawfully in existence, to obtain permission from the State authorities to acquire [their] legal personality";

(d) judgment no. 45/1931 of the Court of Appeal of the Aegean Islands, in which it was held that Catholic parish churches were represented by persons appointed by the Pope, according to canon law;

(e) judgment no. 1885/1946 of the Athens Court of Appeal (the first to be given on the subject after the Civil Code of the same year had come into force), in which the court held that legal persons constituted before 1946 were accorded full recognition under sec. 13 of the Introductory Law to the Civil Code; as regards, more specifically, Catholic Church foundations in Greece, it was held in the same judgment that Catholic bishops had „special" power to constitute them by means of a unilateral decision, without any need for that decision to take any particular form or to be subject to any prior authorisation;

(f) judgment no. 2716/1973 of the Second Division of the Supreme Administrative Court, whereby that court recognised the legal personality of the Catholic convent of the Ursuline Sisters on the island of Tinos, established by law in 1865 and to which was attached the Catholic school operating in Athens under the same name;

(g) judgment no. 1292/1977 of a full court of the Supreme Administrative Court, whereby the court recognised the legal personality of the parish church of St John the Baptist on the island of Thera in a case of expropriation in the public interest;

(h) judgment no. 101/1979 of the Court of Appeal of the Aegean Islands, delivered in a case of unlawful interference with the rights of possession and ownership of the same parish church of the island of Thera, whose capacity to bring and defend legal proceedings was formally confirmed.

On the other hand, following judgment no. 360/1994 delivered by the Court of Cassation in the present case, the Crete Court of Appeal dismissed an action brought jointly by the Episcopal Catholic Church of Crete and the applicant church for recovery of possession of a rented property, holding that the plaintiffs had no standing as they did not have legal personality (judgment no. 408/1995).

[17] The Government cited a judgment of the Supreme Administrative Court (no. 239/1966) in which it was held that a monastery founded in 1963 by a decision of the Catholic bishop of Greece had not by virtue of that fact alone acquired legal personality. The Supreme Administrative Court said:

„The Third Protocol of London adopted by the protecting powers on 3 February 1830, and ratified in Greece by the Greek Senate's Memorandum of 10 April 1830, ... was intended to ensure that the Catholics living in Greece enjoyed freedom of religion and freedom of worship and it did not confer on the bishops of the Western Church any jurisdiction other than spiritual and administrative, that is to say relating to that Church's domestic order, and the provisions of the canon law that governs the Roman Catholic Church which attribute legal personality to convents and other Church establishments founded by decisions of the bishops of that Church were not adopted. The legal personality of Church establishments is a question which does not relate to worship or the Church's domestic order but primarily concerns the legal order of the State and consequently cannot exist unless it is recognised by law."

[18] Lastly, in a judgment (no. 1099/1985) of 1985 the Court of Cassation held that the abbot of a monastic establishment of the Roman Catholic Church is empowered to represent it in legal proceedings concerning its property without the written authorisation of the local bishop as provided in canon 1526.

C. Administrative and notarial practice

[19] According to the applicant church, numerous notarial acts to which the Catholic Church of Greece and/or Catholic parish churches, duly represented by authorised agents in accordance with Catholic canon law, were parties unequivocally attest that as regards their property, the churches' legal personality has never been challenged. By way of example, it has produced the following documents:

(a) contract of sale no. 17955/1915, whereby the Catholic Cathedral of Athens, duly represented by the Archbishop of the Greek Catholics, purchased 12,500 square metres of land in the Athens suburb of Iraklion. Attached to this contract is an Athens Mortgage Registry certificate dated 13 June 1997 confirming that the contract was registered according to the rules in force;

(b) contract of sale no. 5027/1936, whereby the applicant church, duly represented, purchased a shop in the centre of Canea;

(c) contract of sale no. 271/1955, whereby the Catholic Cathedral of Athens, duly represented, purchased a four-storey building in the centre of Athens. Attached to this contract is an Athens Mortgage Registry certificate dated 13 June 1997 confirming that the contract was registered according to the rules in force;

(d) contract of sale no. 2084/1981, whereby the applicant church sold to the city council of Canea 4,231.75 square metres of land in the city centre; in this document the church of Canea was represented by its bishop, appointed by papal decree;

(e) contract of sale no. 53844/1981, whereby the applicant church, expressly described as a private-law entity and a religious foundation of the Catholic Church, purchased a flat in the Athens suburb of Maroussi;

(f) contract of sale no. 1817/1992, whereby the Catholic Cathedral of Athens sold a flat in Athens which it had acquired by gift in 1980. This notarial act mentions (i) the foundation of the vendor cathedral in 1865 by unilateral act of the Bishop of Syros and (ii) the papal bull of 1973 whereby its representative was appointed according to the rules of Catholic canon law. Attached to this contract is an Athens Mortgage Registry certificate dated 13 June 1997 confirming that it was registered according to the rules in force.

In all these contracts it is expressly stated that the appropriate transfer tax was duly paid; and the contracts were all registered with the appropriate mortgage registries. Furthermore, as may be seen from the tax returns duly completed and submitted by the applicant church for the years 1994, 1995 and 1996, its rent income from its properties, including some of the above-mentioned properties, was exempt from income tax because of the landlord's status as a religious legal entity. In addition, two inheritance certificates issued by the clerk of the Athens Court of First Instance on an application by the Catholic Cathedral of Athens (the first certificate) and the Catholic parish church of Phira on the island of Thera (the second certificate) attest that these churches were recognised as the sole heirs of persons who died in 1988 and 1990.

PROCEEDINGS BEFORE THE COMMISSION

(...)

[20] The Commission declared the application (no. 25528/94) admissible on 15 January 1996.

(...)

AS TO THE LAW

I. Preliminary issues

[21] The Government disputed the standing of the Right Reverend Frangiskos Papamanolis, Roman Catholic Bishop of the Islands of Syros, Milos and Thera and Acting Bishop of Crete, to represent the applicant church and thus apply to the Commission; they pointed out that it was Abbot Roussos who had brought the proceedings in question in the national courts. Canea Catholic Church had not provided any explanation as to this change of representative. If Bishop Papamanolis had lodged the application as the statutory representative of the church as a legal entity, the application was inadmissible since the legal entity he claimed to represent did not in fact exist. If, on the other hand, he had acted as the representative of a union of persons, in particular the parishioners who used the church for worship, it had to be concluded that domestic remedies had not been exhausted as the community of parishioners had not, in its own name and in accordance with art. 62 of the Code of Civil Procedure, carried out the necessary formalities to secure adequate legal protection (see par. 18 above).

[22] The Commission considered that the application should be treated as having been submitted by the church itself (see par. 26 above), which it classed as a „non-governmental organisation" within the meaning of art. 25 of the Convention.

[23] The Court likewise considers that Canea Catholic Church validly applied to the Commission through Bishop Papamanolis; it notes in this connection that the Court of Cassation itself had already held, in judgments nos. 142/1889 and 1099/1985, that the Catholic bishop in charge of the churches in his diocese and the abbots in charge of Catholic monastic establishments were alone empowered to represent those churches and establishments in legal proceedings concerning any claim or issue relating to their property (see par. 21 and 23 above).

II. General observation

[24] The applicant church said that the refusal of the Canea Court of First Instance sitting as an appellate court and of the Court of Cassation to recognise it as a legal person with capacity to bring or defend legal proceedings breached art. 6 and 9 of the Convention and art. 1 of Protocol No. 1, each taken either alone or in combination with art. 14 of the Convention.

[25] Unlike the Commission, the Court considers that the applicant church's complaints mainly concern a restriction on the exercise of its right of access to a court. Accordingly, it will consider first the issues relating to art. 6 of the Convention.

III. Alleged violation of Art. 6 § 1 of the Convention

[26] The relevant part of art. 6 § 1 of the Convention reads as follows:

> „*In the determination of his civil rights and obligations ..., everyone is entitled to a ... hearing ... by [a] ... tribunal ...*"

[27] The applicant church alleged that the Court of Cassation's judgment had been an unexpected and unjustified reversal of case-law going back more than a century in which the legal personality of the Catholic Church in general or the various parish churches in particular had never been called in question; the judgment had also evidenced a selective and partial administration of justice as it had permanently deprived the applicant church of the right to take legal proceedings to protect its property, on the sole ground that the church served the Catholic faith. In its submission, a church, of whatever denomination, should enjoy protection appropriate to its nature and to the purpose for which it was intended. By virtue of the act of its foundation according to the rules of the religion to which it was dedicated, a church like the applicant church had the continuity which the law normally ascribed to legal persons; it therefore did not need to produce a document proving that it had acquired legal personality in accordance with the formalities laid down by law before the Civil Code was introduced in Greece or thereafter and constituting recognition of an association, non-commercial partnership or a foundation as a legal person. In short, the applicant church, like all the other churches existing in Greece before the Civil Code was brought in, had legal personality *sui generis*.

[28] The Government maintained that the applicant church had not *ipso facto* acquired legal personality, because it had not complied with the relevant national legislation. Nor was legal personality conferred on it by the Third Protocol of London, because the Catholic Church of the Virgin Mary had been reopened in 1879, that is to say after the adoption

of that protocol, at a time when Crete belonged to the Ottoman Empire; in any case, the protocol only guaranteed religious freedom of minorities and did not settle the question of relations between the Catholic Church established in Greece and the State. Certainly political, religious or other groups were free to determine their own internal management and organisation, but as regards their relations with the State, it was obvious that they had to comply with national legislation. Only theocracies allowed the representatives of the Church to ignore secular laws and gave the Church temporal powers in defiance of the law. It was inconceivable that Orthodox priests or leaders of other faiths and sects should quite simply be able, on their own authority, to disregard provisions making it necessary for that type of legal personality to be registered. Greek law afforded religious communities a sufficient number of possibilities for organising their activities and accordingly for fully and efficiently managing their relations with the outside world, and in particular invoking the aid of the courts to protect such of their property as was intended to provide financial support for their objectives or was used for worship. Religious communities were thereby empowered to set up, on their own initiative, separate, independent legal entities like the associations, religious foundations and partnerships referred to in art. 784 of the Civil Code or, if they did not wish to do so, to operate as unions of persons and protect their property by virtue of that status (art. 61 of the Civil Code and art. 62 of the Code of Civil Procedure). The fact that the applicant church had chosen the wrong means for maintaining that it had acquired legal personality was the sole responsibility of the religious community to which it belonged, and any adverse consequences for its interests - which were, at all events, provisional as all the above-mentioned possibilities still remained open to it - could not be imputed to the State.

[28] The Commission, having expressed the opinion that there had been a violation of art. 9 of the Convention taken together with art. 14, did not consider it necessary to consider the case under art. 6.

[29] In the Golder v. the United Kingdom judgment of 21 February 1975 and the Ashingdane v. the United Kingdom judgment of 28 May 1985 (Series A no. 18, p. 18, § 36, and no. 93, pp. 24-25, § 57) the Court held that art. 6 § 1 secures to everyone the right to have any claim relating to his civil rights and obligations brought before a court or tribunal; in this way the article embodies the „right to a court", of which the right of access, that is the right to institute proceedings before courts in civil matters, constitutes one aspect. The right is not, however, an absolute one; since, by its very nature, it calls for regulation by the State, it may be subject to limitations, although these must not restrict or reduce access in such a way or to such an extent that the very essence of the right is impaired.

[30] It is apparent from the evidence before the Court that the legal personality of the Greek Catholic Church and of the various parish

churches has never been called in question since the creation of the
Greek State either by the administrative authorities or by the courts.
Those churches - including the applicant church - have in their own
name acquired, used and freely transferred movable and immovable
property, concluded contracts and taken part in, among others, notarial
transactions, whose validity has always been recognised. As regards
taxation, they have also enjoyed the exemptions provided in Greek legislation on charitable foundations and non-profit-making associations (see
par. 21 and 24 above).

[31] The Court cannot accept the Government's argument that the applicant church should have carried out the formalities necessary for acquiring one or other form of legal personality provided for in the Civil
Code as there was nothing to suggest that it would one day be deprived
of access to a court in order to defend its civil rights. Settled case-law and
administrative practice had, over the course of the years, created legal
certainty, both in property matters and as regards the representation of
the various Catholic parish churches in legal proceedings, and the applicant church could reasonably rely on that. In this connection, the Court
notes that in the instant case the Canea District Court gave no consideration to the question of legal personality (see par. 9 above) and the reporting judge of the Court of Cassation - relying on the well-established
case-law - had invited that court to quash the judgment of the Court of
First Instance sitting as an appellate court (see par. 12 above). As to the
possibility - which the Government maintained still existed - of the applicant church's acquiring such a personality or constituting itself as a union of persons in order to be able to bring or defend legal proceedings in
the future, in accordance with art. 62 of the Code of Civil Procedure, the
Court shares the reservations expressed by counsel for the applicant
church. Quite apart from the difficulties of adapting a church to that
kind of structure and the procedural problems which might arise in the
event of litigation, such late compliance with the relevant rules of domestic law might be interpreted as an admission that countless acts of the
applicant church in the past were not valid. Furthermore, the Court of
Cassation's judgment would make it problematical to transfer the applicant church's property to a new legal entity which would take the place
of the church, hitherto the owner of its property.

[32] In holding that the applicant church had no capacity to take legal
proceedings, the Court of Cassation did not only penalise the failure to
comply with a simple formality necessary for the protection of public order, as the Government maintained. It also imposed a real restriction on
the applicant church preventing it on this particular occasion and for the
future from having any dispute relating to its property rights determined
by the courts; in this connection, the Court notes that on 31 May 1995
the Crete Court of Appeal, relying on the Court of Cassation's judgment,
dismissed two actions brought by the applicant church against the les-

sees of a business it owned, on the ground that it did not have legal personality (see par. 21 above).

[33] Such a limitation impairs the very substance of the applicant church's „right to a court" and therefore constitutes a breach of art. 6 § 1 of the Convention.

IV. Alleged violation of Art. 14 of the Convention taken together with Art. 6 § 1

[34] Art. 14 of the Convention provides:

„The enjoyment of the rights and freedoms set forth in [the] Convention shall be secured without discrimination on any ground such as sex, race, colour, language, religion, political or other opinion, national or social origin, association with a national minority, property, birth or other status."

[35] The applicant church maintained that it was the victim of discrimination incompatible with that provision, since the removal of its right to bring or defend legal proceedings was based exclusively on the criterion of religion.

[36] The Government argued that no religious community in Greece was entitled to establish a legal entity automatically without complying with the laws of the State. The applicant church had not even alleged that it was a public-law entity, one of whose characteristics lay in its constitution under a law which made provision for its objects, powers and mode of administration and functioning. Even the Orthodox Church, which had existed in Greece since the first century, had not been regarded as a public-law entity *ipso jure*; its status, its organisation and everything to do with its functioning had been laid down in several enactments, the most important being Law no. 590/1977 on the Charter of the Church of Greece (see par. 19 above). The administrative unity of the Catholic Church was scarcely compatible with the obligations entailed in Greece by being a public-law entity like the Orthodox Church, notably acceptance of the fact that the Government, the administrative authorities and the courts played a role in the temporal organisation and running of it. Furthermore, the Church of Greece's personality in public law stemmed from the close and very old relations between it and the State, the overwhelming majority of whose citizens were of the Orthodox faith. As to the personality in public law of Greece's Jewish community, this was explained by the fact that the community was not only a religious organisation but also a union of persons who managed their own affairs and had a number of features in common, including their religion.

[37] The Commission, having expressed the opinion that there had been a violation of art. 9 taken together with art. 14, did not consider it

necessary to examine the case under art. 14 taken together with art. 6 of the Convention.

[38] It is not for the Court to rule on the question whether personality in public law or personality in private law would be more appropriate for the applicant church or to encourage it or the Greek Government to take steps to have one or the other conferred. The Court does no more than note that the applicant church, which owns its land and buildings, has been prevented from taking legal proceedings to protect them, whereas the Orthodox Church or the Jewish community can do so in order to protect their own property without any formality or required procedure. Having regard to its conclusion under art. 6 § 1 of the Convention, the Court considers that there has also been a breach of art. 14 taken together with art. 6 § 1 as no objective and reasonable justification for such a difference of treatment has been put forward.

V. Alleged violations of Art. 9 of the Convention and Art. 1 of Protocol No. 1, each taken alone or together with Art. 14 of the Convention

[39] The applicant church complained of a breach of its right to freedom of religion and of its right to the peaceful enjoyment of its possessions. It relied on art. 9 of the Convention and art. 1 of Protocol No. 1 respectively, each taken either alone or together with art. 14 of the Convention.art. 9 of the Convention and art. 1 of Protocol No. 1 provide:

Art. 9 of the Convention
„1. Everyone has the right to freedom of thought, conscience and religion; this right includes freedom to change his religion or belief and freedom, either alone or in community with others and in public or in private, to manifest his religion or belief, in worship, teaching, practice and observance.
2. Freedom to manifest one's religion or beliefs shall be subject only to such limitations as are prescribed by law and are necessary in a democratic society in the interests of public safety, for the protection of public order, health or morals, or for the protection of the rights and freedoms of others."
Art. 1 of Protocol No. 1
„Every natural or legal person is entitled to the peaceful enjoyment of his possessions. No one shall be deprived of his possessions except in the public interest and subject to the conditions provided for by law and by the general principles of international law.
The preceding provisions shall not, however, in any way impair the right of a State to enforce such laws as it deems necessary to control the use of property in accordance with the general interest or to secure the payment of taxes or other contributions or penalties."

Under art. 9 of the Convention and art. 1 of Protocol No. 1 taken alone, the applicant church maintained that the refusal to acknowledge that it had legal personality so that it could take legal proceedings to protect its property, even if such property was not directly used for religious purposes, infringed its freedom of religion and deprived it of any possibility of applying to the courts in the event of arbitrary dispossession of its property or expropriation. Under art. 14 of the Convention taken together with the foregoing articles, it argued that it had suffered discrimination on the ground of religion.

[40] The Commission expressed the opinion that there had been a violation of art. 9 taken together with art. 14 but no violation of art. 9 taken alone, and considered it unnecessary to examine the case additionally under the other articles.

[41] Having regard to its conclusions in par. 42 and 47 above, the Court holds that it is not necessary to rule on the complaints based on these articles.

VI. Application of Art. 50 of the Convention *(Entschädigung etc. wird zuerkannt)*

For these reasons, the Court unanimously

1. *Holds that the applicant church validly applied to the Commission through Bishop Papamanolis;*
2. *Holds that there has been a breach of art. 6 § 1 of the Convention;*
3. *Holds that there has been a breach of art. 14 of the Convention taken together with art. 6 § 1;*
4. *Holds that it is unnecessary to rule on the complaints based on art. 9 of the Convention and art. 1 of Protocol No. 1, each taken alone or combined with art. 14 of the Convention.*

46

Unter den besonderen Bedingungen des Militärdienstes kann es geboten sein, religiöse Abwerbung (Proselytismus) unter Soldaten disziplinarisch zu ahnden.

Art. 9, 10, 14 EMRK

EGMR, Urteil vom 24. Februar 1998 - No. 140/1996/759/958-960
(Larissis u.a. ./. Griechenland)[1] -

---

[1] RJD 1998-I.

AS TO THE FACTS

I. The circumstances of the case

[7] The first applicant, Mr Dimitrios Larissis, was born in 1949 and lives in Tanagra Viotias. The second applicant, Mr Savvas Mandalarides, was born in 1948 and lives at Agria Volou. The third applicant, Mr Ioannis Sarandis, was born in 1951 and lives in Kamatero Attikis. At the time of the events in question, the three applicants were officers in the same unit of the Greek air force. They were all followers of the Pentecostal Church, a Protestant Christian denomination which adheres to the principle that it is the duty of all believers to engage in evangelism.

A. The alleged acts of proselytism

The alleged proselytising of airman Georgios Antoniadis by the first and second applicants

[8] In the evidence he gave for the purposes of the prosecution against the applicants (see par. 13 below), airman Antoniadis said that he was transferred to the applicants' unit in 1986, two months after joining the air force, and was placed under the command of the second applicant in the teletyping service. On approximately seven occasions the first and second applicants engaged him in religious discussions, reading aloud extracts from the Bible and encouraging him to accept the beliefs of the Pentecostal Church. The second applicant told him that some members of the sect were able to speak in foreign languages with the assistance of divine power. Whenever airman Antoniadis returned from leave, the second applicant asked him if he had visited the Pentecostal Church. The former testified that he felt obliged to take part in these discussions because the applicants were his superior officers. The alleged proselytising of airman Athanassios Kokkalis by the first and third applicants.

[9] In his statement before the Athens Permanent Air Force Court (see par. 13 below), airman Kokkalis testified that he served in the applicants' unit between spring 1987 and October 1988, although he was not under the direct command of any of them. During that time the first applicant engaged him in theological discussions on approximately thirty occasions, and the third applicant on approximately fifty occasions, initially concealing the fact that they were not Orthodox Christians but subsequently criticising some of the tenets of that faith and urging airman Kokkalis to accept their beliefs. The third applicant repeatedly asked him to visit the Pentecostal Church in Larissa while he was on leave, telling him that miracles took place there including the acquisition by believers of the ability to speak in foreign languages, and gave him the Pentecostal newspaper *Christianismos* to read. The applicants were very good officers and were always polite to him, but their approaches

bothered him nonetheless. The alleged proselytising of airman Nikolaos Kafkas by the first and third applicants

[10] Airman Nikolaos Kafkas was unable to give evidence at the first-instance hearing because his wife was ill, but he told the Courts-Martial Appeal Court (see par. 21 below) that he had served in the same unit as the applicants, under the command of the third applicant, between winter 1988 and August 1989. The applicants did not put any pressure on him to become a member of the Pentecostal Church. He himself approached the third applicant and asked why he was so peaceful, to which the latter replied that this was the result of reading the Gospel. When, at the suggestion of the first and third applicants, he started to read the Bible, he noticed a number of points of divergence between it and the teachings of the Orthodox Church. He did not have any discussions with the applicants concerning the Orthodox and Pentecostal Churches, although he did seek their advice whenever he had any questions concerning the Bible and always found their replies convincing. They never gave him any Pentecostal literature or told him to go to the Pentecostal Church. The third applicant never authorised his absence for purposes related to the Pentecostal Church, which he had visited for the first time in September 1989, after he had been discharged from the armed forces. Airman Kafkas's father, Mr Alexandros Kafkas, told the first-instance court that his son had been converted from the Orthodox to the Pentecostal Church while serving in the air force under the orders of the third applicant. According to his father, shortly after he joined the unit his behaviour changed. He stopped seeing his friends, spent long periods of time in his room studying the Bible and listening to taped sermons and brought back from the barracks his television and radio sets and the books from which he used to study for university entrance examinations. He told his father that he had met two officers who were real Christians, unlike his father. When his parents followed him on one of his visits to the Pentecostal Church, he left home and went to live in Athens. He returned after twenty days, when he reconverted to the Orthodox Church, explaining to his father that the first and third applicants had converted him to the Pentecostal Church, taking advantage of their rank to exert pressure on him and using special skills of persuasion. They had told him that he would be given leave of absence if he promised to visit their church. When Alexandros Kafkas left to go on a trip, Nikolaos reconverted to the Pentecostal Church. His father concluded that his son had no will of his own and always did as he was told by other members of the Pentecostal Church. The alleged proselytising of the Baïramis family and their neighbours by the second applicant

[11] According to the statement of Captain Ilias Baïramis, his brother-in-law, Mr Charalampos Apostolidis, a member of the Pentecostal Church, began one day to rage at his wife, telling her that he saw Satan in her. The second applicant was summoned, and as soon as he arrived

Mr Apostolidis became calmer. The second applicant then preached a sermon to the members of the Baïramis family and some neighbours who had come to see what was going on, in the course of which he urged them all to convert to the Pentecostal religion. The alleged proselytising of Mrs Anastassia Zounara by the second and third applicants

[12] In a statement prepared for the purposes of an administrative inquiry against the applicants, Mrs Anastassia Zounara explained that her husband had joined the Pentecostal Church, which led to the breakdown of her family life with him. In an attempt to understand her husband's behaviour, Mrs Zounara visited the Pentecostal Church and the applicants' homes on several occasions over a period of about five months. During this time the applicants, particularly the second and third applicants, used to visit her and urge her to join their Church. They told her that they had received signs from God and could predict the future, and that Mrs Zounara and her children were possessed by the devil. Eventually she developed psychological problems and severed all links with the applicants and the Pentecostal Church.

B. The trial at first instance

[13] On 18 May 1992, the applicants appeared before the Permanent Air Force Court (*Diarkes Stratodikio Aeroporias*) in Athens, composed of one officer with legal training and four other officers. They were tried for various offences of proselytism, under sec. 4 of Law no. 1363/1938 as amended (henceforth, „sec. 4" - see par. 27 below).

[14] In a decision delivered on the day of the hearing (no. 209/92), the court rejected the defence's argument that the law against proselytism was unconstitutional, finding that no issue could arise under the principle *nullum crimen sine lege certa* because of the non-exhaustive enumeration in the statute of the means by which an intrusion on another person's religious beliefs could be brought about. It found all three applicants guilty of proselytism, holding in particular as follows.

1. The first applicant

[15] In respect of the first applicant, the court observed:

„The accused, while he was a military officer ... serving in Unit X, committed the offence of proselytism in the military camp of this unit between November 1986 and December 1987 by engaging in several acts which ... gave rise to a single, albeit continuing, breach of the relevant criminal provision. He acted with the aim of intruding on and changing the religious beliefs of airman Georgios Antoniadis, an Orthodox Christian who served in the same unit. Abusing the trust placed in him by airman Antoniadis, who was his hierarchical subordinate, the accused tried on approximately twenty occasions to persuade airman Antoniadis to become a member of the sect of the Pentecostal Church by engaging in discussions *on theology with him in the course of which the accused contested the correctness of the teachings of the university department of theology concerning God and the Orthodox dogma. He also encouraged airman Antoniadis to read the Bible in the light of the accused's own beliefs as a member of the Pentecostal Church, questioned the holy traditions and recommended that he visit the church of the Pentecostal sect in Athens.*

Acting in the same capacity, the accused committed the offence of proselytism between May 1987 and February 1988 by engaging in several acts which ... gave rise to a single, albeit continuing, breach of the relevant criminal provision. He acted with the aim of intruding on and changing the religious beliefs of airman Athanassios Kokkalis, an Orthodox Christian who served in the same unit. On approximately thirty occasions the accused tried to persuade airman Kokkalis to become a member of the sect of the Church of Pentecost by engaging, persistently and importunately, in discussions with him about the correctness of his beliefs as a member of the sect of the Pentecostal Church, questioning the holiness of the Christian Orthodox Church and inviting airman Kokkalis to listen to taped recordings on the beliefs of the Pentecostal sect. The accused took advantage of the trust inherent in the relationship between a subordinate and a superior and of airman Kokkalis's naïvety, inexperience and youth, telling him that in his Church some people started speaking foreign languages under the effect of the Holy Spirit.

Acting in the same capacity, the accused committed the offence of proselytism between spring 1989 and 18 August 1989, in the place mentioned above, by ... acting with the aim of intruding on and changing the religious beliefs of airman Nikolaos Kafkas, who served under his orders in the same unit. Taking advantage of the trust inherent in the relationship between a subordinate and a superior, and of the young man's naïvety and inexperience, the accused tried to persuade airman Kafkas to become a member of the sect of the Church of Pentecost by continually, persistently and importunately expounding on his beliefs concerning the sect of the Pentecostal Church, reading and explaining the Bible in the light of his beliefs and providing him with copies of a tract entitled Christianismos. The accused succeeded in converting airman Kafkas by taking advantage of the latter's inexperience in theological matters and the influence he had on him due to his position and rank."

The court also found the first applicant guilty of proselytising another airman, Stefanos Voikos.

[16] It sentenced him to five months' imprisonment for proselytising airman Antoniadis, five months' imprisonment for proselytising airman Kokkalis, five months' imprisonment for proselytising airman Voikos and seven months' imprisonment for proselytising airman Kafkas. Overall, however, because some of these periods were to run concurrently, the first applicant was ordered to spend thirteen months in prison. The court ordered that these penalties be converted to fines and not enforced provided the applicant did not commit new offences in the following three years.

2. The second applicant

[17] In respect of the second applicant, the court held as follows:

„*The accused, while he was a military officer ... serving in Unit X, committed the offence of proselytism in the military camp of this unit between November 1986 and December 1987 by engaging in several acts which ... gave rise to a single, albeit continuing, breach of the relevant criminal provision. He took advantage of the authority exercisable by him due to the difference in rank over airman Georgiades Antoniadis, who served in the same unit. On approximately seven occasions, on dates which have not been specified, the accused tried to intrude on and change the religious beliefs of airman Antoniadis by means of skilful discussions with him concerning religion. The accused urged airman Antoniadis, because of his youth, to study nothing but the Gospel, where he told him he would find the truth, which differed from the Orthodox dogma. He also tried, by means of skilful interpretation of extracts from the Holy Gospel in accordance with the beliefs of the sect of the Pentecost, to convince him that the Orthodox faith was not correct and that he should adopt the beliefs of the accused, urging him at the same time in a pressing manner to visit during his leave the church of the Pentecostal sect in Athens.*

The accused also committed the offence of proselytism in Vólos in 1988 by ... taking advantage of the inexperience and intellectual weakness of Mrs Anastassia Zounara. He tried on several occasions, on dates which have not been specified, to intrude on and change her religious beliefs by engaging in a skilful analysis of the beliefs of the sect of the Pentecost and their difference from those of the Orthodox faith. Elaborating on the correctness of the former, he tried persistently to convince her that the followers of the Pentecostal Church bore marks given to them by God, that they could prophesy the future, that she and her children were possessed by the devil who was fighting to keep control over her, that she worshipped idols and demons and that the Pentecostal Church held the truth. He also urged her in a pressing manner to be baptised and become a member of the Pentecostal Church.

The accused also committed the offence of proselytism in Vólos on a date which has not been specified towards the beginning of June 1989. Having been summoned by Captain Ilias Baïramis, the accused went to the house of Mr Apostolos Baïramis, Captain Baïramis's brother, where Mr Charalampos Apostolidis, the brother-in-law of the Baïramis brothers and a follower of the sect of the Pentecostal Church, was in a delirious state under the influence of his religious beliefs. He was foaming at the mouth, invoking Christ's name and saying ,Thank you Christ, because I have known the truth, I see the devil in my wife's and children's faces'. The mere fact of the accused's presence calmed Mr Apostolidis, and the former skilfully took advantage of this by attempting to intrude upon and change the religious beliefs of Apostolos Baïramis and Marigoula, Sotirios and Evangelis Baïrami, who were present during the incident and had been impressed by it, and of a number of neighbours who gathered afterwards. He preached to them, elaborating on the beliefs of the sect of the Pentecostal Church and telling them that these, and not those of the Orthodox Church, were correct and that in 1992 the world would come to an end and the Church would be ,captured'. He urged them persistently and importunately to believe in the true Christ and told them that, by virtue of being Christian Orthodox, they had taken sides with the devil."

[18] The second applicant was sentenced to five months' imprisonment for proselytising airman Antoniadis, five months' imprisonment for proselytising Mrs Zounara, and eight months' imprisonment for proselytising the Baïramis family and their neighbours, although he was only to serve twelve months overall. The court ordered that these penalties be converted to fines and not enforced provided the applicant did not commit new offences in the following three years.

3. The third applicant

[19] In respect of the third applicant, the court held as follows:

„*The accused, while he was a military officer ... serving in Unit X, committed the offence of proselytism in the military camp of this unit between May 1987 and February 1988 by engaging in several acts which ... gave rise to a single, albeit continuing, breach of the relevant criminal provision. He acted with the aim of intruding on and changing the religious beliefs of airman Athanassios Kokkalis, an Orthodox Christian who served in the same unit. Taking advantage of the trust inherent in the relationship between a subordinate and a superior, the accused tried more than fifty times to convince airman Kokkalis that the teachings of the Orthodox faith were not correct on a number of issues, such as the virginity of the Holy Mother, the ranks of the priests and the power of the Holy Spirit. He engaged with airman Kokkalis in persistent and importunate discussions regarding the teachings of the sect of the Pentecostal Church, of which the accused was a follower, telling him that the teachings of the sect, rather than those of the Orthodox Church, were correct. He urged him to visit a place in Larissa where the followers of the Pentecostal Church used to gather and to become a member of the sect and he gave him a free copy of a periodical published by the followers of the Pentecostal Church entitled Christianismos. In the course of these encounters the accused intentionally failed to reveal to airman Kokkalis that he was a member of the Pentecostal sect.*

Acting in the same capacity, the accused committed the offence of proselytism in the same place for a period of four to five months in 1988, ... acting with the aim of intruding on and changing the religious beliefs of Mrs Anastassia Zounara, an Orthodox Christian. He skilfully took advantage of her inexperience in religious matters and her intellectual weakness, resulting from her low level of education, and tried importunately to persuade her to be baptised and become a member of the sect of the Pentecostal Church. He told her constantly that she bore signs given to him by God, that he could foresee the future and that she and her children were possessed. His intention was to undermine her faith in Orthodoxy and convert her to the sect of the Pentecostal Church.

Acting in the same capacity, the accused committed the offence of proselytism in the same place between spring 1989 and 18 August 1989, ... acting with the aim of intruding on and changing the religious beliefs of airman Nikolaos Kafkas, an Orthodox Christian who served in the same unit. Taking advantage of the trust inherent in the relationship between a subordinate and a superior and of airman Kafkas's naïvety and inexperience, the accused tried to persuade him to adhere to the sect of the Pentecostal Church. He engaged in continual, persistent and importunate analysis of his beliefs regarding the sect of the Pentecostal Church, continually reading the Gospel which he interpreted in accordance with his beliefs. He gave airman Kafkas publications of his sect and took him to his place of worship. In this way, he succeeded in converting airman Kafkas, taking advantage of his inexperience in religious matters and the influence he had on him because of his position and rank."

The court also found that the third applicant had engaged in the proselytising of a warrant officer, Adjutant Theophilos Tsikas.

[20] He was sentenced to eight months' imprisonment for proselytising airman Kokkalis, five months' imprisonment for proselytising Mrs Zounara, five months' imprisonment for proselytising Adjutant Tsikas and seven months' imprisonment for proselytising airman Kafkas. He was to serve fourteen months overall. The court ordered that these penalties be converted to fines and not enforced provided the applicant did not commit new offences in the following three years.

C. The appeal to the Courts-Martial Appeal Court

[21] The applicants appealed immediately to the Courts-Martial Appeal Court (*Anatheoritiko Dikastirio*), a court composed of five military judges. Their appeal was heard on 7 October 1992.

[22] In a judgment pronounced immediately after the hearing (no. 390/1992), the Appeal Court rejected the defence's argument to the effect that the accused had merely exercised a constitutional right and upheld most of their convictions, using the same reasoning as the first-instance court. It did, however, reverse the conviction of the first applicant for proselytising airman Voikos and that of the third applicant for proselytising Adjutant Tsikas (see par. 15 and 19 above).

[23] The Appeal Court maintained the penalties imposed by the first-instance court on the first and third applicants in respect of the convictions it had upheld. However, because of the quashing of the two convictions, their overall sentences were reduced to eleven and twelve months respectively. It reduced the second applicant's sentence to four months' imprisonment for proselytising airman Antoniadis, four months for proselytising Mrs Zounara, and six months for proselytising the Baïramis family and neighbours. His overall sentence was reduced to ten months' imprisonment.

[24] As none of the overall sentences imposed involved more than one year's imprisonment, they were automatically converted by the court into pecuniary penalties of 1,000 drachmas per day. The court ordered that the penalties should not be enforced provided that the applicants did not commit new criminal offences in the following three years.

D. The appeal to the Court of Cassation

[25] The applicants appealed in cassation.

In a judgment delivered on 30 July 1993 (no. 1266/1993), the Court of Cassation (*Arios Pagos*) found as follows:

„*It follows from sec. 4 (1) and (2) of Law no. 1363/1938 [see par. 27 below] that in order for the crime of proselytism ... to be established, there must be a direct or indirect attempt to intrude on the religious beliefs of a person of a different religious persuasion with the aim of undermining those beliefs, provided that the attempt is made using the means enumerated in a non-exhaustive fashion in the above-mentioned section, namely by any kind of inducement or promise of an inducement or moral support or material assistance, or by fraudulent means or by taking advantage of the other person's inexperience, trust, need, low intelligence or naïvety.*

The above-mentioned provisions of this section ... are not contrary to [the provisions of the Greek Constitution guaranteeing the principle nullum crimen, nulla poena sine lege]; moreover, they are perfectly consistent with art. 13 of the Constitution [see par. 26 below], which provides that all known religions are free since, under art. 13, proselytism is prohibited ... The argument to the contrary finds no support in the fact that under [the previous Constitutions] the prohibition of proselytism was designed to protect the then (and still) dominant religion, whereas under the present Constitution that prohibition is associated with freedom of conscience in religious matters relating to all known religions. This reasoning is undeniably consistent with both the letter and the spirit [of sec. 4], pursuant to which protection from proselytism employing the unlawful means set out therein is provided for the religious convictions of all persons of different persuasions, i.e. all those belonging to a religion or dogma other than that of the author of the proselytism, and not exclusively those professing the principles of the Orthodox Church.

Furthermore, freedom of conscience in religious matters and of thought, protected as a human right by the present Constitution and by art. 18 and 19 of the United Nations' Universal Declaration and art. 9 and 14 of the European Convention on Human Rights, is not undermined by the above-mentioned criminal provision, since it does not sanction the holding of religious beliefs, which is completely free, but only any attempt to intrude on another person's religious beliefs with the aim of changing them. Such attempts are quite incompatible with religious freedom, which creates an obligation to respect the religious convictions of all those who hold different beliefs."

The court therefore dismissed the applicants' appeal.

II. Relevant domestic law

The right to religious freedom under the Greek Constitution

[26] Art. 13 of the Greek Constitution provides, as relevant:

„*1. Freedom of conscience in religious matters is inviolable. The enjoyment of personal and political rights shall not depend on an individual's religious beliefs.*

2. There shall be freedom to practise any known religion; individuals shall be free to perform their rites of worship without hindrance and under the protection of the law. The performance of rites of worship must not prejudice public order or public morals. Proselytism is prohibited."

The law on proselytism

[27] Sec. 4 of Law no. 1363/1938, as amended by Law no. 1672/1939, provides as follows:

„1. Anyone engaging in proselytism shall be liable to imprisonment and a fine of between 1,000 and 50,000 drachmas; he shall, moreover, be subject to police supervision for a period of between six months and one year to be fixed by the court when convicting the offender.
2. By ‚proselytism' is meant, in particular, any direct or indirect attempt to intrude on the religious beliefs of a person of a different religious persuasion (eterodoxos), with the aim of undermining those beliefs, either by any kind of inducement or promise of an inducement or moral support or material assistance, or by fraudulent means or by taking advantage of the other person's inexperience, trust, need, low intellect or naïvety.
3. The commission of such an offence in a school or other educational establishment or philanthropic institution shall constitute a particularly aggravating circumstance."

There is a considerable body of case-law interpreting and applying this section: see the Court's Kokkinakis v. Greece judgment of 25 May 1993, Series A no. 260-A, pp. 13-15, §§ 17-21, KirchE-EU S. 202.

PROCEDINGS BEFORE THE COMMISSION

[28] In their applications lodged with the Commission on 28 January 1994 (nos. 23372/94, 26377/94 and 26378/94), Mr Larissis, Mr Mandalarides and Mr Sarandis claimed that sec. 4 of Law no. 1363/1938 was too broad and vague to be compatible with the requirements of legal certainty under art. 7, 9 § 2 and 10 § 2 of the Convention. In addition, they complained that their convictions for proselytism amounted to violations of their rights to freedom of religion and expression under art. 9 and 10 of the Convention, and were discriminatory, contrary to art. 14 taken in conjunction with art. 9.

[29] On 27 November 1995, the Commission ordered the joinder of the three applications under Rule 35 of its Rules of Procedure and declared them admissible.

(...)

FINAL SUBMISSIONS TO THE COURT

(...)

AS TO THE LAW

I. Alleged violation of Art. 7 of the convention

[32] The applicants contended that the law against proselytism failed to comply with art. 7 of the Convention, which provides:

> „*1. No one shall be held guilty of any criminal offence on account of any act or omission which did not constitute a criminal offence under national or international law at the time when it was committed. Nor shall a heavier penalty be imposed than the one that was applicable at the time the criminal offence was committed.*
>
> *2. This article shall not prejudice the trial and punishment of any person for any act or omission which, at the time when it was committed, was criminal according to the general principles of law recognised by civilised nations.*"

They argued that the Greek law violated the principle enshrined in art. 7 that only the law can define a crime and prescribe a penalty (*nullum crimen, nulla poena sine lege*), since it was impossible to predict whether certain types of behaviour would lead to a prosecution for proselytism. They contended that this deficiency in the law was evident both from the text of sec. 4 (2) (see par. 27 above) and the jurisprudence which had arisen from it. For example, the use of the words „in particular" implied that the subsequent definition was only one form of proselytism punishable under the statute, and other expressions employed, such as „direct or indirect" and „any kind of inducement or promise of an inducement or moral support or material assistance" were so broad and vague as to embrace almost any form of practical evangelism. The case-law which had grown out of sec. 4 (see the examples set out in the Court's Kokkinakis v. Greece judgment of 25 May 1993, Series A no. 260-A, p. 13, § 18, KirchE-EU S. 202), showed that no one in Greece could possibly determine in advance whether or not his religious actions would constitute the offence of proselytism.

[33] The Government and the Commission, referring to the above-mentioned Kokkinakis judgment, were both of the opinion that there had been no violation of this provision.

[34] The Court recalls its finding in the above-mentioned Kokkinakis case (op. cit., p. 22, § 52) that the definition of the offence of proselytism contained in sec. 4, together with the settled body of national case-law interpreting and applying it, satisfied the conditions of certainty and foreseeability prescribed by art. 7. It is not persuaded that the position in Greek law has become any less clear in the period of under five years since that evaluation. Bearing in mind that the need to avoid excessive rigidity and to keep pace with changing circumstances means that many laws are inevitably couched in terms which, to a greater or lesser extent,

are vague (ibid., p. 19, § 40), it sees no reason to reverse its previous decision.

[35] It follows that there has been no violation of art. 7 of the Convention.

II. Alleged violation of Art. 9 of the convention

[36] The applicants claimed that their prosecution, conviction and punishment for proselytism amounted to violations of art. 9 of the Convention, which states:

> „1. Everyone has the right to freedom of thought, conscience and religion; this right includes freedom to change his religion or belief and freedom, either alone or in community with others and in public or in private, to manifest his religion or belief, in worship, teaching, practice and observance.
> 2. Freedom to manifest one's religion or beliefs shall be subject only to such limitations as are prescribed by law and are necessary in a democratic society in the interests of public safety, for the protection of public order, health or morals, or for the protection of the rights and freedoms of others."

The Government denied that there had been any such breach. The Commission found that there had been no violation with regard to the measures taken against the applicants for the proselytising of the airmen, although it found that art. 9 had been violated in so far as the proselytising of civilians was concerned (see par. 31 above).

[37] The Court must consider whether the applicants' art. 9 rights were interfered with and, if so, whether such interference was „prescribed by law", pursued a legitimate aim and was „necessary in a democratic society" within the meaning of art. 9 § 2.

A. Interference

[38] The Court considers, and indeed it was not disputed by those appearing before it, that the prosecution, conviction and punishment of the applicants for offences of proselytism amounted to interferences with the exercise of their rights to „freedom ... to manifest [their] religion or belief" (see the Kokkinakis judgment cited at par. 32 above, p. 18, § 36).

B. „Prescribed by law"

[39] The applicants, for the same reasons they had advanced in support of a finding of violation of art. 7 (see par. 32 above), contended that the measures taken against them were not „prescribed by law", as required by art. 9 § 2. The Government and the Commission were of the contrary opinion, again relying on the Court's Kokkinakis judgment.

[40] The Court recalls that the expression „prescribed by law" in art. 9 § 2 requires, *inter alia,* that the law in question must be both adequately accessible to the individual and formulated with sufficient precision to enable him to regulate his conduct (see, *mutatis mutandis,* the *Sunday Times* v. the United Kingdom (no. 1) judgment of 26 April 1979, Series A no. 30, p. 31, § 49).

[41] It refers to its finding in the above-mentioned Kokkinakis case that the measures taken against that applicant under sec. 4 were „prescribed by law" (op. cit., pp. 19-20, §§ 40-41). As the Court has already concluded in relation to art. 7 (see par. 34-35 above), it is not satisfied that the position in Greek law has changed subsequently or that it should depart from its earlier assessment for any other reason.

[42] In conclusion, the measures in question were „prescribed by law" within the meaning of art. 9 § 2.

C. *Legitimate aim*

[43] The Government, with whom the Commission agreed, reasoned that the relevant action was taken against the applicants with the aim of protecting the rights and freedoms of others and also, as far as the measures taken following the proselytising of the airmen were concerned, with the aim of preventing disorder in the armed forces and thus protecting public safety and order. The applicants made no particular submission in this connection.

[44] Having regard to the circumstances of the case and, particularly, the terms of the national courts' decisions, the Court considers that the impugned measures essentially pursued the legitimate aim of protecting the rights and freedoms of others (see also the above-mentioned Kokkinakis judgment, p. 20, § 44, KirchE-EU S. 202).

D. *„Necessary in a democratic society"*

[45] The Court emphasises at the outset that while religious freedom is primarily a matter of individual conscience, it also implies, *inter alia,* freedom to „manifest [one's] religion", including the right to try to convince one's neighbour, for example through „teaching" (ibid., p. 17, § 31).art. 9 does not, however, protect every act motivated or inspired by a religion or belief. It does not, for example, protect improper proselytism, such as the offering of material or social advantage or the application of improper pressure with a view to gaining new members for a Church (ibid., p. 21, § 48).

[46] The Court's task is to determine whether the measures taken against the applicants were justified in principle and proportionate. In order to do this, it must weigh the requirements of the protection of the rights and liberties of others against the conduct of the applicants (ibid.,

p. 21, § 47). Since different factors come into the balance in relation to the proselytising of the airmen and that of the civilians, it will assess the two matters separately.

1. The proselytising of the airmen

[47] The Government contended that the applicants had abused the influence they enjoyed as air force officers and had committed the acts in question in a systematic and repetitive manner. The measures taken against them were justified by the need to protect the prestige and effective operation of the armed forces and to protect individual soldiers from ideological coercion.

[48] The applicants submitted that the practice of evangelism within a superior/subordinate relationship could not without more be equated to an abuse of trust. They emphasised that the airmen were adults, able to die for their country, and that there was no evidence that the applicants had used their positions to coerce or override the wills of their subordinates. To interpret art. 9 so as to restrict evangelism to „equals" would be a severe limitation of religious freedom, both within the armed forces and in other contexts.

[49] The Commission found that the interference could be justified as ensuring that the three airmen's religious beliefs were respected, in view in particular of the special character of the relationship between a superior and a subordinate in the armed forces, which rendered the subordinate more susceptible to influence in a variety of matters including religious beliefs.

[50] The Court observes that it is well established that the Convention applies in principle to members of the armed forces as well as to civilians. Nevertheless, when interpreting and applying its rules in cases such as the present, it is necessary to bear in mind the particular characteristics of military life and its effects on the situation of individual members of the armed forces (see the Engel and Others v. the Netherlands judgment of 8 June 1976, Series A no. 22, p. 23, § 54, and, *mutatis mutandis*, the Grigoriades v. Greece judgment of 25 November 1997, RJD 1997-VII, pp. 2589-90, § 45).

[51] In this respect, the Court notes that the hierarchical structures which are a feature of life in the armed forces may colour every aspect of the relations between military personnel, making it difficult for a subordinate to rebuff the approaches of an individual of superior rank or to withdraw from a conversation initiated by him. Thus, what would in the civilian world be seen as an innocuous exchange of ideas which the recipient is free to accept or reject, may, within the confines of military life, be viewed as a form of harassment or the application of undue pressure in abuse of power. It must be emphasised that not every discussion about religion or other sensitive matters between individuals of unequal rank

will fall within this category. Nonetheless, where the circumstances so require, States may be justified in taking special measures to protect the rights and freedoms of subordinate members of the armed forces.

[52] The Court refers to the evidence adduced in the domestic proceedings (see par. 8-10 above). It notes that airmen Antoniadis and Kokkalis testified that the applicants approached them on a number of occasions in order to persuade them to convert and to visit the Pentecostal Church. Mr Antoniadis stated that he felt obliged to take part in the discussions because the applicants were his superior officers, and Mr Kokkalis said that the applicants' approaches bothered him. As the Commission found, there is no evidence that the applicants used threats or inducements. Nonetheless, it appears that they were persistent in their advances and that these two airmen felt themselves constrained and subject to a certain degree of pressure owing to the applicants' status as officers, even if this pressure was not consciously applied.

[53] The Court notes that, contrary to the evidence given by his father at first instance, airman Kafkas testified before the Courts-Martial Appeal Court that the applicants did not apply any pressure to him to become a member of the Pentecostal Church and that he himself initiated the religious discussions that took place between them (see par. 10 above). However, the Appeal Court, having had the opportunity to assess the evidence, including Mr Kafkas's demeanour and credibility, upheld the first-instance court's decision that the first and third applicants had unlawfully taken advantage of the influence they had over Mr Kafkas due to their position and rank (see par. 15, 18 and 22 above). The Court, considering that the domestic courts were better placed than itself to determine the facts of the case, and taking into account the matters referred to in par. 51 above, is of the view that Mr Kafkas, like the other two airmen, must have felt to a certain extent constrained, perhaps obliged to enter into religious discussions with the applicants, and possibly even to convert to the Pentecostal faith.

[54] In view of the above, the Court considers that the Greek authorities were in principle justified in taking some measures to protect the lower ranking airmen from improper pressure applied to them by the applicants in their desire to promulgate their religious beliefs. It notes that the measures taken were not particularly severe and were more preventative than punitive in nature, since the penalties imposed were not enforceable if the applicants did not reoffend within the following three years (see par. 16, 18, 20 and 24 above). In all the circumstances of the case, it does not find that these measures were disproportionate.

[55] It follows that there has been no violation of art. 9 with regard to the measures taken against the first applicant for the proselytising of airmen Antoniadis, Kokkalis and Kafkas, those taken against the second applicant for the proselytising of airman Antoniadis or those taken

against the third applicant for the proselytising of airmen Kokkalis and Kafkas.

2. The proselytising of the civilians

[56] The Government reminded the Court that under sec. 4, only improper proselytism is punishable. They contended that the second and third applicants had systematically exploited the family problems and psychological distress suffered by the Baïramis family and Mrs Zounara and had thus applied unlawful pressure. Furthermore, the penalties imposed on them were not particularly onerous.

[57] The Commission, with whom the applicants agreed, considered that the circumstances leading to the conviction of the second and third applicants for proselytising the Baïramis family and Mrs Zounara were similar to those of the Kokkinakis case (cited at par. 32 above), in that the „targets" of the proselytism were not military personnel and the domestic courts established the defendants' guilt by reciting the words of sec. 4 without adequately explaining in what way the methods employed by the accused had been „improper". It had not been satisfactorily demonstrated that their convictions on these counts were „necessary in a democratic society".

[58] The Court recalls that the second applicant was convicted under sec. 4 for preaching on a single occasion to the Baïramis family and their neighbours, following an incident when he had managed to calm a member of the Baïramis family who was in a delirious state. Together with the third applicant, he was also convicted for the proselytising of Mrs Zounara, whom they had attempted to convert on a number of occasions during a period when she was experiencing marital problems (see par. 11, 12, 17 and 19 above).

[59] The Court finds it of decisive significance that the civilians whom the applicants attempted to convert were not subject to pressures and constraints of the same kind as the airmen. With regard to the Baïramis family and their neighbours, none of the evidence indicates that they felt obliged to listen to the applicant or that his behaviour towards them was improper in any way. As for Mrs Zounara, it was not disputed before the domestic courts that she initially sought out the applicants in an attempt to understand the reasons behind her husband's behaviour. Whilst it is clear that during the period she was in contact with them she was in a state of distress brought on by the breakdown of her marriage, the Court does not find it established that her mental condition was such that she was in need of any special protection from the evangelical activities of the applicants or that they applied improper pressure to her, as was demonstrated by the fact that she was able eventually to take the decision to sever all links with the Pentecostal Church.

[60] For the above reasons, the Court does not consider that the second and third applicants' convictions on the charges in question were justified in the circumstances of the case.

[61] It follows that there has been a violation of art. 9 with regard to the measures taken against the second applicant for the proselytising of the Baïramis family and their neighbours and those taken against the second and third applicants for the proselytising of Mrs Zounara.

III. Alleged violation of Art. 10 of the convention

[62] The applicants claimed that the measures taken against them had also interfered with their rights to freedom of expression, in breach of art. 10 of the Convention, which states, as relevant:

„1. Everyone has the right to freedom of expression. This right shall include freedom to hold opinions and to receive and impart information and ideas without interference by public authority ...

2. The exercise of these freedoms, since it carries with it duties and responsibilities, may be subject to such formalities, conditions, restrictions or penalties as are prescribed by law and are necessary in a democratic society, in the interests of national security, territorial integrity or public safety, for the prevention of disorder or crime, for the protection of health or morals, for the protection of the reputation or rights of others, for preventing the disclosure of information received in confidence, or for maintaining the authority and impartiality of the judiciary."

[63] The Commission, with whom the Government agreed, found that no separate issue arose under this provision.

[64] Having regard to its scrutiny of this case in the context of art. 9, the Court also agrees that no separate issue arises in relation to art. 10.

IV. Alleged violation of Art. 14 of the convention taken together with Art. 9

[65] The applicants alleged that they had been the victims of discrimination contrary to art. 14 of the Convention, which provides:

„The enjoyment of the rights and freedoms set forth in [the] Convention shall be secured without discrimination on any ground such as sex, race, colour, language, religion, political or other opinion, national or social origin, association with a national minority, property, birth or other status."

They contended that the law against proselytism was applied only to members of religious minorities in Greece, no follower of the Orthodox Church ever having been convicted of the offence under sec. 4.

[66] The Government made no particular submission in relation to this complaint.

[67] The Commission found that no separate issue arose under art. 9 and 14 taken together in relation to the measures directed against the second and third applicants for the proselytising of the civilians. As far as the measures taken against the applicants for the proselytising of the airmen were concerned, since no material was provided to substantiate the complaint under art. 9 and 14, it reached a finding of no violation.

[68] The Court notes that the applicants alleged in their memorial that the Greek law against proselytism was applied in a discriminatory manner. However, they have not produced any evidence to suggest that an officer in the armed forces who attempted to convert his subordinates to the Orthodox Church in a manner similar to that adopted by the applicants would have been treated any differently. It follows that no violation of art. 9 and 14 taken together has been established in connection with the proselytising of the airmen.

[69] Having found a violation of art. 9 with regard to the measures taken against the second and third applicants for the proselytising of the Baïramis family and Mrs Zounara, the Court considers that no separate issue arises in that connection under art. 9 and 14 taken together.

V. Application of Art. 50 of the convention

[70] The applicants requested just satisfaction under art. 50 of the Convention, which provides:

>*„If the Court finds that a decision or a measure taken by a legal authority or any other authority of a High Contracting Party is completely or partially in conflict with the obligations arising from the ... Convention, and if the internal law of the said Party allows only partial reparation to be made for the consequences of this decision or measure, the decision of the Court shall, if necessary, afford just satisfaction to the injured party.“*

A. Non-pecuniary damage

[71] The applicants sought 500,000 drachmas (GRD) each to compensate them for moral and material prejudice. This was the amount that the Court had awarded to Mr Kokkinakis in 1993 (op. cit., p. 23, § 60, KirchE-EU S. 202).

[72] At the hearing before the Court, the Government submitted that, in the event of the Court finding a violation, such finding would in itself constitute sufficient just satisfaction.

[73] On the same occasion, the Commission's Delegate commented that the fact that the domestic courts had not sought to take the Court's case-law into account was a particular element to be taken into consideration under art. 50.

[74] The Court observes that it has found violations of the Convention in respect only of the measures taken against the second applicant for

the proselytising of the Baïramis family and the second and third applicants for the proselytising of Mrs Zounara (see par. 58-61 above). The first applicant is not, therefore, entitled to any just satisfaction under art. 50. Making its assessment on an equitable basis, it awards GRD 500,000 each to Mr Mandalarides and Mr Sarandis.

B. Costs and expenses (...)

For these reasons, the Court

1. *Holds by eight votes to one that there has been no violation of art. 7 of the Convention;*
2. *Holds by eight votes to one that there has been no violation of art. 9 of the Convention with regard to the measures taken against the first, second and third applicants for the proselytising of airmen Antoniadis and Kokkalis;*
3. *Holds by seven votes to two that there has been no violation of art. 9 with regard to the measures taken against the first and third applicants for the proselytising of airman Kafkas;*
4. *Holds by seven votes to two that there has been a violation of art. 9 with regard to the measures taken against the second and third applicants for the proselytising of the civilians;*
5. *Holds unanimously that no separate issue arises under art. 10 of the Convention;*
6. *Holds unanimously that there has been no violation of art. 9 and 14 of the Convention taken together in relation to the measures taken against the first, second and third applicants for the proselytising of the airmen;*
7. *Holds unanimously that no separate issue arises under art. 9 and 14 taken together in relation to the measures taken against the second and third applicants for the proselytising of the civilians;*
8. *Holds by seven votes to two*
   (a) that the respondent State is to pay to the second and third applicants, within three months, in respect of compensation for non-pecuniary damage, 500,000 (...) drachmas each;
   (b) ... (Kosten und Auslagen);
   (c) ... (Zinsen)
9. *Dismisses unanimously the remainder of the claim for just satisfaction.*

CONCURRING OPINION OF JUDGE DE MEYER

The law in issue in the present case is contrary to the Convention in its very principle, since it directly encroaches on the very essence of the freedom everyone must have to manifest his religion.

However, in so far as it was applied to attempts to convert servicemen made by their superior officers, those officers cannot have been victims of an infringement of the freedom concerned since in the present case they had abused their position and rank.

PARTLY DISSENTING OPINION OF JUDGE VALTICOS, JOINED BY JUDGE MORENILLA

The instant case, like various others, bears strong similarities, although attended by aggravating circumstances, to the Kokkinakis v. Greece case (judgment of 25 May 1993, Series A no. 260-A, KirchE-EU S. 202), which gave rise to a variety of opinions within the Court. I will not reiterate in detail the position I adopted on that occasion, but I refer the reader to it.

As in the Kokkinakis case, I maintain that any attempt going beyond a mere exchange of views and deliberately calculated to change an individual's religious opinions constitutes a deliberate and, by definition, improper act of proselytism, contrary to „freedom of thought, conscience and religion" as enshrined in art. 9 of the Convention. Such acts of proselytism may take forms that are straightforward or devious, that may or may not be an abuse of the proselytiser's authority and may be peaceful or - and history has given us many bloodstained examples of this - violent. Attempts at „brainwashing" may be made by flooding or drop by drop, but they are nevertheless, whatever one calls them, attempts to violate individual consciences and must be regarded as incompatible with freedom of opinion, which is a fundamental human right.

The measures taken nationally to prohibit and, if need be, punish them cannot therefore be regarded as amounting to breaches of the Convention.

In the instant case I concur in part of the Court's judgment and share its opinion that there has been no violation of the Convention as regards the punishment of the officers' attempted proselytising of soldiers who could have been influenced in part by the officers' authority over them.

However, I consider that even in the case of these officers' attempts to proselytise civilians, the penalties to which these gave rise were justified since the prestige of the officers' uniform may have had an effect even on civilians and, at all events, such deliberate acts of proselytism are contrary to the respect for freedom of conscience and religion guaranteed in the Convention.

PARTLY DISSENTING OPINION OF JUDGE REPIK

I regret that I am unable to agree with the majority about compliance with art. 7 or the conclusion that the interference with the applicants' exercise of their right to manifest their religion was „prescribed by law".

Compliance with Art. 7

It is true that in the Kokkinakis v. Greece case (judgment of 25 May 1993, Series A no. 260-A, p. 22, §§ 52-53, KirchE-EU S. 202), the Court ruled that sec. 4 of Law no. 1363/1938 on the offence of proselytism was compatible with art. 7 of the Convention. However, the nature of the problem has changed since then.

As I understand it, the Court was saying in its judgment in that case that the Greek law in question satisfied the requirements of art. 7 of the Convention only with the assistance provided by the case-law of the Greek courts, which, being published and accessible, complemented the letter of sec. 4 and enabled individuals to regulate their conduct in this respect. The law itself was one of those which, to a greater or lesser extent, were couched in vague terms and whose interpretation and application depended on practice (ibid., pp. 19 and 22, §§ 40 and 52).

However, albeit in connection with the necessity of the interference rather than its legality, the Court laid down the principle that there was a need to distinguish between Christian witness, which was the true form of evangelism and an essential duty of every believer and every Church, on the one hand, and improper proselytism, which was not compatible with the respect due to others' freedom of thought, conscience and religion, on the other. And it went on to add a proviso, namely that the criteria adopted by the Greek legislature were reconcilable with that distinction *if and in so far as* (my emphasis) they were designed only to punish improper proselytism (ibid., p. 21, § 48). It was apparently up to the courts to draw this distinction by means of an appropriate interpretation of the terms of the law. In the case concerned, the Court noted that in finding Mr Kokkinakis guilty the Greek courts had done no more than reproduce the wording of the law, without sufficiently specifying in what way he had attempted to convince his neighbour by improper means (ibid., p. 21, § 49).

I leave aside the question which suggests itself immediately, that is, whether in a system of written law the principle that offences and penalties must be defined by law is respected where the line separating what is criminal conduct from what is merely the normal exercise of a freedom guaranteed by the Constitution and the Convention is drawn by judges rather than by statute. Does that not put the judge in the position where he is required not just restrictively to interpret the law, but instead himself to define an offence which, as drafted, is so broad as to embrace conduct which ought to remain lawful?

Although the case-law of the Greek courts, which was scrutinised by the Court in the Kokkinakis judgment (op. cit., pp. 13-14, §§ 17-21, KirchE-EU S. 202), is not by any means of one piece and contains contradictions, the Court's expectation that conviction would ensue only in cases of improper proselytism could justifiably be based on the fact that in a judgment of 1975, in which it reversed its previous case-law, the Court of Cassation had removed the effects of certain vague terms in the law, notably the words „in particular". But that expectation has not been fulfilled. As the Commission observed in par. 69-70 of its report and as its Delegate pointed out at the hearing, the Court of Cassation in the present case adopted an approach markedly different from the Court's, failing to distinguish between the use of proper and improper means and reverting to its previous case-law to the effect that the means set out in the law were not exhaustively listed and, a fact which to my mind is even more significant, emphasising the subjective elements of the offence, namely the so-called intrusion or attempt to intrude, directly or indirectly, on the religious beliefs of another with the aim of undermining those beliefs. The Court, by drawing a distinction between proper and improper means, has endeavoured to identify some objective element which, in a given individual's conduct, would be the only criterion capable of providing anything like a reliable indication whether a criminal offence has been committed. The Court of Cassation, on the other hand, has once more shifted its emphasis onto subjective elements, which do not provide a suitable criterion for distinguishing between proper and improper proselytism. In the instant case the Court has not taken into account this change of position on the part of the Court of Cassation.

Is it the fault of the law or rather of its interpretation and application by the Greek courts that the limits of its scope have again become considerably more obscure, as Mrs Liddy rightly pointed out in her dissenting opinion annexed to the Commission's report. The difficulty of applying the law in such a way so as not to encroach unduly on the freedoms guaranteed by the Convention is obvious. It is no less obvious that the domestic courts did not succeed in making up for the deficiencies of the law. The case-law, including the case-law of the highest Greek court, is very inconsistent; far too frequently there are prosecutions and even convictions for conduct about which there is nothing improper (for example, the distribution of religious literature). It is the Strasbourg Court which has striven, after the event, to draw certain distinctions in this area, but those distinctions do not flow necessarily from the law, and in fact the domestic courts still fail to discern them in it.

That being the case, a believer who tries to spread his religious beliefs can never be certain whether his conduct is illegal or not. The law is not sufficiently precise and its effects are therefore not sufficiently foreseeable; it cannot guarantee legal certainty or equality of treatment, nor can it afford protection against arbitrary measures by the authorities responsible for applying it. I am unable to conclude that the law in question satisfies the requirements of art. 7 and I accordingly consider that this provision has been breached.

Art. 9

For the same reasons, I am not convinced that the interference with the applicants' exercise of their right to manifest their religion was „prescribed by law" within the meaning of art. 9 § 2. There is nothing in Greek legislation or the case-law of the Greek courts pertaining to religious discussion in the armed forces. Nor do the decisions of the domestic courts concerned draw any distinction between proselytising of servicemen and proselytising of civilians. Once again it was the Court, following the Commission's example, which introduced this distinction after the event. I do not see how the applicants could have foreseen with the requisite degree of certainty that their conduct towards the servicemen would be illegal whereas their conduct towards other persons would not.

PARTLY DISSENTING OPINION OF JUDGE VAN DIJK

I felt unable to join the majority in one part of their conclusion, namely that concerning the compatibility with art. 9 of the Convention of the conviction of the first and third applicants for allegedly proselytising airman Kafkas.

I agree with the general reasoning, contained in par. 51 of the judgment, especially the statement that what would in the civilian world be seen as an innocuous exchange of ideas which the recipient is free to accept or reject, may, within the confines of military life, be viewed as a form of harassment or the application of undue pressure in abuse of power. However, in that same paragraph the Court points to the fact that not every discussion about religion or other sensitive matters between individuals of unequal rank will fall within this category.

Like Mr Schermers and the four other members of the Commission who attached a partly dissenting opinion to the Commission's report in this case, I am of the opinion that it should be possible to rebut the assumption of undue influence exercised by a higher ranking over a lower ranking person in the army. Whereas the testimonies of airmen Antoniadis and Kokkalis before the domestic courts confirmed the said assumption, airman Kafkas testified before the Appeal Court that he made the initial contact with the third applicant; that, later on, it was he who sought the first and third applicants' advice; and that no pressure was ever put on him (see par. 10 of the judgment).

The majority refer to the way in which the Appeal Court assessed this evidence, „including Mr Kafkas's demeanour and credibility", and accept it, „considering that the domestic courts were better placed than itself to determine the facts of the case" (see par. 53 of the judgment). The Court was competent, however, when assessing the proportionality of the limitation, to give its view on the fact that the Appeal Court, although it heard Mr Kafkas's own testimony, adopted the reasoning of the first-instance court which had not heard airman Kafkas as a witness but only his father. In that same context, the majority should also have given their view as to why airman Kafkas's „demeanour and credibility" were in issue - presumably because he had been converted to the Pentecostal Church in the meantime - while the same was not true for his father as a witness, although the latter may be assumed to have been displeased by his son's conversion. At the very least, it would seem unsatisfactory that the Appeal Court did not deem it necessary to assess the statements of these two witnesses in relation to each other. All in all, I find it difficult to understand why the Court should accept, without any examination and supervision, the domestic courts' findings with regard to the proselytising of the airmen, while taking a critical view towards their findings concerning the proselytising of the civilians. I am of the opinion that, in these circumstances, the Court should not have deferred to the domestic courts on the question of the evidence of airman Kafkas and his father and should, in the absence of any counter-indication, have given greater weight to the testimony of the alleged victim of the proselytism than to that of a witness whose testimony was based upon hearsay information.

Since in the material submitted to the Court I cannot find any overriding evidence that airman Kafkas's discussions on religion and subsequent conversion were not prompted by his own free will, I cannot join the majority's conclusion that there was a pressing social need to prosecute and punish those whose guidance he sought on that road, albeit that they were his military superiors.

47

Parlamentsabgeordneten darf nicht zwingend auferlegt werden, den wahlgesetzlich vorgeschriebenen Abgeordneteneid in religiöser Form zu leisten.

Art. 9 EMRK
EGMR, Urteil vom 18. Februar 1999 - No. 24645/94
(Buscarini u.a. ./. San Marino)[1] -

THE FACTS

The circumstances of the case

[1] The applicants were elected to the General Grand Council (the parliament of the Republic of San Marino) in elections held on 30 May 1993.

---

[1] CEDH/ECHR 1999-I; EuGRZ 1999, 213; NJW 1999, 2957; ÖJZ 1999, 852.

[2] Shortly afterwards, they requested permission from the Captains-Regent, who act as the heads of government in San Marino, to take the oath required by sec. 55 of the Elections Act (Law no. 36 of 1958) without making reference to any religious text. The Act in question referred to a decree of 27 June 1909, which laid down the wording of the oath to be taken by members of the Republic's parliament as follows:

„I, ..., swear on the Holy Gospels ever to be faithful to and obey the Constitution of the Republic, to uphold and defend freedom with all my might, ever to observe the Laws and Decrees, whether ancient, modern or yet to be enacted or issued and to nominate and vote for as candidates to the Judiciary and other Public Office only those whom I consider apt, loyal and fit to serve the Republic, without allowing myself to be swayed by any feelings of hatred or love or by any other consideration."

[3] In support of their request the applicants referred to art. 4 of the Declaration of Rights of 1974, which guarantees the right to freedom of religion, and art. 9 of the Convention.

[4] At the General Grand Council session of 18 June 1993 the applicants took the oath in writing, in the form of words laid down in the decree of 27 June 1909 save for the reference to the Gospels, which they omitted. At the same time, the first applicant drew attention to the obligations undertaken by the Republic of San Marino when it became a party to the European Convention on Human Rights.

[5] On 12 July 1993 the Secretariat of the General Grand Council gave an opinion, at the request of the Captains-Regent, on the form of the oath sworn by the applicants, to the effect that it was invalid, and referred the matter to the Council.

[6] At its session of 26 July 1993 the General Grand Council adopted a resolution proposed by the Captains-Regent ordering the applicants to retake the oath, this time on the Gospels, on pain of forfeiting their parliamentary seats.

[7] The applicants complied with the Council's order and took the oath on the Gospels, albeit complaining that their right to freedom of religion and conscience had been infringed.

[8] Subsequently - before ever the applicants applied to the Commission - Law no. 115 of 29 October 1993 („Law no. 115/1993") introduced a choice for newly elected members of the General Grand Council between the traditional oath and one in which the reference to the Gospels was replaced by the words „on my honour". The traditional wording is still mandatory for other offices, such as that of Captain-Regent or of a member of the government.

PROCEEDINGS BEFORE THE COMMISSION

[9] Mr Buscarini, Mr Della Balda and Mr Manzaroli applied to the Commission on 17 November 1995. Relying on art. 9 of the Convention, they complained of an infringement of their right to freedom of religion and conscience.

[100] The Commission declared the application (no. 24645/94) admissible on 7 April 1997. In its report of 2 December 1997 (former art. 31 of the Convention), it concluded unanimously that there had been a violation of art. 9 (...)

FINAL SUBMISSIONS TO THE COURT

[11] The Government raised three preliminary objections and asked the Court to declare the application inadmissible or, in the alternative, to dismiss it as ill-founded and devoid of purpose.

[12] Mr Buscarini and Mr Della Balda requested the Court to dismiss the Government's objections to admissibility and to find that there had been a breach of art. 9 of the Convention.

THE LAW

I. Alleged violation of Art. 9 of the convention

A. *The Government's preliminary objections*
(...)

B. *Compliance with Art. 9 of the Convention*

[13] Art. 9 of the Convention provides:

„*1. Everyone has the right to freedom of thought, conscience and religion; this right includes freedom to change his religion or belief and freedom, either alone or in community with others and in public or private, to manifest his religion or belief, in worship, teaching, practice and observance.*
2. Freedom to manifest one's religion or beliefs shall be subject only to such limitations as are prescribed by law and are necessary in a democratic society in the interests of public safety, for the protection of public order, health or morals, or for the protection of the rights and freedoms of others."

[14] Mr Buscarini and Mr Della Balda submitted that the obligation which the General Grand Council imposed on them on 26 July 1993 demonstrated that in the Republic of San Marino at the material time the exercise of a fundamental political right, such as holding parliamentary office, was subject to publicly professing a particular faith, in breach of art. 9.

[15] The Commission agreed with that analysis; the Government contested it.

[16] The Government maintained that the wording of the oath in question was not religious but, rather, historical and social in significance and based on tradition. The Republic of San Marino had, admittedly, been founded by a man of religion but it was a secular State in which freedom of religion was expressly enshrined in law (art. 4 of the Declaration of Rights of 1974). The form of words in issue had lost its original religious character, as had certain religious feast-days which the State recognised as public holidays.

The act complained of therefore did not amount to a limitation on the applicants' freedom of religion.

[17] The applicants and the Commission rejected that assertion.

[18] The Court reiterates that: „As enshrined in art. 9, freedom of thought, conscience and religion is one of the foundations of a ‚democratic society' within the meaning of the Convention. It is, in its religious dimension, one of the most vital elements that go to make up the identity of believers and their conception of life, but it is also a precious asset for atheists, agnostics, sceptics and the unconcerned. The pluralism indissociable from a democratic society, which has been dearly won over the centuries, depends on it" (see the Kokkinakis v. Greece judgment of 25 May 1993, Series A no. 260-A, p. 17, § 31). That freedom entails, *inter alia*, freedom to hold or not to hold religious beliefs and to practise or not to practise a religion. In the instant case, requiring Mr Buscarini and Mr Della Balda to take an oath on the Gospels did indeed constitute a limitation within the meaning of the second paragraph of art. 9, since it required them to swear allegiance to a particular religion on pain of forfeiting their parliamentary seats. Such interference will be contrary to art. 9 unless it is „prescribed by law", pursues one or more of the legitimate aims set out in par. 2 and is „necessary in a democratic society".

1. „Prescribed by law"

[19] As the Commission noted in its report (par. 38), „the interference in question was based on sec. 55 of the Elections Act, Law no. 36 of 1958, which referred to the decree of 27 June 1909 laying down the wording of the oath to be sworn by members of parliament ... Therefore, it was ‚prescribed by law' within the meaning of the second paragraph of art. 9 of the Convention". That point was not disputed.

2. Legitimate aim and whether „necessary in a democratic society"

[20] The Government emphasised the importance, in any democracy, of the oath taken by elected representatives of the people, which, in their view, was a pledge of loyalty to republican values. Regard being had to

the special character of San Marino, deriving from its history, traditions and social fabric, the reaffirmation of traditional values represented by the taking of the oath was necessary in order to maintain public order. The history and traditions of San Marino were linked to Christianity, since the State had been founded by a saint; today, however, the oath's religious significance had been replaced by „the need to preserve public order, in the form of social cohesion and the citizens' trust in their traditional institutions". It would therefore be inappropriate for the Court to criticise the margin of appreciation which San Marino had to have in this matter. In any event, the Government maintained, the applicants had had no legal interest in pursuing the Strasbourg proceedings since the entry into force of Law no. 115 of 29 October 1993 („Law no. 115/1993"), which did not require persons elected to the General Grand Council to take the oath on the Gospels.

[21] According to Mr Buscarini and Mr Della Balda, the resolution requiring them to take the oath in issue was in the nature of a „premeditated act of coercion" directed at their freedom of conscience and religion. It aimed to humiliate them as persons who, immediately after being elected, had requested that the wording of the oath should be altered so as to conform with, inter alia, art. 9 of the Convention.

[22] The Court considers it unnecessary in the present case to determine whether the aims referred to by the Government were legitimate within the meaning of the second paragraph of art. 9, since the limitation in question is in any event incompatible with that provision in other respects.

[23] The Court notes that at the hearing on 10 December 1998 the Government sought to demonstrate that the Republic of San Marino guaranteed freedom of religion; in support of that submission they cited its founding Statutes of 1600, its Declaration of Rights of 1974, its ratification of the European Convention in 1989 and a whole array of provisions of criminal law, family law, employment law and education law which prohibited any discrimination on the grounds of religion. It is not in doubt that, in general, San Marinese law guarantees freedom of conscience and religion. In the instant case, however, requiring the applicants to take the oath on the Gospels was tantamount to requiring two elected representatives of the people to swear allegiance to a particular religion, a requirement which is not compatible with art. 9 of the Convention. As the Commission rightly stated in its report, it would be contradictory to make the exercise of a mandate intended to represent different views of society within Parliament subject to a prior declaration of commitment to a particular set of beliefs.

[24] The limitation complained of accordingly cannot be regarded as „necessary in a democratic society". As to the Government's argument that the application ceased to have any purpose when Law no. 115/1993

was enacted, the Court notes that the oath in issue was taken before the passing of that legislation.

[25] In the light of the foregoing, there has been a violation of art. 9 of the Convention.

II. Application of Art. 41 of the Convention

[26] Art. 41 of the Convention provides:

„*If the Court finds that there has been a violation of the Convention or the Protocols thereto, and if the internal law of the High Contracting Party concerned allows only partial reparation to be made, the Court shall, if necessary, afford just satisfaction to the injured party.*"

A. Damage

[27] Mr Buscarini and Mr Della Balda claimed no more than one Italian lira for the damage which they alleged they had suffered as a result of being required to take the oath on the Gospels.

[28] The Government did not express a view on this point.

[29] Although the applicants did not expressly say so, their claim obviously relates to non-pecuniary damage. Like the Delegate of the Commission, the Court considers that in the circumstances of the case the finding of a violation of art. 9 of the Convention constitutes sufficient just satisfaction under art. 41.

B. Costs and expenses

[30] The applicants also sought reimbursement of their costs and expenses but did not specify an amount.

[31] The Government did not make any submissions on this point. The Delegate of the Commission wished to leave the matter to the Court's discretion.

[32] By Rule 60 § 2 of the Rules of Court, itemised particulars of any claim made under art. 41 of the Convention must be submitted, together with the relevant supporting documents or vouchers, „failing which the Chamber may reject the claim in whole or in part". Since the applicants did not quantify their claim, the Court dismisses it.

For these reasons, the Court unanimously
1. *Dismisses the Government's preliminary objections;*
2. *Holds that there has been a violation of art. 9 of the Convention;*
3. *Holds that this judgment constitutes in itself sufficient just satisfaction as to the alleged non-pecuniary damage;*
4. *Dismisses the remainder of the claim for just satisfaction.*

48

Religionsfreiheit rechtfertigt nicht einen Anspruch auf generelle Unterrichtsbefreiung für Siebenten-Tags-Adventisten am Sonnabend.

Art. 9, 35 § 3 EMRK
EGMR, Beschluss vom 27. April 1999 - No. 44888/98
(Martins Casimiro u.a. ./. Luxemburg) -

EN FAIT

Le premier requérant est un ressortissant portugais, né en 1955. La seconde requérante, son épouse est une ressortissante portugaise, née en 1961. Ils résident à St. (Luxembourg). Les requérants, ainsi que leur enfant mineur F. sont membres de l'Église adventiste du 7ème Jour.

Le 18 septembre 1993, ils introduisirent une demande auprès du bourgmestre de la commune de St. afin que leur fils soit dispensé de fréquenter son établissement scolaire le samedi, conformément à la norme religieuse de leur culte, qui prescrit le repos absolu le samedi. Par courrier du 29 septembre 1993, le bourgmestre rejeta leur demande au vu de l'avis négatif de l'inspecteur et au motif que la „loi scolaire [n'autorisait] ni le bourgmestre, ni le collège des bourgmestres et échevins, ni le conseil communal et ni la commission scolaire à prendre une décision en ce qui concerne des absences systématiques d'un jour de semaine dans les cours scolaires", que „seul le législateur [était] autorisé à régler ces absences", susceptibles de „gêner considérablement l'instruction" du fils des requérants.

Les requérants décidèrent toutefois de passer outre, et ne conduisirent plus leur fils à l'école le samedi. Ils furent poursuivis pour cette raison devant le tribunal de la jeunesse, lequel par décision du 6 décembre 1994, sursit à statuer afin de permettre aux requérants de formuler une nouvelle demande, adressée à l'autorité compétente.

Sollicité par le conseil des requérants, le ministre de l'Éducation nationale se déclara incompétent pour connaître de la demande en dispense, dans une lettre du 12 décembre 1994, et attira l'attention des requérants sur l'art. 7 de la loi scolaire du 10 août 1912 qui attribue cette compétence aux autorités communales, dès lors que la dispense porte sur une durée d'au moins huit jours consécutifs.

Aussi les requérants adressèrent-ils, par lettre du 18 décembre 1994, une demande en dispense au conseil communal de St., lequel, s'estimant toujours incompétent, refusa de statuer par décision du 28 décembre 1994.

Les requérants renouvelèrent leur demande, jusqu'à ce que le conseil communal accepte finalement de procéder à son examen. Par décision du 6 mars 1995, il refusa, sur le fondement des avis négatifs de la commission scolaire et de l'inspecteur, d'accorder la dispense.

Le 3 juillet 1995, les requérants demandèrent l'annulation de cette décision. Ils formèrent par ailleurs le 3 octobre 1995, un deuxième recours en annulation contre une seconde décision du conseil communal de St. en date du 3 juillet 1995, qui retenait dans son dispositif que la dispense sollicitée était refusée au motif que „des convictions religieuses ne sauraient déroger au principe de la scolarité obligatoire dans l'enseignement primaire (...), alors que la dispense sollicitée ne remplit pas les conditions de l'art. 7 de la loi scolaire du 10 août 1912 qui confère au conseil communal la compétence pour accorder, sur avis conforme de l'inspecteur et la commission scolaire, des exemptions qui réunies ne peuvent excéder trente jours par année scolaire".

Le 16 février 1998, le tribunal administratif, après avoir ordonné la jonction des deux recours, considéra les demandes recevables, mais mal fondées, au motifs suivants:

„Il est en effet constant que l'école publique gratuite, obligatoire et ouverte à tous, symbolise la démocratie et constitue un des pivots des institutions collectives nationales en ce qu'elle a pour but de conférer à tous les citoyens un minimum uniforme d'éducation. Ainsi, le droit à l'éducation fait partie des droits fondamentaux dans un Etat démocratique et constitue partant un droit digne de protection, susceptible de restreindre la liberté de manifester sa religion ou ses convictions, au sens du 2ème alinéa de l'art. 9 précité de la Convention européenne. Il en découle qu'une mesure qui s'avère nécessaire dans une société démocratique pour protéger le droit à l'éducation est de nature à s'inscrire dans les prévisions dudit alinéa (...)

Il y a lieu de retenir que s'il doit en principe être possible aux élèves qui en font la demande de bénéficier individuellement et ponctuellement des dispenses de l'enseignement scolaire nécessaires à l'exercice d'un culte ou de la célébration d'une fête religieuse, cette possibilité doit rester relativisée dans la mesure de la compatibilité des absences qui en découlent avec l'accomplissement des tâches inhérentes aux études (...). Or, dans la mesure où (...) la journée du samedi couvre en fait une partie significante de l'emploi du temps normal dans l'enseignement primaire qui peut comporter notamment des contrôles de connaissances ou l'intervention de titulaires différents, une dérogation systématique, sinon du moins quasi-systématique, à l'obligation de présence pendant une journée déterminée de la semaine, en l'occurrence le samedi, est en l'espèce susceptible de désorganiser démesurément les programmes scolaires aussi bien du point de vue du bénéficiaire du régime ainsi dérogatoire que des responsables de classe, de même que des autres élèves (...) notamment au regard des adaptations de l'emploi du temps et de l'évacuation des programmes ainsi engendrés."

Les requérants firent appel de ce jugement le 27 mars 1998. La cour administrative du Grand-Duché de Luxembourg rejeta leurs prétentions par arrêt du 2 juillet 1998, et confirma le jugement du 16 février 1998 dans toutes ses dispositions.

GRIEF

Invoquant l'art. 9 de la Convention, les requérants estiment que le refus d'accorder la dispense de l'obligation scolaire le samedi qu'ils avaient présentée au nom de leur fils, constitue une atteinte au droit de pratiquer librement leur religion.

EN DROIT

Les requérants estiment que le refus d'accorder à leur fils une dispense de l'obligation scolaire le samedi constitue une atteinte au droit de pratiquer librement sa religion, tel que garanti par l'art. 9 de la Convention, dont les dispositions pertinentes sont ainsi rédigées:

„1. Toute personne a droit à la liberté (...) de religion; ce droit implique la liberté (...) de manifester sa religion (...) individuellement ou collectivement, en public ou en privé, par le culte, l'enseignement, les pratiques et l'accomplissement des rites.
2. La liberté de manifester sa religion (...) ne peut faire l'objet d'autres restrictions que celles qui, prévues par la loi, constituent des mesures nécessaires, dans une société démocratique, à la sécurité publique, à la protection de l'ordre, de la santé ou de la morale publiques, ou à la protection des droits et libertés d'autrui."

La Cour rappelle en premier lieu sa jurisprudence, en vertu de laquelle la liberté de pensée, de conscience et de religion, qui se trouve consacrée à l'art. 9 de la Convention, représente l'une des assises d'une „société démocratique" au sens de la Convention. Elle est, dans sa dimension religieuse, l'un des éléments les plus vitaux contribuant à former l'identité des croyants et leur conception de la vie, mais elle est aussi un bien précieux pour les athées, les agnostiques, les sceptiques ou les indifférents. Il y va du pluralisme - chèrement conquis au cours des siècles - consubstantiel à pareille société. Si la liberté religieuse relève d'abord du for intérieur, elle implique de surcroît, notamment, celle de manifester sa religion. Le témoignage, en paroles et en actes, se trouve lié à l'existence de convictions religieuses (CourEuDH, arrêts Kokkinakis c. Grèce du 25 mai 1993, série A n° 260-A, p. 17, § 31, KirchE-EU S. 202); Otto-Preminger-Institut c. Autriche du 20 septembre 1994, série A n° 295-A, p. 17, § 47, KirchE-EU S. 248).

La Cour relève que les décisions du conseil communal et celles du tribunal administratif et de la cour administrative, qui ont maintenu le refus du conseil communal d'octroyer la dispense, peuvent s'analyser en une restriction au droit de manifester librement leur religion.

Selon sa jurisprudence constante, la Cour reconnaît aux Etats parties à la Convention une certaine marge d'appréciation pour juger de l'existence et de l'étendue de la nécessité d'une ingérence, mais elle va de pair avec un contrôle européen portant à la fois sur la loi et sur les décisions qui l'appliquent. La tâche de la Cour consiste à rechercher si les mesures prises au niveau national se justifient dans leur principe et sont proportionnées (CourEuDH, arrêts Manoussakis et autres c. Grèce du 26 septembre 1996, *Recueil des arrêts et décisions*, 1996-IV, p. 1364, § 44, KirchE-EU S. 263; Kokkinakis précité, p. 21 § 47, KirchE-EU S. 202).

La Cour constate à cet égard que pour rejeter la demande de dispense, les autorités luxembourgeoises ont considéré que si l'art. 7 de la loi scolaire du 10 août 1912 permet au conseil communal d'accorder une dispense de fréquentation scolaire de huit jours au moins et trente jours au plus aux élèves qui en font la demande, les dispenses qui peuvent être ainsi accordées, ponctuellement, pour la célébration des rites religieux propres à certains cultes, ne doivent pas revêtir un caractère général tel qu'elles aboutissent à porter atteinte au droit à l'instruction, protégé par l'art. 2 du Protocole n° 1 à la Convention, et dont l'importance dans une société démocratique ne saurait être méconnue. Or, la dispense sollicitée par les requérants avait pour objet de soustraire l'enfant au rythme normal de la scolarité, le samedi étant un jour à part entière dans le programme d'enseignement, dans la mesure où il comporte notamment des leçons ainsi que des devoirs sur table rédigés en classe. Le tribunal administratif a aussi soutenu, dans son jugement du 16 février 1998, qu'une telle dispense porterait également atteinte aux droits des autres élèves, compte tenu de la désorganisation du système scolaire que cette mesure serait susceptible d'engendrer.

La Cour rappelle à cet égard que l'Etat a le devoir de veiller à ce que les enfants puissent exercer leur droit à l'instruction (CourEuDH, arrêt Costello-Roberts c. Royaume Uni du 25 mars 1993, série A n° 247-C, § 27). Par ailleurs, lorsqu'au lieu de le conforter, le droit des parents au respect de leurs convictions religieuses entre en conflits avec le droit de l'enfant à l'instruction, les intérêts de l'enfant priment (CommEuDH, N° 13887, déc. 5.2.90, DR 64, p. 158; N° 17187/90, déc. 8.9.93, DR 75, p. 65).

Dans ces conditions, la Cour estime que le refus prévu par la loi d'octroyer aux requérants une dispense générale de cours le samedi pour leur fils mineur se justifiait dans leur principe pour la protection des droits et libertés d'autrui, et en particulier du droit à l'instruction, et qu'elles ont respecté un rapport raisonnable de proportionnalité entre les moyens employés et le but visé. Elles ont donc constitué une restriction du droit des requérants à la liberté de manifester leur religion conforme à l'art. 9 § 2 de la Convention.

Il s'ensuit que la requête doit être rejetée comme étant manifestement mal fondée, au sens de l'art. 35 § 3 de la Convention.

Par ces motifs, la Cour, à l'unanimité, déclare la requête irrecevable.

49

Dem Inhaber eines privaten Sicherheitsdienstes (agence de sécurité privée) kann die behördliche Betriebserlaubnis entzogen werden, wenn er sich aktiv für eine Sekte betätigt, deren Verlautbarungen im Widerspruch zu den Belangen der öffentlichen Sicherheit und Ordnung und den Rechten und Freiheiten anderer stehen.

Art. 9 § 2, 35 § 3 EMRK
EGMR, Beschluss vom 14. Oktober 1999 - No. 40130/98
(C.R. ./. Schweiz) -

EN FAIT

Le requérant est un ressortissant français, né en 1946 et résidant à Carouge en Suisse.

A. Circonstances particulières de l'affaire

Par arrêté du 19 janvier 1988, le requérant fut autorisé par le Département cantonal genevois de justice et police (ci-après: Département cantonal) à exploiter, en qualité de sous-directeur, une agence de sécurité privée dans le canton de Genève, pour le compte d'une société privée.

Le requérant et certains de ses collaborateurs quittèrent cette agence le 8 avril 1991 et constituèrent l'équipe dirigeante d'une nouvelle agence de sécurité privée, la société U.

Par arrêté du 12 juillet 1991, P.B., un des collaborateurs du requérant dans l'agence qu'il exploita entre janvier 1988 et avril 1991, fut autorisé par le Département cantonal à exploiter cette agence, dont le but statutaire était la „prestation de services dans le domaine de la sécurité des personnes et des biens, installation d'appareils d'alarmes et de sécurité, ainsi que de toutes installations électriques et téléphoniques connexes". La société U. regroupait une quarantaine d'agents de sécurité privés dont la majorité étaient titulaires d'un permis de port d'arme.

Par un arrêté du Département cantonal du 29 octobre 1991, le requérant fut autorisé à diriger cette nouvelle agence.

Le 24 octobre 1991 une chaîne de télévision française diffusa une émission sur la secte O., installée en France et dirigée par B. Le requérant et P.B. apparaissaient sur les images à plusieurs reprises, vêtus de capes bleu clair lors des scènes d'intérieur et de vestes de camouflage lors des scènes d'extérieur.

Le 5 mars 1992, le requérant fut entendu par la police au sujet de cette émission. Il confirma avoir pris part à la manifestation filmée et ce, afin d'assurer la sécurité du leader de la secte sollicité en cela par des amis qu'il refusa de nommer. Il nia que lui ou ses collaborateurs aient fait partie de la secte. En 1994, des articles sur les liens entre la société U. et la secte parurent dans la presse locale. Le 18 avril notamment fut publié un article où l'un des cinq membres de l'équipe dirigeante de l'agence, V., annonçait sa qualité de membre actif („prêtre") de la secte.

Le 2 juin 1995, le requérant fut interpellé à la frontière par la douane française en possession de documents relatifs à la „croisade" de la secte et des films offset destinés à la fabrication d'un livre écrit par B.

Par courrier spontané du 19 juin 1995, le requérant, au nom de son agence, avertit le Département cantonal qu'il venait de licencier le directeur adjoint en raison de ses liens avec la secte et afin de „dissiper tout éventuel malentendu concernant l'indépendance de l'agence vis-à-vis de quiconque et notamment de [la secte]".

Le 30 juin 1995, le Département cantonal avertit le requérant de son intention de lui retirer l'autorisation à l'exploitation de l'agence sécurité privée et les autorisations afférentes au motif qu'il ne répondait plus au critère d'honorabilité, condition posée par la loi sur la profession d'agent de sécurité privé du 15 mars 1985. Ce courrier invitait néanmoins le requérant à formuler une réponse écrite aux griefs avant le 10 juillet 1995.

Le 14 juillet 1995, par une décision motivée, le Département cantonal disposa que le requérant ne répondant plus à la condition légale d'honorabilité, l'autorisation du 29 octobre 1991 était caduque. Le Département cantonal faisait état de la longue et minutieuse enquête menée par les services de police depuis 1991 et qui permettait de conclure formellement à l'existence de nombreux liens entre le requérant et la secte, et notamment à son appartenance à ladite secte. Il concluait que „la totale inféodation [du requérant et de toute l'agence] par rapport à la secte (...) constitue manifestement une menace pour la sécurité et l'ordre publics".

Le requérant forma un recours devant le tribunal administratif du canton de Genève (ci-après: le tribunal administratif), qui tint plusieurs audiences du 13 juin 1996 au 16 juillet 1996. Le requérant et de nombreux témoins y furent interrogés.

Le 29 septembre 1996, le tribunal administratif rejeta le recours.

Le tribunal administratif précisa d'abord la notion d'honorabilité. Se référant notamment à l'exposé des motifs de la loi et à son commentaire, il s'exprima en ces termes:

„d. L'exposé des motifs de la LPASP et le commentaire des premiers articles de la loi, cités ci-dessus, donnent quant à eux des indications claires sur l'esprit qui anime cette législation. La commission du Grand Conseil chargée d'étudier le projet a souligné que l'on ne devait pas attribuer une arme à n'importe qui, et qu'il fallait donner à la police la possibilité d'exercer une stricte surveillance sur

toutes les agences de sécurité et, de surcroît, sur toutes les personnes exerçant la fonction d'agent (Mémorial 1985 I, p. 1364).

Il faut également constater, dans la systématique de la LPASP, que parmi toutes les conditions posées pour l'octroi de l'autorisation d'exploiter une agence selon l'art. 3 alinéa 1 (nationalité ou permis de séjour, exercice des droits civils, solvabilité, couverture d'assurance-responsabilité civile et réussite d'examens portant sur la législation touchant à l'exercice de la profession), la condition d'honorabilité est la seule avec celle de solvabilité qui permette, dès lors qu'elle est remplie, d'écarter le risque que l'exploitant se serve de sa situation à une fin contraire à l'ordre public, ce qui était le principal souci du législateur.

Force est par conséquent d'admettre que la notion d'honorabilité peut être interprétée de manière très large et qu'elle doit permettre à l'autorité de restreindre la liberté du commerce et de l'industrie (art. 31 al. 1 constitution fédérale) chaque fois que l'ordre public est menacé pour des raisons ayant trait aux antécédents ou au comportement d'une personne, quelle que soit la nature de cette menace. Le respect du principe de proportionnalité s'opère à travers l'appréciation qui doit être faite quant au caractère concret de cette menace.

Enfin, il faut souligner que la notion d'honorabilité n'est pas une et unique, mais qu'elle est susceptible de varier en fonction du cadre dans lequel elle est évoquée. Il va de soi par exemple que les risques que cherche à écarter la loi sur le commerce d'objets usagés ou de seconde main du 16 juin 1988 (I/3/19) sont essentiellement liés au recel. Dans ce cas, par conséquent, on pourra se montrer moins exigeant quant aux antécédents ou au comportement d'une personne que lorsque les risques sont susceptibles de s'étendre à une atteinte à l'intégrité corporelle ou à un homicide."

Après avoir constaté que le requérant et P.B. avaient déclaré avoir travaillé bénévolement pour la secte car, sans en être membres mais seulement sympathisants, le Tribunal releva que ces deux personnes avaient également reconnu avoir payé une cotisation à la secte, avaient reçu des noms initiatiques, habituellement réservés aux membres ayant une ancienneté de dix à quinze ans. Se fondant aussi sur les déclarations de divers témoins ayant travaillé pour une des agences de sécurité précitées ou ayant été membre de la secte, le tribunal conclut que le requérant était entré dans une relation de soumission par rapport à B., lequel était une personnalité dangereuse dont la doctrine tournait autour de la survenance de l'apocalypse et qui pourrait conduire ses adeptes au suicide.

Pour arriver à cette dernière conclusion, le Tribunal se fonda notamment sur les déclarations de B. reproduites dans un compte rendu écrit de l'émission du 24 octobre 1991. Il en cita le texte suivant:

„B. gagne son trône, élève son sceptre. (...) Je suis la réincarnation de Jésus-Christ, de Gengis-Khan, de Saint-Louis et de Napoléon. (...) Un jour, j'ai liquidé dix milliards de Lémuriens et dix milliards d'Atlantes pour ne pas envenimer la situation. (...) Un autre jour, j'ai anéanti, en vingt minutes à peine, quinze mille aéronefs de Lémuriens, lancés vers nous du sud-ouest de la France. (...) Une fois, j'ai dû faire tuer un chien parce qu'un général lémurien, et pas n'importe lequel, avait pris possession de son corps. Je parle aux pierres. J'ai fait tomber le mur de

Berlin. J'ai permis le voyage de milliers de bouddhas itinérants à travers le monde.“

Il cita également une déclaration de B. faite au public à Noël 1990, par l'intermédiaire du journal 24 Heures (édition du 25 décembre 1990):

„Cette Couronne de Feu sur ma Tête symbolise le pouvoir que le Père Céleste M'a confié pour ramener l'Age d'Or sur Terre. Cette Couronne de Feu, c'est le signe que nous approchons de la fin du monde. Un choix s'impose à l'humanité entière et ce choix est terrible, car de lui dépend la survie de la Terre et de ses 5 milliards de Terriens. (...) DIEU M'a investi du pouvoir total de création et de destruction. (...) Milliards d'humains de cette Terre, quelles que soient vos religions, vos traditions, vos civilisations, si par malheur vous faisiez le mauvais choix, alors sachez-le, Je jugerai la Terre selon son choix collectif.“

Le tribunal estima que par le fait d'adhérer à un mouvement et à des idées telles, le requérant avait adopté un comportement qui ne permettait plus „de lui accorder la confiance complète nécessaire pour exploiter une agence de sécurité privée“, ce qui justifiait le constat que les conditions de la délivrance de l'autorisation n'étaient plus remplies.

Le tribunal administratif estima enfin qu'il n'y avait pas atteinte à la liberté de croyance du requérant dans la mesure où le requérant pouvait demeurer membre de la secte, mais que la décision litigieuse portait atteinte à la garantie du commerce et de l'industrie, soulignant que „le fait d'exploiter une agence de sécurité n'implique évidemment pas en soi l'exercice d'une religion“.

Le 7 novembre 1996, le requérant forma un recours de droit public auprès du Tribunal fédéral. Il se plaignait d'une violation de la liberté du commerce et de l'industrie, d'une part, et de la violation de la liberté de conscience et de croyance, d'autre part.

Par un arrêt du 2 septembre 1997, le Tribunal fédéral rejeta ce recours. S'agissant de la liberté du commerce et de l'industrie, il rappela que ladite liberté n'était pas absolue, que la condition légale de réunir „toute garantie d'honorabilité“ posée à son exercice pour les agents de sécurité privée était satisfaite pour les personnes „particulièrement dignes de confiance, qualité qui dépasse la simple honorabilité ou la bonne réputation garantie par le certificat de bonne vie et mœurs“.

Il s'expliqua en ces termes sur cette considération:

„bb) Ni la loi sur la profession d'agent de sécurité privé (art. 3 LPASP a contrario), ni son règlement n'exigent la production d'un certificat de bonne vie et moeurs pour la délivrance de l'autorisation d'exploiter une agence de sécurité ou d'être engagé par une telle agence. De plus, les termes utilisés indiquent au contraire que le degré d'honorabilité exigé pour le certificat est moindre que celui requis d'un agent de sécurité. En effet, celui dont l'honorabilité ,ne peut être déniée avec certitude' (art. 10 al. 1 de la loi sur les certificats de bonne vie et

*moeurs) n'offre pas nécessairement „toute garantie d'honorabilité' (art. 3 LPASP).
Une interprétation littérale amène donc à exclure que le certificat de bonne vie et
moeurs démontre une honorabilité suffisante au sens de l'art. 3 LPASP, bien qu'il
puisse constituer un indice sérieux à cet égard.*

*cc) Une interprétation téléologique conduit à la même conclusion. En effet, la pro-
fession d'agent de sécurité implique de tels risques, à la fois pour l'agent lui-
même, pour l'agence qui l'emploie, pour les clients et pour les tiers, que, l'autorité
ne saurait se contenter de la production d'un certificat de bonne vie et moeurs
pour en autoriser l'exercice. L'agent de sécurité dispose d'un accès privilégié aux
biens et aux personnes qu'il est chargé de protéger, voire à des informations
confidentielles. Il existe donc un certain danger qu'il utilise cet avantage à des
fins délictueuses. De plus, cette activité implique par définition un risque accru
d'atteinte disproportionnée à l'intégrité corporelle - voire à la vie - de ceux qui
sont susceptibles de porter préjudice aux objets de la protection. Le péril est
d'autant plus grand à cet égard que l'agent de sécurité est souvent porteur d'une
arme, même s'il doit être au bénéfice du permis (cf. art. 13 LPASP). Or, tout citoyen peut, même lorsqu'il se comporte de manière correcte, être directement
confronté à un agent de sécurité, par exemple lors d'un contrôle à l'entrée d'un bâtiment, d'un aéroport ou d'une manifestation. Enfin, dans la mesure où l'agent de
sécurité est généralement en uniforme (même si, conformément à l'art. 12 LPASP,
cet habit doit se distinguer nettement de celui utilisé par les agents des corporations de droit public) et qu'il exerce en principe des tâches similaires à celles dévo-
lues à la police, il dispose de fait d'un pouvoir et d'une autorité supérieurs à ceux
du citoyen ordinaire, dont il peut abuser (à ce sujet, cf. Peter Hilfiker, Das Recht
des privaten Ueberwachungspersonals, thèse, Zurich 1984, en particulier
p. 146 ss). Les agents de sécurité et, d'autant plus, celui qui dirige une agence en
ce domaine doivent donc donner toute garantie qu'ils „exerceront leur profession
dans le strict respect de la législation" (cf. art. 10 al 2 LPASP) et qu'ils
n'utiliseront pas leur activité à des fins contraires à al sécurité et à l'ordre publics."*

Le Tribunal fédéral disposa, qu'en l'espèce, les faits et les témoignages
étaient suffisamment nombreux et concordants pour estimer qu'il y avait
un risque d'atteintes graves à l'ordre et à la sécurité publics et que dès
lors le requérant ne pouvait être considéré comme „particulièrement digne de confiance". Il constata notamment que selon les déclarations
d'anciens adeptes, B. exigeait de ses adeptes une allégeance absolue allant jusqu'au sacrifice suprême et à „l'élimination" de personnes si nécessaire et qu'il semblait prêt à utiliser tous les moyens pour éliminer ses
ennemis. Il en conclut „que dans ces conditions, il existe un risque certain que B. décide de dépasser le stade des incantations maléfiques et
d'ordonner à ses adeptes - qui lui sont inféodés jusqu'à la mort - de se livrer à des activités criminelles à l'encontre de ses opposants. Le danger
est d'autant plus grand à cet égard que l'approche de l'an 2000, ainsi que
l'intensification des interventions officielles à l'encontre de G.B., sont
propres à cristalliser les passions."

Le Tribunal fédéral considéra que la mesure satisfaisait à l'exigence de
proportionnalité. Il releva, d'une part, que si aucun manquement profes-

sionnel n'avait été relevé à l'encontre du requérant et aucune plainte formulée contre lui, la mesure attaquée n'était pas une mesure répressive mais préventive. Il constata, d'autre part, que la mesure était certes sévère mais estima que „l'intérêt à supprimer un risque élevé d'atteintes graves à l'ordre et à la sécurité publics" l'emportait sur l'intérêt privé du requérant à exploiter l'agence. Il déclara enfin qu'aucune mesure moins sévère n'était envisageable pour sauvegarder les intérêts publics. En particulier, subordonner l'autorisation à la condition de la rupture des liens avec la secte, serait inopérant puisque le requérant persistait à nier l'étroitesse des liens.

S'agissant de la liberté de croyance garantie par la Constitution et l'art. 9 de la Convention, le Tribunal fédéral reconnut que la décision attaquée portait atteinte à la liberté religieuse du requérant, le retrait du droit d'exercer sa profession en raison de ses liens avec la secte constituant un préjudice pour des motifs religieux. Certes, la décision ne l'obligeait pas à abandonner ses convictions, mais exerçait une contrainte indirecte en ce sens. Le Tribunal fédéral constata l'existence d'une base légale à la décision attaquée en se référant à ses constatations relatives à l'obligation de réunir „toutes garanties d'honorabilité". Il releva que, par ailleurs, la mesure en question ne se fondait pas sur ses convictions religieuses proprement dites, mais uniquement sur la gravité des risques objectifs pour l'ordre et la sécurité publics que pouvaient entraîner, avec un degré de probabilité élevé, les actes inspirés par la doctrine de la secte. La décision attaquée n'impliquait pas de parti pris sur la doctrine de la secte mais se limitait à constater l'incompatibilité de l'appartenance à cette secte avec l'exploitation d'une agence de sécurité privée. Enfin le Tribunal fédéral estima que la mesure respectait le principe de proportionnalité en ce qu'elle permettait au requérant de rester membre de la secte, de conserver ses convictions ou de les manifester et qu'elle ne constituait qu'une contrainte indirecte à cet égard. Il conclut en conséquence que l'intérêt public à supprimer le risque d'atteinte à l'ordre public l'emporte sur l'intérêt privé à ne pas subir de contrainte indirecte sur ses croyances.

B. Droit interne pertinent

L'art. 2 alinéa 1 de la loi cantonale sur la profession d'agent de sécurité privé du 15 mars 1985 est ainsi libellé:

> *„L'exploitation d'une agence de sécurité privée sur le territoire du canton est soumise à l'autorisation préalable du département de justice et police (...)."*

L'alinéa 1 lettre d de l'art. 3 de cette loi se lit comme suit:

„L'autorisation d'exploiter une agence de sécurité privée est délivrée à la condition que le requérant offre, par ses antécédents et son comportement, toute garantie d'honorabilité."

Enfin, aux termes de l'alinéa 2 de l'art. 3 de la loi:

„L'autorisation d'exploiter peut être refusée si l'honorabilité du conjoint du requérant ou des personnes majeures faisant ménage commun avec lui doit être déniée. Il faut cependant que cette situation permette, compte tenu des circonstances, de conclure à l'existence d'une menace pour l'ordre public."

GRIEFS

1. Invoquant l'art. 9 de la Convention, le requérant se plaint de ce que le retrait de l'autorisation d'exploiter l'agence par le Département cantonal constitue une ingérence dans sa liberté de religion, non justifiée au regard de l'art. 9 § 2.

A ce titre il allègue en premier lieu que l'ingérence n'était pas „prévue par la loi" dans la mesure où la condition d'honorabilité est une notion floue et indéterminée, qui a pu de ce fait être étendue à l'appartenance à des mouvements religieux.

Il se plaint en second lieu de ce que la mesure ne poursuivait pas un but légitime, car ni lui en tant que tel, ni même la secte dont il n'était qu'un sympathisant, ne représentent un danger pour l'ordre public.

Enfin il estime que la mesure n'était pas nécessaire dans une société démocratique car s'il y avait eu dangerosité réelle, l'Etat aurait eu les moyens d'intervenir pénalement ou civilement, or tel n'a pas été le cas.

2. Invoquant l'art. 18, le requérant se plaint de ce que l'ingérence dans la liberté de religion a été disproportionnée, au vu notamment du fait qu'aucune infraction ne lui a été reprochée.

EN DROIT

1. Le requérant se plaint de ce que le retrait de l'autorisation d'exploiter l'agence par le Département cantonal constitue une ingérence dans sa liberté de religion. Il invoque l'art. 9 de la Convention libellé comme suit:

„1. Toute personne a droit à la liberté de pensée, de conscience et de religion; ce droit implique la liberté de changer de religion ou de conviction, ainsi que la liberté de manifester sa religion ou sa conviction individuellement ou collectivement, en public ou en privé, par le culte, l'enseignement, les pratiques et l'accomplissement des rites.
2. La liberté de manifester sa religion ou ses convictions ne peut faire l'objet d'autres restrictions que celles qui, prévues par la loi, constituent des mesures nécessaires, dans une société démocratique, à la sécurité publique, à la protection

de l'ordre, de la santé ou de la morale publiques, ou à la protection des droits et libertés d'autrui."

La Cour rappelle en premier lieu sa jurisprudence, en vertu de laquelle la liberté de pensée, de conscience et de religion, qui se trouve consacrée à l'art. 9 de la Convention, représente l'une des assises d'une „société démocratique" au sens de la Convention. Elle est, dans sa dimension religieuse, l'un des éléments les plus vitaux contribuant à former l'identité des croyants et leur conception de la vie, mais elle est aussi un bien précieux pour les athées, les agnostiques, les sceptiques ou les indifférents. Il y va du pluralisme - chèrement conquis au cours des siècles - consubstantiel à pareille société (CourEuDH, arrêts Kokkinakis c. Grèce du 25 mai 1993, série A n° 260-A, p. 17, § 31, KirchE-EU S. 202; Otto-Preminger-Institut c. Autriche du 20 septembre 1994, série A n° 295-A, p. 17, § 47, KirchE-EU S. 248). Si la liberté religieuse relève d'abord du for intérieur, elle implique de surcroît, notamment, celle de manifester sa religion, non seulement de manière collective, en public et dans le cercle de ceux dont on partage la foi: on peut aussi s'en prévaloir individuellement et en privé. L'art. 9 énumère diverses formes que peut prendre la manifestation d'une religion ou d'une conviction, à savoir le culte, l'enseignement, les pratiques et l'accomplissement des rites (CourEuDH, arrêt Kalaç c. Turquie du 1er juillet 1997, RJD 1997-IV, p. 1209, § 27; KirchE-EU S. 312).

La Cour n'estime pas nécessaire de se prononcer sur le point de savoir si le retrait de l'autorisation constitue une ingérence dans les droits garantis par l'art. 9 § 1, dans la mesure où elle estime qu'à supposer l'ingérence établie, elle serait justifiée au regard du par. 2 de cette disposition.

La Cour relève tout d'abord que l'autorisation a été retirée au motif que le requérant ne satisfaisait plus la condition d'offrir „toute garantie d'honorabilité", condition posée par la loi cantonale du 15 mars 1985. Le requérant argue, à cet égard, du caractère indéterminé de la notion „d'honorabilité". Dans l'arrêt Sunday Times c/ Royaume-Uni (arrêt du 26 avril 1976, série A n° 30, p. 31, § 49), la Cour s'est exprimée comme suit à propos des termes „prévues par la loi" repris au par. 2 de l'art. 9:

„Aux yeux de la Cour, les deux conditions suivantes comptent parmi celles qui se dégagent des mots ‚prévues par la loi'. Il faut d'abord que la ‚loi' soit suffisamment accessible: le citoyen doit pouvoir disposer de renseignements suffisants, dans les circonstances de la cause, sur les normes juridiques applicables à un cas donné. En second lieu, on ne peut considérer comme une ‚loi' qu'une norme énoncée avec assez de précision pour permettre au citoyen de régler sa conduite; en s'entourant au besoin de conseils éclairés, il doit être à même de prévoir, à un degré raisonnable dans les circonstances de la cause, les conséquences de nature à dériver d'un acte déterminé."

Le libellé de bien des lois ne présente pas une précision absolue. Beaucoup d'entre elles, en raison de la nécessité d'éviter une rigidité excessive et de s'adapter aux changements de situation, se servent par la force des choses de formules plus ou moins floues. L'interprétation et l'application de pareils textes dépendent de la pratique (CourEuDH, arrêt Kokkinakis c. Grèce du 25 mai 1993, série A n° 260-A, p. 19, § 40; KirchE-EU S. 202).

Ayant examiné les considérations développées à propos des termes „toute garantie d'honorabilité" par le tribunal administratif et le Tribunal fédéral qui se basèrent notamment sur les autres dispositions de la loi et son exposé des motifs, la Cour constate que l'art. 2 de la loi du 15 mars 1985 était suffisamment précis pour permettre aux personnes intéressées de régler leur conduite. La mesure critiquée était donc prévue par la loi au sens de l'art. 9 § 2 de la Convention.

Le requérant fait aussi valoir en outre que la mesure ne poursuivait pas un but légitime au motif que ni lui-même ni la secte ne représentaient un danger pour l'ordre public. Eu égard aux circonstances de la cause et aux termes mêmes des décisions des trois autorités compétentes, la Cour est d'avis que la mesure poursuivait des buts légitimes au sens de l'art. 9 § 2: la sécurité publique, la protection de l'ordre et la protection des droits et libertés d'autrui.

Enfin le requérant allègue que la mesure n'était pas „nécessaire dans une société démocratique". La Cour rappelle que selon sa jurisprudence constante, il faut reconnaître aux Etats contractants une certaine marge d'appréciation pour juger de l'existence et de l'étendue de la nécessité d'une ingérence, mais elle va de pair avec un contrôle européen portant à la fois sur la loi et sur les décisions qui l'appliquent, même quand elles émanent d'une juridiction indépendante. La tâche de la Cour consiste à rechercher si les mesures prises au niveau national se justifient dans leur principe, c'est-à-dire si les motifs invoqués pour les justifier apparaissent „pertinents et suffisants", et sont proportionnées au but légitime poursuivi (arrêt Sunday Times c. Royaume-Uni du 26 novembre 1991, série A n° 217, pp. 28-29, § 50). Pour statuer sur ce dernier point, il y a lieu de mettre en balance les exigences de la protection des droits et libertés d'autrui avec le comportement reproché au requérant. Dans l'exercice de son pouvoir de contrôle, la Cour doit considérer les décisions judiciaires litigieuses sur la base de l'ensemble du dossier (arrêt Kokkinakis c. Grèce du 25 mai 1993, série A n° 260-A, p. 21, § 47; KirchE-EU S. 202).

Appliquant ces principes au cas d'espèce la Cour relève que le Tribunal fédéral a justifié la mesure prise, d'une part, par la gravité des risques que le comportement du requérant engendrait eu égard à la préservation de l'ordre public, à la sécurité publique et la protection des droits et libertés d'autrui. A cet égard, il a tenu compte de la nature même de la profession d'agent de sécurité privée, qui se distingue d'autres professions, notamment du fait que les personnes l'exerçant sont souvent titulaires d'un permis de port d'arme. Il a noté, d'autre part, que la mesure litigieuse ne contraint pas le requérant à abandonner ses convictions, à modifier ou abandonner sa pratique active au sein de la secte. S'agissant de la proportionnalité de la mesure, il a par ailleurs considéré qu'une mesure moins sévère, comme la subordination de l'octroi de l'autorisation à la rupture des liens avec la secte, n'aurait pas permis d'atteindre l'objectif de protection de l'ordre et de la sécurité publics, et ce, en raison du comportement même du requérant qui persistait à nier son appartenance à ladite secte. Il en ressort que les éventuelles convictions religieuses ont été pleinement prises en compte face aux impératifs de la préservation de l'ordre et de la sécurité publics et la protection des droits et libertés d'autrui. Il est également clair que ce sont ces impératifs qui fondaient la décision de retrait de l'autorisation d'exploitation de l'agence et non des objections aux convictions religieuses du requérant. Eu égard aux circonstances de l'espèce, il ne saurait en outre être reproché aux autorités nationales, comme le fait le requérant, d'avoir adopté une mesure préventive sans attendre que le danger que pouvait représenter la poursuite par le requérant de ses activités professionnelles ne soit avéré par la commission d'une infraction.

Partant la mesure litigieuse s'analyse en une mesure justifiée dans son principe et proportionnée à l'objectif visé de protection de l'ordre public et de la sécurité publique. En conséquence la Cour estime que le retrait de l'autorisation constituait une mesure „nécessaire dans une société démocratique".

Il s'ensuit que cette partie de la requête est manifestement mal fondée au sens de l'art. 35 § 3 et doit être rejetée en application de l'art. 35 § 4 de la Convention.

2. Le requérant se plaint que le retrait de l'autorisation a été disproportionné, au vu notamment du fait qu'aucune infraction ne lui a été reprochée. Il invoque l'art. 18 libellé comme suit:

„Les restrictions qui, aux termes de la présente Convention, sont apportées aux droits et libertés garantis par elle ne peuvent être appliquées que dans le but pour lequel elles ont été prévues".

A cet égard, la Cour rappelle que l'art. 18 de la Convention n'a pas un rôle indépendant et qu'il ne peut être appliqué que conjointement à d'autres articles de la Convention. Il découle en outre des termes de l'art. 18 qu'il ne saurait y avoir de violation que si le droit ou la liberté en question peut être soumis à des restrictions aux termes de la Convention (ComEuDH, décision N°9009/80, Bozano c. Suisse du 12 juillet 1984, DR 39, p. 58).

Tel est le cas de la liberté de religion puisque ce droit peut être restreint conformément au par. 2.

En l'espèce cependant, la Cour relève que le requérant ne fait état d'aucun élément montrant que les autorités auraient retiré l'autorisation pour des motifs différents de ceux avancés par elles et examinés ci-dessus. Partant, aucun détournement de pouvoir ne peut être établi et il n'y a donc aucune apparence de violation de l'art. 18 de la Convention combiné à l'art. 9.

Il s'ensuit que cette partie de la requête est manifestement mal fondée au sens de l'art. 35 § 3 et doit être rejetée conformément à l'art. 35 § 4 de la Convention.

Par ces motifs, la Cour, à l'unanimité, déclare la requête irrecevable.

50

Zur Frage des Eingriffs in Freiheitsrechte, wenn eine erwachsene Person, die sich einer sog. Psycho-Sekte angeschlossen hat, zwangsweise einer „Deprogrammierung" zugeführt wird.

Art. 5 EMRK
EGMR, Urteil vom 14. Oktober 1999 - No. 37680/97
(Riera Blume ./. Spanien)[1] -

THE FACTS

I. The circumstances of the case

[12] The applicants, Ms Elena Riera Blume, Ms Concepción Riera Blume, Ms María Luz Casado Perez, Ms Daría Amelía Casado Perez, Ms María Teresa Sales Aige and Mr Javier Bruna Reverter, were born in 1954, 1952, 1950, 1950, 1951 and 1957 respectively and live in Valencia (Spain).

[13] At an unknown date in 1983 the Public Safety Department („the *DGSC"*) of the *Generalitat* (government) of Catalonia received through *Pro Juventud* („Pro Youth"), an association formed to fight against sects, a request for help from several people who alleged that members of their families had been ensnared by a group known by the name of *CEIS* (*Centro Esotérico de Investigaciones*). According to the families' complaints, those who ran the *CEIS* managed to bring about a complete change of personality in their followers, leading them to break off ties with their family and friends and inciting them to prostitution and other activities designed to obtain money for the organisation. The *DGSC* infiltrated an officer into the *CEIS* to check the truth of the complaints and, in the light of the findings, brought the facts to the attention of the Principal Public Prosecutor at the Barcelona *Audiencia Territorial*, who forwarded the complaints and the information gathered to the judicial authorities. Acting on this information, Barcelona investigating court no. 6 opened a

---

[1] CEDH/ECHR 1999-VII.

preliminary investigation in June 1984 and ordered searches of the homes of members of the *CEIS*, including the applicants. The searches took place on 20 June 1984 and numerous people were arrested, including the applicants. After the applicants were arrested, they were transferred to the seat of the investigating court. In the light of information from A.T.V., an official at the *DGSC*, which was confirmed by the prosecuting authorities, there was a danger that the members of the sect would react unpredictably if they were released, and might even commit suicide. The duty judge nevertheless decided to release the applicants but gave oral instructions to the police that those detained, including the applicants, should be handed over to their families, to whom it should be suggested that it would be as well to have them interned in a psychiatric centre, on a voluntary basis as regards the persons of full age, in order for them to recover their psychological balance. The judge in question confirmed his oral instruction in a decision of 26 June 1984. In that decision he also ordered the chief of the Catalan police (*mossos d'esquadra*) to interview and question all those detained during the searches who had subsequently been released.

[14] Later, on the orders of L.R.F., the Director-General of Public Safety, the applicants were transferred to the premises of the *DGSC*. From there, on 21 June 1984, they were taken by members of the Catalan police in official vehicles to a hotel some thirty kilometres from Barcelona, where they were handed over to their families with a view to their recovering their psychological balance. Once at the hotel, the applicants were taken to individual rooms under the supervision of persons recruited for the purpose, one of whom remained permanently in each room, and they were not allowed to leave their rooms for the first three days. The windows were firmly closed with wooden planks and the panes of glass had been taken out. While at the hotel the applicants were allegedly subjected to a process of „deprogramming" by a psychologist and a psychiatrist at the request of *Pro Juventud*. On 29 and 30 June 1984, after being informed of their rights, they were questioned by C.T.R., the Assistant Director-General of Public Safety, aided by A.T.V., in the presence of a lawyer not appointed by the applicants. On 30 June 1984 the applicants left the hotel.

[15] As soon as they had regained their freedom, the applicants lodged a criminal complaint alleging false imprisonment, offences against the exercise of personal rights, falsification of documents, usurpation of functions and misappropriation of goods against A.T.V., C.T.R. and L.R.F., the latter as Director-General of Public Safety, and against all other persons who had taken part in depriving them of their liberty. In the criminal proceedings thus instituted the prosecuting authorities filed submissions against the persons mentioned above accusing them of false imprisonment.

[16] In a judgment of 7 March 1990 the Barcelona *Audiencia Provincial* acquitted the accused, holding that the acts complained of had been prompted by a philanthropic, legitimate and well-intentioned motive and that there had been no intention of depriving the applicants of their liberty, so that the offence of false imprisonment was not made out.

[17] The prosecution and the applicants lodged appeals on points of law, which were dismissed by the Supreme Court on 23 March 1993. In its judgment the Supreme Court held, *inter alia*:

„... A detailed examination of the facts held to have been proved shows that there is no doubt that the appellants were placed in detention [detención] (the expression ,administrative detention' [retención] has no validity, since it is not defined in our legal order), but the detention took place with the sole aim - a very laudable and plausible one - of avoiding worse evils than those complained of by the appellants, so that there was no unlawfulness strictly and properly understood.
... Furthermore, that there was no unlawfulness, the criterion required by law, is all the plainer if it is borne in mind that it was the appellants themselves, together with the closest members of their families, who consented to undergo deprogramming tests which logically required them to be physically isolated initially. That isolation lasted for a very limited time and, it must be emphasised, with the agreement of those concerned and their families. ... It cannot be maintained, in order to argue the contrary, that the wishes of the persons who underwent deprogramming could only have been overridden by the members of their families after proceedings to establish incapacity, seeing that the position of those concerned called for immediate treatment, without any delay, as appears from the judgment under appeal, which refers to fears that the members of the sect might commit suicide.
In conclusion, the offence of false imprisonment cannot be said to have been committed since, firstly, there was no intention on the part of the defendants to deprive anybody of his or her liberty and, on the contrary, their intention, which has been fully proved, was to prevent imminent and very serious harm befalling the persons concerned, such that the mens rea for the offence was lacking. In the second place, the requirement of ,unlawfulness' was lacking inasmuch as the defendants' conduct was in keeping with what society and the legal order, taken as a whole, require in situations and at times such as those of the instant case.“

[18] The applicants lodged an appeal (*recurso de amparo*) with the Constitutional Court. In their appeal they alleged violations of the right to religious freedom (art. 16 of the Constitution), the right to liberty (art. 17 of the Constitution), the right to freedom of movement (art. 19 of the Constitution), the rights of the defence during their detention (art. 24 § 2 of the Constitution) and the right to a fair trial (art. 24 § 1 of the Constitution). They asked the Constitutional Court to quash the judgments of the *Audiencia Provincial* and the Supreme Court, to order the officials complained of to pay five million pesetas as compensation for the damage sustained and to make a declaration to the effect that the *Generalitat* of Catalonia was liable in default.

[19] In the proceedings in the Constitutional Court Mr José Victor Riera Blume was held to have withdrawn on account of failure, through his own fault, to comply with a formal requirement.

[20] On 10 March 1997 the Constitutional Court dismissed the *amparo* appeal. In sec. 2 of the „As to the law" part of the judgment the court first examined a preliminary objection raised by Crown Counsel that appropriate remedies had not been used, namely a habeas corpus application or contentious-administrative proceedings, in the following terms:

„This Court, while holding that a person in possession of a fundamental right could choose the most effective remedy for infringement of that right ..., has also stated that that had to be understood ,subject, of course, to the possibilities afforded by each class of court'. Consequently, in order to resolve the issue raised by Crown Counsel, it would be necessary to determine what those possibilities were in the criminal courts. In the instant case, however, it is not necessary to do so since the appeal is being brought not against administrative acts but against judicial decisions. That being so, the issue is not - and cannot be - whether or not use was made of an effective judicial remedy (sec. 43 (1) of the CCA [Constitutional Court Act]) but whether the remedies afforded by the judicial process chosen (sec. 44 (1)(a) CCA) have been exhausted, an issue that has not been canvassed and could not be since the appellants went to the highest court, the Supreme Court, which heard the appeal on points of law in the case."

[21] That being said, the Constitutional Court pointed out, firstly, that there was no fundamental right to have a person convicted and, secondly, that it could not protect fundamental rights by quashing final substantive judgments whereby defendants had been acquitted. It also pointed out that, according to its case-law, the Constitution did not confer, as such, a right to secure criminal convictions of third parties. Furthermore, decisions of criminal courts were never decisions affecting fundamental rights of the prosecuting party. The court added that the decisions being challenged had not infringed any of the rights relied on by the five remaining appellants, seeing that they were limited to declaring that the acts with which the defendants were charged did not amount to the offences for which they were being prosecuted.

II. Relevant domestic law

[22] Several provisions of the Spanish Constitution are relevant:

Art. 16
„1. Freedom of ideas, religion and worship shall be guaranteed to individuals and communities without any restrictions on its expression other than those necessary for the maintenance of public order as protected by law.
2. No one shall be required to declare his ideological, religious or other beliefs.
3. ..."
Art. 17

„*1. Everyone shall have the right to freedom and security of person. No one may be deprived of his liberty other than in accordance with the provisions of this article and in the circumstances and form provided by law.*
2. ...
3. Everyone who is arrested must be informed immediately, and in a manner he can understand, of his rights and of the reasons for his arrest and cannot be required to make a statement. The assistance of a lawyer is guaranteed to persons detained in police investigations or criminal prosecutions, as provided by law.
4. A habeas corpus procedure shall be established by law for immediately bringing before a judge any person arrested unlawfully. ..."
Artículo 16
„*1. Se garantiza la libertad ideológica, religiosa y de culto de los individuos y las comunidades sin más limitación, en sus manifestaciones, que la necesaria para el mantenimiento del orden público protegido por la ley.*
2. Nadie podrá ser obligado a declarar sobre su ideología, religión o creencias.
3. ..."
Artículo 17
„*1. Toda persona tiene derecho a la libertad y a la seguridad. Nadie puede ser privado de su libertad, sino con la observancia de lo establecido en este artículo y en los casos y en la forma previstos en la ley.*
2. ...
3. Toda persona detenida debe ser informada de forma inmediata, y de modo que le sea comprensible, de sus derechos y de las razones de su detención, no pudiendo ser obligado a declarar. Se garantiza la asistencia de abogado al detenido en las diligencias policiales y judiciales, en los términos que la ley establezca.
4. La ley regulará un procedimiento de hábeas corpus para producir la inmediata puesta a disposición judicial de toda persona detenida ilegalmente.
..."

FINAL SUBMISSIONS TO THE COURT

[23] In their memorial the applicants asked the Court to hold that the respondent State had failed to discharge the obligations imposed on it by art. 5 and 9 of the Convention.

[24] The Government asked the Court to dismiss the applicants' application with regard to the complaints under art. 5 and 9 of the Convention as disclosing no violation of those provisions.

THE LAW

I. Alleged violation of Art. 5 § 1 of the convention

[25] The applicants alleged that the deprivation of liberty of which they had been the victims from 20 to 30 June 1984 had given rise to a violation of art. 5 § 1 of the Convention, which provides:

„1. Everyone has the right to liberty and security of person. No one shall be deprived of his liberty save in the following cases and in accordance with a procedure prescribed by law:
(a) the lawful detention of a person after conviction by a competent court;
(b) the lawful arrest or detention of a person for non-compliance with the lawful order of a court or in order to secure the fulfilment of any obligation prescribed by law;
(c) the lawful arrest or detention of a person effected for the purpose of bringing him before the competent legal authority on reasonable suspicion of having committed an offence or when it is reasonably considered necessary to prevent his committing an offence or fleeing after having done so;
(d) the detention of a minor by lawful order for the purpose of educational supervision or his lawful detention for the purpose of bringing him before the competent legal authority;
(e) the lawful detention of persons for the prevention of the spreading of infectious diseases, of persons of unsound mind, alcoholics or drug addicts or vagrants;
(f) the lawful arrest or detention of a person to prevent his effecting an unauthorised entry into the country or of a person against whom action is being taken with a view to deportation or extradition. "

[26] The applicants maintained that there had been a violation of that provision on account of their having been transferred to a hotel by Catalan police officers and handed over to others to be „deprogrammed" from their membership of a „sect" of which they were alleged to be members. They submitted that they were deprived of their liberty without any legal basis under either domestic or international law.

[27] The Government did not dispute that the applicants had been deprived of their liberty. However, the deprivation could not be attributed to the Catalan police officers, whose role had been limited to carrying out in good faith the investigating judge's instruction to hand the applicants over to their families and suggest that it would be as well to intern them in a psychiatric centre, on a voluntary basis as regards persons of full age, in order for them to recover their emotional balance. In the Government's submission, the responsibility for the alleged deprivation of liberty lay with the members of the applicants' families and with the persons belonging to the *Pro Juventud* private association and not at all with the authorities and officials of the Catalan government. In support of their contention they argued, in particular, that the hotel rooms had been reserved and paid for by the association, that it was the same association that had recruited and paid the young people responsible for supervising the applicants and that the applicants' families had not left the hotel during the period of „deprogramming". As to the applicants' transfer from the Catalan police premises to the hotel, the Government pointed out that during it the applicants had been treated like people at liberty; at no time had they been handcuffed or made to submit to any other measure appropriate for people under arrest.

[28] The Court reiterates that in proclaiming the right to liberty, par. 1 of art. 5 contemplates the physical liberty of the person; its aim is to ensure that no one should be deprived of that liberty in an arbitrary fashion. In order to determine whether someone has been deprived of his liberty within the meaning of art. 5, the starting-point must be his concrete situation, and account must be taken of a whole range of criteria such as the type, duration and manner of implementation of the measure in question (see the following judgments: Engel and Others v. the Netherlands, 8 June 1976, Series A no. 22, p. 24, §§ 58-59; Guzzardi v. Italy, 6 November 1980, Series A no. 39, p. 33, § 92) and Amuur v. France, 25 June 1996, RJD 1996-III, p. 848, § 42).

[29] In the instant case the Court notes that during a preliminary investigation directed by Barcelona investigating court no. 6, after the applicants' homes had been searched, the duty judge decided to release the applicants but gave oral instructions to the Catalan police officers to hand them over to their families and suggest that it would be as well to intern them in a psychiatric centre, on a voluntary basis as regards the persons of full age, so that they could recover their psychological balance. Those instructions were confirmed in a decision of the investigating judge dated 26 June 1984. From the undisputed account of the facts it appears that, in accordance with the judge's instructions, the applicants were transferred by Catalan police officers in official vehicles to a hotel about thirty kilometres away from Barcelona. There they were handed over to their families and taken to individual rooms under the supervision of people recruited for that purpose, one of whom remained permanently in each room, and they were not allowed to leave their rooms for the first three days. The windows of their rooms were firmly closed with wooden planks and the panes of glass had been taken out. While at the hotel the applicants were allegedly subjected to a „deprogramming" process by a psychologist and a psychiatrist at *Pro Juventud's* request. On 29 and 30 June 1984, after being informed of their rights, they were questioned by C.T.R., the Assistant Director-General of Public Safety, aided by A.T.V., in the presence of a lawyer not appointed by the applicants. On 30 June 1984 the applicants left the hotel.

[30] The Court concludes that the applicants' transfer to the hotel by the Catalan police and their subsequent confinement to the hotel for ten days amounted in fact, on account of the restrictions placed on the applicants, to a deprivation of liberty.

[31] It remains to be ascertained whether that deprivation was compatible with art. 5 § 1. The Court reiterates that art. 5 § 1 refers essentially to national law and lays down an obligation to comply with its substantive and procedural rules. It requires, however, that any measure depriving the individual of his liberty must be compatible with the purpose of art. 5, namely to protect the individual from arbitrariness (see, for example, the Van der Leer v. the Netherlands judgment of 21 Febru-

ary 1990, Series A no. 170-A, p. 12, § 22). By laying down that any deprivation of liberty should be „in accordance with a procedure prescribed by law", art. 5 § 1 requires, firstly, that any arrest or detention should have a legal basis in domestic law. The applicants maintained that their detention had no legal basis either in Spanish law or in international law. The Government did not deny that there was no legal basis for the deprivation of liberty. That being said, they argued that the measure in issue could not in any circumstances be attributed to the Catalan police officers, as the responsibility was that of the applicants' families, who had organised their reception and detention at the hotel and their supervision.

[32] It is therefore necessary to consider the part played by the Catalan authorities in the deprivation of liberty complained of by the applicants and to determine its extent. In other words, it must be ascertained whether, as the applicants maintained, the contribution of the Catalan police had been so decisive that without it the deprivation of liberty would not have occurred.

[33] The Court notes, firstly, that it was officers of the autonomous Catalan police who, acting on the instructions of their superiors and, partly, those of the investigating judge, transferred the applicants in official vehicles from the premises of the Catalan police to the hotel. From the applicants' statements it appears that their transfer to the hotel by the police did not take place with their consent but was imposed on them. The fact that they were not handcuffed during the journey cannot alter the fact that they were transferred under duress. Once they had been handed over to their families, the applicants underwent detention similar to false imprisonment, which ended only on 30 June 1984, when they were allowed to leave the hotel. In this connection, the Court notes that on 29 and 30 June 1984, that is to say at a time when the applicants were still being held at the hotel, police officers questioned them in the presence of a lawyer after informing them of their rights. That shows that the Catalan authorities knew all the time that the applicants were still held at the hotel and did nothing to put an end to the situation.

[34] Nor could the police officers be unaware that, in order to be able to derive benefit from the psychiatric assistance recommended by the investigating judge, the applicants were going to be under constant supervision. They thus did not fully comply with the judge's order, according to which the psychiatric assistance that would enable them to recover their psychological balance had to be provided on a voluntary basis as regards the persons of full age, which is what all the applicants were. At all events, even supposing that there was a danger of suicide, a risk of that kind did not justify such a major deprivation of liberty. The fact that, once free, the applicants lodged a criminal complaint alleging false imprisonment and other offences against officials of the Catalan govern-

ment and all others responsible clearly shows that they had been confined in the hotel against their will.

[35] In the light of the foregoing, the Court considers that the national authorities at all times acquiesced in the applicants' loss of liberty. While it is true that it was the applicants' families and the *Pro Juventud* association that bore the direct and immediate responsibility for the supervision of the applicants during their ten days' loss of liberty, it is equally true that without the active cooperation of the Catalan authorities the deprivation of liberty could not have taken place. As the ultimate responsibility for the matters complained of thus lay with the authorities in question, the Court concludes that there has been a violation of art. 5 § 1 of the Convention.

II. Alleged violation of Art. 9 of the convention

[36] The applicants argued that the „deprogramming" measures to which they were subjected during their detention amounted to a violation of art. 9 of the Convention, which provides:

„1. Everyone has the right to freedom of thought, conscience and religion; this right includes freedom to change his religion or belief and freedom, either alone or in community with others and in public or private, to manifest his religion or belief, in worship, teaching, practice and observance.
2. Freedom to manifest one's religion or beliefs shall be subject only to such limitations as are prescribed by law and are necessary in a democratic society in the interests of public safety, for the protection of public order, health or morals, or for the protection of the rights and freedoms of others."

[37] The Government disputed that there had been any such breach as no Catalan police officer or other authority had taken part at any time in the alleged „deprogramming". Moreover, the applicants themselves admitted that fact.

[38] The Court observes that the applicants' detention is at the core of the complaints under consideration. Having held that it was arbitrary and hence unlawful for the purposes of art. 5 § 1 of the Convention (see par. 34 and 35 above), the Court does not consider it necessary to undertake a separate examination of the case under art. 9 (see the Tsirlis and Kouloumpas v. Greece judgment of 29 May 1997, RJD 1997-III, p. 926, § 70).

III. Application of Art. 41 of the Convention (...)

For these reasons, the Court unanimously
1. Holds that there has been a violation of art. 5 § 1 of the Convention;

2. *Holds that it is unnecessary to examine separately the complaint based on art. 9 of the Convention;*
3. *Holds*
   (a) that the respondent State is to pay, within three months from the date on which the judgment becomes final according to art. 44 § 2 of the Convention,
   (i) 250,000 pesetas to each of the applicants for non-pecuniary damage;
   (ii) ... (Kosten und Auslagen);
   (b) ... (Zinsen)
4. *Dismisses the remainder of the claim for just satisfaction.*

51

Konflikte innerhalb einer Religionsgemeinschaft, die ohne Auswirkungen auf deren Status nach weltlichem Recht sind, können in einem demokratischen Gemeinwesen nur aus zwingendem gesellschaftlichen Anlass („pressing social need") Gegenstand staatlicher Maßnahmen sein (hier verneint für strafrechtliche Sanktionen gegen einen Mufti wegen Amtsanmaßung).

Art. 9, 10, 41 EMRK
EGMR, Urteil vom 14. Dezember 1999 - No. 38178/99
(Serif ./. Griechenland)[1] -

THE FACTS

I. The circumstances of the case

[7] The applicant is a Greek citizen, born in 1951. He is a theological school graduate and resides in Komotini.

A. The background of the case

[8] In 1985 one of the two Muslim religious leaders of Thrace, the Mufti of Rodopi, died. The State appointed a mufti *ad interim*. When he resigned, a second mufti *ad interim*, Mr M.T., was appointed. On 6 April 1990 the President of the Republic confirmed M.T. in the post of Mufti of Rodopi.

[9] In December 1990 the two independent Muslim Members of Parliament for Xanthi and Rodopi requested the State to organise elections for the post of Mufti of Rodopi, as the law then in force provided. They

---

[1] CEDH/ECHR 1999-IX.

also requested that elections be organised by the State for the post of the other Muslim religious leader of Thrace, the Mufti of Xanthi. Having received no reply, the two independent MPs decided to organise elections themselves at the mosques on Friday 28 December 1990, after prayers.

[10] On 24 December 1990 the President of the Republic, on the proposal of the Council of Ministers and under art. 44 § 1 of the Constitution, adopted a legislative decree by which the manner of selection of the muftis was changed.

[11] On 28 December 1990 the applicant was elected Mufti of Rodopi by those attending Friday prayers at the mosques. Together with other Muslims, he challenged the lawfulness of M.T.'s appointment before the Supreme Administrative Court. These proceedings are still pending.

[12] On 4 February 1991 Parliament enacted Law no. 1920, thereby retroactively validating the legislative decree of 24 December 1990.

B. The criminal proceedings against the applicant

[13] The Rodopi public prosecutor instituted criminal proceedings against the applicant under art. 175 and 176 of the Criminal Code for having usurped the functions of a minister of a „known religion" and for having publicly worn the dress of such a minister without having the right to do so. On 8 November 1991 the Court of Cassation, considering that there might be disturbances in Rodopi, decided, under art. 136 and 137 of the Code of Criminal Procedure, that the case should be heard in Salonika.

[14] On 5 March 1993 the Salonika public prosecutor summoned the applicant to appear before the Salonika Criminal Court sitting at first instance and composed of a single judge to be tried for the offences provided for under art. 175 and 176 of the Criminal Code.

[15] The applicant was tried by the Salonika Criminal Court on 12 December 1994 ... The court heard a number of prosecution and defence witnesses. Although one witness attested that the applicant had taken part in religious ceremonies, none of the witnesses stated that the applicant had purported to discharge the judicial functions with which muftis are entrusted in Greek law. Moreover, a number of witnesses attested that no official dress for muftis existed. However, one prosecution witness declared that, although in principle all Muslims were allowed to wear the black gown in which the applicant had been appearing, according to local custom this had become the privilege of muftis.

[16] On 12 December 1994 the court found the applicant guilty of the offences provided for under art. 175 and 176 of the Criminal Code. According to the court, these offences had been committed between 17 January and 28 February 1991, a period during which the applicant had discharged the entirety of the functions of the Mufti of Rodopi by officiating at weddings, „christening" children, preaching and engaging in

administrative activities. In particular, the court found that on 17 January 1991 the applicant had issued a message to his fellow Muslims about the religious significance of the Regaib Kandil feast, thanking them at the same time for his election as mufti. On 15 February 1991, in the capacity of a mufti, he had attended the inauguration of the hall of the „Union of the Turkish Youth of Komotini" wearing clothes which, according to Muslim custom, only muftis were allowed to wear. On 27 February 1991 he had issued another message on the occasion of the Berat Kandil feast. Finally, on 28 February 1991 and in the same capacity, he had attended a religious gathering of 2,000 Muslims at Dokos, a village in Rodopi, and had delivered the keynote speech. Moreover, the court found that the applicant had repeatedly worn the official dress of a mufti in public. The court imposed on the applicant a commutable sentence of eight months' imprisonment.

[17] The applicant appealed. The hearing before the Salonika Criminal Court sitting on appeal and composed of three judges was adjourned on 24 May 1995 and 30 April 1996 because, *inter alia*, M.T., the appointed mufti, who had been called by the prosecution, did not appear to testify. M.T. was fined. The appeal was heard on 21 October 1996. In a decision issued on the same date the court upheld the applicant's conviction and imposed on him a sentence of six months' imprisonment to be commuted to a fine.

[18] The applicant paid the fine and appealed on points of law. He submitted, *inter alia*, that the appellate court had interpreted art. 175 of the Criminal Code erroneously when it considered that the offence was made out even where a person claimed to be a minister of a „known religion" without, however, discharging any of the functions of the minister's office. Moreover, the court had been wrong to disregard expert testimony that no official mufti dress existed. The applicant had the right under art. 10 of the Convention to make the statements for which he had been convicted. „The office of the mufti represented the free manifestation of the Muslim religion", the Muslim community had the right under the Treaty of Peace of Athens of 1913 to elect its muftis and, therefore, his conviction violated art. 9 and 14 of the Convention.

[19] On 2 April 1997 the Court of Cassation dismissed the applicant's appeal. It considered that the offence in art. 175 of the Criminal Code was made out „where somebody appeared in public as a minister of a ,known religion' and discharged the functions of the minister's office, including any of the administrative functions pertaining thereto". The court considered that the applicant had committed this offence because he had behaved and appeared in public as the Mufti of Rodopi, wearing the dress which, in people's minds, was that of a mufti. In particular, the court referred to the incidents of 17 January and 15, 27 and 28 February 1991. The Court of Cassation did not specifically address the applicant's arguments under art. 9, 10 and 14 of the Convention.

II. Relevant law and practice

A. International treaties

[20] Art. 11 of the Treaty of Peace of Athens between Greece and others, on the one hand, and the Ottoman Empire, on the other, which was concluded on 17 May 1913 and ratified by the Greek parliament by a law published in the Official Gazette on 14 November 1913, provides as follows:

> „The life, property, honour, religion and customs of the inhabitants of the districts ceded to Greece who will remain under Greek administration shall be scrupulously respected.
>
> They shall enjoy in full the same civil and political rights as the subjects of Greek origin. Muslims shall be entitled to freedom and to practise their religion openly.
> ...
> There shall be no interference with the autonomy or hierarchical organisation of existing or future Muslim communities or in the management of their funds or property.
> ...
> Each mufti shall be elected by Muslim voters in his own constituency.
> ...
> In addition to their authority in purely religious matters and in the supervision of the management of vacouf property, the muftis shall have jurisdiction as between Muslims in the spheres of marriage, divorce, maintenance (nefaca), guardianship, administration, capacity of minors, Islamic wills and succession to the office of mutevelli (Tevliét).
> Judgments delivered by the muftis shall be enforced by the competent Greek authorities.
> As regards successions, any interested Muslim party may with prior agreement submit a dispute to the mufti as arbitrator. Unless the agreement expressly provides otherwise, all avenues of appeal to the Greek courts shall lie against an arbitral award.“

[21] On 10 August 1920 Greece concluded two treaties with the principal Allied Powers at Sèvres. By the first treaty the Allied Powers transferred to Greece all the rights and titles which they had acquired over Thrace by virtue of the peace treaty they had signed with Bulgaria at Neuilly-sur-Seine on 27 November 1919. The second treaty concerned the protection of minorities in Greece. Art. 14 § 1 of the second treaty provides as follows:

> „Greece agrees to take all necessary measures in relation to the Muslims to enable questions of family law and personal status to be regulated in accordance with Muslim usage.“

[22] On 30 January 1923 Greece and Turkey signed a treaty for the exchange of populations. On 24 July 1923 Greece and others, on the one hand, and Turkey, on the other, signed the Treaty of Peace of Lausanne. art. 42 and 45 of this treaty gave the Muslim minority of Greece the same protection as art. 14 § 1 of the Sèvres Treaty for the Protection of Minorities. On the same day Greece signed a protocol with the principal Allied Powers bringing into force the two treaties concluded at Sèvres on 10 August 1920. The Greek parliament ratified the three above-mentioned treaties by a law published in the Official Gazette on 25 August 1923.

[23] In its decision no. 1723/80 the Court of Cassation considered that it was obliged to apply Islamic law in certain disputes between Muslims by virtue of the Treaty of Peace of Athens of 1913, the Treaty for the Protection of Minorities of Sèvres of 1920 and the Treaty of Peace of Lausanne of 1923.

B. The legislation on the muftis

[24] Law no. 2345/1920 provided that the muftis, in addition to their religious functions, had competence to adjudicate on family and inheritance disputes between Muslims to the extent that these disputes were governed by Islamic law. It also provided that the muftis were directly elected by the Muslims who had the right to vote in the national elections and who resided in the prefectoral district in which the muftis would serve. The elections were to be organised by the State and theological school graduates had the right to be candidates. Sec. 6 (8) of the Law provided for the promulgation of a royal decree to make detailed arrangements for the elections of the muftis.

[25] Such a decree was never promulgated. The State appointed a mufti in Rodopi in 1920 and another one in March 1935. In June 1935 a mufti *ad interim* was appointed by the State. In the course of the same year the State appointed a regular mufti. This mufti was replaced by another in 1941, when Bulgaria occupied Thrace. He was reappointed by the Greek State in 1944. In 1948 the Greek authorities appointed a mufti *ad interim* until 1949, when a regular mufti was appointed. The latter served until 1985, when he died.

[26] Under the legislative decree of 24 December 1990 the functions and qualifications of the muftis remain largely unchanged. However, provision is made for the appointment of the muftis by presidential decree following a proposal by the Minister of Education who, in turn, must consult a committee composed of the local prefect and a number of Muslim dignitaries chosen by the State. The legislative decree expressly abrogates Law no. 2345/1920 and provides that it should be ratified by law in accordance with art. 44 § 1 of the Constitution.

[27] Law no. 1920/1991 retroactively validated the legislative decree of 24 December 1990.

C. Legislative decrees under Art. 44 § 1 of the Constitution

[28] Art. 44 § 1 of the Constitution provides as follows:

> „In exceptional circumstances, when an extremely urgent and unforeseeable need arises, the President of the Republic may, on the proposal of the Council of Ministers, adopt legislative acts. These acts must be submitted to Parliament for approval ... within forty days ..."

D. Art. 175 and 176 of the Criminal Code

[29] Art. 175 of the Criminal Code provides as follows:

> „1. A person who intentionally usurps the functions of a State or municipal official shall be liable to a term of imprisonment not exceeding one year or a fine.
> 2. This provision also applies where a person usurps the functions of a lawyer or a minister of the Greek Orthodox Church or another known religion."

[30] The Court of Cassation considered that this provision applied in the case of a former priest of the Greek Orthodox Church who continued to wear the priests' robes (judgment no. 378/80). The priest in question had been defrocked after joining the Old Calendarists, a religious movement formed by Greek Orthodox priests who wanted the Church to maintain the Julian calendar. In judgment no. 454/66 the Court of Cassation considered that the offence in art. 175 of the Criminal Code was also committed by a person who purported to discharge the administrative functions of a priest. In judgments nos. 140/64 and 476/71 the Court of Cassation applied art. 175 of the Code to cases of persons who had purported to exercise the religious functions of an Orthodox priest by conducting services, „christening" children, etc.

[31] Art. 176 of the Criminal Code provides as follows:

> „A person who publicly wears the dress or the insignia of a State or municipal official or of a minister of a religion referred to in art. 175 § 2 without having the right to do so ... shall be liable to a term of imprisonment not exceeding six months or a fine."

E. The legislation on ministers of „known religions"

[32] Ministers of the Greek Orthodox Church and other „known religions" enjoy a number of privileges under domestic law. *Inter alia*, the religious weddings they celebrate produce the same legal effects as civil weddings and they are exempt from military service.

THE LAW

I. Alleged violation of Art. 9 of the Convention

[33] The applicant complained that his conviction amounted to a violation of art. 9 of the Convention, which provides as follows:

> „*1. Everyone has the right to freedom of thought, conscience and religion; this right includes freedom to change his religion or belief and freedom, either alone or in community with others and in public or private, to manifest his religion or belief, in worship, teaching, practice and observance.*
> *2. Freedom to manifest one's religion or beliefs shall be subject only to such limitations as are prescribed by law and are necessary in a democratic society in the interests of public safety, for the protection of public order, health or morals, or for the protection of the rights and freedoms of others.*"

[34] The Government denied that there had been any such breach. In their view, there had been no interference with the applicant's right to freedom of religion. Even if there had been an interference, the Government argued that it would have been justified under the second paragraph of art. 9 of the Convention.

[35] The Court must consider whether the applicant's art. 9 rights were interfered with and, if so, whether such interference was „prescribed by law", pursued a legitimate aim and was „necessary in a democratic society" within the meaning of art. 9 § 2 of the Convention.

A. Existence of an interference

[36] The applicant argued that his conviction amounted to an interference with his right to be free to exercise his religion together with all those who turned to him for spiritual guidance.

[37] The Government submitted that there had been no interference with the applicant's right to freedom of religion because art. 9 of the Convention did not guarantee for the applicant the right to impose on others his understanding as to Greece's obligations under the Treaty of Peace of Athens.

[38] The Court recalls that, while religious freedom is primarily a matter of individual conscience, it also includes, *inter alia*, freedom, in community with others and in public, to manifest one's religion in worship and teaching (see, *mutatis mutandis*, the Kokkinakis v. Greece judgment of 25 May 1993, Series A no. 260-A, p. 17, § 31; KirchE-EU S. 202).

[39] The Court further recalls that the applicant was convicted for having usurped the functions of a minister of a „known religion" and for having publicly worn the dress of such a minister without having the right to do so. The facts underlying the applicant's conviction, as they transpire from the relevant domestic court decisions, were issuing a message about

the religious significance of a feast, delivering a speech at a religious gathering, issuing another message on the occasion of a religious holiday and appearing in public wearing the dress of a religious leader. In these circumstances, the Court considers that the applicant's conviction amounts to an interference with his right under art. 9 § 1 of the Convention, „in community with others and in public ..., to manifest his religion ... in worship [and] teaching".

B. „Prescribed by law"

[40] The Government submitted that the applicant's conviction was provided by law, namely art. 175 and 176 of the Criminal Code. Given the manner in which these provisions had been interpreted by the courts, the outcome of the proceedings against the applicant was foreseeable. In the Government's view, the issue of whether the applicant's conviction was prescribed by law was not related to Law no. 2345 on the election of the muftis or the Treaty of Peace of Athens. In any event, the Government argued that Law no. 2345 had fallen into disuse. Moreover, the provisions of the Treaty of Peace of Athens, which had been concluded when Thrace was not part of Greece, became devoid of purpose after the compulsory exchange of populations in 1923. This was when Greece exchanged all the Muslims who were living on the territories in its possession when the Treaty of Peace of Athens had been concluded. In the alternative, the Government argued that the provisions of the Treaty of Peace of Athens had been superseded by the provisions of the Treaty of Sèvres for the Protection of Minorities in Greece and the Treaty of Peace of Lausanne, and these treaties made no provision for the election of the muftis.

[41] The applicant disagreed. He considered that the Treaty of Peace of Athens remained in force. The Greek Prime Minister had accepted that at the Diplomatic Conference leading to the 1923 Treaty of Peace of Lausanne. Moreover, the Court of Cassation had confirmed the continued validity of the Treaty of Peace of Athens and legal scholars held the same view. The Muslims had never accepted the abrogation of Law no. 2345.

[42] The Court does not consider it necessary to rule on the question whether the interference in issue was „prescribed by law" because, in any event, it is incompatible with art. 9 on other grounds (see the Manoussakis and Others v. Greece judgment of 26 September 1996, RJD 1996-IV, p. 1362, § 38; KirchE-EU S. 263).

C. Legitimate aim

[43] The Government argued that the interference served a legitimate purpose. By protecting the authority of the lawful mufti the domestic courts sought to preserve order in the particular religious community

and in society at large. They also sought to protect the international relations of the country, an area over which States exercise unlimited discretion.

[44] The applicant disagreed.

[45] The Court accepts that the interference in question pursued a legitimate aim under art. 9 § 2 of the Convention, namely „to protect public order". It notes in this connection that the applicant was not the only person claiming to be the religious leader of the local Muslim community. On 6 April 1990 the authorities had appointed another person as Mufti of Rodopi and the relevant decision had been challenged before the Supreme Administrative Court.

D. „Necessary in a democratic society"

[46] The Government submitted that the interference was necessary in a democratic society. In many countries, the muftis were appointed by the State. Moreover, muftis exercised important judicial functions in Greece and judges could not be elected by the people. As a result, the appointment of a mufti by the State could not in itself raise an issue under art. 9.

[47] Moreover, the Government submitted that the Court of Cassation had not convicted the applicant simply because he had appeared in public as the mufti. The court considered that the offence in art. 175 was made out where somebody actually discharged the functions of a religious minister. The court also considered that the acts that the applicant engaged in fell within the administrative functions of a mufti in the broad sense of the term. Given that there were two muftis in Rodopi at the time, the courts had to convict the spurious one in order to avoid the creation of tension among the Muslims, between the Muslims and Christians and between Turkey and Greece. The applicant had questioned the legality of the acts of the lawful mufti. In any event, the State had to protect the office of the mufti and, even if there had not existed a lawfully appointed mufti, the applicant would have had to be punished. Finally, the „election" of the applicant had been flawed because it had not been the result of a democratic procedure and the applicant had been used by the local Muslim MP for party political purposes.

[48] The applicant considered that his conviction was not necessary in a democratic society. He pointed out that the Christians and Jews in Greece had the right to elect their religious leaders. Depriving the Muslims of this possibility amounted to discriminatory treatment. The applicant further contended that the vast majority of Muslims in Thrace wanted him to be their mufti. Such an interference could not be justified in a democratic society, where the State should not interfere with individual choices in the field of personal conscience. His conviction was just

one aspect of the policy of repression applied by the Greek State *vis-à-vis* the Turkish-Muslim minority of western Thrace.

[49] The Court recalls that freedom of thought, conscience and religion is one of the foundations of a „democratic society" within the meaning of the Convention. The pluralism indissociable from a democratic society, which has been dearly won over the centuries, depends on it. It is true that in a democratic society it may be necessary to place restrictions on freedom of religion to reconcile the interests of the various religious groups (see the Kokkinakis judgment cited above, pp. 17 and 18, §§ 31 and 33; KirchE-EU S. 202). However, any such restriction must correspond to a „pressing social need" and must be „proportionate to the legitimate aim pursued" (see, among others, the Wingrove v. the United Kingdom judgment of 25 November 1996, RJD 1996-V, p. 1956, § 53; KirchE-EU S. 278).

[50] The Court also recalls that the applicant was convicted under art. 175 and 176 of the Criminal Code, which render criminal offences certain acts against ministers of „known religions". The Court notes in this connection that, although art. 9 of the Convention does not require States to give legal effect to religious weddings and religious courts' decisions, under Greek law weddings celebrated by ministers of „known religions" are assimilated to civil ones and the muftis have competence to adjudicate on certain family and inheritance disputes between Muslims. In such circumstances, it could be argued that it is in the public interest for the State to take special measures to protect from deceit those whose legal relationships can be affected by the acts of religious ministers. However, the Court does not consider it necessary to decide this issue, which does not arise in the applicant's case.

[51] The Court notes in this connection that, despite a vague assertion that the applicant had officiated at wedding ceremonies and engaged in administrative activities, the domestic courts that convicted him did not mention in their decisions any specific acts by the applicant with a view to producing legal effects. The domestic courts convicted the applicant on the following established facts: issuing a message about the religious significance of a feast, delivering a speech at a religious gathering, issuing another message on the occasion of a religious holiday and appearing in public in the dress of a religious leader. Moreover, it has not been disputed that the applicant had the support of at least part of the Muslim community in Rodopi. However, in the Court's view, punishing a person for merely acting as the religious leader of a group that willingly followed him can hardly be considered compatible with the demands of religious pluralism in a democratic society.

[52] The Court is not oblivious of the fact that in Rodopi there existed, in addition to the applicant, an officially appointed mufti. Moreover, the Government argued that the applicant's conviction was necessary in a democratic society because his actions undermined the system put in

place by the State for the organisation of the religious life of the Muslim community in the region. However, the Court recalls that there is no indication that the applicant attempted at any time to exercise the judicial and administrative functions for which the legislation on the muftis and other ministers of „known religions" makes provision. As for the rest, the Court does not consider that, in democratic societies, the State needs to take measures to ensure that religious communities remain or are brought under a unified leadership.

[53] It is true that the Government argued that, in the particular circumstances of the case, the authorities had to intervene in order to avoid the creation of tension among the Muslims in Rodopi and between the Muslims and the Christians of the area as well as Greece and Turkey. Although the Court recognises that it is possible that tension is created in situations where a religious or any other community becomes divided, it considers that this is one of the unavoidable consequences of pluralism. The role of the authorities in such circumstances is not to remove the cause of tension by eliminating pluralism, but to ensure that the competing groups tolerate each other (see, *mutatis mutandis*, the Plattform „Ärzte für das Leben" v. Austria judgment of 21 June 1988, Series A no. 139, p. 12, § 32). In this connection, the Court notes that, apart from a general reference to the creation of tension, the Government did not make any allusion to disturbances among the Muslims in Rodopi that had actually been or could have been caused by the existence of two religious leaders. Moreover, the Court considers that nothing was adduced that could warrant qualifying the risk of tension between the Muslims and Christians or between Greece and Turkey as anything more than a very remote possibility.

[54] In the light of all the above, the Court considers that it has not been shown that the applicant's conviction under art. 175 and 176 of the Criminal Code was justified in the circumstances of the case by „a pressing social need". As a result, the interference with the applicant's right, in community with others and in public, to manifest his religion in worship and teaching was not „necessary in a democratic society ..., for the protection of public order" under art. 9 § 2 of the Convention. There has, therefore, been a violation of art. 9 of the Convention.

II. Alleged violation of Art. 10 of the Convention

[55] The applicant complained that, since he had been convicted for certain statements he had made and for wearing certain clothes in public, there had also been a violation of art. 10 of the Convention, which provides as follows:

„*1. Everyone has the right to freedom of expression. This right shall include freedom to hold opinions and to receive and impart information and ideas without interference by public authority and regardless of frontiers ...*
2. The exercise of these freedoms, since it carries with it duties and responsibilities, may be subject to such formalities, conditions, restrictions or penalties as are prescribed by law and are necessary in a democratic society, in the interests of national security, territorial integrity or public safety, for the prevention of disorder or crime, for the protection of health or morals, for the protection of the reputation or rights of others, for preventing the disclosure of information received in confidence, or for maintaining the authority and impartiality of the judiciary."

[56] The Government argued that there had been no violation because the applicant had not been punished for expressing certain views but for usurping the functions of a mufti.

[57] Given its finding that there has been a violation of art. 9 of the Convention, the Court does not consider it necessary to examine whether art. 10 was also violated, because no separate issue arises under the latter provision.

III. Application of Art. 41 of the Convention

[58] Art. 41 of the Convention provides:

„*If the Court finds that there has been a violation of the Convention or the Protocols thereto, and if the internal law of the High Contracting Party concerned allows only partial reparation to be made, the Court shall, if necessary, afford just satisfaction to the injured party.*"

A. Damage

[59] The applicant claimed repayment of the fine he had paid as a result of his conviction, which was approximately 700,000 drachmas (GRD). He also claimed GRD 10,000,000 for non-pecuniary damage.

[60] The Government did not accept these claims.

[61] The Court recalls its finding that the applicant's conviction amounted to a violation of art. 9 of the Convention. It therefore awards the applicant as compensation for pecuniary damage the equivalent of the fine he had to pay, namely GRD 700,000. The Court further considers that, as a result of the above violation, the applicant has suffered non-pecuniary damage for which the finding in this judgment does not afford sufficient satisfaction. Making its assessment on an equitable basis, the Court awards the applicant GRD 2,000,000 in this respect.

B. Costs and expenses

[62] The applicant did not make any claim in respect of costs and expenses.

[63] The Court, having regard to the above and to the fact that the applicant had the benefit of legal aid in the proceedings before it, does not consider it appropriate to make an award in this connection.

C. Default interest (...)

For these reasons, the Court unanimously

1. *Holds that there has been a violation of art. 9 of the Convention;*
2. *Holds that no separate issue arises under art. 10 of the Convention;*
3. *Holds that the respondent State is to pay the applicant, within three months from the date on which the judgment becomes final according to art. 44 § 2 of the Convention, 2,700,000 drachmas for damage (...);*
4. *Dismisses the remainder of the applicant's claim for just satisfaction.*

52

Zur Frage der Zuständigkeit staatlicher Gerichte für die Überprüfung von Entscheidungen, die ein Gericht einer Religionsgemeinschaft (hier: Schieds- und Verwaltungsgericht beim Zentralrat der Juden in Deutschland) erlassen hat.

Art. 9, 35 § 3 EMRK
EGMR, Beschluss vom 23. März 2000 - No. 47021/99
(Kohn ./. Deutschland) -

EN FAIT

Le requérant est un ressortissant allemand, né en 1928 et résidant à Hanovre.

A. Circonstances particulières de l'affaire

Les faits de la cause, tels qu'ils ont été exposés par le requérant, peuvent se résumer comme suit.

Le requérant était membre du conseil d'administration (*Vorstand*) de la communauté juive de Hanovre jusqu'en 1995.

Des élections en vue de désigner les membres de ce conseil d'administration se déroulèrent en 1995 et le requérant fut l'un des candidats. A la suite d'un litige sur la remise de l'urne électorale, qui alla jusque devant la Cour fédérale de justice (*Bundesgerichtshof*), l'issue des élections ne fut finalement connue que le 22 avril 1998. Les nouveaux membres du conseil d'administration ainsi élus étaient M. Kune, Mme Kontsour et Mme Thierkopf, qui demandèrent alors en vain au requérant de restituer et de quitter les locaux qu'il avait occupés jusqu'alors en tant que membre du conseil d'administration.

Par une ordonnance de référé (*einstweilige Anordnung*) du 20 mai 1998, le tribunal d'arbitrage et administratif auprès du Consistoire central des juifs en Allemagne (*Schieds- und Verwaltungsgericht beim Zentralrat der Juden in Deutschland*) indiqua que les membres du conseil d'administration élus le 22 avril 1998 étaient désormais les seuls représentants de la communauté juive de Hanovre, et ce jusqu'à ce que le tribunal d'arbitrage rende sa décision dans cette affaire sur le fond, alors que le requérant ne l'était plus. Le tribunal d'arbitrage demanda également à ce dernier de restituer et de quitter immédiatement les locaux.

Le 26 mai 1998, le tribunal d'arbitrage déclara l'ordonnance immédiatement exécutoire et demanda à un huissier de procéder à son exécution, ce que ce dernier fit le 28 mai 1998.

Dans la nuit du 29 au 30 mai 1998, le requérant réintégra les locaux de la communauté juive de Hanovre et changea toutes les serrures.

Une nouvelle demande d'exécution échoua, car le 19 juin 1998, sur opposition du requérant, le tribunal d'instance (*Amtsgericht*) de Hanovre indiqua que la décision du tribunal d'arbitrage n'était pas exécutoire tant qu'elle n'avait pas été entérinée par les pouvoirs publics.

La communauté juive de Hanovre demanda donc au tribunal administratif (*Verwaltungsgericht*) de Hanovre de déclarer la décision du tribunal d'arbitrage exécutoire, mais sa demande échoua définitivement par une décision du 20 octobre 1998 de la cour administrative d'appel (*Oberverwaltungsgericht*).

La communauté juive de Hanovre, corporation de droit public (*Körperschaft des öffentlichen Rechts*), s'adressa alors au tribunal régional (*Landgericht*) de Hanovre, au motif qu'une voie de recours existait exceptionnellement auprès des juridictions civiles allemandes, car il s'agissait d'un droit à l'expulsion (*Räumung*) et à la restitution (*Herausgabe*) sur le terrain du droit civil de protection d'une possession (*zivilrechtlicher Besitzschutz*). La communauté juive serait empêchée, pour l'instant, de pratiquer sa religion et son culte, et c'est pourquoi il était urgent que l'ordonnance du tribunal d'arbitrage fût rendue exécutoire, afin d'éviter des dommages supplémentaires et la disparition d'éléments de preuve, car il y avait eu des malversations de la part des anciens membres du conseil d'administration.

Le requérant, quant à lui, fit valoir que les personnes nouvellement élues n'étaient pas les représentants légitimes de la communauté juive de Hanovre, car la décision du tribunal d'arbitrage méconnaissait l'ordre public et n'était pas valable. Par ailleurs, le tribunal régional n'était pas compétent pour statuer dans ce genre de litige.

Par un jugement du 2 décembre 1998, après avoir tenu une audience, le tribunal régional de Hanovre fit droit à la demande de la communauté juive de Hanovre et ordonna l'expulsion du requérant.

Le tribunal régional estima que la requête était recevable et qu'il était compétent pour statuer dans ce litige, étant donné qu'il s'agissait avant tout d'une ordonnance de référé pour „trouble de la possession" (*Besitzstörung*), alors que la question de la représentation légitime (*ordnungsgemäße Vertretung*) de la communauté juive n'était qu'une question préliminaire, qui avait été provisoirement clarifiée au sein de la communauté religieuse (*innerkirchlich*) par la décision du tribunal d'arbitrage. Le tribunal régional précisa que la communauté juive de Hanovre disposait d'un droit à l'évacuation des lieux en vertu des art. 861 et 858 du code civil, car la décision du tribunal d'arbitrage, d'après laquelle M. Kune et autres étaient provisoirement les seuls représentants légitimes de cette communauté, liait le tribunal. En effet, des mesures internes à une communauté religieuse (*innerkirchliche Maßnahmen*), comme la tenue d'élections, ne pouvaient être contrôlées par les tribunaux étatiques, car ces derniers devaient respecter l'autonomie des corporations religieuses (*Autonomie der Religionskörperschaften*). Cependant, le tribunal d'arbitrage ne pouvait lui-même faire exécuter la décision d'expulsion, et c'est pourquoi il devait s'adresser aux tribunaux étatiques, car l'Etat avait le monopole de l'utilisation de la force.

D'après le tribunal régional, en faisant droit à la demande de la communauté juive de Hanovre, il ne s'immisçait pas dans le droit à l'autonomie de cette dernière, qui était garanti par la Constitution, mais remplissait son devoir de protection (*Schutzpflicht*) à l'égard de la demanderesse et son devoir de rendre la justice (*Justizgewährungspflicht*) pour assurer l'exécution d'une décision prise au sein d'une communauté religieuse. Il n'y avait d'ailleurs pas d'indices indiquant que la décision ait méconnu l'ordre public.

Le tribunal régional ajouta que les conditions de l'art. 861 du code civil étaient réunies, eu égard au fait que le requérant s'était introduit de manière illégale (*im Wege verbotener Eigenmacht*) dans les locaux de la communauté juive dans la nuit du 29 au 30 juin 1998. Le requérant ne pouvait faire valoir que les représentants de cette communauté ne disposaient pas d'un droit de possession, car il n'avait pas lui-même respecté la décision du tribunal d'arbitrage, sans contester la compétence de ce dernier. D'après le tribunal régional, les conditions de l'art. 940 du code de procédure civile étaient également réunies, car la communauté religieuse, par le biais de la déclaration sous serment de son représentant, M. Kune, avait indiqué qu'en raison de l'occupation des locaux, elle n'était pas en mesure de pratiquer sa religion et son culte, et qu'il y avait un danger de disparition d'éléments de preuve.

Par une lettre adressée par télécopie au tribunal régional le 7 décembre 1998, M. Sichrovsky, membre du Parlement européen au titre du parti libéral autrichien (FPÖ - Freiheitliche Partei Österreichs) et président de l'Association des communautés juives, fidèles à la loi, en Allemagne (*Bund gesetzestreuer jüdischer Gemeinden in Deutschland*) informa celui-ci que le tribunal rabbinique (*Rabbinatsgericht*) BEIT DIN avait décidé le 6 décembre 1998 que les anciens membres du conseil d'administration, dont le requérant faisait partie, étaient les seuls représentants légitimes de la communauté juive de Hanovre. Il ajouta que le tribunal rabbinique avait annulé la décision du 20 mai 1998 du tribunal d'arbitrage. D'après M. Sichrovsky, la communauté juive de Hanovre n'était pas soumise à la juridiction de ce tribunal d'arbitrage, car le tribunal rabbinique, en tant qu'organe suprême en matière de litiges de nature religieuse ou juridique au sein de la communauté juive, avait relevé que la décision du tribunal d'arbitrage avait méconnu les principes fondamentaux de la doctrine religieuse et juridique juive et qu'elle devait donc être annulée.

Par une décision du 11 janvier 1999, la Cour constitutionnelle fédérale (*Bundesverfassungsgericht*), statuant en comité de trois membres, rejeta la demande du requérant quant à la suspension de la mesure d'exécution décidée par le tribunal régional.

La Cour constitutionnelle rappela tout d'abord que la question de savoir à quelles conditions des personnes peuvent se présenter à des élections au sein d'une communauté religieuse relevait de l'organisation interne de celle-ci. En l'espèce, le tribunal d'arbitrage avait tranché provisoirement la question de savoir qui étaient les représentants légitimes de la communauté juive de Hanovre, par ses ordonnances des 20 et 26 mai 1998, et avait également demandé l'expulsion du requérant des locaux. Or, conformément à l'art. 140 de la Loi fondamentale (*Grundgesetz*) combiné avec l'art. 137 de la Constitution de la République de Weimar, les juridictions civiles n'avaient pas à contrôler ces décisions internes à la communauté religieuse.

Par un arrêt du 17 février 1999, la cour d'appel (*Oberlandesgericht*) de Celle rejeta le recours du requérant et confirma le jugement du tribunal régional pour les mêmes motifs.

Le 23 mars 1999, le conseil du requérant saisit la Cour européenne des Droits de l'Homme afin qu'elle demande aux autorités allemandes de surseoir à l'exécution de la mesure d'expulsion, prévue pour le 25 mars 1999, conformément à l'art. 39 du règlement de la Cour. D'après lui, la décision d'expulsion des juridictions allemandes reposait sur une décision illégale du tribunal d'arbitrage, et il soumit une attestation d'un psychiatre indiquant que le requérant, survivant de l'holocauste, risquait de subir de dommages psychiques irréparables en cas d'expulsion.

Le même jour, le président de la quatrième section décida de ne pas appliquer l'art. 39 du règlement.

B. Droit interne pertinent

L'art. 140 de la Loi fondamentale combiné avec l'art. 137 de la Constitution de la République de Weimar garantit la liberté de religion et l'indépendance des corporations religieuses en Allemagne.

GRIEFS

1. Le requérant soutient qu'il est le seul représentant de la communauté juive de Hanovre et que son expulsion des locaux de cette communauté, suite à la décision du tribunal d'arbitrage auprès du consistoire central des juifs en Allemagne, a méconnu son droit à la liberté de religion et à l'indépendance des communautés religieuses par rapport à l'Etat garanti à l'art. 9 de la Convention.

2. Il se plaint également de ce que les tribunaux allemands n'ont pas pris en compte le fait que le tribunal rabbinique BEIT-DIN était le seul tribunal compétent pour trancher ce genre de litige.

3. Il allègue également une atteinte à sa dignité contraire à l'art. 3 de la Convention.

EN DROIT

1. Le requérant soutient qu'il est le seul représentant légitime de la communauté juive de Hanovre et que son expulsion des locaux de cette communauté, suite à la décision du tribunal d'arbitrage auprès du consistoire central des juifs en Allemagne, a méconnu son droit à la liberté de religion et à l'indépendance des communautés religieuses par rapport à l'Etat garanti à l'art. 9 de la Convention, ainsi libellé:

„1. Toute personne a droit à la liberté de pensée, de conscience et de religion; ce droit implique la liberté de changer de religion ou de conviction, ainsi que la liberté de manifester sa religion ou sa conviction individuellement ou collectivement, en public ou en privé, par le culte, l'enseignement, les pratiques et l'accomplissement des rites.
2. La liberté de manifester sa religion ou ses convictions ne peut faire l'objet d'autres restrictions que celles qui, prévues par la loi, constituent des mesures nécessaires, dans une société démocratique, à la sécurité publique, à la protection de l'ordre, de la santé ou de la morale publiques, ou à la protection des droits et libertés d'autrui."

Le requérant reproche aux juridictions allemandes une ingérence dans les affaires internes de la communauté juive de Hanovre, car ces dernières ont exécuté une décision illégale du tribunal d'arbitrage, alors que le seul tribunal compétent pour trancher ce genre de litige était le tribunal rabbinique BEIT DIN.

La Cour rappelle que, d'après la jurisprudence des organes de la Convention, l'intervention de l'Etat dans l'organisation d'une communauté religieuse ou dans la gestion de leurs biens peut constituer une ingérence dans les droits protégés par l'art. 9 de la Convention (voir notamment le rapport de la Commission du 26 octobre 2000, requête n° 30985/96, § 81; KirchE-EU S. 444).

En l'espèce cependant, la Cour estime qu'il n'y a pas eu ingérence de l'Etat dans les droits du requérant protégés par cet article.

En effet, comme l'a précisé la Cour constitutionnelle fédérale, les tribunaux allemands ont au contraire souligné qu'il ne leur appartenait pas de s'immiscer dans les affaires internes de la communauté juive de Hanovre, en vertu du principe de l'autonomie des corporations religieuses inscrit dans la Loi fondamentale, et ils ont simplement pris acte de la décision du tribunal d'arbitrage auprès du Consistoire central des juifs en Allemagne désignant les représentants légitimes de cette communauté. Les tribunaux allemands ont ensuite procédé à l'exécution d'une décision prise par ce tribunal en vertu du droit civil allemand, et là aussi, ils n'avaient pas à vérifier le bien-fondé de cette décision interne à la communauté.

Il s'ensuit que ce grief est manifestement mal fondé au sens de l'art. 35 § 3 de la Convention.

2. *(Verletzung der Art. 3 und 6 EMRK wird geprüft und verneint)*

Par ces motifs, la Cour, à l'unanimité, déclare la requête irrecevable.

53

Die Gewährleistung von Religionsfreiheit verbietet es, eine Zugangssperre für bestimmte Berufe wegen Vorstrafen auch auf Bewerber anzuwenden, die aufgrund ihrer religiösen Überzeugung bestraft worden sind (hier: Zugang zum Beruf eines vereidigten Wirtschaftsprüfers für einen Zeugen Jehovas, der wegen eines wehrstrafrechtlichen Delikts belangt worden war).

Art. 9, 14 EMRK
EGMR, Urteil vom 6. April 2000 - No. 34369/97
(Thlimmenos ./. Griechenland)[1] -

---

[1] CEDH/ECHR 2000-IV.

THE FACTS

I. The circumstances of the case

A. The applicant's conviction for insubordination

[1] On 9 December 1983 the Athens Permanent Army Tribunal (*Diarkes Stratodikio*), composed of one career military judge and four other officers, convicted the applicant, a Jehovah's Witness, of insubordination for having refused to wear the military uniform at a time of general mobilisation. However, the tribunal considered under art. 70 (b) of the Military Criminal Code and under art. 84 § 2 (a) of the Criminal Code that there were extenuating circumstances and sentenced the applicant to four years' imprisonment. The applicant was released on parole after two years and one day.

B. The refusal to appoint the applicant to a chartered accountant's post

[2] In June 1988 the applicant sat a public examination for the appointment of twelve chartered accountants, a liberal profession in Greece. He came second among sixty candidates. However, on 8 February 1989 the Executive Board of the Greek Institute of Chartered Accountants (hereinafter „the Board") refused to appoint him on the ground that he had been convicted of a serious crime (*kakuryima*).

C. The proceedings before the Supreme Administrative Court

[3] On 8 May 1989 the applicant seised the Supreme Administrative Court (*Simvulio Epikratias*) invoking, *inter alia*, his right to freedom of religion and equality before the law, as guaranteed by the Constitution and the Convention. The applicant also claimed that he had not been convicted of a crime but of a less serious offence.

[4] On 18 April 1991 the Third Chamber of the Supreme Administrative Court held a hearing. On 25 May 1991 it decided to refer the case to the plenary court because of the important issues it raised. The Chamber's own view was that art. 10 of Legislative Decree no. 3329/1955 provided that a person who would not qualify for appointment to the civil service could not be appointed a chartered accountant. Moreover, according to art. 22 § 1 of the Civil Servants' Code, no person convicted of a serious crime could be appointed to the civil service. However, this provision referred to convictions by courts established in accordance with art. 87 § 1 of the Constitution. This was not the case with the permanent military courts, because the majority of their members were not career judges enjoying the same guarantees of independence as their civilian

colleagues, as envisaged by art. 96 § 5 of the Constitution. As a result, the applicant's conviction by the Athens Permanent Army Tribunal could not be taken into consideration and the Board's decision not to appoint the applicant a chartered accountant had to be quashed.

[5] On 21 January 1994 a hearing was held before the Supreme Administrative Court, sitting in plenary. On 11 November 1994 the court decided that the Board had acted in accordance with the law when, for the purposes of applying art. 22 § 1 of the Civil Servants' Code, it had taken into consideration the applicant's conviction for serious crime by the Athens Permanent Army Tribunal. Art. 96 § 5 of the Constitution provided that the military courts would continue functioning as they had before until the enactment of a new law which would change their composition. Such a law had not yet been enacted. The Supreme Administrative Court further decided to refer the case back to the Third Chamber and ordered it to examine the remaining issues.

[6] The decision of 11 November 1994 was taken by a majority. The minority considered that, since nine years had passed since the Constitution had entered into force without the law envisaged in art. 96 § 5 thereof having been enacted, the guarantees of independence required from civilian judges had to be afforded by the existing military courts. Since that was not the case with the Athens Permanent Army Tribunal, Mr Thlimmenos's application for judicial review had to be allowed.

[7] On 26 October 1995 the Third Chamber held a further hearing. On 28 June 1996 it rejected Mr Thlimmenos's application for judicial review, considering, *inter alia*, that the Board's failure to appoint him was not related to his religious beliefs but to the fact that he had committed a criminal offence.

II. Relevant domestic law

A. Appointment to a chartered accountant's post

[8] Until 30 April 1993 only members of the Greek Institute of Chartered Accountants could provide chartered accountants' services in Greece.

[9] Art. 10 of Legislative Decree no. 3329/1955, as amended by art. 5 of Presidential Decree no. 15/1989, provided that a person who did not qualify for appointment to the civil service could not be appointed a chartered accountant.

[10] According to art. 22 § 1 of the Civil Servants' Code, no person convicted of a serious crime can be appointed to the civil service.

[11] On 30 April 1993 the monopoly of the Institute of Chartered Accountants was abolished. Most chartered accountants became members of the Chartered Auditors' Company Ltd.

B. The criminal offence of insubordination

[12] Art. 70 of the Military Criminal Code in force until 1995 provided:

> "*A member of the armed forces who, having been ordered by his commander to perform a duty, refuses or fails to execute the order shall be punished -*
> *(a) if the act is committed in front of the enemy or armed insurgents, with death;*
> *(b) in times of war or armed insurgency or during a state of siege or general mobilisation, with death or, if there are extenuating circumstances, with life imprisonment or imprisonment of at least five years and*
> *(c) in all other circumstances, with imprisonment between six months and two years.*"

[13] By virtue of Presidential Decree no. 506/1974, at the time of the applicant's arrest Greece was deemed to be in a state of general mobilisation. This decree is still in force.

[14] Art. 84 § 2 (a) of the Criminal Code provides that a lesser penalty shall be imposed on persons who, prior to the crime, had led an honest life.

[15] Under art. 1 of the Military Criminal Code in force until 1995, offences punishable with a sentence of at least five years' imprisonment were considered to be serious crimes (*kakuryimata*). Offences punishable with a sentence of up to five years' imprisonment were considered misdemeanours (*plimmelimata*).

[16] Under the new Military Criminal Code of 1995 insubordination not committed in time of war or in front of the enemy is considered a misdemeanour.

C. The right to conscientious objection to military service

[17] Under sec. 2 (4) of Law no. 731/1977, those who refused to perform unarmed military service on the basis of their religious beliefs were sentenced to imprisonment of a duration equivalent to that of the unarmed service, that is, less than five years.

[18] Law no. 2510/1997, which entered into force on 27 June 1997, gives conscientious objectors the right to perform civilian, instead of military, service. Under sec. 23 (1) and (4) of this law, persons who had been convicted of insubordination in the past were given the possibility of applying for recognition as conscientious objectors. One of the effects of such recognition was having the conviction expunged from one's criminal record.

[19] Applications under sec. 23 (1) and (4) of Law no. 2510/1997 had to be lodged within a period of three months starting from 1 January 1998. They were examined by the commission that advises the Minister of National Defence on the recognition of conscientious objectors. The commission had to apply sec. 18 of Law no. 2510/1997, which provides:

„*Persons who invoke their religious or ideological beliefs in order not to fulfil their military obligations for reasons of conscience may be recognised as conscientious objectors ...*"

THE LAW

I. Scope of the case

[20] In his original application to the Commission the applicant had complained under art. 9 and 14 of the Convention about the failure of the authorities to appoint him to a post of chartered accountant and under art. 6 § 1 about the proceedings he had instituted in this connection. Only in his observations in reply to the Government's observations on the admissibility and merits of the application did the applicant also complain of a violation of art. 1 of Protocol No. 1. The Commission declared the latter complaint inadmissible on the ground that it had not been submitted within the six-month time-limit provided by the Convention.

[21] In his memorial before the Court the applicant contended that the Court was competent to examine his complaint under art. 1 of Protocol No. 1. Although this complaint had not been expressly raised in the application form, the facts underlying it had been set out therein. The Convention organs were free to give them the proper legal qualification.

[22] The Court recalls that the scope of its jurisdiction is determined by the Commission's decision declaring the originating application admissible (see *Sürek v. Turkey (no. 1)* [GC], no. 26682/95, § 40, ECHR 1999-IV). Moreover, it considers, as the Commission did, that the complaint under art. 1 of Protocol No. 1 was separate from the complaints declared admissible. It follows that the Court has no jurisdiction to entertain this complaint.

II. The Government's Preliminary Objection

(wird zurückweisend beschieden)

III. Alleged violation of Art. 14 of the convention taken in conjunction with Art. 9

[23] The Court notes that the applicant did not complain about his initial conviction for insubordination. The applicant complained that the law excluding persons convicted of a serious crime from appointment to a chartered accountant's post did not distinguish between persons convicted as a result of their religious beliefs and persons convicted on other grounds. The applicant invoked art. 14 of the Convention taken in conjunction with art. 9, which provide:

Art. 14

„*The enjoyment of the rights and freedoms set forth in [the] Convention shall be secured without discrimination on any ground such as sex, race, colour, language, religion, political or other opinion, national or social origin, association with a national minority, property, birth or other status.*"

Art. 9

„*1. Everyone has the right to freedom of thought, conscience and religion; this right includes freedom to change his religion or belief and freedom, either alone or in community with others and in public or private, to manifest his religion or belief, in worship, teaching, practice and observance.*

2. Freedom to manifest one's religion or beliefs shall be subject only to such limitations as are prescribed by law and are necessary in a democratic society in the interests of public safety, for the protection of public order, health or morals, or for the protection of the rights and freedoms of others."

A. Arguments before the Court

[24] The applicant submitted that his non-appointment to a post of chartered accountant was directly linked to the manifestation of his religious beliefs and fell within the ambit of art. 9 of the Convention. He pointed out in this connection that he had not been appointed because he had refused to serve in the armed forces; by refusing to do so, he had manifested his religious beliefs as a Jehovah's Witness. The applicant further argued that it could not serve any useful purpose to exclude someone from the profession of chartered accountants for having refused to serve in the armed forces on religious grounds. In the applicant's view, the law should not have excluded every person convicted of a serious crime. The legitimacy of the exclusion depended on the nature of the post and of the offence, including the motives of the offender, the time elapsed since the offence and the offender's conduct during that time. Seen in this light, the authorities' failure to appoint the applicant was not necessary. The class of persons to which the applicant belonged, namely male Jehovah's Witnesses whose religion involved compelling reasons for refusing to serve in the armed forces, was different from the class of most other criminal offenders. The Government's failure to take account of this difference amounted to discrimination not tolerated by art. 14 of the Convention taken in conjunction with art. 9.

[25] The Government argued that art. 14 of the Convention did not apply because the facts of the case did not fall within the ambit of art. 9. The authorities that refused to appoint the applicant a chartered accountant had no option but to apply a rule that excluded all persons convicted of a serious crime from such a post. The authorities could not inquire into the reasons that had led to a person's conviction. Because of its generality, the law in question was neutral. Moreover, it served the public interest. A person convicted of a serious offence could not be appointed to the civil service and, by extension, to a post of chartered accountant.

This prohibition had to be absolute and no distinction could be made on a case-by-case basis. States had a wide margin of appreciation in the characterisation of criminal offences as serious crimes or otherwise. The applicant had committed a serious offence by refusing to perform unarmed military service at a time of general mobilisation because he had tried to avoid a very important obligation towards society and the State, linked with the defence, safety and independence of the country. As a result, the sanction was not disproportionate.

[26] The Government also stressed that the Court had no competence to examine the applicant's initial conviction. In any event, this had nothing to do with his religious beliefs. The obligation to do military service applied to all Greek males without any exceptions on grounds of religion or conscience. Moreover, the applicant had been convicted of insubordination. Discipline in the army could not be made to depend on whether a soldier agreed with the orders given to him.

[27] In the light of all the above, the Government argued that, even if art. 14 applied, there would exist an objective and reasonable justification for the failure to distinguish between the applicant and other persons convicted of a serious crime. There was no need to point out that Greek Orthodox or Catholic Christians would also be excluded from the profession of chartered accountants if they had committed a serious crime.

[28] The Commission considered that art. 14 applied because it was sufficient that the facts of the case fell within the ambit of art. 9, and, in its opinion, there had been an interference with the rights protected by that article in the present case. The Commission further considered that the right not to be discriminated against in the enjoyment of the rights guaranteed under the Convention was violated not only when States treated differently persons in analogous situations without providing an objective and reasonable justification, but also when States, without an objective and reasonable justification, failed to treat differently persons whose situations were different. In the circumstances of the case, there was no objective and reasonable justification for the failure of the drafters of the rules governing access to the profession of chartered accountants to treat differently persons convicted for refusing to serve in the armed forces on religious grounds from persons convicted of other serious crimes.

B. The Court's assessment

[29] The Court considers that the applicant's complaint falls to be examined under art. 14 of the Convention taken in conjunction with art. 9 for the following reasons.

[30] The Court recalls that art. 14 of the Convention has no independent existence, since it has effect solely in relation to the rights and free-

doms safeguarded by the other substantive provisions of the Convention and its Protocols. However, the application of art. 14 does not presuppose a breach of one or more of such provisions and to this extent it is autonomous. For art. 14 to become applicable it suffices that the facts of a case fall within the ambit of another substantive provision of the Convention or its Protocols (see the Inze v. Austria judgment of 28 October 1987, Series A no. 126, p. 17, § 36).

[31] The Court notes that the applicant was not appointed a chartered accountant as a result of his past conviction for insubordination consisting in his refusal to wear the military uniform. He was thus treated differently from the other persons who had applied for that post on the ground of his status as a convicted person. The Court considers that such difference of treatment does not generally come within the scope of art. 14 in so far as it relates to access to a particular profession, the right to freedom of profession not being guaranteed by the Convention.

[32] However, the applicant does not complain of the distinction that the rules governing access to the profession make between convicted persons and others. His complaint rather concerns the fact that in the application of the relevant law no distinction is made between persons convicted of offences committed exclusively because of their religious beliefs and persons convicted of other offences. In this context the Court notes that the applicant is a member of the Jehovah's Witnesses, a religious group committed to pacifism, and that there is nothing in the file to disprove the applicant's claim that he refused to wear the military uniform only because he considered that his religion prevented him from doing so. In essence, the applicant's argument amounts to saying that he is discriminated against in the exercise of his freedom of religion, as guaranteed by art. 9 of the Convention, in that he was treated like any other person convicted of a serious crime although his own conviction resulted from the very exercise of this freedom. Seen in this perspective, the Court accepts that the „set of facts" complained of by the applicant - his being treated as a person convicted of a serious crime for the purposes of an appointment to a chartered accountant's post despite the fact that the offence for which he had been convicted was prompted by his religious beliefs - „falls within the ambit of a Convention provision", namely art. 9.

[33] In order to reach this conclusion, the Court, as opposed to the Commission, does not find it necessary to examine whether the applicant's initial conviction and the authorities' subsequent refusal to appoint him amounted to interference with his rights under art. 9 § 1. In particular, the Court does not have to address, in the present case, the question whether, notwithstanding the wording of art. 4 § 3 (b), the imposition of such sanctions on conscientious objectors to compulsory military service may in itself infringe the right to freedom of thought, conscience and religion guaranteed by art. 9 § 1.

[34] The Court has so far considered that the right under art. 14 not to be discriminated against in the enjoyment of the rights guaranteed under the Convention is violated when States treat differently persons in analogous situations without providing an objective and reasonable justification (see the Inze judgment cited above, p. 18, § 41). However, the Court considers that this is not the only facet of the prohibition of discrimination in art. 14. The right not to be discriminated against in the enjoyment of the rights guaranteed under the Convention is also violated when States without an objective and reasonable justification fail to treat differently persons whose situations are significantly different.

[35] It follows that art. 14 of the Convention is of relevance to the applicant's complaint and applies in the circumstances of this case in conjunction with art. 9 thereof.

[36] The next question to be addressed is whether art. 14 of the Convention has been complied with. According to its case-law, the Court will have to examine whether the failure to treat the applicant differently from other persons convicted of a serious crime pursued a legitimate aim. If it did the Court will have to examine whether there was a reasonable relationship of proportionality between the means employed and the aim sought to be realised (see the Inze judgment cited above, ibid.).

[37] The Court considers that, as a matter of principle, States have a legitimate interest to exclude some offenders from the profession of chartered accountant. However, the Court also considers that, unlike other convictions for serious criminal offences, a conviction for refusing on religious or philosophical grounds to wear the military uniform cannot imply any dishonesty or moral turpitude likely to undermine the offender's ability to exercise this profession. Excluding the applicant on the ground that he was an unfit person was not, therefore, justified. The Court takes note of the Government's argument that persons who refuse to serve their country must be appropriately punished. However, it also notes that the applicant did serve a prison sentence for his refusal to wear the military uniform. In these circumstances, the Court considers that imposing a further sanction on the applicant was disproportionate. It follows that the applicant's exclusion from the profession of chartered accountants did not pursue a legitimate aim. As a result, the Court finds that there existed no objective and reasonable justification for not treating the applicant differently from other persons convicted of a serious crime.

[38] It is true that the authorities had no option under the law but to refuse to appoint the applicant a chartered accountant. However, contrary to what the Government's representative appeared to argue at the hearing, this cannot absolve the respondent State from responsibility under the Convention. The Court has never excluded that legislation may be found to be in direct breach of the Convention (see, *inter alia, Chassagnou and Others v. France* [GC], nos. 25088/94, 28331/95 and

28443/95, ECHR 1999-III). In the present case the Court considers that it was the State having enacted the relevant legislation which violated the applicant's right not to be discriminated against in the enjoyment of his right under art. 9 of the Convention. That State did so by failing to introduce appropriate exceptions to the rule barring persons convicted of a serious crime from the profession of chartered accountants.

[39] The Court concludes, therefore, that there has been a violation of art. 14 of the Convention taken in conjunction with art. 9.

IV. Alleged violation of Art. 9 of the convention

[40] The applicant argued that both his initial conviction for insubordination and the authorities' resultant refusal to appoint him as a chartered accountant constituted interference with his right to manifest his religious beliefs under art. 9 of the Convention. The Commission's case-law to the effect that the Convention did not guarantee the right to conscientious objection to military service had to be reviewed in the light of present-day conditions. Virtually all Contracting States now recognised the right to alternative civilian service. Although the Court was admittedly not competent to examine the interference arising out of the applicant's initial conviction, the applicant submitted that the interference arising out of his non-appointment could not be deemed necessary in a democratic society.

[41] The Government argued that the authorities' refusal to appoint the applicant did not constitute an interference with his right under art. 9 of the Convention. In any event, it was necessary in a democratic society. At the time when the applicant refused to serve in the armed forces, Greek law only recognised the possibility of unarmed military service because it was considered that giving everybody the right to alternative civilian service could give rise to abuses. As a result, the sanction imposed on him was not disproportionate and the rule excluding persons convicted of a serious crime from certain positions had to be applied without any distinctions.

[42] The Commission did not consider it necessary to address the issue.

[43] The Court considers that, since it has found a breach of art. 14 of the Convention taken in conjunction with art. 9 and for the reasons set out in par. 43 above, it is not necessary also to consider whether there has been a violation of art. 9 taken on its own.

V. Alleged violation of Art. 6 § 1 of the convention

[44] The applicant also complained that the length of the proceedings he instituted before the Supreme Administrative Court to challenge his non-appointment gave rise to a violation of art. 6 § 1 of the Convention, the relevant part of which provides:

„In the determination of his civil rights and obligations ..., everyone is entitled to a ... hearing within a reasonable time by [a] ... tribunal ..."

(...)

[45] The Court concludes, therefore, that there has been a violation of art. 6 § 1 of the Convention

VI. Application of Art. 41 of the convention (...)

For these reasons, the court unanimously
1. *Dismisses the Government's preliminary objection;*
2. *Holds that there has been a violation of art. 14 of the Convention taken in conjunction with art. 9;*
3. *Holds that it is not necessary to examine whether there has been a violation of art. 9 of the Convention taken on its own;*
4. *Holds that there has been a violation of art. 6 § 1 of the Convention;*
5. *Holds*
   (a) that the respondent State is to pay the applicant, within three months, the following amounts:
   (i) GRD 6,000,000 for non-pecuniary damage;
   (ii) ... (Kosten und Auslagen);
   (b) ... (Zinsen)
6. *Dismisses the remainder of the applicant's claim for just satisfaction.*

54

Der Staat ist nicht gehindert, im öffentlichen Schulwesens in objektiver, kritischer und pluralistischer Weise auch Informationen und Kenntnisse, die religiöse Sachverhalte berühren (hier: Sexualkundeunterricht), zu vermitteln. Er hat dabei das Recht der Eltern auf Erziehung ihres Kindes nach den eigenen religiösen oder weltanschaulichen Vorstellungen zu respektieren. Diese Gewährleistung des elterlichen Erziehungsrechts begründet - insbesondere in Anbetracht wählbarer Privatschulen - im Bereich des öffentlichen Schulwesens keinen Anspruch auf eine unterschiedliche erzieherische Behandlung der Schüler nach Maßgabe der religiösen oder weltanschaulichen Vorstellungen ihrer Eltern.

Art. 14, 27 § 3 EMRK, 2 Erstes Zusatzprotokoll
EGMR, Beschluss vom 25. Mai 2000 - No. 51188/99
(Jiménez u.a. ./. Spanien) -

THE FACTS

The applicants [Mr Alejandro Jiménez Alonso and Pilar Jiménez Merino] are two Spanish nationals, born in 1948 and 1983 respectively. They live in Lamadrid (Santander Province). The first applicant is the father of the second applicant.

A. The circumstances of the case

During the school year 1996-97 the second applicant, Pilar Jiménez Merino, then aged 13-14, was in the eighth year of compulsory primary and secondary education (*Enseñanza General Obligatoria*) in a state school of Treceño, a village situated in a rural area of the Cantabria region. The first applicant, her father, was a teacher at the school and her personal tutor during that school year.

In May 1997, towards the end of the school year, the Natural Sciences teacher held classes on human sexuality as part of the „Vital Functions" syllabus. As a teaching aid, the teacher distributed to the pupils a 42-page booklet from a publication edited in 1994 by the Department of Education of the Autonomous Government of the Canary Islands. The booklet in question comprised the following chapters:

„Concept of sexuality";
„We are sexual beings";
„Body awareness and sexual development";
„Fertilisation, pregnancy and childbirth";
„Contraception and abortion";
„Sexually transmitted diseases and Aids".

Those chapters included comprehension questions and basic terminology.

The first applicant, who considered that the contents of the booklet went well beyond the scope of Natural Sciences and contained actual guidelines on sexuality which were contrary to his moral and religious convictions, informed the headmaster of the school that his daughter would not be attending the sex education classes. He referred, in his capacity as parent, to his constitutional right to choose his daughter's moral education. The second applicant did not attend the classes in question and refused to answer the questions when she sat the final examination in the subject. Consequently, she failed the examination and had to repeat the school year. The first applicant then lodged an administrative application with the Ministry of Education and Culture. In a decision of 22 July 1997, the provincial director of the Ministry rejected the application. On 12 December 1997 the applicant lodged a special appeal for protection of fundamental rights with the High Court of Justice (Administrative Division) of Cantabria. He complained, *inter alia*, of the lack of consultation with parents regarding the content of the sex education classes; of the clearly moral component of the course; of an infringement of his right to freedom of choice of education guaranteed by art. 27 § 3 of the Constitution; of an infringement of the principle of non-discrimination proclaimed by art. 14; and an infringement of the right to freedom of religion and thought laid down in art. 16 of the Constitution.

In a judgment delivered on 23 March 1997, after a hearing in which both parties had made submissions, the Cantabria High Court of Justice dismissed the appeal. It held that the Ministry's decision had been in conformity with the fundamental rights enshrined in the Constitution. Referring to various applicable international provisions, such as Protocol No. 1 to the European Convention on Human Rights, the UNESCO Convention of 14 December 1960 against Discrimination in Education, the 1989 Convention on the Rights of the Child and the case-law of the Constitutional Court, the court held, *inter alia,*:

„... The right of parents to provide their children with an education in accordance with their convictions presupposes, in a pluralist society, the right to choose, that right being linked to the freedom to establish schools so that parents can choose one adapted to their beliefs and ideas. However, that does not presuppose, nor can it presuppose, the right to impose one's personal convictions on others or to request different treatment in accordance with such convictions.

... The enunciation of respect for personal convictions, in the form of the right to freely choose a school, derives from and is based on certain legal provisions and statements of the Constitutional Court and the Supreme Court.

... Sec. 4 of Institutional Act 8/1985 of 3 July on the right to education states: „parents or guardians shall be entitled, in accordance with the legal provisions:

(a) to provide their children ... with an education in conformity with the aims laid down in the Constitution and the present Act.

(b) to choose a different school from those set up by the public authorities.

(c) to provide ... their children with religious and moral education in conformity with their own convictions."

There is, accordingly, a clear legal link between the right to choose a different school from those set up by the public authorities and the right to an education in conformity with one's own convictions.

...

In conclusion, the right of parents to educate their children in accordance with their own moral, religious and ideological convictions is not an absolute right, but must be determined in relation to the rights which the Constitution guarantees to other partners in the educational community, so that it is not fair to attempt to impose a difference of treatment or positive discrimination on the basis of one's own ideas, or to choose or predetermine, on the basis of one's particular ideas, the contents of a school curriculum in a state establishment, since the right to a particular type of education is ensured by means of the right to establish [private] schools; the latter can offer a special curriculum, unlike the position in state schools in a pluralist State, and parents have the right to choose the type of education which they wish their children to receive."

The first applicant lodged an *amparo* appeal against that judgment with the Constitutional Court. He relied on art. 27 § 3 (right of parents to choose their children's religious and moral education), 14 (principle of non-discrimination) and 24 (right to a fair trial) of the Constitution. In a decision of 11 March 1999, the Constitutional Court declared the appeal inadmissible on the ground that it was manifestly ill-founded, for the following reasons:

> *„Art.* 27 *of the Spanish Constitution recognises rights in favour of all those who participate in the education system, which presupposes that, in the event of dispute, a balance has to be struck between the different interests in issue. In the instant case, the trial court adequately weighed the various conflicting interests while stressing that state education was involved. In the context of that type of education, ideological neutrality has to be preserved, as the court affirmed ... In the instant case, neutrality was preserved, with the result that the trial court's decision was neither arbitrary nor absurd and thus cannot be reviewed in amparo proceedings. ... Nor has there been an infringement of the principle of equality laid down in art. 14 since no relevant term of comparison has been submitted in support of the appeal."*

B. Relevant domestic law

The Constitution

Art. 27
„1. Everyone has a right to education. The freedom of teaching is hereby recognised.
2. The purpose of education is the full development of the human personality in a manner consistent with the democratic principles of coexistence and fundamental rights and freedoms.
3. The public authorities shall guarantee the right of parents to provide their children with a religious and moral education in accordance with their own convictions.
...
6. Natural and legal persons shall have the right to set up teaching institutions in a manner consistent with constitutional principles.
...
9. The public authorities shall assist teaching institutions satisfying the conditions established by law.
..."

Institutional Law 1/1999 of 3 October on the General Planning of the Educational System

Preamble
„... The Constitution confers on all Spaniards a right to education. It guarantees freedom of teaching ... and of setting up schools, and the right to receive religious and moral instruction in accordance with personal convictions. It recognises the

right of parents, teachers and pupils to participate in the supervision and management of publicly funded schools.
...*"*

Sec. 1
„The Spanish education system, established in accordance with the principles and values of the Constitution and founded on the respect of the rights and liberties recognised by the Constitution and by Law 8/1985 of 3 July on the right to education, shall be geared towards the achievement of the following aims set forth in the above-mentioned Act ..."

In accordance with the above-mentioned constitutional and legislative provisions, there is a wide network of State-subsidised private schools in Spain, which coexist with the state school system.

COMPLAINTS

The applicants complained that both the administrative and judicial decisions dismissing their appeals against the decision failing the second applicant in her Natural Sciences examinations on account of her refusal to attend the sex education class infringed art. 2 of Protocol No. 1 to the Convention.

The applicants also complained that the fact that the second applicant had been obliged to sit an end-of-year exam in Natural Sciences despite having passed all her mid-term examinations, whereas no other pupil in her class had been made to sit it, constituted a violation of the principle of non-discrimination guaranteed by art. 14 of the Convention.

Relying on art. 6 § 1 of the Convention, the applicants complained of the domestic courts' assessment of the evidence in the case and submitted that they had not been given a fair hearing.

THE LAW

1. The applicants complained that both the administrative and judicial decisions dismissing their appeals against the decision failing the second applicant in her Natural Sciences examinations on account of her refusal to attend the sex education class infringed art. 2 of Protocol No. 1 to the Convention, which provides:

„No person shall be denied the right to education. In the exercise of any functions which it assumes in relation to education and to teaching, the State shall respect the right of parents to ensure such education and teaching in conformity with their own religious and philosophical convictions."

The Court reiterates that, according to its case-law, the second sentence of art. 2 is binding on the Contracting States in the exercise of each and every function that they undertake in the sphere of education and teaching, including that consisting of the organisation and financing of public education. Furthermore, the second sentence of art. 2 must be read together with the first which enshrines the right of everyone to education. It is on to this fundamental right that is grafted the right of parents to respect for their religious and philosophical convictions, and the first sentence does not distinguish, any more than the second, between State and private teaching. The second sentence of art. 2 aims in short at safeguarding the possibility of pluralism in education, which possibility is essential for the preservation of the „democratic society" as conceived by the Convention. In view of the power of the modern State, it is above all through State teaching that this aim must be realised (see the Kjeldsen, Busk Madsen and Pedersen v. Denmark judgment of 7 December 1976, Series A, no. 23, pp. 24-25, § 50; KirchE-EU S. 181).

The Court also reiterates that the setting and planning of the curriculum fall in principle within the competence of the Contracting States. This mainly involves questions of expediency on which it is not for the Court to rule and whose solution may legitimately vary according to the country and the era. Moreover, the second sentence of art. 2 of the Protocol does not prevent States from imparting through teaching or education information or knowledge of a directly or indirectly religious or philosophical kind. However, in fulfilling the functions assumed by it in regard to education and teaching, the State must take care that information or knowledge included in the curriculum is conveyed in an objective, critical and pluralistic manner. The State is forbidden to pursue an aim of indoctrination that might be considered as not respecting parents' religious and philosophical convictions. That is the limit that must not be exceeded (ibid., pp. 26-27, § 53).

In the instant case the Court notes that the sex education class in question was designed to provide pupils with objective and scientific information on the sex life of human beings, venereal diseases and Aids. The booklet tried to alert them to unwanted pregnancies, the risk of pregnancy at an increasingly young age, methods of contraception and sexually transmitted diseases. That was information of a general character which could be construed as of a general interest and which did not in any way amount to an attempt at indoctrination aimed at advocating particular sexual behaviour. Furthermore, that information did not affect the right of parents to enlighten and advise their children, to exercise with regard to their children natural parental functions as educators, or to guide their children on a path in line with the parents' own religious or philosophical convictions (ibid., pp. 27-28, § 54).

Besides that, the Court notes that the Constitution guarantees to all natural and legal persons the right to establish schools in a manner consistent with constitutional principles, and the right to everyone to receive a religious and moral education in accordance with their own convictions. As the High Court of Justice of Cantabria stressed in its judgment, that freedom presupposes „in a pluralist society, the right to choose, that right being linked to the freedom to establish schools so that parents can choose one adapted to their beliefs and ideas". In accordance with the constitutional provisions, there is a wide network of private schools in Spain which coexist with the State-run system of public education. Parents are thus free to enrol their children in private schools providing an education better suited to their faith or opinions. In the instant case, the applicants have not referred to any obstacle preventing the second applicant from attending such a private school. Insofar as the parents opted for a state school, the right to respect their beliefs and ideas as guaranteed by art. 2 of Protocol No. 1 cannot be construed as conferring on them the right to demand different treatment in the education of their daughter in accordance with their own convictions.

Having regard to the foregoing, the Court considers that this part of the application must be rejected as manifestly ill-founded under art. 35 § 3 of the Convention.

2. The applicants also complained that the fact that the second applicant had been obliged to sit an end-of-year examination in Natural Sciences despite having passed all her mid-term examinations, whereas no other pupil in her class had been obliged to sit it, infringed the principle of non-discrimination guaranteed by art. 14 of the Convention.

The Court considers that the fact that the second applicant was obliged to sit an examination in a subject which was part of the school curriculum on account of her deliberate absence from part of the course did not constitute in itself discriminatory treatment contrary to art. 14 of the Convention. It follows that this complaint must be rejected as manifestly ill-founded in accordance with art. 35 § 3 of the Convention.

3. Relying on art. 6 § 1 of the Convention, the applicants complained of the assessment of the evidence in the case by the domestic courts and submitted that they had not had a fair hearing. (*wird ausgeführt und zurückgewiesen*)

For these reasons, the Court unanimously declares the application inadmissible.

55

Das rituelle Schlachten und die Einhaltung der erforderlichen Hygiene können durch den Staat geregelt und überwacht werden.
Die Feststellung, dass das Fleisch von rituell geschlachteten Tieren eine bestimmte Qualität mit Glaubensbezug („glatt") hat, kann einer Religionsgemeinschaft übertragen werden.

Diese Übertragung verletzt die Rechte Dritter jedenfalls dann nicht, wenn in der Feststellung die Auffassung der Mehrheit der Mitglieder dieser Religionsgemeinschaft zum Ausdruck kommt. **Art. 9 EMRK garantiert nicht das Recht, selbst eine rituelle Schlachtung vorzunehmen, wenn die Möglichkeit eines Bezugs von Fleisch der religionsrechtlich vorgegebenen Qualität besteht.**

Art. 9 EMRK
EGMR, Urteil vom 27. Juni 2000 - No. 27417/95
(Cha'are Shalom ./. Frankreich)[1] -

THE FACTS

I. The circumstances of the case

A. Context of the case

1. Ritual slaughter

[13] Kashrut is the name given to all the Jewish laws on the types of food which may be eaten and how to prepare them. The main principles applying to kosher food are to be found in the Torah, the holy scripture comprising the first five books of the Bible - the Pentateuch - namely Genesis, Exodus, Leviticus, Numbers and Deuteronomy.

[14] At the Creation only food from plants could be eaten by man (Gen. i, 29). Eating meat was not authorised until after the Flood (Gen. ix, 3) and then only under very strict conditions. The Torah absolutely forbids the consumption of blood, since blood is the medium of life and life must not be absorbed with flesh but poured on the earth like water (Deut. xii, 23 and 24). In addition, certain animals are regarded as unclean and consumption of certain parts of animals is also forbidden.

[15] Among quadrupeds, for example, only animals that are both cloven-hoofed and ruminants may be eaten; that excludes solidungulates like horses and camels and non-ruminating quadrupeds like pigs and rabbits (Lev. xi; Deut. xiv). Among aquatic species, only fishes with both fins and scales may be eaten, but not crustaceans or shellfish. Among flying creatures, only non-carnivorous birds, such as grain-eating, farmyard fowls and some types of game may be eaten. Insects and reptiles are totally forbidden.

[16] The Torah (Lev. vii, 26 and 27; xvii, 10-14) prohibits consumption of the blood of authorised mammals and birds, and slaughter must be carried out „as the [Lord has] commanded" (Deut. xii, 21). It is forbidden

---

[1] CEDH/ECHR 2000-VII; ÖJZ 2001, 774.

to eat meat from animals that have died of natural causes or have been killed by other animals (Deut. xiv, 21). It is likewise forbidden to eat meat from an animal showing signs of disease or blemishes at the time of slaughter (Num. xi, 22). Meat and other products of permitted animals (such as milk, cream or butter) must be eaten and prepared separately, in and with separate utensils, because the Torah prohibits the cooking of a kid in its mother's milk (Exod. xxii; Deut. xiv, 21).

[17] With a view to ensuring compliance with all the prohibitions laid down in the Torah, later commentators established very detailed rules concerning, in particular, the approved method of slaughter, initially by handing down the oral tradition but later by compiling an encyclopaedic collection of commentaries - the Talmud.

[18] Observance of the above rules on the eating of meat necessitates special slaughter processes. As it is forbidden for Jews to eat any blood whatsoever, animals for slaughter, after being blessed, must have their throats slit; more precisely, they must be killed with a single stroke of a very sharp knife in such a way that an immediate, clean and deep cut is made through the trachea, the oesophagus, the carotid arteries and the jugular veins, so that the greatest possible quantity of blood will flow. The meat must then be steeped in water and salted, still with the aim of removing any trace of blood. Certain organs, like the liver, must be grilled to remove blood from them. Other parts, like the sciatic nerve, blood vessels or the fat around the vital organs, must be removed.

[19] In addition, immediately after slaughter, the animal must be examined for any signs of disease or anomaly; if there is the slightest doubt on that point, the meat is declared unfit for consumption. Ritual slaughter - *shechitah* - may be performed only by a *shochet*, who must be a devout man of unimpeachable moral integrity and scrupulous honesty. Lastly, until it comes to be sold, the meat must be kept under the supervision of a *kashrut* inspector. The competence and personal integrity of ritual slaughterers and *kashrut* inspectors are subject to continuous appraisal by a religious authority. In order to guarantee consumers that their meat has been slaughtered in accordance with the prescriptions of Jewish law, the religious authority certifies it as „kosher". Such certification gives rise to the levying of a tax known as slaughter tax or rabbinical tax.

[20] In France, as in many other European countries, the ritual slaughter required by Jews and Muslims for religious reasons comes into conflict with the principle that an animal to be slaughtered, after being restrained, must first be stunned, that is plunged into a state of unconsciousness in which it is kept until death intervenes, in order to spare it any suffering. Ritual slaughter is nevertheless authorised under French law and by the Council of Europe Convention for the Protection of Animals for Slaughter and the European Directive of 22 December 1993 (see „Relevant law and practice" below).

[21] Ritual slaughter is regulated in French law by Decree no. 80-791 of 1 October 1980, promulgated to implement art. 276 of the Countryside Code, as amended by Decree no. 81-606 of 18 May 1981. Art. 10 of the decree provides:

„*It is forbidden to perform ritual slaughter save in a slaughterhouse. Subject to the provisions of the fourth paragraph of this article, ritual slaughter may be performed only by slaughterers authorised for the purpose by religious bodies which have been approved by the Minister of Agriculture, on a proposal from the Minister of the Interior. Slaughterers must be able to show documentary proof of such authorisation.*

The approved bodies mentioned in the previous paragraph must inform the Minister of Agriculture of the names of authorised persons and those from whom authorisation has been withdrawn. If no religious body has been approved, the prefect of the département in which the slaughterhouse used for ritual slaughter is situated may grant individual authorisations."

2. The Jewish Consistorial Association of Paris

[22] On 1 July 1982 the approval necessary for power to authorise slaughterers was granted to the Joint Rabbinical Committee alone. The Joint Rabbinical Committee is part of the Jewish Consistorial Association of Paris („the *ACIP*"), which is an offshoot of the Central Consistory, the institution set up by Napoleon I by means of the Imperial Decree of 17 March 1808 to administer Jewish worship in France. Following the separation of the Churches and the State in 1905, the Jewish congregations of France, numbering some 700,000 faithful, formed themselves into Jewish liturgical associations (see „Relevant law and practice" below) under an umbrella organisation called the Union of Jewish Congregations of France, which kept the name Central Consistory.

[23] Under art. 1 of its statute, the aims of the Central Consistory are to serve the general interests of Jewish worship, to safeguard the freedom needed to take part in it, to defend the rights of the congregations and to see to the founding, survival and development of joint institutions and services for the benefit of affiliated bodies. It also seeks to preserve the independence and dignity of the rabbinate, to ensure the permanence of the office of Chief Rabbi of France, to encourage recruitment of rabbis by organising the Jewish Seminary of France and to ensure, by general rules applicable to all the affiliated bodies, the preservation of unity, discipline and orderliness in the performance of acts of worship. It represents the general interests of French Judaism and is dedicated to maintaining and preserving spiritual ties with Israel and Jewish congregations throughout the world.

[24] The Consistory includes congregations representing most of the main denominations within Judaism, with the exception of the liberals, who believe that the Torah should be interpreted in the light of present-

day living conditions, and the ultra-orthodox, who advocate, on the contrary, a strict interpretation of the Torah.

[25] The Joint Rabbinical Committee is composed of the Chief Rabbi of Paris, from the *ACIP*, whose registered office is in the rue Saint-Georges, Paris, the rabbi of the orthodox congregation of the rue Pavée, the rabbi of the Jewish congregation of strict observance and the rabbi of the traditionalist congregation of the rue de Montevideo. It is empowered to issue the authorisations needed to obtain a card permitting access to the slaughterhouses. The rabbinical court, or Beth Din, which rules on questions of religious law (marriage, divorce and conversions), supervises observance of the dietary laws and appoints and monitors the *kashrut* slaughterers and inspectors employed by the Consistory.

[26] Since sec. 2 of the 1905 Act provides that the Republic may not recognise, pay stipends to or subsidise any religious denomination (except in the three *départements* of Bas-Rhin, Haut-Rhin and Moselle, where the 1801 Concordat still applies), the income of all the liturgical associations in France, of whatever denomination, is derived from the contributions and gifts of their adherents. According to the Government, approximately half of the Central Consistory's resources comes from the slaughter tax, which is levied at the rate of about 8 French francs (FRF) per kilo of beef sold.

3. The liturgical association Cha'are Shalom Ve Tsedek

[27] The liturgical association Cha'are Shalom Ve Tsedek is an association declared on 16 June 1986 with its registered office in the rue Amelot, Paris. According to its statute, the applicant association's aims are „to organise, subsidise, encourage, revive, assist, promote and finance, in France, public Jewish worship and any other related or connected activities of a religious nature which might, directly or indirectly, lead towards the object it pursues". In addition, „It will seek to co-ordinate the spiritual actions of other Jewish liturgical associations, particularly those aimed at fostering observance of *kashrut*. It will assist with the promotion and creation of all social, educational, cultural and spiritual activities as far as its means permit and provide both moral and financial support to poor families belonging to the congregation or those experiencing temporary difficulties."

[28] The Cha'are Shalom Ve Tsedek association now has six hundred subscribing members and approximately forty thousand adherents, some of whom run a total of twenty butcher's shops, nine restaurants and five caterers in the Paris region alone. In addition it has more than eighty outlets for the sale of deep-frozen food in the Paris region, Lyons and Marseilles.

[29] The association publishes Jewish calendars, has a Kollel (study centre for young rabbis), two centres for the study of the Torah and two

synagogues, in Paris and Sarcelles. It is administered by a rabbinical committee which has sole jurisdiction over religious issues and is composed of chief rabbis, rabbis, well-known members of the congregation and *kashrut* slaughterers and inspectors.

[30] Originally, the applicant association came into being as a minority movement which split away from the Jewish Central Consistory of Paris. Its members are determined to practise their religion in the strictest orthodoxy. In particular, the applicant association wishes to perform ritual slaughter according to stricter rules than those followed by the slaughterers authorised by the Paris Central Consistory as regards examination of slaughtered animals for any signs of disease or anomalies.

[31] The prescriptions concerning kosher meat, derived from Leviticus, were codified in a compendium called Shulchan Aruch (The Laid Table) written by Rabbi Yosef Caro (1488-1575), which lays down very strict rules. However, some later commentators accepted less constraining rules, particularly with regard to examination of the lungs of slaughtered animals. But a number of orthodox Jews, particularly those who belong to Sephardic congregations originally from North Africa, including the members of the applicant association, wish to eat meat from animals slaughtered according to the most stringent requirements of the Shulchan Aruch. This type of meat is referred to by the Yiddish word „*glatt*", meaning „smooth".

[32] For meat to qualify as „*glatt*", the slaughtered animal must not have any impurity, or in other words any trace of a previous illness, especially in the lungs. In particular, there must be no filamentary adhesions between the pleura and the lung. This requirement of purity mainly concerns adult sheep and cattle, which are more likely to have contracted disease at some point of their existence. But, according to the applicant association, the ritual slaughterers under the authority of the Beth Din, the rabbinical court of the *ACIP*, the only body to have been approved - on 1 July 1982 - by the Ministry of Agriculture, now no longer make a detailed examination of the lungs and are less exacting about purity and the presence of filaments so that, in the applicant association's submission, butchers selling meat certified as kosher by the Central Consistory are selling meat which its members consider impure and therefore unfit for consumption.

[33] The applicant association submitted that it was therefore obliged, in order to be able to make „*glatt*" kosher meat available to its adherents, to slaughter illegally and to obtain supplies from Belgium.

[34] The Government, for their part, produced a certificate from the Chief Rabbi of France to the effect that there were butcher's shops supervised by the Consistory where the members of the Cha'are Shalom association could obtain „*glatt*" meat. In addition, according to figures supplied by the Government, the applicant association, which has nine employees, including six ritual slaughterers, had a turnover of FRF

4,900,000 in 1993, despite refusal of authorisation to perform ritual slaughter, and more than FRF 3,800,000 of this sum came from slaughter tax. In 1994 the turnover was FRF 4,600,000, of which FRF 3,700,000 came from the slaughter tax, and in 1995 the income from the slaughter tax came to more than FRF 4,000,000. The tax levied by the applicant association for slaughter amounted to FRF 4 for each kilo of kosher meat sold.

B. The proceedings which gave rise to the application

1. The first set of proceedings

[35] Between 1984 and 1985, when it was registered only as a cultural (rather than liturgical) association, the applicant association certified as being „glatt" kosher the meat sold in the butcher's shops of its members. This meat was either imported from Belgium or came from animals slaughtered in France in accordance with its own religious prescriptions, and therefore without certification from the Paris Beth Din. Civil proceedings were brought against it by the ACIP, which alleged that it had given a misleading description of goods offered for sale, since it had fraudulently labelled the meat sold as kosher. However, the ACIP's action was dismissed by the Paris Court of Appeal in a judgment of 1 October 1987, later upheld by the Court of Cassation, on the ground that the 1905 Act on the separation of the Churches and the State did not allow the courts to rule on the question whether a liturgical association like the applicant was empowered to guarantee that meat offered for sale was kosher; on the other hand, the Court of Appeal noted that it had not been contested that the applicant association had complied with the strict rules concerning ritual slaughter and inspection.

2. The second set of proceedings

[36] On 11 February 1987 the applicant association asked the Minister of the Interior to propose its approval with a view to practising ritual slaughter. This application was refused by a decision of 7 May 1987 on the grounds that the association was not sufficiently representative within the French Jewish community and was not a religious association within the meaning of Part IV of the Act of 9 December 1905 on the separation of the Churches and the State.

[37] The applicant association appealed to the Paris Administrative Court, pleading an infringement of freedom of religion, guaranteed both by sec. 1 of the Act of 9 December 1905 on the separation of the Churches and the State and by art. 9 of the European Convention on Human Rights.

[38] On 28 June 1989 the Paris Administrative Court dismissed the association's appeal, giving the following reasons:

„...

The grounds given for the impugned decision were that the association was not sufficiently representative within the Jewish community and that it was not a liturgical association within the meaning of Part IV of the Act of 9 December 1905. In making that decision the Minister of the Interior refused to accept that the association was a religious body coming within the scope of the above-mentioned provisions.

Although art. 1 of the appellant's statute describes it as a liturgical association governed by the provisions of the Act of 9 December 1905, ... [the applicant association] has not established, as the evidence stands at present, that it subsidises or that it is an offshoot of an association which subsidises the continuation of and public participation in Jewish worship. The fact that it makes kosher meat available for sale in more than twenty retail butcher's and eighty outlets for the sale of deep-frozen food is not sufficient to give the association the character of a religious body which may be proposed by the Minister of the Interior for approval by the Minister of Agriculture ... The Minister of the Interior was thus able to take the impugned decision without committing any error as to the facts or the law or any manifest error of assessment, nor did he infringe the freedom of worship, since he did no more than verify the status of the appellant organisation in the interests of public policy and pursuant to the provisions referred to above.

Lastly, it has not been established that the Minister's decision was taken on grounds that had nothing to do with public policy requirements and was prompted by a desire to reserve the benefit of approval for the only Jewish religious body which has obtained it ...“

[39] The applicant association appealed against this judgment to the *Conseil d'Etat*. In a judgment of 25 November 1994 the *Conseil d'Etat* dismissed the appeal on the following grounds:

„...

... The documents in the file do not establish that the Jewish liturgical association Cha'are Shalom Ve Tsedek, which does not organise any worship or dispense any teaching, has on account of its activities the character of a ‚religious body‘ for the purposes of art. 10 ... of the decree of 1 October 1980. Consequently, by refusing to propose it for approval by the Minister of Agriculture, the Minister of the Interior did not commit any error of law and gave sufficient grounds for his decision.

[Lastly,] in taking the impugned decision the Minister of the Interior only used the powers conferred on him by the above-mentioned provisions with a view to ensuring that ritual slaughter is performed in conditions consistent with public policy requirements, public hygiene and respect for public freedoms. Accordingly, the appellant association may not validly maintain that the Minister interfered in the functioning of a religious body or that he infringed the freedom of religion guaranteed in particular by the Declaration of the Rights of Man and the European Convention [on] Human Rights ...“

3. The third set of proceedings

[40] Concurrently with its application of 11 February 1987 for approval as a religious body, the applicant association submitted on the same day to the prefect of the *département* of Deux-Sèvres an application on behalf of three ritual slaughterers who were members of the association, and were authorised by it, for specific individual authorisations to perform ritual slaughter in an establishment in that *département*.

[41] On 29 April 1987 the prefect refused this application on the grounds that art. 10 § 3 of Decree no. 80-791 of 1 October 1980 empowered prefects to authorise individual slaughterers only where no religious body had been approved for the religion in question and that it was clear that the Joint Rabbinical Ritual Slaughter Committee had been given the approval concerned.

[42] The applicant association appealed against this decision to the Poitiers Administrative Court.

[43] In a judgment of 10 October 1990 the Poitiers Administrative Court dismissed the appeal against the prefect's decision on the following grounds:

„... *The evidence placed before the Court shows, and this has not been contested, that by a decision of 1 July 1982 the Minister of Agriculture, acting on the basis of art. 10 § 2 of the above-mentioned decree of 1 October 1980, approved the ‚Joint Rabbinical Committee' as a body empowered to appoint ritual slaughterers authorised to perform ritual slaughter in the manner prescribed by the Jewish religion. That approval prevents prefects from issuing individual authorisations under art. 10 § 4 permitting persons or institutions adhering to the religion concerned to perform ritual slaughter. It is clear, particularly in the light of art. 2 of its statute, that the cultural association ‚Cha'are Shalom Ve Tsedek' proclaims its adherence to the Jewish religion. Consequently, and even though the association apparently refuses for religious reasons to recognise the authority of the ‚Joint Rabbinical Committee', the individual application it made for a derogation authorising it to perform ritual slaughter in a slaughterhouse in the département of Deux-Sèvres could only be refused. Accordingly, when the prefect of Deux-Sèvres, in refusing the application on 29 April 1987, applied these legal rules, as he was required to do, without becoming involved in the internal dissensions of the Jewish religion, he did not infringe the principle of equality in the application of administrative rules or the principle of freedom of worship set forth in the Act of 9 December 1905 on the separation of the Churches and the State or the freedom of conscience and religion enunciated ... in art. 9 of the Convention for the protection of Human Rights and Fundamental Freedoms.*"

[44] In a judgment of 25 November 1994 the *Conseil d'Etat* upheld the above judgment on appeal, giving the following reasons:

„*The provisions ... of the third paragraph of art. 10 of the decree of 1 October 1980 give prefects the power to authorise ritual slaughterers only where no reli-*

gious body has been approved for the religion concerned under the first paragraph of the same article. It is clear that the Joint Rabbinical Ritual Slaughter Committee has obtained the approval in question. Consequently, the prefect of Deux-Sèvres was required to refuse, as he did, the application made by the appellant association."
..."

II. Relevant law and practice

A. Domestic law

[45] Art. 2 of the 1958 Constitution provides:

„France is a secular Republic; it shall ensure the equality before the law of all citizens, without distinction as to origin, race or religion. It shall respect all beliefs."

[46] The relevant provisions of the Act of 9 December 1905 on the separation of the Churches and the State (in the version applicable at the material time) is worded as follows:

Sec. 1
„The Republic shall ensure freedom of conscience. It shall guarantee free participation in religious worship, subject only to the restrictions laid down hereinafter in the interest of public order."
Sec. 2
„The Republic shall not recognise, pay stipends to or subsidise any religious denomination. Consequently, from 1 January in the year following promulgation of this Act all expenditure relating to participation in worship shall be removed from State, département and municipality budgets. However, these budgets may include appropriations for expenditure on chaplaincy services intended to ensure freedom of worship in public institutions such as senior and junior high schools, primary schools, hospices, mental hospitals and prisons ..."
Sec. 18
„Associations formed in order to meet the costs of a religious denomination, to ensure its continued existence or to foster participation in public acts of worship shall be constituted in accordance with sec. 5 et seq. of Part 1 of the Act of 1 July 1901. They shall, in addition, be subject to the provisions of the present Act."
Sec. 19
„These associations must have as their sole object participation in religious worship and be composed of at least
- seven persons in municipalities with a population of less than 1,000;
- fifteen persons in municipalities with a population of between 1,000 and 20,000;
- twenty-five adults permanently or temporarily resident in the religious district concerned in municipalities with a population of more than 20,000;
...

Associations may in addition receive contributions as provided in sec. 6 of the Act of 1 July 1901 and the proceeds from collections held to meet the costs of worship and may levy charges for: religious ceremonies and services even in the form of an endowment; renting of benches and seats; provision of objects intended for use in funeral services in religious buildings and for the decoration of such buildings ... Under the conditions laid down by sec. 7 and 8 of the Act of 4 February 1901/8 July 1941, on administrative supervision of donations and bequests, liturgical associations may receive testamentary gifts and donations inter vivos intended to help them achieve their objects or subject to religious or liturgical obligations ... They may not, in any form whatsoever, receive subsidies from the State, the départements or municipalities. Sums allotted for repairs to the buildings used for public worship shall not be considered subsidies, whether or not those buildings are listed as historic monuments."

Sec. 20

„These associations may, in the forms laid down by sec. 7 of the Act of 16 August 1901, set up unions with a central administrative service or governing body ..."

[47] Art. 276 of the Countryside Code provides:

„It is an offence to ill-treat domestic animals or wild animals that have been tamed or are being held in captivity."

[48] The relevant provisions of Decree no. 80-791 of 1 October 1980, promulgated to implement art. 276 of the Countryside Code, are worded as follows:

Art. 7
„The provisions of art. 8 and 9 below shall be applicable in establishments for the slaughter of oxen, sheep, goats, pigs, horses, poultry, domestic rabbits and game."
Art. 8
„All animals must be restrained before slaughter. In the case of ritual slaughter this must be done before the throat is slit.
Restraint techniques must be designed and used in such a way as to avoid all unnecessary suffering, excitement and injury to the animals. Halters may not be tightened by means of twisting-sticks.
It is forbidden to hang animals up before they have been stunned, or, in the case of ritual slaughter, before their throats have been slit.
The provisions of the present article shall not apply to the slaughter of poultry, domestic rabbits and small game where these are stunned after being hung up."
Art. 9
„Stunning, that is the use of an authorised technique which immediately plunges animals into a state of unconsciousness, shall be compulsory before slaughter, save in the following cases:
...
4. ritual slaughter."
Art. 10
„It is forbidden to perform ritual slaughter save in a slaughterhouse (Decree no. 81-606, 18 May 1989, art. 1). Subject to the provisions of the fourth paragraph of this article, ritual slaughter may be performed only by slaughterers authorised for the purpose by religious bodies which have been approved by the Minister of Agriculture, on a proposal from the Minister of the Interior. Slaughterers must be able to show documentary proof of such authorisation.

The approved bodies mentioned in the previous paragraph must inform the Minister of Agriculture of the names of authorised persons and those from whom authorisation has been withdrawn.
If no religious body has been approved, the prefect of the département in which the slaughterhouse used for ritual slaughter is situated may grant individual authorisations on application from the persons concerned."

B. International law

1. The Council of Europe

[49] The European Convention for the Protection of Animals for Slaughter, of 10 May 1979, provides, *inter alia*:

Art. 1
„1. This Convention shall apply to the movement, lairaging, restraint, stunning and slaughter of domestic solipeds, ruminants, pigs, rabbits and poultry.
..."
Art. 12
„Animals shall be restrained where necessary immediately before slaughtering and, with the exceptions set out in art. 17, shall be stunned by an appropriate method."
Art. 13
„In the case of the ritual slaughter of animals of the bovine species, they shall be restrained before slaughter by mechanical means designed to spare them all avoidable pain, suffering, agitation, injury or contusions."
Art. 17
„1. Each Contracting Party may authorise derogations from the provisions concerning prior stunning in the following cases:
- slaughtering in accordance with religious rituals;
..."
Art. 18
„1. Each Contracting Party shall make certain of the skill of persons who are professionally engaged in the restraint, stunning and slaughter of animals.
2. Each Contracting Party shall ensure that the instruments, apparatus or installations necessary for the restraint and stunning of animals comply with the requirements of the Convention."
Art. 19
„Each Contracting Party permitting slaughter in accordance with religious ritual shall ensure, when it does not itself issue the necessary authorisations, that animal sacrificers are duly authorised by the religious bodies concerned."

[50] Recommendation no. R (91) 7 of the Committee of Ministers to member States on the slaughter of animals (adopted by the Committee of Ministers on 17 June 1991 at the 460th meeting of the Ministers' Deputies) includes the following provision:

„...

Recommends to the Governments of the member States:
...
vii. if they authorise slaughter in accordance with religious rites without prior stunning, to take all possible measures to protect the welfare of the animals concerned by ensuring that such slaughter is carried out in appropriate slaughterhouses by trained personnel, who observe as far as possible the provisions in the Code of Conduct.
..."

2. The European Union

[51] The European Directive of 18 November 1974 on stunning of animals before slaughter provides, *inter alia*:

„Whereas ... the practice of stunning animals by appropriate recognised techniques should be generalised;
Whereas, however, it is necessary to take account of the particular requirements of certain religious rites;
..."

Art. 4 of the Directive provides:

„The present Directive does not affect national provisions related to special methods of slaughter which are required for particular religious rites."

[52] The European Directive of 22 December 1993 on the protection of animals at the time of slaughter or killing provides, *inter alia*:

„Whereas at the time of slaughter or killing animals should be spared any avoidable pain or suffering;
Whereas, however, it is necessary ... to take account of the particular requirements of certain religious rites;
..."

C. Case-law

[33] In a judgment of 2 May 1973 (*Association cultuelle des israélites nord-africains de Paris* - Liturgical Association of North-African Jews in Paris, *Rec.* p. 312), the *Conseil d'Etat* held:

„... In requiring ritual slaughter performed under conditions derogating from the provisions of ordinary law to be carried out only by ritual slaughterers authorised by religious bodies approved by the Minister of Agriculture on a proposal by the Minister of the Interior, the Prime Minister did not interfere in the affairs of religious bodies and did not infringe the freedom of worship but took the measures needed for exercise of that freedom in a manner consistent with public policy
..."

THE LAW

I. Preliminary question

[54] Under the terms of art. 37 § 1 (a) of the Convention, the Court may decide, at any time in the proceedings, to strike a case out of its list where the circumstances lead to the conclusion that the applicant does not intend to pursue his application.

[55] In the present case, by a letter of 27 October 1999, the president of the applicant association, Rabbi David Bitton, told the Court that he wished purely and simply to withdraw the application. However, the lawyer of the applicant association contested the validity of this withdrawal, arguing, with supporting documentary evidence, that Mr Bitton had resigned from the office of president of the association on 26 February 1999 and that a new president had been elected by the governing body as far back as 2 March, this election being confirmed by an extraordinary general meeting on 10 March 1999 (see par. 7 to 11 above).

[56] At the hearing on 8 December 1999 the French Government made the preliminary observation that it was for the Court to rule on the validity of the last-minute withdrawal by Mr Bitton and stated that they would not object, should it be adjudged valid, if the Court were to grant his request. They also produced a copy of a letter from the applicant association, dated 24 November 1999, in which it informed the Paris police authority that, following a meeting of its executive committee on 23 September 1999, the association had decided to amend its statute, with regard in particular to its registered office and the composition of the executive committee.

[57] In the absence of an express request by the Government for it to strike the case out of its list, the Court does not consider it necessary to examine of its own motion the question whether, as a matter of domestic law, the new president elected in March 1999 may validly act on behalf of the applicant association, since in the light of the documentary evidence produced by the association's lawyer the Court considers that it has been established that the applicant association intends to pursue its application. There is therefore no reason to strike the case out of the list.

II. Alleged Violation of Art. 9 of the Convention, taken alone and conjunction with Art. 14

[58] The applicant association, whose arguments were endorsed by the Commission, submitted that by refusing it the approval necessary for it to authorise its own ritual slaughterers to perform ritual slaughter, in accordance with the religious prescriptions of its members, and by granting such approval to the *ACIP* alone, the French authorities had infringed in a discriminatory way its right to manifest its religion through

observance of the rites of the Jewish religion. It relied on art. 9 of the
Convention, taken alone and in conjunction with art. 14.

[59] Art. 9 of the Convention provides:

> „1. Everyone has the right to freedom of thought, conscience and religion; this
> right includes freedom to change his religion or belief and freedom, either alone
> or in community with others and in public or private, to manifest his religion or
> belief, in worship, teaching, practice and observance.
> 2. Freedom to manifest one's religion or beliefs shall be subject only to such limi-
> tations as are prescribed by law and are necessary in a democratic society in the
> interests of public safety, for the protection of public order, health or morals, or
> for the protection of the rights and freedoms of others."

The relevant part of art. 14 of the Convention for the purposes of the
present case provides:

> „Enjoyment of the rights and freedoms set forth in [the] Convention shall be se-
> cured without discrimination on any ground such as ... religion ..."

[60] In the submission of the applicant association, the conditions for
ritual slaughter, as performed at present by the ritual slaughterers
authorised by the ACIP, to which the French government granted in
1982 the exclusive privilege of carrying out Jewish ritual slaughter, no
longer satisfied the very strict requirements of the Jewish religion, as set
forth in the Book of Leviticus and codified in the Shulchan Aruch. Since
the ritual slaughterers of the ACIP no longer carried out a thorough inspection of the lungs of slaughtered oxen or sheep, the meat from animals slaughtered in those conditions could not be regarded in the eyes of
the ultra-orthodox, or in any event of the Jews who belonged to the association, as perfectly pure, or „glatt", from the religious point of view.
However, what the Jews who belonged to the applicant association were
asserting was the right not to consume meat if they could not be certain -
because it was not from animals slaughtered and, above all, examined by
their own ritual slaughterers - that it was perfectly pure, or „glatt". In
the applicant association's submission, there had accordingly been a clear
interference with its right to manifest its religion through observance of
the religious rite of ritual slaughter.

[61] The applicant association submitted that the refusal to approve it
could not be justified by any of the legitimate aims set out in art. 9 § 2 of
the Convention and that it was disproportionate and discriminatory for
the purposes of art. 14. It emphasised that it was not contested that the
ritual slaughterers it employed were just as scrupulous as those of the
ACIP in complying with the hygiene regulations in force in slaughterhouses and that the Government could not therefore seriously maintain

that the refusal to approve the association pursued the legitimate aim of „protection of public health".

[62] The applicant association further submitted that it was indeed a „religious body" for the purposes of the 1980 decree regulating ritual slaughter, just like the *ACIP*, since both were liturgical associations within the meaning of the 1905 Act on the separation of the Churches and the State. The only difference lay in the relative size of these two liturgical associations, since the *ACIP* numbered among its adherents the majority of the Jews from the various branches of Judaism in France, with an annual budget of approximately 140,000,000 French francs (FRF) at its disposal, whereas the applicant association had only about 40,000 members, all ultra-orthodox, and had a budget of approximately FRF 4-5,000,000. While it might appear legitimate for a government to seek to establish especially close relations with the most representative trade unions, political parties or even religious associations, it nevertheless remained true, above all in a secular State like France, that the authorities had a duty to respect the rights of minorities. The applicant association emphasised in that connection that the French authorities had been very open-handed in granting approvals for ritual slaughter by Muslims, first to the Paris Central Mosque, and later to the mosques of Lyons and Evry, without the number of such approvals endangering public order or public health in any way whatsoever.

[63] Lastly, the applicant association submitted that the fact that, in order to be able to pay its ritual slaughterers, it levied a slaughter tax of about FRF 4 per kilo of meat certified as being „*glatt*" kosher in the butcher's shops which claimed allegiance to it had no bearing on the strictly religious problem of the ritual slaughter in respect of which it had sought approval. It further observed that the *ACIP* also levied a slaughter tax, of about FRF 8 per kilo of meat sold, and that the income from that tax represented about half of the *ACIP*'s resources.

[64] The Government did not contest the fact that Jewish dietary prohibitions and prescriptions formed part of the practice of Judaism by its adherents, but argued that although the religious rules imposed a certain type of diet on Jews they did not by any means require them to take part themselves in the ritual slaughter of the animals they ate. Accordingly, a refusal of approval was capable of affecting the practice of their religion by Jews only if it was impossible for them, on account of that refusal, to find meat compatible with the religious prescriptions they wished to follow.

[65] Yet that was not the position in the present case, in the Government's submission, because it was quite plain from the documents in the file that certain butcher's shops sold meat certified „*glatt*" from slaughterhouses controlled by the *ACIP*, that the shops of the applicant association, which obtained part of their supplies in Belgium, also sold such meat and that there would be nothing to prevent the applicant associa-

tion from reaching an agreement with the *ACIP* in order to have animals slaughtered by its own religious slaughterers, and according to the methods it defined, under the cover of the approval granted to the *ACIP*. In that connection the Government referred to the agreements reached between the *ACIP* and other very orthodox congregations such as the Lubavitch movement or the congregation of the rue Pavée.

[66] Admittedly, the applicant association denied that meat from the *ACIP* slaughterhouses was truly „*glatt*", criticising the inadequacy of the inspection of the lungs of slaughtered animals by *ACIP* slaughterers, but the Government noted that in doing so the applicant association was challenging the findings of the legitimate and independent religious authorities who personified the religion it professed. The Government emphasised that it was not for the French authorities, bound as they were to respect the principle of secularism, to interfere in a controversy over dogma, but observed that it could not be contested that the Chief Rabbi of France, whose opinion on the matter was based on the rulings of the Beth Din (the rabbinical court), was qualified to say what was or was not compatible with Jewish observance.

[67] In the Government's submission, there had been, in the final analysis, no interference with the right to freedom of religion, since in the present case the only impact of the refusal to approve the applicant association lay in the fact that it was impossible for Jews, given meat of equal quality, to choose meat from animals slaughtered by the applicant association, which differed from the meat offered for sale by the *ACIP* only in its price, since the slaughter tax levied by the applicant association was lower by half than the tax levied by the *ACIP*. In the Government's view, this freedom of choice was an economic, not religious freedom. That was evidenced by the fact that, according to the *ACIP*, the applicant association had at one time tried to obtain a kind of delegated authority from the *ACIP* allowing it to perform ritual slaughter itself, under cover of the approval granted to the *ACIP*, but that approach had come to nothing for lack of agreement on the financial terms of the contract.

[68] Even supposing that there had been interference with the applicant association's right to manifest its religion, the Government maintained that such interference was prescribed by law, namely the 1980 decree regulating slaughterhouse practice, and that it pursued a legitimate aim, that of protecting order and public health. In that connection, the Government argued that ritual slaughter derogated very markedly from the principles underpinning the domestic and international legal rules applicable to the protection of animals and public hygiene. The written law in force prohibited ill-treatment of animals and required them to be stunned before slaughter to spare them any suffering. Similarly, health considerations required slaughter to be carried out in a slaughterhouse and, in the case of ritual slaughter, by slaughterers duly authorised by the religious bodies concerned in order to prevent the exercise of freedom

of religion giving rise to practices contrary to the essential principles of hygiene and public health. Ritual slaughter could therefore be authorised only by way of a radical derogation.

[69] With regard to the reasons which had prompted the French authorities to refuse the approval sought by the applicant association, the Government mentioned two factors, which came within the margin of appreciation the Convention left to Contracting States. In the first place, the Minister of the Interior had taken the view that the applicant association's activity was essentially commercial, and only religious in an accessory way, since it mainly sought to supply meat from animals slaughtered by its ritual slaughterers which was certified „*glatt*", and that it could therefore not be considered a „religious body" within the meaning of the 1980 decree. Secondly, account had been taken of the limited support for the applicant association, which had approximately 40,000 adherents; this was not comparable with that for the *ACIP*, which had 700,000. In view of the exceptional nature of the practice of ritual slaughter, the refusal of approval had therefore been necessary to avoid a proliferation of approved bodies, which would undoubtedly have come about if the threshold of the guarantees required to be given by associations seeking approval had been too low.

[70] Lastly, the Government maintained that there had not been discrimination for the purposes of art. 14 of the Convention either. In the first place, the applicant association and the *ACIP*, on account of their respective activities and levels of support, were not in comparable positions; secondly, even supposing that there had been a difference in treatment, that difference was the expression of the relationship of proportionality between the aim pursued and the means employed. In that connection, the Government again emphasised that the effects of the refusal of approval were very limited for the adherents of the applicant association, and even non-existent in view of the fact that slaughter did not directly affect their freedom of religion.

[71] As to the veiled criticism that a monopoly on slaughter had been given to the *ACIP* in 1982 and was not without advantages for the public authorities, the Government observed that the *ACIP*, an offshoot of the Central Consistory, which had been administering Jewish worship in France for two hundred years, was indeed a legitimate negotiating partner, since it was an umbrella organisation for nearly all the Jewish associations in France and thus guaranteed protection of the interests of the community and respect for the rules dictated by public policy, particularly where health was concerned. The *de facto* monopoly enjoyed by the *ACIP* with regard to ritual slaughter was not, however, the result of any deliberate intention on the part of the State, which would not have failed to grant the approval sought by the applicant association if it had been able to prove that it was essentially a religious body and had wider support within the Jewish community.

[72] The Court considers, like the Commission, that an ecclesiastical or religious body may, as such, exercise on behalf of its adherents the rights guaranteed by art. 9 of the Convention (see, *mutatis mutandis*, the Canea Catholic Church v. Greece judgment of 16 December 1997, RJD 1997-VIII, p. 2856, § 31, KirchE-EU S. 319). In the present case, a community of believers - of whatever religion - must, under French law, be constituted in the form of a liturgical association, as is the applicant association.

[73] The Court next reiterates that art. 9 lists a number of forms which manifestation of one's religion or belief may take, namely worship, teaching, practice and observance (see the Kalaç v. Turkey judgment of 1 July 1997, RJD 1997-IV, p. 1209, § 27; KirchE-EU S. 312). It is not contested that ritual slaughter, as indeed its name indicates, constitutes a rite or „*rite*" (the word in the French text of the Convention corresponding to „observance" in the English), whose purpose is to provide Jews with meat from animals slaughtered in accordance with religious prescriptions, which is an essential aspect of practice of the Jewish religion. The applicant association employs ritual slaughterers and *kashrut* inspectors who slaughter animals in accordance with its prescriptions on the question, and it is likewise the applicant association which, by certifying as „*glatt*" kosher the meat sold in its members' butcher's shops, exercises religious supervision of ritual slaughter.

[74] It follows that the applicant association can rely on art. 9 of the Convention with regard to the French authorities' refusal to approve it, since ritual slaughter must be considered to be covered by a right guaranteed by the Convention, namely the right to manifest one's religion in observance, within the meaning of art. 9.

[75] The Court will first consider whether, as the Government submitted, the facts of the case disclose no interference with the exercise of one of the rights and freedoms guaranteed by the Convention.

[76] In the first place, the Court notes that by establishing an exception to the principle that animals must be stunned before slaughter, French law gave practical effect to a positive undertaking on the State's part intended to ensure effective respect for freedom of religion. The 1980 decree, far from restricting exercise of that freedom, is on the contrary calculated to make provision for and organise its free exercise.

[77] The Court further considers that the fact that the exceptional rules designed to regulate the practice of ritual slaughter permit only ritual slaughterers authorised by approved religious bodies to engage in it does not in itself lead to the conclusion that there has been an interference with the freedom to manifest one's religion. The Court considers, like the Government, that it is in the general interest to avoid unregulated slaughter, carried out in conditions of doubtful hygiene, and that it is therefore preferable, if there is to be ritual slaughter, for it to be performed in slaughterhouses supervised by the public authorities. Accord-

ingly, when in 1982 the State granted approval to the *ACIP*, an offshoot of the Central Consistory, which is the body most representative of the Jewish communities of France, it did not in any way infringe the freedom to manifest one's religion.

[78] However, when another religious body professing the same religion later lodges an application for approval in order to be able to perform ritual slaughter, it must be ascertained whether or not the method of slaughter it seeks to employ constitutes exercise of the freedom to manifest one's religion guaranteed by art. 9 of the Convention.

[79] The Court notes that the method of slaughter employed by the ritual slaughterers of the applicant association is exactly the same as that employed by the *ACIP*'s ritual slaughterers, and that the only difference lies in the thoroughness of the examination of the slaughtered animal's lungs after death. It is essential for the applicant association to be able to certify meat not only as kosher but also as „*glatt*" in order to comply with its interpretation of the dietary laws, whereas the great majority of practising Jews accept the kosher certification made under the aegis of the *ACIP*.

[80] In the Court's opinion, there would be interference with the freedom to manifest one's religion only if the illegality of performing ritual slaughter made it impossible for ultra-orthodox Jews to eat meat from animals slaughtered in accordance with the religious prescriptions they considered applicable.

[81] But that is not the case. It is not contested that the applicant association can easily obtain supplies of „*glatt*" meat in Belgium. Furthermore, it is apparent from the written depositions and bailiffs' official reports produced by the interveners that a number of butcher's shops operating under the control of the *ACIP* make meat certified „*glatt*" by the Beth Din available to Jews.

[82] It emerges from the case file as a whole, and from the oral submissions at the hearing, that Jews who belong to the applicant association can thus obtain „*glatt*" meat. In particular, the Government referred, without being contradicted on this point, to negotiations between the applicant association and the *ACIP* with a view to reaching an agreement whereby the applicant association could perform ritual slaughter itself under cover of the approval granted to the *ACIP*, an agreement which was not reached, for financial reasons (see par. 67 above). Admittedly, the applicant association argued that it did not trust the ritual slaughterers authorised by the *ACIP* as regards the thoroughness of the examination of the lungs of slaughtered animals after death. But the Court takes the view that the right to freedom of religion guaranteed by art. 9 of the Convention cannot extend to the right to take part in person in the performance of ritual slaughter and the subsequent certification process, given that, as pointed out above, the applicant association and its members are not in practice deprived of the possibility of obtaining and eating

meat considered by them to be more compatible with religious prescriptions.

[83] Since it has not been established that Jews belonging to the applicant association cannot obtain „*glatt*" meat, or that the applicant association could not supply them with it by reaching an agreement with the *ACIP*, in order to be able to engage in ritual slaughter under cover of the approval granted to the *ACIP*, the Court considers that the refusal of approval complained of did not constitute an interference with the applicant association's right to the freedom to manifest its religion.

[84] That finding absolves the Court from the task of ruling on the compatibility of the restriction challenged by the applicant association with the requirements laid down in the second paragraph of art. 9 of the Convention. However, even supposing that this restriction could be considered an interference with the right to freedom to manifest one's religion, the Court observes that the measure complained of, which is prescribed by law, pursues a legitimate aim, namely protection of public health and public order, in so far as organisation by the State of the exercise of worship is conducive to religious harmony and tolerance. Furthermore, regard being had to the margin of appreciation left to Contracting States (see the Manoussakis and Others v. Greece judgment of 26 September 1996, RJD 1996-IV, p. 1364, § 44, KirchE-EU S. 263), particularly with regard to establishment of the delicate relations between the Churches and the State, it cannot be considered excessive or disproportionate. In other words, it is compatible with art. 9 § 2 of the Convention.

[85] There has accordingly been no violation of art. 9 of the Convention taken alone.

[86] As regards the applicant association's allegation that it suffered discriminatory treatment on account of the fact that approval was granted to the *ACIP* alone, the Court reiterates that, according to the established case-law of the Convention institutions, art. 14 only complements the other substantive provisions of the Convention and the Protocols. It has no independent existence since it has effect solely in relation to „the enjoyment of the rights and freedoms" safeguarded by those provisions. Although the application of art. 14 does not presuppose a breach of those provisions - and to that extent it is autonomous - there can be no room for its application unless the facts at issue fall within the ambit of one or more of the latter.

[87] The Court notes that the facts of the present case fall within the ambit of art. 9 of the Convention (see par. 74 above) and that therefore art. 14 is applicable. However, in the light of its findings in par. 83 above concerning the limited effect of the measure complained of, findings which led the Court to conclude that there had been no interference with the applicant association's freedom to manifest its religion, the Court considers that the difference of treatment which resulted from the meas-

ure was limited in scope. It further observes that, for the reasons set out in par. 84, in so far as there was a difference of treatment, it pursued a legitimate aim, and that there was „a reasonable relationship of proportionality between the means employed and the aim sought to be realised" (see, among other authorities, the Marckx v. Belgium judgment of 13 June 1979, Series A no. 31, p. 16, § 33). Such difference of treatment as there was therefore had an objective and reasonable justification within the meaning of the Court's consistent case-law.

[88] There has accordingly been no violation of art. 9 of the Convention taken in conjunction with art. 14.

For these reasons the Court holds
1. *Holds by twelve votes to five that there has been no violation of art. 9 of the Convention taken alone;*
2. *Holds by ten votes to seven that there has been no violation of art. 9 of the Convention taken in conjunction with art. 14.*

JOINT DISSENTING OPINION OF JUDGES SIR NICOLAS BRATZA, FISCHBACH, THOMASSEN, TSATSA-NIKOLOVSKA, PANTÎRU, LEVITS AND TRAJA (TRANSLATION)

To our great regret, we cannot agree with either the reasoning or the conclusion of the majority in the present case.

1. With regard to the question whether or not there was interference with the applicant association's right to freedom of religion, we can agree with par. 76 and 77; it is quite correct to say that by granting approval to the *ACIP* in 1982 the State authorities, far from impairing freedom of religion, on the contrary gave practical effect to a positive commitment intended to permit the free exercise of that freedom. On the other hand, we cannot concur with the majority's assertion in par. 78 that it is necessary to ascertain whether or not an application for approval made subsequently by another religious body involves exercise of the right to the freedom to manifest one's religion.

The mere fact that approval has already been granted to one religious body does not absolve the State authorities from the obligation to give careful consideration to any later application made by other religious bodies professing the same religion. In the present case, the applicant association's application was prompted by the fact that, in its submission, the *ACIP*'s ritual slaughterers no longer made a sufficiently thorough examination of the lungs of slaughtered animals, so that meat certified as kosher by the *ACIP* could not be considered „glatt". But the Jews who belong to the applicant association consider that meat which is not „glatt" is impure and therefore not compatible with Jewish dietary laws. There is therefore disagreement on that point between the *ACIP* and the applicant association.

We consider that, while it is possible for tension to be created where a community, and a religious community in particular, is divided, this is one of the unavoidable consequences of the need to respect pluralism. In such a situation the role of the public authorities is not to remove any cause of tension by eliminating pluralism, but to take all necessary measures to ensure that the competing groups tolerate each other (see *Serif v. Greece*, no. 38178/97, § 53, ECHR 1999-IX, KirchE-EU S. 385). We therefore find it particularly inappropriate to mention, as the majority do in par. 82 of the judgment, that the applicant association could have reached an agreement with the *ACIP* in order to perform ritual slaughter under cover of the approval granted to the *ACIP*. That argument amounts to discharging the State, the only entity empowered to grant approval, from the obligation to respect freedom of religion. But the *ACIP* represents the majority current in the Jewish community and as such is the least well-placed to assess the validity of minority claims and act as arbiter on the question.

We also consider that the fact that the applicant association is able to import „*glatt*" meat from Belgium does not justify in this case the conclusion that there was no interference with the right to the freedom to practise one's religion through performance of the rite of ritual slaughter; the same applies to the fact that Jews are able to obtain supplies of „*glatt*" meat, if necessary, from the few butcher's shops run by the *ACIP* which sell it under the aegis of the Beth Din.

Art. 10 of the 1980 decree expressly provides that an approved religious body may authorise ritual slaughterers to perform ritual slaughter and that the necessary approval is to be given by the Minister of Agriculture on a proposal by the Minister of the Interior. By denying the applicant association the status of a „religious body" and by rejecting its application for approved status on that account, the French authorities therefore restricted its freedom to manifest its religion.

In our view, the possibility of obtaining „*glatt*" meat by other means is irrelevant for the purpose of assessing the scope of an act or omission on the part of the State aimed, as in the present case, at restricting exercise of the right to freedom of religion (see, *mutatis mutandis*, the *Observer* and *Guardian* v. the United Kingdom judgment of 26 November 1991, Series A no. 216, pp. 34-35, § 69). We cannot therefore follow the majority's finding that there was no violation of art. 9 taken alone because there had been no interference.

2. With regard to justification of the interference with the right to freedom of religion, we take the view that the main problem in the present case lies in the discrimination of which the applicant association complained.

In that connection, we consider that the reasoning of the majority, as set out in par. 87, is inadequate. In our opinion, in order to find that there had been no violation of art. 9 of the Convention taken in conjunction with art. 14, the majority should not have confined their reasons to the assertion that the interference was of „limited effect" and that the difference of treatment was „limited in scope". Where freedom of religion is concerned, it is not for the European Court of Human Rights to substitute its assessment of the scope or seriousness of an interference for that of the persons or groups concerned, because the essential object of art. 9 of the Convention is to protect individuals' most private convictions.

For our part, we consider it indispensable to examine the question whether, by granting the approval in issue to the *ACIP* while refusing it to the applicant association in 1987, the State authorities secured to the applicant association, without discrimination, in accordance with art. 14 of the Convention, enjoyment of the right to freedom of religion it was afforded under art. 9. In the present case we consider that there has been a violation of art. 14 of the Convention taken in conjunction with art. 9, for the following reasons.

In the first place, we observe that for the purposes of art. 14 the notion of discrimination ordinarily includes cases where States treat persons or groups in analogous situations differently without providing an objective and reasonable justification. According to the case-law of the Convention institutions, a difference of treatment is discriminatory for the purposes of art. 14 if it „has no objective and reasonable justification", that is if it does not pursue a „legitimate aim" or if there is not a „reasonable relationship of proportionality between the means employed and the aim sought to be realised". The Court reaffirmed this recently in *Thlimmenos v. Greece* ([GC], no. 34369/97, ECHR 2000-IV).

The Court should first have considered therefore whether the applicant association was in an analogous situation to that of the *ACIP*. In that connection, we observe that it is not contested that the legal status of the applicant association is that of a liturgical association, within the meaning of the 1905 Act on the separation of the Churches and the State, just like the *ACIP*. Moreover, art. 10 of the decree of 1 October 1980 gives no definition whatsoever of the term „religious body" and lays down no criterion, such as representativeness within the religion concerned, whereby the point can be assessed. Nor has it been contested that the applicant association has two synagogues where acts of worship are regularly celebrated and training establishments for rabbis or that it carries out, in practice, religious supervision over a number of butcher's shops and sales outlets for „*glatt*" kosher meat.

The fact that this movement is a minority within the Jewish community as a whole is not in itself sufficient to deprive it of the character of a religious body. We therefore consider that in the light of its statute and activities there is at first sight no reason to doubt that the applicant association is a „religious body", just like the *ACIP*. We further note that, as regards the practice of ritual slaughter, it is not contested either that the *ACIP* slaughterers and those of the applicant association use exactly the same method of slaughter by throat-slitting, the only difference residing in the scope of the examination of the lungs of the slaughtered animals after death. Here again, therefore, the applicant association is in an analogous situation to that of the *ACIP*.

The Government submitted that the difference in treatment between the *ACIP* and the applicant association was justified by the fact that the applicant association was actually engaged in a purely commercial activity, namely the slaughter, certification and sale of „*glatt*" kosher meat, as evidenced by the fact that more than half of its income came from levying a slaughter tax. The Government argued on that basis that the applicant association was not engaged in truly religious activity comparable to that of the *ACIP*. However, we would observe that the *ACIP* likewise levies a rabbinical tax on slaughter and that it can be seen from the accounts submitted by the third-party interveners that more than half of the *ACIP*'s income also comes from this same tax. That being so, we fail to see in what way the applicant association's activity is more „commercial" than the activity carried on by the *ACIP* in this area.

With regard to the legitimate aims capable of justifying the difference in treatment, the Government relied on the need to protect public health. However, there is nothing to suggest that the ritual slaughterers employed by the applicant association do not comply just as well as those of the *ACIP* with the rules of hygiene imposed by the regulations governing slaughterhouses, a point which was also acknowledged by the domestic courts (see par. 35 of the judgment).

Lastly, the Government referred to the low level of support for the applicant association, which has only about 40,000 adherents, all ultraorthodox Jews, out of 700,000 Jews living in France. Its representativeness, in their submission, could not be compared with that of the *ACIP*, which represented nearly all the Jews in France. The refusal to approve the applicant association had therefore been necessary, they argued, for the protection of public order, with a view to avoiding the proliferation of approved bodies which did not provide the same safeguards as the *ACIP*.

We certainly do not disregard the interest the authorities may have in dealing with the most representative organisations of a specific community. The fact that the State wishes to avoid dealing with an excessive number of negotiating partners so as not to dissipate its efforts and in order to reach concrete results more easily, whether in its relations with trade unions, political parties or religious denominations, is not illegitimate in itself, or disproportionate (see, *mutatis mutandis*, the Swedish Engine Drivers' Union v. Sweden judgment of 6 February 1976, Series A no. 20, p. 17, § 46).

In the present case, however, the dispute submitted to the French authorities did not concern the applicant association's representativeness within the Jewish community and the applicant association has by no means challenged the role and function of the *ACIP*, the Central Consistory or other bodies representing the interests of the Jewish communities in France as the State's preferred interlocutors. For the applicant association, it was solely a matter of obtaining approval to practise ritual slaughter, on which subject it disagrees with the *ACIP.*

We consider that the organisation of ritual slaughter is only one aspect of the relations between the various religious bodies and the State and do not see how granting the approval in question could have threatened to undermine public order. With regard to the Muslim communities living in France, which also practise ritual slaughter but are less well structured than the Jewish communities, it should be noted that the applicant association asserted, without being contradicted on this point by the Government, that approval had been granted fairly liberally by the authorities to a number of different bodies, notably the mosques of Paris, Evry and Lyons, without it even being alleged that the number of approved bodies was such as to threaten public order or health.

In concluding, in par. 87 of the judgment, that there was in the present case a reasonable relationship of proportionality between the means employed and the aim sought to be realised, the majority of the Court refer to par. 84 and to the Manoussakis and Others v. Greece judgment (judgment of 26 September 1996, RJD 1996-IV), stressing the margin of appreciation left to States, „particularly with regard to establishment of the delicate relations between the Churches and the State".

While we accept that States enjoy a margin of appreciation in this area, we observe that in the same judgment the Court went on to emphasise that in delimiting the extent of the margin of appreciation concerned it had to have regard to what was at stake, namely the need to secure true religious pluralism, which is an inherent feature of the notion of a democratic society (loc. cit., p. 1364, § 44).

We consider that similar reasoning is applicable in the present case. In our view, withholding approval from the applicant association, while granting such approval to the *ACIP* and thereby conferring on the latter the exclusive right to authorise ritual slaughterers, amounted to a failure to secure religious pluralism or to ensure a reasonable relationship of proportionality between the means employed and the aim sought to be achieved.

In the light of the foregoing considerations, we consider that the difference in treatment between the applicant association and the *ACIP* - one of which received the approval that the other was denied - had no objective and reasonable justification and was disproportionate. There has therefore been a violation of art. 14 of the Convention taken in conjunction with art. 9.

56

Die interne Organisation einschließlich der Bestimmung der Funktionsträger ist eine eigene Angelegenheit der Religionsgemeinschaft.

Art. 6, 9, 11, 13 EKMR, 1 Erstes Zusatzprotokoll
EGMR, Urteil vom 26. Oktober 2000 - No. 30985/96
(Hasan u.a. ./. Bulgarien)[1] -

THE FACTS

I. The circumstances of the case

A. The applicants

[9] Mr Fikri Sali Hasan („the first applicant") was Chief Mufti of the Bulgarian Muslims from 1992 until the events complained of. Mr Ismail Ahmed Chaush („the second applicant") was formerly a teacher at the Islamic Institute in Sofia.

In his submissions to the Court the second applicant stated that from February 1995 he had also worked on a part-time basis as secretary to the Chief Mufti's Office (...), the national leadership of the Muslim religious organisation, and editor of *Musulmanin*, its newspaper. The Government disputed these assertions.

B. Background to the case

[10] At the end of 1989 a process of democratisation commenced in Bulgaria. Soon thereafter some Muslim believers and activists of the Muslim religion in the country sought to replace the leadership of their religious organisation. They considered that Mr Gendzhev, who was the Chief Mufti at that time, and the members of the Supreme Holy Council (...) had collaborated with the communist regime. The old leadership, with Mr Gendzhev as Chief Mufti of the Bulgarian Muslims, also had supporters. This situation caused divisions and internal conflict within the Muslim community in Bulgaria.

[11] Following general elections held in Bulgaria in October 1991 a new government, formed by the Union of Democratic Forces (СДС) and the Movement for Rights and Freedoms (ДПС), took office towards the end of 1991.

On 10 February 1992 the Directorate of Religious Denominations (...), a governmental agency attached to the Council of Ministers, declared the

---

[1] CEDH/ECHR 2000-XI.

election of Mr Gendzhev in 1988 as Chief Mufti of the Bulgarian Muslims null and void and proclaimed his removal from that position. On 21 February 1992 the Directorate registered a three-member Interim Holy Council as a temporary governing body of the Muslims' religious organisation, pending the election of a new permanent leadership by a national conference of all Muslims.

[12] Following these events Mr Gendzhev, who claimed that he remained Chief Mufti of the Bulgarian Muslims, challenged the decision of 10 February 1992 before the Supreme Court. On 28 April 1992 the Supreme Court rejected his appeal. The court found that the decision of the Directorate of Religious Denominations was not subject to judicial appeal. The ensuing petition for review, submitted by Mr Gendzhev against the Supreme Court's decision, was examined by a five-member Chamber of the Supreme Court. On 7 April 1993 the Chamber dismissed the petition. While confirming the rejection of Mr Gendzhev's appeal, the Chamber also discussed the merits of the appeal. It found, *inter alia*, that the Directorate's decision to declare Mr Gendzhev's election null and void had been within its competence. In so far as the impugned decision had also proclaimed „the removal" of Mr Gendzhev from his position of Chief Mufti, this had been *ultra vires*. However, it was unnecessary to annul this part of the Directorate's decision as in any event it had no legal consequences.

[13] The National Conference of Muslims, organised by the interim leadership, took place on 19 September 1992. It elected Mr Fikri Sali Hasan (the first applicant) as Chief Mufti of the Bulgarian Muslims and also approved a new Statute of the Religious Organisation of Muslims in Bulgaria (...). On 1 October 1992 the Directorate of Religious Denominations registered the statute and the new leadership in accordance with sec. 6 and 16 of the Religious Denominations Act.

C. Events of 1994 and early 1995

[14] While the leadership dispute between Mr Gendzhev and Mr Hasan continued, the official position of the Directorate of Religious Denominations, throughout 1993 and at least the first half of 1994, remained that the first applicant was the legitimate Chief Mufti of the Bulgarian Muslims.

[15] On 29 July 1994 the Directorate of Religious Denominations wrote a letter to Mr Hasan urging him to organise a national conference of all Muslims to solve certain problems arising from irregularities in the election of local religious leaders. The irregularities in question apparently concerned alleged inconsistencies with the internal statute of the Muslim religious organisation, and not breaches of the law.

[16] On 2 November 1994 the supporters of Mr Gendzhev held a national conference. The conference proclaimed itself the legitimate repre-

sentative of Muslim believers, elected an alternative leadership and adopted a statute. Mr Gendzhev was elected President of the Supreme Holy Council. After the conference the newly elected leaders applied to the Directorate of Religious Denominations for registration as the legitimate leadership of the Bulgarian Muslims.

[17] On 3 January 1995 the Supreme Holy Council presided over by the first applicant decided to convene a national conference on 28 January 1995.

[18] At the end of 1994, parliamentary elections took place in Bulgaria. The Bulgarian Socialist Party (БСП) obtained a majority in Parliament and formed a new government, which took office in January 1995.

[19] On 16 January 1995 the Directorate of Religious Denominations wrote a letter to the first applicant in his capacity of Chief Mufti urging him to postpone the conference. The letter stated, *inter alia*:

> „As the Directorate of Religious Denominations was concerned with [the] irregularities [as regards the election of local muftis] as early as the middle of 1994, it repeatedly ... urged the rapid resolution of the problems ... Unfortunately no specific measures were undertaken ... As a result the conflicts in the religious community deepened, and discontent among Muslims increased, leading to the holding of an extraordinary national conference on 2 November 1994. This brought to light a new problem, related to the shortcomings of the statute of the Muslim religious community ... [The statute] does not clarify the procedure for convening a national conference ... Issues concerning the participants, and the manner in which they are chosen ..., are not regulated.
>
> Therefore, for the executive branch of the State it becomes legally impossible to decide whether the national conference is in conformity with the statute [of the Muslim religion] and, accordingly, whether its decisions are valid. These decisions, quite understandably, could be challenged by some of the Muslims in Bulgaria. Any other national conference, except one organised by a joint committee [of the rival leaderships], would raise the same problem. Moreover, the decision of 3 January 1995 of the Supreme Holy Council to hold an extraordinary national conference on 28 January 1995 is signed only by six legitimate members of the Holy Council ... [and] ... cannot be regarded as being in conformity with the statute.
>
> The Directorate of Religious Denominations cannot disregard the findings of the [Chamber of the] Supreme Court in its decision of 7 [April] 1993. It is mentioned therein that the Directorate had acted ultra vires when removing Mr Gendzhev from his position of Chief Mufti and that the decision of the Directorate of 10 February 1992 could not have legal consequences.
>
> Extremely worried as regards the current situation and deeply concerned over the well-being of the Muslims in Bulgaria, the Directorate of Religious Denominations supports the opinion of the Chief Mufti [the first applicant] that it is not advisable to rush ahead with the holding of an extraordinary conference before overcoming the conflicts in the religious community ...
>
> Firmly convinced that the disputed questions in the religious community should not be decided by administrative means by the executive branch of the State ...

the Directorate appeals to you to show good will and reach a consensus for the holding of a united conference ..."

[20] On 27 January 1995 the Supreme Holy Council presided over by Mr Hasan announced that it had postponed the national conference until 6 March 1995.

D. Removal of the first applicant from his position of Chief Mufti

[21] On 22 February 1995 Mr Shivarov, Deputy Prime Minister of Bulgaria, issued Decree R-12, which reads as follows:

„In accordance with Decree KV-15 of 6 February 1995 of the Council of Ministers read in conjunction with sec. 6 of the Religious Denominations Act, I approve the statute of the Muslim religion in Bulgaria, based in Sofia."

[22] The statute of the Muslim religion in Bulgaria mentioned in the decree was apparently the one adopted at the rival national conference, organised by Mr Gendzhev and held on 2 November 1994. Decree KV-15, referred to in Decree R-12, determined that Deputy Prime Minister Shivarov should be in charge of supervising the activity of the Directorate of Religious Denominations.

[23] On 23 February 1995 the Directorate of Religious Denominations of the Council of Ministers issued a decision which stated that, in accordance with sec. 6, 9 and 16 of the Religious Denominations Act and Decree R-12 of the Deputy Prime Minister, it had registered a new leadership of the Bulgarian Muslim community. The leadership thus registered included Mr Gendzhev as President of the Supreme Holy Council and, apparently, those elected at the conference of 2 November 1994.

[24] Neither Decree R-12 nor the decision of the Directorate of Religious Denominations gave any reasons or any explanation regarding the procedure followed. The decisions were not formally served on Mr Hasan, who learned about them from the press.

[25] On 27 February 1995 the newly registered leadership of the Muslim community accompanied by private security guards entered the premises of the Chief Mufti's Office in Sofia, forcibly evicted the staff working there, and occupied the building. The applicants submit that the police, who arrived after the surprise action, immediately stepped in to protect the new occupants of the building. Following the action of 27 February 1995 the new leadership took over all documents and assets belonging to the religious organisation of Bulgarian Muslims in Sofia and, in the months which followed, in various other towns in the country. The Directorate of Religious Denominations allegedly sent letters to the banks where the Muslim religious organisation had its accounts, informing them of the change of leadership. In the following weeks several mu-

nicipalities, allegedly upon the instructions of the Directorate, registered new regional muftis. Also, the staff of the Chief Mufti's Office and ten Islamic teachers, the second applicant among them, were allegedly dismissed *de facto* as they were prevented from continuing their work.

[26] On 27 February 1995, immediately after the take-over, the first applicant submitted to the Chief Public Prosecutor's Office (...) a request for assistance, stating that there had been an unlawful mob action and that the persons who had occupied the building of the Chief Mufti's Office were squatters who had to be evicted. By decisions of 8 and 28 March 1995 the prosecuting authorities refused to take action. They found, *inter alia*, that the new occupants of the building had legal grounds to stay there as they were duly registered by the Directorate of Religious Denominations and represented the religious leadership of the Muslim community in the country.

E. The appeal to the Supreme Court against Decree R-12

[27] On 23 March 1995, apparently in reply to a request from the first applicant, the Directorate of Religious Denominations sent him, in his capacity as a private person, a letter which stated, *inter alia*:

> „*The Muslim religious community in Bulgaria ... has, in 1888, 1891, 1919, 1949, 1986, 1992 and 1995, repeatedly changed its statute as concerns its organisational structure ..., but never as regards its religious foundation. Decree R-12 of 22 February 1995 ... sanctions an [organisational] change, which the religious community itself wished to undertake ...*"

This letter was apparently the first document originating from the competent State bodies which implied clearly that the statute of the Muslim religious community approved by Decree R-12 had replaced the previous statute and that the new registered leadership had replaced the first applicant.

[28] On 18 April 1995 the first applicant, acting on behalf of the Chief Mufti's Office which he headed, lodged an appeal against Decree R-12 with the Supreme Court. He stated that, on the face of it, Decree R-12 stipulated nothing more than the registration of a new religious organisation. However, from the decisions and the letter of the Directorate of Religious Denominations which had followed, it had become clear that what had taken place was the replacement of the statute and the leadership of an existing religious denomination. Furthermore, it transpired that the motivation behind this act had been the understanding that the Muslim religion in Bulgaria could have only one leadership and one statute. The State did not have the right to impose such a view on Muslims, multiple religious organisations of one and the same religion being normal in other countries, as in Bulgaria. Therefore the Council of Ministers had acted beyond its powers. The resulting interference in the internal

disputes of the Muslim religious community was unlawful. At the oral hearing held by the Supreme Court the first applicant also stated that there had been an unlawful interference with Muslims' religious liberties, as enshrined in the Constitution.

[29] The first applicant also submitted that the conference of 2 November 1994 had been organised by people outside the Muslim religious organisation over which he presided. Accordingly, they could register their own religious organisation but could not claim to replace the leadership of another. The second applicant asked the Supreme Court either to declare Decree R-12 null and void as being against the law, or to declare that it constituted the registration of a new religious community, the existing Muslim organisation being unaffected.

[30] On 27 July 1995 the Supreme Court dismissed the appeal. The court stated that under the Religious Denominations Act the Council of Ministers enjoyed full discretion in its decision as to whether or not to register the statute of a given religion. The Supreme Court's jurisdiction was therefore limited to an examination of whether the impugned decision had been issued by the competent administrative organ and whether the procedural requirements had been complied with. In that respect Decree R-12 was lawful. As regards the request for interpretation of Decree R-12, it was not open to the Supreme Court, in the framework of those particular proceedings, to state its opinion as to whether it had the effect of creating a new legal person, or introducing changes, and whether after this decision there existed two parallel Muslim religious organisations.

F. The national conference of 6 March 1995 and the appeal to the Supreme Court against the Council of Ministers' refusal to register its decisions

[31] The national conference of Muslims in Bulgaria organised by Mr Hasan took place as planned on 6 March 1995. The minutes of the conference establish that it was attended by 1,553 persons, of whom 1,188 were official delegates with voting rights. These were representatives of eleven local chapters and of the central leadership. The conference adopted some amendments of the statute of the Muslim community and elected its leadership. The first applicant was re-elected Chief Mufti.

[32] On 5 June 1995 the first applicant, acting as Chief Mufti, submitted a petition to the Council of Ministers requesting the registration of the new statute and leadership of Muslims in Bulgaria, as adopted by the conference of 6 March 1995. On 6 October 1995 he repeated the request. However, there was no response from the Council of Ministers.

[33] On an unspecified date the first applicant appealed to the Supreme Court against the tacit refusal of the Council of Ministers to register the decisions of the March 1995 conference.

[34] On 14 October 1996 the Supreme Court delivered its judgment. It noted that in 1992 the Chief Mufti's Office as represented by Mr Hasan had been duly registered as a religious denomination under sec. 6 of the Religious Denominations Act and had thus obtained legal personality of which it had not been subsequently deprived. Therefore the Council of Ministers was under an obligation, pursuant to sec. 6 and 16 of the Act, to examine a request for registration of a new statute or of changes in the leadership in the existing religious denomination. Accordingly, the Supreme Court ruled that the tacit refusal of the Council of Ministers had been unlawful and ordered the transmission of the file to the Council of Ministers, which was required to examine it.

[35] On 19 November 1996 Deputy Prime Minister Shivarov refused to register the 1995 statute and leadership of the Chief Mufti's Office as represented by Mr Hasan. He sent him a letter stating, *inter alia*, that the Council of Ministers had already registered a leadership of the Muslim community in Bulgaria, which was that elected by the November 1994 conference with Mr Gendzhev as President of the Supreme Holy Council. The Deputy Prime Minister concluded that the first applicant's request "[could not] be granted as it [was] clearly contrary to the provisions of the Religious Denominations Act".

[36] On 5 December 1996 the first applicant, acting as Chief Mufti, appealed to the Supreme Court against the refusal of the Deputy Prime Minister.

[37] On 13 March 1997 the Supreme Court quashed that refusal on the ground that it was unlawful and contrary to art. 13 of the Constitution. The refusal constituted „an unlawful administrative intervention into the internal organisation of [a] religious community". The Supreme Court again ordered the transmission of the file to the Council of Ministers for registration.

[38] Despite these Supreme Court judgments the Council of Ministers did not grant registration to the religious leadership headed by Mr Hasan.

G. The 1997 unification conference and subsequent events

[39] In February 1997 the government of the Bulgarian Socialist Party stepped down and an interim cabinet was appointed. At the general elections which followed in April 1997 the Union of Democratic Forces obtained a majority in Parliament and formed a new government.

[40] On 24 March 1997 the first applicant again requested the Council of Ministers to register the 1995 statute and leadership. There followed informal contacts between the Muslim leadership of Mr Hasan and representatives of the government. The applicants were allegedly told that the government would only agree to register a new leadership of the Muslims if it was elected at a unification conference.

[41] The Directorate of Religious Denominations urged the two rival leaderships of Mr Hasan and of Mr Gendzhev to negotiate a solution. On

12 September 1997 the leadership headed by Mr Hasan decided to accept the holding of a unification conference under certain conditions. A five-member contact group was appointed to hold negotiations. On 30 September 1997 representatives of the two rival leaderships signed an agreement to convene a national conference of all Muslim believers on 23 October 1997. The agreement, which was also signed by Deputy Prime Minister Metodiev and the Director of Religious Denominations, provided, *inter alia*, that the parties would not obstruct the unification process, failing which the Directorate would take appropriate administrative measures. In addition, the leadership of Mr Gendzhev undertook not to dispose of any Muslim property or assets before the conference.

[42] The Directorate of Religious Denominations took an active part in organising the national conference. The mayors in many localities distributed to the local chapters forms bearing the seal of the Directorate. These forms were filled out at the meetings of the local chapters which elected delegates to the national conference and were certified by the mayors' signatures.

[43] On 23 October 1997, 1,384 delegates attended the conference. Only delegates whose election had been certified by the mayors were allowed to participate. The conference adopted a new statute of the Muslim denomination in Bulgaria and elected a new leadership comprising members of the leadership of Mr Hasan and others. Mr Hasan apparently attended the conference and approved of the new leadership. Six leaders of the group led by him were elected to the new Supreme Holy Council. Mr Hasan was not among them. On 28 October 1997 the government registered the newly elected leadership.

[44] Although the religious community which accepted Mr Gendzhev's authority was involved in the unification process, Mr Gendzhev himself and some of his supporters did not sign the agreement of 30 September 1997 and did not attend the conference, considering that it was manipulated by the State. The conference voted a resolution authorising the new leadership to conduct an audit and seek the prosecution of Mr Gendzhev for alleged unlawful transactions.

[45] Mr Gendzhev, who claimed that he remained the Chief Mufti, appealed to the Supreme Administrative Court (...) against the government's decision to register the new leadership. By a judgment of 16 July 1998 the Supreme Administrative Court rejected the appeal as being inadmissible. It found that the Chief Mufti's Office of Mr Gendzhev had no *locus standi* to lodge an appeal as it had never been validly registered. Decree R-12 of 22 February 1995 had been signed by Deputy Prime Minister Shivarov, who had not been duly authorised by the Council of Ministers. Decree KV-15 did not contain an express authorisation for the Deputy Prime Minister to approve the statutes of religious denominations. As a result the Chief Mufti's Office of Mr Gendzhev had never legally existed and all its acts between 1995 and 1997 were null and void.

II. Relevant domestic law and practice

[46] The relevant provisions of the 1991 Constitution read as follows:

Art. 13
„(1) Religions shall be free.
(2) Religious institutions shall be separate from the State.
(3) Eastern Orthodox Christianity shall be considered the traditional religion in the Republic of Bulgaria.
(4) Religious institutions and communities, and religious beliefs shall not be used for political ends."
Art. 37
„(1) The freedom of conscience, the freedom of thought and the choice of religion or of religious or atheistic views shall be inviolable. The State shall assist in the maintenance of tolerance and respect between the adherents of different denominations, and between believers and non-believers.
(2) The freedom of conscience and religion shall not be exercised to the detriment of national security, public order, public health and morals, or of the rights and freedoms of others."

[47] The Constitutional Court's judgment no. 5 of 11 June 1992 provides a legally binding interpretation of the above provisions. It states, *inter alia*, that the State must not interfere with the internal organisation of religious communities and institutions, which must be regulated by their own statutes and rules. The State may interfere with the activity of a religious community or institution only in the cases contemplated in art. 13 § 4 and 37 § 2 of the Constitution. An assessment as to whether there is such a case may also be undertaken at the time of registration of a religious community or institution.

[48] The Religious Denominations Act came into force in 1949 and has been amended several times since then. The relevant provisions of the Act, as in force at the time of the events at issue, read as follows.

Sec. 6
„(1) A religious denomination shall be considered recognised and shall become a legal person upon the approval of its statute by the Council of Ministers, or by a Deputy Prime Minister authorised for this purpose.
(2) The Council of Ministers, or a Deputy Prime Minister authorised for this purpose, shall revoke the recognition, by a reasoned decision, if the activities of the religious denomination breach the law, public order or morals."
Sec. 9
„(1) Every religious denomination shall have a leadership accountable to the State.
(2) The statute of the religious denomination shall establish its governing and representative bodies and the procedure for their election and appointment ..."
Sec. 16
„(1) The national governing bodies of the religious denominations shall register with the Directorate of Religious Denominations of the Council of Ministers, and

local governing bodies with the local municipalities, and they shall submit a list of the names of all members of these governing bodies."

[49] The Act also lays down rules regarding the activities of a religious denomination, imposes requirements as regards its clergy and gives the Directorate of Religious Denominations certain supervisory functions. In its judgment no. 5 of 11 June 1992 the Constitutional Court, while agreeing that certain provisions of the Religious Denominations Act were clearly unconstitutional, found that it was not its task to repeal legal provisions adopted prior to the entry into force of the 1991 Constitution, the ordinary courts being competent to declare them inapplicable.

[50] The applicants contended that as a consequence of the provisions of sec. 6 of the Act, and since there is no public register for recognised religious denominations, in practice a religious community can establish its existence as a legal entity only by producing a copy of a letter or a decision to that effect issued by the Directorate of Religious Denominations. The same applies to the leader of a religious denomination when he needs to provide accreditation.

[51] Under Decree no. 125 of the Council of Ministers of 6 December 1990, as amended, the competence of the Directorate of Religious Denominations includes „contacts between the State and religions denominations", assistance to central and local administrative authorities in solving problems which involve religious matters and assistance to religious organisations as regards education and publications.

[52] There are no procedural provisions under Bulgarian law specifically applicable to the examination by the Council of Ministers, or by a deputy prime minister, of a petition for authorisation of a religious denomination. Sec. 3 of the Administrative Procedure Act (...), which contains a general legal regime on the procedure for the issuing of and appeal against administrative decisions, provides that the Act is not applicable as regards decisions of the Council of Ministers.

THE LAW

I. The government's preliminary objections

[53] Before the Court the Government maintained that the application should be rejected for failure to exhaust domestic remedies, regard being had to the fact that the domestic judicial appeals had been submitted by the first applicant on behalf of the Chief Mufti's Office, and not in his individual capacity. The applicants stated that they had no standing to institute proceedings in their individual capacity. The only possibility was an appeal on behalf of the community. Furthermore, the appeals on behalf of the Chief Mufti's Office had proved to be ineffective. The applicants referred to their complaint under art. 13 of the Convention.

[54] The Court reiterates that objections of the kind now made by the Government should be raised before the admissibility of the application is considered (see, among other authorities, the Campbell and Fell v. the United Kingdom judgment of 28 June 1984, Series A no. 80, p. 31, § 57; the Artico v. Italy judgment of 13 May 1980, Series A no. 37, pp. 13-14, § 27; and *Brumărescu v. Romania* [GC], no. 28342/95, §§ 52-53, ECHR 1999-VII). However, the Government's objection was first raised on 25 August 1998, after the Commission's decision declaring the application admissible (see par. 12 of the Commission's report of 26 October 1999). There is, therefore, estoppel.

II. Alleged violation of Art. 9 of the convention

[55] The applicants complained that the alleged forced replacement of the leadership of the Muslim religious community in Bulgaria in 1995 and the ensuing events up to October 1997 had given rise to a violation of their rights under art. 9 of the Convention. Art. 9 reads as follows:

„1. *Everyone has the right to freedom of thought, conscience and religion; this right includes freedom to change his religion or belief and freedom, either alone or in community with others and in public or private, to manifest his religion or belief, in worship, teaching, practice and observance.*
2. *Freedom to manifest one's religion or beliefs shall be subject only to such limitations as are prescribed by law and are necessary in a democratic society in the interests of public safety, for the protection of public order, health or morals, or for the protection of the rights and freedoms of others.*"

A. Applicability of Art. 9

1. Arguments before the Court

(a) The applicants

[56] The applicants maintained that the right to manifest one's religion in community with others meant that the community should be allowed to organise itself according to its own rules. In their view any interference in the internal life of the organisation was a matter of concern not only to the organisation but also to every person who belonged to the religious community and, in particular, to those directly involved in the religious or organisational leadership. The applicants stated that for a religious community the organisational structure was not simply a form of their existence, but had a substantive meaning. The identity of the leaders of the community was crucial, history abounding with examples of religious leaders converting believers or founding new religions. No less important for the individual believer was the way in which the organisation managed its places of worship and its property. The applicants were

thus of the opinion that the alleged forced removal of the leadership of their religious community concerned their individual rights protected by art. 9 of the Convention, the more so given the first applicant's position of Chief Mufti and the second applicant's involvement in the life of the community.

(b) The Government

[57] The Government maintained that in the Convention organs' practice an application submitted in terms of art. 9 together with other provisions of the Convention would normally be examined under the other provisions relied on. They therefore concentrated in their memorial on art. 11 of the Convention. In their view not every act motivated by religious belief could constitute a manifestation of religion, within the meaning of art. 9.

[58] The Government further submitted that in Bulgaria freedom of religion was guaranteed by the Constitution. Religious institutions being independent, the State had a duty to maintain a climate of tolerance and mutual respect between them without interfering in their internal organisational life. Thus, the Muslim religion was officially registered under the Religious Denominations Act. Muslim believers attended more than 1,000 mosques in the country. They had several religious schools and a newspaper, and maintained international contacts freely.

Against that background the Government asserted that the facts relied on by the applicants had no bearing on their right to practise their religion, individually or collectively, in private or in public, to observe religious holidays, or to teach in schools.

(c) The Commission

[59] The Commission considered that the organisation of a religious community was an important part of religious life and that participation therein is a manifestation of one's religion. The applicants' complaints therefore fell within the ambit of art. 9 of the Convention.

2. The Court's assessment

[60] The Court recalls that freedom of thought, conscience and religion is one of the foundations of a democratic society within the meaning of the Convention. The pluralism indissociable from a democratic society, which has been dearly won over the centuries, depends on it (see *Serif v. Greece*, no. 38178/97, § 49, ECHR 1999-IX, KirchE-EU S. 385, and the Kokkinakis v. Greece judgment of 25 May 1993, Series A no. 260-A, pp. 17-18, §§ 31 and 33, KirchE-EU S. 202). While religious freedom is primarily a matter of individual conscience, it also implies, *inter alia*, freedom to manifest one's religion, alone and in private, or in community

with others, in public and within the circle of those whose faith one shares. Art. 9 lists a number of forms which manifestation of one's religion or belief may take, namely worship, teaching, practice and observance. Nevertheless, art. 9 does not protect every act motivated or inspired by a religion or belief (see the Kalaç v. Turkey judgment of 1 July 1997, RJD 1997-IV, p. 1209, § 27; KirchE-EU S. 312).

[61] In the present case the parties differ on the question whether or not the events under consideration, which all relate to the organisation and leadership of the Muslim community in Bulgaria, concern the right of the individual applicants to freedom to manifest their religion and, consequently, whether or not art. 9 of the Convention applies. The applicants maintained that their religious liberties were at stake, whereas the Government analysed the complaints mainly from the angle of art. 11 of the Convention.

[62] The Court recalls that religious communities traditionally and universally exist in the form of organised structures. They abide by rules which are often seen by followers as being of a divine origin. Religious ceremonies have their meaning and sacred value for the believers if they have been conducted by ministers empowered for that purpose in compliance with these rules. The personality of the religious ministers is undoubtedly of importance to every member of the community. Participation in the life of the community is thus a manifestation of one's religion, protected by art. 9 of the Convention. Where the organisation of the religious community is at issue, art. 9 of the Convention must be interpreted in the light of art. 11, which safeguards associative life against unjustified State interference. Seen in this perspective, the believers' right to freedom of religion encompasses the expectation that the community will be allowed to function peacefully, free from arbitrary State intervention. Indeed, the autonomous existence of religious communities is indispensable for pluralism in a democratic society and is thus an issue at the very heart of the protection which art. 9 affords. It directly concerns not only the organisation of the community as such but also the effective enjoyment of the right to freedom of religion by all its active members. Were the organisational life of the community not protected by art. 9 of the Convention, all other aspects of the individual's freedom of religion would become vulnerable.

[63] There is no doubt, in the present case, that the applicants are active members of the religious community. The first applicant was an elected Chief Mufti of the Bulgarian Muslims. The Court need not establish whether the second applicant, who used to work as an Islamic teacher, was also employed as a secretary to the Chief Mufti's Office, it being undisputed that Mr Chaush is a Muslim believer who actively participated in religious life at the relevant time.

[64] It follows that the events complained of concerned both applicants' right to freedom of religion, as enshrined in art. 9 of the Convention. That provision is therefore applicable.

[65] Further, the Court does not consider that the case is better dealt with solely under art. 11 of the Convention, as suggested by the Government. Such an approach would take the applicants' complaints out of their context and disregard their substance.

The Court finds, therefore, that the applicants' complaints fall to be examined under art. 9 of the Convention. In so far as they touch upon the organisation of the religious community, the Court reiterates that art. 9 must be interpreted in the light of the protection afforded by art. 11 of the Convention.

B. Compliance with Art. 9

1. Arguments before the Court

(a) The applicants

[66] The applicants contended that the State authorities had interfered twice with the organisational life of the Muslim community. Firstly, in February 1995, they had replaced the legitimate leadership of the community led by the first applicant and then, in the following years, they had refused recognition of the re-elected leadership of the first applicant. In the applicants' view the measures undertaken by the State had profound consequences and amounted to replacement of the whole organisational structure of the Muslim community and a complete destruction of normal community life. All income was frozen, offices were seized by force, control over mosques was transferred, and any use of the communities' documents and property by the leadership of the first applicant was made impossible. Mr Hasan was thus compelled to continue his activities as head of the second largest religious community in Bulgaria „from the street, with zero financial resources". Moreover, following the registration in February 1995 by the Directorate of Religious Denominations of Mr Gendzhev's leadership, no court, government body or indeed no person would recognise Mr Hasan as a legitimate representative of the Muslim believers.

[67] The applicants further maintained that State interference with the internal affairs of the religious community had not been based on clear legal rules. They considered that the law in Bulgaria, in matters concerning religious communities, did not provide clarity and guarantees against abuse of administrative discretion. In their view the relations between the State and religious communities in Bulgaria were governed not by law, but by politics. Indeed, the replacement of the leadership of the Muslim religious community had curiously coincided with the change

of government in Bulgaria. The relevant law, which had remained unchanged since the events complained of, provided for a discretionary power of the government to change religious leaderships at will. In the absence of a clear procedure in this respect or a public register of the by-laws and the representation of religious denominations, the system of *ad hoc* letters, issued by the Directorate of Religious Denominations to confirm the representation of the community to interested third parties and even to courts, created vast opportunities for arbitrary exercise of powers. In the applicant's view the authorities had failed in their duty to enact an adequate legal framework in this respect.

[68] The applicants further claimed that Decree R-12 was in breach of the relevant law as it sanctioned a leadership which had not been elected in accordance with the statute and the by-laws of the Muslim community. These rules provided for a procedure for the election of leaders at a national conference convened by decision of the Supreme Holy Council, the Chief Mufti, and the Control Commission. Having recognised these rules in 1992, the authorities should not have registered leaders elected in breach thereof. Furthermore, in the applicants' view the replacement of the leadership had been achieved through arbitrary decrees which gave no reasons and had been issued without the parties concerned even being informed. The refusal of the Council of Ministers to comply with two judgments of the Supreme Court had been another arbitrary interference with the internal life of the community. The prosecuting authorities' refusal to intervene and remedy what the applicants saw as a blatant criminal act, namely the forcible eviction of the first applicant and the staff from the building of the Chief Mufti's Office on 27 February 1995 had also been a clear breach of domestic law.

[69] The applicants further asserted that the interference with their rights under art. 9 of the Convention had no legitimate aim. It could not be argued seriously that the government's purpose was to ensure clarity as to the representation of the Muslim religious community. Its actions at the material time had replaced one leadership of the community with another.

(b) The Government

[70] The Government submitted that there had not been any interference with the applicants' rights under art. 9 of the Convention. The acts of the Directorate of Religious Denominations were of a declarative nature. They did not give rise to rights and obligations and consequently were not capable of affecting the legal rights of others. According to the Court's case-law a registration requirement in religious matters was not as such incompatible with the Convention.

[71] In the Government's view nothing prevented the applicants from freely participating in the organisation of the Muslim community during

the period of time under consideration. There was no evidence that the applicants could not hold meetings or could not be elected to the leadership of the Muslim community. Indeed, on 6 March 1995 they had freely organised a new national conference at which the first applicant had been re-elected Chief Mufti. The fact that there was another national conference, that of 2 November 1994, which elected other leaders, could not be imputed to the State. It had been an expression of the free exercise of the right to freedom of association. Therefore, in the Government's view, it was not the State that had replaced the first applicant as Chief Mufti, but the independent will of the Muslim believers. In fact, Mr Hasan did not meet the age and qualification requirements for the position of Chief Mufti, as provided for in the statute of the Muslim religion in Bulgaria.

[72] The Government also submitted that the State had continued to pay subsidies to the Muslim community. The question of who managed these funds had been decided freely by the community. The Government further rejected as unsubstantiated and ill-founded the first applicant's allegation that he could not address the faithful through the media on the occasion of religious holidays, the media being free and independent from the State. In the Government's view all complaints concerning the alleged indirect effects of the registration of another leadership were ill-founded.

[73] In the Government's opinion the applicants were pursuing their own personal career by falsely presenting before the Court the events complained of as involving human rights issues. If their logic was followed, every leader of a religious community who had lost the confidence of the believers could lodge an application. That would create a dangerous precedent. The Government urged the Court to distance itself from such essentially political disputes. They reiterated that the Parliamentary Assembly of the Council of Europe had noted the progress made in Bulgaria in respect of religious freedoms and informed the Court that a new law on religious denominations was being drafted.

(c) The Commission

[74] The Commission found unanimously that there had been an unlawful State interference with the internal organisation of the Muslim community and the applicants' right to freedom of religion.

2. The Court's assessment

(a) Whether there has been an interference

[75] The Court must examine whether there has been State interference with the internal organisation of the Muslim community and, consequently, with the applicants' right to freedom of religion.

[76] The Government's position was entirely based on the assertion that the impugned acts of the Directorate of Religious Denominations could not be regarded as an interference with the internal organisation of the community as they had been of a purely declaratory nature and had constituted nothing more than an administrative registration. The applicants alleged that these acts had had serious legal and practical consequences and had been aimed directly at removing the legitimate leadership of the Muslim community and replacing it by leaders politically associated with the government of the day.

[77] The Court does not deem it necessary to decide *in abstracto* whether acts of formal registration of religious communities and changes in their leadership constitute an interference with the rights protected by art. 9 of the Convention.

[78] Nevertheless, the Court considers, like the Commission, that facts demonstrating a failure by the authorities to remain neutral in the exercise of their powers in this domain must lead to the conclusion that the State interfered with the believers' freedom to manifest their religion within the meaning of art. 9 of the Convention. It recalls that, but for very exceptional cases, the right to freedom of religion as guaranteed under the Convention excludes any discretion on the part of the State to determine whether religious beliefs or the means used to express such beliefs are legitimate. State action favouring one leader of a divided religious community or undertaken with the purpose of forcing the community to come together under a single leadership against its own wishes would likewise constitute an interference with freedom of religion. In democratic societies the State does not need to take measures to ensure that religious communities are brought under a unified leadership (see *Serif*, cited above, § 52).

[79] In the present case the Court notes that by virtue of Decree R-12 and the decision of the Directorate of Religious Denominations of 23 February 1995 the executive branch of government in Bulgaria proclaimed changes in the leadership and statute of the Muslim religious community. No reasons were given for this decision. There was no explanation why preference was to be given to the leaders elected at the national conference of 2 November 1994, which was organised by Mr Gendzhev's followers, and not to the first applicant, who had the support of another part of the community, as evidenced by the results of the national conference held on 6 March 1995. The Court further observes that in Bulgaria

the legitimacy and representation powers of the leadership of a religious denomination are certified by the Directorate of Religious Denominations. The first applicant was thus deprived of his representation powers in law and in practice by virtue of the impugned decisions of February 1995. He was refused assistance by the prosecuting authorities against the forced eviction from the offices of the Chief Mufti precisely on the ground that Decree R-12 proclaimed another person as the Chief Mufti. He was apparently not able to retain control over at least part of the property belonging to the community, although Mr Hasan undoubtedly had the support of a significant proportion of its members. The impugned decisions thus clearly had the effect of putting an end to the first applicant's functions as Chief Mufti, removing the hitherto recognised leadership of the religious community and disallowing its statute and by-laws. The resulting situation remained unchanged throughout 1996 and until October 1997 as the authorities repeatedly refused to give effect to the decisions of the national conference organised by the first applicant on 6 March 1995.

[80] It is true that in its judgments of 14 October 1996 and 13 March 1997 the Supreme Court implicitly refused to accept that the registration of a new leadership of the divided religious community had the effect of removing the previously recognised leadership of the rival faction. It therefore found that the Council of Ministers was under an obligation to examine the first applicant's request for registration of a new statute. However, those judgments did not have any practical effect, the Council of Ministers having refused to comply with them.

[81] The Government's argument that nothing prevented the first applicant and those supporting him from organising meetings is not an answer to the applicants' grievances. It cannot be seriously maintained that any State action short of restricting the freedom of assembly could not amount to an interference with the rights protected by art. 9 of the Convention even though it adversely affected the internal life of the religious community.

[82] The Court therefore finds, like the Commission, that Decree R-12, the decision of the Directorate of Religious Denominations of 23 February 1995, and the subsequent refusal of the Council of Ministers to recognise the existence of the organisation led by Mr Hasan were more than acts of routine registration or of correcting past irregularities. Their effect was to favour one faction of the Muslim community, granting it the status of the single official leadership, to the complete exclusion of the hitherto recognised leadership. The acts of the authorities operated, in law and in practice, to deprive the excluded leadership of any possibility of continuing to represent at least part of the Muslim community and of managing its affairs according to the will of that part of the community. There was therefore an interference with the internal organisation of the Muslim

religious community and with the applicants' right to freedom of religion as protected by art. 9 of the Convention.

[83] Such an interference entails a violation of that provision unless it is prescribed by law and necessary in a democratic society in pursuance of a legitimate aim (see *Cha'are Shalom Ve Tsedek v. France* [GC], no. 27417/95, §§ 75 and 84, ECHR 2000-VII).

(b) Whether the interference was justified

[84] The Court reiterates its settled case-law according to which the expressions „prescribed by law" and „in accordance with the law" in art. 8 to 11 of the Convention not only require that the impugned measure should have some basis in domestic law, but also refer to the quality of the law in question. The law should be both adequately accessible and foreseeable, that is, formulated with sufficient precision to enable the individual - if need be with appropriate advice - to regulate his conduct (see the *Sunday Times* v. the United Kingdom (no. 1) judgment of 26 April 1979, Series A no. 30, p. 31, § 49; the Larissis and Others v. Greece judgment of 24 February 1998, RJD 1998-I, p. 378, § 40; *Hashman and Harrup v. the United Kingdom* [GC], no. 25594/94, § 31, ECHR 1999-VIII; and *Rotaru v. Romania* [GC], no. 28341/95, § 52, ECHR 2000-V). For domestic law to meet these requirements it must afford a measure of legal protection against arbitrary interferences by public authorities with the rights safeguarded by the Convention. In matters affecting fundamental rights it would be contrary to the rule of law, one of the basic principles of a democratic society enshrined in the Convention, for a legal discretion granted to the executive to be expressed in terms of an unfettered power. Consequently, the law must indicate with sufficient clarity the scope of any such discretion conferred on the competent authorities and the manner of its exercise (see *Rotaru*, cited above, § 55). The level of precision required of domestic legislation - which cannot in any case provide for every eventuality - depends to a considerable degree on the content of the instrument in question, the field it is designed to cover and the number and status of those to whom it is addressed (see *Hashman and Harrup*, cited above, § 31, and the Groppera Radio AG and Others v. Switzerland judgment of 28 March 1990, Series A no. 173, p. 26, § 68).

[85] The Court notes that in the present case the relevant law does not provide for any substantive criteria on the basis of which the Council of Ministers and the Directorate of Religious Denominations register religious denominations and changes of their leadership in a situation of internal divisions and conflicting claims for legitimacy. Moreover, there are no procedural safeguards, such as adversarial proceedings before an independent body, against arbitrary exercise of the discretion left to the executive. Furthermore, Decree R-12 and the decision of the Directorate were never notified to those directly affected. These acts were not rea-

soned and were unclear to the extent that they did not even mention the first applicant, although they were intended to, and indeed did, remove him from his position as Chief Mufti. The Court has already found that these acts and the subsequent refusal of the Council of Ministers to recognise the leadership of Mr Hasan had the effect of arbitrarily favouring one faction of the divided religious community. It is noteworthy in this context that the replacement of the community's leadership in 1995, as well as in 1992 and 1997, occurred shortly after a change of government.

[86] The Court finds, therefore, that the interference with the internal organisation of the Muslim community and the applicants' freedom of religion was not „prescribed by law" in that it was arbitrary and was based on legal provisions which allowed an unfettered discretion to the executive and did not meet the required standards of clarity and foreseeability.

[87] The Court further agrees with the Commission that the repeated refusal of the Council of Ministers to comply with the judgments of the Supreme Court of 1996 and 1997 was a clearly unlawful act of particular gravity. The rule of law, one of the fundamental principles of a democratic society, is inherent in all articles of the Convention and entails a duty on the part of the State and any public authority to comply with judicial orders or decisions against it (see the Hornsby v. Greece judgment of 19 March 1997, RJD 1997-II, pp. 510-11, §§ 40-41, and *Iatridis v. Greece* [GC], no. 31107/96, § 58, ECHR 1999-II).

[88] In view of these findings the Court deems it unnecessary to continue the examination of the applicants' complaints in respect of the „legitimate aim" and „necessary in a democratic society" requirements. Such an examination can only be undertaken if the aim of the interference is clearly defined in domestic law.

[89] There has, therefore, been a violation of art. 9 of the Convention.

III. Alleged violation of Art. 11 of the convention

[90] The applicants complained that the State interference with the internal organisation of the Muslim religious community also violated their rights under art. 11 of the Convention. The Government denied that the Muslim community was an „association" and maintained that in any event there had not been any State interference with rights protected by that article. The Commission considered that it was not necessary to examine the applicants' complaints under art. 11 of the Convention separately.

[90] The Court, like the Commission, considers that no separate issue arises under art. 11 of the Convention. It has already dealt with the complaint concerning State interference with the internal organisation of the Muslim religious community under art. 9 of the Convention, interpreted in the light of art. 11 (see par. 62 and 65 above).

IV. Alleged violation of Art. 13 of the convention

[92] The applicants complained that they did not have an effective remedy against the interference with their right to freedom of religion. They relied on art. 13 of the Convention, which reads as follows:

> „*Everyone whose rights and freedoms as set forth in [the] Convention are violated shall have an effective remedy before a national authority notwithstanding that the violation has been committed by persons acting in an official capacity.*"

1. Arguments before the Court

[93] The applicants submitted, *inter alia*, that the procedure before the Supreme Court, which ended with a judgment of 27 July 1995, was not an effective remedy. Although the Supreme Court could have granted appropriate relief by quashing Decree R-12, it had chosen not to deal with the applicants' arguments on the merits. This had been the consequence of what the applicants described as „the doctrine of full discretion". In the applicants' submission the Bulgarian Supreme Court had repeatedly adhered to the position that in numerous areas the executive enjoyed full discretion which was not subject to judicial review.

[94] The Government replied that the applicants had not instituted any proceedings in their capacity as individuals. In these circumstances they could not claim *in abstracto* that the law did not guarantee effective remedies. In the Government's view the applicants could have requested the institution of criminal proceedings under art. 164 and 165 of the Criminal Code, which concern hate speech and impeding the free manifestation of religion through force or duress.

[95] The Commission considered that the applicants did not have an effective remedy and that there had been a violation of art. 13 of the Convention.

2. The Court's assessment

[96] The Court recalls that art. 13 guarantees the availability at national level of a remedy in respect of grievances which can be regarded as „arguable" in terms of the Convention. Such a remedy must allow the competent domestic authority both to deal with the substance of the relevant Convention complaint and to grant appropriate relief, although Contracting States are afforded some discretion as to the manner in which they discharge their obligations under art. 13. The remedy required by art. 13 must be „effective" in practice as well as in law, in particular in the sense that its exercise must not be unjustifiably hindered by the acts or omissions of the authorities of the respondent State (see *Çakıcı v. Turkey* [GC], no. 23657/94, § 112, ECHR 1999-IV).

[97] In the present case the Court has found that the applicants' rights under art. 9 of the Convention were infringed. They therefore had an arguable claim within the meaning of the Court's case-law.

[98] The Court further considers that the scope of the obligation under art. 13 varies depending on the nature of the Convention right relied on. Like the Commission, it takes the view that in the context of the present case art. 13 cannot be seen as requiring a possibility for every believer, such as the second applicant, to institute in his individual capacity formal proceedings challenging a decision concerning the registration of his religious community's leadership. Individual believers' interests in this respect can be safeguarded by their turning to their leaders and supporting any legal action which the latter may initiate.

[99] The Court thus finds that in such a case the State's obligation under art. 13 may well be discharged by the provision of remedies which are only accessible to representatives of the religious community aggrieved by a State interference with its internal organisation. In the present case the first applicant, Mr Hasan, was the leader of the faction of the Muslim organisation which was replaced through the State decisions complained of. The Court will therefore examine whether effective remedies existed for the first applicant in his capacity as religious leader.

[100] The Court observes that Mr Hasan, acting as Chief Mufti, attempted to obtain a remedy against the interference with the internal organisation of the religious community by challenging Decree R-12 before the Supreme Court. The Supreme Court did not question Mr Hasan's *locus standi* and accepted the case for examination. A representative of the religious community was thus provided access to a judicial remedy. However, the Supreme Court refused to study the substantive issues, considering that the Council of Ministers enjoyed full discretion whether or not to register the statute and leadership of a religious denomination, and only ruled on the formal question whether Decree R-12 was issued by the competent body. The appeal to the Supreme Court against Decree R-12 was not, therefore, an effective remedy.

[101] The other two appeals to the Supreme Court, which were submitted by the first applicant against the refusal of the Council of Ministers to register the results of the national conference of 6 March 1995, were not effective remedies either. Although the Supreme Court upheld these appeals, the Council of Ministers refused to comply with its judgments.

[102] The Government suggested that the applicants could have requested the institution of criminal proceedings against persons who might have impeded the exercise of their freedom of religion. The Court observes, however, that the first applicant did in fact turn to the prosecuting authorities for assistance, but to no avail (see par. 26 above). Furthermore, the Government have not indicated how criminal proceedings, if instituted, could have led to an examination of the substance of the applicants' complaints, which concern decisions issued by a Deputy Prime

Minister and the Directorate of Religious Denominations and found by the Supreme Court, in its judgment of 27 July 1995, to have been formally lawful. It is unclear how such proceedings could have remedied the situation complained of.

[103] The Government have not indicated any other remedy which could be used by the applicants or other representatives of the religious community.

[104] The Court finds, therefore, that the leadership of the faction led by Mr Hasan were unable to mount an effective challenge to the unlawful State interference in the internal affairs of the religious community and to assert their right to organisational autonomy, as protected by art. 9 of the Convention. It follows that neither applicant had an effective remedy in respect of the violation of art. 9. There has, therefore, been a violation of art. 13 of the Convention.

V. Alleged violation of Art. 6 of the convention

[105] The applicants complained that they did not have access to a court for the determination of certain civil rights. In their view Decree R-12 was decisive for some of their civil rights. These were the first applicant's right, in his capacity of Chief Mufti, to manage the religious affairs of the community, to administer its funds and property, and his right to remuneration for his services as Chief Mufti, and the second applicant's right to continue his job of an Islamic teacher, from which he was allegedly *de facto* dismissed. The applicants asserted that the determination of their civil rights without them having been parties to any proceedings, and without the Supreme Court having examined in substance the challenge against Decree R-12, was contrary to art. 6 of the Convention.

[106] The Government submitted that the misfortunes in the applicants' careers were not the consequence of the impugned decisions. The applicants had not been parties to the proceedings before the Supreme Court against Decree R-12. Furthermore, if the second applicant had had an employment contract, he could have challenged its termination before the courts.

[107] The Commission considered that the applicants' complaints under art. 6 were unsubstantiated.

[108] The Court notes that the applicants have not substantiated the legal basis and the content of their alleged civil rights. Furthermore, they have not shown that there existed any obstacles preventing them from bringing civil actions before the courts in respect of their alleged right to remuneration. The Court therefore finds that there has been no violation of art. 6 of the Convention.

VI. Alleged violation of Art. 1 of protocol Nr. 1

[109] The Court notes that the applicants did not reiterate their complaints made before the Commission under art. 1 of Protocol No. 1. In those circumstances the Court sees no reason to deal with them of its own motion.

VII. Application of Art. 41 of the convention (...)

For these reasons, the Court
1. *Dismisses unanimously the Government's preliminary objection;*
2. *Holds unanimously that there has been a violation of art. 9 of the Convention;*
3. *Holds unanimously that no separate issue arises under art. 11 of the Convention;*
4. *Holds unanimously that there has been a violation of art. 13 of the Convention;*
5. *Holds unanimously that there has been no violation of art. 6 of the Convention;*
6. *Holds unanimously that it is not necessary to examine the complaints under art. 1 of Protocol No. 1;*
7. *Holds unanimously that the respondent State is to pay within three months to the first applicant, for non-pecuniary damage, BGN 10,000;*
8. *Holds by eleven votes to six that the finding of violations of the Convention constitutes sufficient just satisfaction in respect of the second applicant;*
9. *... (Kosten und Auslagen);*
10. *... (Zinsen)*
11. *Dismisses unanimously the remainder of the applicants' claims for just satisfaction.*
(...)

JOINT PARTLY DISSENTING OPINION OF JUDGES TULKENS AND CASADEVALL JOINED BY JUDGES BONELLO, STRÁŽNICKÁ, GREVE AND MARUSTE

[1] We do not agree with the majority regarding point 8 of the operative provisions on just satisfaction for the second applicant in respect of non-pecuniary damage.

[2] Since the freedom of thought, conscience and religion protected by art. 9 of the Convention is one of the foundations of a democratic society, as the judgment quite rightly points out, we consider that the mere finding of a violation of that provision does not in itself constitute sufficient just satisfaction.

[3] In the present case there is no doubt that both the first and the second applicants were victims of the violations alleged and that they were both „active members of the religious community ...". Moreover, it is undisputed that the second applicant, Mr Chaush, who used to work as a Muslim teacher, „is a ... believer who actively participated in religious life at the relevant time" (see par. 63 of the judgment), and he „continued to work facing enormous difficulties" for nearly three years (see par. 119 *in fine*).

[4] That being so, we think that the second applicant also suffered distress and sustained non-pecuniary damage, certainly less serious damage than the first applicant, but damage which nevertheless warranted an award of just satisfaction to Mr Chaush under art. 41 of the Convention.

57

Zur Frage der Verfügungsfreiheit einer römisch-katholischen Ordensgemeinschaft in der Türkei hinsichtlich ihres Grundvermögens.

Art. 9 EMRK
EGMR, Beschluss vom 14. Dezember 2000 - No. 26308/95
(Institut de Prêtres français u.a. ./. Türkei) -

EN FAIT

[9] L'acte de fondation (*le firman*) accordé par le Sultan ottoman autorisa en 1859 l'archevêque de la communauté catholique (Institut de Prêtres français dénommés les Augustins de l'Assomption, branche turque de la Congrégation des Augustins de l'Assomption, institution de droit canon) à construire une église et d'autres locaux de culte sur un terrain situé à Kadıköy (Istanbul).

[10] Une chapelle et un bâtiment de séminaire furent érigés sur le domaine. Le 20 septembre 1910, le domaine fut enregistré au nom des Augustins de l'Assomption, comme lieu de culte, séminaire et monastère. Par l'accord franco-turc du 18 décembre 1913, l'Institut fut reconnu par le gouvernement turc comme établissement religieux français. Une lettre annexée au Traité de Lausanne du 24 juillet 1923 assura la reconnaissance et la protection des institutions religieuses françaises, entre autres l'Institut de Prêtres français. Elle précisa que ces institutions devaient être „traitées sur un pied d'égalité avec les institutions similaires turques".

[11] Le 30 mai 1982, en vue de trouver des moyens financiers pour l'entretien des lieux de culte, l'Institut loua une partie du jardin et des locaux à une société privée.

[12] Le 7 novembre 1988, le Trésor public intenta une action devant le tribunal de grande instance de Kadıköy, tendant à l'annulation du titre de propriété de l'Institut et à la restitution du domaine. Il soutenait que l'Institut n'avait pas le droit de procéder sur les lieux à des activités lucratives. Il exposa qu'en louant certaines parties du domaine, l'Institut ne poursuivait plus de but religieux.

[13] Par un jugement du 6 juin 1989, le tribunal de grande instance de Kadıköy rejeta la demande du Trésor. Il considéra notamment que „les Augustins de l'Assomption, Institut de Prêtres français, font partie des institutions françaises reconnues et protégées par le Traité de Lausanne, et que l'utilisation des lieux à but lucratif ne confère pas le droit de restitution de ces lieux au Trésor".

[14] Sur pourvoi du Trésor, la Cour de cassation, par un arrêt du 18 mai 1990, cassa le jugement du 6 juin 1989 et renvoya l'affaire devant la juridiction de première instance. Elle considéra que „l'autorisation d'acquisition des biens immobiliers accordée par l'Empire ottoman en vertu d'une loi promulguée en 1868, aux personnes morales étrangères pour la construction d'édifices religieux, scolaires, de bienfaisance, tels églises, couvents, écoles, hôpitaux, dispensaires, presbytères, est donnée à condition d'utiliser lesdits lieux conformément au but initial relatif à leur utilisation". Elle estima aussi que ces institutions étrangères devaient avoir, avant le 30 octobre 1914 et actuellement, la personnalité juridique reconnue par la législation. Elle jugea également que les institutions en question ne devaient pas se livrer à des activités et utilisations lucratives. Elle constata qu'en l'espèce, contrairement à l'art. 3 de la loi sur le registre foncier de 1934 (*Tapu Kanunu*), l'Institut n'avait pas de personnalité juridique et n'était pas reconnu par l'Etat turc.

[15] Par un jugement du 5 avril 1993, se conformant à l'arrêt de la Cour de cassation, le tribunal de grande instance de Kadıköy donna gain de cause au Trésor. Il ordonna l'inscription du domaine au nom du Trésor. Il considéra en outre qu'une partie du domaine litigieux devait être inscrite au nom de la Direction générale des fondations (*Vakıflar Genel Müdürlüğü*) qui était intervenue dans la procédure engagée par le Trésor.

[16] L'Institut forma un pourvoi en cassation contre ce jugement. A l'issue d'une audience le 12 avril 1994, la Cour de cassation confirma le jugement attaqué.

[17] Le 19 septembre 1994, la Cour de cassation rejeta le recours en rectification de l'Institut.

EN DROIT

[18] Le 15 novembre 2000, la Cour a reçu la déclaration suivante, signée par le représentant des requérants:

„J'ai l'honneur de vous informer qu'en date d'aujourd'hui (le 14 novembre 2000) le Gouvernement vient de me communiquer le texte d'un règlement amiable susceptible de mettre fin à l'affaire citée en marge.

J'en ai aussitôt informé mon client le Père Alain Fontaine afin d'avoir son acquiescement. Le Père Alain Fontaine m'a déclaré que le texte proposé donne satisfaction aux souhaits de l'Eglise auparavant formulés.

Le texte présenté en annexe contient notamment:

1. Les titulaires actuels du terrain, respectivement le Trésor et la Direction générale des fondations, reconnaissent le droit d'usufruit en faveur des prêtres en charge dans l'Institut requérant. Le droit d'usufruit comprend la pleine utilisation et la jouissance des lieux et des bâtiments qui s'y trouvent. Cela implique aussi que l'Institut pourra louer le terrain [à des] fins lucratives pour subvenir à ses besoins. L'Institut consent au prélèvement d'une somme raisonnable sur le revenu provenant des loyers au profit du Trésor et de la Direction générale des fondations. Les deux administrations consentent à [remplir] les formalités pour inscrire leurs déclarations respectives sur le registre immobilier en vue du renouvellement du droit d'usufruit en faveur des prêtres qui vont remplacer [les] actuels titulaires du droit d'usufruit.

2. Le Trésor accepte la première disposition pour ce qui le concerne.

3. La Direction générale des fondations renonce à son droit de créance de 41 670 USD en charge de l'Institut requérant pour la collecte des loyers survenue dans les cinq ans après l'annulation du titre de propriété.

Mon client, croyant que le Gouvernement va rester fidèle à son engagement, considère désormais l'affaire réglée par ces dispositions [dont] les parties sont convenues.“

[19] Toujours le 15 novembre 2000, la Cour a reçu du Gouvernement la déclaration suivante:

„J'ai le plaisir de vous informer par la présente que le Gouvernement turc est parvenu à un règlement amiable avec les requérants. Je joins en annexe la déclaration relative au règlement amiable.

En outre, le Gouvernement s'engage à ne pas demander le renvoi de l'affaire à la Grande Chambre conformément à l'ar. 43 de la Convention.“

Annexe

„1. Mettre en place un droit à l'usufruit au profit des Prêtres de l'Assomption sur la partie de l'immeuble utilisée à des fins commerciales qui comprend une église et un terrain, enregistrés au registre foncier au nom de la Direction générale des fondations suite à un arrêt judiciaire devenu définitif sous condition de céder en contrepartie, une partie des revenus qui seront perçus, à déterminer par accord entre les parties, à la direction générale des fondations, conformément à l'art. 57/g de la loi sur les appels d'offre; reconnaître le droit à l'usufruit de la partie du terrain qui comprend exclusivement l'église et ses dépendances aux prêtres qui les utilisent en vue du seul usage religieux, assurant leur entretien et les travaux de réparation et autres; enregistrer l'ensemble des inscriptions nécessaires à cet effet au registre foncier et conférer la garantie jugée comme appropriée afin d'assurer la même facilité à ceux qui, en cas de décès, succéderont aux prêtres dans leurs fonctions.

2. Assurer la solution adéquate concernant le droit à l'usufruit pour la partie de l'église transférée au Trésor en vertu d'un arrêt judiciaire définitif conformément à la [réglementation émanant de] la Direction générale des domaines nationaux.

3. Renonciation de la part de la Direction générale des fondations, dans le cadre du règlement amiable, à sa créance de 41 670 USD y compris les intérêts moratoires légaux découlant des suites de l'action intentée concernant le terrain utilisé par les Prêtres (ce point a été admis par l'arrêt no. 2000/80 rendu par la première chambre du Conseil d'Etat le 19 avril 2000)."

[20] La Cour prend acte du règlement amiable auquel sont parvenues les parties (art. 39 de la Convention). Elle est assurée que ce règlement s'inspire du respect des droits de l'homme tels que les reconnaissent la Convention ou ses Protocoles (art. 37 § 1 *in fine* de la Convention et 62 § 3 du règlement).

[21] Partant, il convient de rayer l'affaire du rôle.

Par ces motifs, la Cour, à unanimité, décide de rayer l'affaire du rôle.

58

Die Verbreitung von Propagandamaterial der Front Islamique du Salut (FIS) ist nicht Ausdruck einer religiösen Überzeugung im Sinne von Art. 9 EMRK.

Zur Frage der Zulässigkeit einer Beschränkung des Zugangs zu Kommunikationsmedien aus Gründen der öffentlichen Sicherheit und Ordnung.

Art. 9, 10, 35 §§ 3, 4 EMRK
EGMR, Beschluss vom 18. Januar 2001 - No. 41615/98
(Zaoui u.a. ./. Schweiz) -

EN FAIT

Le requérant est un ressortissant algérien, né en 1960 et résidant à Ouagadougou au Burkina Faso.

A. Les circonstances de l'espèce

Le requérant était à Alger l'un des membres du conseil consultatif national du Front Islamique du Salut (FIS). Il fut élu député du FIS lors des élections de décembre 1991. Il quitta l'Algérie dans le courant du mois de juillet 1993 pour se rendre au Maroc. Il apprit ultérieurement qu'il y avait été condamné à mort par contumace.

Par la suite, le requérant se réfugia d'abord en France, puis en Belgique où il déposa deux demandes d'asile politique qui furent rejetées. En raison de ses activités politiques, il fut condamné en appel à une peine de

4 ans d'emprisonnement avec sursis pour „association de malfaiteurs", en raison de son appartenance à un groupe d'islamistes. La nuit du 2 novembre 1997, le requérant quitta clandestinement le territoire belge où il avait fait l'objet d'une assignation à résidence et entra illégalement en Suisse le même jour. Il demanda l'asile politique aux autorités suisses.

Lors de son séjour en Suisse, le requérant a publié trois communiqués de propagande du Conseil de coordination à l'étranger du FIS (CCFIS), outre celui du 5 octobre 1997, rédigé alors qu'il se trouvait encore en Belgique. Dans ces communiqués, il annonçait la constitution du CCFIS, la composition de son bureau provisoire, déclarait s'écarter de la ligne du FIS et exposait les objectifs du CCFIS. Il appelait par ailleurs l'ensemble des partisans du projet islamique à se regrouper autour du CCFIS, dénonçait le pouvoir dictatorial en Algérie et soutenait la résistance populaire à l'intérieur du pays.

En raison de ces publications, le Conseil fédéral, par ordonnance du 27 avril 1998, décida d'interdire à Ahmed Zaoui et aux personnes mandatées par lui:

> „- de créer des organisations qui, par leur propagande, justifient, prônent, encouragent ou soutiennent matériellement des actes terroristes ou extrémistes à caractère violent ou toutes autres violences, ou de participer à de telles organisations qui visent notamment à perturber l'ordre étatique par la violence en Algérie;
> - de faire de la propagande pour de telles organisations, en particulier pour celles qui appellent indirectement à la violence ou à son soutien, ou qui justifient ou prônent le recours à la violence."

Dans la même décision, le Conseil fédéral ordonna, en application des art. 70, 102 chiffres 8 et 10 de la Constitution fédérale, la saisie, par la police, des télécopieurs du requérant, le blocage de ses raccordements à la messagerie électronique et à Internet qui avaient servi à la diffusion de ses communiqués, ainsi que la saisie de ses appareils téléphoniques s'il n'obtempérait pas à la décision.

B. Le droit interne pertinent

L'art. 70 de la Constitution fédérale prévoit:

> „La Confédération a le droit de renvoyer de son territoire les étrangers qui compromettent la sûreté intérieure ou extérieure de la Suisse".

L'art. 102 chiffres 8 et 10 de la Constitution fédérale dispose:

> „Les attributions et les obligations du Conseil fédéral, dans les limites de la présente constitution, sont notamment les suivantes:
> (...)

8. Il veille aux intérêts de la Confédération au dehors, notamment à l'observation de ses rapports internationaux, et il est, en général, chargé des relations extérieures;
(...)
10. Il veille à la sûreté intérieure de la Confédération, au maintien de la tranquillité et de l'ordre. (...)"
L'art. 53 de la Loi fédérale suisse sur l'asile dispose également:
„L'asile n'est pas accordé au réfugié qui en est indigne en raison d'actes répréhensibles, qui a porté atteinte à la sûreté intérieure ou extérieure de la Suisse ou qui la compromet".

GRIEFS

Invoquant les art. 9 et 10 de la Convention, le requérant se plaint de ce que la décision du Conseil fédéral de saisir les moyens de communication à sa disposition, de bloquer l'accès à la messagerie électronique et à Internet ainsi que la menace de la saisie de ses appareils téléphoniques constitue une entrave à sa liberté religieuse et une violation de son droit à la liberté d'expression.

EN DROIT

1. Le requérant se plaint de ce que la décision du Conseil fédéral de confisquer les moyens de communication dont il disposait a violé l'art. 9 de la Convention, ainsi libellé:

„1. Toute personne a droit à la liberté de pensée, de conscience et de religion; ce droit implique la liberté de changer de religion ou de conviction, ainsi que la liberté de manifester sa religion ou sa conviction individuellement ou collectivement, en public ou en privé, par le culte, l'enseignement, les pratiques et l'accomplissement des rites.
2. La liberté de manifester sa religion ou ses convictions ne peut faire l'objet d'autres restrictions que celles qui, prévues par la loi, constituent des mesures nécessaires, dans une société démocratique, à la sécurité publique, à la protection de l'ordre, de la santé ou de la morale publiques, ou à la protection des droits et libertés d'autrui."

La Cour rappelle que l'art. 9 de la Convention protège avant tout le domaine des convictions personnelles et des croyances religieuses; c'est-à-dire ce qui relève du for intérieur. De plus, cette disposition protège les actes intimement liés à ces comportements, tels les actes de culte ou de dévotion qui sont des aspects de la pratique d'une religion ou d'une croyance reconnues (CommEuDH, N° 11308/84, décision du 13 avril 1986, DR 46, p. 200).

En l'espèce, la Cour observe que les activités du requérant visaient principalement à diffuser des messages de propagande en faveur du FIS et ne constituaient pas l'expression d'une conviction religieuse au sens de l'art. 9 de la Convention. La Cour constate dès lors que la confiscation des moyens de communication utilisés à des fins de propagande politique ne met pas en cause la liberté de religion.

Dans ces conditions, le présent grief doit être rejeté comme manifestement mal fondé au sens de l'art. 35 § 3 et en application de l'art. 35 § 4 de la Convention.

2. Le requérant allègue également que la saisie de ses télécopieurs, le blocage de ses raccordements à la messagerie électronique et à Internet ainsi que la menace de la saisie de ses appareils téléphoniques constituent une violation de l'art. 10 de la Convention selon lequel:

„1. Toute personne a droit à la liberté d'expression. Ce droit comprend la liberté d'opinion et la liberté de recevoir ou de communiquer des informations ou des idées sans qu'il puisse y avoir ingérence d'autorités publiques et sans considération de frontière. Le présent article n'empêche pas les Etats de soumettre les entreprises de radiodiffusion, de cinéma ou de télévision à un régime d'autorisations.

2. L'exercice de ces libertés comportant des devoirs et des responsabilités peut être soumis à certaines formalités, conditions, restrictions ou sanctions prévues par la loi, qui constituent des mesures nécessaires, dans une société démocratique, à la sécurité nationale, à l'intégrité territoriale ou à la sûreté publique, à la défense de l'ordre et à la prévention du crime, à la protection de la santé ou de la morale, à la protection de la réputation ou des droits d'autrui, pour empêcher la divulgation d'informations confidentielles ou pour garantir l'autorité et l'impartialité du pouvoir judiciaire."

a) Concernant la menace de saisie des appareils téléphoniques, la Cour constate que le requérant ne peut se prétendre victime au sens de l'art. 34 de la Convention, car il s'agit uniquement d'une sanction hypothétique qui n'a, de surcroît, jamais été effective et mise en œuvre par les autorités fédérales.

b) En ce qui concerne la confiscation des télécopieurs et le blocage des raccordements à Internet, la condamnation litigieuse s'analyse en une „ingérence" dans l'exercice par l'intéressé de sa liberté d'expression. Pareille immixtion enfreint l'art. 10, sauf si elle est „prévue par la loi", dirigée vers un ou des buts légitimes au regard du par. 2 et „nécessaire" dans une société démocratique pour les atteindre.

1. „Prévue par la loi"

La Cour considère que l'ingérence est „prévue par la loi", à savoir l'art. 102 ch. 8 et 10 de la Constitution fédérale.

2. Buts légitimes

La Cour constate que selon l'art. 102 ch. 10 de la Constitution fédérale, une des attributions du Conseil fédéral consiste à veiller à la sûreté intérieure de la Confédération, au maintien de la tranquillité et de l'ordre. Dès lors, l'ingérence apparaît légitime puisqu'elle a pour but de protéger la sécurité nationale, la sûreté publique et la défense de l'ordre en Suisse.

3. „Nécessaire dans une société démocratique"

La Cour doit rechercher si ladite ingérence était „nécessaire", dans une société démocratique, pour atteindre ces buts.

La Cour rappelle que la liberté d'expression constitue l'un des fondements essentiels d'une société démocratique. Sous réserve du par. 2 de l'art. 10, elle vaut non seulement pour les „informations" ou „idées" accueillies avec faveur ou considérées comme inoffensives ou indifférentes, mais aussi pour celles qui heurtent, choquent ou inquiètent: ainsi le veulent le pluralisme, la tolérance et l'esprit d'ouverture sans lesquels il n'est pas de „société démocratique" (arrêts Handyside c. Royaume-Uni du 7 décembre 1976, série A n° 24, p. 23, § 49, et Jersild c. Danemark du 23 septembre 1994, série A n° 298, p. 26, § 37).

D'une manière générale, la „nécessité" d'une quelconque restriction à l'exercice de la liberté d'expression doit se trouver établie de façon convaincante (arrêt Sunday Times c. Royaume-Uni (n° 2) du 26 novembre 1991, série A n° 217, pp. 28-29, § 50). Certes, il revient en premier lieu aux autorités nationales d'évaluer s'il existe un „besoin social impérieux" susceptible de justifier cette restriction, exercice pour lequel elles bénéficient d'une certaine marge d'appréciation.

La Cour n'a pas pour tâche, lorsqu'elle exerce son contrôle, de se substituer aux juridictions internes, mais elle doit vérifier, sous l'angle de l'art. 10 de la Convention, les décisions qu'elles ont rendues en vertu de leur pouvoir d'appréciation. Pour cela, la Cour doit considérer „l'ingérence" litigieuse à la lumière de l'ensemble de l'affaire pour déterminer si les motifs invoqués par les autorités nationales pour la justifier apparaissent „pertinents et suffisants" (arrêt Goodwin c. Royaume-Uni du 27 mars 1996, RJD 1996-II, pp. 500-501, § 40).

En l'espèce, la Cour observe que la mesure prise par le Conseil fédéral visait selon lui à confisquer les moyens de communication rapides tels que télécopieurs et messagerie électronique afin d'empêcher le requérant de poursuivre de la propagande politique au niveau international.

Avant de s'établir sur le territoire helvétique, le requérant séjournait en Belgique où il était assigné à résidence et faisait l'objet de contrôles stricts. Il avait également été condamné avec sursis pour „association de malfaiteurs". Malgré toutes les mesures de surveillance mises en place, le requérant a quitté clandestinement la Belgique, sans disposer de documents d'identité, afin de se rendre illégalement en Suisse pour y déposer une demande d'asile.

De plus, la décision du 27 avril 1998 du Conseil fédéral était fondée sur le fait que le requérant s'était adonné à des actes de propagande politique

alors que sa demande d'asile était pendante. Or, en vertu de l'art. 53 de
la Loi fédérale suisse sur l'asile, la Confédération est en droit de refuser
l'asile à un réfugié qui menace la sûreté intérieure ou extérieure de la
Suisse ou qui la compromet.

En l'occurrence, il est difficile pour un Etat tiers d'évaluer la situation
politique régnant en Algérie, de déterminer l'influence des partis politiques et des groupes armés et de mesurer le risque et l'impact des activités exercées à l'étranger par des personnalités appartenant à l'opposition
islamique. Toutefois, compte tenu du contexte dans lequel le requérant a
quitté l'Algérie où il avait été condamné à mort par contumace, de son activité liée à l'opposition islamique, de sa condamnation en Belgique, des
circonstances dans lesquelles il est entré en Suisse, des raisons de son séjour et de ses agissements dans ce pays d'accueil, la saisie des moyens de
communication afin d'empêcher le requérant de poursuivre de la propagande pour le CCFIS peut être justifiée comme nécessaire dans une société démocratique à la sécurité nationale et à la sûreté publique.

Par conséquent, le grief tiré de l'art. 10 de la Convention est manifestement mal fondé au sens de l'art. 35 § 3 et doit être rejeté conformément
à l'art. 35 § 4 de la Convention.

Par ces motifs, la Cour, à l'unanimité, déclare la requête irrecevable.

59

**Zur Frage der Einschränkung des staatlichen Rechtsschutzes bei
Streitigkeiten wegen Beendigung des kirchlichen Dienstverhältnis-
ses eines Geistlichen.**

Art. 6 Abs. 1, 35 §§ 1, 4 EMRK
EGMR, Beschluss vom 30. Januar 2001 - No. 40224/98
(Dudova u.a. ./. Tschechische Republik)[1] -

EN FAITS

Les requérants sont des ressortissants tchèques, nés respectivement en
1954 et 1958 et résidant à Prague.

A. Les circonstances de l'espèce

Depuis le 1er février 1993, les requérants exerçaient leur profession de
prêtre auprès de l'Église tchécoslovaque hussite *(Církev Československá
husitská)* („l'Église") à Křemž et České Budějovice - Rožnov, respectivement. Leur rapport de service *(služební poměr)* avec l'Église était basé

---

[1] öarr 2003, 149 (LS).

sur deux décrets de désignation du conseil du diocèse *(diecézní rada)* de Plzeň du 28 janvier 1993. Le conseil du diocèse leur payait également leur salaire.

Les 21 juin et 1ᵉʳ juillet 1993, les requérants demandèrent à interrompre leur service ecclésiastique alléguant que les relations de travail avec leurs collègues n'étaient pas satisfaisantes. Par deux décisions du 20 juillet 1993, le conseil du diocèse constata que les requérants avaient quitté leur appartement de service le 22 juin 1993 et que depuis, ils n'avaient pas rempli leur mission ecclésiastique. Le conseil informa également les requérants qu'il ne pouvait pas répondre favorablement à leur demande d'interrompre le service ecclésiastique. Par ailleurs, le Statut de l'Eglise *(organizační řád)* n'autorisant pas une telle interruption, leur rapport de service prit fin à la date de la notification de ces décisions.

Le 17 janvier 1994, les requérants engagèrent une procédure civile contre l'archevêque de l'Administration ecclésiastique du diocèse de l'Eglise tchécoslovaque hussite de Plzeň *(Duchovní správa diecéze církve Československé husitské)*. Ils demandèrent que la fin de leur rapport de service constatée dans la décision du 20 juillet 1993 soit annulée *ex tunc* et qu'une somme de CZK 37,380 et de CZK 35,980 leurs soit payée au titre des salaires perdus.

Par jugement du 8 septembre 1994, le tribunal de district de Plzeň-město *(okresní soud)* rejeta l'action des requérants en relevant en particulier que ces derniers n'avaient pas été en rapport de service avec l'archevêque qui ne pouvait pas être partie à la procédure.

Par arrêt du 28 mars 1995, la cour régionale de Plzeň *(krajský soud)* annula le jugement du tribunal de district et suspendit la procédure. La cour releva entre autre:

„L'objet de la procédure, tel qu'il avait été formulé par les requérants, était la question de savoir si leur rapport de service en tant que prêtres de l'Eglise tchécoslovaque hussite avait été rompu valablement. Selon l'art. 7 du code de procédure civile, les tribunaux civils examinent et décident des affaires concernant les relations juridiques, de travail, familiales, de coopérative ainsi que les relations commerciales sauf si elles sont examinées et réglées, conformément à la loi, par d'autres autorités. (...) Par conséquent, les litiges entre un prêtre et l'Eglise sont exclus de la compétence des tribunaux, ce qui est, par ailleurs, souligné par la loi sur la liberté de religion et sur la position des Eglises et communautés religieuses (loi n° 308/1991). Selon l'art. 5-2 de cette loi, les Eglises et communautés religieuses gèrent leurs affaires; en particulier, elles désignent leurs organes, prêtres et institutions indépendamment à des autorités d'État. Selon l'art. 7, les personnes exerçant des activités ecclésiastiques, sont mandatées par l'Eglise ou la communauté religieuse qui évaluent leur capacité à exercer de telles activités (...).
Dans ces circonstances, il est évident qu'une décision des tribunaux sur l'existence d'un rapport de service entre un prêtre et l'Église aurait constitué une atteinte inadmissible à l'autonomie interne de cette dernière et à son indépendance décisionnelle. Une telle atteinte aurait été en contradiction avec la loi constitutionnelle n° 23/1993 sur la Charte des droits et libertés fondamentaux qui, dans son

*art. 16-2, stipule (...) que les Eglises et communautés religieuses gèrent leurs af-
faires, particulièrement, elles nomment leurs organes et prêtres indépendamment
aux autorités d'Etat. Les tribunaux ne peuvent même pas examiner [l'affaire des
requérants] au regard du Chapitre V du code de procédure civile relatif à la justice administrative (...) car leur compétence ne porte que sur les décisions en matière d'administration publique, par opposition au domaine privé dont relève
l'administration interne des Eglises.
La cour d'appel donc a constaté que l'affaire des requérants ne relève pas de la
compétence des tribunaux. En conséquence, la cour (...) a annulé le jugement de
première instance et a suspendu la procédure. En même temps, elle a transmis le
dossier à l'autorité compétente. En fait, conformément à l'art. 34 du Statut de
l'Église tchécoslovaque hussite, le rapport de service d'un prêtre avec l'Église est
rompue par libération du rapport de service par le Conseil central qui est (...) ap-
pelé à résoudre cette affaire."*
*Le 11 avril 1995, les requérants saisirent le tribunal d'arrondissement de Prague
6 (obvodní soud) d'une action contre le Conseil central de l'Eglise tchécoslovaque
hussite (Ústřední rada Církve Československé husitské) tendant à ce que le tribunal lui ordonne de rompre valablement le rapport de service des requérants et de
leur délivrer leurs fiches de service (zápočtové listy). Ils firent valoir que leur demande d'interruption du rapport de service du 23 juin 1993 n'avait pas été examinée par le Conseil central, tandis que le conseil du diocèse de Plzeň y avait ré-
pondu par rupture du rapport de service, ce que les requérants considèrent être
une violation de l'art. 34a du Statut car le conseil du diocèse n'était pas compétent pour prendre une telle décision. Les requérants demandèrent également à ce
que des dommages et intérêts correspondant à leurs salaires perdus leur soient
payés.*
*Le 11 mai 1995, les requérants complétèrent leur action par une demande ten-
dant à ce que le tribunal d'arrondissement déclare que la rupture du rapport de
service du 20 juillet 1993 était un acte nul ex tunc.*
*Le 8 janvier 1996, le tribunal d'arrondissement de Prague 6 suspendit la procé-
dure en transmettant l'affaire au Conseil central de l'Eglise. Le tribunal releva,
en particulier:*
*„Selon l'art. 33 du Statut de l'Église tchécoslovaque hussite, le rapport de service
d'un prêtre en tant qu'employé de l'Eglise débute par son accueil par le Conseil
central. La relation de service commence par l'entrée sur les postes de services
auprès des unités d'organisation de l'Eglise (...). Les unités d'organisation (...)
sont - vis-à-vis des prêtres - en position d'employeur. Selon l'art. 34, le rapport de
service entre le prêtre et l'Eglise hussite peux être interrompu par libération du
prêtre des services de l'Eglise, par perte des capacités d'exercer le service ecclésiastique, par acceptation d'une résignation, départ à la retraite, par abandon de
l'Eglise et par décès.*
*Selon ces dispositions, il n'y a pas de doutes que le rapport de service des prêtres
avec l'Eglise est gouverné uniquement par le Statut de l'Eglise et non par le code
du travail. (...) Selon l'ar. 65 [du code du travail], le rapport de travail, établi par
élection ou désignation, commence le jour fixé comme l'entrée aux fonctions. Il
s'agit donc de l'établissement du rapport de travail sur la base de l'élection ou désignation. Selon les dispositions du Statut ainsi que les dispositions de la loi
n° 308/1991, le rapport de service des prêtres ne commence en aucun cas comme
il a été indiqué dans l'art. 65 du code du travail (...). Les prêtres sont accueillis
dans le service de l'Eglise par un acte interne d'un organe qui, conformément au*

Statut, est compétent à accueillir des personnes physiques dans le service ecclésiastique. L'intervention de la part de l'Etat aurait constitué une restriction des compétences des Eglises dans un contexte où la liberté de religion est garantie (...). Une décision judiciaire sur la continuation du rapport de service d'un prêtre avec l'Eglise aurait été une atteinte inadmissible à l'autonomie interne de l'Eglise, à son indépendance décisionnelle qui est garantie par la loi n° 23/1991 sur la Charte des droits et libertés fondamentaux ainsi que par la loi n° 308/1991."

Par arrêt du 30 avril 1996, la cour municipale de Prague *(městský soud)* confirma le jugement de première instance.

Le 29 juillet 1996, les requérants introduisirent un recours constitutionnel *(ústavní stížnost)* alléguant que par décisions des tribunaux ordinaires, leurs droits garanti par les art. 26 §§ 1 et 3 et 36 §§ 1 et 2 de la Charte des droits et libertés fondamentaux *(Listina základních práv a svobod)* avaient été violés. Ils alléguèrent également que la Conseil central de l'Eglise, par l'intermédiaire de l'archevêque de Plzeň, avait rompu le rapport de service des requérants avec l'Eglise en violation de l'art. 34 du Statut de l'Eglise. Ils firent valoir que la terminaison de leur relation de service n'était pas valide et que le Conseil central de l'Eglise devait immédiatement mettre fin au rapport de service de façon valable, rembourser aux requérants leurs salaires perdus depuis le 1er juillet 1993, et leur délivrer leurs fiches de service.

Le 26 mars 1997, la Cour constitutionnelle *(Ústavní soud)* adopta un arrêt annulant le jugement du tribunal d'arrondissement de Prague 6 du 8 janvier 1996 ainsi que l'arrêt de la cour municipale de Prague du 30 avril 1996 dans la mesure où ils concernaient la suspension de la procédure quant à la demande des requérants de payer des dommages et intérêts correspondant à leurs salaires perdus. Pour le surplus, la Cour constitutionnelle rejeta le recours des requérants. Elle releva en particulier:

„En ce qui concerne la question d'établir la nullité de la rupture du rapport de service, la Cour constitutionnelle a conclu, à l'instar de la cour d'appel, que selon l'art. 16 § 2 de la Charte des droits et libertés fondamentaux, les Eglises gèrent leurs affaires, fondant en particulier leurs organes, accueillant leurs prêtres et créant leurs institutions indépendamment aux autorités d'Etat. Selon les art. 7-1 et 7-2 de la loi n° 308/1991 sur la liberté de religion et la position des Eglises et communautés religieuses, les personnes exerçant les activités ecclésiastiques agissent au nom des Eglises et des communautés religieuses conformément aux règles internes et aux actes législatifs. (...)
Les tribunaux ordinaires ont relevé à juste titre qu'une décision sur la continuation du rapport de service du prêtre aurait constitué une atteinte inadmissible à l'autonomie de l'Eglise et à son indépendance décisionnelle, telle qui est décrite dans l'art. 34 du Statut de l'Église tchécoslovaque hussite, selon lequel le rapport de service entre le prêtre et l'Eglise peut être rompu par sa libération des services de l'Eglise faite par le Conseil central. (...)

Dans la mesure où le recours constitutionnel des requérants concerne le payement de leurs salaires perdus et autres prétentions pécuniaires, [la Cour constitutionnelle] estime que ces affaires ne constituent pas une atteinte à l'autonomie interne de l'Eglise et à son pouvoir de décision. Ici, l'Eglise représente une personne légale ayant un caractère privé et des obligations envers des tiers (...). Selon l'art. 7 du code de procédure civile, les tribunaux examinent et décident des affaires relevant des relations du droit civil, du travail [etc.]. Dans ce cas, les tribunaux doivent déterminer, sur la base des documents juridiques produits par les parties, s'ils examinent l'affaire conformément aux dispositions du code civile ou du code de travail (l'art. 7 de la loi n° 308/1991), et puis prendre une décision sur les griefs des requérants, ce qu'ils n'ont pas encore fait.

Par conséquent, dans la mesure où les tribunaux ordinaires ont relevé leur incompétence pour examiner le cas d'espèce, ils ont violé les droits et libertés fondamentaux des requérants garantis par l'art. 36 § 1, selon lequel toute personne a droit de faire examiner son affaire devant un tribunal indépendant et impartial, ainsi par l'art. 90 de la Constitution, selon lequel les tribunaux sont appelés en particulier à protéger les droits suivant la voie légale (...)"

Le 8 janvier 1998, le tribunal d'arrondissement de Prague 6 rejeta l'action des requérants tendant à ce que le Conseil central de l'Eglise tchécoslovaque hussite leur paie respectivement CZK 423,388 et CZK 407,765 avec des intérêts, à titre de salaires perdus.

Le 16 juin 1998, la cour municipale de Prague annula le jugement du tribunal d'arrondissement et renvoya l'affaire à ce tribunal pour un nouveau jugement.

Par jugement du 26 février 1999, le tribunal d'arrondissement de Prague 6 ordonna que le Conseil central verse la somme de CZK 118,480 avec intérêts à la requérante et la somme de CZK 114,080 avec intérêts au requérant, au titre de leurs salaires perdus entre 20 juillet 1993 et 30 avril 1995. Le tribunal fit droit aux requérants dans la mesure où il constata que l'Eglise avait violé son Statut quand le rapport de service avec les requérants avait été terminé par le conseil du diocèse et non par le Conseil central. Il releva néanmoins que les requérants n'avaient le droit au paiement de dommages et intérêts qu'en ce qui concerne la période du 20 juillet 1993 et 30 avril 1995 car, ayant reçu leurs listes blanches le 15 avril 1995, ils pouvaient conclure un nouveau contrat de travail depuis cette date.

Par arrêt du 24 septembre 1999, la cour municipale de Prague confirma le jugement de la première instance.

B. Le droit interne pertinent

Charte des droits et libertés fondamentaux

Selon l'art. 3 § 1 de la Charte, les droits et libertés fondamentaux sont garantis à tous, sans distinction de sexe, de race, de couleur, de croyance et de religion, d'opinion politique ou autre, d'origine nationale ou sociale, d'appartenance à une minorité nationale ou ethnique, de fortune, de naissance ou d'autre situation. L'art. 9 dispose entre autres que nul ne sera astreint à accomplir des travaux ou services forcés. Ne constituent pas les travaux ou services forcés les travaux imposés en vertu de la loi aux personnes qui purgent une peine privative de liberté ou une autre peine remplaçant une peine privative de liberté, le service militaire ou un autre service prévu par la loi à la place du service militaire obligatoire, le service requis en vertu de la loi dans le cas de calamités, de sinistres ou d'autres dangers qui menacent la vie, la santé ou des biens importants, ou les actions imposées par la loi afin de protéger la vie, la santé ou les droits d'autrui.

Selon l'art. 15 § 1, la liberté de pensée, de conscience et de croyance religieuse est garantie. Chacun a le droit de changer de religion ou de croyance ou de ne pas avoir de croyance religieuse.

L'art. 16 dispose que chacun a le droit de manifester librement sa religion ou sa croyance individuellement ou en commun avec d'autres, en privé ou en public par le culte, l'enseignement, les pratiques religieuses et l'accomplissement des rites. Les églises et les sociétés religieuses gèrent leurs affaires; elles mettent notamment en place leurs autorités, désignent les ecclésiastiques et fondent leurs ordres et autres institutions religieuses indépendamment des organes de l'Etat. L'exercice de ces droits peut être limité par la loi s'il s'agit de mesures nécessaires, dans une société démocratique, à la protection de la sûreté publique et de l'ordre, de la santé et de la morale ou des droits et libertés d'autrui.

Selon l'art. 26, chacun a droit au libre choix de sa profession et à la formation professionnelle, ainsi qu'à entreprendre et à réaliser une autre activité économique. Néanmoins, la loi peut imposer des conditions et des restrictions à l'exercice de certaines professions ou activités. Chacun a également le droit de se procurer les moyens de couvrir ses besoins par le travail. L'État garantit matériellement ce droit, dans une étendue adéquate, aux citoyens hors d'état de l'exercer pour des raisons qui ne leur sont pas imputables; les conditions en sont établies par la loi.

L'art. 36 dispose que chacun a droit de demander justice, suivant une procédure définie, auprès d'un tribunal indépendant et impartial et, dans des cas déterminés, auprès d'une autre autorité. Par ailleurs, celui qui affirme avoir été lésé dans ses droits par une décision d'une autorité administrative peut s'adresser au tribunal en lui demandant de réexaminer la légalité d'une telle décision à moins que la loi n'en dispose autrement. Toutefois, le réexamen des décisions relatives aux droits et libertés fondamentaux selon la Charte ne peut pas être exclu des pouvoirs du tribunal. Chacun a également droit à la réparation du préjudice causé par une décision illégale d'un tribunal ou d'une autre autorité de l'Etat ou d'une autorité administrative ou par une procédure officielle incorrecte. Les conditions et détails sont fixés par la loi.

GRIEF

Invoquant l'art. 6 § 1 de la Convention, les requérants se plaignent de la violation de leur droit d'accès au tribunal dans la mesure où tant les tribunaux ordinaires que la Cour constitutionnelle n'auraient pas examiné la question de la validité de la terminaison du rapport de service des requérants avec l'Eglise tchécoslovaque hussite.

Ils se plaignent également, sous l'angle de l'art. 4 § 2 de la Convention, de ce que la pratique juridique des tribunaux tchèques dans les affaires concernant les questions de rapports de service conclus entre des prêtres et les Eglises donne à l'activité ecclésiastique le caractère d'un travail forcé.

Invoquant l'art. 9 de la Convention, les requérants allèguent qu'ils auraient été privés de leur liberté d'exercer l'activité de prêtres de l'Eglise et, par conséquent, de manifester leur religion collectivement par la liturgie et les pratiques religieuses, et par l'éducation religieuse.

Enfin, les requérants se plaignent d'avoir été discriminés par rapport à d'autres employés dont les rapports de travail sont régis par le code de travail et dont litiges éventuels avec leurs employeurs tombent dans la compétence des tribunaux nationaux. Ils invoquent à cet égard l'art. 14 de la Convention.

EN DROIT

1. Invoquant l'art. 6 § 1 de la Convention, les requérants se plaignent de la violation de leur droit d'accès au tribunal dans la mesure où tant les tribunaux ordinaires que la Cour constitutionnelle n'auraient pas statué sur la question de la validité de la terminaison de leur rapport de service avec l'Eglise tchécoslovaque hussite.

L'art. 6 § 1 dispose notamment que:

> *„Toute personne a droit à ce que sa cause soit entendue équitablement (...), par un tribunal (...) qui décidera (...) des contestations sur ses droits et obligations de caractère civil (...)"*

A titre préliminaire, la Cour estime nécessaire de déterminer si les juridictions tchèques étaient saisies d'une contestation portant sur un „droit" que l'on peut dire, de manière défendable, reconnu en droit interne au sens de l'art. 6 § 1 de la Convention.

La Cour rappelle à cet égard que l'art. 6 § 1 ne vise pas à créer de nouveaux droits matériels qui n'ont pas de fondement légal dans l'Etat considéré, mais à fournir une protection procédurale aux droits reconnus en droit interne. Ainsi, l'art. 6 § 1 de la Convention régit uniquement les „contestations" relatives à des droits et obligations de caractère civil que l'on peut dire, au moins de manière défendable, reconnus en droit interne; il n'assure par lui-même aux droits et obligations de caractère civil aucun contenu matériel déterminé dans l'ordre juridique des Etats contractants. Les contestations peuvent concerner aussi bien l'existence même d'un droit que son étendue ou ses modalités d'exercice. L'issue de la procédure doit être directement déterminante pour le droit en question. La Cour a toujours considéré qu'un lien ténu ou des répercussions lointaines ne suffisent pas à faire entrer en jeu l'art. 6 § 1 (voir les arrêts suivants: Le Compte, Van Leuven et De Meyere c. Belgique du 23 juin 1981, série A n° 43, pp. 21-22, § 47; W. c. Royaume-Uni du 8 juillet 1987, série A n° 121, p. 32 et suivant, § 73; Fayed c. Royaume-Uni du 21 septembre 1994, série A n° 294-B, pp. 45-46, § 56; Masson et Van Zon c. Pays-Bas du 28 septembre 1995, série A n° 327-A, p. 17, § 44; Balmer-Schafroth et autres précité, p. 1357, § 32; Le Calvez c. France du 29 juillet 1998, Recueil des arrêts et décisions 1998-V, p. 1899, § 56).

La Cour constate que les requérants, exerçant le métier de prêtres auprès de l'Eglise tchécoslovaque hussite, et licenciés par une décision du conseil du diocèse, sans aucune intervention d'une décision d'une autorité publique, ont fait valoir devant les juridictions tchèques que la terminaison de leur rapport de service avec l'Eglise était nulle car décidée par une autorité de l'Eglise incompétente. Les requérants sollicitaient, par ailleurs, une indemnisation du préjudice subi du fait de leur licenciement et de la non-délivrance de leurs fiches de service. La Cour observe cependant que ladite indemnisation leur a été accordée. Il s'agit donc de déterminer si un „droit" à l'examen de la validité de la terminaison du rapport de service d'un prêtre avec l'Eglise, réclamé par les requérants pouvait, de manière défendable, passer pour reconnu en droit interne.

La Cour note que la première action des requérants dirigée contre l'archevêque de l'Administration ecclésiastique du diocèse de l'Eglise tchécoslovaque hussite de Plzeň s'est terminée par la constatation de l'incompétence par la cour régionale de Plzeň qui a relevé entre autres que les litiges entre un prêtre et l'Eglise sont exclus de la compétence des tribunaux civils. En fait, selon les art. 5-2 et 7 de la loi sur la liberté de religion et sur la position des Eglises et communautés religieuse n° 308/1991, les Eglises et communautés religieuses gèrent leurs affaires indépendamment des autorités d'Etat, et les personnes exerçant des activités ecclésiastiques sont mandatées par l'Eglise ou la communauté religieuse qui évaluent leur capacité à exercer de telles activités. La cour régionale a conclu qu'une décision des tribunaux sur l'existence d'un rapport de service entre un prêtre et l'Eglise aurait constitué une atteinte inadmissible à l'autonomie interne de cette dernière ainsi qu'à son indépendance décisionnelle, en violation de l'art. 16-2 de la Charte des droits et libertés fondamentaux.

La seconde action des requérants, dirigée cette fois-ci contre le Conseil central de l'Eglise tchécoslovaque hussite, fut également rejetée par le tribunal d'arrondissement de Prague 6 dont le jugement fut confirmé par la cour municipale de Prague. Les deux juridictions ont relevé en particulier que les rapports de service des prêtres avec l'Eglise sont gouvernés uniquement par le Statut de l'Eglise, ne commençant de la même manière qu'un rapport de travail établi par élection ou désignation en vertu du code de travail. Les prêtres sont accueillis dans le service de l'Eglise par un acte interne émanant d'un organe qui, conformément au Statut, est compétent à accueillir des personnes physiques dans le service ecclésiastique. Les deux tribunaux ont constaté, à l'instar de l'opinion des juridictions exprimée dans la procédure précédente, qu'une décision judiciaire sur la continuation du rapport de service d'un prêtre avec l'Eglise aurait constitué une atteinte inadmissible à l'autonomie interne de l'Eglise, à son indépendance décisionnelle qui est garantie par la Charte des droits et libertés fondamentaux ainsi que par la loi sur la liberté de religion et sur la position des Eglises et communautés religieuses. La Cour constitutionnelle a confirmé le raisonnement des tribunaux ordinaires.

Dans ces circonstances, la Cour considère que les procédures engagées par les requérants ne portaient nullement sur un „droit" que l'on pouvait prétendre, de manière défendable, reconnu en droit tchèque.

Il est vrai que le tribunal d'arrondissement de Prague 6 ainsi que la cour municipale de Prague, en examinant ensuite la demande des requérants visant le versement d'une indemnisation au titre de leurs salaires perdus, ont constaté que l'Eglise avait violé son Statut quand le rapport de service avec les requérants avait été terminé par le conseil du diocèse et non par le Conseil central. Néanmoins, cette constatation n'a aucunement affecté l'incompétence des juridictions tchèques pour statuer sur la validité ou la nullité de la terminaison du rapport de service des requérants en tant que prêtres auprès de l'Eglise tchécoslovaque hussite.

Cela étant, l'art. 6 § 1 de la Convention n'était pas applicable à la procédure en cause. Partant, cette partie de la requête doit être rejetée comme étant incompatible *ratione materiae* en application des dispositions de l'art. 35 §§ 3 et 4 de la Convention.

2. Les requérants se plaignent également de ce que les décisions des tribunaux nationaux équivalent à une violation de leur droit de ne pas être soumis à un travail forcé ou obligatoire au sens de l'art. 4 § 2 de la Convention, de leur droit de liberté de religion garanti par l'art. 9 de la Convention, ainsi que de leur droit de ne pas être discriminé au sens de l'art. 14 de la Convention.

Toutefois, la Cour n'est pas appelée à se prononcer sur le point de savoir si les faits allégués par les requérants révèlent l'apparence d'une violation de ces dispositions. En effet, aux termes de l'art. 35 § 1 de la Convention, „la Cour ne peut être saisie qu'après l'épuisement des voies de recours internes, tel qu'il est entendu selon les principes de droit international généralement reconnus". Le fondement de la règle de l'épuisement des voies de recours internes consiste en ce qu'avant de saisir un tribunal international, le requérant doit avoir donné à l'Etat responsable la faculté d'éviter, de redresser ou de remédier aux violations alléguées par des moyens internes, en utilisant les ressources judiciaires offertes par la législation nationale pourvu qu'elles se révèlent efficaces et suffisantes (voir, par exemple, l'arrêt Cardot c. France du 9 mars 1991, série A n° 200, p. 19, § 36). La Cour note que la Convention forme partie intégrante du système juridique tchèque où elle prime la loi. Elle relève en outre que ses art. 4, 9 et 14 revêtent un caractère directement applicable; les requérants auraient donc pu se prévaloir de ces dispositions devant les juridictions nationales ordinaires et, en particulier, devant la Cour constitutionnelle, et plaider qu'elles se trouvaient violées dans leur chef. Or les requérants ne se sont appuyés, à aucun moment devant les instances judiciaires nationales, sur les art. 4, 9 et 14 de la Convention ni sur des moyens d'effet équivalent ou similaire fondés sur le droit interne, en l'occurrence les art. 3, 9, 15 et 16 de la Charte des droits et libertés fondamentaux.

Tant devant les tribunaux ordinaires que devant la Cour constitutionnelle, les requérants se sont bornés à démontrer la violation de leur droit au libre choix de leur profession, leur droit de se procurer les moyens de couvrir leurs besoins par le travail, ainsi que leur droit à la protection judiciaire et juridique en invoquant expressément l'art. 26 §§ 1 et 3, ainsi que l'art. 36 §§ 1 et 2 de la Charte. A cet égard, la présente affaire se distingue nettement de l'affaire Castells c. Espagne où le requérant avait invoqué devant la Cour suprême et le Tribunal constitutionnel l'article pertinent de la Constitution espagnole (arrêt du 23 avril 1992, série A n° 236, p. 20, § 31).

A supposer même que les juridictions tchèques aient pu, voire dû, examiner d'office le litige sous l'angle d'une disposition particulière de la Convention, cela ne saurait avoir dispensé les requérants de s'appuyer devant elles sur ce traité ou de leur présenter des moyens d'effet équivalent ou similaire et attirer ainsi leur attention sur le problème dont ils entendaient saisir après coup, au besoin, la Cour (voir, l'arrêt Van Oosterwijck c. Belgique du 6 novembre 1980, série A n° 40, p. 19, par. 39).

Dans ces circonstances, la Cour estime que le requérant n'a pas satisfait à la condition relative à l'épuisement des voies de recours internes et que cette partie de sa requête doit être rejetée conformément à l'art. 35 §§ 1 et 4 de la Convention.

Par ces motifs, la Cour, à la majorité, déclare la requête irrecevable.

60

Die Schulbehörde des Kantons Genf hat ihren Beurteilungsspielraum nicht überschritten, als sie unter Abwägung der Religionsfreiheit der Lehrkräfte gegenüber dem Schutz des religiösen Friedens einer Lehrerin muslimischen Glaubens insbesondere wegen

**des Alters der Kinder untersagte, während des Unterrichts an einer
öffentlichen Grundschule ein Kopftuch zu tragen.**

Art. 9, 14, 35 EMRK

EGMR, Beschluss vom 15. Februar 2001 - No. 42393/98

(Dahlab ./. Schweiz)[1] -

THE FACTS

The applicant [Lucia Dahlab], a Swiss national born in 1965, is a
primary-school teacher and lives in Geneva (Switzerland).

A. The circumstances of the case

The applicant was appointed as a primary-school teacher by the Geneva cantonal government (Conseil d'Etat) on 1 September 1990, having
taught at Châtelaine Primary School in the Canton of Geneva since the
1989-90 school year.

After a period of spiritual soul-searching, the applicant abandoned the
Catholic faith and converted to Islam in March 1991. On 19 October 1991
she married an Algerian national, Mr A. Dahlab. The marriage has produced three children, born in 1992, 1994 and 1998.

The applicant began wearing an Islamic headscarf in class towards the
end of the 1990-91 school year, her intention being to observe a precept
laid down in the Koran whereby women were enjoined to draw their veils
over themselves in the presence of men and male adolescents.

The applicant went on maternity leave from 21 August 1992 to 7 January 1993 and from 12 January 1994 to 1 June 1994.

In May 1995 the schools inspector for the Vernier district informed the
Canton of Geneva Directorate General for Primary Education that the
applicant regularly wore an Islamic headscarf at school; the inspector
added that she had never had any comments from parents on the subject.

On 27 June 1996 a meeting was held between the applicant, the Director General of Primary Education („the Director General") and the head
of the teaching-personnel department concerning the fact that the applicant wore a headscarf. In a letter of 11 July 1996 the Director General
confirmed the position she had adopted at the meeting, requesting the
applicant to stop wearing the headscarf while carrying out her professional duties, as such conduct was incompatible with sec. 6 of the Public
Education Act.

In a letter of 21 August 1996 the applicant requested the Director General to issue a formal ruling on the matter.

---

[1] CEDH/ECHR 2001-V; EuGRZ 2003, 595; KuR 2001, 189 (LS); NJW 2001,
2871; NVwZ 2001, 1389 (LS); Schweizerisches Jahrbuch für Kirchenrecht 2001,
111.

On 23 August 1996 the Directorate General for Primary Education confirmed its previous decision. It prohibited the applicant from wearing a headscarf in the performance of her professional duties on the grounds that such a practice contravened sec. 6 of the Public Education Act and constituted „an obvious means of identification imposed by a teacher on her pupils, especially in a public, secular education system".

On 26 August 1996 the applicant appealed against that decision to the Geneva cantonal government.

The cantonal government dismissed the appeal in an order of 16 October 1996, on the following grounds:

> „Teachers must ... endorse both the objectives of the State school system and the obligations incumbent on the education authorities, including the strict obligation of denominational neutrality (...)
>
> The clothing in issue ... represents ..., regardless even of the appellant's intention, a means of conveying a religious message in a manner which in her case is sufficiently strong ... to extend beyond her purely personal sphere and to have repercussions for the institution she represents, namely the State school system."

On a public-law appeal lodged by the applicant on 25 November 1996, in which she had alleged a violation of art. 9 of the Convention and submitted that the prohibition on wearing a headscarf interfered with the „inviolable core of her freedom of religion", the Federal Court upheld the Geneva cantonal government's decision in a judgment of 12 November 1997, which was served on 18 November 1997.

It held, in particular:

> „Firstly, it should be observed that the appellant's main argument is that her clothing, consisting of items that may be purchased at the hypermarket, should be treated not as a religious symbol but in the same way as any other perfectly inoffensive garments that a teacher may decide to wear for his or her own reasons, notably for aesthetic reasons or in order to emphasise or conceal part of his or her anatomy (a scarf around the neck, a cardigan, a hat, etc.). She accordingly submits that the impugned decision is tantamount to prohibiting teachers, without sufficient justification, from dressing as they please.
>
> However, there is no doubt that the appellant wears the headscarf and loose-fitting clothes not for aesthetic reasons but in order to obey a religious precept which she derives from the following passages of the Koran. (...)
>
> The wearing of a headscarf and loose-fitting clothes consequently indicates allegiance to a particular faith and a desire to behave in accordance with the precepts laid down by that faith. Such garments may even be said to constitute a ‚powerful' religious symbol - that is to say, a sign that is immediately visible to others and provides a clear indication that the person concerned belongs to a particular religion.
>
> What is in issue, therefore, is the wearing of a powerful religious symbol by a teacher at a State school in the performance of her professional duties. No restrictions have been imposed on the appellant as regards her clothing when she is not

teaching. Nor does the case concern the wearing of a religious attribute by a pupil or the wearing of outlandish or unusual clothing with no religious connotations by a teacher at school.

...

Similarly, by art. 9 § 2 of the European Convention on Human Rights, freedom to manifest one's religion or beliefs may be subject to restrictions (see the European Court of Human Rights' judgment of 25 May 1993 in the case of Kokkinakis v. Greece, Series A no. 260-A, § 33, and Frowein and Peukert, Europäische Menschenrechtskonvention, 2nd ed., 1996, note 1 on art. 9, p. 368). Conversely, freedom of thought is absolute; since it cannot by nature give rise to any interference with public order, it is not subject to any restrictions (see Velu and Ergec, La Convention européenne des droits de l'homme, Brussels, 1990, note 714, p. 584).

In the instant case, even if it is particularly important to the appellant and does not merely represent an expression of a particular religious belief but complies with an imperative requirement of that belief, the wearing of a headscarf and loose-fitting clothes remains an outward manifestation which, as such, is not part of the inviolable core of freedom of religion.(...)

3. The appellant maintains that the impugned order does not have a sufficient basis in law.(...)

Serious interferences with constitutional freedoms must be clearly and unequivocally provided for, as to their substance, by a law in the strict sense (ATF [Arrêts du Tribunal fédéral suisse], vol. 122 I, p. 360, ground 5(b)(bb), at p. 363, and vol. 118 Ia, p. 305, ground 2(a), at pp. 309-10). However, where interference with freedom of conscience and belief results from a rule of conduct that is very specific or would be regarded by the average citizen as being of minor importance (in this case, prohibiting a teacher from wearing a headscarf at school), the requisite basis in law cannot be too precise. In such circumstances it is sufficient for the rule of conduct to derive from a more general obligation laid down by the law in the strict sense.

Furthermore, the decision appealed against concerns the appellant in her capacity as a civil servant of the Canton of Geneva. Civil servants are bound by a special relationship of subordination to the public authorities, a relationship which they have freely accepted and from which they benefit; it is therefore justifiable that they should enjoy public freedoms to a limited extent only. In particular, the legal basis for restrictions on such freedoms does not have to be especially precise. The manifold, varying nature of daily relations between a civil servant and the authority to which he or she is answerable means that it is impossible to lay down an exhaustive list of types of conduct to be restricted or prohibited. It is therefore sufficient for the law to give a general indication, by means of indeterminate legal concepts, of the values which must be adhered to and which may subsequently be made explicit in an order or in an individual decision. However, as to their substance, any restrictions on public freedoms must be justified by the aim pursued and by the proper functioning of the institution. Lastly, observance of the principles of public interest and proportionality is to be monitored all the more rigorously where the interference with the civil servant's interests is serious and the basis in law imprecise (ATF, vol. 120 Ia, p. 203, ground 3(a), at p. 205; vol. 119 Ia, p. 178, ground 6(b), at p. 188; vol. 101 I a, p. 172, ground 6, at p. 181; SJ [La Semaine Judiciaire], 1995, p. 681, ground 3; ZBl [Schweizerisches Zentralblatt für Staats- und Verwaltungsrecht] 85/1984, p. 308, ground 2(b); Pierre Moor, Droit administratif, Berne, vol. III, 1992, note 5.1.2.3., pp. 213-14, and note 5.3.1.2., pp. 223-24; vol. I, 1994, note 4.2.4.5., pp. 362 et seq.; Thomas Wyss, Die dienstrechtliche Stellung des Volksschullehrers im Kanton Zürich, thesis, Zürich, 1986, pp. 224 et seq.; Paul Richli, ,Grundrechtliche Aspekte der Tätigkeit von Lehrkräften', in PJA [Pratique juridique actuelle] 6/93, pp. 673 et seq., in particular p. 677).

In Geneva, sec. 6 of the cantonal Public Education Act of 6 November 1940 provides: ,The public education system shall ensure that the political and religious beliefs of pupils and parents are respected'. It also follows from art. 164 et seq. of the cantonal Constitution that there is a clear separation between Church and State in the canton, the State being secular (Ueli Friederich, Kirchen und Glaubensgemeinschaften im pluralistischen Staat, thesis, Berne, 1993, p. 239, and Häfelin, op. cit. [Commentaire de la Constitution fédérale], notes 26-27 on art. 49). In the education system, this separation is given practical effect by sec. 120 (2) of the Public Education Act, which provides: ,Civil servants must be lay persons; derogations from this provision shall be permitted only in respect of university teaching staff'.

In the instant case the measure prohibiting the appellant from wearing a headscarf that clearly identified her as a member of a particular faith reflects an increasing desire on the part of the Geneva legislature, as expressed in the provisions cited above, to ensure that the education system observes the principles of denominational neutrality (cf. art. 27 § 3 of the Constitution) and of separation between Church and State. Accordingly, even if the impugned order entailed serious interference with the appellant's freedom of religion, it had a sufficient basis in law.(...)

4. (a) The appellant further submits that there were no public-interest grounds for the impugned decision.

In displaying a powerful religious attribute on the school premises - indeed, in the classroom - the appellant may have interfered with the religious beliefs of her pupils, other pupils at the school and the pupils' parents. Admittedly, there have been no complaints from parents or pupils to date. But that does not mean that none of them has been affected. Some may well have decided not to take any direct action so as not to aggravate the situation, in the hope that the education authorities will react of their own motion. Moreover, the matter has caused a stir among the public, the appellant has given numerous interviews and the Grand Council [cantonal parliament] has passed a resolution along the same lines as the decision taken by the cantonal government. In addition, while it is true that the education authorities did not intervene by taking a decision immediately after the inspector had informed them of the appellant's clothing, that attitude should not be construed as implicit approval. It is understandable that the authorities should first have attempted to settle the matter without resorting to confrontation.

The impugned decision is fully in accordance with the principle of denominational neutrality in schools, a principle that seeks both to protect the religious beliefs of pupils and parents and to ensure religious harmony, which in some respects is still fragile. In this connection, it should be noted that schools would be in danger of becoming places of religious conflict if teachers were allowed to manifest their religious beliefs through their conduct and, in particular, their clothing.

There are therefore significant public-interest grounds for prohibiting the appellant from wearing an Islamic headscarf.

(b) It remains to be determined whether the impugned order observes the principle of proportionality; the interests at stake must be weighed up with the utmost care (Häfelin, op. cit., note 139 on art. 49).

Here, the appellant's freedom of conscience and belief should be weighed against the public interest in ensuring the denominational neutrality of the school system; in other words, the appellant's interest in obeying a precept laid down by her faith should be set against the interest of pupils and their parents in not being influenced or offended in their own beliefs, and the concern to maintain religious harmony in schools. Lastly, regard must also be had to the need for tolerance - a further element of the principle of denominational neutrality - between members of different religious faiths ...

It should, however, be emphasised at the outset that religious freedom cannot automatically absolve a person of his or her civic duties - or, as in this case, of the duties attaching to his or her post (ATF, vol. 119 Ia, p. 178, ground 7(a), at p. 190). Teachers must tolerate proportionate restrictions on their freedom of religion (Hafner, La liberta religiosa chiede la tolleranza per i simboli religiosi, J+P Text 2/95, note III/D4, p. 9; Thomas Wyss, op. cit., p. 232).

(aa) Before the points in issue are examined in greater detail, it may be helpful to consider the solutions adopted by other countries in identical cases or by the Federal Court in similar cases.(...)

Freedom of conscience and belief requires the State to observe denominational and religious neutrality; citizens may assert individual rights in this domain (ATF, vol. 118 Ia, p. 46, ground 3(b) at p. 53, and ground 4(e)(aa) at p. 58; vol. 113 Ia, p. 304, ground 4c at p. 307). There may be an infringement of freedom of religion where the State unlawfully takes sides in religious or metaphysical disputes, in particular by offering financial support to one of the protagonists (ATF, vol. 118 Ia, p. 46, ground 4(e)(aa) at p. 58). However, the neutrality requirement is not absolute, as is illustrated by the fact that national churches recognised by public law are allowed to exist (ATF, vol. 118 Ia, p. 46, ground 4(e)(aa) at p. 58; vol. 116 Ia, p. 252, ground 5(d) at pp. 258-59). Neutrality does not mean that all religious or metaphysical aspects are to be excluded from the State's activities; however, an attitude that is anti-religious, such as militant secularism, or irreligious does not qualify as neutral. The principle of neutrality seeks to ensure that consideration is given, without any bias, to all conceptions existing in a pluralistic society. The principle that the State may not discriminate in favour of or against anybody on religious grounds is general in scope and results directly from art. 49 and 50 of the Constitution (ATF, vol. 118 Ia, p. 46, ground 4(e)(aa) at p. 58; Karlen, ,Umstrittene Religionsfreiheit', op. cit. [in Revue du droit suisse (,RDS') 1997 I, p. 193] at pp. 199-200; idem, Das Grundrecht [der Religionsfreiheit in der Schweiz], op. cit. [Zürich, 1988], p. 188). Lastly, the secular nature of the State entails an obligation to remain neutral, which means that in all official dealings it must refrain from any denominational or religious considerations that might jeopardise the freedom of citizens in a pluralistic society (ATF, vol. 116 Ia, p. 252, ground 5(e) at p. 260, and the references cited). In that respect, the principle of secularism seeks both to preserve individual freedom of religion and to maintain religious harmony in a spirit of tolerance (see Gut, op. cit. [,Kreuz und Kruzifix in öffentlichen Räumen im säkularen Staat', in RDS 1997 I, p. 63], note 11 at p. 76; and Martin Philipp Wyss, op. cit. [,Glaubens- und Religionsfreiheit zwischen Integration und Isolation', in ZBl 95/1994, p. 385], at pp. 400-01).

This neutrality assumes particular importance in State schools, because educa-
tion is compulsory for all, without any distinction being made between different
faiths. In this respect, art. 27 § 3 of the Federal Constitution, according to
which 'it shall be possible for members of all faiths to attend State schools with-
out being affected in any way in their freedom of conscience or belief', is the corol-
lary of freedom of conscience and belief. (...)
Accordingly, the attitude of teachers plays an important role. Their mere conduct
may have a considerable influence on their pupils; they set an example to which
pupils are particularly receptive on account of their tender age, their daily contact
with them - which, in principle, is inescapable - and the hierarchical nature of
this relationship. Teachers are both participants in the exercise of educational
authority and representatives of the State, which assumes responsibility for their
conduct. It is therefore especially important that they should discharge their du-
ties - that is to say, imparting knowledge and developing skills - while remaining
denominationally neutral."

After a lengthy discussion of the scope of the neutrality requirement,
the Federal Court concluded as follows:

„(cc) In the instant case, on the one hand, as was outlined above, prohibiting the
appellant from wearing a headscarf forces her to make a difficult choice between
disregarding what she considers to be an important precept laid down by her re-
ligion and running the risk of no longer being able to teach in State schools.
On the other hand, however, the headscarf is a manifest religious attribute in this
case. Furthermore, the appellant teaches in a primary school; her pupils are
therefore young children who are particularly impressionable. Admittedly, she is
not accused of proselytising or even of talking to her pupils about her beliefs.
However, the appellant can scarcely avoid the questions which her pupils have
not missed the opportunity to ask. It would seem somewhat awkward for her to
reply by citing aesthetic considerations or sensitivity to the cold - the approach
she claims to have adopted to date, according to the file - because the children
will realise that she is evading the issue. It is therefore difficult for her to reply
without stating her beliefs. However, the appellant participates in the exercise of
educational authority and personifies school in the eyes of her pupils; as a result,
even if other teachers from the same school display different religious views, the
manifestation of such an image of oneself appears hard to reconcile with the
principle of non-identification with a particular faith in so far as her status as a
civil servant means that the State must assume responsibility for her conduct.
Lastly, it should be emphasised that the Canton of Geneva has opted for a clear
separation between Church and State, reflected in particular by the distinctly
secular nature of the State education system.
It must also be acknowledged that it is difficult to reconcile the wearing of a
headscarf with the principle of gender equality (see Sami Aldeeb, ,Musulmans en
terre européenne', in PJA 1/96, pp. 42 et seq., in particular sec. (d) at p. 49),
which is a fundamental value of our society enshrined in a specific provision of
the Federal Constitution (art. 4 § 2) and must be taken into account by schools.
Furthermore, religious harmony ultimately remains fragile in spite of everything,
and the appellant's attitude is likely to provoke reactions, or even conflict, which
are to be avoided. When the various interests at stake are weighed up, regard

must also be had to the fact that allowing headscarves to be worn would result in the acceptance of garments that are powerful symbols of other faiths, such as soutanes or kippas (in this connection, the principle of proportionality has led the cantonal government to allow teachers to wear discreet religious symbols at school, such as small pieces of jewellery - an issue that does not require further discussion here). Such a consequence might undermine the principle of denominational neutrality in schools. Lastly, it may be observed that it is scarcely conceivable to prohibit crucifixes from being displayed in State schools and yet to allow the teachers themselves to wear powerful religious symbols of whatever denomination."

B. Relevant domestic law

Sec. 6 of the Canton of Geneva Public Education Act of 6 November 1940 provides:

„The public education system shall ensure that the political and religious beliefs of pupils and parents are respected."

Sec. 120 (2) of the Public Education Act provides:

„Civil servants must be lay persons; derogations from this provision shall be permitted only in respect of university teaching staff."

Art. 27 § 3 of the Federal Constitution of 29 May 1874 reads:

„It shall be possible for members of all faiths to attend State schools without being affected in any way in their freedom of conscience or belief."

COMPLAINT

1. The applicant submitted that the measure prohibiting her from wearing a headscarf in the performance of her teaching duties infringed her freedom to manifest her religion, as guaranteed by art. 9 of the Convention. She further complained that the Swiss courts had erred in accepting that the measure had a sufficient basis in law and in considering that there was a threat to public safety and to the protection of public order. She observed that the fact that she wore an Islamic headscarf had gone unnoticed for four years and did not appear to have caused any obvious disturbance within the school.

2. In conjunction with art. 9, the applicant submitted that the prohibition imposed by the Swiss authorities amounted to discrimination on the ground of sex within the meaning of art. 14 of the Convention, in that a man belonging to the Muslim faith could teach at a State school without being subject to any form of prohibition.

THE LAW

1. The applicant submitted that the measure prohibiting her from wearing a headscarf in the performance of her teaching duties infringed her freedom to manifest her religion, as guaranteed by art. 9 of the Convention, the relevant parts of which provide:

„1. *Everyone has the right to freedom of ... religion; this right includes ... freedom, either alone or in community with others and in public or private, to manifest his religion ... in worship, teaching, practice and observance.*
2. Freedom to manifest one's religion ... shall be subject only to such limitations as are prescribed by law and are necessary in a democratic society in the interests of public safety, for the protection of public order, health or morals, or for the protection of the rights and freedoms of others."

The Government made the preliminary observation that, in the opinion of the applicant herself, the Islamic headscarf was a powerful religious symbol and was directly recognisable by others. They further noted that the scope of the present case was delimited by the Federal Court's judgment of 12 November 1997, which drew a fundamental distinction between the wearing of a religious attribute by a teacher and similar conduct on the part of a pupil. The Federal Court had held that the prohibition on wearing an Islamic headscarf applied solely to the applicant in her capacity as a teacher at a State school and could not extend to the alleged effects on the freedom of conscience and religion of pupils who wore veils.

In their analysis, the Government stated that the measure prohibiting the applicant from wearing a headscarf in her capacity as a teacher at a State school did not amount to interference with her right to freedom of religion. In that connection, they drew attention to the principle that State schools were non-denominational, as laid down in art. 27 § 3 of the Federal Constitution, a principle that applied in every State school in Switzerland. In the Canton of Geneva, that constitutional guarantee was given effect by sec. 6 and 120 (2) of the Public Education Act. In the instant case the applicant had chosen to pursue her profession as a teacher at a State school, an institution that was required to observe the principle of secularism in accordance with the provisions cited above. She had satisfied that requirement when she had been appointed on a permanent basis in December 1990. At that time she had been a member of the Catholic faith and had not manifested her religious beliefs by wearing any conspicuous religious symbols. It was after her appointment that she had decided, on 23 March 1991, to convert to Islam and to go to school wearing a headscarf.

The Government submitted that the applicant was qualified to teach children aged between four and eight and that she accordingly had the option of teaching infant classes at private schools; such classes, of which there were many in the Canton of Geneva, were not bound by the requirement of secularism.

In the eventuality of the Court's holding that the measure in issue amounted to interference with the applicant's right to freedom of religion, the Government submitted, in the alternative, that the interference was justified under par. 2 of art. 9 of the Convention.

The interference, they maintained, had a basis in law. Art. 27 § 3 of the Federal Constitution made it compulsory to observe the principle of denominational neutrality in schools. Sec. 6 of the Public Education Act established the principle that the State education system had to respect the religious beliefs of pupils and parents, and sec. 120 (2) of the Act laid down the rule that civil servants had to be lay persons. Furthermore, even before the applicant had decided to convert to Islam in March 1991, the Federal Court had ruled on the scope of the secularism requirement in art. 27 § 3 of the Constitution. In particular, in a published judgment of 26 September 1990 it had held that the presence of a crucifix in State primary-school classrooms fell foul of the requirement of denominational neutrality (ATF, vol. 116 Ia, p. 252).

The Government argued that the aims pursued in the instant case were undeniably legitimate and were among those listed in the second par. of art. 9 of the Convention. In their submission, the measure prohibiting the applicant from wearing an Islamic headscarf was based on the principle of denominational neutrality in schools and, more broadly, on that of religious harmony.

Lastly, the prohibition was necessary in a democratic society. In the Government's view, where an applicant was bound to the State by a special status, the national authorities enjoyed a wider margin of appreciation in restricting the exercise of a freedom. As a teacher at a State school, the applicant had freely accepted the requirements deriving from the principle of denominational neutrality in schools. As a civil servant, she represented the State; on that account, her conduct should not suggest that the State identified itself with one religion rather than another. That was especially valid where allegiance to a particular religion was manifested by a powerful religious symbol, such as the wearing of an Islamic headscarf.

The Government pointed out that the State's neutrality as regards religious beliefs was all the more valuable as it made it possible to preserve individual freedom of conscience in a pluralistic democratic society. The need to preserve such pluralism was even more pressing where the pupils came from different cultural backgrounds. In the applicant's case, her class comprised pupils of a wide range of nationalities. Lastly, it should not be forgotten that teachers were important role models for their pupils, especially when, as in the applicant's case, the pupils were very young children attending compulsory primary school. Experience showed that such children tended to identify with their teacher, particularly on account of their daily contact and the hierarchical nature of their relationship.

In the light of those considerations, the Government were satisfied that the Swiss authorities had not exceeded the margin of appreciation which they enjoyed in the light of the Court's case-law.

In the applicant's submission, the secular nature of State schools meant that teaching should be independent of all religious faiths, but did not prevent teachers from holding beliefs or from wearing any religious symbols whatever. She argued that the measure prohibiting her from wearing a headscarf amounted to manifest interference with her right to freedom of conscience and religion.

The applicant pointed out that, after her appointment as a civil servant in the public education service, she had converted to Islam in March 1991 following a period of spiritual soul-searching. Since that time, she had worn a headscarf in class, a fact that had not bothered the school's head teacher, his immediate superior or the district inspector whom she had met regularly. Furthermore, her teaching, which was secular in nature, had never given rise to the slightest problem or to any complaints from pupils or their parents. The Geneva authorities had consequently been in full knowledge of the facts in endorsing, until June 1996, the applicant's right to wear a headscarf. Only then, without stating any reasons, had the authorities required her to stop wearing the headscarf.

The applicant further maintained that, contrary to the Government's submissions, she had no choice but to teach within the State school system. In practice, State schools had a virtual monopoly on infant classes. Private schools, of which there were not many in the Canton of Geneva, were not non-denominational and were governed by religious authorities other than those of the applicant; accordingly, they were not accessible to her. Lastly, the applicant contended that it had never been established that her clothing had had any impact on pupils. The mere fact of wearing a headscarf was not likely to influence the children's beliefs. Indeed, some of the children or their parents wore similar garments, both at home and at school.

Under the second paragraph of art. 9 of the Convention, the applicant submitted that the interference in question infringed her freedom of religion because it had no basis in law and was not justified. She pointed out that sec. 6 of the Public Education Act referred expressly to the education system alone and not to teachers themselves, and that sec. 120 (2) of the Act did not clarify the situation.

Furthermore, the fact that no complaints had been made by pupils or parents during a period of more than five years constituted sufficient proof that the religious beliefs of others had been respected. Lastly, religious harmony had never been disturbed within the school, because the applicant had always shown tolerance towards her pupils, all the more so as they encompassed a wide range of nationalities and were therefore particularly accustomed to diversity and tolerance.

The Court refers, in the first place, to its case-law to the effect that freedom of thought, conscience and religion, as enshrined by art. 9 of the Convention, represents one of the foundations of a „democratic society" within the meaning of the Convention. In its religious dimension, it is one of the most vital elements that go to make up the identity of believers and their conception of life, but it is also a precious asset for atheists, agnostics, sceptics and the unconcerned. The pluralism indissociable from a democratic society, which has been dearly won over the centuries, depends on it. While religious freedom is primarily a matter of individual conscience, it also implies freedom to manifest one's religion. Bearing witness in words and deeds is bound up with the existence of religious convictions (see Kokkinakis v. Greece, 25 May 1993, Series A no. 260-A, p. 17, § 31, and Otto-Preminger-Institut v. Austria, 20 September 1994, Series A no. 295-A, p. 17, § 47).

The Court further observes that in democratic societies, in which several religions coexist within one and the same population, it may be necessary to place restrictions on this freedom in order to reconcile the interests of the various groups and ensure that everyone's beliefs are respected (see Kokkinakis, cited above, p. 18, § 33).

The applicant argued, firstly, that the impugned measure did not have a sufficient basis in law. In The Sunday Times v. the United Kingdom (no. 1) (26 April 1979, Series A no. 30, p. 31, § 49) the Court made the following observations about the expression „prescribed by law" in par. 2 of art. 9:

> „In the Court's opinion, the following are two of the requirements that flow from the expression ‚prescribed by law'. Firstly, the law must be adequately accessible: the citizen must be able to have an indication that is adequate in the circumstances of the legal rules applicable to a given case. Secondly, a norm cannot be regarded as a ‚law' unless it is formulated with sufficient precision to enable the citizen to regulate his conduct: he must be able - if need be with appropriate advice - to foresee, to a degree that is reasonable in the circumstances, the consequences which a given action may entail."

The wording of many statutes is not absolutely precise. The need to avoid excessive rigidity and to keep pace with changing circumstances means that many laws are inevitably couched in terms which, to a greater or lesser extent, are vague. The interpretation and application of such enactments depend on practice (see Kokkinakis, cited above, p. 19, § 40). Having examined the Federal Court's reasoning on this point, the Court observes that sec. 6 and 120 (2) of the cantonal Act of 6 November 1940 were sufficiently precise to enable those concerned to regulate their conduct. The measure in issue was therefore prescribed by law within the meaning of art. 9 § 2 of the Convention.

The applicant further argued that the measure did not pursue a legitimate aim. Having regard to the circumstances of the case and to the actual terms of the decisions of the three relevant authorities, the Court considers that the measure pursued aims that were legitimate for the purposes of art. 9 § 2, namely the protection of the rights and freedoms of others, public safety and public order.

Lastly, as to whether the measure was „necessary in a democratic society," the Court reiterates that, according to its settled case-law, the Contracting States have a certain margin of appreciation in assessing the existence and extent of the need for interference, but this margin is subject to European supervision, embracing both the law and the decisions applying it, even those given by independent courts. The Court's task is to determine whether the measures taken at national level were justified in principle - that is, whether the reasons adduced to justify them appear „relevant and sufficient" and are proportionate to the legitimate aim pursued (see The Sunday Times v. the United Kingdom (no. 2), 26 November 1991, Series A no. 217, pp. 28-29, § 50). In order to rule on this latter point, the Court must weigh the requirements of the protection of the rights and liberties of others against the conduct of which the applicant stood accused. In exercising its supervisory jurisdiction, the Court must look at the impugned judicial decisions against the background of the case as a whole (see Kokkinakis v. Greece, cited above, p. 21, § 47).

Applying these principles in the instant case, the Court notes that the Federal Court held that the measure by which the applicant was prohibited, purely in the context of her activities as a teacher, from wearing a headscarf was justified by the potential interference with the religious beliefs of her pupils, other pupils at the school and the pupils' parents, and by the breach of the principle of denominational neutrality in schools. In that connection, the Federal Court took into account the very nature of the profession of State school teachers, who were both participants in the exercise of educational authority and representatives of the State, and in doing so weighed the protection of the legitimate aim of ensuring the neutrality of the State education system against the freedom to manifest one's religion. It further noted that the impugned measure had left the applicant with a difficult choice, but considered that State school teachers had to tolerate proportionate restrictions on their freedom of religion. In the Federal Court's view, the interference with the applicant's freedom to manifest her religion was justified by the need, in a democratic society, to protect the right of State school pupils to be taught in a context of denominational neutrality. It follows that religious beliefs were fully taken into account in relation to the requirements of protecting the rights and freedoms of others and preserving public order and safety. It is also clear that the decision in issue was based on those requirements and not on any objections to the applicant's religious beliefs.

The Court notes that the applicant, who abandoned the Catholic faith and converted to Islam in 1991, by which time she had already been teaching at the same primary school for more than a year, wore an Islamic headscarf for approximately three years, apparently without any action being taken by the head teacher or the district schools inspector or any comments being made by parents. That implies that during the period in question there were no objections to the content or quality of the teaching provided by the applicant, who does not appear to have sought to gain any kind of advantage from the outward manifestation of her religious beliefs.

The Court accepts that it is very difficult to assess the impact that a powerful external symbol such as the wearing of a headscarf may have on the freedom of conscience and religion of very young children. The applicant's pupils were aged between four and eight, an age at which children wonder about many things and are also more easily influenced than older pupils. In those circumstances, it cannot be denied outright that the wearing of a headscarf might have some kind of proselytising effect, seeing that it appears to be imposed on women by a precept which is laid down in the Koran and which, as the Federal Court noted, is hard to square with the principle of gender equality. It therefore appears difficult to reconcile the wearing of an Islamic headscarf with the message of tolerance, respect for others and, above all, equality and non-discrimination that all teachers in a democratic society must convey to their pupils.

Accordingly, weighing the right of a teacher to manifest her religion against the need to protect pupils by preserving religious harmony, the Court considers that, in the circumstances of the case and having regard, above all, to the tender age of the children for whom the applicant was responsible as a representative of the State, the Geneva authorities did not exceed their margin of appreciation and that the measure they took was therefore not unreasonable.

In the light of the above considerations and those set out by the Federal Court in its judgment of 12 November 1997, the Court is of the opinion that the impugned measure may be considered justified in principle and proportionate to the stated aim of protecting the rights and freedoms of others, public order and public safety. The Court accordingly considers that the measure prohibiting the applicant from wearing a headscarf while teaching was „necessary in a democratic society."

It follows that this part of the application is manifestly ill-founded within the meaning of art. 35 § 3 of the Convention and must be rejected in accordance with art. 35 § 4.

2. In conjunction with the alleged violation of art. 9 of the Convention, the applicant submitted that the prohibition amounted to discrimination on the ground of sex within the meaning of art. 14 of the Convention, in that a man belonging to the Muslim faith could teach at a State school without being subject to any form of prohibition, whereas a woman hold-

ing similar beliefs had to refrain from practising her religion in order to be able to teach.

Art. 14 of the Convention provides:

> *„The enjoyment of the rights and freedoms set forth in [the] Convention shall be secured without discrimination on any ground such as sex, race, colour, language, religion, political or other opinion, national or social origin, association with a national minority, property, birth or other status."*

The Court reiterates that the Convention institutions have consistently held that art. 14 affords protection against different treatment, without an objective and reasonable justification, of persons in similar situations (see Observer and Guardian v. the United Kingdom, 26 November 1991, Series A no. 216, p. 35, § 73, and The Sunday Times v. the United Kingdom (no. 1), cited above, p. 43, § 70). For the purposes of art. 14 a difference in treatment is discriminatory if it does not pursue a legitimate aim or if there is not a relationship of proportionality between the means employed and the aim sought to be realised. Moreover, the Contracting States enjoy a margin of appreciation in assessing whether and to what extent differences in otherwise similar situations justify a different treatment (see Van Raalte v. the Netherlands, 21 February 1997, RJD 1997-I, p. 186, § 39).

The Court also reiterates that the advancement of the equality of the sexes is today a major goal in the member States of the Council of Europe. This means that very weighty reasons would have to be advanced before a difference in treatment on the ground of sex could be regarded as compatible with the Convention (see Abdulaziz, Cabales and Balkandali v. the United Kingdom, 28 May 1985, Series A no. 94, p. 38, § 78, and Schuler-Zgraggen v. Switzerland, 24 June 1993, Series A no. 263, pp. 21-22, § 67).

The Court notes in the instant case that the measure by which the applicant was prohibited, purely in the context of her professional duties, from wearing an Islamic headscarf was not directed at her as a member of the female sex but pursued the legitimate aim of ensuring the neutrality of the State primary-education system. Such a measure could also be applied to a man who, in similar circumstances, wore clothing that clearly identified him as a member of a different faith.

The Court accordingly concludes that there was no discrimination on the ground of sex in the instant case.

It follows that this part of the application is manifestly ill-founded within the meaning of art. 35 § 3 of the Convention and must be rejected in accordance with art. 35 § 4.

For these reasons, the Court, by a majority, declares the application inadmissible.

61

Das demokratische Prinzip gebietet eine weitreichende Gewähr-leistung der Meinungsfreiheit für Äußerungen von Abgeordneten im Rahmen einer Ratssitzung (hier: über sog. Psychosekten). Zur Abgrenzung von Tatsachenbehauptungen und Werturteilen.

Art. 10 EMRK
EGMR, Urteil vom 27. Februar 2001 - No. 26958/95
(Jerusalem ./. Österreich)[1] -

THE FACTS

I. The circumstances of the case

[1] The applicant is an Austrian citizen, residing in Vienna. At the relevant time she was a member of the Vienna Municipal Council (Gemeinderat), which also acts as the Regional Parliament (Landtag).

[2] On 11 June 1992, in the course of a session of the Vienna Municipal Council, the applicant, in her function as member of the Municipal Council, gave a speech. The debate related to the granting of subsidies by the municipality to an association which assists parents whose children had become involved in sects. In this context the applicant made the following statement:

„Like everyone else, I know that today a sect no longer means a small group that breaks away from a big church ..., but a psycho-sect.
These psycho-sects also exist in Vienna. They have common features. One aspect they have in common is their totalitarian character. Moreover, in their ideology, they show fascist tendencies and often have hierarchical structures. In general, a person who gets involved with such a sect loses his identity and submits to the group ...“

After having commented on the activities of an association she considered a sect, the applicant continued as follows:

„... the sect IPM [Institut zur Förderung der Psychologischen Menschenkenntnis - Institute for a Better Understanding of Human Psychology], which has not long been in existence in Austria but which has existed for several years in Switzerland, where it is called the VPM [Verein zur Förderung der Psychologischen Menschenkenntnis - Association for a Better Understanding of Human Psychology] has had a certain influence on the drugs policy of the Austrian People's Party.“

---

[1] CEDH/ECHR 2001-II; dt. Übersetzungen: Medien und Recht 2001, 89 (LS); ÖJZ 2001, 693.

[3] The applicant then stated that the Austrian People's Party had issued a publication on drugs policy in cooperation with the IPM, and had organised information activities involving public discussions together with the IPM. The applicant then requested a resolution by the Municipal Council that, before granting subsidies to an association, the question whether that association was a sect should be examined.

[4] The debate in the Municipal Council then turned to the drugs policy and the applicant, in a further speech, criticised the cooperation between the Austrian People's Party and the IPM, and made further statements on the nature and activities of the IPM.

[5] On 27 October 1992 the IPM, an association established under Austrian law, and the VPM, an association established under Swiss law, filed a civil-law action under art. 1330 of the Austrian Civil Code against the applicant with the Vienna Regional Court for Civil Matters (Landesgericht für Zivilrechtssachen). The associations requested the court to issue an injunction against the applicant prohibiting her from repeating the statement that the IPM was a sect, ordering her to retract this statement and directing the publication of the applicant's retraction in several Austrian newspapers.

[6] On 2 February 1993 the applicant commented on the action. She submitted that the term „sect" used by her was a value judgment and not a statement of fact. It had been used in the context of a political debate. If the court, however, was of the opinion that the term „sect" was a statement of fact, she was willing to prove that this statement was true, and proposed documentary evidence and the hearing of witnesses to confirm that the plaintiffs were sects. As documentary evidence, the applicant proposed a decision by a German court and seven articles from newspapers and periodicals on the internal structure and activities of the plaintiffs. She proposed that four witnesses be heard. She also requested that the court obtain an expert report.

[7] On 16 February 1993 the IPM and the VPM altered their injunction claim to include the following statement made by the applicant on 11 June 1992:

> „One aspect they have in common is their totalitarian character. Moreover, in their ideology, they show fascist tendencies and often have hierarchical structures. In general, a person who gets involved with such a sect loses his identity and submits to the group ..."

[8] On 18 February 1993 the applicant confirmed that she had received the plaintiffs' amended claim. She submitted a transcript of the session of the Vienna Municipal Council of 11 June 1992, and argued that the modification of the action merely referred to a general explanation of the term „psycho-sect" and had no direct relation to the plaintiffs. She fur-

ther referred to her previous statements and the evidence proposed therein.

[9] On 22 February 1993 a hearing took place before the Regional Court. The court accepted several documents submitted by the parties, closed the taking of evidence and rejected all requests for the taking of other evidence as irrelevant because the documents submitted had clarified the issues sufficiently.

[10] On 8 April 1993 the Regional Court granted the injunction. It ordered the applicant not to repeat her statements that the IPM and the VPM were sects of a totalitarian character. Furthermore, the court ordered the applicant to retract these statements, the retraction to be published in several newspapers. The Regional Court found that, contrary to the applicant's opinion, her statements were not value judgments, but statements of fact. Having regard to the statutes of the associations and other evidence before it, the Regional Court considered that the applicant's statements had proved to be untrue. The applicant had disseminated unfounded assumptions as proven fact and had therefore acted negligently. As the damage to the plaintiff associations' earnings and livelihood was manifest, the Court granted the requested injunction under art. 1330 § 2 of the Civil Code.

[11] On 12 July 1993 the applicant appealed. She submitted that the Regional Court had failed to take the evidence requested by her. She contended in particular that the real activities of the plaintiffs and their (totalitarian) methods could not be seen from their statutes. In particular, the internal organisational structure (hierarchical structure), their conduct against critics (exhibiting a totalitarian character and an ideology with fascist features) and the effect on the personality of the persons concerned (loss of identity and submission to the group) should have been examined. Only a report by an expert using sociological and psychological methods, or interviews with the persons affected, could have clarified these issues. In any event, the applicant's statements were value judgments made in the context of a political debate and not statements of fact. The injunction therefore violated her right to freedom of expression under art. 10 of the Convention.

[12] On 16 November 1993 the Vienna Court of Appeal (Oberlandesgericht) upheld the Regional Court's decision in so far as it concerned the prohibition on repetition, but quashed the order for a retraction and its publication.

[13] It confirmed the Regional Court's view that the applicant's allegations were statements of fact. Contrary to the opinion of the Regional Court, the Court of Appeal considered that the applicant's allegations amounted to an insult and fell not only within the scope of the second but also within the scope of the first paragraph of art. 1330 of the Civil Code. In that case, the applicant had to prove the truth of her allegations.

[14] With regard to the applicant's complaint that the Regional Court had refused to take the evidence she had proposed in order to prove that the plaintiffs were sects, the Court of Appeal found that such evidence was irrelevant to the proceedings. According to the Court of Appeal's legal point of view, the applicant's statements had to be seen as a whole. Thus, the use of the term „sect" was not decisive, but the allegation of fascist tendencies was of primary importance. This latter statement amounted to an insult going beyond justified criticism. Since the applicant had not offered any evidence with regard to this definition of a psycho-sect, but only with regard to the question whether the plaintiffs were sects, she had failed to prove its truth, as required by art. 1330 § 1 of the Civil Code. The Court of Appeal also found that the request for a retraction of the statement and its publication in several newspapers had to be dismissed because the plaintiffs had failed to specify the addressees of the retraction, even though the applicant's statements had been reported in the newspapers.

[15] On 18 August 1994 the Supreme Court (Oberster Gerichtshof) rejected as inadmissible the applicant's further appeal on points of law (Revision). It confirmed, however, that the statements such as „fascist tendencies" or „totalitarian character" were statements of fact which the applicant had failed to prove. Referring to its previous case-law, it stated that disparagement by means of untrue statements, even though it was made in the course of a political debate, went beyond acceptable political criticism and could not be justified by a weighing of interests or by the right to freedom of expression.

II. Relevant domestic law

[16] Art. 1330 of the Austrian Civil Code (Allgemeines Bürgerliches Gesetzbuch) provides as follows:

> „(1) Everyone who has suffered material damage or loss of profit because of an insult may claim compensation.
> (2) The same applies if anyone disseminates statements of fact which jeopardise another person's credit, income or livelihood and if the untruth of the statement was known or must have been known to him. In such a case the public retraction of the statement may also be requested ..."

[17] Members of the Vienna Municipal Council enjoy a limited parliamentary immunity. They are exempt from legal proceedings for anything said by them in the course of debates in the Municipal Council in so far as the Municipal Council sits as the Parliament of a Land (art. 57, 58 and 96 of the Federal Constitution). However, this privilege does not extend to sessions of the Municipal Council sitting as the local council. The reason is that Vienna, under the Austrian Constitution, has a dual func-

tion, being at the same time a Land and a local council (art. 108 of the Federal Constitution).

THE LAW

I. Alleged violation of Art. 10 of the convention

[18] The applicant alleged a breach of art. 10 of the Convention, which reads as follows:

> „1. Everyone has the right to freedom of expression. This right shall include freedom to hold opinions and to receive and impart information and ideas without interference by public authority and regardless of frontiers. ...
> 2. The exercise of these freedoms, since it carries with it duties and responsibilities, may be subject to such formalities, conditions, restrictions or penalties as are prescribed by law and are necessary in a democratic society ... for the protection of the reputation or rights of others ...“

[19] The applicant contests the necessity of the interference with her right to freedom of expression. The incriminated statements had been made in the course of a session of the Vienna Municipal Council and concerned a political issue, namely the granting of public subsidies to associations and, in particular, an association of parents whose children had become involved with sects. In this context the applicant had pointed out that sects were gaining influence in politics and had cited the plaintiff associations as examples because of their cooperation with the Austrian People's Party. The applicant had not been involved in a direct dispute with the VPM (Verein zur Förderung der Psychologischen Menschenkenntnis - Association for a Better Understanding of Human Psychology) or the IPM (Institut zur Förderung der Psychologischen Menschenkenntnis - Institute for a Better Understanding of Human Psychology). Rather, her statements were a critical comment on the drug policy of another political party, and could not be understood as an attack on the plaintiffs' reputation. In any event, the IPM itself had repeatedly made public statements on AIDS prevention as well as on drug policy, and the applicant was therefore entitled to comment on that. Finally, the applicant submitted that the statements at issue were value judgments. This opinion was not shared by the Austrian courts, which qualified them as statements of fact, the truth of which had to be proved. Nevertheless, she had offered evidence to prove their truth, but the Austrian courts had refused it. Thus, it was not her fault that she had not succeeded in proving the truth of her statements.

[20] The Government accept that the injunction interfered with the applicant's right to freedom of expression. However, in their view, the measure at issue was justified under par. 2 of art. 10 as it was „pre-

scribed by law", namely art. 1330 of the Civil Code, and pursued the legitimate aim of protecting the reputation and rights of others. Moreover, it was necessary in a democratic society in the interests of that aim. In this respect the Government submit that the limits of acceptable criticism are wider in respect of a politician than in respect of a private individual. In the present case, however, the applicant had not attacked a politician but had raised serious accusations against private bodies, whose political function, if any, was merely a consultative one. In her capacity as member of the Municipal Council, the applicant had attacked the associations in circumstances which prevented them from defending themselves in the same way, at the same place and before the same audience. Moreover, the interference was not disproportionate since the impugned judicial proceedings were not instituted ex officio by the State but by private organisations, and the proceedings were not criminal in nature but civil.

[21] The Government submit further that the Austrian courts had correctly qualified the applicant's remarks as statements of fact. Thus, the applicant had the opportunity to prove the truth of her statements, which she failed to do.

[22] The Court notes that it was common ground between the parties that the injunction constituted an interference with the applicant's right to freedom of expression, as guaranteed by art. 10 § 1 of the Convention. Furthermore, there was no dispute that the interference was prescribed by law and pursued a legitimate aim, namely the protection of the reputation or rights of others, within the meaning of art. 10 § 2. The Court endorses this assessment.

[23] The dispute in the case relates to the question whether the interference was „necessary in a democratic society".

[24] According to the Court's well-established case-law, freedom of expression constitutes one of the essential foundations of a democratic society and one of the basic conditions for its progress and for individual self-fulfilment. Subject to par. 2 of art. 10, it is applicable not only to „information" or „ideas" that are favourably received or regarded as inoffensive or as a matter of indifference, but also to those that offend, shock or disturb. Such are the demands of pluralism, tolerance and broadmindedness, without which there is no „democratic society". As set forth in art. 10, this freedom is subject to exceptions, which must, however, be construed strictly, and the need for any restrictions must be established convincingly.

[25] The test of „necessity in a democratic society" requires the Court to determine whether the „interference" complained of corresponded to a „pressing social need", whether it was proportionate to the legitimate aim pursued and whether the reasons given by the national authorities to justify it are relevant and sufficient (see The Sunday Times v. the United Kingdom (no. 1), judgment of 26 April 1979, Series A no. 30, p. 38, § 62).

In assessing whether such a „need" exists and what measures should be adopted to deal with it, the national authorities are left a certain margin of appreciation. This power of appreciation is not, however, unlimited but goes hand in hand with a European supervision by the Court, whose task it is to give a final ruling on whether a restriction is reconcilable with freedom of expression as protected by art. 10 (see, among many other authorities, Nilsen and Johnsen v. Norway [GC], no. 23118/93, § 43, ECHR 1999-VIII).

[26] The Court's task in exercising its supervisory function is not to take the place of the national authorities but rather to review under art. 10, in the light of the case as a whole, the decisions they have taken pursuant to their power of appreciation (ibid.).

[27] In examining the particular circumstances of the case, the Court will take the following elements into account: the position of the applicant, the position of the associations which instituted the injunction proceedings and their activities, and the subject matter of the debate before the Vienna Municipal Council.

[28] As regards the applicant's position, the Court observes that she was an elected politician sitting as a member of the Vienna Municipal Council. As such, the applicant enjoyed limited parliamentary immunity (see par. 25 above). However, the session of the Municipal Council during which the applicant made her speech was one of the local council and not the Land Parliament. In the latter instance, any statement made by the applicant would have been protected by parliamentary immunity and an action for an injunction would have been impossible. In this respect the Court recalls that while freedom of expression is important for everybody, it is especially so for an elected representative of the people. He or she represents the electorate, draws attention to their preoccupations and defends their interests. Accordingly, interferences with the freedom of expression of an opposition member of parliament, like the applicant, call for the closest scrutiny on the part of the Court (see Castells v. Spain, judgment of 23 April 1992, Series A no. 236, pp. 22-23, § 42).

[29] As regards the position of the IPM and the VPM, the applicant's opponents in the injunction proceedings, the Government submitted that the associations were private bodies and could not, for the purposes of art. 10, be compared with politicians.

[30] The Court recalls that the limits of acceptable criticism are wider with regard to politicians acting in their public capacity than in relation to private individuals, as the former inevitably and knowingly lay themselves open to close scrutiny of word and deed by both journalists and the public at large. Politicians must display a greater degree of tolerance, especially when they themselves make public statements that are susceptible to criticism.

However, private individuals or associations lay themselves open to scrutiny when they enter the arena of public debate. In the case of Nilsen and Johnsen, cited above, § 52, the Court found that Mr Bratholm, a government expert involved in a dispute with Mr Nilsen and Mr Johnsen, could not, on account of that position, be compared to a politician who had to display a greater degree of tolerance. However, the Court found that Mr Bratholm's participation in a public debate was a relevant factor.

[31] In the present case the Court observes that the IPM and the VPM were associations active in a field of public concern, namely drug policy. They participated in public discussions on this matter and, as the Government conceded, cooperated with a political party. Since the associations were active in this manner in the public domain, they ought to have shown a higher degree of tolerance to criticism when opponents considered their aims as well as to the means employed in that debate.

[32] As regards the impugned statements of the applicant, the Court observes that they were made in the course of a political debate within the Vienna Municipal Council. It is not decisive that this debate occurred before the Vienna Municipal Council sitting as the local council and not as the Land Parliament. Irrespective of whether the applicant's statements were covered by parliamentary immunity, the Court finds that they were made in a forum which was at least comparable to Parliament as concerns the public interest in protecting the participants' freedom of public expression. In a democracy, Parliament or such comparable bodies are the essential for a for political debate. Very weighty reasons must be advanced to justify interfering with the freedom of expression exercised therein.

[33] The debate in the Municipal Council related to the granting of public subsidies to associations and the applicant commented on one particular item on the agenda, namely the granting of subsidies to an association which assisted parents whose children had become involved in sects (der Selbsthilfegruppen von Sektenopfern). The purpose of the applicant's speech was to emphasise the necessity for such assistance by describing the dangers of groups which, with a connotation quite distinct from that attaching to the words in past religious controversies, were commonly referred to as sects. In this context - in which the IPM and the VPM were not mentioned - she explained the term „sect" and expressed the opinion that one aspect which these sects have in common is their totalitarian character. Her further elaboration of the point was fully in line with general definitions of totalitarianism. It was only later in her speech that the applicant criticised connections between the Austrian People's Party and the IPM and the VPM.

[34] In the present case, the Austrian courts qualified the applicant's statements as statements of fact. Accordingly, the applicant was obliged to prove their truth in order to avoid an injunction. In this respect the Court recalls that in the cases of Lingens v. Austria (judgment of 8 July 1986, Series A no. 103, p. 28, § 46), and Oberschlick v. Austria (no. 1) (judgment of 23 May 1991, Series A no. 204, pp. 27-28, § 63), the Court

has distinguished between statements of fact and value judgments. The existence of facts can be demonstrated, whereas the truth of value judgments is not susceptible of proof. The requirement to prove the truth of a value judgment is impossible to fulfil and infringes freedom of opinion itself, which is a fundamental part of the right secured by art. 10.

[35] However, the Court further recalls that, even where a statement amounts to a value judgment, the proportionality of an interference may depend on whether there exists a sufficient factual basis for the impugned statement, since even a value judgment without any factual basis to support it may be excessive (see De Haes and Gijsels v. Belgium, judgment of 24 February 1997, RJD 1997-I, p. 236, § 47, and Oberschlick v. Austria (no. 2), judgment of 1 July 1997, RJD 1997-IV, p. 1276, § 33).

[36] The Court finds that, contrary to the view of the Austrian Courts, the impugned statements in the present case, reflecting as they did fair comment on matters of public interest by an elected member of the Municipal Council, are to be regarded as value judgments rather than statements of fact (see Lingens, cited above, p. 28, § 46, and Wabl v. Austria, no. 24773/94, § 36, 21 March 2000, unreported).

[37] The question remains whether there existed a sufficient factual basis for such value judgments. In this regard, the Court notes that the applicant offered documentary evidence, especially articles from newspapers and magazines, on the internal structure and the activities of the plaintiffs, as well as a German court judgment on this matter. In the Court's view, such material may have been relevant to show a prima facie case that the value judgment expressed by the applicant was fair comment. Apart from that documentary evidence, which was accepted by the Regional Court, the applicant also proposed the evidence of four witnesses and suggested that an expert opinion be sought. Nevertheless, the Regional Court refused to take this evidence because, as the Court of Appeal explained, it merely related to the term „sect" and not to that term as explained by the applicant in her speech, namely a body having a totalitarian character, showing fascist tendencies and having hierarchical structures with a resultant adverse impact on the psychological situation of its members or followers. Such evidence was therefore deemed irrelevant. No comment was made as to its availability.

However, the Court considers that the distinction drawn between the term „sect" and „psycho-sect showing totalitarian features" was artificial and disregarded the true nature of the debate in which the applicant was involved. It is struck by the inconsistent approach of the domestic courts on the one hand requiring proof of a statement and on the other hand refusing to consider all available evidence.

[38] The Court finds that, in requiring the applicant to prove the truth of her statements, while at the same time depriving her of an effective opportunity to adduce evidence to support her statements and thereby show that they constituted fair comment, the Austrian courts over-

stepped their margin of appreciation and that the injunction granted against the applicant amounted to a disproportionate interference with her freedom of expression.

II. Alleged violation of Art. 6 of the convention (...)

For these reasons, the Court unanimously
1. *Holds that there has been a violation of art. 10 of the Convention;*
2. *Holds that it is not necessary to examine separately whether there has been a violation of art. 6 of the Convention;*
3. *Holds that the finding of a violation in itself constitutes sufficient just satisfaction for any non-pecuniary damage sustained by the applicant.*

62

Solange eine Religionsgemeinschaft nicht von der Möglichkeit Gebrauch macht, an einem steuerrechtlich gestützten System der Kirchenfinanzierung (hier: Zuweisung eines Einkommenssteueranteils als Kultussteuer nach Wahl des Steuerpflichtigen) teilzunehmen, haben deren Mitglieder keinen Anspruch auf steuerrechtliche Gleichbehandlung mit Steuerpflichtigen, deren Religionsgemeinschaft eine entsprechende Vereinbarung mit dem Staat herbeigeführt hat.

Art. 9 § 1, 14, 35 § 3 EMRK
EGMR, Beschluss vom 14. Juni 2001 - No. 53072/99 (Alujer ./. Spanien)[1] -

THE FACTS

The applicants are Spanish nationals and live at A. (Valencia).

A. The circumstances of the case

The applicants are Protestants and members of the Baptist Evangelical Church in Valencia, which is on the official register of religious institutions kept by the Ministry of Justice, and a member of the Federation of Evangelical Churches of Spain (*FEREDE*).

In their income-tax returns for 1988, the applicants were given a choice between allocating part of their income tax to financial support for the Catholic Church or for other charitable purposes.

---

[1] CEDH/ECHR 2001-VI.

Since it was not legally possible for them to allot part of their income tax to financial support for their own Church, the applicants used a remedy afforded by Law no. 62/1978 on Judicial Protection of the Fundamental Rights of the Person and lodged an administrative appeal with the Valencia High of Justice challenging the Law on the State Budget 1988 on the ground that it contravened art. 14 (principle of equality) and 16 (right to freedom of conscience and religion) of the Constitution. In their appeal, they sought a declaration that the system implemented through the income-tax returns for 1988 was invalid, as it denied them a right enjoyed by Spaniards of the Catholic faith.

The Valencia High Court of Justice dismissed that appeal in a judgment of 22 April 1990, notably on the following grounds:

Three: The issue to be resolved in the present appeal ultimately amounts to deciding whether or not the difference in tax treatment complained of is based on unjustified discrimination prohibited by the Constitution that invalidates the impugned acts ...

Four: As the Constitutional Court has said many times, a finding of discrimination contrary to the principle of equality will be made only if in normative cases that are identical in substance a difference in legal treatment has no objective or reasonable justification, since it lacks a rational basis ...

Five: In the present case, the Court finds no violation of the principle of equality as, in accordance with art. 133.3 of the Constitution, any fiscal privilege concerning State taxes must be provided for by statute. In the instant case, sec. 7 (2) of Institutional Law no. 7/1980 of 5 July 1980 on Religious Freedom, which implements the said art. 16 of the Spanish Constitution, makes legal recognition of tax privileges laid down by general legislation in favour of non-profit making associations and other charitable bodies conditional on entry into agreements or conventions that must not only abide by the principle of equality but also, by virtue of sub-par. 1 of that article, take religious beliefs existing in Spanish society into account. That provision complies with the content of art. 16.3 of the Constitution.

However, in practice the situation of the Catholic Church, which has entered into a subsisting convention with the Spanish State and has the largest number of practising members and responsibility for a vast historical and cultural heritage, is different to that of the Baptist Evangelical Church, which has no convention or cooperation agreement with the Spanish State and does not satisfy the other condition.

Naturally, under no circumstances should that be taken to mean that this Division entertains any doubts as to the constitutionality of any agreement implementing the right sought by the appellants and, while it is not for this Division to decide issues that are within the sole discretion of the legislature, it is obvious that it would be more consistent with the principle of religious freedom and equality for such a right to be made available ...

Six: As to the alleged violation of the right not to reveal one's religious convictions, it is obvious that there has been no such violation in the instant case as no declaration was made in the impugned document. Furthermore, the fact that tax is allocated to the Catholic faith, which in any event will in principle only be the case with Catholics, does not infringe the right concerned either since, as with all fundamental rights, it is subject to limitations. In the instant case, the declaration predetermining expenditure is both justified and reasonable ... Furthermore, opting to predetermine expenditure does not necessarily mean that the taxpayer adheres to that religion, as the possibility that he or she has so opted for other reasons such, for instance, ... as the exercise of an adequate social activity, cannot be excluded."

The applicants appealed against that judgment to the Supreme Court, which declared their appeal inadmissible in a decision of 26 March 1992. The applicants lodged an *amparo* appeal with the Constitutional Court, which on 20 June 1994 ordered the Supreme Court to declare the appeal admissible and to rule on the merits. On 20 October 1997 the Supreme Court examined the appeal and dismissed it on the merits, upholding the judgment appealed against.

Relying on art. 14, 16 and 24 of the Constitution, the applicants lodged an *amparo* appeal with the Constitutional Court, which in a decision of 13 May 1992, dismissed it for the following reasons:

„There has been no violation in the instant case of the constitutional rights to equality before the law without discrimination based on religion (art. 14 of the Spanish Constitution), not to be required to reveal one's religion or beliefs (art. 16.2 of the Constitution) and to the effective protection of the courts (art. 24.1 of the Constitution) ...

A decision by a taxpayer not to complete the section of the income-tax return for the fixed statutory percentage of tax that may be allocated to religious ends or other charitable interests in the absence of an alternative allowing an allocation in favour of the taxpayer's own Church does not entail even an indirect violation of the constitutional guarantee of the right not to reveal one's religion or beliefs (art. 16.2 of the Constitution).

Furthermore, the court cannot find any discrimination based on religion violating the right to equality of treatment before the law (art. 14 of the Constitution), since a rational and objective basis exists for setting up a specific scheme of financial support for the Catholic Church through additional clause 5 (4) of Law no. 33/97... and the principle that the State is non-denominational is supplemented by the mandate which art. 16.3 of the Constitution gives the public authorities to establish „appropriate cooperation with the Catholic Church and the other denominations", having regard to the religious beliefs of Spanish society. It is within that institutional framework that the cooperation agreements have been entered into. These include ... an agreement on financial questions entered into with the Holy See by which the State undertakes to assist with the financial support of the Catholic Church. Thus, in the absence of any similar undertaking in favour of other denominations, the proposed basis for comparison is not adequate and the difference in treatment made by the legislature is neither arbitrary nor unjustified. Furthermore, art. 16.3 of the Constitution does not establish any directly enforceable fundamental right to compel the public authorities to set up a system enabling the alleged right to allocate a percentage of one's income tax to the support of one's own Church and the constitutional remedy of amparo is not

the appropriate remedy for calling into question the constitutionality of the (alleged deficiencies) in the law.
Lastly, the judgments appealed against provided a reasoned and legally founded answer to the issues raised by the applicants ..."

B. Relevant domestic law

1. Constitution

Art. 14
„*Spanish nationals shall be equal before the law and may not be discriminated against in any way on account of birth, race, sex, religion, opinion or any other condition or personal or social circumstance.*"
Art. 16
„*1. Freedom of ideology, religion and worship is guaranteed for private individuals and communities without any limitation on its expression other than as shall be necessary to maintain public order protected by law.*
2. No one may be required to reveal their ideology, religion or beliefs.
3. No denomination shall be treated as the religion of the State. Public authorities shall take into account the religious beliefs of the Spanish society and shall accordingly seek to cooperate with the Catholic Church and the other denominations."

Under Institutional Law no. 7/1980 on Freedom of Religion, the State may enter into cooperation agreements - providing, *inter alia*, tax exemptions - with Churches. The arrangements will depend on the number of members the Church has, the extent to which it is established in Spanish society and the beliefs of the majority of Spaniards.

2. Law no. 33/1987 of 23 December 1987 on the State Budget for 1988

Supplemental provision no. 5
„*Pursuant to the provision set out in art. II of the Agreement on Financial Matters entered into by the Spanish State and the Holy See on 3 January 1979...,
from 1988 onwards a percentage of the income tax paid by private individuals will be allocated to religious ends or other ends in the interest of society.*
2. The said percentage shall be determined in each annual budget and shall apply to the tax levied on the basis of the annual returns made by taxpayers.
...
4. Taxpayers may indicate in their tax return their wish for a percentage of their income tax to be allocated to:
(a) providing financial support for the Catholic Church; or
(b) other ends set out in subpar. 1 of this provision.
Anyone who does not expressly state their preference shall be deemed to have opted for the ends referred to in subpar. (b)."

3. Law of 10 November 1992 establishing a cooperation agreement between the State and the Federation of Evangelical Churches in Spain (FEREDE)

The Law of 10 November 1992, which was published in the State Official Gazette of 12 November 1992, governs the following matters:

(i) the status of ministers of the evangelical church;

(ii) legal protection for places of worship;

(iii) recognition under the civil law of marriages celebrated according to Evangelical rite;

(iv) religious assistance in public centres or institutions;

(v) Evangelical religious teaching in schools;

(vi) tax privileges applicable to certain assets and activities of Churches that are members of the *FEREDE*.

Further, supplemental provision no. 2 of the Law provides that the agreement may be varied in whole or in part on the initiative of either party. Supplemental provision no. 3 establishes a joint committee comprising representatives of the State and of the *FEREDE*.

According to information provided in February 2001 by the Director of Religious Affairs at the Ministry of Justice, a meeting of the joint committee (State-*FEREDE*) was held on 15 April 1999. During the course of the committee's examination of the problem of financial cooperation with the State regarding certain activities of the Evangelical Churches, the State representative asked *FEREDE* for its view on the system of allocation of income tax. In reply to that question, the executive secretary of the *FEREDE* replied: „after various consultations, it was discovered that the opinion of the Churches within the Federation is divided, such that a final view has yet to be reached; it will be announced once it has been determined by negotiation". Consequently, the 1992 agreement has not been amended and, to date, the *FEREDE* has not requested any amendment to it.

COMPLAINT

The applicants alleged that, as members of the Evangelical Baptist Church and unlike Spaniards of the Catholic faith, they were unable when completing their income-tax returns to allocate part of their income tax directly for the financial support of their own Church. They considered that difference in treatment to constitute discrimination contrary to art. 14 and 9 § 1 of the Convention.

THE LAW

Relying on art. 14 and 9 § 1 of the Convention, the applicants alleged that, as members of the Evangelical Baptist Church and unlike Spaniards of the Catholic faith, they were unable when completing their income-tax returns to allocate part of their income tax directly for the financial support of their own Church.

The relevant provisions read as follows:

Art. 14
„*The enjoyment of the rights and freedoms set forth in [the] Convention shall be secured without discrimination on any ground such as ... religion ...*"
Art. 9
„*1. Everyone has the right to freedom of thought, conscience and religion; this right includes freedom to change his religion or belief and freedom, either alone or in community with others and in public or private, to manifest his religion or belief, in worship, teaching, practice and observance.*
2. Freedom to manifest one's religion or beliefs shall be subject only to such limitations as are prescribed by law and are necessary in a democratic society in the interests of public safety, for the protection of public order, health or morals, or for the protection of the rights and freedoms of others."

The Government explained at the outset that the applicants' alleged inability to allocate part of their income tax directly for the financial support of their own Church was not attributable to any statutory provision but simply to the fact that neither the Valencia Baptist Evangelical Church nor the *FEREDE* had yet sought to benefit from such a system of financing.

They said that, in accordance with art. 16 and 14 of the Constitution, art. 9 and 14 of the Convention and the Law of 5 July 1980 on Freedom of Religion, everyone in Spain enjoyed freedom of religion and the right not to be discriminated against in the exercise of that freedom. Furthermore, under the cooperation agreement that had been entered into by the State and the *FEREDE*, as stipulated in the Law of 10 November 1992, members of the Evangelical Churches had been granted other rights.

The Government explained that the applicants, as private individuals, could make donations to their Church or to any other Church, and that such donations were eligible for tax relief. As regards public financing for the Church, the Government pointed out that that issue depended first and foremost on the stance taken by the Church as a religious group. In that connection, the Government observed that Spain had entered into financial agreements with the Catholic Church in 1979. It was pursuant to those agreements that the possibility of an allocation of income tax in favour of the Catholic Church had been established in 1987, by means of a specific allocation of a percentage of income tax. In the instant case, however, the Government noted that the applicants were not acting as representatives of a Church, but solely as members of the Valencia Baptist Evangelical Church, in which the first applicant was a deacon of music. Thus, neither the Valencia Baptist Evangelical Church nor the *FEREDE* had ever sought to benefit from the possibility of receiving an allocation of tax resources from the State. In that connection, the Government noted that the Evangelical Churches had formed a Federation (the *FEREDE*) to represent them through the medium of the joint committee set up in conjunction with the State. However, as the information received from the Director of Religious Affairs of the Ministry of Justice showed, at a meeting on 15 April 1999 the representative of the *FEREDE* had declined to make a request enabling its member Churches to benefit from tax resources through a special allocation of part of the revenue from income tax.

In conclusion, the Government submitted that the application was manifestly ill-founded.

The applicants contested the Government's argument and explained that they sought neither public financing for their Church nor an agreement with the Protestant Churches. On the other hand, they could not accept that the agreement on financial matters entered into on 3 January 1979 by the Spanish State and the Holy See should mandatorily apply to them. What they were seeking was a personal right, in common with Catholics, to be able to decide on the use to which their money should be put by allocating part of their income tax to their own Church. However, in their submission, it was not necessary to have an agreement between the State and the Protestant Churches for that purpose.

The Court considered that the issue in the instant case was whether the applicants were victims of treatment that amounted to discrimination contrary to art. 9 § 1 of the Convention taken together with art. 14.

The Court reiterates that art. 14 does not prohibit every difference of treatment in the exercise of the recognised rights and freedoms. A difference in treatment will only be discriminatory if it has no objective and reasonable justification, that is if it does not pursue a legitimate aim and if there is no reasonable relationship of proportionality between the means employed and the aim sought to be realised (*Case „relating to certain aspects of the laws on the issue of languages in education in Belgium" (Merits)*, 23 July 1968, Series A no. 6 § 10; and *Darby v. Sweden*, 24 September 1990, Series A no. 187, p. 12, § 31).

The Court points out that the power of taxation is expressly recognised by the Convention system and is ascribed to the State by art. 1 of Protocol No. 1 (see C. v. the United Kingdom, application no. 10358/83, Commission decision of 15 December 1983, DR 37, p. 147). In addition, freedom of religion does not entail Churches or their members being given a different tax status to that of other taxpayers. However, the conclusion of agreements between the State and a particular Church establishing a special tax regime in favour of the latter does not, in principle, contravene the requirements of art. 9 and 14 of the Convention, provided that there is an objective and reasonable justification for the difference in treatment and that similar agreements may be entered into by other Churches wishing to do so. On this point, the Court notes that Law no. 7/1980 on Freedom of Religion allows agreements to be made between the State and various Churches or religious associations, according to the number of members they have and the beliefs of the majority of Spanish society. By virtue of that statute, the State and the *FEREDE* entered into a cooperation agreement that was implemented by the Law of 10 November 1992. The agreement covered various aspects of the exercise of evangelical worship in Spain and of legal protection for such worship. In that connection, the Court observes that the agreement is an open-ended one, since supplemental provision no. 2 to the Law provides that it may be amended on the initiative of either party. However, the court notes that neither the Church to which the applicants belonged nor the *FEREDE* wished to enter into an agreement with the Spanish State regarding the allocation of part of the revenue raised by income tax to the applicants' Church.

The Court observes that the special tax treatment enjoyed by the Catholic Church in Spain is contained in supplemental provision no. 5 to the Law of 23 December 1987 on the State Budget for 1988 and arises out of the agreements made on 3 January 1979 between Spain and the Holy See, which impose reciprocal obligations on both parties. Thus, for instance, the Catholic Church has undertaken to place at the service of Spanish society as a whole its historic, artistic and documentary heritage (art. XV of the Agreement on Teaching and Cultural Affairs), while at the same time an exemption from tax operates in favour of its places of worship (by virtue of art. IV of the Agreement on Financial Matters). The Court notes that the applicants do not contest, in itself, the compatibility with the Convention of the statutory choice available to members of the Catholic Church to allocate a percentage of their income tax for the financing of their Church. Their complaint is that they are unable to act in a like manner in favour of their own Church without a prior agreement with the Spanish State. However, the obligation imposed on Churches to reach an agreement with the State in order to be eligible to receive part of the revenue from income tax does not appear to the Court to be unfounded or disproportionate. Furthermore, regard being had to the margin of appreciation left to Contracting States (*Manoussakis and Others v. Greece*, 29 September 1996, RJD 1996-IV, p. 1364, § 44; KirchE-EU S. 263), particularly as regards the building the fragile relations that exist between the State and religions, it cannot be considered as amounting to discriminatory interference with the applicants' right to freedom of religion (*Cha'are Shalom Ve Tsedek c. France* [GC], no. 27417/95 § 84, ECHR 2000-VII; KirchE-EU S. 418). Indeed, such a margin of appreciation is all the more warranted in that there is no common European standard governing the financing of churches or religions, such questions being closely related to the history and traditions of each country. Furthermore, the Court notes that taxpayers are not obliged by Spanish tax law to pay any part of their tax to the Catholic Church and are free to allot the percentage of their tax determined by the Law on the State Budget to purposes in the social or general interest. The Court also notes that, according to the Government, the Spanish legislation in force allows taxpayers to make private donations to the Church of their choice on fiscally advantageous terms.

In the light of the foregoing, the Court considers that the applicants' complaint must be dismissed as being manifestly ill-founded within the meaning of art. 35 § 3 of the Convention.

For these reasons, the Court unanimously declares the application inadmissible.

63

Die Erteilung eines Schulzeugnisses mit der formularmäßigen Rubrik „Religion/Ethik", aber ohne Eintrag einer Note verletzt nicht die Religionsfreiheit des Schülers.

Art. 9, 35 §§ 3, 4 EMRK
EGMR, Beschluss vom 26. Juni 2001 - No. 40319/98
(Saniewski ./. Polen) -

THE FACTS

The applicant is a Polish national, born in 1980 and living in Pionki.

A. The circumstances of the case

On 20 June 1997 the applicant obtained a school report for the school year 1996/97. He attended a State secondary school in Pionki. The report contained a list of courses that he had followed during this year, including „religion/ethics", and marks obtained for his progress. The place reserved for „religion/ethics" contained no mark, but was left blank. Likewise, places reserved for certain other subjects such as „informatics", „music" and „fine arts" were left blank.

B. Relevant domestic law and practice

1. Freedom of religion and conscience

Art. 53 of the Constitution of Poland, adopted on 2 April 1997, provides that freedom of faith and religion shall be ensured to everyone. Pursuant to this article, freedom of religion shall include the freedom to profess or to accept a religion by personal choice as well as to manifest such religion, either individually or collectively, publicly or privately, by worshipping, praying, participating in ceremonies, performing rites or teaching.

Freedom of religion shall also include the possession of sanctuaries and other places of worship as well as the right of individuals, wherever they may be, to benefit from religious services.

According to this article, parents shall have the right to ensure their children's moral and religious upbringing and teaching in accordance with their convictions.

The religion of a church or other legally recognised religious organisation may be taught in schools, but the freedom of religion and conscience of others shall not be infringed thereby.

The freedom to express publicly one's religion may be limited only by means of statute and only where this is necessary for the defence of State security, public order, health, morals or the rights and freedoms of others.

No one shall be compelled to participate in religious practices or prevented from such participation. No one may be compelled by the organs of a public authority to disclose his philosophy of life, religious convictions or beliefs.

Other provisions on freedom of religion and conscience are laid down in the Freedom of Conscience and Religion Act of 17 May 1989, as amended, which reads as follows:

> *Art. 1*
> „*1. Poland (...) shall secure to its citizens freedom of conscience and religion.*
> *2. Freedom of conscience and religion includes freedom to choose one's religion or belief and freedom to manifest one's religion or belief, either alone or in community with others, in private and in public. (...)"*
> *Art. 2*
> „*In the exercise of their freedom of conscience and religion, citizens may in particular: (...)*
> *2 a) belong, or not belong, to churches or other religious communities;*
> *3) express their religious opinions;*
> *4) raise their children in conformity with their religious convictions;*
> *5) remain silent as to their religion or convictions, ..."*

2. Legal basis for religious instruction in schools

The majority of schoolchildren attend State schools. In August 1990 the Ministry of Education issued two Ordinances, introducing religious instruction in Roman Catholicism and other religions into public schools on a voluntary basis. A declaration was to be made by parents in primary schools, and pupils in secondary schools, to confirm whether the pupils wished to attend. Separate school reports were to be issued with marks for religious instruction.

The Ombudsman lodged a constitutional complaint with the Constitutional Court (*Trybunał Konstytucyjny*), challenging the conformity of certain provisions of those Ordinances with the law. The Ombudsman considered that they breached the statutory guarantee of the right to remain silent with regard to one's religion and convictions, as provided for in the Freedom of Conscience and Religion Act of 1989. He contended that the Ordinances disclosed a breach of this guarantee as their implementation would result in an obligation to reveal the religious convictions of parents and children.

In a decision of 30 January 1991, the Constitutional Court found that voluntary religious tuition at school was not in breach of the Freedom of Conscience and Religion Act. The court considered that by allowing a child to attend religious instruction a parent is not obliged to reveal his or her beliefs, since a non-believer could agree to the child attending such classes whereas a believer could refuse. It further considered that the right to remain silent with regard to one's religion and convictions could not be interpreted as an obligation to remain silent. The Court stressed that neither declaring one's wish to attend religious instruction nor the instruction itself was mandatory.

On 15 April 1992 the Minister of Education enacted a new Ordinance on the organisation of religious instruction in public schools. The Ordinance replaced the 1990 Ordinance referred to above. It provides for participation in religious instruction on a voluntary basis, a course on ethics being organised on the same voluntary basis for those pupils who do not wish to attend such instruction. It further provided for marks for „religious instruction/ethics" to be included in the official school reports. Art. 9 of the Ordinance provides that the school report should not contain any data which would disclose whether a pupil attended a course in any particular religion or in ethics „in order to eliminate any possible opportunities for intolerance" (...).

In August 1992 the Ombudsman filed a constitutional complaint against this Ordinance with the Constitutional Court. The Ombudsman submitted that including marks for religious instruction in an official school report breaches the principle of the separation of churches and the State, and infringes the right to remain silent about one's beliefs and convictions, guaranteed by law.

In a decision given on 30 April 1993, the Constitutional Court found that including marks for „religion/ethics" in official school reports did not reveal whether a pupil had attended one course or the other. Therefore, the court found it unnecessary to examine the question whether the impugned Ordinance had infringed the right to remain silent regarding one's religion and convictions.

On 14 April 1997 Poland ratified the concordat with the Vatican. Art. 12 (1) of the concordat reads as follows:

> „The State, respecting the right of parents to ensure the religious education of their children and the principle of tolerance, shall guarantee that public primary and secondary schools and pre-school establishments, run by the State and local government administration, organise, if interested persons so wish, courses in religious education within the framework of school and pre-school curricula."

3. Constitutional complaints before the Constitutional Court

In accordance with art. 33a of the Constitution of 2 April 1997, the Constitutional Court rules on the conformity of statutes and other normative acts enacted by the main and central State organs with the Constitution, and establishes a universally binding interpretation of laws.

Pursuant to art. 79 of the Constitution, everyone whose constitutional rights or freedoms have been infringed shall have the right to request a ruling by the Constitutional Court as to the conformity with the Constitution of a statute or another normative act, on the basis of which a court or organ of public administration has given a final decision impinging upon the complainant's constitutional rights or freedoms.

Under art. 188 of the Constitution, the Constitutional Court shall give rulings concerning, *inter alia*, the conformity of statutes and international agreements with the Constitution, and also the conformity of provisions enacted by central State organs with the Constitution, as well as that of ratified international agreements and statutes.

Under the provisions of the Constitutional Court Act of 1 August 1987, a constitutional complaint should not be directed against an individual act of application of legal provisions, such as an administrative decision or a judicial decision. Its purpose and scope should be limited to challenge the compatibility with the Constitution of legal provisions which served as a legal basis for such an individual act.

The complaint shall indicate which constitutional rights or freedoms have been violated by a statute, ordinance, order, or other normative act complained of, and contain a description of the alleged violation.

It should be lodged with the court within three months after a final individual decision has been served on the complainant.

COMPLAINTS

The applicant complains about the contents of his school report for the 1996/97 school year. He asserts that his freedom of thought and conscience was breached since the absence of a mark for the course in religion reveals that he did not follow this course. He is obliged thereby to make a public statement as to his beliefs. He submits that he is an atheist and in Poland, which is a Catholic country where manifestations of religious intolerance are frequent, his chances of obtaining a place at university or a good job are seriously diminished thereby.

The applicant argues that the interference with his rights guaranteed by art. 9 of the Convention was not necessary in a democratic society and was not justified by any of legitimate aims listed in this provision.

He further complains on behalf of his parents, invoking art. 2 of Protocol No. 1 to the Convention, that the contents of the impugned school report breached their right to ensure his education and teaching in conformity with their religious and philosophical convictions.

THE LAW

1. The applicant complains under art. 9 of the Convention about the contents of his school report for the 1996/97 school year. He asserts that his freedom of thought and conscience was breached since the absence of a mark for the course in religion reveals that he did not follow this course. He is obliged thereby to make a public statement as to his beliefs.

Art. 9 of the Convention reads:

> „1. Everyone has the right to freedom of thought, conscience and religion; this right includes freedom to change his religion or belief and freedom, either alone or in community with others and in public or private, to manifest his religion or belief, in worship, teaching, practice and observance.
>
> 2. Freedom to manifest one's religion or beliefs shall be subject only to such limitations as are prescribed by law and are necessary in a democratic society in the interests of public safety, for the protection of public order, health or morals, or for the protection of the rights and freedoms of others. "

The Court recalls that freedom of thought, conscience and religion is one of the foundations of a „democratic society" within the meaning of the Convention. It is, in its religious dimension, one of the most vital elements that go to make up the identity of believers and their conception of life, but it is also a precious asset for atheists, agnostics, sceptics and the unconcerned. The pluralism indissociable from a democratic society, which has been dearly won over the centuries, depends on it (the Kokinnakis v. Greece judgment of 25 May 1993, Series A no. 260-A, p. 17, § 31; KirchE-EU S. 202; *Hasan and Chaush v. Bulgaria*, [GC], no. 30985/96, § 60, ECHR 2000 [26.10.00], KirchE-EU S. 444).

The Court further recalls that, according to the case-law of the Convention organs, art. 9 of the Convention affords protection against religious indoctrination by the State. Art. 9 primarily protects the sphere of personal beliefs and religious creeds, i.e. the area which is sometimes called the *forum internum*. However, it also recalls the case-law of the European Commission of Human Rights which found that there was no interference with the rights safeguarded by art. 9 of the Convention where voluntary religious education had been organised in State schools, or exemptions were possible from compulsory religious education, or when marks for attendance at such courses or alternative ethics courses were foreseen in school reports (EuCommHR, no. 23380/94, Decision 16.1.96, DR 84-A, p. 46; no. 10491/83, Decision 3.12.86, DR 51 p. 41).

As regards the facts of the present case, the Court first notes that, even assuming that the applicant may be said to have exhausted domestic remedies, he was not obliged to attend religious instruction, as it was organised on a voluntary basis. It is not alleged that he had to participate in any school activities of a religious character which were incompatible with his views. Neither was he prevented from expressing his opinions in respect of religion.

Secondly, leaving open the question whether art. 9 of the Convention guarantees a right to remain silent as to one's religious beliefs, the Court notes that the applicant complains about the contents of his second year school report in a secondary school when he was sixteen years old. This report covered only one school year when he was young and the applicant does not contend that he would have to show it to any higher educational establishment in the framework of an admissions procedures, or to submit it to any future employer. He has thus not substantiated his claim that the report might prejudice his future educational or employment prospects. Consequently, the Court does not find it established that the impugned school report had, or would have, any material impact on the applicant's interests.

The Court also notes that on the impugned school report places reserved for marks for certain other subjects such as „informatics", „music" and „fine arts" were also left blank. Therefore, no conclusion can be drawn on the basis of the report as to whether the applicant refused to attend the courses for which there was no mark on the report, or whether these courses simply were not organised in his school in this school year.

Thirdly, the Court notes that discrimination on religious grounds is illegal in Poland, being prohibited by domestic law and the Conventions of the International Labour Organisation. The applicant would, therefore, have a remedy against the apparently minimal risk of any prejudice the school report might engender in the future in the context of private employment.

Moreover, the applicant has not contended that he suffered any specific problems as a result of the impugned school report. In particular, he did not refer to any hostile remarks being made to him, or other manifestations of intolerance. He does not allege that he has suffered discrimination on account of his atheism, either on the part of any public authority, or on the part of any private person or entity.

The Court concludes that the applicant has not shown that he has suffered such consequences from the school report which could be said to amount to an interference with his rights and freedoms guaranteed by art. 9 of the Convention.

It follows that this part of the application is to be rejected as being manifestly ill-founded pursuant to art. 35 §§ 3 and 4 of the Convention.

2. (...)

For these reasons, the Court unanimously declares the application inadmissible.

64

Zur Frage der Beachtung raumordnungsrechtlicher, insbesondere naturschutzrechtlicher Vorschriften bei Planungsvorhaben von Religionsgemeinschaften (hier: Anlage einer Kapelle und eines Friedhofs).

Art. 9 Abs. 2, 35 § 3 EMRK
EGMR, Beschluss vom 10. Juli 2001 - No. 41754/98
(Johannische Kirche u.a. ./. Deutschland)[1] -

THE FACTS

The first applicant [Johannische Kirche] is a Christian religious community (Free Church) with public-law corporation status (*Körperschaft des öffentlichen Rechts*) whose governing board (*Vorstand*) is based in Berlin. The second applicant [Horst Peters] is a German national (...)

The facts of the case, as submitted by the applicants, may be summarised as follows.

In July 1991 the first applicant requested a permit to build a chapel and cemetery on land belonging to it.

Its request was rejected by the administrative authorities, whereupon the first applicant lodged an application with the Bayreuth Administrative Court. At the public hearing before that court it requested an adjournment of the proceedings concerning the cemetery.

On 20 December 1993, after visiting the site of the planned building, the Administrative Court rejected the application concerning the chapel on the grounds that the site where it was to be built was in an undeveloped protected zone (*Außenbereich*) and that it was not certain that public services (*Erschließung*) could be installed.

On 10 August 1994, after hearing submissions from, among others, the public-health department, the water resources office (*Wasserwirtschaftsamt*), the town of Waischenfeld (on whose territory the first applicant's land was) and other departments which had not given their consent or had done so only on certain conditions, the Bayreuth administrative authorities rejected the request concerning the cemetery, in respect of which the proceedings had been resumed after the Administrative Court had given judgment, on the ground that the proposed site was in an undeveloped protected zone and it was not certain that services could be installed on the land because the town of Waischenfeld refused to grant the first applicant a right of access over the adjoining municipal land to the site of the planned cemetery.

---

[1] CEDH/ECHR 2001-VIII; öarr 2003, 151 (LS).

On 15 December 1994 the Bayreuth Administrative Court dismissed the application mainly on the same grounds as those set out in the judgment of 20 December 1993, to which it referred at length moreover.

On 4 July 1996, after visiting the site of the planned cemetery, the Bavaria Administrative Court of Appeal upheld the judgment of the Bayreuth Administrative Court of 15 December 1994. It noted, among other things, that construction of the planned cemetery was incompatible with the nature of the environment surrounding the site in question, particularly as, since the entry into force on 14 July 1995 of the legislative decree on the creation of Franconian Switzerland Wildlife Park (*Naturpark Fränkische Schweiz*), any act such as to disfigure the character of the wildlife park - even locally - was prohibited. The fact that the first applicant was a religious community did not alter that finding because it could build the cemetery on other land less affected by environmental restrictions. The Court of Appeal also noted that the lack of services on the land in question was an additional factor militating against the first applicant's project.

The Court of Appeal also decided not to grant leave to appeal on points of law. The first applicant appealed against that decision.

On 7 March 1997 the Federal Administrative Court (3 B 173.96; KirchE 35, 93) dismissed the appeal on the ground that it did not raise an issue of fundamental importance. It noted that freedom of religion was limited by the values laid down in the Constitution itself. Among those constitutional values was the protection of life's natural sources (*natürliche Lebensgrundlagen*), as declared in sec. 20(a) of the Basic Law, which included the creation of protected zones. Additionally, the provisions relating to planning matters applied to everyone without distinction and did not impose more restrictions on religious communities than on other persons or groups of persons. As far as the provisions relating to cemeteries were concerned, it was indisputable that the creation of a cemetery was subject to laws relating to public health and the management of water resources. The freedom of a religious community subject to public law to practise its religion did not compel the authorities to grant that community an exemption from the statutory restrictions relating to the protection of the environment and the countryside. Besides that, the question as to whether such an exemption should have been granted, under the legislative decree of 14 July 1995 relating to the creation of Franconian Switzerland Wildlife Park, concerned provisions adopted by the Bavarian legislature, that is to say by a *Land*, and could not therefore be relied on before the Federal Administrative Court.

On 14 October 1997 the Federal Constitutional Court, ruling as a panel of three judges, decided not to uphold the first applicant's constitutional appeal. It noted, *inter alia*, that freedom of religion and freedom to manifest it was not unlimited and could be balanced against other constitutional values, of which sec. 20(a) of the Basic Law was one. It also noted that the first applicant could build the cemetery on other land which was less affected by regulatory restrictions.

COMPLAINT

Relying on art. 9 of the Convention, the applicants complained that the German authorities had breached their right to freedom of religion when they dismissed the first applicant's request. Their religion was characterised by the belief that after death there was no further difference in social class and that human beings would all be equal before God. That belief found its expression in the very natural layout of the planned cemetery in that all the tombstones had to be laid on their side and be uniform in size, even if the burial of a member of the first applicant in a traditional cemetery was not prohibited.

THE LAW

The applicants submitted that the German authorities' refusal to grant the first applicant planning permission to build a cemetery was contrary to art. 9 of the Convention, the relevant parts of which provide:

> „1. Everyone has the right to freedom ... of religion; this right includes freedom ... either alone or in community with others and in public or private, to manifest his religion or belief, in worship, teaching, practice and observance.
> 2. Freedom to manifest one's religion or beliefs shall be subject only to such limitations as are prescribed by law and are necessary in a democratic society in the interests of public safety, for the protection of public order, health or morals, or for the protection of the rights and freedoms of others."

According to the applicants, the construction and upkeep of a cemetery were not only the expression of freedom to practise one's religion but were part of the very freedom of religion.

The Court points out at the outset that the second applicant, who was not a party to the proceedings before the German authorities and courts, described himself as an „intervener" (Streithelfer) in the present application. The Court does not consider it necessary to rule on the issue whether this means that the second applicant does not qualify as an applicant for the purposes of art. 34 of the Convention because the application must in any event be declared inadmissible for the following reasons.

The Court reiterates that freedom of thought, conscience and religion is one of the foundations of a democratic society within the meaning of the Convention. While religious freedom is primarily a matter of individual conscience, it also implies, inter alia, freedom to manifest one's religion alone and in private, or in community with others, in public and within the circle of those whose faith one shares. Art. 9 of the Convention lists a number of forms which manifestation of one's religion or belief may take, namely worship, teaching, practice and observance. Nevertheless, art. 9 does not protect every act motivated or inspired by a religion or belief (see *Hassan and Tchaouch v. Bulgaria* [GC], no. 30985/96, § 60, ECHR 2000-XI, KirchE-EU S. 444; *Cha'are Shalom Ve Tsedek v. France* [GC], no. 27417/95, § 73, ECHR 2000-VII, KirchE-EU S. 418; and the Kalaç v. Turkey judgment of 1 July 1997, RJD 1997-IV, p. 1209, § 27, KirchE-EU S. 312).

The Court notes that the impugned decisions of the German authorities can be construed as a restriction of the right to manifest one's religion within the meaning of art. 9 § 2 of the Convention in so far as the manner of burying the dead and cemetery layout represents an essential aspect of the religious practice of the first applicant and its members (see, *mutatis mutandis*, the *Cha'are Shalom Ve Tsedek v. France* judgment cited above, §§ 73-74).

The Court also notes that the interference in question was prescribed by law, which the first applicant did not dispute moreover.

The Court next reiterates that the Contracting States enjoy a certain margin of appreciation in assessing the existence and extent of the necessity of an interference, but this margin is subject to European supervision, embracing both the legislation and the decisions applying it. The Court's task is to determine whether the measures taken at national level were justified in principle and proportionate (see the Kokkinakis v. Greece judgment of 25 May 2993, Series A no. 260-A, p. 21, § 47, KirchE-EU S. 202, and the Manoussakis and Others v. Greece judgment of 26 September 1996, RJD 1996-VI, p. 1364, § 44, KirchE-EU S. 263).

The Court notes in the instant case that the authorities justified their refusal to authorise construction of the cemetery on the basis of provisions relating to planning, environmental protection and services, and particularly by the fact that there was no other building in the zone in question.

It is true that the administrative authority and the Bayreuth Administrative Court did not make any allusion to the fact that the first applicant was a religious community, and it was only before the Bavaria Administrative Court of Appeal that a possible interference with the first applicant's right to religious freedom was examined.

However, the Administrative Court of Appeal noted that the status of the first applicant did not give it the right to build a cemetery on a site specially protected by the legislative decree on the creation of Franconian Switzerland Wildlife Park. With regard to the federal courts, the Court notes that they duly explained how and to what extent a right to freedom of religion, guaranteed by the Basic Law without express restrictions, was limited by the rights of others and constitutional values such as the protection of life's natural sources, as declared in sec. 20(a) of the Basic Law. These decisions show that the German authorities did not aim their decision to dismiss the application at the first applicant as a religious community; the prohibition on building applied to any person applying for a building permit in the zone in question.

In the light of the foregoing, and having regard to the wide margin of appreciation of the Contracting States in planning matters (see, *mutatis mutandis*, the Sporrong and Lönnroth v. Sweden judgment of 23 September 1982, Series A no. 52, p. 26, § 6, and application no. 20490/92, Iskcon and Others v. the United Kingdom, Commission decision of 8 March 1994, DR 76, p. 91), the Court considers that the measure complained of amounts to a restriction of the first applicant's right to freedom to manifest its religion which is justified in principle and proportionate to the aim pursued (protection of the rights and freedoms of others) and, accordingly, to an interference which is in conformity with art. 9 § 2 of the Convention.

It follows that the application is manifestly ill-founded within the meaning of art. 35 § 3 of the Convention and must be rejected in accordance with art. 35 § 4 of the Convention.

For these reasons, the Court unanimously declares the application inadmissible.

65

Ein Gesetz, das von Bewerbern um öffentliche Ämter die Erklärung der Nichtmitgliedschaft in einer Freimaurerloge verlangt, verstößt gegen die Vereinigungsfreiheit nach Art. 11 EMRK.
Zur Beschwerdebefugnis einer Freimaurerloge.

EGMR, Urteil vom 2. August 2001 - No. 35972/97
(Grande Oriente d'Italia di Palazzo Giustiniani ./. Italien)[1] -

---

[1] CEDH/ECHR 2001-VIII, 499. Deutsche Übersetzungen: EzAR 935 Nr 11; Inf-AuslR 2001, 476; ZAR 2003, 366 (LS). Vgl. auch EGMR, Urteil vom 2.8.2001 - No. 37119/97 (N.F. ./. Italien) - Slg. 2001-IX, Beschwerde betr. Disziplinarmaßnahme gegen einen Richter wegen Mitgliedschaft in einer Freimaurerloge. Das Gericht gibt der Beschwerde statt, weil bereits eine für den Betroffenen ersichtliche und „vom Gesetz vorgesehene" Einschränkung der Vereinigungsfreiheit (Art. 11 § 2 EMRK) als Rechtsgrundlage der Disziplinarmaßnahme nicht festgestellt werden konnte. Die ebenfalls gerügte Verletzung von Art. 8, 9, 10 u. 14 EMRK bedurfte dann keiner Sachprüfung.

THE FACTS

I. The circumstances of the case

[8] The applicant association is an Italian masonic association which groups together several lodges. It has been in existence since 1805 and is affiliated to Universal Freemasonry. In Italian law the applicant association has the status of an unrecognised private-law association under art. 36 of the Civil Code. It therefore does not have legal personality. It has filed its articles of Association with a notary (notaio) and anyone can have access to them. By Regional Law no. 34 of 5 August 1996 („the 1996 Law"), published in the Official Gazette of 14 August of the same year, the Marches Region („the Region") laid down the rules to be followed for nominations and appointments to public office for which the Region was the appointing authority (Norme per le nomine e designazioni di spettanza della Regione). Before the Court the applicant association complained of the damage allegedly sustained by it as a result of the content of sec. 5 of the 1996 Law. Sec. 1 of the 1996 Law provides that the rules shall apply to all nominations and appointments by the bodies constituted according to the Region's Statute pursuant to laws, rules, statutes and agreements to posts in „departments of public-law and private-law authorities and bodies other than the Region". It also provides that the rules shall likewise apply to nominations to fifteen regional bodies (listed in Schedule A to the 1996 Law) and, in some cases, to other regional bodies for which the Regional Council is the appointing authority (Schedule B to the 1996 Law). Sec. 5 of the Law sets out the terms and conditions for submitting applications for nominations and appointments. It provides, inter alia, that candidates must not be Freemasons. It is worded as follows:

Sec. 5
Applications
„*1. Applications may be submitted by regional councillors and council groups and by professional bodies, organisations and associations active in the fields concerned to the President of the Regional Council and the President of the Regional Government respectively until thirty days before the period allowed for a nomination or appointment expires.*
2. Applications must be accompanied by a statement of supporting reasons and a report containing the following particulars:
(a) municipality of residence, date and place of birth;
(b) qualifications;
(c) career to date, usual occupation, list of currently and previously held public offices or positions in majority State-owned companies and publicly registered private companies;
(d) lack of conflict of interest with the office proposed;
(e) declaration of non-membership of a masonic lodge;

(f) declaration, signed by the candidate, accepting the public office and stating that there is nothing to debar him from office on criminal, civil or administrative grounds.

3. The declaration of acceptance signed by the candidate must be certified authentic and contain a statement by him of any grounds of incompatibility and of the absence of any grounds debarring him from applying or making it impossible for him to do so, regard being had also to sec. 15 of Law no. 55 of 19 March 1990 as subsequently amended."

[9] In June 1999 the first committee of the Marches Regional Council rejected a regional bill (no. 352/98) proposing amendments and additions to Law no. 34 of 1996. The bill was intended, among other things, to abolish the declaration provided for in sec. 5 of the 1996 Law.

II. Relevant domestic law

[10] Art. 18 of the Constitution provides:

„Citizens may form associations freely, without authorisation, for purposes not prohibited for individuals by the criminal law.
Secret associations and associations pursuing, even indirectly, a political aim through organisations of a military nature shall be prohibited."

Law no. 17 of 25 January 1982 contains the implementing provisions for art. 18 of the Constitution with regard to secret associations and provided for the dissolution of the association called „P2 Lodge". Sec. 1 lays down the criteria for regarding an association as being a secret one. Sec. 4 sets out the measures to be taken in respect of persons employed in the civil service or appointed to a public office who are suspected of belonging to a secret association. That section also provides that the regions shall enact regional laws for their officials and persons nominated or appointed by a region to a public office. These regional laws must respect principles laid down in the same provision. According to the information supplied to the Court by the applicant association, such laws have been enacted by the regions of Tuscany (Law no. 68 of 29 August 1983), Emilia-Romagna (Law no. 34 of 16 June 1984), Liguria (Law no. 4 of 22 August 1984), Piedmont (Law no. 65 of 24 December 1984) and Lazio (Law no. 23 of 28 February 1985). Two of these regional laws provide that persons nominated or appointed to public office must name the associations to which they belong (sec. 12 of the Tuscany law and sec. 8 of the Lazio law). The other laws lay down the penalties to be imposed on persons so nominated or appointed if it transpires that they are members of a secret association (sec. 7 of the Emilia-Romagna law, sec. 8 of the Liguria law and sect. 8 of the Piedmont law). The Emilia-Romagna law also contains a prohibition on nominating or appointing persons affiliated to secret associations (sec. 7 of the Emilia-Romagna law).

THE LAW

I. The government's preliminary objection

*[11]*When the admissibility of the application was being examined, the Government maintained that the applicant association could not claim to be a victim of the breaches it alleged. Sec. 5 of the 1996 Law did not, they argued, jeopardise either the applicant association's existence or its activities. The alleged breach applied only to individuals and affected a member of the association only if he applied for a public office. It could not concern an association. In its decision of 21 October 1999 the Court upheld the Government's objection with regard to the complaints under art. 8, 9 and 10 of the Convention and declared them inadmissible. However, with regard to the complaint under art. 11, it considered that „an examination of the status of victim [was] in this case closely linked to an examination of the merits of the complaint, and in particular to the question of the existence of an interference with the applicant association's right". It will therefore come back to this issue later (see par. 16 below).

II. Alleged violation of Art. 11 of the Convention

[12] The applicant association submitted that sec. 5 of the 1996 Law infringed its right to freedom of association as guaranteed by art. 11 of the Convention, which provides:

> „1. Everyone has the right to freedom of peaceful assembly and to freedom of association with others, including the right to form and to join trade unions for the protection of his interests.
> 2. No restrictions shall be placed on the exercise of these rights other than such as are prescribed by law and are necessary in a democratic society in the interests of national security or public safety, for the prevention of disorder or crime, for the protection of health or morals or for the protection of the rights and freedoms of others. This article shall not prevent the imposition of lawful restrictions on the exercise of these rights by members of the armed forces, of the police or of the administration of the State."

According to the applicant association, sec. 5 of the 1996 Law forced its members to choose between two alternatives: either renounce membership or forgo public office in a regional body. It thus restricted not only the freedom of association of every member, but also that of the association itself.

A. Whether there was interference

[13] The applicant association submitted that the obligation on candidates to declare that they were not members of a masonic lodge was a

twofold interference. Firstly, it was an interference with the right to freedom of association taken as the right of any social group to exist and act without unjustified restrictions being imposed on it or its members by the authorities. Requiring the applicant association's members to declare that they were not Freemasons deprived them of access to numerous public offices at regional level. That constituted interference with the applicant association's activities because either it resulted in a loss of members - where they decided to leave the association, not from conviction but on account of a statutory obligation, in order to apply for public office in the Marches Region - or it imposed an unreasonable sacrifice on the applicant association's members where they decided to remain members of the applicant association rather than apply for public office. The obligation in question also created a negative image of the association. Sec. 5 of the 1996 Law gave the impression that Freemasonry was a criminal association or, at any rate, one that did not comply with Italian law. Yet not only had Freemasonry been recognised as a lawful association by the courts and by a parliamentary investigating committee, but, above all, it was covered by the guarantees set forth in art. 2 and 18 of the Constitution. The applicant association deduced from the foregoing that it directly suffered the detrimental effects of sec. 5 of the 1996 Law.

[14] For their part, the Government disputed that there was any interference. They submitted that the right to freedom of association could be relied on by an individual who wanted to join an association, but not by an association, which, they maintained, was the product of the exercise of that freedom. Secondly, even supposing that the guarantees of art. 11 did apply to associations, the disqualifications affecting one of the association's members on account of his or her membership of it could not be challenged by the association because they did not concern it.

[15] The Court reiterates that art. 11 applies to associations, including political parties (see United Communist Party of Turkey and Others v. Turkey, judgment of 30 January 1998, RJD 1998-I, and Socialist Party and Others v. Turkey, judgment of 25 May 1998, RJD 1998-III). It has indicated in general that „an association, including a political party, is not excluded from the protection afforded by the Convention simply because its activities are regarded by the national authorities as undermining the constitutional structures of the State and calling for the imposition of restrictions" (see United Communist Party of Turkey and Others, cited above, p. 17, § 27). The Court is of the opinion that this reasoning applies all the more to an association which, like the applicant association, is not suspected of undermining the constitutional structures. Additionally, and above all, the Court accepts that the measure in question may cause the applicant association - as it submits - damage in terms of loss of members and prestige.

[16] The Court therefore concludes that there has been interference. It follows that the applicant association can claim to be a victim of the al-

leged violation and that, accordingly, the Government's objection must be dismissed.

B. Whether the interference was justified

1. In the light of the first sentence of Par. 2 of Art. 11

[17] Such interference will constitute a breach of art. 11 unless it was „prescribed by law", pursued one or more legitimate aims under par. 2 and was „necessary in a democratic society" for the achievement of those aims.

(a) „Prescribed by law"

[18] The applicant association did not dispute that the interference was „prescribed by law", seeing that the impugned measure was based on a regional law (see par. 16-17 above).

(b) Legitimate aim

[19] The Government did not indicate which aim among those referred to in par. 2 was pursued by the measure in question. However, after asserting that the system of allocating public offices needed to be credible and required confidence in the persons chosen, they referred to suspicion among the public that some candidates might have been appointed because they were Freemasons. The harm caused by such suspicions had to be avoided at all costs, bearing in mind the role certain Freemasons had played in Italy's democracy, contributing to blacken the image of Italian public life, as had been shown by parliamentary and judicial inquiries.

[20] The applicant association submitted that the interference did not pursue any of the legitimate aims referred to in the first sentence of par. 2. In particular, the Government could not rely on the prevention of disorder or crime as justifications, because the applicant association was not a secret or criminal association on which it was necessary to impose prohibitions for preventive or punitive purposes.

[21] The Court notes that, according to the Government, sec. 5 of the 1996 Law was introduced to „reassure" the public at a time when there was controversy surrounding the role played by certain Freemasons in the life of the country. The Court therefore accepts that the interference was intended to protect national security and prevent disorder.

(c) „Necessary in a democratic society"

(i) The parties' submissions

[22] The applicant association submitted that the restriction on freedom of association was not reasonable and proportionate, and that the interference complained of was consequently not necessary in a democratic society. It cited as evidence the fact that the Marches Region was the only region which had made use of the powers delegated in sec. 4 of Law no. 17 of 1982, which sought to debar members of secret associations (see par. 10 above) by introducing an obligation on candidates to declare that they were not Freemasons. Moreover, that obligation did not even exist at central government level, so there was nothing to prevent a prime minister, a minister, a senior official or even the President of the Republic from being a Freemason. The applicant association also pointed out that, according to the Court's case-law, a judge could be a Freemason without this casting doubt on his or her objective impartiality (see Kiiskinen v. Finland (dec.), no. 26323/95, ECHR 1999-V). Additionally, the debate which had taken place in Parliament after the enactment of the 1996 Law had shown the unreasonable nature of the measure in question. Lastly, the applicant association pointed out that it had been a private-law association since 1805, that it had acted within the law since then and that, even if there was a move in Italy to „outlaw" Freemasonry, the association was still one which pursued a moral aim, was protected by art. 18 of the Constitution and should not be confused with a secret or criminal association. Even if there had been improper activities within Freemasonry, these had not concerned the applicant association and were not sufficient to demonise Freemasonry as a whole.

[23] The Government pointed out that there was no restriction on freedom of association, but only a potential disability. Further, the measure in question had been introduced by a law relating to the organisation of the region and therefore fell within the powers devolved to the regions by art. 117 of the Constitution.

(ii) Decision of the Court

[24] The Court has examined the impugned measure in the light of the case as a whole in order to determine, in particular, whether it was proportionate to the legitimate aim pursued.

[25] The proportionality principle demands that a balance be struck between the requirements of the purposes listed in art. 11 § 2 of the Convention and those of the free exercise of freedom of association. The pursuit of a just balance must not result in individuals being discouraged, for fear of having their applications for office rejected, from exercising their right of association on such occasions.

[26] Compared with the total number of members of the applicant association, the number of actual or potential members of the association who may be confronted with the dilemma of choosing between being Freemasons and competing for the public offices referred to in sec. 5 of the 1996 Law cannot be said to be large. Consequently, the damage which the applicant association may suffer is likewise limited. The Court considers, however, that freedom of association is of such importance that it cannot be restricted in any way, even in respect of a candidate for public office, so long as the person concerned does not himself commit any reprehensible act by reason of his membership of the association. It is also clear that the association will suffer the consequences of its members' decisions. In short, the prohibition complained of, however minimal it might be for the applicant association, does not appear „necessary in a democratic society".

2. In the light of the second sentence of Par. 2 of Art. 11

[27] Having arrived at that conclusion, the Court must determine whether the prohibition in issue was justified by the last sentence of art. 11 § 2, since this empowers States to impose „lawful restrictions" on the exercise of the right to freedom of association by the members of certain groups, including „the administration of the State".

[28] The applicant association maintained that the interference was not justified by the second sentence of art. 11 § 2 because it was not „lawful". In its submission, sec. 5 of the 1996 Law contravened art. 2, 3, 18 and 117 of the Constitution; exceeded the limits laid down by Law no. 17 of 1982, sec. 4 of which provided that rules could be laid down debarring from public office civil servants who were members of secret associations; and, lastly, breached art. 8, 11 and 14 of the Convention, which was an integral part of Italian domestic law. The applicant association also disputed that the offices for which it was necessary to make the declaration required by sec. 5 formed part of „the administration of the State" strictly speaking. These were offices of assorted categories, including professional bodies and associations working in the relevant fields. Likewise concerned were private-law associations or, at any rate, associations having substantial autonomy (universities, leisure, cultural or sports associations, etc.) vis-à-vis the regional bodies.

[29] For their part, the Government considered that the expression „administration of the State" had to be understood in a broad sense and extended to administrative authorities as a whole.

[30] The Court reiterates that the term „lawful" in the second sentence of art. 11 § 2 alludes to the same concept of lawfulness as that to which the Convention refers elsewhere when using the same or similar expressions, notably the expression „prescribed by law" found in the second paragraphs of art. 9 to 11. The concept of lawfulness used in the Conven-

tion, apart from positing conformity with domestic law, also implies qualitative requirements in the domestic law such as foreseeability and, generally, an absence of arbitrariness (see Rekvényi v. Hungary [GC], no. 25390/94, § 59, ECHR 1999-III). In so far as the applicant association criticised the basis of the impugned restriction in domestic law, the Court reiterates that it is primarily for the national authorities to interpret and apply domestic law, especially if there is a need to elucidate doubtful points (see S.W. v. the United Kingdom, judgment of 22 November 1995, Series A no. 335-B, p. 42, § 36). In the present case, however, the applicant association could not challenge the constitutionality of the impugned provision in the courts, a fact which was not disputed by the Government. That being so, the Court concludes that the legal position was sufficiently clear to enable the applicant association to regulate its conduct and that the requirement of foreseeability was consequently satisfied. The contested restriction was therefore „lawful" within the meaning of art. 11 § 2.

[31] As to whether the offices covered by sec. 5 of the 1996 Law fall within the scope of „the administration of the State", the Court notes that the offices listed in Schedules A and B to the 1996 Law were not part of the organisational structure of the Region, but fell into two other categories: regional organisations and nominations and appointments for which the Regional Council was responsible. According to the Court's case-law, „the notion of ,administration of the State' should be interpreted narrowly, in the light of the post held by the official concerned" (see Vogt v. Germany, judgment of 26 September 1995, Series A no. 323, p. 31, § 67). The Court reiterates that in Vogt it did not consider it necessary to determine the issue whether a teacher - a permanent civil servant - was part of the administration of the State (ibid., p. 31, § 68). In the present case it notes on the basis of the evidence before it that the link between the offices referred to in Schedules A and B to the 1996 Law and the Marches Region is undoubtedly looser than the link which existed between Mrs Vogt, a permanent teacher, and her employer.

[32] Accordingly, the interference in question cannot be justified under the second sentence of art. 11 § 2 either.

[33] In conclusion, there has been a breach of art. 11 of the Convention.

III. Alleged violation of Art. 13 and 14 of the convention taken in conjunction with Art. 11

[34] The applicant association also alleged a breach of art. 13 and 14 of the Convention, taken in conjunction with art. 11. As its complaints related to the same facts as those examined under art. 11, the Court does not consider it necessary to examine them separately.

(...)

For these reasons, the court unaninimously
1. *Dismisses the Government's preliminary objection;*
2. *Holds that there has been a violation of art. 11 of the Convention;*
3. *Holds that it is not necessary to examine the case under art. 13 and 14 of the Convention taken in conjunction with art. 11.*

66

Die Heranziehung von Nichtmitgliedern zu einer herabgesetzten Kirchensteuer (dissenter tax) im Hinblick auf die von der Kirche im Allgemeininteresse wahrgenommenen Aufgaben (u.a. die Unterhaltung von Friedhöfen) verstößt nicht gegen Art. 9 EMRK.

Art. 9, 35 § 3 EKMR
EGMR, Beschluss vom 28. August 2001 -No. 36846/97
(Lundberg ./. Schweden)[1] -

THE FACTS

The applicant is a Swedish national, born in 1949 and living in Vällingby.

A. The circumstances of the case

The facts of the case, as submitted by the parties, may be summarised as follows.

The applicant, who is not a member of the Lutheran Church of Sweden, requested in his tax returns for the income years 1992-94 to be exempted from church tax. He claimed that the levying of church tax on a nonmember of the Church of Sweden contravened, inter alia, the Swedish Constitution and art. 9 of the Convention. He also stated that the municipality of Stockholm and not the relevant parish of the Church, Brännkyrka, was financing the construction and maintenance of burialgrounds and the maintenance of churchyards in the area where he lived.

The tax authorities rejected the applicant's request and decided to charge him approximately 425, 362 and 385 Swedish *kronor* (SEK) respectively for the three years in church tax, totalling SEK 1,172. This corresponded to 0.156 per cent of his taxable income for 1992 and 0.13 per cent for 1993 and 1994. The decision was taken in accordance with sec. 1 of the Act on Reduction of Tax Liability of Persons Not Members of

---

[1] Vgl. Zu demselben Gegenstand auch EGMR, Urteil vom 23.10.1990 No. 11581/85 (Darby ./. Schweden), dt. Übersetzung: EuGRZ 1990, 504, NJW 1991, 1404; ÖJZ 1991, 392; EGMR, Beschluss vom 28.8.2001 No. 32196/96 (Bruno ./. Schweden).

the Church of Sweden (*Lag om viss lindring i skattskyldigheten för den som icke tillhör svenska kyrkan*, 1951:691; hereinafter „the Dissenter Tax Act") which provided that, of the ordinary church tax, a non-member of the Church of Sweden should pay 30 per cent for 1992 and 25 per cent for 1993 and 1994.

The applicant appealed to the County Administrative Court (*länsrätten*) of the County of Stockholm but did not request an oral hearing. On 30 December 1994 the Court rejected his appeal as far as it concerned 1993 and, on 11 September 1996, it rejected his appeal with regard to 1992 and 1994.

The applicant appealed to the Administrative Court of Appeal (*kammarrätten*) in Stockholm. Again, he did not request an oral hearing. On 14 February 1997 his appeals were rejected.

On 23 April 1997 the Supreme Administrative Court (*Regeringsrätten*) refused the applicant leave to appeal. In his appeal to that court he had requested an oral hearing.

B. Relevant domestic law and practice

1. The activities of the Church of Sweden

According to the Burial Act (*Begravningslagen*, 1990:1144), the parishes within the Church of Sweden are obliged to construct and maintain public burial-grounds, unless the Government decide in the case of a specific municipality that this task shall be performed by the municipality itself (chapter 2, sec. 1). The right to be buried in a public burial-ground is not dependent on the deceased being a member of a particular religious community (chapter 2, sec. 4). However, the responsible organ, whether it be the local parish or the municipality, is obliged to provide for separate burial-grounds for those who are not members of any Christian community. The construction and maintenance of such burial-grounds are done in consultation with the religious communities concerned (chapter 2, sec. 2). Decisions taken under the Act by the parish or the municipality may be appealed against to the County Administrative Board (*länsstyrelsen*) (previously regulated in chapter 9 of the Act, now in chapter 11). In the municipality where the applicant was liable to pay tax the burial administration was - and still is - the responsibility of the municipality.

When the responsibility for the keeping of population records was transferred from the Church of Sweden to the local tax authorities in July 1991 (see further below), it was decided that the parishes should take care of population records made before that date until these old records have been transferred to the State archives (sec. 10 of the Act on Promulgation of the Population Registration Act; *Lagen om införande av folkbokförings-lagen*, 1991:481). It was estimated that it would take up to twenty years before all old records had been so transferred.

The Church Act (*Kyrkolagen*, 1992:300) also specifically stipulated that a parish may, *inter alia*, use its financial means to acquire and maintain church buildings and other ecclesiastical property.

2. Church tax

At the material time, a church tax was collected together with the ordinary municipal tax. Chapter 21, sec. 1 of the Church Act referred in this respect to the provisions of the Municipal Tax Act (*Kommunalskatte-lagen*, 1928:370). The rate was determined by the local parish council which, under the transitional provisions of the 1974 Constitution (*Rege-ringsformen*), had a status similar to that of the municipalities, including the right of taxation. This system had a long tradition, based on the fact that the Lutheran Church of Sweden is the established church. In 1990 the rates applied by the parishes varied between 0.56 and 2.64 per cent of the taxpayer's taxable income. The lowest rates were applied by the parishes of Stockholm where it is the municipality - and not the parishes - that has the responsibility for the burial administration (cf. *Svenska kyrkans ekonomi, Statskontoret* 1991:12, p. 9, a report on the economy of the Church of Sweden made by the National Agency for Administrative Development). In 1992-94, the relevant years in the present case, the rate applied in the parish of Brännkyrka, where the applicant lived, was 0.52 per cent.

3. Dissenter tax

The Dissenter Tax Act stipulated that a person who was not a member of the Church of Sweden should pay a reduced church tax, the so-called dissenter tax. The reduction was motivated by the fact that non-members, referred to as dissenters, should pay the share of the tax that corresponded to the costs relating to the civil, i.e. non-religious, activities of the parish. The dissenter tax, like the church tax, was collected by the local tax authority and forwarded to the relevant parish.

Originally, the dissenter tax amounted to 60 per cent of the ordinary church tax. In 1974 it was reduced to 30 per cent of what the members of the Church of Sweden had to pay. The rationale behind this change was that the share of the costs for the civil tasks performed by the Church - the keeping of population records and the maintenance of churchyards and public burial-grounds - amounted on average to approximately 30 per cent of the Church's total costs (cf. Government Bill 1973:184, pp. 3-5).

On 1 July 1991 the responsibility for the keeping of population records was transferred to the local tax authorities. With effect as from 1993, the dissenter tax was consequently further decreased, this time to 25 per cent of the amount paid by the members of the Church of Sweden. It was considered that this percentage corresponded to the average costs of the parishes for the burial of the deceased (cf. Government Bill 1991/92:100, appendix 8, p. 141). Reference was made to the above-mentioned report on the economy of the Church of Sweden, according to which 1.25 billion SEK, or about 24 per cent of the Church's total costs, related to the burial of the deceased.

4. Tax equalisation

Under Chapter 42 of the Church Act the tax revenue of the different parishes was to a certain extent equalised through payments to and subsidies from the so-called Church Fund. Poor parishes received a general equalisation subsidy which was not ear-marked for any particular purpose. They could also be granted extra subsidies for specific purposes.

5. Reforms

On 1 January 2000 the relations between the Swedish State and the Church of Sweden were changed, involving in practice a separation between the State and the Church. The Church Act and the Dissenter Tax Act were abolished.

The parishes' right of taxation, previously regulated in the Church Act and the Municipal Tax Act, was replaced with an obligation, laid down in sec. 7 of the new Act on the Swedish Church (*Lagen om svenska kyrkan*, 1998:1591), on persons belonging to the Church to pay a church fee.

According to the new chapter 9 of the Burial Act, every person who is registered as resident in Sweden has to pay a burial fee to defray the costs of the burial of the deceased (sec. 1). The fee is based on the taxpayer's taxable income (sec. 3) and is paid to the organ - parish or municipality - responsible for burials at the place where the individual is registered (sec. 2 § 1). In the municipalities where the local parishes are responsible for burials, the fee of the members of the Church of Sweden is to be included in the church fee (sec. 2 § 2). According to the Burial Fee Ordinance (*Förordningen om begravningsavgift*, 1999:729), the burial fee of non-members is fixed by the National Judicial Board for Public Lands and Funds (*Kammarkollegiet*) following a proposal by the Church of Sweden. The Church of Sweden and the municipalities responsible for burials are obliged to provide the tax authorities and - in the case of the Church - the National Judicial Board with the information needed to calculate and collect the fees. Under the new chapter 10 of the Burial Act, the relevant County Administrative Board supervises the parishes' burial administration in respect of persons who are not members of the Church of Sweden.

As the parishes continue to be responsible for the care and maintenance of church buildings and other ecclesiastical property of historic
value, the Church of Sweden is to receive certain financial compensation
from the State for the performance of this task.

COMPLAINTS

1. The applicant claims that the levying of church tax on him, who is
not a member of the Church of Sweden, violated his freedom of religion
as protected by art. 9 of the Convention.
2. He further complains that the administrative courts were not independent and impartial tribunals as required by art. 6 § 1 of the Convention and that no oral hearing was held.

THE LAW

1. The applicant complains of a violation of his right to freedom of
religion under art. 9 of the Convention. This provision reads as follows:

> „1. Everyone has the right to freedom of thought, conscience and religion; this
> right includes freedom to change his religion or belief and freedom, either alone
> or in community with others and in public or private, to manifest his religion or
> belief, in worship, teaching, practice and observance.
> 2. Freedom to manifest one's religion or beliefs shall be subject only to such limi-
> tations as are prescribed by law and are necessary in a democratic society in the
> interests of public safety, for the protection of public order, health or morals, or
> for the protection of the rights and freedoms of others."

The respondent Government submit that the present complaint is
manifestly ill-founded. They state that the obligation of non-members to
pay church tax, i.e. dissenter tax, to the Church of Sweden was based on
the notion that the Church had been entrusted with certain tasks carried
out in the interest of everyone - members as well as non-members -
including the legal obligation to provide a final resting-place in public
burial-grounds for both members and non-members. Although the burial
administration no doubt is the most costly non-religious task entrusted
with the Church, it also performs other civil activities in the interest of
society as a whole, inter alia the care and maintenance of old church
buildings and other ecclesiastical property and the care of old population
records. Considering that religious buildings and property form part of
the Swedish cultural heritage which should be preserved for future
generations and that the old population records are of importance to
researchers and to the general public, the Government submit that it has
been natural to demand financial contributions from both members and
non-members of the Church of Sweden for the performance of those
tasks.

The Government state that the dissenter tax was designed to cover only the civil activities of the parishes. The 30 and 25 per cent rates fixed by the Dissenter Tax Act was based on investigations into the economy of the Church of Sweden. They refer to the above-mentioned Government Bills and the report by the National Agency for Administrative Development.

Noting that the parish of Brännkyrka, where the applicant lived, was not responsible for the burial administration in its area, the Government assert that that parish was still contributing to the burial administration in the country in general by means of contributions to the Church Fund. They state that the parish paid more than SEK five million to the Church Fund in 1994. The Government also point out that the rate applied by the parish for the church tax - and consequently for the dissenter tax - was very low due to the fact that it was not responsible for the burial administration but only for its other civil activities.

The applicant maintains that his obligation to pay tax to the Church of Sweden has violated his right to freedom of religion. He points out that the relevant parish had no costs for the burial of the deceased, as this task was the responsibility of the municipality of Stockholm. Further, as the cost of keeping population records could be estimated at 5 per cent of the parishes' tax income on account of the corresponding reduction of the dissenter tax when this task was transferred to the tax authorities, the cost of taking care of old population records must be only a fraction of those 5 per cent. As regards the care and maintenance of church buildings, the applicant asserts that the property is used exclusively by the Church of Sweden and, thus, the need for care and maintenance is mainly caused by religious activities.

Moreover, the applicant claims that, as the parish of Brännkyrka was a net payer to the Church Fund and the tax equalisation system covers all expenses of the receiving parishes, the dissenter tax he paid went to religious activities, not only in the parish of Brännkyrka but in other parishes as well. He also submits that, although non-members pay the dissenter tax, they have no influence on the tax rates to be applied since, as non-members, they cannot be elected to the local parish council deciding on the rates.

The Court notes that the issue at stake is whether the applicant's rights under art. 9 of the Convention have been violated due to the fact that he had to pay a special tax to the Church of Sweden although he is not a member of that Church. Considering that the payment of a tax cannot be characterised as a „manifestation" of one's religion, the Court will examine this complaint under the first limb of art. 9 § 1 which concerns the general right to freedom of religion.

This general right protects everyone from being compelled to be involved in religious activities against his will without being a member of the religious community carrying out those activities. The payment of a specific tax to a church for its religious activities may, in certain circumstances, be seen as such involvement (see the Darby v. Sweden judgment of 23 October 1990, Series A no. 187, opinion of the Commission, p. 19, § 51).

In the present case, the Court agrees with Government that the administration of burials, the care and maintenance of church property and buildings of historic value and the care of old population records can reasonably be considered as tasks of a non-religious nature which are performed in the interest of society as a whole. It must be left to the State to decide who should be entrusted with the responsibility of carrying out these tasks and how they should be financed. While it is under an obligation to respect the individual's right to freedom of religion, the State has a wide margin of appreciation in making such decisions.

In the present case, the Court recalls that the applicant, not being a member of the Church of Sweden, did not have to pay the full church tax but only a portion thereof - 30 or 25 per cent of the full amount depending on the year - as a dissenter tax. As has been noted above, the rationale behind the obligation to pay the dissenter tax was that non-members should contribute to the non-religious activities of the Church. The 25 per cent tax rate was determined on the basis of an investigation of the economy of the Church of Sweden, which showed that the costs for the burial of the deceased amounted to about 24 per cent of the Church's total costs. The reduction from 30 to 25 per cent as from 1993 was due to the transfer from the Church to the tax authorities of the task of keeping population records, the cost of which apparently amounted to about 5 per cent of the Church's total costs.

It is thus apparent that the dissenter tax paid to the Church of Sweden was proportionate to the costs of its civil responsibilities. It is true that the relevant parish of Brännkyrka was not responsible for the local burial administration, which is undoubtedly the most costly civil activity of the Church of Sweden. However, through payments to the Church Fund in accordance with the tax equalisation scheme under chapter 42 of the Church Act, that parish contributed to the overall costs of the Church of Sweden, including the burial administration in other parts of Sweden. Having found that the rate of the dissenter tax in general corresponded to the costs of the Church's civil responsibilities, the Court cannot find that the fact that the parish of Brännkyrka did not concern itself with the burial administration meant that the applicant, by being obliged to pay the dissenter tax, was compelled to contribute to the religious activities of the Church. In this connection, the Court further notes that the rate of the applicant's dissenter tax was considerably lower than the rates applied in most other parishes, apparently on account of the burial administration having been entrusted with the municipality rather than the parish.

Moreover, the fact that the Church of Sweden has been entrusted with the tasks in question cannot in itself be considered to violate art. 9 of the Convention. In this respect, it should be noted that the Church was in charge of keeping population records for many years and it is thus natural that it takes care of those records until they have been finally transferred to the State archives. Also, the administration of burials and the maintenance of old church property are tasks that may reasonably be entrusted with the established church in the country. The Court further takes into account that the payment of the dissenter tax and the performance of the civil activities of the Church were overseen by public authorities, including the tax authorities and the County Administrative Board.

The Court therefore concludes that the applicant's obligation to pay the dissenter tax did not contravene his right to freedom of religion under art. 9 of the Convention.

It follows that this part of the application is manifestly ill-founded within the meaning of art. 35 § 3 of the Convention.

2. The applicant complains also that his rights under art. 6 § 1 of the Convention were violated in the court proceedings.

(...)

It follows that this part of the application must be rejected as being incompatible *ratione materiae* with the provisions of the Convention within the meaning of art. 35 § 3 of the Convention.

For these reasons, the Court by a majority declares the application inadmissible.

67

Zur Frage der Ausschöpfung des nationalen Rechtsschutzes gegen die Verweigerung einer Befreiung vom Ethikunterricht und gegen einen Religionseintrag im Personalausweis.

Art. 9, 35 §§ 1, 4 EMRK
EGMR, Beschluss vom 11. September 2001 - No. 26328/95
(Erdem ./. Türkei)[1] -

EN FAIT

Le requérant est un ressortissant turc, né en 1953 et résidant à Denizli. Il est pédiatre à l'hôpital public de Denizli. Il a introduit la requête à son nom, ainsi qu'au nom de ses deux enfants, Ö.E. et Öz. E., âgés de quinze et dix-sept ans lors de l'introduction de la requête.

---

[1] RJD 2001-VII; EuGRZ 2005, 474; NJW 2003, 1439.

A. Les circonstances de l'espèce

Le requérant a deux enfants d'âge scolaire. Ils fréquentaient l'école publique Anadolu Lisesi à Denizli. A l'époque des faits, le premier était au premier cycle du secondaire, le deuxième était au deuxième cycle du secondaire (lycée). Pendant l'année scolaire 1993-1994, ils ont suivi des cours de „culture religieuse et d'éthique".

Le 14 septembre 1994, le requérant demanda au ministère de l'Education nationale que ses deux enfants fussent dispensés des cours d'éducation religieuse.

Par une lettre du 6 octobre 1994, la section de l'éducation religieuse auprès du ministère de l'Education nationale informa le requérant que „l'enseignement de la culture religieuse et de l'éthique, selon l'art. 24 de la Constitution, figure au nombre des matières obligatoires enseignées dans les établissements scolaires du primaire et du premier cycle du secondaire", et pour cette raison refusa la dispense.

Le 20 septembre 1994, le requérant présenta une requête au président de l'Assemblée nationale. Il demanda la radiation de la mention „islam" sur sa carte d'identité ainsi que sur celles de ses enfants, la dispense de ses enfants des cours de culture religieuse et d'éthique.

Le 10 novembre 1994, la présidence de la Commission de pétition auprès de l'Assemblée nationale indiqua au requérant, quant à sa première demande, qu'il lui incombait de saisir les instances judiciaires et que ses autres griefs nécessitaient une révision législative.

B. Le droit et la pratique internes pertinents

1. L'art. 24 de la Constitution turque, dans sa partie pertinente, est ainsi libellé:

„(...) Toute personne a liberté de conscience et de religion.
Nul ne peut être forcé de participer aux cultes et aux cérémonies religieuses et de relever ses convictions religieuses et ses croyances. Nul ne peut être accusé en raison de ses convictions religieuses et ses croyances.
„L'éducation et l'instruction religieuse et éthique se font sous la surveillance et le contrôle de l'Etat. L'enseignement de la culture religieuse et de l'éthique figure au nombre des matières obligatoires enseignées dans les établissements scolaires du primaire et du premier cycle du secondaire. En dehors de ces cas, l'éducation et l'instruction religieuses sont subordonnées à la demande de chacun et pour les mineurs, à celle de leur représentant légal."

2. L'art. 43 de la loi n° 1587 du 5 mai 1972 sur l'état civil dispose que les prénom, nom et sexe des membres de la famille, les prénom et nom des parents, les lieu et date de naissance, la religion, l'état civil et autres renseignements seront inscrits sur le registre familial. En vertu de l'art. 46 de cette loi, le tribunal de grande instance saisi par les personnes ou par le procureur de la République d'une demande de rectification de registre juge et décide de l'opportunité de la demande. La décision est rendue en présence du procureur de la République et du directeur de l'état civil ou d'un fonctionnaire de l'état civil. La décision du tribunal de grande instance est susceptible d'être attaquée devant la Cour de cassation.

3. Les recours contentieux en droit administratif turc

En droit administratif turc, il existe deux principaux recours contentieux, l'un pour excès de pouvoir, l'autre de pleine juridiction. Dans le recours pour excès de pourvoir, la question soulevée devant le juge par la partie demanderesse est celle de la légalité d'un acte administratif et de la violation par cet acte d'une règle de droit général et impersonnel. Quant au recours de pleine juridiction, la question posée par la partie demanderesse porte sur l'existence ou l'étendue d'une situation juridique individuelle subjective à laquelle le requérant prétend. L'intéressé, se prétendant victime d'un dommage dont il attribue la responsabilité à l'administration, lui réclame une indemnité.

4. Jurisprudence administrative et constitutionnelle soumise par le Gouvernement

Le Gouvernement a produit un arrêt du Conseil d'Etat daté du 25 octobre 1995 ayant pour objet le refus par le tribunal administratif d'Izmir de la demande d'une personne voulant faire inscrire „Bahai" comme religion sur sa carte d'identité. Estimant l'art. 43 de la loi n° 1587 contraire à la liberté de religion, le Conseil d'Etat saisit d'office la Cour constitutionnelle. Dans son arrêt du 21 juin 1995, vu le caractère formel et démographique d'une telle mention, cette dernière conclut à la conformité d'une telle disposition avec la Constitution et releva que des personnes demandant la rectification de leur registre de famille pouvaient saisir le tribunal de grande instance compétent d'une demande de rectification.

Le Gouvernement produit également un arrêt du Conseil d'Etat daté du 10 février 1987 ayant pour objet une demande d'annulation d'une exclusion temporaire imposée à un élève. Dans cet arrêt, le Conseil d'Etat s'est prononcé en ces termes:

„(...) Il est évident que les intéressés peuvent intenter une action si le contenu des cours d'éthique et de religion dépasse les limites de la culture religieuse (...)".

GRIEFS

Le requérant soutient que le refus par l'administration de sa demande de dispense de ses enfants de suivre des cours de culture religieuse et d'éthique constitue une atteinte à sa liberté de conscience et de religion garantie par l'art. 9 de la Convention. Il fait valoir qu'en participant à ces cours, ses enfants font l'objet d'un endoctrinement religieux.

Dans le contexte de la liberté de conscience, il se plaint également de l'existence de la mention „islam" sur sa carte d'identité ainsi que sur celles de ses enfants.

EN DROIT

1. Le requérant soutient qu'en participant à des cours obligatoires de culture religieuse et d'éthique, ses enfants font l'objet d'un endoctrinement religieux en faveur de la tendance majoritaire de l'islam.

L'art. 9 de la Convention, dans sa partie pertinente, dispose:

> „1. Toute personne a droit à la liberté (...) de religion; ce droit implique la liberté (...) de manifester sa religion (...) individuellement ou collectivement, en public ou en privé, par le culte, l'enseignement, les pratiques et l'accomplissement des rites. (...)"

Le Gouvernement soutient, à titre principal, que le requérant n'a pas épuisé les voies de recours internes, faute d'avoir soumis le grief qu'il soulève devant la Cour à l'examen des tribunaux administratifs. Selon le Gouvernement, le requérant aurait pu introduire une action en annulation de la réponse du ministère de l'Education qui constitue un acte administratif. De plus, s'appuyant sur la jurisprudence du Conseil d'Etat rendue le 10 février 1987, il ajoute que les parents estimant leurs enfants victimes d'un endoctrinement peuvent intenter une action si le contenu des cours d'éthique et de religion dépasse les limites de la culture religieuse.

Le requérant rétorque que le recours en annulation n'est pas un recours efficace en matière d'une pratique conforme à la Constitution.

La Cour rappelle que la finalité de l'art. 35 est de ménager aux Etats contractants l'occasion de prévenir ou redresser les violations alléguées contre eux avant que ces allégations ne lui soient soumises (voir, par exemple, les arrêts Hentrich c. France du 22 septembre 1994, série A n° 296-A, p. 18, § 33, et Remli c. France du 23 avril 1996, *Recueil des arrêts et décisions* 1996-II, p. 571, § 33). Ainsi, le grief dont on entend saisir la Cour doit d'abord être soulevé, au moins en substance, dans les formes et délais prescrits par le droit interne, devant les juridictions nationales appropriées. Néanmoins, les dispositions de l'art. 35 de la Convention ne prescrivent l'épuisement que des recours à la fois relatifs aux violations incriminées, disponibles et adéquats. Ils doivent exister à un degré suffisant de certitude, non seulement en théorie mais aussi en pratique, sans quoi leur manquent l'effectivité et l'accessibilité voulues; il incombe à l'Etat défendeur de démontrer que ces exigences se trouvent réunies (voir, en dernier lieu, *Civet c. France [GC]*, n° 29340/95, § 41, CEDH 1999-VI).

En l'espèce, la Cour observe que le grief dont elle est saisie ne concerne pas l'incompatibilité de l'enseignement obligatoire de la culture de la religion et de l'éthique avec les dispositions de la Convention, mais porte pour l'essentiel sur une prétendue pratique d'endoctrinement en faveur d'une religion déterminée dans l'enseignement de la culture de la religion et de l'éthique, qui contredirait non seulement les art. 9 de la Convention et 2 du Protocole n° 1 (voir, *mutatis mutandis,* l'arrêt Kjeldsen, Busk Madsen et Petersen c. Danemark du 7 décembre 1976, série A n° 23, pp. 24-25, § 50, KirchE-EU S. 181) mais également l'art. 24 de la Constitution turque. Dès lors, la Cour estime qu'un recours contentieux devant les tribunaux administratifs par lequel le requérant, dénonçant la pratique incriminée, aurait pu soulever la responsabilité de l'Etat avait pu avoir une chance de succès. De surcroît, la Cour constate que le requérant ne fournit aucun argument qui rend les voies de recours invoquées par le Gouvernement sujettes à caution.

En conclusion, en n'utilisant pas la voie du recours contentieux devant les tribunaux administratifs, le requérant n'a pas donné aux juridictions turques l'occasion que l'art. 35 a pour finalité de ménager en principe aux Etats contractants: éviter ou redresser les violations alléguées contre eux (voir, entre autres, les arrêts Guzzardi c. Italie du 6 novembre 1980, série A n° 39, p. 27, § 72, et Cardot c. France du 19 mars 1991, série A n° 200, p. 19, § 36).

L'exception de non-épuisement des voies de recours internes se révèle donc fondée. Il s'ensuit que cette partie de la requête doit être rejetée en application de l'art. 35 § 1 et 4 de la Convention.

2. Le requérant se plaint également de l'existence de la mention „islam" sur sa carte d'identité ainsi que sur celles de ses enfants. Il invoque à cet égard l'art. 9 de la Convention.

Le gouvernement défendeur soulève une exception d'irrecevabilité tirée du non-épuisement des voies de recours internes. Il expose à cet égard que le requérant aurait pu saisir le tribunal de grande instance d'une demande de modification de la mention „islam" inscrite sur le registre de l'état civil. A l'appui de sa thèse, le Gouvernement fournit à la Cour l'arrêt de la Cour constitutionnelle turque rendu le 21 juin 1995 dans lequel cette dernière, vu le caractère formel et démographique d'une telle mention, a conclu à la conformité de cette disposition à la Constitution et relevé que des personnes demandant la rectification de leur registre de famille peuvent saisir le tribunal de grande instance compétent d'une demande de rectification.

Le requérant s'oppose à la thèse du Gouvernement et soutient que cette voie de recours est inefficace. Selon lui, la République de Turquie est un Etat théocratique qui privilégie la primauté de la branche sunnite de l'islam, et impose ainsi aux citoyens une version officielle de la religion. Tout système judiciaire fonctionne de manière à garder ces privilèges.

La Cour observe d'emblée qu'en dénonçant catégoriquement le „régime de Turquie", le requérant ne donne aucun argument ni précision quant à l'inefficacité de la voie de recours invoquée par le Gouvernement. Il n'a pas non plus expliqué pourquoi, s'il s'estime victime direct de cet acte, il n'avait pas saisi le tribunal compétent d'un recours tendant à supprimer cette mention sur sa carte d'identité ou sur celles de ses enfants.

L'exception de non-épuisement des voies de recours internes soulevée par le Gouvernement se révèle donc fondée. Il s'ensuit que cette partie de la requête doit être rejetée en application de l'art. 35 § 1 et 4 de la Convention.

Par ces motifs, la Cour, à l'unanimité, déclare la requête irrecevable.

68

Die durch Art. 9 Abs. 1 EMRK gewährleistete Freiheit religiöser Praxis (practice) umfasst nicht jedwede Verhaltensweise, die durch Religion oder Weltanschauung motiviert oder inspiriert ist (hier: Weigerung eines Apothekers, empfängnisverhütende Präparate abzugeben).

Art. 9, 35 § 3 EKMR
EGMR, Beschluss vom 2. Oktober 2001 - No. 49853/99
(Pichon u.a. ./. Frankreich) -

THE FACTS

The applicants are French nationals, who were born in 1955 and 1949 respectively and live in S. (Gironde).

A. The circumstances of the case

The applicants are the joint owners of a pharmacy in S.

On 9 June 1995 three women arrived at the same time at the applicants' pharmacy to be told in turn that they could not be supplied with the contraceptives prescribed to each of them by their doctors in prescriptions whose validity has never been called into question.

On the same day the three women in question filed a complaint against the applicants for refusing to sell contraceptives on a doctor's prescription, an offence provided for and punished by art. 33, par. 1 of Decree no. 86-1309 of 29 December 1986 and art. L 122-1 of the Consumer Code. They lodged a civil-party claim in which they were joined by an association.

The applicants argued before the Bordeaux Police Court that the refusal to sell of which they were accused was justified on the legitimate ground that no statutory provision required pharmacists to supply contraceptives or abortifacients. They relied on art. L 645 of the Public Health Code, under which pharmacists were not required to supply single or compound preparations based on oestrogens.

In a judgment of 16 November 1995 the Bordeaux Police Court found the applicants guilty of the offences of which they had been accused. The Police Court noted the following: „art. L 645, on which the defendants rely, does not in any way concern contraceptive medicines but only abortifacients"; the products that the applicants had refused to supply were contraceptive medicines „which [could] not be regarded as the equivalents of abortifacients". The Police Court added: „Ethical or religious principles are not legitimate grounds to refuse to sell a contraceptive. There is no legislation which authorises pharmacists to refuse to supply contraceptives, unlike the provisions relating to doctors, midwives and nurses as regards the termination of pregnancy (art. L 602-8 of the Public Health Code)". In conclusion the Police Court held as follows: „Consequently, as long as the pharmacist is not expected to play an active part in manufacturing the product, moral grounds cannot absolve anyone from the obligation to sell imposed on all traders by the law (art. L 122-1 of the Consumer Code)". The applicants were sentenced to a fine of 5,000 French francs (FRF) each and ordered to pay, jointly and severally, FRF 1,000 in damages to the three complainants.

The applicants appealed against that judgment. In a decision of 14 January 1997, the Bordeaux Court of Appeal upheld the Police Court's judgment. It noted that the applicants had never disputed that they had committed the acts of which they were accused and that they had stated that their conduct was dictated by religious reasons. It further observed: „The offences of refusing to sell for which the defendants stood trial did not stem in any way from a practical impossibility to satisfy their customers but were committed in the name of religious convictions which cannot be interpreted as a legitimate reason within the meaning of art. L 122-1 of the Consumer Code. Thus the failure to stock this type of product in their dispensary was not the cause but indeed the consequence of this refusal on principle". The Court of Appeal also noted that the defendants' pharmacy was the only one in Salleboeuf. It upheld the Police Court's finding that the products which the applicants had refused to sell were not covered by art. L 645 of the Public Health Code.

The applicants lodged an appeal on points of law against that judgment. They relied in particular on art. 9 of the Convention, asserting that the freedom to manifest one's religion implied that a pharmacist was entitled not to stock contraceptives whose use amounted to an interference with their religious beliefs. In a judgment of 21 October 1998 the Court of Cassation dismissed that appeal. It agreed with the Court of

Appeal's finding that „personal convictions ... [could] not constitute for pharmacists, who have the exclusive right to sell medicines, a legitimate reason within the meaning of art. L 122-1". The Court of Cassation's decision was served on the applicants by a letter from the prosecuting authorities of the Bordeaux Court of Appeal dated 4 December 1998 and posted on 7 December 1998.

B. Relevant domestic law

Art. L 122-1 of the Consumer Code
„It is prohibited to refuse to sell a product or provide a service to a customer for no legitimate reason, to make the sale of a product conditional on the purchase of a compulsory quantity or the concomitant purchase of another product or payment for another service or to make the provision of a service conditional on the provision of another service or the purchase of a product.
This provision shall apply to all the activities contemplated in the last paragraph of art. L 113-2."
Art. L 113-2 of the Consumer Code
„The rules relating to the scope of Ordinance no. 86-1243 of 1 December 1986 cited above are laid down by art. 53 of that Ordinance, which provides as follows:
„Art. 53: The rules laid down in the present ordinance apply to all production, distribution, and service activities, including those that are carried out by public bodies, particularly under agreements on the delegation of public service activities."
NB: Art. 53 of Ordinance no. 86-1243 of 1 December 1986 as set out above was repealed by Ordinance no. 2000-912 of 18 September 2000."
Art. 33 of Decree no. 86-1309 of 29 December 1986
Amended by Decree no. 97-298 of 27 March 1999, art. 5, Official Gazette of the French Republic (JORF), 3 April 1997
„The offer for sale of products or provision of services in breach of the provisions of art. 37 of Ordinance no. 86-1243 of 1 December 1986 shall be punishable by the fines applicable to minor offences (contraventions) of the fifth class.
If the offence is repeated, the fines imposed for repeated minor offences of the fifth class shall be applicable."
(Transferred into R113-1 and R121-13 of the Consumer Code).
Art. L 645 of the Public Health Code
„It is prohibited for any person in any way whatsoever to display, offer, cause to be offered, sell, put on sale, distribute or cause to be distributed the medicines or substances, intra-uterine probes or other similar objects capable of causing or facilitating abortion listed in a decree issued after consultation of the Conseil d'Etat.
Pharmacists may, however, sell the medicines, substances and objects specified above but only on a medical prescription which must be transcribed into a numbered register initialled by the mayor or the police superintendent. ..."

COMPLAINT

The applicants complained under art. 9 of the Convention that their right to freedom of religion had been disregarded by the domestic courts.

THE LAW

The applicants complained that they had been convicted for refusing to sell contraceptive pills whereas they considered that that amounted to a manifestation of their freedom of religion. They relied on art. 9 of the Convention which provides:

> „1. *Everyone has the right to freedom of thought, conscience and religion; this right includes freedom to change his religion or belief and freedom, either alone or in community with others and in public or private, to manifest his religion or belief, in worship, teaching, practice and observance.*
> 2. *Freedom to manifest one's religion or beliefs shall be subject only to such limitations as are prescribed by law and are necessary in a democratic society in the interests of public safety, for the protection of public order, health or morals, or for the protection of the rights and freedoms of others."*

The Court would point out that the main sphere protected by art. 9 is that of personal convictions and religious beliefs, in other words what are sometimes referred to as matters of individual conscience. It also protects acts that are closely linked to these matters such as acts of worship or devotion forming part of the practice of a religion or a belief in a generally accepted form.

The Court also reiterates that art. 9 lists a number of forms which manifestation of one's religion or belief may take, namely worship, teaching, practice and observance (see the Kalaç v. Turkey judgment of 1 July 1997, RJD 1997-IV, p. 1209, § 27, KirchE-EU S. 312, and Cha'are Shalom Ve Tsedek v. France [GC] no. 27417/95, 27 June 2000, ECHR 2000-VII, § 73, KirchE-EU S. 418).

However, in safeguarding this personal domain, art. 9 of the Convention does not always guarantee the right to behave in public in a manner governed by that belief. The word „practice" used in art. 9 § 1 does not denote each and every act or form of behaviour motivated or inspired by a religion or a belief.

The Court notes that in the instant case the applicants, who are the joint owners of a pharmacy, submitted that their religious beliefs justified their refusal to sell contraceptive pills in their dispensary. It considers that, as long as the sale of contraceptives is legal and occurs on medical prescription nowhere other than in a pharmacy, the applicants cannot give precedence to their religious beliefs and impose them on others as justification for their refusal to sell such products, since they can manifest those beliefs in many ways outside the professional sphere.

It follows that the applicants' conviction for refusal to sell did not interfere with the exercise of the rights guaranteed by art. 9 of the Convention and that the application is manifestly ill-founded within the meaning of art. 35 § 3 of the Convention.

For these reasons, the Court, by a majority, declares the application inadmissible.

69

Zur Frage, inwieweit parlamentarische Kommissionsberichte und gesetzgeberische Maßnahmen, die die Betätigung sog. Sekten betreffen, deren Religionsfreiheit und Anspruch auf gerichtlichen Rechtsschutz berühren. Die Fédération Chrétienne des Témoins de Jéhovah de France ist nicht Verletzte (victim) im Sinne von Art. 34 EMRK.

Art. 6, 9, 13, 14, 35 §§ 1, 3 u. 4 EMRK
EGMR, Beschluss vom 6. November 2001 - No. 53430/99 (Fédération
Chrétienne des Témoins de Jéhovah de France ./. Frankreich)[1] -

THE FACTS

The applicant association [the Fédération Chrétienne des Témoins de Jéhovah de France - the Christian Federation of Jehovah's Witnesses in France] was founded in accordance with the provisions of sec. 20 of the Act of 9 December 1905 on the separation of the churches and the State.

A. The circumstances of the case

The applicant association provides representation and legal protection for 1,149 local associations for the religion of Jehovah's Witnesses. Its purpose is to „contribute to the practice of the Jehovah's Witnesses' religion, meet its costs and provide for its maintenance. It is committed to coordinating and developing the activities of the member associations, whose purpose is to ensure that Jehovah's Witnesses can worship and can practise their faith." (art. 2 of its articles of association). It „shall act to protect and defend Jehovah's Witnesses from attacks on their religious convictions, in particular by combating any form of segregation or ostracism. The Federation may act by all legal means and, in particular, by taking court proceedings, to protect both individual interests and the collective interests of its members." (art. 3).

There have been Jehovah's Witnesses in France since the beginning of the twentieth century and, according to the applicant association, they are the country's third Christian denomination. At the most recent celebration of the Memorial of Christ's death on 1 April 1999, 249,918 believers, including both regular and occasional worshippers, gathered in their places of worship. Since 1906, when the first local association was registered at a prefecture, Jehovah's Witnesses have been able to exercise their religion in France freely and in peace.

---

[1] RJD 2001-XI.

On 29 June 1995 the National Assembly adopted a draft resolution for the establishment of a parliamentary commission of inquiry „to study the phenomenon of sects and, if appropriate, propose changes to existing legal provisions". The commission was set up on 11 July 1995 and decided to hold its hearings in camera. It held twenty hearings „lasting for a total of twenty-one hours". On 22 December 1995 it published Report no. 2468, entitled Les sectes en France („Sects in France") and better known as the Gest/Guyard Report.

In the report the parliamentarians acknowledged that it was difficult to define the word „sect". On page 14 they stated: „The difficulty of defining the word „sect", which will nevertheless be used in the rest of this report, led the Commission to consider a whole range of criteria, each of which could give rise to lengthy discussion. It has therefore preferred, at the risk of offending many people's susceptibilities or making an incomplete analysis of the real situation, to adopt the ordinary meaning that the public attributes to the word."

Among the indicators „from which it is possible to infer that there might be some truth in suspicions which lead people to describe as a sect a movement presenting itself as a religious movement" the commission decided to adopt the criteria used by the Police Intelligence Branch (Direction centrale des Renseignements Généraux), namely mental destabilisation, exorbitant financial demands, inducing people to sever their ties with their home environment, bodily harm, indoctrination of children, more or less antisocial views, prejudicing public order, numerous lawsuits, possible misuse of traditional financial channels and attempts to infiltrate public authorities.

According to the Police Intelligence Branch, 172 movements had been identified as fulfilling one of its criteria of dangerousness. Those movements had been separately listed as „sects". Jehovah's Witnesses appear on the list, which was published as an integral part of the commission's report.

The Gest/Guyard Report was widely circulated not only among public authorities (government, civil service, local councillors, etc.) but also among the public at large. A commercial version for the general public was published and distributed by a commercial company. However, after submitting their report, the members of the National Assembly who had made up the first study group on sects undertook new activities with a view to broadening the investigations into sects.

An Interministerial Observatory on Sects was set up by a decree of 9 May 1996. This body, answerable to the Prime Minister, was charged with studying the phenomenon of sects and making proposals to the Government for improving the means of combating them. It was replaced on 7 October 1998 by the Interministerial Task Force for Action to Combat Sects, which is empowered to report offences committed by sectarian

movements to public prosecutors where they are capable of being catego-
rised as criminal offences.

On 15 December 1998 a new resolution intended to broaden investigations was adopted by the National Assembly. A new commission, chaired
by Mr Jacques Guyard, the former rapporteur of the first commission,
and with Mr Jean-Pierre Brard as its rapporteur, was given six months
to carry out its inquiry. According to the report of proceedings in the National Assembly on 10 December 1998, Mr Guyard said:

> *„If the work carried out by the commission of inquiry in 1995 served a purpose, it
> was largely because the commission published a list of sectarian movements, giv-
> ing it a degree of publicity which nobody dared to do for fear of being prosecuted.
> We accepted that responsibility collectively, irrespective of our political sympa-
> thies, and that helped to give the information wide circulation. I am pleased that
> the 1995 Report is the Assembly's best-selling report. More than ten thousand
> copies have had to be printed to meet the demand from members of the public
> who wanted to be informed. "*

The new commission expressly confirmed that it was continuing the
work carried out by the 1995 commission. Its aim was to examine the financial, property and tax situation of sects as well as their business activities and their relations with business and financial circles. Its report
was registered on 10 June 1999.

Initially the commission sought help from the Police Intelligence
Branch. Police investigators asked associations for important documents
and sensitive information informally and even orally without giving details. The parliamentary commission sent a questionnaire to some sixty
associations, including the applicant association, in a letter of 19 March
1999 requesting a reply by 24 April 1999 at the latest. The applicant association sent a comprehensive reply to the commission by the appointed
date, together with nine boxes of documents.

The commission's report, entitled „Sects and money", was published on
17 June 1999; it is better known as the Guyard/Brard Report. In its conclusions the commission noted, in particular: „The right to be different
must also be protected. However, it is unacceptable for the exercise of
that right to jeopardise certain principles, chief among which is the right
to protection of the weakest members of society. ... The preservation of
freedom of conscience cannot be based on disregard for basic individual
liberties - the freedom to come and go as we please, to own property and
have the enjoyment of it, to keep ourselves fit and healthy, to be protected from abuses of power, to defend ourselves against damage to our
pecuniary and non-pecuniary interests ..." An annexe to the report contained information on the organisation, financial influence and economic
network of thirty or so associations representative of sectarian movements, including the applicant association.

According to the applicant association, the commission's report contained numerous inaccurate and defamatory statements about Jehovah's Witnesses. For example, it was asserted that Jehovah's Witnesses were engaged in criminal activities amounting to tax evasion (pages 219 to 224).

In a letter of 20 July 1999 to the Speaker of the National Assembly, the applicant association made a formal request for the parts of the Guyard/Brard Report that contained inaccuracies to be purely and simply deleted. It also sent the Speaker of the National Assembly a file on Jehovah's Witnesses and their funding and the Guyard/Brard Report. The file contained documents analysing the allegations and the accusations disseminated in the parliamentary commission's report under the responsibility of the National Assembly - accusations which the applicant association said were false. To date, the Speaker of the National Assembly has not taken any action on either of those letters.

The applicant association maintained that on the basis of the work carried out by the parliamentary commissions, the State had embarked on a policy of repression and oppression of the groups mentioned, in particular Jehovah's Witnesses, the largest of them. It submitted that the following measures taken by the State had formed part of that policy:

(a) On 29 February 1996 the Minister of Justice had sent to Principal Public Prosecutors throughout the country a circular containing the list of „dangerous sects" that had been published in the Gest/Guyard Report, a list that had been supplied by the Police Intelligence Branch. The need to „combat" those movements was urged. The Minister of Justice requested Principal Public Prosecutors to „apply the existing law more strictly" and make full use of „the existing legal arsenal" by exercising „unfailing vigilance" and „particular severity". They were also to consult anti-sect organisations for information purposes as some of the members of those organisations were former adherents of the groups referred to (Minister of Justice's Circular no. 92 F24 C, 29 February 1996).

(b) On 9 May 1996 the State had issued a decree to set up an Interministerial Observatory on Sects. That body had been composed of representatives from most of the major government departments. Its purpose had been to assist the Prime Minister in his campaign against sects (Decree no. 96-387 of 9 May 1996).

(c) On 7 October 1998 the State had issued a decree to set up an interministerial task force on combating sects. The task force was empowered to train public officials to combat sects and inform the public about the dangers they posed (Decree no. 98-890 of 7 October 1998).

(d) On 1 December 1998 the Ministry of Justice, noting that it had not received a sufficient number of complaints about sects and was thus not in a position to prosecute them, had instructed Principal Public Prosecutors to work with anti-sect organisations to encourage complaints against minority groups. The aim of that collaboration had been to obtain information in order to prosecute individuals belonging to one of the 172 minority groups regarded as „dangerous sects" (Minister of Justice's Circular, CRIM. 98-11/G3, 1 December 1998).

(e) On 3 October 2000 the Ministry of Employment and Solidarity had issued Circular no. 2000-501 on abuses by sects. It laid down that Ministry's administrative action when dealing with sectarian practices, clarifying its legal framework, and described the type of administrative organisation that had been adopted. It made direct reference to the criteria used by the 1996 parliamentary commission of inquiry for defining a sect.

The applicant association submitted that although the reports of parliamentary commissions were supposed to be merely information documents without any legal effect, that had not been true of the Gest/Guyard and Guyard/Brard reports. It alleged that the two reports had given rise to the following measures infringing rights and liberties:

(a) Refusals to grant the organisation exemption from property tax on its places of worship (in judgments delivered by the Clermont-Ferrand Administrative Court on 26 May 1999 and the Rennes Administrative Court on 12 May 1999).

(b) A major tax inspection from 1995 to 1997. (It had been established that Jehovah's Witnesses' activities were non-profit-making, disinterested and non-commercial.) As a consequence of the tax inspection, believers' offerings received by the applicant association over the previous four years, totalling 297,403,534 French francs (or 45,335,904 euros), had been taxed at a rate of 108%.

(c) Refusal by the health-insurance office for the clergy to register members of the Christian Community of the Bethelites (one of the applicant association's member associations), with explicit reference to the Guyard Report.

(d) An inspection by the social-security-contribution collection agency, the URSSAF, and an investigation by the labour inspectorate.

(e) The seizure on 6 June 1998, following the imposition of tax by the authorities, of all the movable and immovable property used by the applicant association.

(f) Investigations by the Police Intelligence Branch into all the local associations of Jehovah's Witnesses.

As a consequence of the Gest/Guyard Report and the resulting recommendations, numerous administrative decisions had been taken that adversely affected the Jehovah's Witnesses and some of their registered associations. For example, a series of measures had been taken on grounds that referred expressly to the Report, which maintained that Jehovah's Witnesses were a „dangerous sect":

(a) Local authorities had refused to let municipal rooms to local associations because they belonged to the applicant church, as in Lyons

(15 September 1997 and 18 November 1999), Annecy (27 January 1998) and Saint-Genis-Laval (27 November 1998).

(b) State representatives had refused to renew the administrative certification of childminders who were Jehovah's Witnesses, causing them to lose their jobs (administrative decisions by the councils of the départements of Cher (26 August 1996, 27 August 1997 and 5 June 1998), Pas-de-Calais (16 July 1997), Yonne (7 August 1997) and Haute-Marne (11 December 1998)).

(c) A mother's custody and care of a child had been called in question on the sole ground that she was a Jehovah's Witness (judgment of the Foix tribunal de grande instance, 5 October 1998).

(d) Local authorities had refused planning permission for places of worship (in municipal decisions of the mayor of Beuvillers (département of Moselle), 29 September 1997, and the mayor of Sainte-Hélène (département of Morbihan) on 26 June 1999).

(e) Fifty-six prefectures consulted by the main tax office in each of their départements had given a negative ruling on whether Jehovah's Witnesses' places of worship should be exempted from property tax.

(f) Judgments had been delivered in cases relating to press law in which the classification of offences as insult or defamation had been rejected because of an explicit reference by courts of first instance and courts of appeal to the Guyard Report (judgment of the Rennes Court of Appeal of 10 March 1998).

(g) On 15 November 1999 the governor of Bapaume Prison had refused to allow publications by the Jehovah's Witnesses in the prison „in view of the sectarian nature of the movement as recognised by the parliamentary commission".

(h) The authorisation for a childminder in Blagnac to mind a child in her care had been withdrawn because she was a Jehovah's Witness.

(i) On 12 May 2000 the family-affairs judge at the Colmar tribunal de grande instance had made an order referring directly to the parliamentary reports of 1996 and 1998 (which described the movement as a sect), prohibiting a child's father from making him take part in events organised by Jehovah's Witnesses.

The applicant association further alleged that the Guyard Report had also given rise to a series of hostile reactions to Jehovah's Witnesses, including:

(a) Public impugning, by school parents' associations, of teachers who were Jehovah's Witnesses by means of leaflets and denunciation, calling for the teachers in question to be dismissed because they belonged to a „dangerous sect".

(b) Criticism of the Jehovah's Witnesses, who had been depicted as forming a „dangerous sect" in the course of awareness-raising activities and discussions on sects held in schools, with the result that the children belonging to that faith had been stigmatised and marginalised.

(c) The setting up of residents' action groups objecting, often with the support of the local mayor, to the establishment in their community of Jehovah's Witnesses wishing to build a place of worship.

(d) Damage to Jehovah's Witnesses' places of worship and intimidating and threatening letters.

(e) A veritable press campaign attacking the Jehovah's Witnesses, who had been subjected to an avalanche of negative and detrimental articles (some 700 recorded between 1996 and 1999) and comments simply because they had been listed as a „dangerous sect" in the Gest/Guyard Report and accused of tax evasion in the Guyard/Brard Report.

B. Relevant domestic law and practice

Under the second paragraph of subsec. (1) of sec. 6 of Ordinance no. 58-1100 of 17 November 1958 on the functioning of the parliamentary assemblies, commissions of inquiry „shall be formed to collect information on specific matters or on the management of public services or State-owned companies with a view to submitting their findings to the assembly which set them up". The task of these commissions of inquiry comes to an end when they submit their report. The commissions may hold hearings, which are public unless the decision is taken that they should be held in private.

According to the applicant association, the decisions of parliamentary commissions of inquiry could not be challenged in the courts. Although their modus operandi was nowhere laid down, they had wide inquisitorial powers. They could arbitrarily decide to hold hearings in camera without any justification, and no appeal lay against such decisions. Evidence from doubtful sources could be gathered and even used against individuals or groups, who had no right to be heard in their own defence. Refusal to cooperate with a commission could lead to criminal proceedings resulting in fines and imprisonment. It was not possible to challenge either the procedure followed by such commissions or their findings (sec. 6 of Ordinance no. 58-1100 of 17 November 1958, as amended by Law no. 91-698 of 20 July 1991).

The applicant association observed more particularly that in the case of the Gest/Guyard and Guyard/Brard reports, parliamentary immunity meant that there was no domestic remedy that would enable it to put an end to the discrimination, the violation of freedom of conscience and the other alleged infringements of its believers' fundamental rights by the State. There was no national authority which could deal with such a complaint.

The applicant association attributed the failure of its attempts to settle the case to the total immunity from legal proceedings enjoyed by parliamentary commissions. For example, on 7 March 1997 the rapporteur of the commission which adopted the Guyard/Brard Report, Mr Jean-Pierre

Brard, a member of the National Assembly, wrote to the applicant association. In his letter he referred to „Jehovah's Witnesses' criminal nature" and suggested: „If you wish to establish contact with representatives of the State, I would strongly recommend the officers of the national police force or the members of the public prosecutor's office of the département of Hauts-de-Seine."

On 22 June 2000 the National Assembly adopted document no. 546 on a bill tabled by Mr Nicolas About, a member of the Senate, designed to strengthen preventive and punitive action against sectarian groups. This bill added an article to the Criminal Code on the judicial dissolution of „any legal entity, whatever its legal form or purpose, which engaged in activities whose aim or effect was to bring about or exploit the psychological or physical dependence of persons taking part in [certain] activities". It also included provisions placing restrictions on the establishment or advertising of sectarian groups (clauses 6 and 8 of the bill). The National Assembly further proposed an offence of mental manipulation but on the second reading of the bill in the Senate it was rejected. On the other hand, it was decided to supplement the offence of fraudulent abuse of a state of ignorance or weakness provided for by art. 313-4 of the Criminal Code, which currently appears in the part of the Code relating to interference with property and covers only minors and persons who are particularly vulnerable because of a physical or mental deficiency.

On 12 June 2001 Law no. 2001-504 „to strengthen preventive and punitive action against sectarian movements infringing human rights and fundamental freedoms" was enacted (it was published in Official Gazette no. 135 of 13 June 2001). Sec. 1 provides as follows:

Any legal entity, whatever its legal form or purpose, which engages in activities whose aim or effect is to bring about, perpetuate or exploit the psychological or physical subjection of persons taking part in those activities shall be liable to dissolution as provided in this section where there have been final criminal convictions of the legal entity itself or of those who are de jure or de facto in control of it for one or other of the following offences: (1) Intentional or unintentional homicide, bodily harm or psychological injury; endangering life; deprivation of liberty; undermining human dignity; infringing personal rights; endangering minors; or interfering with the peaceful enjoyment of possessions ..."

Sec. 20 of the Law added a new paragraph to art. 223-15, which provides as follows:

„A sentence of three years' imprisonment and a fine of FRF 2,500,000 shall be imposed for the fraudulent abuse of the state of ignorance or weakness of minors, persons whose particular vulnerability, owing to their age, illness, disability, physical or mental deficiency or pregnancy, is obvious and known to the person committing the abuse, or persons in a state of psychological or physical subjection resulting from the exertion of serious or repeated pressure or techniques likely to affect their

judgment, with the purpose of inducing the minors or persons concerned to act or fail to act in such a manner as to cause them serious harm ..."

Other provisions restrict advertising by sectarian movements in the same circumstances and confer the rights of a civil party in criminal proceedings on any properly registered, State-approved association that proposes in its articles of association to protect and assist individuals or uphold individual and collective rights and freedoms.

COMPLAINT

1. Relying on art. 9 of the Convention, the applicant association alleged that the publication of the two reports of the parliamentary commissions of inquiry and the bill to strengthen preventive and punitive action against sectarian groups had seriously jeopardised the exercise of its freedom of religion.

2. In reliance on art. 13 of the Convention, the applicant association further complained that because of the parliamentary immunity enjoyed by parliamentary commissions of inquiry, it had no remedy before a „national authority" to have its „claim decided and, if appropriate, to obtain redress" for the State's infringement of its right to freedom of religion.

3. The applicant association also alleged a breach of its right of access to a court, guaranteed by art. 6 § 1 of the Convention, because of the judicial immunity covering the content and effects of the reports of parliamentary commissions of inquiry.

4. Lastly, the applicant association submitted that by setting up a commission which was entitled to defame a religious minority such as the Jehovah's Witnesses by declaring that its members were involved in tax-evasion schemes and constituted a dangerous sect and by embarking on a repressive campaign against them, the State had subjected that minority to discriminatory treatment, contrary to art. 14, taken together with art. 6, 9 and 13 of the Convention.

THE LAW

The applicant association alleged a violation of art. 6 § 1 (right of access to a court), art. 9 (right to freedom of religion) and art. 13 (right to an effective remedy before a national authority), taken alone and together with art. 14 (prohibition of discrimination) of the Convention. It emphasised that the novelty of its application lay in the fact that the infringements of the Convention were attributed to acts that were entirely devoid of any direct legal effect inasmuch as the reports of the parliamentary inquiries complained of could not be equated with a law or an enforceable administrative decision or other instrument or a court decision. However, the parliamentary reports had not been without adverse effects on the Jehovah's Witnesses they stigmatised. They established a frame of reference for the administrative, legislative and judicial measures to be taken against Jehovah's Witnesses. They encouraged the relevant authorities and bodies to take those measures as soon as possible. As a result, they created a context of legal and social uncertainty that was incompatible with the principles on which the Convention was based.

In its main plea, the Government asked the Court to reject the application on the ground that the applicant was not a victim within the meaning of art. 34 of the Convention.

The Government emphasised that the applicant association was a legal entity and that, according to the Court's case-law, any legal person constituted in the form of an association had to be the direct and immediate victim of the violation it complained of; it could only allege an infringement of its own rights as an association, not one from which its members had suffered and still less one resulting from an act harming the collective interests which it had set itself the task of protecting. Many of the measures infringing rights and freedoms of which the applicant complained affected not the Federation itself but local associations, affiliated groups or even individual members.

The Government argued that the applicant association could rely neither on the parliamentary reports of 1995 and 1999 nor on the bill to strengthen preventive and punitive action against sectarian groups (Law no. 2001-504 had not yet been adopted when the Government filed their observations) in order to argue that it had been the victim of a violation of the Convention.

As regards the complaints relating to the 1995 report, they were inadmissible for failure to comply with the six-month time-limit. As to the 1999 report, it was nothing more than a document setting out theoretical ideas and prospective studies and could not form the legal basis for any criminal proceedings or administrative decision; there was no follow-up to it and it did not give rise to any implementing or execution measures. The report was a contribution to a public political debate and its content reflected the views of its authors alone, whose aim was to address a complex social issue with a view to combating the abuses of sects more effectively.

Lastly, the Government pointed out that Law no. 2001-504 of 12 June 2001 was designed to afford individuals better protection against illegal activities engaged in by sects that infringed human rights and fundamental freedoms and to punish those who committed such acts. It provided no definition of the word „sect" and was not aimed at all associations that could be described as sects, merely those which infringed human rights. The applicant association could not fall foul of the Law in its criminal aspect simply because it existed as a legal person. The possibility of dissolution and the restrictions on advertising were not dependent on whether a legal person existed but on whether it had had several criminal convictions. Above all, dissolution could only be decided by a court after fully adversarial proceedings.

The applicant association maintained that it was at once a direct, indirect and potential victim of a violation of the Convention.

It alleged that any Jehovah's Witness or association set up for the Jehovah's Witnesses' faith in France was the direct victim of the parliamentary reports on „sects". To accept the Government's argument that the applicant association could not be considered a direct and immediate victim would be tantamount to requiring that 249,918 regular and occasional Jehovah's Witnesses and 1,150 registered associations should each have lodged an application. By virtue of its status as a federation of associations, the applicant association was justified in applying to the Court because the parliamentary reports gave no details as to the legal entities concerned; it only referred to Jehovah's Witnesses in general.

Furthermore, the applicant association submitted that, as a federation of associations bringing together legal and natural persons, it was itself subject to the measures of State repression. The mere fact that it was an association that claimed to belong to the Jehovah's Witnesses movement constituted a convenient and sufficient reason for the State to monitor it through the political department of the Police Intelligence Branch and take action against it by means of the Interministerial Task Force for Action to Combat Sects, answerable to the Prime Minister. It was a federative body which, precisely because of its status as a „sect", was liable to the same measures as all of France's Jehovah's Witnesses and their associations.

Its official status as a „sect" in itself conferred the stamp and the stigma which justified its being monitored by the administrative law-enforcement authorities in the police, social, tax and customs fields. The applicant association relied on all too long a list of complaints and objective, serious infringements pointing in the same direction. The interplay of parliamentary suspicion and political conjecture had prepared the ground for administrative and judicial repression, as was evidenced by the circulars of the Ministries of the Interior and of Justice of 29 February 1996, 17 November 1997 and 1 December 1998 and that of the Minister of Employment and Solidarity of 3 October 2000. When combined, those administrative and political acts had produced a series of prejudicial and discriminatory measures taken by the State.

According to the applicant association, the Government could not seriously maintain that reports of parliamentary inquiries had no legal force. Their legally backed authority, the criminal penalties resulting from a refusal to appear before commissions of inquiry and the very way in which Parliament's work was organised were clear signs of the eminently legal nature of such documents, which preceded the enactment of specific legal provisions by Parliament and the Government.

As to the Law of 12 June 2001, it added in art. 223-15-2 of the Criminal Code a new offence, which defined a new category of vulnerable persons and used vague notions drawn from psychiatry; those notions would have to be assessed by trial courts, which were supposed to „scrutinise intentions and behaviour".

The Court notes that the present application relates to the pernicious effects that the adoption and publication, on 22 December 1995 and 17 June 1999, of two reports of parliamentary commissions of inquiry on sects and the promulgation on 13 June 2001 of Law no. 2001-504 to strengthen preventive and punitive action against sectarian movements infringing human rights and fundamental freedoms allegedly had and continue to have on the applicant association and its members. The applicant association claimed to be both a direct and a potential victim of the reports and the Law.

In the first place, the Court considers that it must confine its consideration of whether the applicant association is a victim to the parliamentary report published on 17 June 1999 and the Law of 12 June 2001. As the application was lodged on 9 December 1999, the complaints in respect of the report published on 22 December 1995 are inadmissible at the outset for failure to comply with the six-month time-limit, in accordance with art. 35 § 1 of the Convention.

The Court reiterates that art. 34 of the Convention requires that an individual applicant should claim to have been actually affected by the violation he alleges. That article does not institute for individuals a kind of actio popularis for the interpretation of the Convention; it does not permit individuals to complain against a law in abstracto simply because they feel that it contravenes the Convention. In principle, it does not suffice for an individual applicant to claim that the mere existence of a law violates his rights under the Convention; it is necessary that the law should have been applied to his detriment (Klass and Others v. Germany, 6 September 1978, Series A no. 28, § 33).

Moreover, the European Commission of Human Rights had considered that it could be observed from the terms „victim" and „violation" and from the philosophy underlying the obligation to exhaust domestic remedies provided for in former art. 26 that in the system for the protection of human rights conceived by the authors of the Convention, the exercise of the right of individual petition could not be used to prevent a potential violation of the Convention: in theory the organs designated by art. 19 to ensure the observance of the engagements undertaken by the Contracting Parties in the Convention could not examine - or, if applicable, find - a violation other than a posteriori, once that violation had occurred. ... It was only in highly exceptional circumstances that an applicant could nevertheless claim to be a victim of a violation of the Convention owing to the risk of a future violation (application no. 28204/95, Noël Narvii

Tauira and 18 Others v. France, Commission decision of 4 December 1995, DR 83, p. 112).

The Court has accordingly accepted the notion of a potential victim in the following cases: where the applicant was not in a position to demonstrate that the legislation he complained of had actually been applied to him because of the secret nature of the measures it authorised (Klass and Others v. Germany, cited above); where a law punishing homosexual acts was likely to be applied to a certain category of the population, to which the applicant belonged (Dudgeon v. the United Kingdom, 22 October 1981, Series A no. 45); and, lastly, where the forced removal of aliens had already been decided on but not yet carried out and enforcement of the measure would have exposed the persons concerned to the risk of treatment contrary to art. 3 in the country of destination (Soering v. the United Kingdom, 7 July 1989, Series A no. 161) or would have infringed the right to respect for family life (Beldjoudi v. France, 26 March 1992, Series A no. 234).

In order for an applicant to claim to be a victim in such a situation, he must, however, produce reasonable and convincing evidence of the likelihood that a violation affecting him personally will occur; mere suspicion or conjecture is insufficient in this respect (see application no. 28204/95, Noël Narvii Tauira and Others v. France, cited above, p. 131).

In the instant case and as regards the parliamentary inquiry report of 17 June 1999, the Court points out that the applicant association complained of a series of hostile reactions to Jehovah's Witnesses (a press campaign, the establishment of civic action groups, the holding of public debates on sects, etc.) and measures such as judicial or administrative decisions allegedly affecting certain Jehovah's Witnesses individually or associations of Jehovah's Witnesses. Even supposing that the applicant association can claim to be directly affected by the measures in question, as the federal body of all Jehovah's Witnesses with responsibility for protecting their interests, the Court notes firstly that some of the measures were not based on the report complained of and secondly that even where reference was made to the report, it was merely a passing mention which could not in any way be regarded as the reason for taking the measure. The Court notes, moreover, like the Government, that a parliamentary report has no legal effect and cannot serve as the basis for any criminal or administrative proceedings.

More specifically, the Court notes that the few court decisions cited by the applicant association were mainly in civil cases and related to facts whose assessment fell within the exclusive jurisdiction of the trial courts. Similarly, certain administrative decisions not to grant or renew certifications related to individual situations and appeals against them could have been lodged with the relevant administrative courts. As to the tax inspections and the social-security inspections by the URSSAF mentioned by the applicant association, the Court does not overlook that such measures can be taken against any member of the public and that the applicant association did not show how they had the purpose or the effect of infringing its rights under the Convention.

As to the Law of 12 June 2001, the Court notes that its aim, as its title indicates, is to strengthen preventive and punitive action against sectarian movements infringing human rights and fundamental freedoms. It is not the Court's task to rule on legislation in abstracto and it cannot therefore express a view as to the compatibility of the provisions of the new legislation with the Convention (Findlay v. the United Kingdom, 25 February 1997, RJD 1997-I, § 67). Admittedly, the impugned Law provides for the possibility of dissolving sects, a term which it does not define, but such a measure can be ordered only by the courts and when certain conditions are satisfied, in particular where there have been final convictions of the sect concerned or of those in control of it for one or more of an exhaustively listed set of offences - a situation in which the applicant association should not normally have any reason to fear finding itself. Impugning Parliament's motives in passing this legislation, when it was concerned to settle a burning social issue, does not amount to proof that the applicant association was likely to run any risk. Moreover, it would be inconsistent for the latter to rely on the fact that it is not a movement that infringes freedoms and at the same time to claim that it is, at least potentially, a victim of the application that may be made of the Law.

It follows that the applicant association cannot claim to be a victim within the meaning of art. 34 of the Convention and that its application must be declared inadmissible in its entirety, pursuant to art. 35 §§ 1, 3 and 4 of the Convention.

For these reasons, the Court unanimously declares the application inadmissible.

70

Zur Frage der Beschränkung der Religionsfreiheit in Zusammenhang mit der staatlichen Anerkennung einer Religionsgemeinschaft.

Art. 9 Abs. 2 EMRK

EGMR, Urteil vom 13. Dezember 2001 - No. 45701/99

(Metropolitan Church of Bessarabia u.a. ./. Moldawien)[1] -

---

[1] RJD 2001-XII; öarr 2003, 157 (LS).

THE FACTS

I. The circumstances of the case

The first applicant, the Metropolitan Church of Bessarabia, is an autonomous Orthodox Church having canonical jurisdiction in the territory of the Republic of Moldova. The other applicants are Moldovan nationals who are members of the eparchic council of the first applicant.

A. Creation of the applicant Church and proceedings to secure its official recognition

1. Creation of the Metropolitan Church of Bessarabia

On 14 September 1992 the applicant natural persons joined together to form the applicant Church - the Metropolitan Church of Bessarabia - a local, autonomous Orthodox Church. According to its articles of association, it took the place, from the canon-law point of view, of the Metropolitan Church of Bessarabia which had existed until 1944. In December 1992 it was attached to the patriarchate of Bucharest.

The Metropolitan Church of Bessarabia adopted articles of association which determined, among other matters, the composition and administration of its organs, the training, recruitment and disciplinary supervision of its clergy, the ecclesiastical hierarchy and rules concerning its assets. In the preamble to the articles of association the principles governing the organisation and operation of the applicant Church are defined as follows:

> „The Metropolitan Church of Bessarabia is a local, autonomous Orthodox Church attached to the patriarchate of Bucharest. The traditional ecclesiastical denomination ‚Metropolitan Church of Bessarabia' is of a historically conventional nature and has no link with current or previous political situations. The Metropolitan Church of Bessarabia has no political activities and will have none in future. It shall carry on its work in the territory of the Republic of Moldova. The Metropolitan Church of Bessarabia shall have the status of an exarchate of the country. According to canon law, communities of the Moldovan diaspora may also become members. No charge shall be made for the accession of individual members and communities living abroad.
> In the context of its activity in the Republic of Moldova, it shall respect the laws of the State and international human rights law. Communities abroad which have adhered for the purposes of canon law to the Metropolitan Church of Bessarabia shall establish relations with the authorities of the States concerned, complying with their legislation and the relevant provisions of international law. The Metropolitan Church of Bessarabia shall cooperate with the authorities of the State in the sphere of culture, education and social assistance. The Metropolitan Church of Bessarabia does not make any claim of an economic or any other kind against other Churches or religious organisations. The Metropolitan Church

of Bessarabia maintains ecumenical relations with other Churches and religious movements and considers that fraternal dialogue is the only proper form of relationship between Churches.
Priests of the Metropolitan Church of Bessarabia working in Moldovan territory shall be Moldovan citizens. When nationals of foreign States are invited to come to Moldova to carry on a religious activity or citizens of the Republic of Moldova are sent abroad for the same purpose, the legislation in force must be complied with.
Members of the Metropolitan Church of Bessarabia shall be citizens of the Republic of Moldova who have joined together on a voluntary basis to practise their religion in common, in accordance with their own convictions, and on the basis of the precepts of the Gospel, the Apostolic Canons, Orthodox canon law and Holy Tradition.
Religious services held in all the communities of the Metropolitan Church of Bessarabia shall include special prayers for the authorities and institutions of the State, couched in the following terms: ,We pray, as always, for our country, the Republic of Moldova, for its leaders and for its army. May God protect them and grant them peaceful and honest lives, spent in obedience to the canons of the Church.'"

To date, the Metropolitan Church of Bessarabia has established 117 communities in Moldovan territory, three communities in Ukraine, one in Lithuania, one in Latvia, two in the Russian Federation and one in Estonia. The communities in Latvia and Lithuania have been recognised by the State authorities and have legal personality.

Nearly one million Moldovan nationals are affiliated to the applicant Church, which has more than 160 clergy. The Metropolitan Church of Bessarabia is recognised by all the Orthodox patriarchates with the exception of the patriarchate of Moscow.

2. Administrative and judicial proceedings to secure official recognition of the applicant Church

Pursuant to the Religious Denominations Act (Law no. 979-XII of 24 March 1992), which requires religious denominations active in Moldovan territory to be recognised by means of a government decision, the applicant Church applied for recognition on 8 October 1992. It received no reply.

It made further applications on 25 January and 8 February 1995. On a date which has not been specified the Religious Affairs Department refused these applications.

On 8 August 1995 the applicant Petru P., relying on art. 235 of the Code of Civil Procedure (which governs judicial review of administrative acts contrary to recognised rights), brought civil proceedings against the government in the Court of First Instance of the Buiucani district of Chişinău. He asked for the decisions refusing to recognise the applicant

Church to be set aside. The court ruled in his favour and, on 12 September 1995, ordered recognition of the Metropolitan Church of Bessarabia.

On 15 September 1995 the Buiucani public prosecutor appealed against the Buiucani Court of First Instance's decision of 12 September 1995.

On 18 October 1995 the Supreme Court of Justice set aside the decision of 12 September 1995 on the ground that the courts did not have jurisdiction to consider the applicant Church's application for recognition.

On 13 March 1996 the applicant Church filed a fresh application for recognition with the government. On 24 May 1996, having received no reply, the applicants brought civil proceedings against the government in the Chişinău Court of First Instance, seeking recognition of the Metropolitan Church of Bessarabia. On 19 July 1996 that court gave judgment against the applicants.

On 20 August 1996 the applicants again filed an application for recognition, which went unanswered.

The applicants appealed to the Chişinău Municipal Court (*Tribunal municipiului*) against the judgment of 19 July 1996. In a judgment of 21 May 1997, against which no appeal lay, the Municipal Court quashed the impugned judgment and allowed the applicants' claim.

However, following a reform of the Moldovan judicial system, the file was sent to the Moldovan Court of Appeal for trial *de novo*.

On 4 March 1997 the applicants again applied to the government for recognition. On 4 June 1997, not having received any reply, they referred the matter to the Court of Appeal, seeking recognition of the Metropolitan Church of Bessarabia, relying on their freedom of conscience and freedom of association for the purpose of practising their religion. The resulting action was joined to the case already pending before the Court of Appeal.

In the Court of Appeal the government alleged that the case concerned an ecclesiastical conflict within the Orthodox Church in Moldova (the Metropolitan Church of Moldova), which could be resolved only by the Romanian and Russian Orthodox Churches, and that any recognition of the Metropolitan Church of Bessarabia would provoke conflicts in the Orthodox community.

The Court of Appeal allowed the applicants' claim in a decision of 19 August 1997. It pointed out, firstly, that art. 31 §§ 1 and 2 of the Moldovan Constitution guaranteed freedom of conscience and that that freedom should be exercised in a spirit of tolerance and respect for others. In addition, the various denominations were free to organise themselves according to their articles of association, subject to compliance with the laws of the Republic. Secondly, it noted that from 8 October 1992 the applicant Church, acting pursuant to sec. 14 and 15 of the Religious Denominations Act, had filed with the government a number of applications for recognition, but that no reply had been forthcoming. By a letter of 19 July 1995 the Prime Minister had informed the applicants that the government could not consider the application of the Metropolitan Church of Bessarabia without interfering with the activity of the Metropolitan Church of Moldova. The Court of Appeal further noted that while the applicant Church's application for recognition had been ignored, the Metropolitan Church of Moldova had been recognised by the government on 7 February 1993, as an eparchy dependent on the patriarchate of Moscow. - The Court of Appeal dismissed the government's argument that recognition of the Metropolitan Church of Moldova made it possible to satisfy the wishes of all Orthodox believers. It pointed out that the term denomination was not to be reserved for catholicism or orthodoxy, but should embrace all faiths and various manifestations of religious feelings by their adherents, in the form of prayers, ritual, religious services or divine worship. It noted that from the point of view of canon law the Metropolitan Church of Moldova was part of the Russian Orthodox Church and therefore dependent on the patriarchate of Moscow, whereas the Metropolitan Church of Bessarabia was attached to the Romanian Orthodox Church and therefore dependent on the patriarchate of Bucharest. - The Court of Appeal held that the government's refusal to recognise the applicant Church was contrary to the freedom of religion, as guaranteed not only by the Religious Denominations Act but also by art. 18 of the Universal Declaration of Human Rights, art. 5 of the International Covenant on Economic, Social and Cultural Rights and art. 18 of the International Covenant on Civil and Political Rights, to all of which Moldova was party. Noting that the representative of the government had taken the view that the applicant Church's articles of association complied with domestic legislation, the Court of Appeal ordered the government to recognise the Metropolitan Church of Bessarabia and to ratify its articles of association.

The government appealed against the above decision on the ground that the courts did not have jurisdiction to try such a case.

In a judgment of 9 December 1997 the Supreme Court of Justice set aside the decision of 19 August 1997 and dismissed the applicants' action on the grounds that it was out of time and manifestly ill-founded. It went on to say that, in any event, the government's refusal of the applicants' application had not infringed their freedom of religion as guaranteed by international treaties, and in particular by art. 9 of the European Convention on Human Rights, because they were Orthodox Christians and could manifest their beliefs within the Metropolitan Church of Moldova, which the government had recognised by a decision of 7 February 1993.

The Supreme Court of Justice considered that the case was simply an administrative dispute within a single Church, which could be settled only by the Metropolitan Church of Moldova, since any interference by the State in the matter might aggravate the situation. It held that the

State's refusal to intervene in this conflict was compatible with art. 9 § 2 of the European Convention on Human Rights.

Lastly, it noted that the applicants could manifest their beliefs freely, that they had access to Churches and that they had not adduced evidence of any obstacle whatsoever to the practice of their religion.

On 15 March 1999 the applicants again applied to the government for recognition.

By a letter dated 20 July 1999 the Prime Minister refused on the ground that the Metropolitan Church of Bessarabia was not a religious denomination in the legal sense but a schismatic group within the Metropolitan Church of Moldova.

He informed the applicants that the government would not allow their application until a religious solution to the conflict had been found, following the negotiations in progress between the patriarchates of Russia and Romania.

On 10 January 2000 the applicants lodged a further application for recognition with the government. The Court has not been informed of the outcome of that application.

3. Recognition of other denominations

Since the adoption of the Religious Denominations Act, the government has recognised a number of denominations, some of which are listed below.

On 7 February 1993 the government ratified the articles of association of the Metropolitan Church of Moldova, attached to the patriarchate of Moscow. On 28 August 1995 it recognised the Orthodox Eparchy of the Old Christian Liturgy of Chişinău, attached to the Russian Orthodox Church of the Old Liturgy, whose head office was in Moscow. On 22 July 1993 the government recognised the „Seventh-Day Adventist Church". On 19 July 1994 it decided to recognise the „Seventh-Day Adventist Church - Reform Movement". On 9 June 1994 the government ratified the articles of association of the „Federation of Jewish (Religious) Communities" and on 1 September 1997 those of the „Union of Communities of Messianic Jews".

4. Reaction of various national authorities

Since it was first set up, the Metropolitan Church of Bessarabia has regularly applied to the Moldovan authorities to explain the reasons for its creation and to seek their support in obtaining official recognition.

The government asked several ministries for their opinion about whether to recognise the applicant Church. On 16 October 1992 the Ministry of Culture and Religious Affairs informed the government that it was favourable to the recognition of the Metropolitan Church of Bessarabia. On 14 November 1992 the Ministry of Financial Affairs informed the government that it could see no objection to the recognition of the Metropolitan Church of Bessarabia. On 8 February 1993 the Ministry of Labour and Social Protection declared that it was favourable to the recognition of the applicant Church. In a letter of 8 February 1993 the Ministry of Education emphasised the need for the rapid recognition of the Metropolitan Church of Bessarabia in order to avoid any discrimination against its adherents, while pointing out that its articles of association could be improved upon. On 15 February 1993 the Secretariat of State for Privatisation stated that it was favourable to the recognition of the Metropolitan Church of Bessarabia, while proposing certain amendments to its articles of association.

On 11 March 1993, in reply to a letter from the Bishop of Bălți, writing on behalf of the Metropolitan of Bessarabia, the Moldovan parliament's Cultural and Religious Affairs Committee noted that the delay in registering the Metropolitan Church of Bessarabia was aggravating the social and political situation in Moldova, even though its actions and articles of association complied with Moldovan legislation. The committee therefore asked the government to recognise the applicant Church.

A memorandum from the Religious Affairs Department, dated 21 November 1994, summarised the situation as follows:

„For nearly two years an ecclesiastical group known under the name of the Metropolitan Church of Bessarabia has been operating illegally in Moldovan territory. No positive result has been obtained in spite of our sustained efforts to put a stop to its activity (discussions between members of the so-called Church, priests, Mr G.E., Mr I.E. ..., representatives of the State and believers from the localities in which its adherents are active, Mr G.G., Minister of State, and Mr N.A., Deputy Speaker; all the organs of local and national administrative bodies have been informed of the illegal nature of the group, etc.).

In addition, although priests and adherents of the Church have been forbidden to take part in divine service, for failure to comply with canon law, they have nevertheless continued their illegal activities in the churches and have also been invited to officiate on the occasion of various public activities organised, for example, by the Ministries of Defence and Health. The management of the Bank of Moldova and the National Customs Service have not acted on our request for liquidation of the group's bank accounts and strict supervision of its priests during their numerous crossings of the border.

The activity of the so-called Church is not limited to attracting new adherents and propagating the ideas of the Romanian Church. It also has all the means necessary for the work of a Church, it appoints priests, including nationals of other States ..., trains clergy, builds churches and many, many other things.

It should also be mentioned that the group's activity (more political than religious) is sustained by forces both from within the country (by certain mayors and their villages, by opposition representatives, and even by some MPs) and from outside (by decision no. 612 of 12 November 1993 the Romanian government granted it 399,400,000 lei to finance its activity ...

The activity of this group is causing religious and socio-political tension in Moldova and will have unforeseeable repercussions ...
The Religious Affairs Department notes:
(a) Within Moldovan territory there is no territorial administrative unit with the name of Bessarabia which might justify setting up a religious group named ‚Metropolitan Church of Bessarabia'. The creation of such a group and recognition of its articles of association would constitute a wrongful anti-State act - a negation of the sovereign and independent State which the Republic of Moldova constitutes.
(b) The Metropolitan Church of Bessarabia was set up to take the place of the former Eparchy of Bessarabia, founded in 1925 and recognised by Decree no. 1942 promulgated on 4 May 1925 by the King of Romania. Legal recognition of the validity of those acts would imply recognition of their present-day effects within Moldovan territory.
(c) All Orthodox parishes in Moldovan territory have been registered as constituent parts of the Orthodox Church of Moldova (the Metropolitan Church of Moldova), whose articles of association were ratified by the government in its decision no. 719 of 17 November 1993.
In conclusion:
1. If nothing is done to put a stop to the activity of the so-called Metropolitan Church of Bessarabia, the result will be destabilisation not just of the Orthodox Church but of the whole of Moldovan society.
2. Recognition of the Metropolitan Church of Bessarabia (Old Style) and ratification of its articles of association by the government would automatically entail the disappearance of the Metropolitan Church of Moldova."

On 20 February 1996, following a question in Parliament asked by the applicant Vlad Cubreacov, a Moldovan MP, the Deputy Prime Minister wrote a letter to the Speaker explaining the reasons for the government's refusal to recognise the Metropolitan Church of Bessarabia. He said that the applicant Church was not a denomination distinct from the Orthodox Church but a schismatic group within the Metropolitan Church of Moldova and that any interference by the State to resolve the conflict would be contrary to the Moldovan Constitution. He pointed out that the political party to which Mr Cubreacov belonged had publicly expressed disapproval of the Supreme Court of Justice's decision of 9 December 1997, that Mr Cubreacov himself had criticised the government for their refusal to recognise „this phantom metropolitan Church" and that he continued to support it by exerting pressure in any way he could, through statements to the media and approaches to the national authorities and international organisations. The letter ended with the assertion that the „feverish debates" about the Metropolitan Church of Bessarabia were purely political.

On 29 June 1998 the Religious Affairs Department sent the Deputy Prime Minister its opinion on the question of recognition of the Metropolitan Church of Bessarabia. It pointed out in particular that not since 1940 had there been an administrative unit in Moldova with the name

„Bessarabia" and that the Orthodox Church had been recognised on 17 November 1993 under the name of the Metropolitan Church of Moldova, of which the Metropolitan Church of Bessarabia was a „schismatic element". It accordingly considered that recognition of the applicant Church would represent interference by the State in the affairs of the Metropolitan Church of Moldova, and that this would aggravate the „unhealthy" situation in which the latter Church was placed. It considered that the articles of association of the applicant Church could not be ratified since they merely „reproduce[d] those of the Orthodox Church of another country".

On 22 June 1998 the Ministry of Justice informed the government that it did not consider the articles of association of the Metropolitan Church of Bessarabia to be contrary to Moldovan legislation.

By letters of 25 June and 6 July 1998 the Ministry of Labour and Social Protection and the Ministry of Financial Affairs again informed the government that they could see no objection to recognition of the Metropolitan Church of Bessarabia.

On 7 July 1998 the Ministry of Education informed the government that it supported recognition of the Metropolitan Church of Bessarabia.

On 15 September 1998 the Cultural and Religious Affairs Committee of the Moldovan parliament sent the government, for information, a copy of a report by the Ministry of Justice of the Russian Federation, which showed that on 1 January 1998 there were at least four different Orthodox Churches in Russia, some of which had their head offices abroad. The Committee expressed the hope that the above-mentioned report would assist the government to resolve certain similar problems, particularly the problem concerning the Metropolitan Church of Bessarabia's application for recognition.

In a letter sent on 10 January 2000 to the applicant Vlad Cubreacov, the Deputy Attorney-General expressed the view that the government's refusal to reply to the Metropolitan Church of Bessarabia's application for recognition was contrary to the freedom of religion and to art. 6, 11 and 13 of the Convention.

In a decision of 26 September 2001 the government approved the amended version of art. 1 of the Metropolitan Church of Moldova's articles of association, worded as follows:

„*The Orthodox Church of Moldova is an independent Church and is the successor in law to ... the Metropolitan Church of Bessarabia. While complying with the canons and precepts of the Holy Apostles, Fathers of the Church and the Ecumenical Synods, and the decisions of the Universal Apostolic Church, the Orthodox Church of Moldova operates within the territory of the State of the Republic of Moldova in accordance with the provisions of the legislation in force.*"

In a letter received by the Court on 21 September 2001 the President of the Republic of Moldova expressed his concern about the possibility that the applicant Church might be recognised. He said that the issue could be resolved only by negotiation between the Russian and Romanian patriarchates, since it would be in breach of Moldovan legislation if the State authorities were to intervene in the conflict. Moreover, if the authorities were to recognise the Metropolitan Church of Bessarabia, this would have unforeseeable consequences for Moldovan society.

5. International reactions

In its Opinion no. 188 (1995) to the Committee of Ministers on Moldova's application for membership of the Council of Europe, the Parliamentary Assembly of the Council of Europe noted the Republic of Moldova's willingness to fulfil the commitments it had entered into when it lodged its application for membership on 20 April 1993. These commitments, which had been reaffirmed before the adoption of the above-mentioned opinion, included an undertaking to „confirm complete freedom of worship for all citizens without discrimination" and to „ensure a peaceful solution to the dispute between the Moldovan Orthodox Church and the Bessarabian Orthodox Church".

In its annual report for 1997 the International Helsinki Federation for Human Rights criticised the Moldovan government's refusal to recognise the Metropolitan Church of Bessarabia. The report stated that as a result of this refusal many churches had been transferred to the ownership of the Metropolitan Church of Moldova. It drew attention to allegations that members of the applicant Church's clergy had been subjected to physical violence without receiving the slightest protection from the authorities.

In its 1998 report the Federation criticised the Religious Denominations Act, and in particular sec. 4 thereof, which denied any protection of the freedom of religion to the adherents of religions not recognised by a government decision. It pointed out that this section was a discriminatory instrument which enabled the government to make it difficult for the adherents of the Metropolitan Church of Bessarabia to bring legal proceedings with a view to reclaiming church buildings which belonged to them. In addition, the report mentioned acts of violence and vandalism to which the applicant Church and its members were subjected.

B. Alleged incidents affecting the Metropolitan Church of Bessarabia and its members

The applicants reported a number of incidents during which members of the clergy or adherents of the applicant Church had allegedly been intimidated or prevented from manifesting their beliefs. The Government did not dispute that these incidents had taken place. (*wird ausgeführt*)

C. Incidents affecting the assets of the Metropolitan Church of Bessarabia (wird ausgeführt)

D. Questions relating to the personal rights of the applicant Church's clergy (wird ausgeführt)

II. Relevant domestic law

A. The Constitution of 29 July 1994

Art. 31 of the Moldovan Constitution, concerning freedom of conscience, provides:

„*1. Freedom of conscience is guaranteed. It must be manifested in a spirit of tolerance and mutual respect.*
2. Freedom of worship is guaranteed. Religious denominations shall organise themselves according to their own articles of association, in compliance with the law.
3. Any manifestation of discord is forbidden in relations between religious denominations.
4. Religious denominations shall be autonomous and separated from the State, and shall enjoy the latter's support, including facilities granted for the purpose of providing religious assistance in the army, hospitals, prisons, mental institutions and orphanages."

B. The Religious Denominations Act (Law no. 979-XII of 24 March 1992)

The relevant provisions of the Religious Denominations Act, as published in the Official Gazette no. 3/70 of 1992, read as follows:

Sec. 1 - Freedom of conscience
„*The State shall guarantee freedom of conscience and freedom of religion within Moldovan territory. Everyone shall have the right to manifest his belief freely, either alone or in community with others, to propagate his belief and to worship in public or in private, on condition that such worship is not contrary to the Constitution, the present Act or the legislation in force.*"
Sec. 4 - Intolerance on denominational grounds
„*Intolerance on denominational grounds, manifested by acts which interfere with the free operation of a religious denomination recognised by the State, shall be an offence punished in accordance with the relevant legislation.*"

Sec. 9 - Religious denominations' freedom of organisation and operation
„*Denominations shall be free to organise and operate freely on condition that their practices and rites do not contravene the Constitution, the present Act or the legislation in force.*
Where that is not the case, denominations shall not qualify for State recognition."
Sec. 14 - Recognition of religious denominations
„*In order to be able to organise and operate, denominations must be recognised by means of a government decision.*
Where a denomination fails to comply with the conditions laid down by the first paragraph of sec. 9 of the present Act, recognition may be withdrawn under the same procedure."
Sec. 15 - Articles of association
„*To qualify for recognition, each denomination shall submit to the Government, for scrutiny and approval, the articles of association governing its organisation and operation. The articles of association must contain information on its system of organisation and administration and on the fundamental principles of its beliefs.*"
Sec. 21 - Associations and foundations
„*Associations and foundations which pursue a religious aim, in whole or in part, shall enjoy religious rights and shall be subject to the obligations arising from the legislation on religious denominations.*"
Sec. 22 - Clergy, invitation and delegation
„*Leaders of denominations having republican and hierarchical rank ..., and all persons employed by religious denominations, must be Moldovan citizens.*
Denominations which wish to take foreign nationals into their employ to conduct religious activities, or to delegate Moldovan citizens to conduct religious activities abroad, must in every case seek and obtain the agreement of the State authorities."
Sec. 24 - Legal personality
„*Denominations recognised by the State shall be legal persons ...*"
Sec. 35 - Publishing and liturgical objects
„*Only denominations recognised by the State and registered in accordance with the relevant legislation may*
(a) produce and market objects specific to the denomination concerned;
(b) found periodicals for the faithful, or publish and market liturgical, theological or ecclesiastical books necessary for practice of the religion concerned;
(c) lay down scales of charges for pilgrimages and touristic activities in the denomination's establishments;
(d) organise, within Moldovan territory or abroad, exhibitions of liturgical objects, including exhibitions of items for sale;
...
For the purposes of the present section, the term ‚liturgical objects' shall mean liturgical vessels, metal and lithographic icons, crosses, crucifixes, church furniture, cross-shaped pendants or medallions framing religious images specific to each denomination, religious objects sold from door to door, etc. The following items shall be assimilated with liturgical objects: religious calendars, religious postcards and leaflets, albums of religious works of art, films and labels portraying places of worship or objects of religious art, other than those which form part of the national cultural heritage, products necessary for worship, such as incense and candles, including decorations for weddings and christenings, material and

embroidery for the production of liturgical vestments and other objects necessary for practice of a religion."

Sec. 44 - Recruitment of clergy and employees by religious denominations
„Bodies affiliated to religious denominations or institutions and enterprises set up by them may engage staff in accordance with labour legislation."

Sec. 45 - Contracts
„Clergy and employees of religious denominations shall be engaged under a written contract ..."

Sec. 46 - Legal status
„Clergy and employees of religious denominations or the institutions and enterprises set up by them shall have the same legal status as the employees of organisations, institutions and enterprises, so that labour legislation shall be applicable to them."

Sec. 48 - State pensions
„Whatever pensions are paid by religious denominations, their clergy and employees shall receive State pensions, in accordance with the Moldovan State Pensions Act."

THE LAW

I. Alleged violation of Art. 9 of the Convention

1. The applicants alleged that the Moldovan authorities' refusal to recognise the Metropolitan Church of Bessarabia infringed their freedom of religion, since only religions recognised by the government could be practised in Moldova. They asserted in particular that their freedom to manifest their religion in community with others was frustrated by the fact that they were prohibited from gathering together for religious purposes and by the complete absence of judicial protection of the applicant Church's assets. They relied on art. 9 of the Convention, which provides:

„1. Everyone has the right to freedom of thought, conscience and religion; this right includes freedom to change his religion or belief and freedom, either alone or in community with others and in public or private, to manifest his religion or belief, in worship, teaching, practice and observance.
2. Freedom to manifest one's religion or beliefs shall be subject only to such limitations as are prescribed by law and are necessary in a democratic society in the interests of public safety, for the protection of public order, health or morals, or for the protection of the rights and freedoms of others."

A. Arguments submitted to the Court

1. The applicants

2. Citing Manoussakis and Others v. Greece (judgment of 26 September 1996, RDJ 1996-IV, p. 1361, § 37, KirchE-EU S. 263), the applicants alleged that the refusal to recognise the applicant Church infringed their freedom of religion, since the lack of authorisation made it impossible to

practise their religion. They submitted that a State could require a prior registration procedure for religious denominations without breaching art. 9 of the Convention provided that registration did not become an impediment to believers' freedom of religion. But in the present case the refusal to recognise did not have any basis which was acceptable in a democratic society. In particular, the applicants asserted that the applicant Church and its members could not be criticised for any activity which was illegal or contrary to public order.

3. The applicants submitted that in a democratic society any group of believers who considered themselves to be different from others should be able to form a new Church, and that it was not for the State to determine whether or not there was a real distinction between these different groups or what beliefs should be considered distinct from others.

Similarly, it was not for the State to favour one Church rather than another by means of recognition, or to censor the name of a Church solely on the ground that it referred to a closed chapter of history.

Consequently, in the present case, the Moldovan State was not entitled to decide whether the applicant Church was a separate entity or a grouping within another Church.

2. The Government

4. The Government accepted that the right to freedom of religion included the freedom to manifest one's religion through worship and observance, but considered that in the present case the refusal to recognise the applicant Church did not amount to a prohibition of its activities or those of its members. The members of the applicant Church retained their freedom of religion, both as regards their freedom of conscience and as regards the freedom to manifest their beliefs through worship and practice.

5. The Government further submitted that the applicant Church, as an Orthodox Christian Church, was not a new denomination, since Orthodox Christianity had been recognised in Moldova on 7 February 1993 at the same time as the Metropolitan Church of Moldova. There was absolutely no difference, from the religious point of view, between the applicant Church and the Metropolitan Church of Moldova.

The creation of the applicant Church had in reality been an attempt to set up a new administrative organ within the Metropolitan Church of Moldova. The State could not interfere in the conflict within the Metropolitan Church of Moldova without infringing its duty of neutrality in religious matters.

At the hearing on 2 October 2001 the Government submitted that this conflict, apparently an administrative one, concealed a political conflict between Romania and Russia; were it to intervene by recognising the applicant Church, which it considered to be a schismatic group, the consequences were likely to be detrimental to the independence and territorial integrity of the young Republic of Moldova.

B. The third party

6. The third party submitted that the present application originated in an administrative conflict within the Metropolitan Church of Moldova. It asserted that the applicant Church had been set up by clergy of the Metropolitan Church of Moldova who, prompted by their personal ambition, had decided to split away from it. As the schismatic activity of the applicant Petru Păduraru had been contrary to the canons of the Russian Orthodox Church, the patriarch of Moscow had forbidden him to conduct divine service. However, in breach of canon law, and without consulting either the patriarchate of Moscow or the Moldovan civil authorities, the patriarchate of Bucharest had decided to recognise the schismatic Church. The conflict thus generated should therefore be resolved only by negotiations between the Romanian and Russian patriarchates.

7. The third party contended that the applicant Church was based on ethnic criteria and that its recognition by the government would therefore not only constitute interference by the State in religious matters but would also have detrimental consequences for the political and social situation in Moldova and would encourage the existing nationalist tendencies there. In addition, such recognition would prejudice the friendly relations between Moldova and Ukraine.

C. The Court's assessment

8. The Court reiterates at the outset that a Church or ecclesiastical body may, as such, exercise on behalf of its adherents the rights guaranteed by art. 9 of the Convention (see Cha'are Shalom Ve Tsedek v. France [GC], no. 27417/95, § 72, ECHR 2000-VII, KirchE-EU S. 418). In the present case the Metropolitan Church of Bessarabia may therefore be considered an applicant for the purposes of art. 34 of the Convention.

1. Whether there was an interference

9. The Court must therefore determine whether there was an interference with the applicants' right to freedom of religion on account of the refusal to recognise the applicant Church.

10. The Government submitted that the refusal to recognise the applicant Church did not prevent the applicants from holding beliefs or manifesting them within the Orthodox Christian denomination recognised by the State, namely the Metropolitan Church of Moldova.

11. The applicants asserted that, according to Moldovan law, only religions recognised by the State may be practised and that refusing to recognise the applicant Church therefore amounted to forbidding it to operate,

both as a liturgical body and as an association. The applicants who are natural persons may not express their beliefs through worship, since only a denomination recognised by the State can enjoy legal protection.

12. The Court notes that, according to the Religious Denominations Act, only religions recognised by government decision may be practised.

In the present case the Court observes that, not being recognised, the applicant Church cannot operate. In particular, its priests may not conduct divine service, its members may not meet to practise their religion and, not having legal personality, it is not entitled to judicial protection of its assets.

The Court therefore considers that the government's refusal to recognise the applicant Church, upheld by the Supreme Court of Justice's decision of 9 December 1997, constituted interference with the right of the applicant Church and the other applicants to freedom of religion, as guaranteed by art. 9 § 1 of the Convention.

13. In order to determine whether that interference entailed a breach of the Convention, the Court must decide whether it satisfied the requirements of art. 9 § 2, that is whether it was „prescribed by law", pursued a legitimate aim for the purposes of that provision and was „necessary in a democratic society".

2. Whether the interference was prescribed by law

14. The applicants accepted that the interference in question was prescribed by the Religious Denominations Act. They asserted nevertheless that the procedure laid down by the Act had been misapplied, since the real reason for refusal to register had been political; the Government had neither submitted nor proved that the applicant Church had failed to comply with the laws of the Republic.

15. The Government made no observation on this point.

16. The Court refers to its established case-law to the effect that the terms „prescribed by law" and „in accordance with the law" in art. 8 to 11 of the Convention not only require that the impugned measures have some basis in domestic law, but also refer to the quality of the law in question, which must be sufficiently accessible and foreseeable as to its effects, that is formulated with sufficient precision to enable the individual - if need be with appropriate advice - to regulate his conduct (see The Sunday Times v. the United Kingdom (no. 1), judgment of 26 April 1979, Series A no. 30, p. 31, § 49; Larissis and Others v. Greece, judgment of 24 February 1998, RJD 1998-I, p. 378, § 40; Hashman and Harrup v. the United Kingdom [GC], no. 25594/94, § 31, ECHR 1999-VIII; and Rotaru v. Romania [GC], no. 28341/95, § 52, ECHR 2000-V).

For domestic law to meet these requirements, it must afford a measure of legal protection against arbitrary interferences by public authorities with the rights guaranteed by the Convention. In matters affecting fundamental rights it would be contrary to the rule of law, one of the basic principles of a democratic society enshrined in the Convention, for a legal discretion granted to the executive to be expressed in terms of an unfettered power. Consequently, the law must indicate with sufficient clarity the scope of any such discretion and the manner of its exercise (see Hasan and Chaush v. Bulgaria [GC], no. 30985/96, § 84, ECHR 2000-XI, KirchE-EU S. 444).

The level of precision required of domestic legislation - which cannot in any case provide for every eventuality - depends to a considerable degree on the content of the instrument in question, the field it is designed to cover and the number and status of those to whom it is addressed (see Hashman and Harrup, cited above, § 31, and Groppera Radio AG and Others v. Switzerland, judgment of 28 March 1990, Series A no. 173, p. 26, § 68).

17. In the present case the Court notes that sec. 14 of the Law of 24 March 1992 requires religious denominations to be recognised by a government decision and that, according to sec. 9 of the same law, only denominations whose practices and rites are compatible with the Moldovan Constitution and legislation may be recognised.

Without giving a categorical answer to the question whether the above-mentioned provisions satisfy the requirements of foreseeability and precision, the Court is prepared to accept that the interference in question was „prescribed by law" before deciding whether it pursued a „legitimate aim" and was „necessary in a democratic society".

3. Legitimate aim

18. At the hearing on 2 October 2001 the Government submitted that the refusal to allow the application for recognition lodged by the applicants was intended to protect public order and public safety. The Moldovan State, whose territory had repeatedly passed in earlier times from Romanian to Russian control and vice versa, had an ethnically and linguistically varied population. That being so, the young Republic of Moldova, which had been independent since 1991, had few strengths it could depend on to ensure its continued existence, but one factor conducive to stability was religion, the majority of the population being Orthodox Christians. Consequently, recognition of the Moldovan Orthodox Church, which was subordinate to the patriarchate of Moscow, had enabled the entire population to come together within that Church. If the applicant Church were to be recognised, that tie was likely to be lost and the Orthodox Christian population dispersed among a number of Churches. Moreover, under cover of the applicant Church, which was subordinate to the patriarchate of Bucharest, political forces were at work, acting hand-in-glove with Romanian interests favourable to reunification between Bessarabia and Romania. Recognition of the applicant

Church would therefore revive old Russo-Romanian rivalries within the population, thus endangering social stability and even Moldova's territorial integrity.

19. The applicants denied that the measure complained of had been intended to protect public order and public safety. They alleged that the Government had not shown that the applicant Church had constituted a threat to public order and public safety.

20. The Court considers that States are entitled to verify whether a movement or association carries on, ostensibly in pursuit of religious aims, activities which are harmful to the population or to public safety (see *Manoussakis and Others, cited* above, p. 1362, § 40, and Stankov and the United Macedonian Organisation Ilinden v. Bulgaria, nos. 29221/95 and 29225/95, § 84, ECHR 2001-IX).

Having regard to the circumstances of the case, the Court considers that the interference complained of pursued a legitimate aim under art. 9 § 2, namely protection of public order and public safety.

4. Necessary in a democratic society

(a) General principles

21. The Court refers to its settled case-law to the effect that, as enshrined in art. 9, freedom of thought, conscience and religion is one of the foundations of a „democratic society" within the meaning of the Convention. It is, in its religious dimension, one of the most vital elements that go to make up the identity of believers and their conception of life, but it is also a precious asset for atheists, agnostics, sceptics and the unconcerned. The pluralism indissociable from a democratic society, which has been dearly won over the centuries, depends on it.

While religious freedom is primarily a matter of individual conscience, it also implies, *inter alia*, freedom to „manifest [one's] religion" alone and in private or in community with others, in public and within the circle of those whose faith one shares. Bearing witness in words and deeds is bound up with the existence of religious convictions. That freedom entails, *inter alia*, freedom to hold or not to hold religious beliefs and to practise or not to practise a religion (see Kokkinakis v. Greece, judgment of 25 May 1993, Series A no. 260-A, p. 17, § 31, KirchE-EU S. 202, and Buscarini and Others v. San Marino [GC], no. 24645/94, § 34, ECHR 1999-I, KirchE-EU S. 356). Art. 9 lists a number of forms which manifestation of one's religion or belief may take, namely worship, teaching, practice and observance. Nevertheless, art. 9 does not protect every act motivated or inspired by a religion or belief (see *Kalaç v. Turkey*, judgment of 1 July 1997, RJD 1997-IV, p. 1209, § 27).

22. The Court has also said that, in a democratic society, in which several religions coexist within one and the same population, it may be nec-

essary to place restrictions on this freedom in order to reconcile the interests of the various groups and ensure that everyone's beliefs are respected (see Kokkinakis, cited above, p. 18, § 33).

23. However, in exercising its regulatory power in this sphere and in its relations with the various religions, denominations and beliefs, the State has a duty to remain neutral and impartial (see *Hasan and Chaush*, cited above, § 78). What is at stake here is the preservation of pluralism and the proper functioning of democracy, one of the principle characteristics of which is the possibility it offers of resolving a country's problems through dialogue, without recourse to violence, even when they are irksome (see United Communist Party of Turkey and Others v. Turkey, judgment of 30 January 1998, RJD 1998-I, p. 27, § 57). Accordingly, the role of the authorities in such circumstances is not to remove the cause of tension by eliminating pluralism, but to ensure that the competing groups tolerate each her (see Serif v. Greece, no. 38178/97, § 53, ECHR 1999-IX, KirchE-EU S. 385).

24. The Court further observes that in principle the right to freedom of religion for the purposes of the Convention excludes assessment by the State of the legitimacy of religious beliefs or the ways in which those beliefs are expressed. State measures favouring a particular leader or specific organs of a divided religious community or seeking to compel the community or part of it to place itself, against its will, under a single leadership, would also constitute an infringement of the freedom of religion. In democratic societies the State does not need to take measures to ensure that religious communities remain or are brought under a unified leadership (see *Serif*, cited above, § 52). Similarly, where the exercise of the right to freedom of religion or of one of its aspects is subject under domestic law to a system of prior authorisation, involvement in the procedure for granting authorisation of a recognised ecclesiastical authority cannot be reconciled with the requirements of par. 2 of art. 9 (see, *mutatis mutandis*, Pentidis and Others v. Greece, judgment of 9 June 1997, RJD 1997-III, p. 995, § 46,.

25. Moreover, since religious communities traditionally exist in the form of organised structures, art. 9 must be interpreted in the light of art. 11 of the Convention, which safeguards associative life against unjustified State interference. Seen in that perspective, the right of believers to freedom of religion, which includes the right to manifest one's religion in community with others, encompasses the expectation that believers will be allowed to associate freely, without arbitrary State intervention. Indeed, the autonomous existence of religious communities is indispensable for pluralism in a democratic society and is thus an issue at the very heart of the protection which art. 9 affords (see *Hasan and Chaush*, cited above, § 62).

In addition, one of the means of exercising the right to manifest one's religion, especially for a religious community, in its collective dimension, is the possibility of ensuring judicial protection of the community, its members and its assets, so that art. 9 must be seen not only in the light of art. 11, but also in the light of art. 6 (see, mutatis mutandis, Sidiropoulos and Others v. Greece, judgment of 10 July 1998, RJD 1998-IV, p. 1614, § 40, and Canea Catholic Church v. Greece, judgment of 16 December 1997, RJD 1997-VIII, pp. 2857 and 2859, §§ 33 and 40-41, and opinion of the Commission, p. 2867, §§ 48-49, KirchE-EU S. 319).

26. According to its settled case-law, the Court leaves to States party to the Convention a certain margin of appreciation in deciding whether and to what extent an interference is necessary, but that goes hand in hand with European supervision of both the relevant legislation and the decisions applying it. The Court's task is to ascertain whether the measures taken at national level are justified in principle and proportionate.

In order to determine the scope of the margin of appreciation in the present case the Court must take into account what is at stake, namely the need to maintain true religious pluralism, which is inherent in the concept of a democratic society (see Kokkinakis, cited above, p. 17, § 31). Similarly, a good deal of weight must be given to that need when determining, as par. 2 of art. 9 requires, whether the interference corresponds to a „pressing social need" and is „proportionate to the legitimate aim pursued" (see, mutatis mutandis, among many other authorities, Wingrove v. the United Kingdom, judgment of 25 November 1996, RJD 1996-V, p. 1956, § 53, KirchE-EU S. 278). In exercising its supervision, the Court must consider the interference complained of on the basis of the file as a whole (see Kokkinakis, cited above, p. 21, § 47).

(b) Application of the above principles

27. The Government submitted that the interference complained of was necessary in a democratic society. In the first place, to recognise the applicant Church the State would have had to give up its position of neutrality in religious matters, and in religious conflicts in particular, which would have been contrary to the Moldovan Constitution and Moldovan public policy. It was therefore in order to discharge its duty of neutrality that the Government had urged the applicant Church to settle its differences with the Metropolitan Church of Moldova first.

Secondly, the refusal to recognise, in the Government's submission, was necessary for national security and Moldovan territorial integrity, regard being had to the fact that the applicant Church engaged in political activities, working towards the reunification of Moldova with Romania, with the latter country's support. In support of their assertions, they mentioned articles in the Romanian press favourable to recognition of the applicant Church by the Moldovan authorities and reunification of Moldova with Romania.

Such activities endangered not only Moldova's integrity but also its peaceful relations with Ukraine, part of whose present territory had been under the canonical jurisdiction of the Metropolitan Church of Bessarabia before 1944.

The Government further asserted that the applicant Church was supported by openly pro-Romanian Moldovan parties, who denied the specificity of Moldova, even sometimes during debates in Parliament, thus destabilising the Moldovan State. In that connection, they mentioned the Christian Alliance for the Reunification of Romania, set up on 1 January 1993, whose affiliates included a number of associations and a political party represented in the Moldovan parliament, the Christian Democratic Popular Front, which had welcomed the reappearance of the Metropolitan Church of Bessarabia.

Thirdly, in the Government's submission, the refusal to recognise the applicant Church had been necessary to preserve social peace and understanding among believers. The aggressive attitude of the applicant Church, which sought to draw other Orthodox Christians to it and to swallow up the other Churches, had led to a number of incidents which, without police intervention, could have caused injury or loss of life.

Lastly, the Government emphasised that, although they had not recognised the Metropolitan Church of Bessarabia, the Moldovan authorities were acting in a spirit of tolerance and permitted the applicant Church and its members to continue their activities without hindrance.

28. The applicants submitted that the refusal to recognise the Metropolitan Church of Bessarabia was not necessary in a democratic society. They asserted that all the arguments put forward by the Government were without foundation and unsubstantiated and that they did not correspond to a „pressing social need". There was nothing in the file to show that the applicants had intended or carried on or sought to carry on activities capable of undermining Moldovan territorial integrity, national security or public order.

They alleged that the government, by refusing recognition even though it had recognised other Orthodox Churches, had failed to discharge its duty of neutrality for preposterously fanciful reasons.

Non-recognition had made it impossible for the members of the applicant Church to practise their religion because, under the Religious Denominations Act, the activities of a particular denomination and freedom of association for religious purposes may be exercised only by a denomination recognised by the State. Similarly, the State provided its protection only to recognised denominations and only those denominations could defend their rights in the courts. Consequently, the clergy and members of the applicant Church had not been able to defend themselves against the physical attacks and persecution which they had suffered, and the applicant Church had not been able to protect its assets.

The applicants denied that the State had tolerated the applicant Church and its members. They alleged, on the contrary, not only that State agents had permitted acts of intimidation which members of the applicant Church had suffered at the hands of other believers but also that in a number of cases State agents had participated in such acts.

29. The Court will examine in turn the arguments put forward by the Government in justification of the interference and the proportionality of that interference in relation to the aims pursued.

(i) Arguments put forward in justification of the interference

(α) Upholding Moldovan law and Moldovan constitutional principles

30. The Court notes that art. 31 of the Moldovan Constitution guarantees freedom of religion and enunciates the principle of religious denominations' autonomy *vis-à-vis* the State, and that the Religious Denominations Act (the Law of 24 March 1992) lays down a procedure for the recognition of religious denominations.

The Government submitted that it was in order to comply with the above principles, including the duty of neutrality as between denominations, that the applicant Church had been refused recognition and instead told first to settle its differences with the already recognised Church from which it wished to split, namely the Metropolitan Church of Moldova.

The Court notes first of all that the applicant Church lodged a first application for recognition on 8 October 1992 to which no reply was forthcoming, and that it was only later, on 7 February 1993, that the State recognised the Metropolitan Church of Moldova. That being so, the Court finds it difficult, at least for the period preceding recognition of the Metropolitan Church of Moldova, to understand the Government's argument that the applicant Church was only a schismatic group within the Metropolitan Church of Moldova, which had been recognised.

In any event, the Court observes that the State's duty of neutrality and impartiality, as defined in its case-law, is incompatible with any power on the State's part to assess the legitimacy of religious beliefs, and requires the State to ensure that conflicting groups tolerate each other, even where they originated in the same group. In the present case, the Court considers that by taking the view that the applicant Church was not a new denomination and by making its recognition depend on the will of an ecclesiastical authority that had been recognised - the Metropolitan Church of Moldova - the State failed to discharge its duty of neutrality and impartiality. Consequently, the Government's argument that refusing recognition was necessary in order to uphold Moldovan law and the Moldovan Constitution must be rejected.

(β) Threat to territorial integrity

31. The Court notes in the first place that in its articles of association, in particular in the preamble thereto, the applicant Church defines itself as an autonomous local Church, operating within Moldovan territory in accordance with the laws of that State, and whose name is a historical one having no link with current or previous political situations. Although its activity is mainly religious, the applicant Church states that it is also prepared to cooperate with the State in the fields of culture, education and social assistance. It further declares that it has no political activity.

The Court considers those principles to be clear and perfectly legitimate.

32. At the hearing on 2 October 2001 the Government nevertheless submitted that in reality the applicant Church was engaged in political activities contrary to Moldovan public policy and that, were it to be recognised, such activities would endanger Moldovan territorial integrity.

The Court reiterates that while it cannot be ruled out that an organisation's programme might conceal objectives and intentions different from the ones it proclaims, to verify that it does not the Court must compare the content of the programme with the organisation's actions and the positions it defends (see Sidiropoulos and Others, cited above, p. 1618, § 46). In the present case it notes that there is nothing in the file which warrants the conclusion that the applicant Church carries on activities other than those stated in its articles of association.

As to the press articles mentioned above, although their content, as described by the Government, reveals ideas favourable to reunification of Moldova with Romania, they cannot be imputed to the applicant Church. Moreover, the Government have not argued that the applicant Church had prompted such articles.

Similarly, in the absence of any evidence, the Court cannot conclude that the applicant Church is linked to the political activities of the abovementioned Moldovan organisations (see par. 120 above), which are allegedly working towards unification of Moldova with Romania. Furthermore, it notes that the Government have not contended that the activity of these associations and political parties is illegal.

As for the possibility that the applicant Church, once recognised, might constitute a danger to national security and territorial integrity, the Court considers that this is a mere hypothesis which, in the absence of corroboration, cannot justify a refusal to recognise it.

(γ) Protection of social peace and understanding among believers

33. The Court notes that the Government did not dispute that incidents had taken place at meetings of the adherents and members of the clergy of the applicant Church (see par. 47-87 above). In particular, con-

flicts have occurred when priests belonging to the applicant Church tried to celebrate mass in places of worship to which the adherents and clergy of the Metropolitan Church of Moldova laid claim for their exclusive use, or in places where certain persons were opposed to the presence of the applicant Church on the ground that it was illegal.

On the other hand, the Court notes that there are certain points of disagreement between the applicants and the Government about what took place during these incidents.

34. Without expressing an opinion on exactly what took place during the events concerned, the Court notes that the refusal to recognise the applicant Church played a role in the incidents.

(ii) Proportionality in relation to the aims pursued

35. The Government submitted that although the authorities had not recognised the applicant Church they acted in a spirit of tolerance and permitted it to continue its activities without hindrance. In particular, its members could meet, pray together and manage assets. As evidence, they cited the numerous activities of the applicant Church.

36. The Court notes that, under Law no. 979-XII of 24 March 1992, only religions recognised by a government decision may be practised in Moldova. In particular, only a recognised denomination has legal personality (sec. 24), may produce and sell specific liturgical objects (sec. 35) and engage clergy and employees (sec. 44). In addition, associations whose aims are wholly or partly religious are subject to the obligations arising from the legislation on religious denominations (sec. 21).

That being so, the Court notes that in the absence of recognition the applicant Church may neither organise itself nor operate. Lacking legal personality, it cannot bring legal proceedings to protect its assets, which are indispensable for worship, while its members cannot meet to carry on religious activities without contravening the legislation on religious denominations.

As regards the tolerance allegedly shown by the government towards the applicant Church and its members, the Court cannot regard such tolerance as a substitute for recognition, since recognition alone is capable of conferring rights on those concerned.

The Court further notes that on occasion the applicants have not been able to defend themselves against acts of intimidation, since the authorities have fallen back on the excuse that only legal activities are entitled to legal protection (see par. 56, 57 and 84 above).

Lastly, it notes that when the authorities recognised other liturgical associations they did not apply the criteria which they used in order to refuse to recognise the applicant Church and that no justification has been put forward by the Government for this difference in treatment.

37. In conclusion, the Court considers that the refusal to recognise the applicant Church has such consequences for the applicants' freedom of religion that it cannot be regarded as proportionate to the legitimate aim pursued or, accordingly, as necessary in a democratic society, and that there has been a violation of art. 9 of the Convention.

II. Alleged violation of Art. 14 of the convention taken in conjunction with Art. 9

38. The applicant Church further submitted that it was the victim of discrimination on account of the authorities' unjustified refusal to recognise it, whereas they had recognised other Orthodox Churches and had also recognised several different associations which all claimed allegiance to a single religion. It relied on art. 14 of the Convention, which provides:

„The enjoyment of the rights and freedoms set forth in [the] Convention shall be secured without discrimination on any ground such as sex, race, colour, language, religion, political or other opinion, national or social origin, association with a national minority, property, birth or other status."

39. According to the Government, as the Orthodox Christian religion had been recognised in the form of the Metropolitan Church of Moldova, there was no justification for recognising in addition the applicant Church, which also claimed allegiance to the Orthodox Christian religion. The applicant Church was not a new denomination but a schismatic group whose beliefs and liturgy did not differ in any way from those of the Metropolitan Church of Moldova. The Government admitted that the Orthodox Eparchy of Chişinău, which was attached to the Russian Orthodox Church of the Old Liturgy, whose head office was in Moscow, had been recognised even though it was not a new denomination, but submitted that the difference in treatment was based on an ethnic criterion, since the adherents and clergy of the Orthodox Eparchy of Chişinău were all of Russian origin.

40. The applicants submitted that the reason given to the applicant Church for refusing to recognise it was neither reasonable nor objective, because when the authorities recognised other denominations they had not applied the criteria of believers' ethnic origins or the newness of the denomination. They pointed out, for instance, that the authorities had recognised two Adventist Churches and two Jewish associations, which were not organised along ethnic lines.

41. The Court considers that the allegations relating to art. 14 of the Convention amount to a repetition of those submitted under art. 9. Accordingly, there is no cause to examine them separately.

For these reasons, the Court unanimously
1. *Holds that there has been a violation of art. 9 of the Convention;*
2. *Holds that it is not necessary to examine the case also from the stand-point of art. 14 of the Convention taken in conjunction with art. 9.*

3. Europäischer Gerichtshof

71

1. Da die Einschränkungen des Grundsatzes der Freizügigkeit der Arbeitnehmer, die der Staat aus Gründen der öffentlichen Ordnung, Sicherheit und Gesundheit einführen kann, einer gerichtlichen Nachprüfung zugänglich sind, hindert der Vorbehalt in Abs. 3 nicht, dass die Bestimmungen des Art. 48 den einzelnen Rechte verleihen, die sie gerichtlich geltend machen können und die die innerstaatlichen Gerichte zu wahren haben.

2. Mit der den Richtlinien durch Art. 189 zuerkannten verbindlichen Wirkung wäre es unvereinbar, grundsätzlich auszuschließen, dass betroffene Personen sich auf die durch die Richtlinie auferlegte Verpflichtung berufen können. Insbesondere in den Fällen, in denen etwa die Gemeinschaftsbehörden die Mitgliedstaaten durch Richtlinie zu einem bestimmten Verhalten verpflichten, würde die nützliche Wirkung („effet utile") einer solchen Maßnahme abgeschwächt, wenn die einzelnen sich vor Gericht hierauf nicht berufen und die staatlichen Gerichte sie nicht als Bestandteil des Gemeinschaftsrechts berücksichtigen könnten. Art. 177, wonach die staatlichen Gerichte befugt sind, den Gerichtshof mit der Gültigkeit und Auslegung aller Handlungen der Organe ohne Unterschied zu befassen, setzt im Übrigen voraus, dass die einzelnen sich vor diesen Gerichten auf die genannten Handlungen berufen können.

Es ist daher in jedem einzelnen Fall zu prüfen, ob die Bestimmung, um die es geht, nach Rechtsnatur, Systematik und Wortlaut geeignet ist, unmittelbare Wirkungen in den Rechtsbeziehungen zwischen den Mitgliedstaaten und den einzelnen zu begründen.

3. Art. 3 Abs. 1 der Richtlinie Nr. 64/221 des Rates vom 25.2.1964 „zur Koordinierung der Sondervorschriften für die Einreise und den Aufenthalt von Ausländern, soweit sie aus Gründen der öffentlichen Ordnung, Sicherheit oder Gesundheit gerechtfertigt sind," begründet Rechte der einzelnen, welche diese in einem Mitgliedstaat gerichtlich geltend machen können und welche die innerstaatlichen Gerichte zu wahren haben.

4. Der Begriff der öffentlichen Ordnung ist im Gemeinschaftsrecht, namentlich wenn er eine Ausnahme von einem wesentlichen Grundsatz des Gemeinschaftsrechts rechtfertigt, eng zu verstehen; daher darf seine Tragweite nicht von jedem Mitgliedstaat einseitig ohne Nachprüfung durch die Organe der Gemeinschaft bestimmt werden. Dennoch können die besonderen Umstände, die möglicherweise die Berufung auf den Begriff der öffentlichen Ordnung rechtfertigen, von Land zu Land und im zeitlichen Wechsel verschieden sein, so dass insoweit den zuständigen innerstaatlichen Behörden ein Beurteilungsspielraum innerhalb der durch den Vertrag gesetzten Grenzen zuzubilligen ist.

5. Art. 48 EWG-Vertrag und Art. 3 Abs. 1 der Richtlinie Nr. 64/221 müssen dahin ausgelegt werden, dass ein Mitgliedstaat, der aus Gründen der öffentlichen Ordnung gerechtfertigte Beschränkungen geltend macht, als persönliches Verhalten des Betroffenen berücksichtigen darf, dass dieser einer Vereinigung oder Organisation (hier: Scientology) angehört, deren Betätigung von dem Mitgliedstaat als eine Gefahr für die Gesellschaft angesehen wird, ohne indessen verboten zu sein; dies gilt auch dann, wenn den eigenen Staatsangehörigen dieses Staates, die eine vergleichbare Beschäftigung aufnehmen wollen, wie sie der Staatsangehörige eines anderen Mitgliedstaats bei denselben Vereinigungen oder Organisationen anstrebt, keine entsprechenden Beschränkungen auferlegt werden.

EuGH, Urteil vom 4. Dezember 1974 - Rs. 41/74
(van Duyn ./. Home Office/Vereinigtes Königreich)[1] -

TATBESTAND

I. Sachverhalt und schriftliches Verfahren

[1] Bei der Church of Scientology handelt es sich um eine in den Vereinigten Staaten von Amerika niedergelassene Vereinigung, die sich im Vereinigten Königreich über eine Bildungsstätte in East Grinstead, Sussex, betätigt. Die britische Regierung sieht in der Betätigung der Church of Scientology einen Verstoß gegen die öffentliche Ordnung. Am 25.7.1968 erklärte der Minister of Health (Gesundheitsminister) vor dem Parlament, die Regierung sei zu der Überzeugung gelangt, dass Scientology sozialschädlich sei. Diese Erklärung enthielt u.a. folgende Bemerkungen:

„Scientology ist ein pseudo-philosophischer Kult ... Die Regierung ist nach Auswertung aller verfügbaren Quellen zu der Überzeugung gekommen, dass Scientology sozialschädlich ist. Sie entfremdet Familienmitglieder untereinander und unterstellt allen ihren Gegnern schmutzige und entehrende Beweggründe; ihre autoritären Grundsätze und Praktiken stellen eine potentielle Bedrohung für Persönlichkeit und Wohlbefinden derjenigen dar, die so irregeführt sind, dass sie ihre Anhänger werden; insbesondere können ihre Methoden zu einer ernsthaften Gefahr für die Gesundheit derjenigen werden, die sich ihnen unterwerfen. Es gibt Beweise dafür, dass jetzt auch Kinder indoktriniert werden. Nach geltendem Recht gibt es keine Grundlage für ein Verbot der Ausübung der Scientology; die Regierung ist jedoch zu dem Ergebnis gekommen, dass dieser Kult so anstößig ist, dass es angezeigt erscheint, alle in ihrer Macht liegenden Schritte zu ergreifen, um sein Anwachsen zu zügeln ... Ausländer kommen ins Land, um Sciento-

---

[1] Amtl. Leitsätze. Slg. 1974, 1337; EuR 1976, 47.

logy zu studieren und um an dem sogenannten College in East Grinstead zu arbeiten. Die Regierung ist nach geltendem Recht in der Lage, dies zu verhindern ..., und hat beschlossen, dies zu tun. Ab sofort werden folgende Maßnahmen ergriffen ...

(e) Arbeitserlaubnisse und Beschäftigungsnachweise werden für die Tätigkeit an einer Scientology-Einrichtung an Ausländer ... nicht mehr ausgegeben."

Es gibt keine gesetzlichen Beschränkungen (abgesehen von einigen unerheblichen Ausnahmen) für die Ausübung der Scientology im Vereinigten Königreich durch britische Staatsbürger, die Mitglieder der Church of Scientology werden oder in ihren Dienst treten wollen. *[2]* Fräulein van Duyn ist Niederländerin. Mit Schreiben vom 4.5.1973 wurde ihr eine Stelle als Sekretärin bei der Church of Scientology an der Bildungsstätte in East Grinstead angeboten. Am 9.5.1973 kam sie mit der Absicht, dieses Stellenangebot anzunehmen, auf dem Flughafen Gatwick an, wo sie von einem Einwanderungsbeamten befragt und ihr die Einreise versagt wurde. Bei ihrer Befragung stellte sich heraus, dass sie in einer Scientology-Einrichtung in Amsterdam sechs Monate lang gearbeitet hatte, eine praktizierende Scientologistin war und beabsichtigte, in einer Scientology-Einrichtung im Vereinigten Königreich zu arbeiten.

Der Grund für die Versagung der Einreiseerlaubnis lautet, wie aus der von dem Einwanderungsbeamten an Fräulein van Duyn ausgehändigten „Versagung der Einreiseerlaubnis" hervorgeht: „Sie haben um die Erlaubnis zur Einreise ins Vereinigte Königreich nachgesucht, um in die Dienste der Church of Scientology zu treten. Der Secretary of State (Innenminister) hält es jedoch für unerwünscht, Personen die Einreise ins Vereinigte Königreich zu gestatten, die für diese Organisation tätig sind oder in ihren Diensten stehen."

Die Befugnis, die Einreise in das Vereinigte Königreich zu gestatten oder zu versagen, steht dem Einwanderungsbeamten gemäß Abschnitt 4 (1) des Immigration Act 1971 zu. Der Einwanderungsbeamte hat die Einreise in Übereinstimmung mit der Regierungspolitik und gemäß Art. 65 der einschlägigen Immigration Rules for Control of Entry versagt, die im Vereinigten Königreich Gesetzeskraft besitzen. Art. 65 lautet:

„Jedem, außer der Ehefrau oder einem Kind unter 18 Jahren einer im Vereinigten Königreich wohnhaften Person, kann die Einreise aus Gründen des öffentlichen Wohls versagt werden, wenn a) der Secretary of State entsprechende Weisungen erteilt hat oder b) aus dem Einwanderungsbeamten verfügbaren Informationen die Versagung der Einreiseerlaubnis aus diesem Grunde berechtigt erscheint - wenn beispielsweise nach Charakter, Führung oder Verbindungen des Reisenden die Erteilung der Einreiseerlaubnis unerwünscht ist."

3. Unter Berufung auf die Vorschriften des Gemeinschaftsrechts über die Freizügigkeit der Arbeitnehmer, insbesondere auf Art. 48 EWG-

Vertrag, auf die Verordnung Nr. 1612/68 und auf Art. 3 der Richtlinie 64/221 („Bei Maßnahmen der öffentlichen Ordnung oder Sicherheit darf ausschließlich das persönliche Verhalten der in Betracht kommenden Einzelperson ausschlaggebend sein") macht die Klägerin des Ausgangsverfahrens geltend, die Versagung der Einreiseerlaubnis sei rechtswidrig gewesen; sie beantragt, der High Court möge feststellen, dass sie berechtigt ist, sich zur Ausübung unselbstständiger Arbeit im Vereinigten Königreich aufzuhalten, und Anspruch auf die Erlaubnis zur Einreise ins Vereinigte Königreich hat.

Vor der weiteren Entscheidung hat der High Court das Verfahren ausgesetzt und dem Gerichtshof nach Art. 177 EWG-Vertrag folgende Fragen zur Vorabentscheidung vorgelegt:

1. Gilt Art. 48 des Vertrages zur Gründung der Europäischen Wirtschaftsgemeinschaft unmittelbar, so dass er Einzelpersonen Rechte verleiht, die sie bei den Gerichten eines Mitgliedstaats geltend machen können?

2. Gilt die am 25.2.1964 gemäß dem Vertrag zur Gründung der Europäischen Wirtschaftsgemeinschaft erlassene Richtlinie 64/221 unmittelbar, so dass sie Einzelpersonen Rechte verleiht, die sie bei den Gerichten eines Mitgliedstaats geltend machen können?

3. Hat ein Mitgliedstaat nach richtiger Auslegung des Art. 48 des Vertrages zur Gründung der Europäischen Wirtschaftsgemeinschaft und des Art. 3 der Richtlinie 64/221/EWG, wenn er eine Maßnahme der öffentlichen Ordnung oder Sicherheit ausschließlich auf das persönliche Verhalten der in Betracht kommenden Einzelperson stützen darf, das Recht, als persönliches Verhalten zu berücksichtigen:

a) dass die betroffene Einzelperson einer Vereinigung oder Organisation angehört oder angehört hat, deren Tätigkeit der Mitgliedstaat als dem öffentlichen Interesse zuwiderlaufend betrachtet, ohne dass sie jedoch in diesem Staat ungesetzlich wäre;

b) dass die betroffene Einzelperson beabsichtigt, in dem Mitgliedstaat in die Dienste einer solchen Vereinigung oder Organisation zu treten, wenn gleichzeitig gegenüber den Angehörigen des Mitgliedstaats, die vergleichbare Tätigkeiten bei einer solchen Vereinigung oder Organisation aufnehmen möchten, keine Beschränkungen bestehen?

II. Beim Gerichtshof eingereichte schriftliche Erklärungen

(...)

Zur dritten Frage

Der erste Teil der Frage unterstellt nach Ansicht der *Klägerin des Ausgangsverfahrens* eine Organisation, die sich in dem Mitgliedstaat in erlaubter Weise betätigt. Die Frage beruhe nicht notwendigerweise auf der Annahme, dass die betreffende Einzelperson beabsichtigt, ihre Mitgliedschaft fortzusetzen. Ihre frühere Mitgliedschaft reiche vielmehr aus. Hierzu trägt Fräulein van Duyn vor, selbst wenn jemand Mitglied einer illegalen Organisation gewesen und wegen seiner damit zusammenhängenden Tätigkeiten strafrechtlich verurteilt worden sei, so reiche dieser Umstand nach Art. 3 Abs. *2* der Richtlinie *64/221* für sich allein nicht aus, den Erlass von ordnungspolizeilichen Maßnahmen durch den Mitgliedstaat mit dem Ziel der Ausweisung zu rechtfertigen.

Gehöre jemand lediglich einer erlaubten Organisation an, ohne sich notwendigerweise an ihrer Tätigkeit zu beteiligen, so kann darin nach Ansicht von Fräulein Duyn kein „Verhalten" erblickt werden, denn Verhalten bedeute „Tätigkeit". Auch könne die Tätigkeit der fraglichen Organisation dem einzelnen nicht bloß deshalb „persönlich" zugerechnet werden, weil er passives Mitglied der Organisation sei oder gewesen sei. Die gegenteilige Auffassung würde bedeuten, dass ein einzelner durch einen Mitgliedstaat lediglich aus dem Grund zurückgewiesen werden könnte, weil er in ferner Vergangenheit einmal für eine kurze Zeit in seinem eigenen Mitgliedstaat vollkommen rechtmäßig Mitglied einer etwas extremen politischen oder religiösen Organisation gewesen ist.

Fräulein van Duyn bemerkt zum zweiten Teil der Frage, dass es sich bei der Freizügigkeit um einen der wesentlichen Vertragsgrundsätze handle und Art. 7 jede Diskriminierung aus Gründen der Staatsangehörigkeit verbiete. Ausnahmen zu diesen Grundsätzen seien eng auszulegen.

Die Frage nehme eine Diskriminierung aus Gründen der Staatsangehörigkeit an und gehe von der Sachlage aus, dass ein einzelner, dessen Verhalten in der Vergangenheit einwandfrei gewesen sei, sich in einen Mitgliedstaat begeben wolle, um dort für eine Organisation zu arbeiten, in deren Dienste die Angehörigen dieses Mitgliedstaats völlig frei eintreten können. Halte ein Mitgliedstaat eine Organisation für mit dem öffentlichen Wohl unvereinbar, so werde er vor eine einfache Entscheidung gestellt: Entweder erlasse er - ohne seine eigenen Staatsangehörigen auszunehmen - ein allgemeines Verbot, in den Dienst dieser Organisation zu treten, oder er dulde eine solche Tätigkeit bei Staatsangehörigen eines anderen Mitgliedstaats in gleicher Weise wie bei seinen eigenen.

Nach Ansicht der *Kommission* sind die Begriffe „öffentliche Ordnung" und „persönliches Verhalten" in Art. *48* Abs. 3 des Vertrages und in Art. 3 der Richtlinie *64/221* Begriffe des Gemeinschaftsrechts. Ihre Auslegung müsse primär nach dem Gemeinschaftsrecht erfolgen, Gesichtspunkte des innerstaatlichen Rechts seien nur für ihre Anwendung erheblich.

Könnte die Auslegung des Begriffs der „öffentlichen Ordnung" von jedem Mitgliedstaat eingegrenzt werden, dann erhielten in der Praxis die auf dem Grundsatz der Freizügigkeit der Arbeitnehmer beruhenden Verpflichtungen in den verschiedenen Mitgliedstaaten einen unterschiedlichen Inhalt. Nur bei einheitlicher Anwendung in allen Mitgliedstaaten könne die Freizügigkeit innerhalb der ganzen Gemeinschaft gewahrt werden. Es verstoße gegen den Vertrag, wenn ein Mitgliedstaat Arbeitnehmer aus einem anderen Mitgliedstaat aufnehme, obgleich seine eigenen Arbeitnehmer durch diesen mit Bezug auf die Anwendung der Vorschriften der öffentlichen Ordnung nicht gleichbehandelt würden.

Diskriminiere ein Mitgliedstaat aus Gründen der öffentlichen Ordnung die Angehörigen eines anderen Mitgliedstaats mit der Begründung, dass sie bei einer Organisation beschäftigt werden wollten, deren Tätigkeit nach seiner Auffassung dem öffentlichen Wohl zuwiderlaufe, obgleich er die Beschäftigung bei einer solchen Organisation seinen eigenen Staatsangehörigen nicht verbiete, so verstoße dies gegen Art. *48* Abs. *2* des Vertrages. Art. *3* Abs. 1 der Richtlinie besage eindeutig, dass bei Maßnahmen der öffentlichen Ordnung ausschließlich das persönliche Verhalten der in Betracht kommenden Einzelpersonen ausschlaggebend sein dürfe. Persönliches Verhalten, das bei Staatsangehörigen eines Mitgliedstaates nicht zu beanstanden sei, könne nach Gemeinschaftsrecht nicht dann beanstandet werden, wenn es von Angehörigen eines anderen Mitgliedstaats an den Tag gelegt werde.

Zu bedenken sei, dass Art. *3* den Mitgliedstaat hindere, sich als allgemeine Vorkehrung gegen eine etwaige Gefahr für die Allgemeinheit auf die öffentliche Ordnung zu berufen, um die Einreise zu versagen, wenn das persönliche Verhalten des Betreffenden weder früher noch im Augenblick der Einreise gegen die öffentliche Ordnung des Mitgliedstaats verstoßen habe. Die Mitgliedschaft in einer militanten im Gastland verbotenen Organisation könne zugegebenermaßen bei der Beurteilung des persönlichen Verhaltens zu berücksichtigen sein, um die Versagung der Einreise aus Gründen der öffentlichen Ordnung oder Sicherheit zu rechtfertigen.

Bei dem ersten Teil der Frage behandelt das *Vereinigte Königreich* drei Probleme. Das erste Problem sei, ob die frühere oder augenblickliche Zugehörigkeit einer Person zu einer Organisation als ein Teil ihres persönlichen Verhaltens angesehen werden könne. Das Vereinigte Königreich hält es für wichtig, dass ein Mitgliedstaat im Zusammenhang mit der öffentlichen Ordnung die Zugehörigkeit einer Person zu einer Vereinigung oder Organisation berücksichtigen dürfe. In geeigneten Fällen müsse der Mitgliedstaat berechtigt sein, diese Person auszuschließen, so zum Beispiel, wenn die Organisation aus Gründen der öffentlichen Ordnung für hinreichend unerwünscht angesehen werde und eine hinreichend enge Verbindung zwischen dieser Person und der Organisation bestehe.

Zweitens trägt das Vereinigte Königreich vor, eine aus Gründen der öffentlichen Ordnung erlassene Maßnahme, welche wegen der Zugehörigkeit zu einer Organisation die Einreise einer Person ausschließe, sei mit Art. *3* Abs. 1 vereinbar. Diese Bestimmung habe zwar Gruppenausweisungen verhindern und die innerstaatlichen Behörden verpflichten wollen, in jedem Einzelfall die persönlichen Umstände zu berücksichtigen. Trotzdem dürfe ein Mitgliedstaat auf die Zugehörigkeit zu einer Organisation abstellen und in geeigneten Fällen die betreffende Person wegen dieser Zugehörigkeit ausschließen. Ob dies in einem bestimmten Fall berechtigt sei, hänge davon ab, wie der Mitgliedstaat die Organisation beurteile.

In der Praxis seien die Verfahren zur Erteilung der Erlaubnis zur Einreise in einen Mitgliedstaat durch eine Vielzahl von Beamten zu handhaben. Von diesen könne nicht erwartet werden, dass sie über eine bestimmte Organisation alles das wüssten, was die Regierung wisse; daher müssten sie zwangsläufig nach Weisungen der Regierung handeln, welche die allgemeinen Grundsätze enthielten, nach denen die Beamten zu verfahren haben. Es sei unvermeidlich, dass derartige Weisungen auch bestimmte Organisationen betreffen könnten, die vielleicht nach Ansicht einer Regierung gegen das öffentliche Wohl verstießen.

Drittens meint das Vereinigte Königreich, die Tatsache, dass die Tätigkeit der Organisation in einem Mitgliedstaat zwar nicht illegal sei, aber doch als dem öffentlichen Wohl zuwiderlaufend angesehen werde, nehme dem Mitgliedstaat nicht das Recht, die Zugehörigkeit des einzelnen zu der Organisation in Rechnung zu stellen. Es müsse der Entscheidung der einzelnen Staaten überlassen bleiben, ob sie die Tätigkeit einer Organisation oder die Organisation selber verböten. Nur der Staat sei zu einer solchen Entscheidung befugt, und er werde sie im Hinblick auf die besondere Sachlage fällen. Wie allgemein bekannt, zeigt das Vereinigte Königreich auf seinem Hoheitsgebiet gegenüber Organisationen im beträchtlichen Maße Toleranz. Die am 25.7.1968 im Parlament abgegebene Stellungnahme habe die Gründe erläutert, warum das Vereinigte Königreich die Betätigung der Anhänger der Scientology als einen Verstoß gegen die öffentliche Ordnung erachte. Das Welthauptquartier dieser Bewegung befinde sich immer noch im Vereinigten Königreich, so dass die Scientology dem Vereinigten Königreich im besonderen Maße Sorge bereite.

Teil b der Frage wirft nach Ansicht des Vereinigten Königreichs zwei Probleme auf.

Erstens, ob es dem persönlichen Verhalten einer Person zuzurechnen sei, dass sie in den Dienst einer solchen Organisation treten wolle. Nach Meinung des Vereinigten Königreichs ist eine derartige Absicht ein ganz wesentlicher Aspekt des persönlichen Verhaltens.

Zweitens, ob es dem Mitgliedstaat verwehrt sei, diese Absicht zu berücksichtigen, weil seine eigenen Staatsangehörigen, die eine derartige Beschäftigung bei einer solchen Organisation aufnehmen wollen, keinen Beschränkungen unterliegen.

Das Vereinigte Königreich weist darauf hin, dass es bei der Einreise in einen Staat unvermeidlich eine gewisse Diskriminierung zugunsten der eigenen Staatsangehörigen geben müsse; denn einem solchen könne, wie erwünscht oder möglicherweise gesellschaftsschädlich seine Einreise auch sein möge, der Zugang zu seinem eigenen Staat nicht versagt werden. Der Staat sei völkerrechtlich verpflichtet, seine eigenen Staatsangehörigen wieder aufzunehmen. Das Vereinigte Königreich verweist unter anderem auf Art. 13 Ziffer 2 der Allgemeinen Erklärung der Menschenrechte, der besagt: „Jeder Mensch hat das Recht, jedes Land, einschließlich seines eigenen, zu verlassen sowie in sein Land zurückzukehren." So dürfe zum Beispiel ein Mitgliedstaat einem drogensüchtigen Angehörigen eines anderen Staates die Einreise verweigern, müsse aber gleichwohl einen Drogensüchtigen seiner eigenen Staatsangehörigkeit aufnehmen.

ENTSCHEIDUNGSGRÜNDE

1/3. Mit Beschluss ihres Vice-Chancellor vom 1.3.1974, beim Gerichtshof eingegangen am 13.6., hat die Chancery-Division des High Court of Justice nach Art. 177 EWG-Vertrag drei Fragen zur Auslegung einiger Vorschriften des Gemeinschaftsrechts auf dem Gebiet der Freizügigkeit der Arbeitnehmer vorgelegt. Diese Fragen sind in einem Rechtsstreit zwischen einer niederländischen Staatsangehörigen und dem Home Office aufgeworfen worden; der Niederländerin war die Genehmigung zur Einreise ins Vereinigte Königreich zu dem Zweck, eine Beschäftigung als Sekretärin bei der „Church of Scientology" zu übernehmen, versagt worden. Dies entsprach der Politik, welche die Regierung des Vereinigten Königreichs gegenüber dieser Organisation verfolgt, deren Praktiken sie für gesellschaftsschädlich hielt.

Zur ersten Frage

4. Mit der ersten Frage wird der Gerichtshof um eine Entscheidung darüber ersucht, ob Art. 48 EWG-Vertrag unmittelbar gilt, so dass er Einzelpersonen Rechte verleiht, die sie bei den Gerichten eines Mitgliedstaats geltend machen können.

(wird ausgeführt und bejaht)

Zur zweiten Frage

9/10. Die zweite Frage geht dahin, ob die Richtlinie des Rates vom 25.2.1964 (64/221) „zur Koordinierung der Sondervorschriften für die Einreise und den Aufenthalt von Ausländern, soweit sie aus Gründen der öffentlichen Ordnung, Sicherheit oder Gesundheit gerechtfertigt sind", unmittelbar gilt, so dass sie Einzelpersonen Rechte verleiht, die diese bei den Gerichten eines Mitgliedstaats geltend machen können. Nach dem Vorlagebeschluss geht es hier nur um Art. 3 Abs. 1 der Richtlinienbestimmung, wonach „bei Maßnahmen der öffentlichen Ordnung oder Sicherheit ... ausschließlich das persönliche Verhalten der in Betracht kommenden Einzelperson ausschlaggebend sein [darf]".

(wird ausgeführt)

15. Die vorgelegte Frage ist also dahin zu beantworten, dass Art. 3 Abs. 1 der Richtlinie 64/221 des Rates vom 25.2.1964 Rechte der einzelnen begründet, welche diese in einem Mitgliedstaat gerichtlich geltend machen können und welche die innerstaatlichen Gerichte zu wahren haben.

Zur dritten Frage

Mit der dritten Frage wird der Gerichtshof ersucht zu entscheiden, ob bei richtiger Anwendung von Art. 48 EWG-Vertrag und Art. 3 der Richtlinie 64/221 ein Mitgliedstaat,

> *„wenn er eine Maßnahme der öffentlichen Ordnung oder Sicherheit ausschließlich auf das persönliche Verhalten der in Betracht kommenden Person stützen darf, das Recht [hat], als persönliches Verhalten zu berücksichtigen:*
> *a) dass die betroffene Einzelperson einer Vereinigung oder Organisation angehört oder angehört hat, deren Tätigkeit der Mitgliedstaat als dem öffentlichen Interesse zuwiderlaufend betrachtet, ohne dass sie jedoch in diesem Staat ungesetzlich wäre;*
> *b) dass die betroffene Einzelperson beabsichtigt, in dem Mitgliedstaat in die Dienste einer solchen Vereinigung oder Organisation zu treten, wenn gleichzeitig gegenüber den Angehörigen des Mitgliedstaats, die vergleichbare Tätigkeiten bei einer solchen Vereinigung oder Organisation aufnehmen möchten, keine Beschränkungen bestehen."*

17. Zunächst ist zu prüfen, ob in der bloßen Tatsache, dass jemand einer Vereinigung oder einer Organisation angehört, ein persönliches Verhalten im Sinne von Art. 3 der Richtlinie 64/221 liegen kann. Wenn auch eine frühere Mitgliedschaft im allgemeinen nicht ausreichen dürfte, um dem Betroffenen die Freizügigkeit innerhalb der Gemeinschaft zu versagen, so kann doch eine bestehende Mitgliedschaft, die eine Beteiligung an den Tätigkeiten der Vereinigung oder Organisation sowie eine Identifizierung mit ihren Zielen und Absichten widerspiegelt, als freiwilliges Tun und damit als Teil des persönlichen Verhaltens im Sinne der genannten Vorschrift gewertet werden.

18/19. In der Vorlagefrage wird sodann das Problem aufgeworfen, wie der Umstand zu werten ist, dass die Tätigkeit der fraglichen Organisation, die nach Ansicht des Mitgliedstaats dem öffentlichen Interesse zuwiderläuft, nach dem innerstaatlichen Recht nicht verboten ist. Der Begriff der öffentlichen Ordnung ist im Gemeinschaftsrecht, namentlich, wenn er eine Ausnahme von dem wesentlichen Grundsatz der Freizügigkeit der Arbeitnehmer rechtfertigt, eng zu verstehen; daher darf seine Tragweite nicht von jedem Mitgliedstaat einseitig ohne Nachprüfung durch die Organe der Gemeinschaft bestimmt werden. Dennoch können die besonderen Umstände, die möglicherweise die Berufung auf den Begriff der öffentlichen Ordnung rechtfertigen, von Land zu Land und im zeitlichen

Wechsel verschieden sein, so dass insoweit den zuständigen innerstaatlichen Behörden ein Beurteilungsspielraum innerhalb der durch den Vertrag gesetzten Grenzen zuzubilligen ist. Haben die zuständigen Behörden eines Mitgliedstaats ihre Haltung gegenüber der Betätigung einer bestimmten Organisation eindeutig festgelegt und diese Betätigung als eine Gefahr für die Gesellschaft bezeichnet, haben sie ferner Verwaltungsmaßnahmen ergriffen, um die genannte Betätigung zu bekämpfen, so ist der Mitgliedstaat also nicht verpflichtet, sie auch noch gesetzlich zu verbieten, um sich auf die öffentliche Ordnung berufen zu können, wenn eine solche Maßnahme den Umständen nach unzweckmäßig erscheint.

20. Schließlich wirft die Vorlagefrage noch das Problem auf, ob ein Mitgliedstaat sich aus Gründen der öffentlichen Ordnung dagegen wehren darf, dass in seinem Hoheitsgebiet ein Staatsangehöriger aus einem anderen Mitgliedstaat bei einer Vereinigung oder Organisation eine entgeltliche Beschäftigung aufnimmt, obgleich seine eigenen Staatsangehörigen keiner vergleichbaren Beschränkung unterliegen.

21/23. Der Vertrag anerkennt zwar den Grundsatz der Freizügigkeit der Arbeitnehmer ohne Diskriminierung zwischen den Angehörigen der einzelnen Mitgliedstaaten, fügt aber in Art. 48 Abs. 3 den aus diesem Grundsatz fließenden Rechten einen Vorbehalt an, der aus Gründen der öffentlichen Ordnung, Sicherheit und Gesundheit gerechtfertigte Beschränkungen betrifft. Danach unterliegen diesem Vorbehalt unter anderem das Recht, sich um tatsächlich angebotene Stellen zu bewerben, das Recht, sich zu diesem Zweck im Hoheitsgebiet der Mitgliedstaaten frei zu bewegen, sowie das Recht, sich in einem Mitgliedstaat aufzuhalten, um dort eine Beschäftigung auszuüben. Der Vorbehalt bewirkt also, dass einem Staatsangehörigen eines Mitgliedstaats die Einreise in das Hoheitsgebiet eines anderen Mitgliedstaats oder der Aufenthalt in diesem Gebiet versagt werden kann, wenn die Voraussetzungen des Vorbehalts gegeben sind. Andererseits besagt ein völkerrechtlicher Grundsatz, den der EWG-Vertrag in den Beziehungen der Mitgliedstaaten zueinander sicherlich nicht außer Acht lassen wollte, dass ein Staat seinen eigenen Staatsangehörigen die Einreise in sein Hoheitsgebiet oder den Aufenthalt in diesem nicht versagen darf. Sonach kann ein Mitgliedstaat aus Gründen der öffentlichen Ordnung gegebenenfalls einem Angehörigen eines anderen Mitgliedstaats die Rechtsvorteile aus der Anwendung des Grundsatzes der Freizügigkeit der Arbeitnehmer im Hinblick auf die Ausübung einer bestimmten entgeltlichen Beschäftigung versagen, obwohl er seinen eigenen Staatsangehörigen keine vergleichbare Beschränkung auferlegt.

24. Auf die Vorlagefrage ist also zu antworten: Art. 48 EWG-Vertrag und Art. 3 Abs. 1 der Richtlinie 64/221 müssen dahin ausgelegt werden, dass ein Mitgliedstaat, der aus Gründen der öffentlichen Ordnung gerechtfertigte Beschränkungen geltend macht, als persönliches Verhalten

des Betroffenen berücksichtigen darf, dass dieser einer Vereinigung oder Organisation angehört, deren Betätigung von dem Mitgliedstaat als eine Gefahr für die Gesellschaft angesehen wird, ohne indessen verboten zu sein; dies gilt auch dann, wenn den eigenen Staatsangehörigen dieses Staates, die eine vergleichbare Beschäftigung aufnehmen wollen, wie sie der Staatsangehörige eines anderen Mitgliedstaats bei denselben Vereinigungen oder Organisationen anstrebt, keine entsprechenden Beschränkungen auferlegt werden.

(...)

TENOR

Aus diesen Gründen hat der Gerichtshof auf die ihm vom High Court of Justice gemäß Beschluss vom 1.3.1974 vorgelegten Fragen für Recht erkannt:

1. Art. 48 EWG-Vertrag erzeugt unmittelbare Wirkungen in den Rechtsordnungen der Mitgliedstaaten und verleiht den einzelnen Rechte, welche die innerstaatlichen Gerichte zu wahren haben.

2. Art. 3 Abs. 1 der Richtlinie 64/221 des Rates vom 25.2.1964 „zur Koordinierung der Sondervorschriften für die Einreise und den Aufenthalt von Ausländern, soweit sie aus Gründen der öffentlichen Ordnung, Sicherheit oder Gesundheit gerechtfertigt sind", begründet Rechte der einzelnen, welche diese in einem Mitgliedstaat gerichtlich geltend machen können und welche die innerstaatlichen Gerichte zu wahren haben.

3. Art. 48 EWG-Vertrag und Art. 3 Abs. 1 der Richtlinie 64/221 müssen dahin ausgelegt werden, dass ein Mitgliedstaat, der aus Gründen der öffentlichen Ordnung gerechtfertigte Beschränkungen geltend macht, als persönliches Verhalten des Betroffenen berücksichtigen darf, dass dieser einer Vereinigung oder Organisation angehört, deren Betätigung von dem Mitgliedstaat als eine Gefahr für die Gesellschaft angesehen wird, ohne indessen verboten zu sein; dies gilt auch dann, wenn den eigenen Staatsangehörigen dieses Staates, die eine vergleichbare Beschäftigung aufnehmen wollen, wie sie der Staatsangehörige eines anderen Mitgliedstaats bei denselben Vereinigungen oder Organisationen anstrebt, keine entsprechenden Beschränkungen auferlegt werden.

SCHLUSSANTRÄGE DES GENERALANWALTS VOM 13.11.1974
(Auszug)

I. Sachverhalt

(...)

Gegenstand der ersten Frage ist die unmittelbare Geltung von Art. 48 EWG Vertrag.

Die zweite Frage zielt dahin, ob auch die Richtlinie Nr. 64/221 des Rates unmittelbare Geltung in dem Sinne besitzt, dass sie Einzelpersonen Rechte verleiht, die sie in einem Mitgliedstaat gerichtlich geltend machen können.

Mit der dritten Frage wird um die Auslegung von Art. 48 EWG-Vertrag und von Art. 3 der Richtlinie ersucht. Der High Court will wissen, ob die zuständige Behörde eines Mitgliedstaats, die aus Gründen der öffentlichen Ordnung einen Gemeinschaftsangehörigen bei der Einreise zurückweist und dies mit dem persönlichen Verhalten des Betreffenden begründet, als persönliches Verhalten berücksichtigen darf:

a) dass der Betroffene einer Organisation angehört oder angehört hat, deren Tätigkeit die Regierung des Mitgliedstaats als dem öffentlichen Interesse zuwiderlaufend betrachtet, ohne dass sie jedoch in diesem Staat ungesetzlich wäre;

b) dass der Betroffene beabsichtigt, in dem Mitgliedstaat in die Dienste einer solchen Organisation zu treten, wenn gleichzeitig die Angehörigen des Mitgliedstaats, die vergleichbare Beschäftigungen aufnehmen möchten, keinen Beschränkungen unterliegen.

II. Erörterung

1. Unmittelbare Geltung von Art. 48 EWG-Vertrag

(wird ausgeführt und bejaht)

2. Unmittelbare Geltung der Richtlinie Nr. 64/221 des Rates

(wird ausgeführt und bejaht)

3. Öffentliche Sicherheit - Begriff des persönlichen Verhaltens

Damit kommen wir zur dritten Frage. Was ist unter einem „persönlichen Verhalten" zu verstehen, das ein Verbot zur Einreise in das Hoheitsgebiet eines Mitgliedstaats rechtfertigt? Wie lässt sich dieser Begriff definieren?

Über die reine Textanalyse hinaus wird die Lösung meines Erachtens von zwei Grundgedanken bestimmt:

- Zum einen gehört die Freizügigkeit der Arbeitnehmer zu den wesentlichen Grundsätzen des Vertrages, und das Verbot jeder auf der Staatsangehörigkeit beruhenden unterschiedlichen Behandlung von Arbeitnehmern der Mitgliedstaaten wird nur durch die in Art. 48 Abs. 3 abschließend aufgezählten Vorbehalte hinsichtlich der öffentlichen Ordnung, Sicherheit und Gesundheit eingeschränkt (EuGH 15.10.1969 - Ugliola, 15/69 - Slg. 1969, 368).

- Zum anderen gibt es zwar eine „öffentliche Ordnung der Gemeinschaft" in den Bereichen, in denen der Vertrag bezweckt oder bewirkt, dass Befugnisse, die früher die Mitgliedstaaten wahrgenommen haben, unmittelbar auf die Gemeinschaftsorgane übergehen, doch kann es sich dabei nur um eine öffentliche Ordnung im wirtschaftlichen Bereich handeln, die sich zum Beispiel auf die gemeinsamen Agrarmarktorganisationen, den Handel, den Gemeinsamen Zolltarif oder das Wettbewerbsrecht bezieht.

Dagegen sind meines Erachtens bei den gegenwärtigen tatsächlichen und rechtlichen Verhältnissen, vorbehaltlich der Regelungen, die sich in bestimmten Rechtsvorschriften der Gemeinschaft, wie der Richtlinie Nr. 64/221, finden, nur die Staaten befugt, die Maßnahmen zu erlassen, die der Schutz der öffentlichen Sicherheit auf ihrem Hoheitsgebiet verlangt, und zu entscheiden, wodurch diese Sicherheit gefährdet werden könnte.

Wenn auch, anders ausgedrückt, der allgemeine Vorbehalt der öffentlichen Ordnung, den sowohl Art. 48 als auch Art. 56 enthält, eine eng auszulegende begrenzte Ausnahmeregelung zu den Grundsätzen des Vertrages über die Freizügigkeit und die Niederlassungsfreiheit darstellt, so glaube ich dennoch im Gegensatz zur Kommission nicht, dass sich ein gemeinschaftsrechtlicher Begriff der öffentlichen Sicherheit herausarbeiten lässt. Dieser Begriff bleibt - zumindest im Augenblick - innerstaatlich, und das entspricht den tatsächlichen Gegebenheiten, da die Erfordernisse der öffentlichen Sicherheit von Land zu Land nach Ort und Zeit verschiedene sein können.

Anhand dieser Grundgedanken ist meines Erachtens die dritte Frage zu beantworten.

Zunächst ist zu klären, inwieweit sich der Begriff „persönliches Verhalten" auf die von dem innerstaatlichen Richter festgestellten Tatsachen anwenden lässt: nämlich auf die Mitgliedschaft eines Gemeinschaftsangehörigen in einer Organisation, deren Betätigung als für die öffentliche Ordnung schädlich angesehen wird, ohne jedoch verboten zu sein, sowie auf die Absicht, bei dieser Organisation eine Beschäftigung aufzunehmen, wobei zu berücksichtigen ist, dass die Angehörigen des Mitgliedstaats für diesen Fall keinen Beschränkungen unterliegen.

Diese Frage hat mich veranlasst, in der Akte des High Court nach Anhaltspunkten für ein besseres Verständnis der Tatsachen zu suchen, die Grund für die Zurückweisung der Klägerin des Ausgangsverfahrens waren.

Aus der Akte geht hervor, dass Fräulein van Duyn sich nicht nur erwiesenermaßen mit der Absicht nach England begab, eine Stelle als Sekretärin bei der Church of Scientology zu übernehmen, sondern dass sie bereits in den vorangegangenen sechs Monaten in den Niederlanden bei einer Einrichtung derselben Organisation gearbeitet hatte, ferner, dass sie die Scientology studiert und praktiziert hatte.

Sicherlich hat die Summe dieser Tatsachen, deren Richtigkeit ich na-
türlich nicht zu beurteilen habe, die britische Einwanderungsbehörde
veranlasst, Fräulein van Duyn die Einreise zu versagen.

Die Akte zeigt weiter, dass der Gesundheitsminister des Vereinigten
Königreichs 1968 in einer Erklärung vor dem Parlament die Meinung
vertrat:

„Scientology ist ein pseudo-philosophischer Kult", dessen Grundsätze
oder Praktiken nach Ansicht der britischen Regierung eine Gefahr sowohl für die öffentliche Sicherheit als auch für die Gesundheit seiner
Anhänger darstellen.

Der Minister teilte sodann die Entscheidung der Regierung mit, sich
im Rahmen ihrer Befugnisse der Tätigkeit dieser Organisation zu wider-
setzen. Wenn auch nach dem geltenden innerstaatlichen Recht die Ausübung der Scientology nicht verboten war, so konnte die Regierung we-
nigstens Ausländern die Einreise versagen, welche am Sitz der Church of
Scientology in England zu arbeiten beabsichtigten.

Es scheint, dass Fräulein van Duyn die Einreise in das Vereinigte Königreich gerade aufgrund dieser Politik versagt wurde, und zwar wegen
der Beziehungen, die sie bereits früher in den Niederlanden mit dieser
sogenannten „Kirche" unterhielt, sowie wegen der Tatsache, dass sie
praktizierende Anhängerin der Scientology war und beabsichtigte, eine
Beschäftigung in Saint Hill Manor aufzunehmen.

Bei diesem Stand der Dinge besteht meines Erachtens kein Zweifel
daran, dass die genannten Tatsachen insgesamt dem Begriff des „persönlichen Verhaltens" im Sinne von Art. 3 Abs. 1 der Richtlinie genügen und
dass die bloße Zugehörigkeit zur Church of Scientology - sei es auch nur
durch einen dazwischengeschobenen Arbeitsvertrag - ein Aspekt des persönlichen Verhaltens ist.

Wie ich bereits dargelegt habe, war Anlass für die fragliche Bestimmung im Wesentlichen die Sorge der Organe der Gemeinschaft, den Mitgliedstaaten den Erlass kollektiver polizeilicher Maßnahmen gegenüber
Gemeinschaftsangehörigen zu untersagen. Diese Bestimmung verlangt,
den Fall einer jeden Person einzeln zu prüfen, gegen die eine Entscheidung ergeht, die mit der Wahrung der öffentlichen Ordnung begründet
wird; die Bestimmung schließt ganz ohne Zweifel, wie hier geschehen,
eine gerichtliche Nachprüfung der Gründe einer solchen Entscheidung
durch die innerstaatlichen Gerichte ein, welche die Möglichkeit - oder in
bestimmten Fällen sogar die Pflicht - haben, wegen der Auslegung des
geltenden Gemeinschaftsrechts den Gerichtshof anzurufen.

In diesem Punkt - und nur in diesem Punkt - wird in dem fraglichen
Bereich die Zuständigkeit der Mitgliedstaaten durch die Richtlinie sicherlich beschränkt.

Als letztes bleibt zu untersuchen, ob die Regierung des Vereinigten
Königreichs, indem sie einem Staatsangehörigen der Gemeinschaft aus
den dargelegten Gründen die Einreise versagte, nicht gegen den Grund-

satz der Nichtdiskriminierung, der Gleichbehandlung mit den eigenen
Staatsangehörigen, verstoßen hat, der die notwendige Ergänzung zur
Freizügigkeit bildet und der, obgleich im Wesentlichen in Art. 7 des Vertrages geregelt, nach Art. 48 ausdrücklich auf die Freizügigkeit der Arbeitnehmer anwendbar ist.

Wenn auch die Church of Scientology nach Meinung der britischen Regierung sozialschädlich ist und folglich ihre Tätigkeiten als der öffentlichen Ordnung zuwiderlaufend angesehen werden, so steht doch fest,
dass diese Tätigkeiten auf dem Gebiet des Vereinigten Königreichs nicht
verboten sind und dass die eigenen Staatsangehörigen Scientology studieren und praktizieren sowie am Sitz der Organisation arbeiten dürfen.

Auf den ersten Blick liegt also eine Diskriminierung in der Behandlung der Staatsangehörigen der übrigen Mitgliedstaaten der Gemeinschaft, und zwar darin, dass ihnen nur deshalb verboten wird, in das britische Hoheitsgebiet einzureisen, weil sie in Saint Hill Manor Scientology
praktizieren und dort eine Beschäftigung übernehmen wollen.

Ich glaube aber nicht, dass diese Diskriminierung gegen den Vertrag
verstößt.

Der Vorbehalt der öffentlichen Ordnung und insbesondere der öffentlichen Sicherheit bewirkt, wie ich bereits dargelegt habe, dass die Mitgliedstaaten ihre Befugnisse in diesem Bereich behalten, jedoch verpflichtet sind, die Maßnahmen aus Gründen der öffentlichen Sicherheit
mit dem persönlichen Verhalten der Betroffenen zu begründen.

Die Mitgliedstaaten behalten aber, was die Feststellung einer Gefähr-
dung ihrer Sicherheit und die Zweckmäßigkeit der gebotenen Maßnahmen anbelangt, eine Befugnis, deren Ausübung den Gleichbehandlungs-
grundsatz nicht berührt, es sei denn, sie machen von ihr zu anderen als
den vorgesehenen Zwecken Gebrauch, zum Beispiel mit dem Ziel, wirtschaftlichen Schutz zu gewähren.

Wie aus den Erklärungen der britischen Regierung hervorgeht, ist -
und war - es nach dem innerstaatlichen Recht nicht möglich, die Sciento-
logy-Vereinigung zu verbieten. Dies ist die Folge eines besonders libera-
len Systems. In anderen Mitgliedstaaten, deren Regierungen etwa die
Tätigkeiten der fraglichen Organisation als der öffentlichen Ordnung
zuwiderlaufend ansähen, könnte sicherlich anders verfahren werden.
Soweit aber die Regierung des Vereinigten Königreichs über die rechtlichen Mittel verfügt zu verhindern, dass Ausländer, seien es auch Ge-
meinschaftsangehörige, auf britischem Hoheitsgebiet die Schar der
Scientology-Anhänger verstärken, kann sie meines Erachtens so vorge-
hen, wie sie es getan hat, ohne dadurch im Sinne von Art. 48 EWG-
Vertrag zu diskriminieren. Die britische Regierung handelt so im Rahmen der staatlichen Befugnisse, die der Vorbehalt der öffentlichen Ordnung in der genannten Bestimmung jedem Mitgliedstaat einräumt.

Daher schlage ich vor, für Recht zu erkennen:
1 *Sowohl Art. 48 des Vertrages als auch Art. 3 Abs. 1 der Richtlinie Nr. 64/221 des Rates gelten unmittelbar in der Rechtsordnung eines jeden Mitgliedstaats und erzeugen Rechte der einzelnen, welche die innerstaatlichen Behörden zu wahren haben.*
2. *Es fällt unter den Begriff des „persönlichen Verhaltens", das geeignet ist, eine Maßnahme der öffentlichen Ordnung oder Sicherheit im Sinne der erwähnten Bestimmung der Richtlinie 64/221 zu rechtfertigen, wenn jemand einer Organisation angehört oder angehört hat, deren Betätigung ein Mitgliedstaat als der öffentlichen Ordnung zuwiderlaufend ansieht; dies gilt selbst dann, wenn diese Betätigung auf dem Hoheitsgebiet dieses Mitgliedstaats nach innerstaatlichem Recht nicht verboten ist.*
3. *Es fällt auch unter den Begriff des „persönlichen Verhaltens", wenn sich jemand in das Hoheitsgebiet des genannten Mitgliedstaats begibt, um dort bei einer Organisation zu arbeiten, deren Betätigung als der öffentlichen Ordnung und Sicherheit zuwiderlaufend angesehen wird, obgleich die Staatsangehörigen dieses Staates, die in den Dienst der genannten Organisation treten wollen, keinen Beschränkungen unterliegen.*

72

1. Bei einem Auswahlverfahren aufgrund von Prüfungen gebietet der Gleichheitssatz, dass die Prüfungen für alle Bewerber unter den gleichen Bedingungen stattfinden, und im Falle schriftlicher Prüfungen ist es wegen der praktischen Schwierigkeit, die Arbeiten der Bewerber zu vergleichen, notwendig, dass diese Prüfungen für alle gleich sind. Es ist deshalb sehr wichtig, dass alle Bewerber die schriftlichen Prüfungen zum gleichen Zeitpunkt ablegen, Im Hinblick auf dieses Erfordernis ist das Interesse der Bewerber daran zu beurteilen, dass die Prüfungen nicht an einem Tage stattfinden, der ihnen ungelegen ist.

2. Teilt ein Bewerber der Anstellungsbehörde mit, dass ihn religiöse Gebote daran hindern, sich an bestimmten Tagen zu Prüfungen einzufinden, so muss die Behörde dem Rechnung tragen und sich bei der Terminbestimmung für die Prüfungen bemühen, diese Daten zu vermeiden. Setzt der Bewerber dagegen die Anstellungsbehörde nicht rechtzeitig von seinen Schwierigkeiten in Kenntnis, so kann diese es ablehnen, einen anderen Termin vorzuschlagen, insbesondere wenn andere Bewerber bereits zu den Prüfungen geladen worden sind.

Art. 9, 14 EMRK
EuGH, Urteil vom 27. Oktober 1976 - Rs. 130/75
(Prais ./. Rat der Europäischen Gemeinschaften)[1] -

SACHVERHALT

Mit Schreiben vom 23.4.1975 hat sich die Klägerin, eine britische Staatsangehörige, auf eine vom Generalsekretariat des Rates der Europäischen Gemeinschaften ausgeschriebene Stelle einer juristischen Übersetzerin beworben. Unter dem 23.4.1975 wurde sie - gleichzeitig mit weiteren Bewerbern - zur Teilnahme an der schriftlichen Einstellungsprüfung auf Freitag, den 16.5.1975, geladen.
Mit Schreiben vom 25.4.1975 bat die Klägerin, zu einem anderen Prüfungstermin geladen zu werden, weil sie jüdischen Glaubens sei und am 16.5., dem ersten Tag des jüdischen Festes Schawuot (Pfingsten), weder reisen noch schreiben dürfe. Der Beklagte lehnte unter dem 5.5.1975 das Terminsverlegungsgesuch ab und führte zur Begründung aus, es sei unbedingt notwendig, dass alle Bewerber am gleichen Tag die gleiche Prüfung ablegten; die Vorbereitungen für den Prüfungstermin am 16.5. seien bereits abgeschlossen.
Mit ihrer nach erfolgloser Beschwerde (complaint gem. Art. 90 Abs. 2 Beamtenstatut) erhobenen Klage gegen den Rat begehrte die Klägerin u.a. die Aufhebung der Entscheidung des Rates vom 5.5.1975 mit der ihr verwehrt worden war, die Einstellungsprüfung an einem anderen Tag abzulegen. Ihren. ursprünglich gestellten Antrag, die Ergebnisse des Auswahlverfahrens vom 16.5.1975 für ungültig zu erklären, hatte die Klägerin in der mündlichen Verhandlung zurückgenommen.
Der Gerichtshof weist die Klägerin mit der Klage ab.

AUS DEN GRÜNDEN

[6/9] Die Klägerin macht zunächst geltend, die Ablehnung ihres Antrags habe bewirkt, dass sie wegen ihrer religiösen Überzeugungen an der Teilnahme am Auswahlverfahren gehindert worden sei, und zwar unter Verletzung von Art. 27 Abs. 2 des Statuts, dem zufolge die Beamten ohne Rücksicht auf Rasse, Glauben oder Geschlecht ausgewählt würden.
Sie trägt ferner vor, das Gemeinschaftsrecht untersage jede Diskriminierung aus Gründen der Religion, da eine solche Diskriminierung gegen die Grundrechte des Menschen verstoße, deren Wahrung der Gerichtshof zu sichern habe.
Außerdem stützt sie sich auf Art. 9 Abs. 2 der Europäischen Konvention zum Schutze der Menschenrechte und Grundfreiheiten ... Da die

---

[1] Amtl. Leitsätze. Slg. 1976, 1589; DÖV 1977, 408; EuGRZ 1976, 426.

Konvention von allen Mitgliedstaaten ratifiziert worden sei, könnten die in ihr enthaltenen Rechte als den Grundrechten zugehörig betrachtet werden, die vom Gemeinschaftsrecht geschützt würden.

Sie macht schließlich geltend, Art. 27 des Beamtenstatuts sei dahin auszulegen, dass der Beklagte den Termin für die von ihm veranstalteten Auswahlverfahren für die Einstellung so bestimmen müsse, dass jeder Bewerber unter Bedingungen an den Prüfungen teilnehmen könne, die seine religiösen Überzeugungen nicht verletzen. Dies gebiete im Übrigen auch das von der genannten Konvention garantierte Recht auf Religionsfreiheit.

[(10/11] Der Beklagte bestreitet nicht, dass die Beamten nach Art. 27 des Statuts ohne Rücksicht auf Rasse, Glauben oder Geschlecht auszuwählen sind; er begehrt auch nicht die Feststellung, dass das Recht auf Religionsfreiheit, so wie es in der Europäischen Menschenrechtskonvention verankert ist, nicht zu den vom Gemeinschaftsrecht anerkannten Grundrechten gehört, wenngleich er hervorhebt, dass weder das Statut noch die Konvention in dem Sinne verstanden werden dürften, dass sie der Klägerin die Rechte gewährten, die sie geltend mache.

Er trägt vor, die in Rede stehende Verpflichtung würde ihn zu umfassenden organisatorischen Maßnahmen zwingen. Art. 27 zähle nicht bestimmte Bekenntnisse auf, auf die sein Anwendungsbereich beschränkt sei, und es wäre daher erforderlich, die Gebräuche aller in den Mitgliedstaaten der Gemeinschaft ausgeübten Religionen zu kennen, um zu vermeiden, dass ein Auswahlverfahren an einem Tag oder zu einer Stunde stattfinde, die mit den Vorschriften einer dieser Religionen unvereinbar sind, und die Bewerber, die diese Religion ausübten, daran gehindert würden, an den Prüfungen teilzunehmen.

[12/19] Nach dem Beamtenstatus erfolgt, wenn eine freie Planstelle zu besetzen ist und beschlossen wurde, sie anders als im Wege der Beförderung oder Versetzung zu besetzen, die Auslese der Bewerber im allgemeinen durch ein Auswahlverfahren auf Grund von Befähigungsnachweisen oder Prüfungen oder auf Grund von Befähigungsnachweisen und Prüfungen. Handelt es sich um ein Auswahlverfahren auf Grund von Prüfungen, so gebietet der Gleichheitsgrundsatz, dass die Prüfungen für alle Bewerber unter den gleichen Bedingungen stattfinden, und im Falle schriftlicher Prüfungen ist es wegen der praktischen Schwierigkeit, die Arbeiten der Bewerber zu vergleichen, notwendig, dass diese Prüfungen für alle gleich sind.

Es ist deshalb sehr wichtig, dass alle Bewerber die schriftlichen Prüfungen zum gleichen Zeitpunkt ablegen. Im Hinblick auf dieses Erfordernis ist das Interesse der Bewerber daran zu beurteilen, dass die Prüfungen nicht an einem Tag stattfinden, der ihnen ungelegen ist.

Teilt ein Bewerber der Anstellungsbehörde mit, dass ihn religiöse Gebote daran hindern, sich an bestimmten Tagen zu den Prüfungen einzufinden, so muss die Behörde dem Rechnung tragen und sich bei der Terminbestimmung für die Prüfungen bemühen, diese Daten zu vermeiden. Setzt der Bewerber dagegen die Anstellungsbehörde nicht rechtzeitig von seinen Schwierigkeiten in Kenntnis, so kann diese es ablehnen, einen anderen Termin vorzuschlagen, insbesondere wenn andere Bewerber bereits zu den Prüfungen geladen worden sind.

Es ist zwar wünschenswert, dass sich die Anstellungsbehörde allgemein über die Daten, die möglicherweise aus religiösen Gründen nicht genehm sind, informiert und die Festsetzung der Prüfungen auf solche Daten zu vermeiden sucht; doch kann aus den vorgenannten Gründen nicht davon ausgegangen werden, dass das Beamtenstatut oder die erwähnten Grundrechte die Anstellungsbehörde verpflichten, einen Konflikt mit einer religiösen Forderung zu vermeiden, von deren Existenz sie nicht unterrichtet worden ist ...

SCHLUSSANTRÄGE DES GENERALANWALTS VOM 22.9.1976
(Auszug)

(...) Frau Prais hat vorgetragen, sie sei aufgrund ihres Glaubensbekenntnisses daran gehindert worden, an dem Auswahlverfahren teilzunehmen. Sie hat sich auf Art. 27 des Beamtenstatuts 3) gestützt, der unter anderem bestimmt, dass Beamte ohne Rücksicht auf Rasse, Glauben oder Geschlecht auszuwählen sind, sowie auf Art. 9 der Europäischen Menschenrechtskonvention ...

Frau Prais hat die Auffassung vertreten, die Achtung der Religionsfreiheit sollte die Bereitschaft einschließen, die notwendigen verwaltungstechnischen Vorkehrungen zu treffen, damit alle Bewerber die Prüfung im Einklang mit ihren religiösen Überzeugungen ablegen könnten ... Die Praxis von Prüfungsausschüssen im Vereinigten Königreich zeige, dass dies möglich sei; der Hinweis auf verwaltungsmäßige Schwierigkeiten sei kein erheblicher Einwand ...

Im Vereinigten Königreich besteht ein Unterschied zwischen der Praxis von beruflichen und akademischen Prüfungsgremien und der Praxis der „Civil Service Commission", die vornehmlich für Einstellungen in den öffentlichen Dienst verantwortlich ist. Es scheint ständige Übung der Berufsund Hochschulausschüsse zu sein, praktizierenden Juden auf Antrag Ersatztermine einzuräumen ... Das gilt jedoch nicht für die Praxis der „Civil Service Commission" ... Eine mögliche Erklärung für diese unterschiedliche Übung ist, dass die Prüfungen der beruflichen und akademischen Ausschüsse nur den Zweck haben festzustellen, ob der Bewerber bestimmte Kenntnisse erlangt hat, die für seine Zulassung zum Beruf oder für die Verleihung des angestrebten Grades erforderlich sind. Eingangsprüfungen für den öffentlichen Dienst haben jedoch Wettbewerbscharakter: Sie sollen die Feststellung ermöglichen, welcher der Bewerber für die ausgeschriebene Stelle am besten geeignet ist. Eure

Lordschaften werden sich erinnern dass der Rat hat vortragen lassen, dass bei einem solchen Auswahlwettbewerb der unmittelbare Vergleich zwischen den Bewerbern erschwert würde, wenn nicht alle gleichzeitig dieselbe Prüfung ablegten, und dass es bei Zulassung besonderer Prüfungstermine für einzelne Bewerber schwierig sein könnte, die Anonymität der Prüfungsarbeiten zu wahren ...

Zwei wichtige Folgerungen können aus den Erkenntnissen über die Praxis im Vereinigten Königreich gezogen werden. Die erste ist, dass sie Frau Prais' Behauptungen ... nicht zu bestätigen vermögen ... Die Praxis der „Civil Service Commission" besagt nicht mehr, als dass „so weit wie möglich" versucht wird, Prüfungen nicht auf Tage anzuberaumen, die „bekannterweise" Schwierigkeiten für „besondere Bewerbergruppen" verursachen. Wenn aber Prüfungstermine einmal festgesetzt sind, werden sie nicht mehr geändert. Die zweite Folgerung ist die Feststellung, dass diese Praxis nicht auf irgendeiner gesetzlichen Regelung beruht, sondern lediglich der Ausdruck von gesundem Menschenverstand und einem Sinn für Fairness ist ...

Art. 27 (des Beamtenstatuts) verbietet einem Bewerber nicht, darauf hinzuweisen - z. B. wenn er seine Bewerbung zur Teilnahme an einem Auswahlverfahren einreicht -, dass er einem Glaubensbekenntnis angehört, das ihm nicht erlaubt, an bestimmten Tagen Prüfungen abzulegen ... Wenn eine Behörde einen solchen Hinweis vor Anberaumung des Prüfungstermins erhält und die Prüfung dennoch mutwillig auf den „verbotenen" Tag ansetzt, macht sie sich meines Erachtens einer rechtswidrigen Diskriminierung schuldig ... Aber ich meine, dass der Rat mit seiner Auffassung, ein solcher Bewerber sei zu diesem Hinweis verpflichtet, zu weit gegangen ist ...

Meines Erachtens irrt auch Frau Prais, wenn sie aus Art. 27 (des Beamtenstatuts) eine Verpflichtung der Gemeinschaftsorgane herleitet, für jede Einstellungsprüfung zu gewährleisten, dass jeder Bewerber, ganz gleich welches seine religiösen Umstände sind, daran teilnehmen kann ... Allen Bewerbern eine solche Möglichkeit einzuräumen, würde einen komplizierten Verwaltungsapparat erfordern ... Er besteht in keinem der Mitgliedstaaten ... Weder die Verfassungen noch die Gesetze der Mitgliedstaaten enthalten eine solche Verpflichtung.

Ich wende mich daher den Art. 9 und 14 der Europäischen Menschenrechtskonvention zu.

Ich möchte gleich betonen, dass ich es bedaure, dass die Konvention weder diesem Gericht noch den nationalen Gerichten die Befugnis einräumt, dem Europäischen Gerichtshof für Menschenrechte Fragen der Auslegung der Konvention im Wege der Vorabentscheidung vorzulegen ...

Unter Berücksichtigung des Wortlauts der Art. 9 und 14 vermag ich nicht festzustellen, dass diese Vorschriften die Wirkung haben, die Frau Prais ihnen beimisst. Ich finde vielmehr das Argument überzeugend, dass, wollte man ihnen diese Wirkung beimessen, man schließen müsste, dass die meisten Mitgliedstaaten der Gemeinschaften die Konvention konsequent verletzt haben ...

Folglich kann meines Erachtens die Klage keinen Erfolg haben ... Man kann nicht zu einem Grundrecht erheben, was - wie ich zu erläutern versucht habe - nicht mehr ist als das Ergebnis der Ausübung von gesundem Menschenverstand verbunden mit einem Sinn für Fairness ..."

73

Der Begriff „Selbstständige" im Sinne von Art. 1 Buchst. a Ziff. IV der Verordnung Nr. 1408/71 in der durch die Verordnung Nr. 1390/81 geänderten Fassung gilt für Personen, die außerhalb eines Arbeitsvertrags oder der Ausübung eines freien Berufs oder des selbstständigen Betriebs eines Unternehmens eine Berufstätigkeit ausüben oder ausgeübt haben, in deren Rahmen sie Leistungen erhalten, die es ihnen ermöglichen, ganz oder teilweise ihren Lebensunterhalt zu bestreiten, auch wenn diese Leistungen von Dritten erbracht werden, zu deren Gunsten ein Priester-Missionar tätig wird.

EuGH, Urteil vom 23. Oktober 1986 - Rs. 300/ 84
(Van Roosmalen ./. Bestuur van de Bedrijfsvereniging/Niederlande)[1] -

AUS DEN GRÜNDEN

Wie sich aus dem Vorlagebeschluss ergibt, ist der Kläger des Ausgangsverfahrens ein römisch-katholischer Priester des auch als Prämonstratenserorden bezeichneten Ordens des Heiligen Norbert. Er ist niederländischer Staatsangehörigkeit und stammt aus der niederländischen Gemeinde Oost-, West- en Middelbeers, wo er bis Dezember 1945 lebte. Nachdem er sich daraufhin in Postel (Belgien), das unmittelbar auf der anderen Seite der niederländisch-belgischen Grenze gelegen ist, niedergelassen hatte, um in einem Kloster seines Ordens zu studieren, wurde er aus dem Einwohnermelderegister seiner Herkunftsgemeinde gestrichen. Von 1955 bis 1980 war er Missionar in Belgisch-Kongo, seit 1960 Zaire.

Während seiner Urlaubszeiten in den Niederlanden in den Jahren 1977 und 1980 ließ sich der Kläger des Ausgangsverfahrens erneut in das Einwohnermelderegister seiner Herkunftsgemeinde eintragen. Während seines Aufenthalts in Zaire unterlag er nicht der niederländischen Einkommen- und/oder Lohnsteuer; dagegen unterlag er während seiner Urlaubszeit in den Niederlanden in Bezug auf die Leistungen, die ihm

---

[1] Auszug aus den amtl. Leitsätzen. Slg. 1986, 3097.

nach dem allgemeinen niederländischen Sozialhilfegesetz (Algemene Bijstandswet, Stb. 1963, 284) gewährt wurden, der Lohnsteuer. Während seines Urlaubs in seiner Herkunftsgemeinde im Jahr 1977 trat er der freiwilligen Versicherung bei, die in Art. 77 der am 1.10.1976 in Kraft getretenen AAW zugunsten derjenigen vorgesehen ist, die Tätigkeiten in einem Entwicklungsland ausüben. Aufgrund dieses Gesetzes ist grundsätzlich jeder versichert, der im Hoheitsgebiet der Niederlande in Europa wohnt. Art. 77 der AAW sieht jedoch vor, dass ehemalige Versicherte, aber auch diejenigen, die vor dem 1.10.1976 und nach Vollendung des 15. Lebensjahres in den Niederlanden gewohnt haben, für die Zeiten, für die sie nicht versichert sind, Beiträge leisten können, wenn sie Tätigkeiten in einem Entwicklungsland ausüben oder ausüben werden. Zaire ist als ein solches Land bezeichnet worden. Nach Art. 13 der königlichen Verordnung vom 19.11.1976 (Stb. 622), der Durchführungsregelung zu Art. 77 der AAW, besteht die Möglichkeit, sich freiwillig im Rahmen der AAW versichern zu lassen, auch für diejenigen, die bereits am 1.10.1976 in einem Entwicklungsland arbeiteten und nach Vollendung des 15. Lebensjahres in den Niederlanden gewohnt haben.

Nachdem sich der Kläger des Ausgangsverfahrens in Zaire eine zur Invalidität führende Krankheit zugezogen hatte und im März 1981 nach Oost-, West- en Middelbeers zurückgekehrt war, erhielt er vom Beklagten des Ausgangsverfahrens ab 12.1.1982 Leistungen wegen Invalidität aufgrund der AAW. Nachdem der Beklagte des Ausgangsverfahrens davon Kenntnis erhalten hatte, dass sich der Kläger des Ausgangsverfahrens am 2.7.1982 endgültig in Postel niedergelassen hatte, setzte er mit Entscheidung vom 8.12.1982 die Gewährung dieser Leistung mit Wirkung vom 1.12.1982 aus und begründete dies damit, dass der Kläger des Ausgangsverfahrens die in Art. 10 der oben genannten königlichen Verordnung vom 19.11.1976 vorgesehene Aufenthaltsvoraussetzung nicht erfülle. Diese Vorschrift hat folgenden Wortlaut:

„1. Wer als versichert gilt, hat abweichend von Art. 6 des Gesetzes erst Anspruch auf eine Leistung wegen Arbeitsunfähigkeit, wenn er 52 Wochen lang ununterbrochen im Inland arbeitsunfähig gewesen ist und die Arbeitsunfähigkeit nach Ablauf dieses Zeitraums noch fortbesteht.
2. Kann zur Überzeugung der Bedrijfsvereniging nachgewiesen werden, dass die Arbeitsunfähigkeit zu einem Zeitpunkt begonnen hat, der vor dem Tag der Rückkehr des als versichert Geltenden in das Inland liegt, so hat dieser Anspruch auf eine Leistung wegen Arbeitsunfähigkeit, wenn er seit dem besagten Zeitpunkt 52 Wochen lang ununterbrochen arbeitsunfähig gewesen ist und die Arbeitsunfähigkeit nach Ablauf dieses Zeitraums noch fortbesteht; diese Leistung wird jedoch in jedem Fall erst ab dem Tag bewilligt, an dem er in die Niederlande zurückgekehrt ist.“

Der Raad van Beroep Utrecht, bei dem der Kläger des Ausgangsverfahrens Anfechtungsklage gegen die oben genannte Entscheidung erhob, hat, da er Zweifel an der Vereinbarkeit dieser Aufenthaltsvoraussetzung mit dem Gemeinschaftsrecht hatte, dem Gerichtshof mit Beschluss vom 11.12.1984 folgende Fragen zur Vorabentscheidung vorgelegt:

Ist Art. 52 oder 53 des Vertrages zur Gründung der EWG oder irgendeine andere Bestimmung des Gemeinschaftsrechts so auszulegen, dass es mit ihnen unvereinbar ist, wenn in Rechtsvorschriften eines Mitgliedstaats, die unter anderem den Angehörigen dieses Mitgliedstaats die Möglichkeit einräumen, sich freiwillig gegen die finanziellen Folgen der Arbeitsunfähigkeit versichern zu lassen, die während einer Tätigkeit in einem außerhalb des Gebiets der EWG gelegenen Entwicklungsland eintritt, als zusätzliche Voraussetzung für den Leistungsanspruch im Hinblick auf die Kontrolle bestimmt wird, dass der Betroffene nach dem Eintritt des Versicherungsfalls erst 52 Wochen lang ununterbrochen im Hoheitsgebiet nur dieses Mitgliedstaats gewohnt oder sich dort aufgehalten haben muss, damit ein Leistungsanspruch besteht, ohne dass das Wohnen oder der Aufenthalt im Hoheitsgebiet eines anderen Mitgliedstaats nach dem Eintritt des Versicherungsfalls mit dem Wohnen oder dem Aufenthalt in dem betreffenden Mitgliedstaat gleichgesetzt wird?

2) Dürfen die in Art. 1 Buchst. a Ziffer ii der Verordnung Nr. 1408/71 genannten Kriterien, zu denen die in Anhang I genannten Kriterien gehören, auch bei der Feststellung, ob eine Person im Sinne von Art. 1 Buchst. a Ziffer ii im Rahmen eines für Einwohner geltenden Systems im Lohn- oder Gehaltsverhältnis beschäftigt ist,, angewandt werden, oder hat dieser Ausdruck eine andere, selbstständige Bedeutung und, wenn ja, welche?

3) Fallen unter den Begriff „Selbstständiger", wie er unter anderem in Art. 1 Buchst. a Ziffer ii der Verordnung Nr. 1408/71 verwendet wird, auch Personen, die im Rahmen eines für alle Einwohner geltenden Systems der sozialen Sicherheit einen Leistungsanspruch aus Arbeitseinkommen herleiten können, das kein Einkommen aus einem Dienstverhältnis oder aus einem selbstständig ausgeübten Beruf oder Gewerbe im Sinne der einzelstaatlichen Rechtsvorschriften ist?

4) Fallen unter den Begriff „Selbstständiger" wie er unter anderem in Art. 1 Buchst. a Ziffer ii der Verordnung Nr. 1408/71 verwendet wird, oder unter den in Art. 1 Buchst. a Ziffer iv enthaltenen Begriff eine selbstständige Tätigkeit ausübt,, auch Personen, die sich im Rahmen eines für alle Einwohner geltenden Systems wegen der Ausübung einer Beschäftigung freiwillig versichern oder weiterversichern lassen können, und zwar auch dann, wenn sie nicht als Arbeitnehmer oder Selbstständiger im Sinne der nationalen Rechtsvorschriften angesehen werden können, aber bezüglich dieser freiwilligen Versicherung dennoch denselben Schutz wie der echte, Arbeitnehmer oder Selbstständige genießen?

5) Sind Rechtsvorschriften, deren Wirkung sich auf Gebiete außerhalb des Gebiets der EWG erstreckt, als Rechtsvorschriften, im Sinne von Art. 2 der Verordnung Nr. 1408/71 anzusehen?

Bei Bejahung dieser Frage: Hat ein Arbeitnehmer oder Selbstständiger, der diesen Rechtsvorschriften ausschließlich wegen einer Tätigkeit außerhalb des Gebiets der EWG unterlag, Anspruch auf den Schutz dieser Verordnung?

6) Wenn aufgrund einer nationalen Rechtsvorschrift eine Leistung nicht bewilligt wird, weil der Betroffene nicht 52 Wochen lang ununterbrochen in dem betreffenden Mitgliedstaat arbeitsunfähig gewesen ist, handelt es sich dann um den Fall

des Art. 2 Abs. 4 der Verordnung Nr. 1390/81, dass eine Leistung wegen des Wohnortes nicht festgestellt worden ist?
Ist die vorstehende Frage anders zu beantworten, wenn dem betreffenden Mitgliedstaat arbeitsunfähig' so zu verstehen ist, dass der Betroffene in diesem Mitgliedstaat seinen Wohnort gehabt haben muss?"

Mit Beschluss vom 26.11.1985 hat der Gerichtshof die Rechtssache an die Zweite Kammer verwiesen.

Die niederländische Regierung und die Kommission der Europäischen Gemeinschaften haben beim Gerichtshof schriftliche Erklärungen eingereicht.

Das vorlegende Gericht hat eine Reihe von Fragen gestellt, die mit der Hauptfrage zusammenhängen, ob eine Aufenthaltsvoraussetzung, an die die Gewährung von Leistungen bei Invalidität geknüpft wird, unter den Umständen des vorliegenden Falles mit dem Gemeinschaftsrecht vereinbar ist. Um dieses Problem, das in der ersten und in der sechsten Frage auftaucht, zu lösen, sind zunächst die Vorfragen zu prüfen, die in der zweiten bis fünften Frage enthalten sind und die sich auf die Definition der Begriffe „Selbstständiger" und „Rechtsvorschriften" im Sinne der Bestimmungen der Verordnung Nr. 1408/71 in ihrer durch die Verordnung Nr. 1390/81 geänderten Fassung beziehen.

(...)

Zur Definition des Begriffes „Selbstständiger" (zweite bis vierte Frage)

Das vorlegende Gericht möchte wissen, ob alle diejenigen, die außerhalb eines Arbeitsvertrags oder eines freien Berufs oder des selbstständigen Betriebs eines Unternehmens irgendeine Tätigkeit ausüben, für die sie als Gegenleistung ein Einkommen beziehen, als „Selbstständige" im Sinne der Verordnung Nr. 1408/71 in ihrer durch die Verordnung Nr. 1390/81 geänderten Fassung anzusehen sind, um entscheiden zu können, ob ein Priester, der keine Bezüge von seinem Orden erhält, sondern von den Angehörigen seiner Gemeinde unterhalten wird, unter diesen Begriff fällt.

Dazu führt das vorlegende Gericht aus, nach niederländischem Steuerrecht seien als „Arbeitseinkünfte" in diesem Zusammenhang Einkünfte aus einer Arbeit anzusehen, die im Wirtschaftsleben ausgeübt werde und bei der ein finanzieller Vorteil erzielt werden solle oder nach den gesellschaftlich anerkannten Regeln vernünftigerweise erwartet werden könne.

Nach ständiger Rechtsprechung des Gerichtshofes gehört dieser Begriff nicht zum nationalen Recht der Mitgliedstaaten, sondern zum Gemeinschaftsrecht und ist in Anbetracht der Zielsetzung des Art. 51 weit auszulegen, die darin besteht, zur Herstellung einer möglichst vollständigen Freizügigkeit der Wanderarbeitnehmer beizutragen, ein Grundsatz, der eines der Fundamente der Gemeinschaft darstellt.

Die niederländische Regierung trägt dazu vor, unter dem Begriff „Selbstständiger" sei, was die Niederlande angehe, im Einklang mit der Regelung in Anhang 1 zur Verordnung Nr. 1408/71 unter I derjenige zu verstehen, der „eine Tätigkeit oder einen Beruf außerhalb eines Arbeitsvertrags ausübt". Es sei also nicht erforderlich, dass das Einkommen, das der Betroffene beziehe, aus einem Arbeitsverhältnis oder der Tätigkeit in einem freien Beruf oder dem selbstständigen Betrieb eines Unternehmens im Sinne der innerstaatlichen Rechtsvorschriften herrühre. Dieser Begriff erfasse daher auch Personen, die im Rahmen eines für alle Einwohner geltenden Systems der sozialen Sicherheit hinsichtlich der Ausübung aller Tätigkeiten in die freiwillige Versicherung aufgenommen werden könnten, selbst wenn sie nicht als Arbeitnehmer oder als Selbstständige im Sinne der nationalen Rechtsvorschriften angesehen werden könnten.

In der Erwägung, dass die Freizügigkeit nicht ausschließlich auf die Arbeitnehmer beschränkt ist, sondern im Rahmen der Niederlassungsfreiheit und des freien Dienstleistungsverkehrs auch die Selbstständigen betrifft, und dass die Koordinierung der Systeme der sozialen Sicherheit für Selbstständige zur Verwirklichung eines der Ziele der Gemeinschaft erforderlich ist, hat der Rat durch die genannte Verordnung Nr. 1390/81 den Anwendungsbereich der Verordnung Nr. 1408/71 generell auf die Selbstständigen und ihre Familienangehörigen ausgedehnt.

Da die Vorschriften der Verordnung Nr. 1390/81 erlassen worden sind, um dieselben Ziele wie die der Verordnung Nr. 1408/71 zu erreichen, soll der Begriff „Selbstständige" diesen denselben sozialen Schutz bieten wie den Arbeitnehmern und ist daher weit auszulegen.

Die niederländische Regierung weist jedoch darauf hin, dass das niederländische Sozialversicherungsrecht zwar nicht zwischen den einzelnen Kategorien von Versicherten unterscheide, dass aber in bestimmten Fällen im Rahmen der AAW ein

Unterschied zwischen Pflichtversicherten und freiwillig Versicherten durch die Festlegung zusätzlicher Voraussetzungen für den Erwerb des Leistungsanspruchs gemacht werde.

Die Kommission ist ebenfalls der Auffassung, dass der Ausdruck „Selbstständiger" sich nicht auf diejenigen beschränken könne, die im Sinne der nationalen Rechtsvorschriften ein Unternehmen betrieben oder einen freien Beruf ausübten, sondern jeden bezeichne, der im Rahmen eines für alle Einwohner geltenden Systems der sozialen Sicherheit Leistungen aufgrund von Einkünften aus einer Arbeit beanspruchen könne, die im Wirtschaftsleben ausgeführt werde und bei der ein finanzieller Vorteil erzielt werden solle oder nach den gesellschaftlich anerkannten Regeln vernünftigerweise erwartet werden könne.

Zur Auslegung des Begriffes „Selbstständiger" ist zunächst festzustellen, dass sich die aufgrund von Art. 51 EWG-Vertrag erlassenen Vorschriften der Verordnung Nr. 1408/71 ursprünglich nur auf den Begriff des „Arbeitnehmers" bezogen.

Was die Definition des Begriffes „Selbstständige" im einzelnen angeht, so ist zu bemerken, dass dieser Ausdruck nach Art. 1 Buchst. a Ziffer iv der Verordnung Nr. 1408/71 in ihrer durch die Verordnung Nr. 1390/81 geänderten Fassung in Bezug auf diejenigen, die, wie der Kläger des Ausgangsverfahrens, freiwillig versichert sind, jede Person bezeichnet, die „eine selbstständige Tätigkeit ausübt". Für diejenigen, die pflichtversichert sind, nimmt Art. 1 Buchst. a Ziffer ii in diesem Zusammenhang entweder auf die „Art der Verwaltung oder der Finanzierung" des anwendbaren Systems der sozialen Sicherheit oder - hilfsweise - auf „die in Anhang I [zur Verordnung] enthaltene Definition" Bezug. Nach Punkt I dieses Anhangs, der sich ausschließlich auf die Niederlande bezieht, gilt als Selbstständiger im Sinne des genannten Artikels, „wer eine Tätigkeit oder einen Beruf außerhalb eines Arbeitsvertrags ausübt".

Daraus folgt, dass der Begriff „Selbstständiger" im Rahmen einer für die Arbeitnehmer oder Selbstständigen oder für alle Einwohner geschaffenen freiwilligen Sozialversicherung durch die Art der Tätigkeit gekennzeichnet ist, die eine Person ausübt oder ausgeübt hat, und dass dies nicht irgendeine Tätigkeit sein kann, sondern dass es sich dabei um eine Berufstätigkeit handeln muss. In Anbetracht der gebotenen weiten Auslegung dieses Begriffes ist es jedoch nicht erforderlich, dass der Selbstständige ein Entgelt als unmittelbare Gegenleistung für seine Tätigkeit erhält; es reicht aus, dass er im Rahmen dieser Tätigkeit Leistungen erhält, die es ihm ermöglichen, ganz oder teilweise seinen Lebensunterhalt zu bestreiten, auch wenn diese Leistungen - wie im vorliegenden Fall - von Dritten erbracht werden, zu deren Gunsten ein Priester-Missionar tätig wird.

Folglich ist zu antworten, dass der Begriff „Selbstständige" im Sinne von Art. 1 Buchst. a Ziffer iv der Verordnung Nr. 1408/71 in der durch die Verordnung Nr. 1390/81 geänderten Fassung für Personen gilt, die außerhalb eines Arbeitsvertrags oder der Ausübung eines freien Berufs oder des selbstständigen Betriebs eines Unternehmens eine Berufstätigkeit ausüben oder ausgeübt haben, in deren Rahmen sie Leistungen erhalten, die es ihnen ermöglichen, ganz oder teilweise ihren Lebensunterhalt zu bestreiten, auch wenn diese Leistungen von Dritten erbracht werden, zu deren Gunsten ein Priester-Missionar tätig wird.

Zum Begriff „Rechtsvorschriften" (fünfte Frage) (*wird ausgeführt*)

74

Art. 2 EWG-Vertrag ist dahin auszulegen, dass die Tätigkeiten der Mitglieder einer auf Religion oder einer anderen Form der Weltanschauung beruhenden Vereinigung im Rahmen der gewerblichen Tätigkeit dieser Vereinigung insoweit einen Teil des Wirtschaftslebens ausmachen, als die Leistungen, die die Vereinigung ihren Mitgliedern gewährt, als mittelbare Gegenleistung für tatsächliche und echte Tätigkeiten betrachtet werden können.

Die Art. 59 und 60 EWG-Vertrag gelten nicht für den Angehörigen eines Mitgliedstaats, der sich in das Hoheitsgebiet eines anderen Mitgliedstaats begibt und dort seinen Hauptaufenthalt nimmt, um dort für unbestimmte Dauer Dienstleistungen zu erbringen oder zu empfangen.

EuGH, Urteil vom 5. Oktober 1988 - Rs. 196/87
(Steymann ./. Staatssecretaris van Justitie/Niederlande)[1] -

SACHVERHALT UND VORLAGEFRAGEN

[3] Der Kläger des Ausgangsverfahrens, Herr Steymann, ist deutscher Staatsangehöriger. Er ließ sich am 26.3.1983 in den Niederlanden nieder. Er arbeitete kurze Zeit als Klempner im Rahmen eines Arbeitsverhältnisses. Später wurde er Mitglied der Religionsgemeinschaft „De Stad Rajneesh Neo-Sannyas Commune" (nachstehend: Bhagwan-Vereinigung), die ihre wirtschaftliche Unabhängigkeit durch gewerbliche Betätigungen wie den Betrieb einer Diskothek, eines Getränkehandels und eines Waschsalons sicherstellt.

[4] Im Rahmen seiner Teilnahme am Leben der Bhagwan-Vereinigung führt der Kläger bestimmte Klempnerarbeiten am Gebäude dieser Vereinigung sowie Hausarbeiten allgemeiner Art durch. Er beteiligt sich im Übrigen an den gewerblichen Betätigungen der Vereinigung. Unabhängig von Art und Umfang seiner Tätigkeit sorgt die Vereinigung in jedem Fall für seinen Lebensunterhalt.

[5] Am 28.8.1984 beantragte der Kläger eine Aufenthaltserlaubnis in den Niederlanden zur Ausübung einer unselbstständigen Beschäftigung. Die Erteilung dieser Erlaubnis lehnte der Leiter der Ortspolizeibehörde ab. Der Kläger beantragte beim Staatssecretaris van Justitie eine Überprüfung dieses ablehnenden Bescheids; mit Bescheid vom 20.12.1985 wurde sein Antrag unter anderem mit der Begründung abgelehnt, er gehe keiner unselbstständigen Beschäftigung nach und sei deshalb nicht als begünstigter EWG-Angehöriger im Sinne des niederländischen Ausländerrechts anzusehen.

---

[1] Slg. 1988, 6159; NVwZ 1990, 53; BayVBl. 1990, 715; NJW 1990, 627 (LS).

[6] Gegen diese Entscheidung erhob der Kläger beim Raad van State Klage mit der Begründung, als Mitglied der Bhagwan-Vereinigung sei er im Verhältnis zu dieser Vereinigung Dienstleistungsempfänger und -erbringer. Das nationale Gericht hat das Verfahren ausgesetzt und dem Gerichtshof folgende Fragen zur Vorabentscheidung vorgelegt:

„1) Kann von einer wirtschaftlichen Betätigung oder von einer Dienstleistung im Sinne des EWG-Vertrags gesprochen werden, wenn es um Tätigkeiten geht, die in der Teilnahme an einer auf Religion oder einer anderen Form der Weltanschauung beruhenden Lebensgemeinschaft - und dem völligen Aufgehen in ihr und der Befolgung von deren Lebensregeln bestehen, wobei man einander Vorteile verschafft?
2) Sind die Art. 59 und 60 EWG-Vertrag dahin auszulegen, dass nicht von der Erbringung von Dienstleistungen im Sinne des Vertrages gesprochen werden kann, wenn sich ein Angehöriger eines Mitgliedstaats zu einem Aufenthalt von unbestimmter Dauer in das Hoheitsgebiet eines anderen Mitgliedstaats begibt - und damit seinen Hauptaufenthalt in diesen Mitgliedstaat verlegt - und sich auch aus der Art der geleisteten Dienste keine zeitliche Begrenzung dieses Aufenthalts ergibt?
3) Sind die Art. 59 und 60 EWG-Vertrag dahin auszulegen, dass nicht vom Empfang von Dienstleistungen im Sinne des Vertrages gesprochen werden kann, wenn sich ein Angehöriger eines Mitgliedstaats zu einem Aufenthalt von unbestimmter Dauer in das Hoheitsgebiet eines anderen Mitgliedstaats begibt - und damit seinen Hauptaufenthalt in diesen Mitgliedstaat verlegt - und sich aus der Art der empfangenen Dienstleistungen keine zeitliche Begrenzung dieses Aufenthalts ergibt?"

ENTSCHEIDUNGSGRÜNDE

Zur ersten Frage

[8] Mit der ersten Frage wird im Wesentlichen Auskunft darüber begehrt, inwieweit die Tätigkeiten der Mitglieder einer auf Religion oder einer anderen Form der Weltanschauung beruhenden Vereinigung im Rahmen der Betätigungen dieser Vereinigung als Teil des Wirtschaftslebens im Sinne des EWG-Vertrags betrachtet werden können.

[9] Hierzu ist vorab festzustellen, dass angesichts der Ziele der Gemeinschaft die Teilnahme an einer auf Religion oder einer anderen Form der Weltanschauung beruhenden Vereinigung nur insoweit in den Anwendungsbereich des Gemeinschaftsrechts fällt, als sie als Teil des Wirtschaftslebens im Sinne von Art. 2 EWG-Vertrag angesehen werden kann.

[10] Wie der Gerichtshof in seinem Urteil vom 14.7.1976 in der Rechtssache 13/76 (Donà, Slg. 1976, 1333) entschieden hat, macht eine entgeltliche Arbeits- oder Dienstleistung einen Teil des Wirtschaftslebens im Sinne dieser Bestimmung des EWG-Vertrags aus.

[11] Die Tätigkeiten, um die es im vorliegenden Ausgangsverfahren geht, umfassen, wie aus den Akten hervorgeht, Arbeiten, die in der

Bhagwan-Vereinigung und für deren Rechnung als Teil der gewerblichen Tätigkeiten dieser Vereinigung verrichtet werden. Es scheint, dass diese Arbeiten einen ziemlich bedeutenden Platz im Leben der Bhagwan-Vereinigung einnehmen und dass die Mitglieder sich ihnen nur unter besonderen Umständen entziehen. Die Bhagwan-Vereinigung sorgt wiederum, unabhängig von Art und Umfang der Arbeiten, die ihre Mitglieder verrichten, für deren Lebensunterhalt und zahlt ihnen ein Taschengeld.

[12] In einem Fall wie dem vom vorlegenden Gericht geschilderten, kann nicht von vornherein ausgeschlossen werden, dass die von den Mitgliedern dieser Vereinigung verrichteten Arbeiten einen Teil des Wirtschaftslebens im Sinne von Art. 2 EWG-Vertrag ausmachen. Soweit nämlich diese Arbeiten, mit denen der Bhagwan-Vereinigung die wirtschaftliche Unabhängigkeit gesichert werden soll, ein wesentliches Element der Teilnahme an dieser Vereinigung darstellen, können die Leistungen, die diese Vereinigung ihren Mitgliedern gewährt, als mittelbare Gegenleistung für deren Arbeiten angesehen werden.

[13] Allerdings muss es sich, wie der Gerichtshof in seinem Urteil vom 23.3.1982 in der Rechtssache 53/81 (Levin, Slg. 1982, 1035) entschieden hat, um tatsächliche und echte Tätigkeiten handeln, die keinen so geringen Umfang haben dürfen, dass sie sich als völlig untergeordnet und unwesentlich darstellen. Das vorlegende Gericht hat festgestellt, dass es sich im vorliegenden Fall um tatsächliche und echte Tätigkeiten handelt.

[14] Unter diesen Umständen ist auf die erste Frage zu antworten, dass Art. 2 EWG-Vertrag dahin auszulegen ist, dass die Tätigkeiten der Mitglieder einer auf Religion oder einer anderen Form der Weltanschauung beruhenden Vereinigung im Rahmen der gewerblichen Tätigkeit dieser Vereinigung insoweit einen Teil des Wirtschaftslebens ausmachen, als die Leistungen, die die Vereinigung ihren Mitgliedern gewährt, als mittelbare Gegenleistung für tatsächliche und echte Tätigkeiten betrachtet werden können.

Zur zweiten und dritten Frage

[15] In der zweiten und dritten Frage geht es im Wesentlichen darum, ob die Art. 59 und 60 EWG-Vertrag für den Angehörigen eines Mitgliedstaats gelten, der sich in das Hoheitsgebiet eines anderen Mitgliedstaats begibt und dort seinen Hauptaufenthalt nimmt, um dort für unbestimmte Dauer Dienstleistungen zu erbringen oder zu empfangen.

[16] Hierzu führen die niederländische Regierung und die Kommission zu Recht aus, dass die Art. 59 und 60 EWG-Vertrag einen solchen Fall nicht erfassen. Bereits aus dem Wortlaut von Art. 60 geht nämlich hervor, dass eine auf Dauer oder jedenfalls ohne absehbare zeitliche Beschränkung ausgeübte Tätigkeit nicht unter die gemeinschaftsrechtlichen Vorschriften über den freien Dienstleistungsverkehr fallen kann.

Solche Tätigkeiten können hingegen je nach Lage des Falles in den Anwendungsbereich der Art. 48 bis 51 und 52 bis 68 EWG-Vertrag fallen.
*[17] Deshalb ist auf die zweite und die dritte Frage zu antworten, dass
die Art. 59 und 60 EWG-Vertrag nicht für den Angehörigen eines Mitgliedstaats gelten, der sich in das Hoheitsgebiet eines anderen Mitgliedstaats begibt und dort seinen Hauptaufenthalt nimmt, um dort für unbestimmte Dauer Dienstleistungen zu erbringen oder zu empfangen.*

SCHLUSSANTRÄGE DES GENERALWANWALTS VOM 5.7.1988
(Auszug)

[1] Unter Berücksichtigung des im Zwischenurteil des niederländischen Raad van State, mit dem Sie befasst sind, dargestellten Sachver-
halts und um diesem Gericht eine sachdienliche Antwort zu geben, halte
ich es für richtig, von vornherein jede Bezugnahme auf die Art. 59 und
60 EWG-Vertrag und allgemein auf den freien Dienstleistungsverkehr,
der Gegenstand der zweiten und der dritten Vorabentscheidungsfrage
ist, auszuschließen. Diese Freiheit betrifft im Wesentlichen die gelegent-
liche und vorläufige Ausübung einer selbstständigen beruflichen Tätigkeit.

[2] Die gemeinschaftsrechtlichen Vorschriften über Dienstleistungen
können nicht auf eine feste und auf unbestimmte Zeit angelegte Situation angewandt werden. Diese Erwägung gilt sowohl für Dienstleistende
als auch für Dienstleistungsempfänger.

[3] Lassen Sie mich darauf hinweisen, dass nach Art. 4 Abs. 2 Unterabs. 1 der Richtlinie 73/148/EWG des Rates vom 21.5.1973 zur Aufhebung der Reise- und Aufenthaltsbeschränkungen für Staatsangehörige
der Mitgliedstaaten innerhalb der Gemeinschaft auf dem Gebiet der Nie-
derlassung und des Dienstleistungsverkehrs (ABl. L 172 vom 28.6.1973,
S. 14) das Aufenthaltsrecht für Leistungserbringer und Leistungsemp-
fänger „der Dauer der Leistung [entspricht]" und dass nach Unterabs. 2
eine Aufenthaltserlaubnis zum Nachweis dieses Rechts ausgestellt wird,
sofern die Dauer der Leistung drei Monate übersteigt.

[4] Um die Dienstleistungsempfänger ging es unter anderem im Urteil
Luisi und Carbone, in dem das Erfordernis der zeitlichen Begrenzung
des Empfangs von Dienstleistungen in Erscheinung tritt. Sie haben dort
nämlich ausgeführt, „dass der freie Dienstleistungsverkehr die Freiheit
der Dienstleistungsempfänger einschließt, sich zur Inanspruchnahme einer Dienstleistung in einen anderen Mitgliedstaat zu begeben ..., und
dass Touristen sowie Personen, die eine medizinische Behandlung in Anspruch nehmen, und solche, die Studien- oder Geschäftsreisen unternehmen, als Empfänger von Dienstleistungen anzusehen sind" (Urteil
vom 31.1.1984 in den verbundenen Rechtssachen 286/82 und 26/83, Slg.
1984, 377, Rn 16).

Es zeigt sich also deutlich, dass eine dauernd oder jedenfalls ohne absehbare zeitliche Beschränkung ausgeführte Tätigkeit nicht unter die gemeinschaftsrechtlichen Vorschriften über Dienstleistungen fallen kann.

[5] Die erste Frage des vorlegenden Gerichts hat hingegen allgemeine Bedeutung und ist unter diesem Gesichtspunkt zu prüfen. Sie werden im Wesentlichen gefragt, inwieweit Betätigungen, die im Rahmen und anlässlich der Teilnahme an einer auf Religion oder einer anderen Form der Weltanschauung beruhenden Gemeinschaft verrichtet werden, als Teil des Wirtschaftslebens im Sinne des EWG-Vertrags angesehen werden können.

[6] Die Auffassung, dass in einem solchen Rahmen verrichtete Tätigkeiten als Teil des Wirtschaftslebens definiert werden können und die aufgrund dessen unter das Gemeinschaftsrecht fallen, lässt sich nicht von vornherein ablehnen. Gleichwohl kann die gestellte Frage nicht abstrakt beantwortet werden. Eine Teilnahme an einer Gemeinschaft, wie sie vom vorlegenden Gericht dargestellt wird, kann die Ausübung bestimmter Berufstätigkeiten, die die Merkmale einer Teilnahme am Wirtschaftsleben im Sinne des Vertrages erfüllen, umfassen. Das nationale Gericht hat in jedem Fall die Natur und die Häufigkeit der betreffenden Tätigkeiten sowie die Beziehung zwischen demjenigen, der sie ausübt, und demjenigen, der sie vergütet, zu berücksichtigen und insbesondere zu beurteilen, ob die empfangene Vergütung unabhängig von ihrer Natur die Gegenleistung für die geleistete Arbeit darstellt.

[7] In einer Situation, die durch ihre unbestimmte Dauer gekennzeichnet ist, kann eine wirtschaftliche Tätigkeit entweder aufgrund der Freizügigkeit der Arbeitnehmer oder aufgrund der Niederlassungsfreiheit ausgeübt werden.

[8] In Ihrem Urteil Walrave und Koch haben Sie in anderem Zusammenhang entschieden: Wenn sich eine Betätigung, die einen Teil des Wirtschaftslebens im Sinne von Art. 2 des Vertrages ausmacht, „als entgeltliche Arbeits- oder Dienstleistung kennzeichnen (lässt), so gelten für sie, je nach Lage des Einzelfalles, die besonderen Vorschriften der Art. 48 bis 51 oder 59 bis 66 des Vertrages") (Urteil vom 12.12.1974 in der Rechtssache 36/74, Slg. 1974, 1405, Rn 5).

Mit anderen Worten, sobald es sich um eine entgeltliche Berufstätigkeit handelt, liegt eine Betätigung vor, die einen Teil des Wirtschaftslebens ausmacht.

[9] Aus den zuvor genannten Gründen ist im vorliegenden Fall jede Verweisung auf die Bestimmungen über den freien Dienstleistungsverkehr auszuschließen. Aus dem genannten Urteil geht hervor - und diese Lösung wird durch das Urteil Donà (Urteil vom 14.7.1976 in der Rechtssache 13/76, Slg. 1976, 1333) bestätigt -, dass eine entgeltliche Betätigung ipso facto einen Teil des Wirtschaftslebens ausmacht.

[10] Um zu entscheiden, ob für den Sachverhalt, über den das vorlegende Gericht zu befinden hat, die Bestimmungen des Gemeinschafts-

rechts über die Niederlassungsfreiheit oder über die Freizügigkeit der Wanderarbeitnehmer gelten, ist darauf hinzuweisen, dass Sie in Ihrem Urteil Lawrie-Blum festgestellt haben, dass der Begriff Arbeitnehmer „anhand objektiver Kriterien zu definieren ist), die das Arbeitsverhältnis im Hinblick auf die Rechte und Pflichten der betroffenen Personen kennzeichnen".

Weiter haben Sie ausgeführt: „Das wesentliche Merkmal des Arbeitsverhältnisses besteht aber darin, dass jemand während einer bestimmten Zeit für einen anderen nach dessen Weisung Leistungen erbringt, für die er als Gegenleistung eine Vergütung erhält" (Urteil vom 3.7.1986 in der Rechtssache 66/85, Slg. 1986, 2121, Rn 17).

[11] Ferner haben Sie unter Hinweis auf Ihr Urteil Levine (Urteil vom 23.3.1983 in der Rechtssache 53/81, Slg. 1982, 1035) ausgeführt, dass „die Begriffe des Arbeitnehmers und der Tätigkeit im Lohn- oder Gehaltsverhältnis so zu verstehen (sind), dass sie auch Personen umfassen, die, weil sie keiner Vollzeitbeschäftigung nachgehen, nur ein Einkommen beziehen, das unter dem für eine Vollzeitbeschäftigung liegt, sofern es sich um die Ausübung tatsächlicher und echter Tätigkeiten handelt" (Urteil in der Rechtssache 66/85, aaO, Rn 21).

[12] Mit anderen Worten, es ist Sache des vorlegenden Gerichts, zu beurteilen, ob die Stellung des Klägers des Ausgangsverfahrens in der betreffenden Gemeinschaft, die von ihm versehenen Aufgaben und die Vergütung, die er für sie erhält, die gemeinschaftsrechtlichen Vorschriften, je nach Lage des Falles über die Freizügigkeit der Arbeitnehmer oder über die Niederlassungsfreiheit, zur Anwendung kommen lassen.

[13] Im vorliegenden Fall ist es jedoch unerheblich, welche dieser Bestimmungen angewandt werden, da Herr Steymann seine Klage gegen den Bescheid richtet, mit dem die Gewährung einer Aufenthaltserlaubnis für ihn abgelehnt worden ist.

[14] Sie haben nämlich in Ihrem Urteil Royer anerkannt, dass die Bestimmungen über diese beiden Freiheiten auf denselben Grundsätzen beruhen, und ausgeführt, dass dies auch zutrifft

„für das Recht der vom Gemeinschaftsrecht geschützten Personen [gilt], in das Hoheitsgebiet der Mitgliedstaaten einzureisen und sich dort aufzuhalten" (Urteil vom 8.4.1976 in der Rechtssache 48/75, Slg. 1976, 497, Rn 12).

[15] Deshalb muss das vorlegende Gericht, um den Rechtsstreit im Ausgangsverfahren zu entscheiden und festzulegen, ob auf den vorliegenden Fall die Vorschriften des Gemeinschaftsrechts über die Freizügigkeit der Personen anzuwenden sind, die Art der vom Kläger verrichteten Tätigkeiten untersuchen und prüfen, inwieweit dieser eine Vergütung als Gegenleistung für seine Arbeit, und nicht unabhängig von dieser, erhält.

[16] Ich schlage deshalb vor, für Recht zu erkennen:

„*Eine in einem Mitgliedstaat von einem Angehörigen eines anderen Mitgliedstaats im Rahmen oder im Dienste einer weltanschaulichen Gemeinschaft ausgeübte Berufstätigkeit kann vom einzelstaatlichen Gericht als Teil des Wirtschaftslebens im Sinne des Vertrages angesehen werden, wenn sie die notwendige Gegenleistung für das Entgelt, unabhängig von dessen Art, darstellt, das der Betroffene von dieser Gemeinschaft erhält.“*

Sachregister

Die Seitenzahlen verweisen jeweils auf die erste Seite der Entscheidung.